Digital Communications
and
Signal Processing

Digital Communications *and* Signal Processing

Second edition

K Vasudevan
Department of Electrical Engineering
Indian Institute of Technology Kanpur
Kanpur 208 016

Universities Press

UNIVERSITIES PRESS (INDIA) PRIVATE LIMITED

Registered Office
3-6-747/1/A & 3-6-754/1, Himayatnagar, Hyderabad 500 029 (A.P.), India
info@universitiespress.com; www.universitiespress.com

Distributed by
Orient Blackswan Private Limited

Registered Office
3-6-752 Himayatnagar, Hyderabad 500 029 (A.P.) India

Other Offices
Bangalore / Bhopal / Bhubaneshwar / Chandigarh / Chennai
Ernakulam / Guwahati / Hyderabad / Jaipur / Kolkata
Lucknow / Mumbai / New Delhi / Noida / Patna

First published in India by
Universities Press (India) Private Limited 2010

ISBN 978 81 7371 710 9

Typeset in Times 10/12 *by*
Krishtel eMaging Solutions Pvt. Ltd
Chennai 600 017

Printed at
Graphica Printers, Hyderabad 500 013

Published by
Universities Press (India) Private Limited
3-6-747/1/A & 3-6-754/1, Himayatnagar,
Hyderabad 500 029 (A.P.), India

The price of the book is inclusive of the CD.

To my family

Contents

Notations

$\{A\} \setminus \{B\}$	Elements of set A minus set B
$a \in \{A\}$	a is an element of set A
$a \notin \{A\}$	a is not an element of set A
$a \wedge b$	Logical AND of a and b
$a \vee b$	Logical OR of a and b
$a \stackrel{?}{=} b$	a may or may not be equal to b
$\exists$	There exists
$\exists!$	There exists uniquely
$\nexists$	Does not exist
$\forall$	For all
$\lfloor x \rfloor$	Largest integer less than or equal to x
$\lceil x \rceil$	Smallest integer greater than or equal to x
j	$\sqrt{-1}$
$\stackrel{\Delta}{=}$	Equal to by definition
$\star$	Convolution
$\delta_D(\cdot)$	Dirac delta function
$\delta_K(\cdot)$	Kronecker delta function
$\tilde{x}$	A complex quantity
$\hat{x}$	Estimate of x
$\mathbf{x}$	A vector or matrix
$\mathbf{I}_M$	An $M \times M$ identity matrix
S	Complex symbol (note the absence of tilde)
$\Re\{\cdot\}$	Real part
$\Im\{\cdot\}$	Imaginary part
x_I	Real or in-phase part of $\tilde{x}$
x_Q	Imaginary or quadrature part of $\tilde{x}$
$E[\cdot]$	Expectation
$\mathrm{erfc}(\cdot)$	Complementary error function
$[x_1, x_2]$	Closed interval, inclusive of x_1 and x_2
$[x_1, x_2)$	Open interval, inclusive of x_1 and exclusive of x_2
(x_1, x_2)	Open interval, exclusive of x_1 and x_2
$P(\cdot)$	Probability
$p(\cdot)$	Probability density function
Hz	Frequency in Hertz

Calligraphic Letters

$\mathscr{A}$	A
$\mathscr{B}$	B
$\mathscr{C}$	C
$\mathscr{D}$	D
$\mathscr{E}$	E
$\mathscr{F}$	F
$\mathscr{G}$	G
$\mathscr{H}$	H
$\mathscr{I}$	I
$\mathscr{J}$	J
$\mathscr{K}$	K
$\mathscr{L}$	L
$\mathscr{M}$	M
$\mathscr{N}$	N
$\mathscr{O}$	O
$\mathscr{P}$	P
$\mathscr{Q}$	Q
$\mathscr{R}$	R
$\mathscr{S}$	S
$\mathscr{T}$	T
$\mathscr{U}$	U
$\mathscr{V}$	V
$\mathscr{W}$	W
$\mathscr{X}$	X
$\mathscr{Y}$	Y
$\mathscr{Z}$	Z

List of Programs

1. Associated with Chapter 2 (Communicating with Points)
   (a) `mdcoho`: Coherent detection of multidimensional orthogonal constellations in AWGN channels.
   (b) `mdnc`: Noncoherent detection of multidimensional orthogonal constellations in AWGN channels.
   (c) `fade`: Coherent detection of M-ary constellations in Rayleigh flat fading channels.
2. Associated with Chapter 3 (Channel Coding)
   (a) `hdclass`: Hard decision decoding of convolutional codes using the Viterbi algorithm.
   (b) `tc12`: MAP decoding of parallel concatenated turbo codes.
   (c) `shellmap`: The shell mapping algorithm.
3. Associated with Chapter 4 (Transmission of Signals through Distortionless Channels)
   (a) `deal1`: A digital communication system employing root-raised cosine pulse shaping, with algorithms for carrier and timing synchronization of uncoded QPSK signals.

Preface to the Second Edition

The second edition of this book is a result of the continuing efforts of the author to unify the areas of discrete-time signal processing and communication. The use of discrete-time techniques allows us to implement the transmitter and receiver algorithms in software.

The additional topics covered in the second edition are:

1. Computing the average probability of error for constellations having non-equiprobable symbols (Chapter 1).
2. Performance analysis of differential detectors in Rayleigh flat fading channels (Chapter 1).
3. Synchronization techniques for linearly modulated signals (Chapter 4).

The additional C programs that are included in the CDROM are:

1. Coherent detection of multidimensional orthogonal constellations in AWGN channels (associated with Chapter 1).
2. Noncoherent detection of multidimensional orthogonal constellations in AWGN channels (associated with Chapter 1).
3. Coherent detection of M-ary constellations in Rayleigh flat fading channels (associated with Chapter 1).
4. Coherent detection of QPSK signals transmitted over AWGN channels. Here, the concepts of pulse shaping, carrier and timing synchronization are involved (associated with Chapter 4).

Many new examples have been added. I hope the reader will find the second edition of the book interesting.

K. Vasudevan
August 2009

Preface to the First Edition

This book has evolved out of the lecture notes prepared for the graduate level course on *Communication Theory* at the IIT Kanpur. It has been written keeping in mind the practical aspects of digital communications, with sufficient emphasis on discrete-time processing of digitally modulated signals. The companion CD-ROM contains C programs on various aspects of digital communications systems.

The topics covered in the book have been presented in a simple and logical manner. Some of the key features of this book include:

1. Expressing the probability of error in terms of the Euclidean distance (which seems more intuitive) instead of the usual E_b/N_0.
2. Computing the average probability of error of constellations having non-equiprobable symbols
3. A new approach to the Viterbi algorithm which does not assume any knowledge of the encoder starting and ending states.
4. A discussion on constellation shaping and the shell mapping algorithm.
5. Special emphasis on the root-raised cosine pulse shaping which is used widely in practical communication systems employing linear modulation.
6. A unified approach to continuous phase frequency modulation, where M-ary FSK and MSK are special cases.
7. Introducing the fractionally-spaced ML detector and demonstrating the equivalence between the fractionally-spaced and symbol-spaced ML detectors.
8. Synchronization techniques for linearly modulated signals that are simple and effective even at low signal-to-noise ratios.

As a prerequisite, the reader must have undergone a first course on digital signal processing and should possess some knowledge of probability theory, random variables and random processes. Specific topics that supplement the material in the text are covered in the appendices. The book is suitable for a senior undergraduate or graduate course, and I hope that students as well as practicing engineers will find it useful.

April 2006 *K. Vasudevan*

Acknowledgements

During the course of my master's degree and PhD at IIT Madras, I had the opportunity to learn the fundamental concepts of digital communications from my instructors, Dr V G K Murthy, Dr V V Rao, Dr K. Radhakrishna Rao, Dr Bhaskar Ramamurthi and Dr Ashok Jhunjhunwalla. It is a pleasure to acknowledge their teaching. I also gratefully acknowledge the guidance of Dr K Giridhar and Dr Bhaskar Ramamurthi, who were jointly my doctoral supervisors. I also wish to thank Dr Devendra Jalihal for introducing me to the LaTeX document processing system, without which this book would not have been completed. I would like to express my gratitude to my instructors at IIT Kharagpur (from where I had completed my undergraduation)—Dr S L Maskara, Dr T S Lamba, Dr R V Rajkumar and Dr S Shanmugavel (now with Anna University, Chennai). I thank Dr Surendra Prasad of IIT Delhi and Dr P Y Kam of the National University of Singapore for encouraging me to write this book.

During the early stages of my career (1991–1992), I was associated with the CAD-VLSI Group of the Indian Telephone Industries, Bangalore. I would like to express my gratitude to K S Raghunathan (formerly Deputy Chief Engineer at the CAD-VLSI Group), for his supervision of the implementation of a statistical fault analyzer for digital circuits. It was from him that I learnt the concepts of good programming, which I cherish and use to this day.

A special mention is also due to Dr Bixio Rimoldi of the Mobile Communications Lab, EPFL Switzerland, and Dr Raymond Knopp, now with Institute Eurecom, Sophia Antipolis, France, for providing me the opportunity to implement the signal processing algorithms discussed in Chapter 4 in real-time for their software radio platform.

I would like to thank many of my students for their valuable feedback on the first edition of this book. Finally, I thank my colleagues at IIT Kanpur; in particular, Dr S C Srivastava, Dr V Sinha (now retired from IIT-K), Dr Govind Sharma, Dr Pradip Sircar, Dr R K Bansal, and Dr A K Chaturvedi, for their support and encouragement. I also wish to thank Universities Press for bringing out the second edition of this book.

In spite of my best efforts, some errors might have gone unnoticed in the book. I would be glad to be notified of the same and welcome suggestions for improving the book.

K Vasudevan

1 Introduction

The basic purpose of communication is to exchange information. The main components of a communication system (whether it is analog or digital) are the source of information, a transmitter that converts the information into a form that is suitable for transmission through a channel, a receiver that performs the reverse function of the transmitter and finally the destination (Figure 1.1). The source of information is usually humans (in the form of voice or pictures) or devices like computers, storage media (in the form of data). The main feature that distinguishes analog from digital communication is that in the former the information is continuous in time as well as in amplitude, whereas in the latter it is discrete.

The main advantages of digital communications over analog communications are listed below

1. Errors can be detected and corrected. This makes the system more reliable.
2. It can be implemented in software, which makes the system flexible.

Error detection and correction is a feature unique to digital communication. The usefulness of a software-based implementation needs no emphasis. Besides providing flexibility, it is also much more reliable than a hardware implementation. Sophisticated signal processing techniques can be used to obtain optimal performance. In today's scenario, software implementation is feasible due to the easy availability of high-speed digital signal processors (DSPs).

The other important features of digital communication include the ability to compress the data and the ability to encrypt the data. The process of compression involves removing the redundancy in the data. This makes the transmission of data more efficient. Encryption of the data makes it immune to eavesdropping by an intruder. This is useful in millitary applications.

The two main resources that are available to a communication system are:

1. Bandwidth of the transmitted signal which is directly proportional to the bit-rate or the symbol-rate. The bandwidth of the transmitted signal is usually governed by the available channel bandwidth.
2. Transmit power.

The performance criteria for a digital communication system is usually the probability of error. There is usually a tradeoff between bandwidth and power, in order to maintain a given probability of error. For example, in satellite or deep space communication, bandwidth (bit-rate) is not a constraint whereas the power available on-board the satellite is limited. Such systems would therefore employ the simplest modulation schemes, namely binary phase

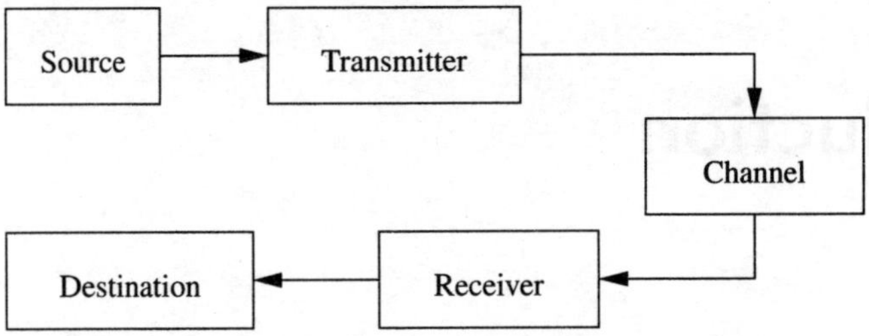

Figure 1.1 *Basic components in a communication system*

shift keying (BPSK) or quadrature phase shift keying (QPSK) that require the minimum power to achieve a given error-rate. The reverse is true for telephone-line communication employing voiceband modems, where power is not a constraint and the available channel bandwidth is limited. In order to maximize the bit-rate, these systems tend to pack more number of bits into a symbol (typically in excess of 10) resulting in large constellations requiring more power.

The channel is an important component of a communication system. They can be classified as follows:

(a) Time-invariant – the impulse response of the channel is invariant to time. Examples are the telephone-line, Ethernet, fiber-optic cable, etc.

(b) Time-variant or fading – the impulse response varies with time, e.g. wireless channels.

Channels can also be classified as

(a) Distortionless – the impulse response of the channel can be modelled as a Dirac-Delta function.

(b) Distorting – the impulse response cannot be modelled as a Dirac-Delta function.

Whether the channel is distortionless or distorting depends on the frequency response of the channel over the bandwidth of the transmitted signal. If the magnitude response of the channel is flat (constant) and the phase response is linear over the transmission bandwidth, then the channel is said to be distortionless, otherwise the channel is distorting. The channel also adds additive white Gaussian noise (AWGN)[1]. A distortionless channel is usually referred to as an AWGN channel.

In wireless communications, commonly encountered channels are:

1. Time-varying distortionless channels, also known as frequency nonselective or flat fading channels.
2. Time-varying distorting channels, also known as frequency selective fading channels.

Finally, the receiver design depends on the transmitter and the channel characteristics. The various topics covered in this book is elaborated in the next section.

1.1 Overview of the Book

Digital communication is all about sending *bits* (1s and 0s) from a transmitter to a receiver through a channel. The number of bits transmitted per second is called the bit rate. In Chapter 2, we assume that the transmitter emits bits, the channel adds additive white Gaussian noise (AWGN) and the receiver tries to optimally detect the bits such that the bit-error-rate (BER) is minimized. The BER is defined as

$$\text{BER} \stackrel{\Delta}{=} \frac{\text{Number of bits in error}}{\text{Total number of bits transmitted}}. \tag{1.1}$$

A more complex transmitter would map a group of bits into a *symbol* and transmit the symbols. The symbols are taken from a *constellation*. A constellation is defined as a set of points in N-dimensional space. Thus a point in the constellation can be represented by a $N \times 1$ column vector. When $N = 2$ we get a 2-D constellation and the symbols are usually represented by a complex number instead of a 2×1 vector.

The number of symbols transmitted per second is called the symbol rate or bauds. The symbol rate or baud rate is related to the bit rate by

$$\text{Symbol rate} \stackrel{\Delta}{=} \frac{\text{Bit rate}}{\text{Number of bits per symbol}}. \tag{1.2}$$

From the above equation it is clear that the transmission bandwidth reduces by grouping bits to a symbol.

The receiver optimally detects the symbols such that the symbol-error-rate (SER) is minimized. The SER is defined as

$$\text{SER} \stackrel{\Delta}{=} \frac{\text{Number of symbols in error}}{\text{Total number of symbols transmitted}}. \tag{1.3}$$

In general, minimizing the SER *does not* imply minimizing the BER. The BER is minimized only when the symbols are Gray-coded.

A receiver is said to be coherent if it knows the constellation points exactly. However, if the received constellation is rotated by an arbitrary phase that is unknown to the receiver, it is still possible to detect the symbols. Such a receiver is called a *noncoherent* receiver. Chapter 2 covers the performance of both coherent as well as noncoherent receivers. The performance of coherent detectors for constellations having non-equiprobable symbols is also described.

In many situations the additive noise is not white, though it may be Gaussian. We devote a section in Chapter 2 for the derivation and analysis of a coherent receiver in coloured Gaussian noise. Finally, we discuss the performance of coherent and differential detectors in fading channels.

Chapter 3 is devoted to forward error correction. We restrict ourselves to the study of convolutional codes and its extensions like trellis coded modulation (TCM). In particular, we show how soft-decision decoding of convolutional codes is about 3 dB better than har d-decision decoding. We also demonstrate that TCM is a bandwidth efficient coding scheme compared to convolutional codes. The Viterbi algorithm for hard- and soft-decision decoding of convolutional codes is discussed. In practice, it is quite easy to obtain a coding gain of about 4 dB by using TCM schemes having reasonable decoding complexity. However, to obtain an additional 1 dB coding gain, a disproportionately large decoding complexity is required. To alleviate this problem, the concept of constellation shaping is introduced. It is quite easy to obtain a shape gain of 1 dB. Thus the net gain that can be attained by using both TCM and constellation shaping is 5 dB. Finally, we conclude the chapter with a discussion on turbo codes and performance analysis of maximum likelihood (ML) decoding of turbo codes. A notable feature in this section is the development of the BCJR algorithm using the MAP (maximum *a posteriori*) detector, unlike the conventional methods in literature where the log-MAP or the max-log-MAP is used.

In Chapter 4 we discuss how the "points" (which may be coded or uncoded) are converted to signals suitable for transmission through a distortionless channel. Though this is an idealized channel model, it helps in obtaining the "best performance limit" of a digital communication system. In fact the performance of a digital communication system through a distorting channel can only be inferior to that of a distortionless channel. This chapter also seeks to justify the communication model used in Chapter 2. Thus Chapters 2 and 4 neatly separate the two important issues in a idealized digital communication system namely, analysis and implementation. Whereas Chapter 2 deals exclusively with analysis, Chapter 4 is devoted mostly to implementation.

Chapter 4 is broadly divided into two parts. The first part deals with linear modulation and the second part deals with nonlinear modulation. Under the heading of linear modulation we discuss the power spectral density of the transmitted signals, the optimum (matched filter) receiver and the Nyquist criterion for zero ISI. The important topic of synchronization of linearly modulated signals is dealt with. The topics covered under nonlinear modulation include strongly and weakly orthogonal signals. We demonstrate that minimum shift keying (MSK) is a particular case of weakly orthogonal signals. The bandpass sampling theorem is also discussed.

In Chapter 5 we deal with the real-life scenario where the channel is non-ideal. In this situation there are two kinds of detection strategies: the first one is based on equalization and the other is based on maximum likelihood (ML) estimation. The approaches based on equalization are simple to implement but are suboptimal in practice due to the use of finite-length (impulse response is of finite duration) equalizers. The approaches based on ML estimation have a high computational complexity but are optimal for finite-length channels. Finally, multi carrier communication as a means of mitigating ISI is presented.

The topics covered under equalization are symbol-spaced, fractionally-spaced and decision-feedback equalizers. We show that the Viterbi algorithm can be used in the receivers based on ML estimation. We also show that the symbol-spaced and fractionally-spaced ML detectors are equivalent.

1.2 Bibliography

There are other books on digital communication which are recommended for further reading. The book by Proakis[2] covers a wide area of topics like information theory, source coding, synchronization, OFDM and wireless communication, and is quite suitable for a graduate level course in communications. In Messerschmitt,[3] special emphasis is given to synchronization techniques. *Communication Systems* by Haykin[4] covers various topics at a basic level and is well suited for a first course in communications. There are also many recent books on specialized topics. Synchronization in digital communication systems is discussed in [5–7]. The book by Hanzo[8] discusses turbo coding and its applications. A good treatment of turbo codes can also be found in [9] and [10]. Space-time codes are addressed in [11]. An exhaustive discussion on the recent topics in wireless communications can be found in [12]. A more classical treatment of wireless communication can be found in [13]. Various wireless communication standards are described in [14]. Besides, the fairly exhaustive list of references at the end of the book is a good source of information to the interested reader.

2 Communicating with Points

This chapter is devoted to the performance analysis of both coherent and non-coherent receivers. We assume a simple communication model: the transmitter emits symbols that is corrupted by additive white Gaussian noise (AWGN) and the receiver tries to optimally detect the symbols. In the later chapters, we demonstrate how a real-life digital communication system can be reduced to the simple model considered in this chapter.

We begin with the analysis of coherent receivers.

2.1 Coherent Detectors for Two-Dimensional Constellations

Consider the digital communication system shown in Figure 2.1. Bit 0 gets mapped to $\tilde{a}_1$ and 1 gets mapped to $\tilde{a}_2$. Thus, the constellation consists of two complex points $\tilde{a}_1$ and $\tilde{a}_2$. The transmitted symbol at time n is given by $S_n^{(i)} \in \{\tilde{a}_1, \tilde{a}_2\}$, where the superscript (i) denotes the ith symbol in the constellation $(1 \leq i \leq 2)$.

The received point is given by

$$\tilde{r}_n = S_n^{(i)} + \tilde{w}_n \tag{2.1}$$

where $\tilde{w}_n$ denotes samples of a wide sense stationary (WSS), additive white Gaussian noise (AWGN) process with zero-mean and variance

$$\sigma_w^2 = \frac{1}{2} E\left[|\tilde{w}_n|^2\right]. \tag{2.2}$$

We assume that the real and imaginary parts of $\tilde{w}_n$ are *statistically independent*, that is

$$E\left[w_{n,\,I} w_{n,\,Q}\right] = E\left[w_{n,\,I}\right] E\left[w_{n,\,Q}\right] = 0 \tag{2.3}$$

since each of the real and imaginary parts have zero mean. Thus (2.2) also implies that

$$E\left[w_{n,\,I}^2\right] = E\left[w_{n,\,Q}^2\right] = \sigma_w^2. \tag{2.4}$$

In general, the autocorrelation of $\tilde{w}_n$ is given by

$$\tilde{R}_{\tilde{w}\tilde{w}}(m) \stackrel{\Delta}{=} \frac{1}{2} E\left[\tilde{w}_n \tilde{w}_{n-m}^*\right] = \sigma_w^2 \delta_K(m) \tag{2.5}$$

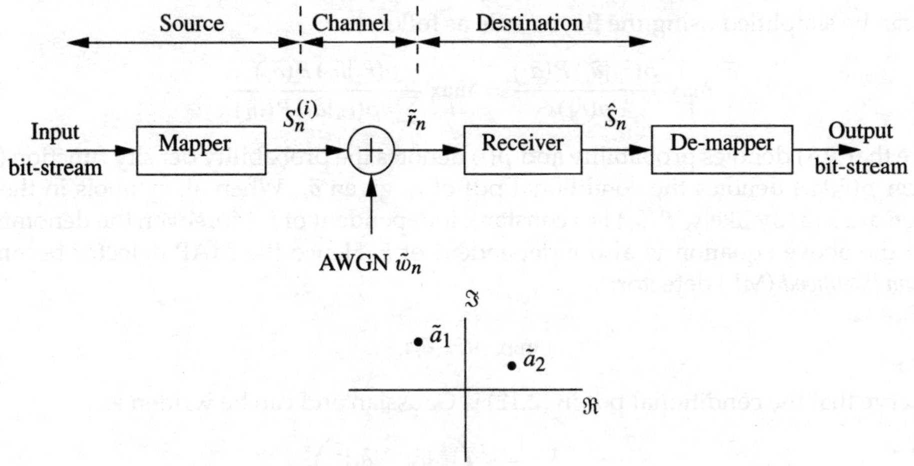

Figure 2.1 *Block diagram of a simple digital communication system. The transmitted constellation is also shown.*

where

$$\delta_K(m) \stackrel{\Delta}{=} \begin{cases} 1 & \text{if } m = 0 \\ 0 & \text{otherwise} \end{cases} \tag{2.6}$$

is the *Kronecker delta* function.

Let us now turn our attention to the receiver. Given the received point $\tilde{r}_n$, the receiver has to decide whether $\tilde{a}_1$ or $\tilde{a}_2$ was transmitted. Let us assume that the receiver decides in favour of $\tilde{a}_i$, $i \in \{1, 2\}$. Let us denote the average probability of error in this decision by $P_e(\tilde{a}_i, \tilde{r}_n)$. Clearly,[15,16]

$$\begin{aligned} P_e(\tilde{a}_i, \tilde{r}_n) &= P\left(\tilde{a}_i \text{ not sent} \,|\tilde{r}_n\right) \\ &= 1 - P\left(\tilde{a}_i \text{ was sent} \,|\tilde{r}_n\right). \end{aligned} \tag{2.7}$$

For brevity, the above equation can be written as

$$P_e(\tilde{a}_i, \tilde{r}_n) = 1 - P\left(\tilde{a}_i|\tilde{r}_n\right). \tag{2.8}$$

Now, if we wish to minimize the probability of error, we must maximize $P(\tilde{a}_i|\tilde{r}_n)$.

Thus the receiver computes the probabilities $P(\tilde{a}_1|\tilde{r}_n)$ and $P(\tilde{a}_2|\tilde{r}_n)$ and decides in favour of the maximum. Mathematically, this operation can be written as:

$$\text{Choose } \hat{S}_n = \tilde{a}_i \text{ if } P(\tilde{a}_i|\tilde{r}_n) \text{ is the maximum.} \tag{2.9}$$

The estimate in the above equation is referred to as the *maximum a posteriori* (MAP) estimate and the receiver is called the MAP receiver. The above equation can be written more succinctly as

$$\max_i P(\tilde{a}_i|\tilde{r}_n) \tag{2.10}$$

which can be simplified using the Bayes' rule as follows

$$\max_i \frac{p(\tilde{r}_n|\tilde{a}_i)P(\tilde{a}_i)}{p(\tilde{r}_n)} = \max_i \frac{p(\tilde{r}_n|\tilde{a}_i)P(\tilde{a}_i)}{\sum_i p(\tilde{r}_n|\tilde{a}_i)P(\tilde{a}_i)}. \tag{2.11}$$

Observe that $P(\cdot)$ denotes probability and $p(\cdot)$ denotes the probability density function (pdf). The term $p(\tilde{r}_n|\tilde{a}_i)$ denotes the conditional pdf of $\tilde{r}_n$ given $\tilde{a}_i$. When all symbols in the constellation are equally likely, $P(\tilde{a}_i)$ is a constant, independent of i. Moreover, the denominator term in the above equation is also independent of i. Hence the MAP detector becomes a *maximum likelihood* (ML) detector:

$$\max_i p(\tilde{r}_n|\tilde{a}_i). \tag{2.12}$$

We observe that the conditional pdf in (2.12) is Gaussian and can be written as

$$\max_i \frac{1}{2\pi\sigma_w^2} \exp\left(-\frac{|\tilde{r}_n - \tilde{a}_i|^2}{2\sigma_w^2}\right). \tag{2.13}$$

Taking the natural logarithm of the above equation and ignoring the constants results in

$$\min_i |\tilde{r}_n - \tilde{a}_i|^2 . \tag{2.14}$$

To summarize, the ML detector decides in favour of that point (or symbol) in the constellation that is nearest to the received point $\tilde{r}_n$. Let us now analyze the performance of the ML detector.

2.1.1 Performance analysis

In this section we compute the probability that the ML detector makes an error, given that the symbol $\tilde{a}_1$ was transmitted. This would happen when

$$|\tilde{r}_n - \tilde{a}_2|^2 < |\tilde{r}_n - \tilde{a}_1|^2 . \tag{2.15}$$

The above equation can be simplified to[3]

$$\begin{aligned} \left|\tilde{d} + \tilde{w}_n\right|^2 &< |\tilde{w}_n|^2 \\ \Rightarrow \left|\tilde{d}\right|^2 + 2\Re\left\{\tilde{d}^* \tilde{w}_n\right\} &< 0 \end{aligned} \tag{2.16}$$

where the superscript '$*$' denotes the complex conjugate and

$$\tilde{d} = \tilde{a}_1 - \tilde{a}_2. \tag{2.17}$$

Let

$$\begin{aligned} Z &= 2\Re\left\{\tilde{d}^* \tilde{w}_n\right\} \\ &= 2\left(d_I w_{n,\,I} + d_Q w_{n,\,Q}\right) \end{aligned} \tag{2.18}$$

where the subscripts I and Q denote the in-phase and quadrature components respectively. It is clear that Z is a real Gaussian random variable, since it is a linear combination of two real Gaussian random variables. The mean and variance of Z is given by

$$\begin{aligned} E[Z] &= 0 \\ E[Z^2] &= 4\sigma_w^2 \left|\tilde{d}\right|^2 \\ &= \sigma_Z^2 \quad \text{(say)}. \end{aligned} \tag{2.19}$$

Thus the required probability of error is given by

$$\begin{aligned} P\left(Z < -\left|\tilde{d}\right|^2\right) &= \int_{Z=-\infty}^{-\left|\tilde{d}\right|^2} \frac{1}{\sigma_Z\sqrt{2\pi}} \exp\left(-\frac{Z^2}{2\sigma_Z^2}\right) dZ \\ &= \frac{1}{2}\operatorname{erfc}\left(\sqrt{\frac{\left|\tilde{d}\right|^2}{8\sigma_w^2}}\right) \end{aligned} \tag{2.20}$$

where

$$\operatorname{erfc}(x) = \frac{2}{\sqrt{\pi}} \int_{y=x}^{\infty} e^{-y^2}\, dy \qquad \text{for } x > 0 \tag{2.21}$$

is the complementary error function.

To summarize, the above equation implies that the probability of error depends only on the squared Euclidean distance, $|\tilde{d}|^2$, between the two points and the noise variance σ_w^2. In other words, the probability of error is independent of the rotation and translation of the constellation. The next important question that needs attention is whether the same performance can be obtained by *minimizing* the transmit power. This aspect is investigated in the next section.

2.1.2 Optimizing the constellation

A constellation is optimized by minimizing its average power for a *given minimum* distance between the points. For the constellation given in Figure 2.1, the conditions can be written as (assuming that $\tilde{a}_1$ and $\tilde{a}_2$ are equiprobable):

$$\min \frac{1}{2}\left(|\tilde{a}_1|^2 + |\tilde{a}_2|^2\right) \text{ subject to the constraint } |\tilde{a}_1 - \tilde{a}_2|^2 = |\tilde{d}|^2. \tag{2.22}$$

The above optimization problem can be solved using the method of *Lagrange multipliers.* Equation (2.22) can be re-written as

$$\min f(\tilde{a}_1, \tilde{a}_2) = \frac{1}{2}\left(|\tilde{a}_1|^2 + |\tilde{a}_2|^2\right) + \lambda\left(|\tilde{a}_1 - \tilde{a}_2|^2 - |\tilde{d}|^2\right). \tag{2.23}$$

Taking partial derivatives with respect to $\tilde{a}_1^*$ and $\tilde{a}_2^*$ (see Appendix A) and setting them equal to zero, we get the conditions:

$$\frac{1}{2}\tilde{a}_1^* + \tilde{\lambda}(\tilde{a}_1 - \tilde{a}_2) = 0,$$

$$\frac{1}{2}\tilde{a}_2^* - \tilde{\lambda}(\tilde{a}_1 - \tilde{a}_2) = 0. \tag{2.24}$$

It is clear from the above equations that the two points $\tilde{a}_1$ and $\tilde{a}_2$ have to be *antipodal*, that is,

$$\tilde{a}_1 = -\tilde{a}_2. \tag{2.25}$$

2.1.3 Union bound on the probability of error for 2-D constellations

In this section we derive a union bound on the probability of error when there are G_0 points at a distance of $|\tilde{d}|$ from the transmitted point $\tilde{a}_0$. This is illustrated in Figure 2.2 for $G_0 = 4$. We assume that $\tilde{a}_0$ has been transmitted. The probability that the ML detector makes an error is equal to the probability of detecting $\tilde{a}_1$ or $\tilde{a}_2$ or $\tilde{a}_3$ or $\tilde{a}_4$. We now invoke the well known axiom in probability, relating to events A and B:

$$\begin{aligned} P(A \text{ or } B) &= P(A) + P(B) - P(A \text{ and } B) \\ &\leq P(A) + P(B). \end{aligned} \tag{2.26}$$

In Figure 2.2, the probability that the received point falls in regions R_1 and R_2 correspond to the events A and B in the above equation. It is clear that the events overlap. It is now easy to conclude that the probability of error given that $\tilde{a}_0$ was transmitted is given by

$$\begin{aligned} P(e|\tilde{a}_0) &\leq G_0 P(\tilde{a}_1|\tilde{a}_0) \\ &= \frac{G_0}{2}\,\text{erfc}\left(\sqrt{\frac{\left|\tilde{d}\right|^2}{8\sigma_w^2}}\right), \end{aligned} \tag{2.27}$$

where we have made use of the expression for *pairwise probability* of error derived in (2.20) and $P(e|\tilde{a}_0)$ denotes the probability of error given that $\tilde{a}_0$ was transmitted. In general, the G_i nearest points equidistant from a transmitted point $\tilde{a}_i$, are called the *nearest neighbours*.

We are now in a position to design and analyze more complex transmitters and receivers. This is explained in the next section.

2.1.4 M-ary signalling schemes

In the previous sections it was assumed that one bit is transmitted at a time. Therefore, the bit rate equals the baud rate. We now consider a more complex transmitter which maps a group of bits into a symbol. The relationship between the bit rate and the baud rate is given by (1.2).

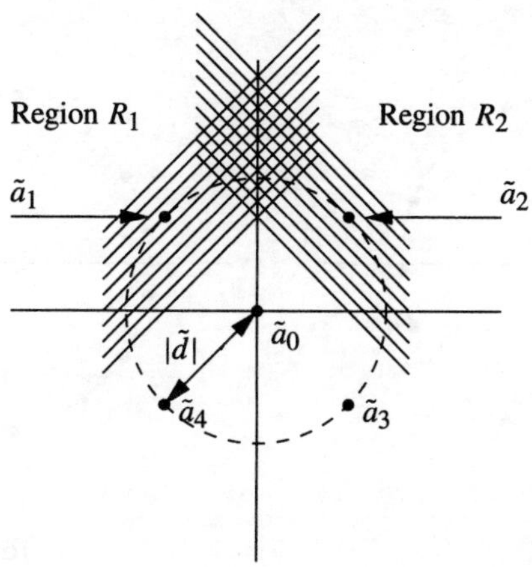

Figure 2.2 *Illustration of the computation of the union bound*

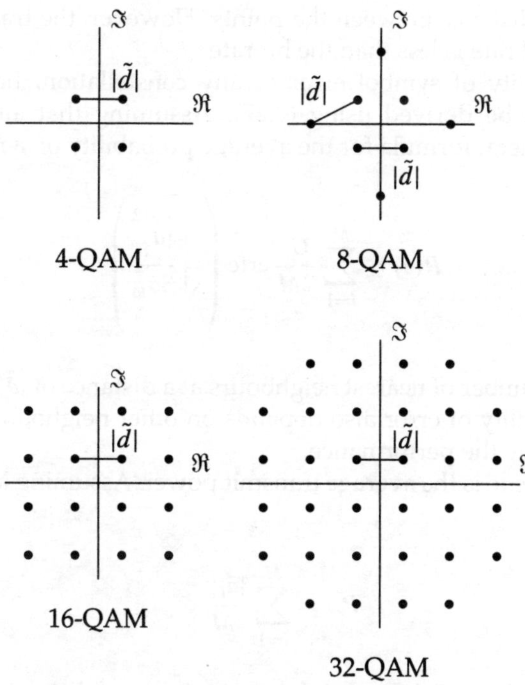

Figure 2.3 *Some commonly used QAM (quadrature amplitude modulation) constellations*

Observe that m bits must get mapped to $M = 2^m$ distinct symbols in the constellation. Some commonly used constellations are shown in Figures 2.3 and 2.4[17]. It is clear that grouping more bits into a symbol increases the size of the constellation (transmit power),

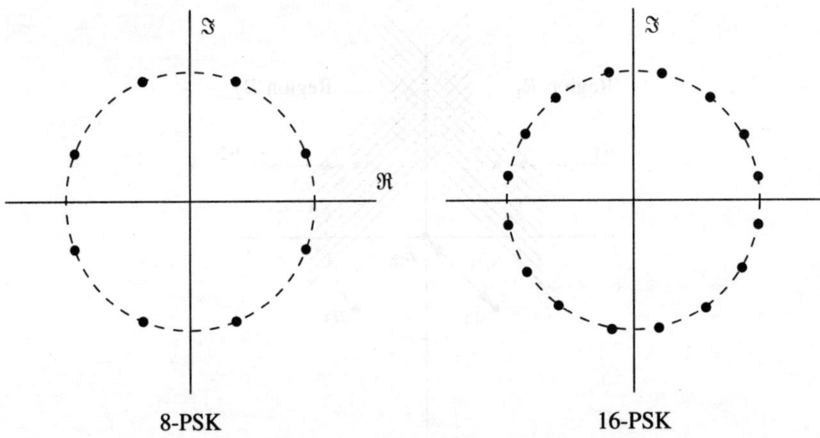

Figure 2.4 *Some commonly used PSK (phase shift keying) constellations*

for the *same* minimum distance between the points. However, the transmission bandwidth decreases since the baud rate is less than the bit rate.

The average probability of symbol error of any constellation, based on the *minimum distance error event*, can be derived using (2.27). Assuming that all symbols occur with probability $1/M$, the general formula for the average probability of symbol error is

$$P(e) \leq \sum_{i=1}^{M} \frac{G_i}{2M} \operatorname{erfc}\left(\sqrt{\frac{|\tilde{d}|^2}{8\sigma_w^2}}\right) \tag{2.28}$$

where G_i denotes the number of nearest neighbours at a distance of $|\tilde{d}|$ from symbol $\tilde{a}_i$. Note that the average probability of error also depends on other neighbours, but it is the *nearest* neighbours that dominate the performance.

The next important issue is the average transmit power. Assuming all symbols are equally likely, this is equal to

$$P_{\text{av}} = \sum_{i=1}^{M} \frac{|\tilde{a}_i|^2}{M}. \tag{2.29}$$

It is clear from Figures 2.3 and 2.4 that for the *same* minimum distance, the average transmit power *increases* as M increases. Having defined the transmit power, it is important to define the average signal-to-noise ratio (SNR). For a two-dimensional constellation, the the average SNR is defined as

$$\text{SNR}_{\text{av}} = \frac{P_{\text{av}}}{2\sigma_w^2}. \tag{2.30}$$

The reason for having the factor of two in the denominator is because the average signal power P_{av} is defined over two dimensions (real and imaginary), whereas the noise power σ_w^2 is over one dimension (either real or imaginary, see equation 2.4). Hence the noise variance over two dimensions is $2\sigma_w^2$.

In general, if we wish to compare the symbol-error-rate performance of different M-ary modulation schemes, say 8-PSK with 16-PSK, then it would be inappropriate to use SNR_{av} as the yardstick. In other words, it would be unfair to compare 8-PSK with 16-PSK for a given SNR_{av} simply because 8-PSK transmits 3 bits per symbol whereas 16-PSK transmits 4 bits per symbol. Hence it seems logical to define the average SNR *per bit* as

$$\text{SNR}_{av,\,b} = \frac{P_{av}}{2\kappa\,\sigma_w^2} \tag{2.31}$$

where $\kappa = \log_2(M)$ is the number of bits per symbol. The error-rate performance of different M-ary schemes can now be compared for a given $\text{SNR}_{av,\,b}$.

It is also useful to define

$$P_{av,\,b} \stackrel{\Delta}{=} \frac{P_{av}}{\kappa} \tag{2.32}$$

where $P_{av,\,b}$ is the average power of the BPSK constellation or the average power per bit.

Example 2.1.1 Compute the average probability of symbol error for 16-QAM using the union bound. Compare the result with the exact expression for the probability of error. Assume that the in-phase and quadrature components of noise are statistically independent and all symbols equally likely.

Solution: In the 16-QAM constellation there are four symbols having four nearest neighbours, eight symbols having three nearest neighbours and four having two nearest neighbours. Thus the average probability of symbol error from the union bound argument is

$$\begin{aligned} P(e) &\le \frac{1}{16}[4\times 4 + 3\times 8 + 4\times 2]\frac{1}{2}\operatorname{erfc}\left(\sqrt{\frac{d^2}{8\sigma_w^2}}\right) \\ &= 1.5\operatorname{erfc}\left(\sqrt{\frac{d^2}{8\sigma_w^2}}\right). \end{aligned} \tag{2.33}$$

Note that for convenience we have assumed $|\tilde{d}| = d$ is the minimum distance between the symbols. To compute the exact expression for the probability of error, let us first consider an innermost point (say $\tilde{a}_i$) which has four nearest neighbours. The probability of correct decision given that $\tilde{a}_i$ was transmitted is

$$\begin{aligned} P(c|\tilde{a}_i) &= P((-d/2 \le w_{n,\,I} < d/2) \text{ AND } (-d/2 \le w_{n,\,Q} < d/2)) \\ &= P(-d/2 \le w_{n,\,I} < d/2)P(-d/2 \le w_{n,\,Q} < d/2), \end{aligned} \tag{2.34}$$

where we have used the fact that the in-phase and quadrature components of noise are statistically independent. The above expression simplifies to

$$P(c|\tilde{a}_i) = [1 - y]^2, \tag{2.35}$$

where

$$y = \operatorname{erfc}\left(\sqrt{\frac{d^2}{8\sigma_w^2}}\right). \tag{2.36}$$

Similarly we can show that for an outer point having three nearest neighbours

$$P(c|\tilde{a}_j) = [1 - y]\left[1 - \frac{y}{2}\right], \tag{2.37}$$

and for an outer point having two nearest neighbours

$$P(c|\tilde{a}_k) = \left[1 - \frac{y}{2}\right]^2. \tag{2.38}$$

The average probability of correct decision is

$$P(c) = \frac{1}{16}\left[4P(c|\tilde{a}_i) + 8P(c|\tilde{a}_j) + 4P(c|\tilde{a}_k)\right]. \tag{2.39}$$

The average probability of error is

$$P(e) = 1 - P(c). \tag{2.40}$$

When $y \ll 1$, the average probability of error reduces to

$$P(e) \approx 1.5y = 1.5 \operatorname{erfc}\left(\sqrt{\frac{d^2}{8\sigma_w^2}}\right), \tag{2.41}$$

which is identical to that obtained using the union bound in (2.33).

In Figure 2.5 we have plotted the theoretical and simulated performance of 16-QAM. The simulations were performed over 10^8 symbols.

Example 2.1.2 Compute the average probability of symbol error for 16-PSK using the union bound. Assume that the in-phase and quadrature components of noise are statistically independent and all symbols are equally likely. Using numerical integration techniques, plot the exact probability of error for 16-PSK.

Solution: In the 16-PSK constellation all symbols have two nearest neighbours. Hence the average probability of error using the union bound is

$$P(e) \le \frac{16 \times 2}{16} \times \frac{1}{2} \operatorname{erfc}\left(\sqrt{\frac{d^2}{8\sigma_w^2}}\right)$$

$$= \operatorname{erfc}\left(\sqrt{\frac{d^2}{8\sigma_w^2}}\right), \tag{2.42}$$

where d is the minimum distance between the symbols.

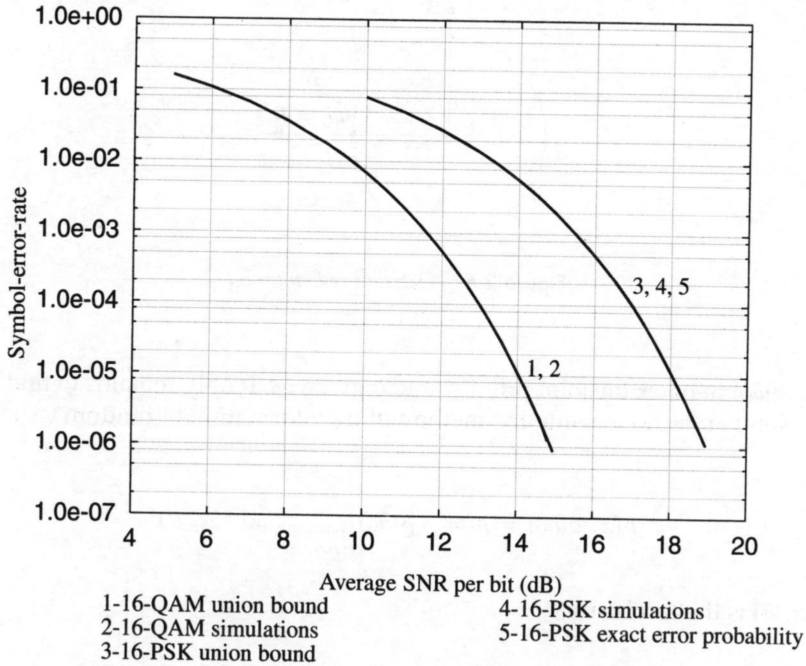

Figure 2.5 *Theoretical and simulation results for 16-QAM and 16-PSK*

We now compute the exact expression for the probability of error assuming an M-ary PSK constellation with radius R. Note that for M-ary PSK, the minimum distance d between symbols is related to the radius R by

$$d = 2R\sin(\pi/M). \tag{2.43}$$

To evaluate the average probability of error, it is convenient to first compute the average probability of correct decision. For convenience, let us assume that $\tilde{a}_0 = R$ was transmitted. Then the received symbol can be denoted by

$$\tilde{r} = r_I + \mathrm{j}\, r_Q = R + w_I + \mathrm{j}\, w_Q = x\mathrm{e}^{\mathrm{j}\,\theta} \quad \text{(say)} \tag{2.44}$$

where we have suppressed the time index n for brevity and w_I and w_Q denote samples of in-phase and quadrature components of the AWGN. The probability of correct decision is the probability that $\tilde{r}$ lies in the triangular decision region ABC, as illustrated in Figure 2.6. Since the decision region can be conveniently represented in polar coordinates, the probability of correct decision given $\tilde{a}_0$ can be written as

$$\begin{aligned} P(c|\tilde{a}_0) &= \int_{\theta=-\pi/M}^{\pi/M} \int_{x=0}^{\infty} p(x,\, \theta|\tilde{a}_0)\, d\theta\, dx \\ &= \int_{\theta=-\pi/M}^{\pi/M} p(\theta|\tilde{a}_0)\, d\theta \end{aligned} \tag{2.45}$$

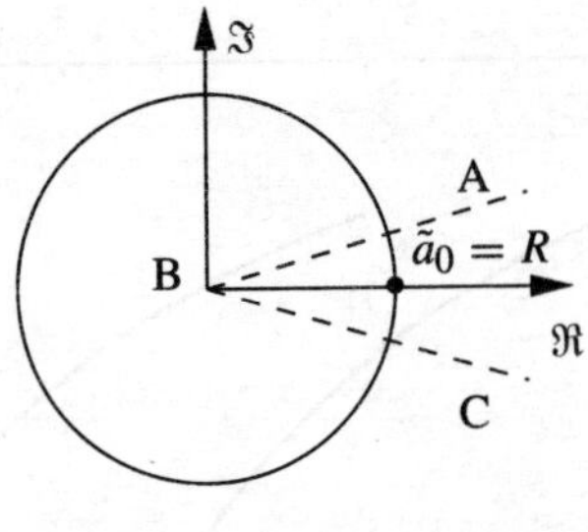

Figure 2.6 *Decision region for* $\tilde{a}_0$

where $p(x, \theta|\tilde{a}_0)$ denotes the joint pdf of x and θ given $\tilde{a}_0$. It only remains to find out the pdf $p(x, \theta|\tilde{a}_0)$. This can be done using the method of transformation of random variables[18]. We have

$$p(x, \theta|\tilde{a}_0) = p(r_I, r_Q|\tilde{a}_0)\big|_{\substack{r_I = x\cos(\theta) \\ r_Q = x\sin(\theta)}} |J(x, \theta)| \tag{2.46}$$

where $J(x, \theta)$ is the Jacobian

$$J(x, \theta) = \begin{vmatrix} \frac{\partial r_I}{\partial x} & \frac{\partial r_Q}{\partial x} \\ \frac{\partial r_I}{\partial \theta} & \frac{\partial r_Q}{\partial \theta} \end{vmatrix} = x. \tag{2.47}$$

Thus (2.46) becomes

$$\begin{aligned} p(x, \theta|\tilde{a}_0) &= \frac{x}{2\pi\sigma_w^2} \exp\left(-\frac{(r_I - R)^2 + r_Q^2}{2\sigma_w^2}\right)\Bigg|_{\substack{r_I = x\cos(\theta) \\ r_Q = x\sin(\theta)}} \\ &= \frac{x}{2\pi\sigma_w^2} \exp\left(-\frac{x^2 + R^2 - 2Rx\cos(\theta)}{2\sigma_w^2}\right) \\ &= \frac{x}{2\pi\sigma_w^2} \exp\left(-\frac{(x - R\cos(\theta))^2 + R^2\sin^2(\theta)}{2\sigma_w^2}\right) \end{aligned} \tag{2.48}$$

where σ_w^2 is the variance of w_I and w_Q. Now,

$$p(\theta|\tilde{a}_0) = \int_{x=0}^{\infty} p(x, \theta|\tilde{a}_0)\, dx. \tag{2.49}$$

Let

$$\frac{R^2}{2\sigma_w^2} = \gamma = \text{SNR}_{\text{av}}$$

$$\frac{x - R\cos(\theta)}{\sigma_w\sqrt{2}} = y$$

$$\Rightarrow \frac{dx}{\sigma_w\sqrt{2}} = dy. \tag{2.50}$$

Therefore

$$p(\theta|\tilde{a}_0) = \frac{1}{2\pi\sigma_w^2}\mathrm{e}^{-\gamma\sin^2(\theta)}\int_{y=-\sqrt{\gamma}\cos(\theta)}^{\infty}(y\sigma_w\sqrt{2} + R\cos(\theta))\mathrm{e}^{-y^2}\sigma_w\sqrt{2}\,dy$$

$$= \frac{1}{\pi}\mathrm{e}^{-\gamma\sin^2(\theta)}\int_{y=-\sqrt{\gamma}\cos(\theta)}^{\infty} y\mathrm{e}^{-y^2}\,dy + \frac{R\cos(\theta)}{\sigma\pi\sqrt{2}}\mathrm{e}^{-\gamma\sin^2(\theta)}\int_{y=-\sqrt{\gamma}\cos(\theta)}^{\infty}\mathrm{e}^{-y^2}\,dy$$

$$= \frac{1}{2\pi}\mathrm{e}^{-\gamma} + \mathrm{e}^{-\gamma\sin^2(\theta)}\sqrt{\frac{\gamma}{\pi}}\cos(\theta)\left[1 - 0.5\,\text{erfc}\left(\sqrt{\gamma}\cos(\theta)\right)\right]. \tag{2.51}$$

Thus $P(c|\tilde{a}_0)$ can be found by substituting the above expression in (2.45). However, (2.45) cannot be integrated in a closed form and we need to resort to numerical integration as follows.

$$P(c|\tilde{a}_0) \approx \sum_{k=0}^{K} p(\theta_0 + k\Delta\theta|\tilde{a}_0)\,\Delta\theta \tag{2.52}$$

where

$$\theta_0 = -\frac{\pi}{M}$$

$$\Delta\theta = \frac{2\pi}{MK}. \tag{2.53}$$

Note that K must be chosen large enough so that $\Delta\theta$ is close to zero.

Due to symmetry of the decision regions

$$P(c|\tilde{a}_0) = P(c|\tilde{a}_i) \tag{2.54}$$

for any other symbol $\tilde{a}_i$ in the constellation. Since all symbols are equally likely, the average probability of correct decision is

$$P(c) = \frac{1}{M}\sum_{i=1}^{M} P(c|\tilde{a}_i) = P(c|\tilde{a}_0). \tag{2.55}$$

The average probability of error is

$$P(e) = 1 - P(c). \tag{2.56}$$

We have plotted the theoretical and simulated curves for 16-PSK in Figure 2.5.

In the next section, we discuss how the average transmit power, P_{av}, can be minimized for an M-ary constellation.

2.1.5 Constellations with minimum average power

Consider an M-ary constellation with the ith symbol denoted by $\tilde{a}_i$. Let the probability of $\tilde{a}_i$ be P_i. The average power of this constellation is given by

$$P_{\text{av}} = \sum_{i=1}^{M} |\tilde{a}_i|^2 \, P_i. \tag{2.57}$$

Consider now a translate of the original constellation, that is, all symbols in the constellation are shifted by a complex constant $\tilde{c}$. Note that the probability of symbol error remains unchanged due to the translation. The average power of the modified constellation is given by

$$\begin{aligned} P_{\text{av}} &= \sum_{i=1}^{M} |\tilde{a}_i - \tilde{c}|^2 \, P_i \\ &= \sum_{i=1}^{M} (\tilde{a}_i - \tilde{c}) \left(\tilde{a}_i^* - \tilde{c}^*\right) P_i. \end{aligned} \tag{2.58}$$

The statement of the problem is: Find out $\tilde{c}$ such that the average power is minimized. The problem is solved by differentiating with respect to $\tilde{c}$ (refer to Appendix A) and setting the result to zero. Thus we get

$$\begin{aligned} \sum_{i=1}^{M} \left(\tilde{a}_i^* - \tilde{c}^*\right) P_i &= 0 \\ \Rightarrow \tilde{c} &= \sum_{i=1}^{M} \tilde{a}_i P_i \\ \Rightarrow \tilde{c} &= E\left[\tilde{a}_i\right]. \end{aligned} \tag{2.59}$$

The above result implies that to minimize the transmit power, the constellation must be translated by an amount equal to the *mean value* of the constellation. This further implies that a constellation with zero mean value has the minimum transmit power.

In Sections 2.1.1 and 2.1.3, we had derived the probability of error for a two-dimensional constellation. In the next section we derive the probability of error for multidimensional orthogonal constellations.

2.1.6 Analysis for non-equiprobable symbols

The earlier sections dealt with the situation where the symbols were equiprobable, therefore the MAP detector reduces to an ML detector. Let us now consider the case where the symbols are non-equiprobable, due to which the MAP detector must be used. We refer back to Figure 2.1 with the additional constraint that the probability of $\tilde{a}_i$ is given by $P(a_i)$. Note that the probabilities of $\tilde{a}_1$ and $\tilde{a}_2$ need not add up to unity. In other words, $\tilde{a}_1$ and $\tilde{a}_2$ could be a part of a larger constellation. Let us now compute the pairwise error probabilities $P(\tilde{a}_1|\tilde{a}_2)$ and $P(\tilde{a}_2|\tilde{a}_1)$.

Using Bayes' rule, the MAP detector can be written as

$$\max_i \; p(\tilde{r}_n|\tilde{a}_i)P(\tilde{a}_i). \tag{2.60}$$

Substituting for the conditional pdf in (2.60), we get

$$\begin{aligned}&\max_i \frac{1}{2\pi\sigma_w^2}\exp\left(-\frac{|\tilde{r}_n-\tilde{a}_i|^2}{2\sigma_w^2}\right)P(\tilde{a}_i)\\ &\Rightarrow \max_i \exp\left(-\frac{|\tilde{r}_n-\tilde{a}_i|^2}{2\sigma_w^2}\right)P(\tilde{a}_i).\end{aligned} \tag{2.61}$$

The MAP detector decides in favour of $\tilde{a}_2$ given that $\tilde{a}_1$ was transmitted when

$$\begin{aligned}&\exp\left(-\frac{|\tilde{r}_n-\tilde{a}_1|^2}{2\sigma_w^2}\right)P(\tilde{a}_1) < \exp\left(-\frac{|\tilde{r}_n-\tilde{a}_2|^2}{2\sigma_w^2}\right)P(\tilde{a}_2)\\ &\Rightarrow |\tilde{r}_n-\tilde{a}_2|^2 - |\tilde{r}_n-\tilde{a}_1|^2 < \mathcal{T}\end{aligned} \tag{2.62}$$

where

$$\mathcal{T} = 2\sigma_w^2 \ln\left(\frac{P(\tilde{a}_2)}{P(\tilde{a}_1)}\right). \tag{2.63}$$

If $\tilde{a}_1$ was transmitted

$$\tilde{r}_n = \tilde{a}_1 + \tilde{w}_n. \tag{2.64}$$

Substituting (2.64) in (2.65) we get

$$\begin{aligned}&|\tilde{d}+\tilde{w}_n|^2 - |\tilde{w}_n|^2 < \mathcal{T}\\ &\Rightarrow Z < \mathcal{T} - |\tilde{d}|^2\end{aligned} \tag{2.65}$$

where $\tilde{d}$ and Z are defined by (2.17) and (2.18) respectively. The mean and variance of Z are given by (2.19). Assuming that

$$\mathcal{T} - |\tilde{d}|^2 < 0 \tag{2.66}$$

we get

$$P(\tilde{a}_2|\tilde{a}_1) = P(Z < \mathscr{T} - |\tilde{d}|^2)$$
$$= \frac{1}{2}\text{erfc}\left(\sqrt{\frac{(|\tilde{d}|^2 - \mathscr{T})^2}{8|\tilde{d}|^2\,\sigma_w^2}}\right). \tag{2.67}$$

Observe that

$$\mathscr{T} - |\tilde{d}|^2 > 0$$
$$\Rightarrow P(\tilde{a}_2|\tilde{a}_1) > 0.5 \tag{2.68}$$

which does not make sense.

It can be similarly shown that when

$$\mathscr{T} + |\tilde{d}|^2 > 0 \tag{2.69}$$

we get the pairwise probability as

$$P(\tilde{a}_1|\tilde{a}_2) = P(Z > \mathscr{T} + |\tilde{d}|^2)$$
$$= \frac{1}{2}\text{erfc}\left(\sqrt{\frac{(|\tilde{d}|^2 + \mathscr{T})^2}{8|\tilde{d}|^2\,\sigma_w^2}}\right). \tag{2.70}$$

Again,

$$\mathscr{T} + |\tilde{d}|^2 < 0$$
$$\Rightarrow P(\tilde{a}_1|\tilde{a}_2) > 0.5 \tag{2.71}$$

which does not make sense. The average probability of error can be written as

$$P(e) = \sum_{i=1}^{M} P(e|\tilde{a}_i)P(\tilde{a}_i) \tag{2.72}$$

where the probability of error given $\tilde{a}_i$ is given by the union bound

$$P(e|\tilde{a}_i) \le \sum_{\tilde{a}_i \in \mathscr{G}_i} P(\tilde{a}_j|\tilde{a}_i) \tag{2.73}$$

where $\mathscr{G}_i$ denotes the set of symbols closest to $\tilde{a}_i$.

2.2 Coherent Detectors for Multidimensional Orthogonal Constellations

In this section we deal with M-dimensional (vector) constellations. Note that

$$M = 2^{\kappa} \tag{2.74}$$

where κ denotes the number of bits per symbol. The ith symbol in an M-dimensional orthogonal constellation is represented by an $M \times 1$ vector

$$\tilde{\mathbf{a}}_i = \begin{bmatrix} 0 \\ 0 \\ \vdots \\ \tilde{a}_{i,\,i} \\ \vdots \\ 0 \end{bmatrix} \qquad \text{for } 1 \le i \le M. \tag{2.75}$$

The following relationship holds:

$$\tilde{\mathbf{a}}_i^H \tilde{\mathbf{a}}_j = \begin{cases} 0 & \text{for } i \neq j \\ \left|\tilde{a}_{i,\,i}\right|^2 = C & \text{(a constant) for } i = j. \end{cases} \tag{2.76}$$

The superscript H in the above equation denotes conjugate transpose.

The received vector can be represented as

$$\tilde{\mathbf{r}}_n = \mathbf{S}_n^{(i)} + \tilde{\mathbf{w}}_n \tag{2.77}$$

where

$$\mathbf{S}_n^{(i)} = \tilde{\mathbf{a}}_i \tag{2.78}$$

and

$$\tilde{\mathbf{w}}_n = \begin{bmatrix} \tilde{w}_{n,\,1} \\ \vdots \\ \tilde{w}_{n,\,M} \end{bmatrix} \tag{2.79}$$

denotes the noise vector. The elements of $\tilde{\mathbf{w}}_n$ are uncorrelated, that is

$$\frac{1}{2} E\left[\tilde{w}_{n,\,i} \tilde{w}_{n,\,j}^*\right] = \begin{cases} \sigma_w^2 & \text{for } i = j \\ 0 & \text{otherwise.} \end{cases} \tag{2.80}$$

Once again, the optimum (MAP) detector maximizes the probability:

$$\max_i P(\tilde{\mathbf{a}}_i|\tilde{\mathbf{r}}_n) \tag{2.81}$$

which reduces to the ML detector which maximizes the joint conditional pdf (when all symbols are equally likely)

$$\max_i p(\tilde{\mathbf{r}}_n|\tilde{\mathbf{a}}_i). \tag{2.82}$$

Substituting the expression for the conditional pdf[19,20] we get

$$\max_i \frac{1}{(2\pi)^M \det(\tilde{\mathbf{R}}_{\tilde{w}\tilde{w}})} \exp\left(-\frac{1}{2}\left(\tilde{\mathbf{r}}_n - \tilde{\mathbf{a}}_i\right)^H \tilde{\mathbf{R}}_{\tilde{w}\tilde{w}}^{-1}\left(\tilde{\mathbf{r}}_n - \tilde{\mathbf{a}}_i\right)\right) \tag{2.83}$$

where $\tilde{\mathbf{R}}_{\tilde{w}\tilde{w}}$ denotes the $M \times M$ conditional covariance matrix (given that symbol $\tilde{a}_i$ was transmitted)

$$\begin{aligned}\tilde{\mathbf{R}}_{\tilde{w}\tilde{w}} &\stackrel{\Delta}{=} \frac{1}{2}E\left[\left(\tilde{\mathbf{r}}_n - \tilde{\mathbf{a}}_i\right)\left(\tilde{\mathbf{r}}_n - \tilde{\mathbf{a}}_i\right)^H\right] = \frac{1}{2}E\left[\tilde{\mathbf{w}}_n\tilde{\mathbf{w}}_n^H\right] \\ &= \sigma_w^2 \mathbf{I}_M\end{aligned} \tag{2.84}$$

where $\mathbf{I}_M$ is an $M \times M$ identity matrix. The maximization in (2.83) can be simplified to

$$\max_i \frac{1}{\left(2\pi\sigma_w^2\right)^M} \exp\left(-\frac{\sum_{l=1}^{M}\left|\tilde{r}_{n,\,l} - \tilde{a}_{i,\,l}\right|^2}{2\sigma_w^2}\right) \tag{2.85}$$

where $\tilde{a}_{i,\,l}$ denotes the lth element of symbol $\tilde{\mathbf{a}}_i$.

Taking the natural logarithm of the above equation and ignoring the constants we get

$$\min_i \sum_{l=1}^{M}\left|\tilde{r}_{n,\,l} - \tilde{a}_{i,\,l}\right|^2. \tag{2.86}$$

Observe that the above expression for the ML detector is valid irrespective of whether the symbols are orthogonal to each other or not. We have not even assumed that the symbols have constant energy. In fact, if we assume that the symbols are orthogonal and have constant energy, the detection rule in (2.86) reduces to

$$\max_i \Re\left\{\tilde{r}_{n,\,i}\tilde{a}_{i,\,i}^*\right\}. \tag{2.87}$$

If we further assume that all samples are real-valued and $\tilde{a}_{i,\,i}$ is positive, then the above detection rule becomes

$$\max_i r_{n,\,i}. \tag{2.88}$$

In the next section, we present the performance analysis of multidimensional orthogonal signalling, where we explicitly assume that the symbols are orthogonal and have constant energy.

2.2.1 Performance analysis

Given that the ith symbol was transmitted, the ML detector decides in favour of the jth $(1 \le i,\ j \le M)$ symbol when

$$\sum_{l=1}^{M} \left|\tilde{r}_{n,\,l} - \tilde{a}_{j,\,l}\right|^2 < \sum_{l=1}^{M} \left|\tilde{r}_{n,\,l} - \tilde{a}_{i,\,l}\right|^2$$

$$\Rightarrow \sum_{l=1}^{M} \left|\tilde{e}_{i,\,j,\,l} + \tilde{w}_{n,\,l}\right|^2 < \sum_{l=1}^{M} \left|\tilde{w}_{n,\,l}\right|^2 \tag{2.89}$$

where

$$\tilde{e}_{i,\,j,\,l} = \tilde{a}_{i,\,l} - \tilde{a}_{j,\,l} \tag{2.90}$$

is an element of the $M \times 1$ vector

$$\tilde{\mathbf{e}}_{i,\,j} = \tilde{\mathbf{a}}_i - \tilde{\mathbf{a}}_j. \tag{2.91}$$

The inequality in (2.89) can be simplified to (due to orthogonality between symbols)

$$2C + 2\Re\left\{\tilde{a}_{i,\,i}^{*}\tilde{w}_{n,\,i} - \tilde{a}_{j,\,j}^{*}\tilde{w}_{n,\,j}\right\} < 0, \tag{2.92}$$

where C is defined in (2.76).

Let

$$\begin{aligned} Z &= 2\Re\left\{\tilde{a}_{i,\,i}^{*}\tilde{w}_{n,\,i} - \tilde{a}_{j,\,j}^{*}\tilde{w}_{n,\,j}\right\} \\ &= 2\left(a_{i,\,i,\,I}w_{n,\,i,\,I} + a_{i,\,i,\,Q}w_{n,\,i,\,Q} - a_{j,\,j,\,I}w_{n,\,j,\,I} - a_{j,\,j,\,Q}w_{n,\,j,\,Q}\right). \end{aligned} \tag{2.93}$$

It is clear that Z is a real Gaussian random variable with mean and variance given by

$$\begin{aligned} E[Z] &= 0 \\ E\left[Z^2\right] &= 8C\sigma_w^2. \end{aligned} \tag{2.94}$$

Thus the required probability of error is given by

$$\begin{aligned} P(Z < -2C) &= \int_{Z=-\infty}^{-2C} \frac{1}{\sigma_Z\sqrt{2\pi}} \exp\left(-\frac{Z^2}{2\sigma_Z^2}\right) \\ &= \frac{1}{2}\operatorname{erfc}\left(\sqrt{\frac{2C}{8\sigma_w^2}}\right). \end{aligned} \tag{2.95}$$

Note that $2C$ is the squared Euclidean distance between symbols $\tilde{\mathbf{a}}_i$ and $\tilde{\mathbf{a}}_j$, that is

$$\tilde{\mathbf{e}}_{i,j}^H \tilde{\mathbf{e}}_{i,j} = 2C. \tag{2.96}$$

Thus, we once again conclude from (2.95) that the probability of error depends on the squared distance between the two symbols and the noise variance. In fact, (2.95) is *exactly* identical to (2.20).

We now compute the average probability of symbol error for M-ary multidimensional orthogonal signalling. It is clear that each symbol has got $M-1$ nearest neighbours at a squared distance equal to $2C$. Hence, using (2.28) we get

$$P(e) \leq \frac{M-1}{2} \operatorname{erfc}\left(\sqrt{\frac{2C}{8\sigma_w^2}}\right). \tag{2.97}$$

The performance of various multidimensional modulation schemes is shown in Figure 2.7. When all the symbols are equally likely, the average transmit power is given by (2.76), that is

$$P_{\text{av}} = \frac{1}{M}\sum_{i=1}^{M} \tilde{\mathbf{a}}_i^H \tilde{\mathbf{a}}_i = C. \tag{2.98}$$

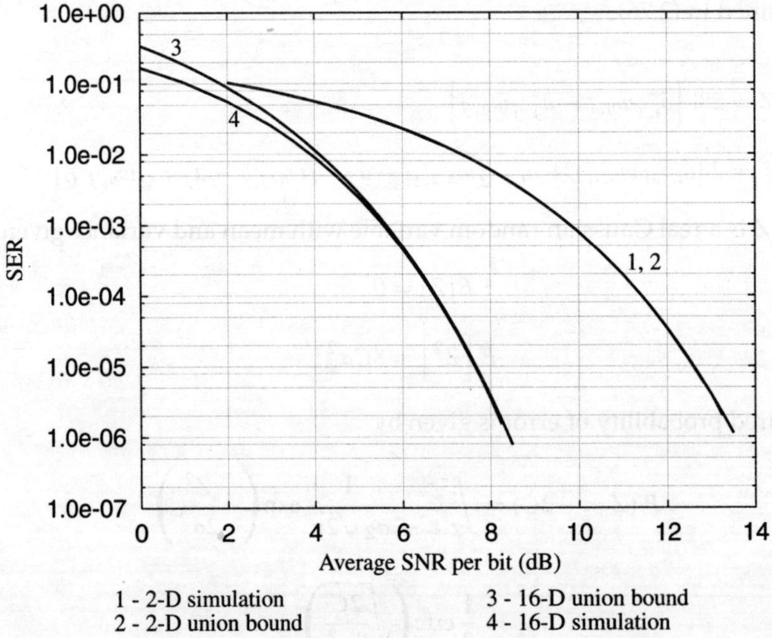

Figure 2.7 *Performance of coherent detectors for various multidimensional constellations*

The average SNR is defined as

$$\text{SNR}_{\text{av}} = \frac{P_{\text{av}}}{2\sigma_w^2} \tag{2.99}$$

which is exactly identical to (2.30) for the two-dimensional case. The average SNR per bit is also the same as that for the two-dimensional case, and is given by (2.31). With the above definitions we are now ready to compute the minimum SNR per bit required to achieve arbitrarily low probability of error for M-ary orthogonal signalling.

2.2.2 Union bound on the probability of error for multi-D constellations

We begin by making use of the Chernoff bound (see Appendix B)

$$\frac{1}{2}\,\text{erfc}\,(y) \le \exp\left(-y^2\right). \tag{2.100}$$

The average probability of error in (2.97) can now be approximated as

$$\begin{aligned} P(e) &\le (M-1)\exp\left(-\frac{2C}{8\sigma_w^2}\right) \\ &< M\exp\left(-\frac{2C}{8\sigma_w^2}\right) \\ &= 2^{\kappa}\exp\left(-\frac{2C}{8\sigma_w^2}\right) \\ &= \exp\left(\kappa\ \ln(2) - \frac{\kappa\ \text{SNR}_{\text{av},\,b}}{2}\right). \end{aligned} \tag{2.101}$$

From the above equation it is clear that as $\kappa \to \infty$ (number of bits per symbol tends to infinity), the average probability of symbol error goes to zero provided

$$\ln(2) < \frac{\text{SNR}_{\text{av},\,b}}{2}. \tag{2.102}$$

Equation (2.102) implies that as long as the SNR per bit is greater than 1.42 dB, the probability of error tends to zero as κ tends to infinity. However, this bound on the SNR is not very tight. In the next section we derive a tighter bound on the minimum SNR required for error-free signalling as $\kappa \to \infty$.

2.2.3 Minimum SNR required for error-free transmission

We begin this section by first deriving an *exact* expression for the probability of correct decision, given that the ith symbol of the M-ary orthogonal constellation has been transmitted. For ease of analysis, we consider only real-valued signals in this section. Let the received signal be denoted by

$$\mathbf{r}_n = \mathbf{S}_n^{(i)} + \mathbf{w}_n \tag{2.103}$$

where

$$\mathbf{r}_n = \begin{bmatrix} r_{n,1} \\ r_{n,2} \\ \vdots \\ r_{n,M} \end{bmatrix}; \quad \mathbf{S}_n^{(i)} = \mathbf{a}_i = \begin{bmatrix} 0 \\ 0 \\ \vdots \\ a_{i,i} \\ \vdots \\ 0 \end{bmatrix} \quad \text{for } 1 \le i \le M \tag{2.104}$$

and

$$\mathbf{w}_n = \begin{bmatrix} w_{n,1} \\ \vdots \\ w_{n,M} \end{bmatrix}. \tag{2.105}$$

Once again, we assume that the elements of $\mathbf{w}_n$ are uncorrelated, that is

$$E\left[w_{n,i} w_{n,j}\right] = \begin{cases} \sigma_w^2 & \text{for } i = j \\ 0 & \text{otherwise.} \end{cases} \tag{2.106}$$

Comparing the above equation with (2.80), we notice that the factor of 1/2 has been eliminated. This is because, the elements of $\mathbf{w}_n$ are *real*.

The exact expression for the probability of correct decision is given by

$$\begin{aligned} P(c|\mathbf{a}_i) = \int_{r_{n,i}=-\infty}^{\infty} & P\left(\left(w_{n,1} < r_{n,i}\right) \text{ AND } \ldots \left(w_{n,i-1} < r_{n,i}\right) \text{ AND}\right. \\ & \left.\left(w_{n,i+1} < r_{n,i}\right) \text{ AND } \ldots \left(w_{n,M} < r_{n,i}\right)\right| r_{n,i},\, a_{i,i}\right) p(r_{n,i}|a_{i,i})\, dr_{n,i}. \end{aligned} \tag{2.107}$$

For convenience, let

$$\begin{aligned} r_{n,i} &= y \\ a_{i,i} &= y_0. \end{aligned} \tag{2.108}$$

We also observe that since the elements of $\mathbf{w}_n$ are uncorrelated, the probability inside the integral in (2.107) is just the product of the individual probabilities. Hence using the notation in equation (2.108), (2.107) can be reduced to

$$P(c|\mathbf{a}_i) = \int_{y=-\infty}^{\infty} \left(P\left(w_{n,1} < y\right| y,\, y_0)\right)^{M-1} p(y|y_0)\, dy. \tag{2.109}$$

Solving the above equation, we get (assuming $y > 0$)

$$\begin{aligned} P\left(w_{n,1} < y \middle| y, y_0\right) &= \frac{1}{\sigma_w\sqrt{2\pi}}\int_{w_{n,1}=-\infty}^{y} \exp\left(-\frac{w_{n,1}^2}{2\sigma_w^2}\right) \\ &= 1 - \frac{1}{2}\operatorname{erfc}\left(\frac{y}{\sigma_w\sqrt{2}}\right). \end{aligned} \tag{2.110}$$

Note that for $y < 0$ in the above equation, we can make use of the relation

$$\operatorname{erfc}(y) = 2 - \operatorname{erfc}(-y). \tag{2.111}$$

Let us make the substitution:

$$z = \frac{y}{\sigma_w\sqrt{2}}. \tag{2.112}$$

Hence (2.110) becomes

$$P\left(w_{n,1} < y \middle| y, y_0\right) = 1 - \frac{1}{2}\operatorname{erfc}(z). \tag{2.113}$$

From (2.112) it is clear that z is a real Gaussian random variable with conditional mean and variance given by

$$\begin{aligned} E[z|y_0] &= E\left[\frac{y}{\sigma_w\sqrt{2}}\right] \\ &= E\left[\frac{y_0 + w_{n,i}}{\sigma_w\sqrt{2}}\right] \\ &= \frac{y_0}{\sigma_w\sqrt{2}} \\ &= m_z \qquad \text{(say).} \\ E\left[(z-m_z)^2 \,|y_0\right] &= \frac{1}{2} \\ &= \sigma_z^2 \qquad \text{(say).} \end{aligned} \tag{2.114}$$

Next, we observe that $p(y|y_0)$ in (2.109) is given by

$$\begin{aligned} p(y|y_0) &= \frac{1}{\sigma_w\sqrt{2\pi}}\exp\left(-\frac{(y-y_0)^2}{2\sigma_w^2}\right) \\ \Rightarrow p(z|y_0) &= \frac{1}{\sigma_z\sqrt{2\pi}}\exp\left(-\frac{(z-m_z)^2}{2\sigma_z^2}\right). \end{aligned} \tag{2.115}$$

Now, substituting (2.112) and (2.115) in (2.109), we get

$$P\left(c|\mathbf{a}_i\right) = \frac{1}{\sigma_Z\sqrt{2\pi}}\int_{z=-\infty}^{\infty}\left(1-\frac{1}{2}\operatorname{erfc}(z)\right)^{M-1}\exp\left(-\frac{(z-m_Z)^2}{2\sigma_Z^2}\right)dz. \tag{2.116}$$

The probability of error given that $\mathbf{a}_i$ has been transmitted is given by

$$P\left(e|\mathbf{a}_i\right) = 1-P(c|\mathbf{a}_i) = \frac{1}{\sigma_Z\sqrt{2\pi}}\int_{z=-\infty}^{\infty}\left(1-\left(1-\frac{1}{2}\operatorname{erfc}(z)\right)^{M-1}\right)\exp\left(-\frac{(z-m_Z)^2}{2\sigma_Z^2}\right)dz. \tag{2.117}$$

It is clear that the above integral cannot be solved in closed form, and some approximations need to be made. We observe that

$$\begin{aligned}
\lim_{z\to-\infty} 1-\left(1-\frac{1}{2}\operatorname{erfc}(z)\right)^{M-1} &= 1 \\
\lim_{z\to\infty} 1-\left(1-\frac{1}{2}\operatorname{erfc}(z)\right)^{M-1} &= \frac{(M-1)}{2}\operatorname{erfc}(z) \\
&\leq (M-1)\exp\left(-z^2\right) \\
&< M\exp\left(-z^2\right).
\end{aligned} \tag{2.118}$$

Notice that we have used the Chernoff bound in the second limit. It is clear from the above equation that the term on the left-hand-side *decreases monotonically* from 1 to 0 as z changes from $-\infty$ to ∞. This is illustrated in Figure 2.8, where the various functions plotted are:

$$\begin{aligned}
f_1(z) &= 1 \\
f_2(z) &= 1-\left(1-\frac{1}{2}\operatorname{erfc}(z)\right)^{M-1} \\
f_3(z) &= M\exp\left(-z^2\right).
\end{aligned} \tag{2.119}$$

We will now make use of the first limit in (2.118) for the interval $(-\infty, z_0]$ and the second limit in (2.118) for the interval $[z_0, \infty)$, for some value of z_0 that needs to be optimized. Note that since

$$\begin{aligned}
& f_1(z) > f_2(z) \qquad \text{for } -\infty < z < \infty \\
\text{and} \quad & f_3(z) > f_2(z) \qquad \text{for } z_0 < z < \infty
\end{aligned} \tag{2.120}$$

$P\left(e|\mathbf{a}_i\right)$ (computed using $f_2(z)$) is *less* than the probability of error computed using $f_1(z)$ and $f_3(z)$. Hence, the optimized value of z_0 yields the *minimum* value of the probability of error

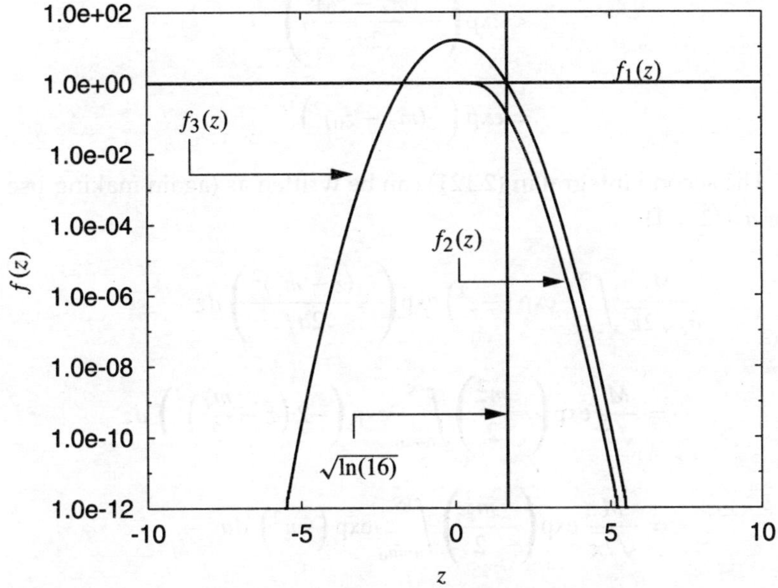

Figure 2.8 *Plots of various functions described in (2.119) for $M = 16$*

that is computed using $f_1(z)$ and $f_3(z)$. To find out the optimum value of z_0, we substitute $f_1(z)$ and $f_2(z)$ in (2.117) to obtain

$$P(e|\mathbf{a}_i) < \frac{1}{\sigma_z\sqrt{2\pi}}\int_{z=-\infty}^{z_0}\exp\left(-\frac{(z-m_z)^2}{2\sigma_z^2}\right)dz$$

$$+\frac{M}{\sigma_z\sqrt{2\pi}}\int_{z=z_0}^{\infty}\exp\left(-z^2\right)\exp\left(-\frac{(z-m_z)^2}{2\sigma_z^2}\right)dz. \tag{2.121}$$

Next, we differentiate the above equation with respect to z_0 and set the result to zero. This results in

$$1 - M\exp\left(-z_0^2\right) = 0$$

$$\Rightarrow z_0 = \sqrt{\ln(M)}. \tag{2.122}$$

We now proceed to solve (2.121). The first integral can be written as (for $z_0 < m_z$)

$$\frac{1}{\sigma_z\sqrt{2\pi}}\int_{z=-\infty}^{z_0}\exp\left(-\frac{(z-m_z)^2}{2\sigma_z^2}\right)dz = \frac{1}{\sqrt{\pi}}\int_{z=-\infty}^{(z_0-m_z)/(\sigma_z\sqrt{2})}\exp\left(-x^2\right)dx$$

$$= \frac{1}{2}\operatorname{erfc}\left(\frac{m_z - z_0}{\sigma_z\sqrt{2}}\right)$$

$$
\begin{aligned}
&< \exp\left(-\frac{(m_z - z_0)^2}{2\sigma_z^2}\right) \\
&= \exp\left(-(m_z - z_0)^2\right)
\end{aligned} \tag{2.123}
$$

since $2\sigma_z^2 = 1$. The second integral in (2.121) can be written as (again making use of the fact that $2\sigma_z^2 = 1$ or $\sigma_z\sqrt{2} = 1$)

$$
\begin{aligned}
&\frac{M}{\sigma_z\sqrt{2\pi}} \int_{z=z_0}^{\infty} \exp\left(-z^2\right) \exp\left(-\frac{(z-m_z)^2}{2\sigma_z^2}\right) dz \\
&= \frac{M}{\sqrt{\pi}} \exp\left(-\frac{m_z^2}{2}\right) \int_{z=z_0}^{\infty} \exp\left(-2\left(z - \frac{m_z}{2}\right)^2\right) dz \\
&= \frac{M}{\sqrt{2\pi}} \exp\left(-\frac{m_z^2}{2}\right) \int_{u=u_0}^{\infty} \exp\left(-u^2\right) du \\
&= I \qquad \text{(say).}
\end{aligned} \tag{2.124}
$$

In the above equation, u_0 is defined as

$$
u_0 \stackrel{\Delta}{=} \sqrt{2}\left(z_0 - \frac{m_z}{2}\right). \tag{2.125}
$$

Now, the term I in (2.124) depends on whether u_0 is positive or negative. When u_0 is positive ($z_0 > m_z/2$), we get

$$
\begin{aligned}
I &= \frac{M}{\sqrt{2}} \exp\left(-m_z^2/2\right) \frac{1}{2} \operatorname{erfc}(u_0) \\
&< \frac{M}{\sqrt{2}} \exp\left(-m_z^2/2\right) \exp\left(-u_0^2\right).
\end{aligned} \tag{2.126}
$$

When u_0 is negative ($z_0 < m_z/2$), we get

$$
\begin{aligned}
I &= \frac{M}{\sqrt{2}} \exp\left(-m_z^2/2\right) \left[1 - \frac{1}{2} \operatorname{erfc}(-u_0)\right] \\
&< \frac{M}{\sqrt{2}} \exp\left(-m_z^2/2\right).
\end{aligned} \tag{2.127}
$$

Using (2.123), (2.126) and (2.127), the probability $P(e|\mathbf{a}_i)$ can be written as

$$
P(e|\mathbf{a}_i) < \begin{cases} \mathrm{e}^{-(m_z - z_0)^2} + \frac{M}{\sqrt{2}} \mathrm{e}^{-(m_z^2/2 + 2(z_0 - m_z/2)^2)} & \text{for } m_z/2 < z_0 < m_z \\ \mathrm{e}^{-(m_z - z_0)^2} + \frac{M}{\sqrt{2}} \mathrm{e}^{-m_z^2/2} & \text{for } z_0 < m_z/2. \end{cases} \tag{2.128}
$$

We now make use of the fact that $M = 2^{\kappa}$ and the relation in (2.122) to obtain

$$M = e^{z_0^2}. \tag{2.129}$$

We substitute the above relation in (2.128) to obtain

$$P(e|\mathbf{a}_i) < \begin{cases} e^{-(m_z - z_0)^2}\left(1 + \frac{1}{\sqrt{2}}\right) & \text{for } m_z/2 < z_0 < m_z \\ \frac{e^{(z_0^2 - m_z^2/2)}}{\sqrt{2}}\left(1 + \sqrt{2}e^{-2(z_0 - m_z/2)^2}\right) & \text{for } z_0 < m_z/2. \end{cases} \tag{2.130}$$

Next, we observe that

$$\text{SNR}_{\text{av}} = \frac{P_{\text{av}}}{2\sigma_w^2} = \frac{y_0^2}{2\sigma_w^2} = m_z^2.$$

$$\text{SNR}_{\text{av},\,b} = \frac{m_z^2}{\kappa}.$$

$$z_0^2 = \kappa \ln(2). \tag{2.131}$$

Substituting for m_z^2 and z_0^2 from the above equation in (2.130), we get for $m_z/2 < z_0 < m_z$ (which corresponds to the interval $\ln(2) < \text{SNR}_{\text{av},\,b} < 4\ln(2)$)

$$P(e|\mathbf{a}_i) < e^{-\left(\sqrt{\kappa \text{SNR}_{\text{av},\,b}} - \sqrt{\kappa \ln(2)}\right)^2}\left(1 + \frac{1}{\sqrt{2}}\right). \tag{2.132}$$

From the above equation it is clear that if

$$\text{SNR}_{\text{av},\,b} > \ln(2), \tag{2.133}$$

the average probability of symbol error tends to zero as $\kappa \to \infty$. This minimum SNR per bit required for error-free transmission is called the Shannon limit.

For $z_0 < m_z/2$ (which corresponds to $\text{SNR}_{\text{av},\,b} > 4\ln(2)$), (2.130) becomes

$$P(e|\mathbf{a}_i) < \frac{e^{(\kappa \ln(2) - \kappa \text{SNR}_{\text{av},\,b}/2)}}{\sqrt{2}}\left(1 + \sqrt{2}e^{-2\left(\sqrt{\kappa \ln(2)} - \sqrt{\kappa \text{SNR}_{\text{av},\,b}/2}\right)^2}\right). \tag{2.134}$$

Thus, for $\text{SNR}_{\text{av},\,b} > 4\ln(2)$, the bound on the SNR per bit for error free transmission is

$$\text{SNR}_{\text{av},\,b} > 2\ln(2), \tag{2.135}$$

which is also the bound derived in the earlier section. It is easy to show that when $z_0 > m_z$ in (2.123) (which corresponds to $\text{SNR}_{\text{av},\,b} < \ln(2)$), the average probability of error tends to one as $\kappa \to \infty$.

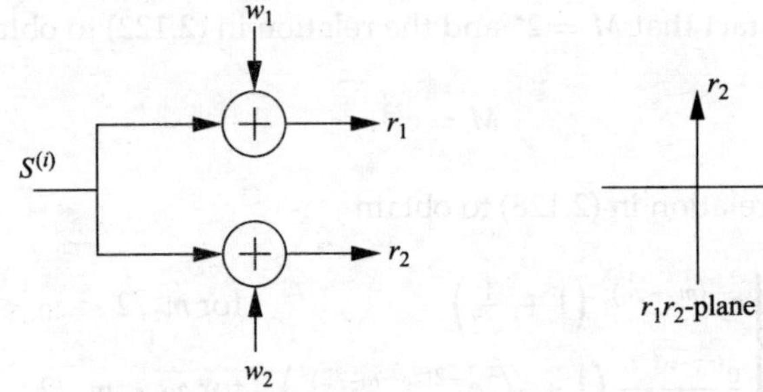

Figure 2.9 *Block diagram of a communication system*

Example 2.2.1 Consider the communication system shown in Figure 2.9[15]. For convenience of representation, the time index n has been dropped. The symbols $S^{(i)}$, $i = 1, 2$, are taken from the constellation $\{\pm A\}$, and are equally likely. The noise variables w_1 and w_2 are statistically independent with pdf

$$p_{w_1}(\alpha) = p_{w_2}(\alpha) = \frac{1}{4}\mathrm{e}^{-|\alpha|/2} \qquad \text{for } -\infty < \alpha < \infty. \tag{2.136}$$

1. Derive the ML detection rule and reduce it to the simplest form.
2. Find the decision region for each of the symbols in the r_1r_2-plane.

Solution: Observe that all variables in this problem are real-valued, hence we have not used the tilde. Though the constellation used in this example is BPSK, we are dealing with a vector receiver, hence we need to use the concepts developed in section 2.2. Note that

$$\mathbf{r} = \begin{bmatrix} r_1 \\ r_2 \end{bmatrix} = \begin{bmatrix} S^{(i)} + w_1 \\ S^{(i)} + w_2 \end{bmatrix}. \tag{2.137}$$

Since w_1 and w_2 are independent of each other, the joint conditional pdf $p(\mathbf{r}|S^{(i)})$ is equal to the product of the marginal conditional pdfs $p(r_1|S(i))$ and $p(r_2|S^{(i)})$ and is given by (see also (2.85))

$$p\left(\mathbf{r}|S^{(i)}\right) = p\left(r_1, r_2|S^{(i)}\right) = \frac{1}{16}\exp\left(-\frac{|r_1 - S^{(i)}| + |r_2 - S^{(i)}|}{2}\right). \tag{2.138}$$

The ML detection rule is given by

$$\max_i p\left(\mathbf{r}|S^{(i)}\right) \tag{2.139}$$

which simplifies to

$$\min_i |r_1 - S^{(i)}| + |r_2 - S^{(i)}| \qquad \text{for } i = 1, 2. \tag{2.140}$$

Therefore, the receiver decides in favour of $+A$ if:

$$|r_1 - A| + |r_2 - A| < |r_1 + A| + |r_2 + A|. \tag{2.141}$$

Note that if

$$|r_1 - A| + |r_2 - A| = |r_1 + A| + |r_2 + A| \tag{2.142}$$

then the receiver can decide in favour of either $+A$ or $-A$.

In order to arrive at the decision regions for $+A$ and $-A$, we note that both r_1 and r_2 can be divided into three distinct intervals:

1. $r_1, r_2 \geq A$
2. $-A \leq r_1, r_2 < A$
3. $r_1, r_2 < -A$.

Since r_1 and r_2 are independent, there are nine possibilities. Let us study each of these cases.

1. Let $r_1 \geq A$ AND $r_2 \geq A$.
   This implies that the receiver decides in favour of $+A$ if
   $$\begin{aligned} r_1 - A + r_2 - A &< r_1 + A + r_2 + A \\ \Rightarrow -2A &< 2A \end{aligned} \tag{2.143}$$
   which is consistent. Hence $r_1 \geq A$ AND $r_2 \geq A$ corresponds to the decision region for $+A$.
2. Let $r_1 \geq A$ AND $-A \leq r_2 < A$.
   This implies that the receiver decides in favour of $+A$ if
   $$\begin{aligned} r_1 - A - r_2 + A &< r_1 + A + r_2 + A \\ \Rightarrow r_2 &> -A \end{aligned} \tag{2.144}$$
   which is consistent. Hence $r_1 \geq A$ AND $-A \leq r_2 < A$ corresponds to the decision region for $+A$.
3. Let $r_1 \geq A$ AND $r_2 < -A$.
   This implies that the receiver decides in favour of $+A$ if
   $$\begin{aligned} r_1 - A - r_2 + A &< r_1 + A - r_2 - A \\ \Rightarrow 0 &< 0 \end{aligned} \tag{2.145}$$
   which is inconsistent. Moreover, since LHS is equal to RHS, $r_1 \geq A$ AND $r_2 < -A$ corresponds to the decision region for both $+A$ and $-A$.
4. Let $-A \leq r_1 < A$ AND $r_2 \geq A$.
   This implies that the receiver decides in favour of $+A$ if
   $$\begin{aligned} -r_1 + A + r_2 - A &< r_1 + A + r_2 + A \\ \Rightarrow r_1 &> -A \end{aligned} \tag{2.146}$$
   which is consistent. Therefore $-A \leq r_1 < A$ AND $r_2 \geq A$ corresponds to the decision region for $+A$.

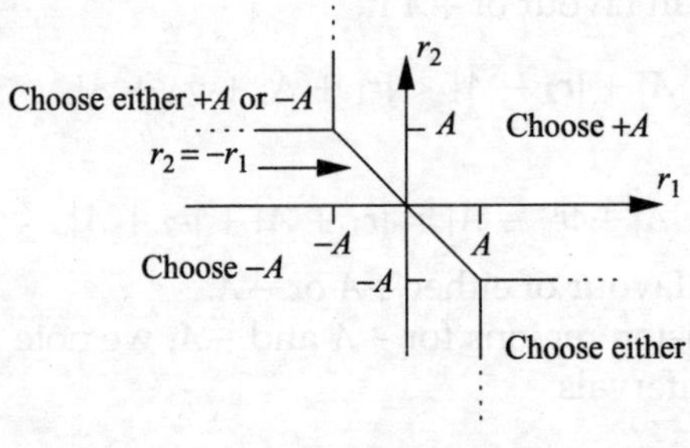

Figure 2.10 *Decision regions for Figure 2.9*

5. Let $-A \leq r_1 < A$ AND $-A \leq r_2 < A$.
This implies that the receiver decides in favour of $+A$ if

$$\begin{aligned} -r_1 + A - r_2 + A &< r_1 + A + r_2 + A \\ \Rightarrow r_1 + r_2 &> 0 \end{aligned} \tag{2.147}$$

which is consistent. This decision region lies above the line $r_2 = -r_1$ in Figure 2.10.
6. Let $-A \leq r_1 < A$ AND $r_2 < -A$.
This implies that the receiver decides in favour of $+A$ if

$$\begin{aligned} -r_1 + A - r_2 + A &< r_1 + A - r_2 - A \\ \Rightarrow r_1 &> A \end{aligned} \tag{2.148}$$

which is inconsistent. Therefore $-A \leq r_1 < A$ AND $r_2 < -A$ corresponds to the decision region for $-A$.
7. Let $r_1 < -A$ AND $r_2 \geq A$.
This implies that the receiver decides in favour of $+A$ if

$$\begin{aligned} -r_1 + A + r_2 - A &< -r_1 - A + r_2 + A \\ \Rightarrow 0 &< 0 \end{aligned} \tag{2.149}$$

which is inconsistent. Moreover, since LHS is equal to RHS, $r_1 < -A$ AND $r_2 \geq A$ corresponds to the decision region for both $+A$ and $-A$.
8. Let $r_1 < -A$ AND $-A \leq r_2 < A$.
This implies that the receiver decides in favour of $+A$ if

$$\begin{aligned} -r_1 + A - r_2 + A &< -r_1 - A + r_2 + A \\ \Rightarrow r_2 &> A \end{aligned} \tag{2.150}$$

which is inconsistent. Hence $r_1 < -A$ AND $-A \leq r_2 < A$ corresponds to the decision region for $-A$.

9. Let $r_1 < -A$ AND $r_2 < -A$.
This implies that the receiver decides in favour of $+A$ if

$$\begin{aligned} -r_1 + A - r_2 + A &< -r_1 - A - r_2 - A \\ \Rightarrow 2A &< -2A \end{aligned} \tag{2.151}$$

which is inconsistent. Hence $r_1 < -A$ AND $r_2 < -A$ corresponds to the decision region for $-A$.
The decision regions for $+A$ and $-A$ are summarized in Figure 2.10.

2.2.4 Binary antipodal and orthogonal constellations

Let us now compare the transmit power for binary antipodal signalling with binary orthogonal signalling, assuming that the minimum squared Euclidean distance is the same in both cases, that is,

$$\left|\tilde{d}\right|^2 \text{ in equation (2.20)} = 2C \text{ in equation (2.95).} \tag{2.152}$$

In the case of M-ary orthogonal signalling, the transmit power is a constant equal to C, *independent* of M. However, for binary antipodal signalling, the transmit power is only

$$\left[\frac{\left|\tilde{d}\right|}{2}\right]^2 = \frac{C}{2}. \tag{2.153}$$

Thus, binary antipodal signalling (BPSK) is 3 dB more efficient than binary orthogonal signalling (binary FSK) for the *same* average error-rate performance.

2.3 Bi-Orthogonal Constellations

The i_+th symbol in an M-dimensional bi-orthogonal constellation is represented by

$$\tilde{\mathbf{a}}_{i_+} = \begin{bmatrix} 0 \\ 0 \\ \vdots \\ +\tilde{a}_{i,\,i} \\ \vdots \\ 0 \end{bmatrix} \quad \text{for } 1 \le i \le M. \tag{2.154}$$

and the ith symbol is denoted by

$$\tilde{\mathbf{a}}_{i-} = \begin{bmatrix} 0 \\ 0 \\ \vdots \\ -\tilde{a}_{i,\,i} \\ \vdots \\ 0 \end{bmatrix} \quad \text{for } 1 \le i \le M. \tag{2.155}$$

Observe that $2M$ distinct symbols can be represented by an M-dimensional bi-orthogonal constellation, as opposed to only M distinct symbols in an M-dimensional orthogonal constellation.

The squared minimum distance between symbols is given by

$$\tilde{\mathbf{e}}_{i+,\,j+}^{H}\,\tilde{\mathbf{e}}_{i+,\,j+} = 2C, \tag{2.156}$$

where

$$\tilde{\mathbf{e}}_{i+,\,j+} = \tilde{\mathbf{a}}_{i+} - \tilde{\mathbf{a}}_{j+}. \tag{2.157}$$

Thus the squared minimum distance is identical to that of the orthogonal constellation. However, the number of nearest neighbours is double that of the orthogonal constellation and is equal to $2(M-1)$. Hence the approximate expression for the average probability of error for the bi-orthogonal constellation is given by

$$P(e) \le (M-1)\,\mathrm{erfc}\left(\sqrt{\frac{2C}{8\sigma_w^2}}\right). \tag{2.158}$$

Note also that the average power of the bi-orthogonal constellation is identical to the orthogonal constellation.

2.4 Simplex Constellations

Consider an M-dimensional orthogonal constellation whose ith symbol is given by (2.75). The mean of the symbols is given by

$$\tilde{\mathbf{m}} = \frac{1}{M}\sum_{i=1}^{M}\tilde{\mathbf{a}}_i = \frac{\tilde{C}}{M}\begin{bmatrix} 1 \\ 1 \\ \vdots \\ 1 \end{bmatrix}. \tag{2.159}$$

where $\tilde{C} = \tilde{a}_{i,\,i}$, for $1 \le i \le M$, is a complex constant. Note that $|\tilde{C}|^2 = C$, where C is defined in (2.76). Define a new symbol set $\mathbf{b}_i$ such that

$$\tilde{\mathbf{b}}_i = \tilde{\mathbf{a}}_i - \tilde{\mathbf{m}}. \tag{2.160}$$

The new constellation obtained is called *simplex* constellation. It is clear that the squared minimum distance between the new set of symbols is identical to that of the orthogonal signal set since

$$\left(\tilde{\mathbf{b}}_i - \tilde{\mathbf{b}}_j\right)^H \left(\tilde{\mathbf{b}}_i - \tilde{\mathbf{b}}_j\right) = \left(\tilde{\mathbf{a}}_i - \tilde{\mathbf{a}}_j\right)^H \left(\tilde{\mathbf{a}}_i - \tilde{\mathbf{a}}_j\right)$$

$$= 2C. \tag{2.161}$$

Hence the average probability of error is again given by (2.97). The average power is given by

$$\frac{1}{M}\sum_{i=1}^{M} \tilde{\mathbf{b}}_i^H \tilde{\mathbf{b}}_i = C - \frac{C}{M} \tag{2.162}$$

which is *less* than the orthogonal signal set.

2.5 Noncoherent Detectors for Multidimensional Orthogonal Constellations

Noncoherent detectors do not require or do not make use of any phase information contained in the received signal. This section is devoted to the study of *optimum* noncoherent detectors for multidimensional orthogonal constellations.

The received signal can be written as

$$\tilde{\mathbf{r}}_n = \mathbf{S}_n^{(i)} \mathrm{e}^{\mathrm{j}\theta} + \tilde{\mathbf{w}}_n \qquad \text{for } 1 \le i \le M \tag{2.163}$$

where θ is a uniformly distributed random variable in the interval $[0, 2\pi)$ and the remaining terms are defined in (2.77). The receiver is assumed to have no knowledge about θ.

The MAP detector once again maximizes the probability

$$\max_i P(\tilde{\mathbf{a}}_i | \tilde{\mathbf{r}}_n) \qquad \text{for } 1 \le i \le M \tag{2.164}$$

which reduces to the ML detector

$$\begin{aligned}
& \max_i p(\tilde{\mathbf{r}}_n | \tilde{\mathbf{a}}_i) \\
\Rightarrow\quad & \max_i \int_{\theta=0}^{2\pi} p(\tilde{\mathbf{r}}_n | \tilde{\mathbf{a}}_i, \theta)\, p(\theta)\, d\theta \\
\Rightarrow\quad & \max_i \frac{1}{(2\pi)^M \det(\tilde{\mathbf{R}}_{\tilde{w}\tilde{w}})} \int_{\theta=0}^{2\pi} \exp\left(-\frac{1}{2}\left(\tilde{\mathbf{r}}_n - \tilde{\mathbf{a}}_i\, \mathrm{e}^{\mathrm{j}\theta}\right)^H \tilde{\mathbf{R}}_{\tilde{w}\tilde{w}}^{-1} \left(\tilde{\mathbf{r}}_n - \tilde{\mathbf{a}}_i\, \mathrm{e}^{\mathrm{j}\theta}\right)\right) \frac{1}{2\pi}\, d\theta
\end{aligned} \tag{2.165}$$

where we have used the fact that

$$p(\theta) = \frac{1}{2\pi} \qquad \text{for } 0 \le \theta < 2\pi \tag{2.166}$$

and $\tilde{\mathbf{R}}_{\tilde{w}\tilde{w}}$ is the $M \times M$ conditional covariance matrix:

$$\tilde{\mathbf{R}}_{\tilde{w}\tilde{w}} \stackrel{\Delta}{=} \frac{1}{2} E\left[\left(\tilde{\mathbf{r}}_n - \tilde{\mathbf{a}}_i \, \mathrm{e}^{\mathrm{j}\theta}\right)\left(\tilde{\mathbf{r}}_n - \tilde{\mathbf{a}}_i \, \mathrm{e}^{\mathrm{j}\theta}\right)^H\right] = \frac{1}{2} E\left[\tilde{\mathbf{w}}_n \tilde{\mathbf{w}}_n^H\right]$$
$$= \sigma_w^2 \mathbf{I}_M. \tag{2.167}$$

Ignoring terms that are independent of i and θ in (2.165), we get

$$\max_i \frac{1}{2\pi} \int_{\theta=0}^{2\pi} \exp\left(-\frac{\sum_{l=1}^{M} |\tilde{r}_{n,\,l} - \tilde{a}_{i,\,l} \, \mathrm{e}^{\mathrm{j}\theta}|^2}{2\sigma_w^2}\right) d\theta. \tag{2.168}$$

We note that $\sum_l |\tilde{r}_{n,\,l}|^2$ and $\sum_l |\tilde{a}_{i,\,l} \exp(\mathrm{j}\theta)|^2$ are independent of i and θ and hence they can be ignored. The maximization in (2.168) can now be written as[21]

$$\max_i \frac{1}{2\pi} \int_{\theta=0}^{2\pi} \exp\left(\frac{\sum_{l=1}^{M} 2\Re\left\{\tilde{r}_{n,\,l} \tilde{a}_{i,\,l}^* \, \mathrm{e}^{-\mathrm{j}\theta}\right\}}{2\sigma_w^2}\right) d\theta$$

$$\Rightarrow \max_i \frac{1}{2\pi} \int_{\theta=0}^{2\pi} \exp\left(\frac{\Re\left\{\mathrm{e}^{-\mathrm{j}\theta} \sum_{l=1}^{M} 2\tilde{r}_{n,\,l} \tilde{a}_{i,\,l}^*\right\}}{2\sigma_w^2}\right) d\theta$$

$$\Rightarrow \max_i \frac{1}{2\pi} \int_{\theta=0}^{2\pi} \exp\left(\frac{\Re\left\{\mathrm{e}^{-\mathrm{j}\theta} A_i \mathrm{e}^{\mathrm{j}\phi_i}\right\}}{2\sigma_w^2}\right) d\theta$$

$$\Rightarrow \max_i \frac{1}{2\pi} \int_{\theta=0}^{2\pi} \exp\left(\frac{A_i \cos(\phi_i - \theta)}{2\sigma_w^2}\right) d\theta$$

$$\Rightarrow \max_i I_0\left(\frac{A_i}{2\sigma_w^2}\right), \tag{2.169}$$

where

$$A_i \mathrm{e}^{\mathrm{j}\phi_i} = \sum_{l=1}^{M} 2\tilde{r}_{n,\,l} \tilde{a}_{i,\,l}^* \tag{2.170}$$

and $I_0(\cdot)$ is the modified Bessel function of the zeroth order. Noting that $I_0(x)$ is a monotonically increasing function of x, the maximization in (2.169) can be written as

$$\begin{aligned}
&\max_i \frac{A_i}{2\sigma_w^2} \\
\Rightarrow\quad &\max_i A_i \\
\Rightarrow\quad &\max_i \left|\sum_{l=1}^{M} \tilde{r}_{n,\,l}\tilde{a}_{i,\,l}^*\right| \\
\Rightarrow\quad &\max_i \left|\sum_{l=1}^{M} \tilde{r}_{n,\,l}\tilde{a}_{i,\,l}^*\right|^2
\end{aligned} \tag{2.171}$$

which is the required expression for a noncoherent ML detector.

Observe that in the above derivation we have *not* made any assumption about the orthogonality of the symbols. We have only assumed that all symbols have equal energy, that is

$$\sum_{l=1}^{M} \left|\tilde{a}_{i,\,l}\right|^2 = C \qquad \text{(a constant independent of } i\text{)}. \tag{2.172}$$

In the next section we present the performance analysis where we assume that the symbols are orthogonal.

2.5.1 Performance analysis

Given that the ith symbol has been transmitted, the ML detector decides in favour of symbol j when

$$\left|\sum_{l=1}^{M} \tilde{r}_{n,\,l}\tilde{a}_{j,\,l}^*\right|^2 > \left|\sum_{l=1}^{M} \tilde{r}_{n,\,l}\tilde{a}_{i,\,l}^*\right|^2. \tag{2.173}$$

Making use of the orthogonality between the symbols and the fact that $\tilde{a}_{i,\,l} = 0$ for $i \neq l$, the above expression simplifies to

$$\begin{aligned}
&\left|\tilde{w}_{n,\,j}\tilde{a}_{j,\,j}^*\right|^2 > \left|C\mathrm{e}^{\mathrm{j}\theta} + \tilde{w}_{n,\,i}\tilde{a}_{i,\,i}^*\right|^2 \\
\Rightarrow\quad &C\left|\tilde{w}_{n,\,j}\right|^2 > C^2 + C\left|\tilde{w}_{n,\,i}\right|^2 + 2C\Re\left\{\tilde{w}_{n,\,i}\tilde{a}_{i,\,i}^*\mathrm{e}^{-\mathrm{j}\theta}\right\} \\
\Rightarrow\quad &\left|\tilde{w}_{n,\,j}\right|^2 > C + \left|\tilde{w}_{n,\,i}\right|^2 + 2\Re\left\{\tilde{w}_{n,\,i}\tilde{a}_{i,\,i}^*\mathrm{e}^{-\mathrm{j}\theta}\right\}.
\end{aligned} \tag{2.174}$$

Let

$$\begin{aligned}
u + \mathrm{j}\,v &= \tilde{w}_{n,\,i}\mathrm{e}^{-\mathrm{j}\theta} \\
&= \left(w_{n,\,i,\,I}\cos(\theta) + w_{n,\,i,\,Q}\sin(\theta)\right) + \mathrm{j}\left(w_{n,\,i,\,Q}\cos(\theta) - w_{n,\,i,\,I}\sin(\theta)\right).
\end{aligned} \tag{2.175}$$

Since θ is uniformly distributed in $[0,\,2\pi)$, both u and v are Gaussian random variables. If we further assume that θ is independent of $\tilde{w}_{n,\,i}$, we then have

$$\begin{aligned} E[u] &= 0 \\ &= E[v] \\ E\left[u^2\right] &= \sigma_w^2 \\ &= E\left[v^2\right] \\ E[uv] &= 0 \end{aligned} \tag{2.176}$$

where we have used the fact that $w_{n,i,I}$ and $w_{n,i,Q}$ are statistically independent. Thus we observe that u and v are uncorrelated and being Gaussian, they are also statistically independent. Note also that

$$\left|\tilde{w}_{n,i}\right|^2 = \left|\tilde{w}_{n,i}\mathrm{e}^{-\mathrm{j}\theta}\right|^2 = u^2 + v^2. \tag{2.177}$$

Let

$$\begin{aligned} Z &= \left|\tilde{w}_{n,j}\right|^2 \\ Y &= C + u^2 + v^2 + 2\Re\left\{(u + \mathrm{j}\,v)\tilde{a}_{i,i}^*\right\} \\ &= f(u,v) \qquad \text{(say)}. \end{aligned} \tag{2.178}$$

It is clear that Z is a Chi-square distributed random variable with two degrees of freedom and pdf given by[2]

$$p(Z) = \frac{1}{2\sigma_w^2}\exp\left(-\frac{Z}{2\sigma_w^2}\right) \qquad \text{for } Z > 0. \tag{2.179}$$

Now, the probability of detecting $\tilde{\mathbf{a}}_j$ instead of $\tilde{\mathbf{a}}_i$ is given by (using the fact that u and v are statistically independent)

$$\begin{aligned} P\left(\tilde{\mathbf{a}}_j|\tilde{\mathbf{a}}_i\right) &= \int_{Y=0}^{\infty} P(Z > Y|Y)p(Y)\,dY \\ &= \int_{u=-\infty}^{\infty}\int_{v=-\infty}^{\infty} P(Z > f(u,v)|u,v)p(u)p(v)\,du\,dv. \end{aligned} \tag{2.180}$$

First, we evaluate $P(Z > Y|Y)$:

$$\begin{aligned} P(Z > Y|Y) &= \frac{1}{2\sigma_w^2}\int_{Z=Y}^{\infty}\exp\left(-\frac{Z}{2\sigma_w^2}\right)dZ \\ &= \exp\left(-\frac{Y}{2\sigma_w^2}\right) \\ &= \exp\left(-\frac{C + u^2 + v^2 + 2(ua_{i,i,I} + va_{i,i,Q})}{2\sigma_w^2}\right). \end{aligned} \tag{2.181}$$

Substituting the above probability into (2.180), we get

$$P\left(\tilde{\mathbf{a}}_j|\tilde{\mathbf{a}}_i\right) = \int_{u=-\infty}^{\infty}\int_{v=-\infty}^{\infty} \exp\left(-\frac{C+u^2+v^2+2(ua_{i,\,i,\,I}+va_{i,\,i,\,Q})}{2\sigma_w^2}\right) p(u)p(v)\,du\,dv. \tag{2.182}$$

Since u and v are Gaussian random variables with zero-mean and variance σ_w^2, the above pairwise probability of error reduces to

$$\begin{aligned} P\left(\tilde{\mathbf{a}}_j|\tilde{\mathbf{a}}_i\right) &= \exp\left(-\frac{C}{2\sigma_w^2}\right)\frac{1}{2}\exp\left(\frac{C}{4\sigma_w^2}\right) \\ &= \frac{1}{2}\exp\left(-\frac{C}{4\sigma_w^2}\right). \end{aligned} \tag{2.183}$$

Using the union bound argument, the average probability of error is upper bounded by

$$P\left(e|\tilde{\mathbf{a}}_i\right) \le \frac{M-1}{2}\exp\left(-\frac{C}{4\sigma_w^2}\right) \tag{2.184}$$

which is less than the union bound obtained for coherent detection (see (2.101))! However, the union bound obtained above is not very tight. In the next section we will obtain the exact expression for the probability of error.

2.5.2 Exact expression for probability of error

Consider equation (2.178). Let

$$Z_j = \left|\tilde{w}_{n,\,j}\right|^2 \qquad \text{for } 1 \le j \le M,\, j \ne i. \tag{2.185}$$

Then, using the fact that the noise terms are uncorrelated and hence also statistically independent, the exact expression for the probability of correct decision is given by

$$\begin{aligned} P\left(c|\tilde{\mathbf{a}}_i\right) &= \int_{Y=0}^{\infty} P\left((Z_1 < Y) \text{ AND } \ldots (Z_{i-1} < Y) \text{ AND } (Z_{i+1} < Y)\right. \\ &\qquad \left.\text{AND} \ldots (Z_M < Y)|Y\right) p(Y)\,dY \\ &= \int_{Y=0}^{\infty} \left(P(Z_1 < Y|Y)\right)^{M-1} p(Y)\,dY \\ &= \int_{u=-\infty}^{\infty}\int_{v=-\infty}^{\infty} \left(P(Z_1 < f(u,\,v)|u,\,v)\right)^{M-1} p(u)p(v)\,du\,dv, \end{aligned} \tag{2.186}$$

where the terms Y, u and v are defined in (2.178). Now, the probability

$$
\begin{aligned}
P(Z < Y|Y) &= \frac{1}{2\sigma_w^2}\int_{Z=0}^{Y} \exp\left(-\frac{Z}{2\sigma_w^2}\right) dZ \\
&= 1 - \exp\left(-\frac{Y}{2\sigma_w^2}\right) \\
&= 1 - \exp\left(-\frac{f(u,\, v)}{2\sigma_w^2}\right). \qquad (2.187)
\end{aligned}
$$

Substituting the above expression in (2.186), we get

$$
\begin{aligned}
P\left(c|\tilde{\mathbf{a}}_i\right) &= \int_{u=-\infty}^{\infty}\int_{v=-\infty}^{\infty}\left(1 - \exp\left(-\frac{f(u,\, v)}{2\sigma_w^2}\right)\right)^{M-1} p(u)p(v)\, du\, dv \\
&= \int_{u=-\infty}^{\infty}\int_{v=-\infty}^{\infty}\left(\sum_{l=0}^{M-1}(-1)^l\binom{M-1}{l}\exp\left(-\frac{f(u,\, v)l}{2\sigma_w^2}\right)\right) p(u)p(v)\, du\, dv \\
&= \sum_{l=0}^{M-1}(-1)^l\binom{M-1}{l}\int_{u=-\infty}^{\infty}\int_{v=-\infty}^{\infty}\exp\left(-\frac{f(u,\, v)l}{2\sigma_w^2}\right) p(u)p(v)\, du\, dv. \qquad (2.188)
\end{aligned}
$$

Once again, we note that u and v are Gaussian random variables with zero-mean and variance σ_w^2. Substituting the expression for $p(u)$, $p(v)$ and Y in the above equation, we get

$$
P\left(c|\tilde{\mathbf{a}}_i\right) = \sum_{l=0}^{M-1}(-1)^l\binom{M-1}{l}\frac{1}{l+1}\exp\left(-\frac{lC}{2(l+1)\sigma_w^2}\right). \qquad (2.189)
$$

The probability of error given that $\tilde{\mathbf{a}}_i$ is transmitted is given by

$$
\begin{aligned}
P\left(e|\tilde{\mathbf{a}}_i\right) &= 1 - P\left(c|\tilde{\mathbf{a}}_i\right) \\
&= \sum_{l=1}^{M-1}(-1)^{l+1}\binom{M-1}{l}\frac{1}{l+1}\exp\left(-\frac{lC}{2(l+1)\sigma_w^2}\right). \qquad (2.190)
\end{aligned}
$$

The performance of noncoherent detectors for 2D and 16D constellations is depicted in Figure 2.11. For the sake of comparison, the performance of the corresponding coherent detectors is shown.

2.6 Noncoherent Detectors for M-ary PSK

In this section we derive the detection rule and the performance of noncoherent detectors for M-ary PSK in AWGN channels. Noncoherent detectors for multilevel signals in fading

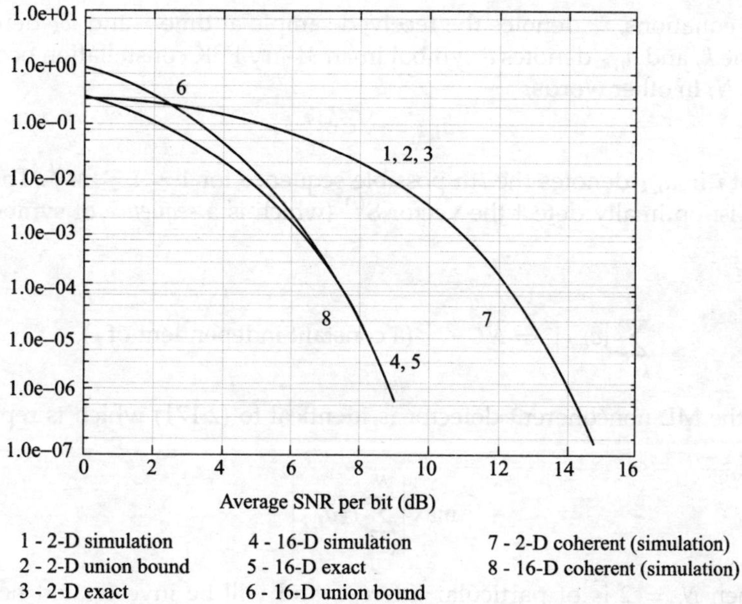

Figure 2.11 *Performance of noncoherent detectors for various multi-dimensional constellations*

channel is addressed in [22–25]. Differentially coherent receivers is discussed in [21–26]. The bit-error-rate performance of differentially coherent feedback detectors is given in [27]. Viterbi decoding (see Section 3.3.1) of differentially encoded BPSK is given in [28,29]. In [30] differential detection of 16-DAPSK (differential amplitude and phase shift keyed) signals is described. Noncoherent detectors for (error control) coded signals is presented in [31]. Various maximum likelihood receivers for M-ary differential phase shift keyed (DPSK) signals is discussed in [32–37]. A differential detector for M-ary DPSK using linear prediction (see Appendix J) is discussed in [38].

Let the received signal be denoted by

$$\tilde{\mathbf{r}} = \mathbf{S}^{(i)} \mathrm{e}^{\mathrm{j}\theta} + \tilde{\mathbf{w}} \tag{2.191}$$

where

$$\tilde{\mathbf{r}} = \begin{bmatrix} \tilde{r}_1 \\ \tilde{r}_2 \\ \vdots \\ \tilde{r}_N \end{bmatrix}; \qquad \mathbf{S}^{(i)} = \tilde{\mathbf{a}}_i = \begin{bmatrix} \tilde{a}_{i,\,1} \\ \tilde{a}_{i,\,2} \\ \vdots \\ \tilde{a}_{i,\,N} \end{bmatrix} \qquad \text{for } 1 \leq i \leq M^N \tag{2.192}$$

and the noise vector is

$$\tilde{\mathbf{w}} = \begin{bmatrix} \tilde{w}_1 \\ \vdots \\ \tilde{w}_N \end{bmatrix}. \tag{2.193}$$

In the above equations, $\tilde{r}_k$ denotes the received sample at time k and $\tilde{w}_k$ denotes the noise sample at time k, and $\tilde{a}_{i,\,k}$ denotes a symbol in an M-ary PSK constellation occurring at time k for $1 \le k \le N$. In other words,

$$\tilde{a}_{i,\,k} = \sqrt{C}\mathrm{e}^{\mathrm{j}\phi_{i,\,k}}. \tag{2.194}$$

The subscript i in $\tilde{a}_{i,\,k}$ denotes the ith possible sequence for $1 \le i \le M^N$. The statement of the problem is: optimally detect the vector $\mathbf{S}^{(i)}$ (which is a *sequence* of symbols) when θ is unknown.

Since

$$\sum_{k=1}^{N} \left|\tilde{a}_{i,\,k}\right|^2 = NC \qquad \text{(a constant independent of } i\text{)}, \tag{2.195}$$

the rule for the ML noncoherent detector is identical to (2.171) which is repeated here for convenience.

$$\max_i \left|\sum_{k=1}^{N} \tilde{r}_k \tilde{a}^*_{i,\,k}\right|^2. \tag{2.196}$$

The case when $N = 2$ is of particular interest, and will be investigated here. The above maximization reduces to

$$\begin{aligned} &\max_i \left|\tilde{r}_1\tilde{a}^*_{i,\,1} + \tilde{r}_2\tilde{a}^*_{i,\,2}\right|^2 \\ \Rightarrow\quad &\max_i \Re\left\{\tilde{r}^*_1\tilde{r}_2\tilde{a}_{i,\,1}\tilde{a}^*_{i,\,2}\right\} \qquad \text{for } 1 \le i \le M^2 \end{aligned} \tag{2.197}$$

where we have made use of the fact that $|\tilde{a}_{i,\,k}|^2 = C$ is a constant independent of i and k. An important point to note in the above equation is that, out of the M^2 possible products $\tilde{a}_{i,\,1}\tilde{a}^*_{i,\,2}$, only M are distinct. Hence $\tilde{a}_{i,\,1}\tilde{a}^*_{i,\,2}$ can be replaced by $C\mathrm{e}^{-\mathrm{j}\phi_\ell}$, where

$$\phi_\ell = \frac{2\pi\ell}{M} \qquad \text{for } 1 \le \ell \le M. \tag{2.198}$$

With this simplification, the maximization rule in (2.197) can be written as

$$\begin{aligned} &\max_\ell \Re\left\{\tilde{r}^*_1\tilde{r}_2 C\mathrm{e}^{-\mathrm{j}\phi_\ell}\right\} \qquad \text{for } 1 \le \ell \le M \\ \Rightarrow\quad &\max_\ell \Re\left\{\tilde{r}^*_1\tilde{r}_2 \mathrm{e}^{-\mathrm{j}\phi_\ell}\right\} \qquad \text{for } 1 \le \ell \le M. \end{aligned} \tag{2.199}$$

The maximization rule in the above equation corresponds to that of a *differential detector* for M-ary PSK. It is clear that information needs to be transmitted in the form of phase difference between successive symbols for the detection rule in (2.199) to be valid. Observe that for M-ary PSK, there are M possible phase differences. The mapping of symbols to phase differences is illustrated in Figure 2.12 for $M = 2$ and $M = 4$. We now evaluate the performance of the differential detector for M-ary PSK.

Bit	Phase change (radians)
0	0
1	π

Differential binary PSK

Dibit	Phase change (radians)
00	0
01	$\pi/2$
11	π
10	$3\pi/2$

Differential 4-ary PSK

Figure 2.12 *Mapping of symbols to phase differences for $M = 2$ and $M = 4$*

2.6.1 Approximate performance analysis of differential M-ary PSK

Let the pair of received points be denoted by

$$\tilde{r}_1 = \sqrt{C}\, e^{j\theta} + \tilde{w}_1,$$
$$\tilde{r}_2 = \sqrt{C}\, e^{j(\theta+\phi_i)} + \tilde{w}_2 \tag{2.200}$$

where ϕ_i is given by (2.198) and denotes the transmitted phase change between consecutive symbols. As before, we assume that θ is uniformly distributed in $[0, 2\pi)$ and is independent of the noise and signal terms. The differential detector makes an error when it decides in favour of a phase change ϕ_j such that

$$\Re\left\{\tilde{r}_1^*\tilde{r}_2 e^{-j\phi_j}\right\} > \Re\left\{\tilde{r}_1^*\tilde{r}_2 e^{-j\phi_i}\right\} \quad \text{for } j \neq i.$$
$$\Rightarrow \Re\left\{\tilde{r}_1^*\tilde{r}_2\left(e^{-j\phi_i} - e^{-j\phi_j}\right)\right\} < 0$$
$$\Rightarrow \Re\left\{\tilde{r}_1^*\tilde{r}_2 e^{-j\phi_i}\left(1 - e^{j\delta_{i,j}}\right)\right\} < 0 \tag{2.201}$$

where

$$\delta_{i,j} = \phi_i - \phi_j. \tag{2.202}$$

Observe that for high SNR,

$$\tilde{r}_1^*\tilde{r}_2 e^{-j\phi_i} = C + \sqrt{C}\,\tilde{w}_2 e^{-j(\theta+\phi_i)} + \sqrt{C}\,\tilde{w}_1^* e^{j\theta} + \tilde{w}_1^*\tilde{w}_2 e^{-j\phi_i}$$
$$\approx C + \sqrt{C}\,\tilde{w}_2 e^{-j(\theta+\phi_i)} + \sqrt{C}\,\tilde{w}_1^* e^{j\theta}. \tag{2.203}$$

Let

$$1 - e^{j\delta_{i,j}} = (1 - \cos(\delta_{i,j})) - j\sin(\delta_{i,j})$$
$$= B e^{j\alpha} \qquad \text{(say)}. \tag{2.204}$$

Making use of (2.203) and (2.204), the differential detector decides in favour of ϕ_j when

$$\begin{aligned}&\Re\left\{\left(C+\sqrt{C}\,\tilde{w}_2\mathrm{e}^{-\mathrm{j}(\theta+\phi_i)}+\sqrt{C}\,\tilde{w}_1^*\mathrm{e}^{\mathrm{j}\theta}\right)B\mathrm{e}^{\mathrm{j}\alpha}\right\}<0\\ \Rightarrow\ &\Re\left\{\left(\sqrt{C}+\tilde{w}_2\mathrm{e}^{-\mathrm{j}(\theta+\phi_i)}+\tilde{w}_1^*\mathrm{e}^{\mathrm{j}\theta}\right)\mathrm{e}^{\mathrm{j}\alpha}\right\}<0\\ \Rightarrow\ &\sqrt{C}\cos(\alpha)+w_{2,\,I}\cos(\theta_1)-w_{2,\,Q}\sin(\theta_1)+w_{1,\,I}\cos(\theta_2)+w_{1,\,Q}\sin(\theta_2)<0\end{aligned}\tag{2.205}$$

where

$$\begin{aligned}\theta_1&=\alpha-\theta-\phi_i\\ \theta_2&=\alpha+\theta.\end{aligned}\tag{2.206}$$

Let

$$Z=w_{2,\,I}\cos(\theta_1)-w_{2,\,Q}\sin(\theta_1)+w_{1,\,I}\cos(\theta_2)+w_{1,\,Q}\sin(\theta_2).\tag{2.207}$$

Now, Z is a Gaussian random variable with mean and variance given by

$$\begin{aligned}E[Z]&=0\\ E\left[Z^2\right]&=2\sigma_w^2.\end{aligned}\tag{2.208}$$

The probability that the detector decides in favour of ϕ_j given that ϕ_i is transmitted is given by

$$\begin{aligned}P(\phi_j|\phi_i)&=P(Z<-\sqrt{C}\cos(\alpha))\\ &=\frac{1}{2}\,\mathrm{erfc}\left(\sqrt{\frac{C\cos^2(\alpha)}{4\sigma_w^2}}\right).\end{aligned}\tag{2.209}$$

Now, the squared distance between the two points in a PSK constellation corresponding to ϕ_i and ϕ_j with radius $\sqrt{C}$ is given by

$$\begin{aligned}d_{i,\,j}^2&=C\left(\cos(\phi_j)-\cos(\phi_j+\delta_{i,\,j})\right)^2+C\left(\sin(\phi_j)-\sin(\phi_j+\delta_{i,\,j})\right)^2\\ &=2C\left(1-\cos(\delta_{i,\,j})\right).\end{aligned}\tag{2.210}$$

This is illustrated in Figure 2.13. From (2.204) we have:

$$\begin{aligned}B^2&=\left(1-\cos(\delta_{i,\,j})\right)^2+\sin^2(\delta_{i,\,j})\\ &=2(1-\cos(\delta_{i,\,j}))\\ &=d_{i,\,j}^2/C.\end{aligned}\tag{2.211}$$

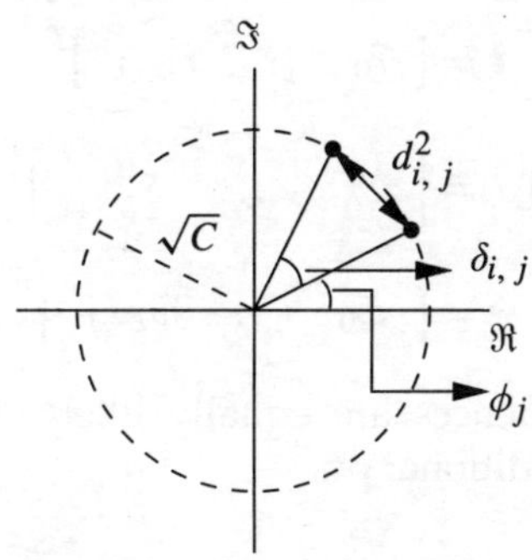

Figure 2.13 *Illustrating the distance between two points in a PSK constellation*

Hence

$$
\begin{aligned}
\cos(\alpha) &= \frac{1 - \cos(\delta_{i,j})}{B} \\
&= \frac{B}{2}.
\end{aligned}
\tag{2.212}
$$

Hence the probability of deciding in favour of ϕ_j is given by

$$
P(\phi_j|\phi_i) = \frac{1}{2}\operatorname{erfc}\left(\sqrt{\frac{d_{i,j}^2}{16\sigma_w^2}}\right). \tag{2.213}
$$

Comparing with the probability of error for coherent detection given by (2.20) we find that the differential detector for M-ary PSK is 3 dB worse than a coherent detector for M-ary PSK.

2.7 Coherent Detectors in Coloured Noise

The reader is advised to go through Chapter 3 and Appendix J before reading this section. So far we have dealt with both coherent as well as noncoherent detection in the presence of AWGN. In this section we discuss coherent detection in the presence of additive coloured (or correlated) Gaussian noise (ACGN)[39,40]. The noise is assumed to be wide sense stationary (WSS).

Assume that L symbols have been transmitted. The symbols are taken from an M-ary two-dimensional constellation. The received signal can be written as

$$
\tilde{\mathbf{r}} = \mathbf{S}^{(i)} + \tilde{\mathbf{w}} \tag{2.214}
$$

where $\tilde{\mathbf{r}}$ is an $L \times 1$ column vector of the received samples, $\mathbf{S}^{(i)}$ is an $L \times 1$ vector of the ith possible symbol sequence ($1 \leq i \leq M^L$) and $\tilde{\mathbf{w}}$ is an $L \times 1$ column vector of correlated Gaussian noise samples. Note that

$$\begin{aligned}\tilde{\mathbf{r}} &= \begin{bmatrix} \tilde{r}_0 & \dots & \tilde{r}_{L-1} \end{bmatrix}^T \\ \mathbf{S}^{(i)} &= \begin{bmatrix} S_0^{(i)} & \dots & S_{L-1}^{(i)} \end{bmatrix}^T \\ \tilde{\mathbf{w}} &= \begin{bmatrix} \tilde{w}_0 & \dots & \tilde{w}_{L-1} \end{bmatrix}^T.\end{aligned} \tag{2.215}$$

Assuming that all symbol sequences are equally likely, the maximum likelihood (ML) detector maximizes the joint conditional pdf

$$\max_j p\left(\tilde{\mathbf{r}}|\mathbf{S}^{(j)}\right) \qquad \text{for } 1 \le j \le M^L \tag{2.216}$$

which is equivalent to

$$\max_j \frac{1}{(2\pi)^L \det\left(\tilde{\mathbf{R}}\right)} \exp\left(-\frac{1}{2}\left(\tilde{\mathbf{r}} - \mathbf{S}^{(j)}\right)^H \tilde{\mathbf{R}}^{-1}\left(\tilde{\mathbf{r}} - \mathbf{S}^{(j)}\right)\right) \tag{2.217}$$

where the covariance matrix conditioned on the jth possible symbol sequence is given by

$$\begin{aligned}\tilde{\mathbf{R}} &\stackrel{\Delta}{=} \frac{1}{2} E\left[\left(\tilde{\mathbf{r}} - \mathbf{S}^{(j)}\right)\left(\tilde{\mathbf{r}} - \mathbf{S}^{(j)}\right)^H \middle| \mathbf{S}^{(j)}\right] \\ &= \frac{1}{2} E\left[\tilde{\mathbf{w}}\tilde{\mathbf{w}}^H\right].\end{aligned} \tag{2.218}$$

Since $\tilde{\mathbf{R}}$ is not a diagonal matrix, the maximization in (2.217) cannot be implemented recursively using the Viterbi algorithm. However, if we perform a Cholesky decomposition (see Appendix J) on $\tilde{\mathbf{R}}$, we get

$$\tilde{\mathbf{R}}^{-1} = \tilde{\mathbf{A}}^H \mathbf{D}^{-1} \tilde{\mathbf{A}} \tag{2.219}$$

where $\tilde{\mathbf{A}}$ is an $L \times L$ lower triangular matrix given by

$$\tilde{\mathbf{A}} \stackrel{\Delta}{=} \begin{bmatrix} 1 & 0 & \dots & 0 \\ \tilde{a}_{1,1} & 1 & \dots & 0 \\ \vdots & \vdots & \vdots & \vdots \\ \tilde{a}_{L-1,L-1} & \tilde{a}_{L-1,L-2} & \dots & 1 \end{bmatrix} \tag{2.220}$$

where $\tilde{a}_{k,p}$ denotes the pth coefficient of the optimal kth-order forward prediction filter. The $L \times L$ matrix $\mathbf{D}$ is a diagonal matrix of the prediction error variance denoted by

$$\mathbf{D} \stackrel{\Delta}{=} \begin{bmatrix} \sigma_{e,0}^2 & \dots & 0 \\ \vdots & \vdots & 0 \\ 0 & \dots & \sigma_{e,L-1}^2 \end{bmatrix}. \tag{2.221}$$

Observe that $\sigma^2_{e,j}$ denotes the prediction error variance for the optimal jth-order predictor ($1 \leq j \leq L$). Substituting (2.219) into (2.217) and noting that $\det \tilde{\mathbf{R}}$ is independent of the symbol sequence j, we get

$$\min_j \left(\tilde{\mathbf{r}} - \mathbf{S}^{(j)}\right)^H \tilde{\mathbf{A}}^H \mathbf{D}^{-1} \tilde{\mathbf{A}} \left(\tilde{\mathbf{r}} - \mathbf{S}^{(j)}\right) \tag{2.222}$$

which is equivalent to

$$\min_j \eta_j = \sum_{k=0}^{L-1} \frac{\left|\tilde{z}_k^{(j)}\right|^2}{\sigma^2_{e,k}} \tag{2.223}$$

where the prediction error at time k for the jth symbol sequence, $\tilde{z}_k^{(j)}$, is an element of $\tilde{\mathbf{z}}^{(j)}$ and is given by

$$\begin{bmatrix} \tilde{z}_0^{(j)} \\ \tilde{z}_1^{(j)} \\ \vdots \\ \tilde{z}_{L-1}^{(j)} \end{bmatrix} \triangleq \tilde{\mathbf{z}}^{(j)} = \tilde{\mathbf{A}} \left(\tilde{\mathbf{r}} - \mathbf{S}^{(j)}\right). \tag{2.224}$$

Note that the prediction error variance is given by

$$\sigma^2_{e,k} \triangleq \frac{1}{2} E\left[\tilde{z}_k^{(j)} \left(\tilde{z}_k^{(j)}\right)^*\right]. \tag{2.225}$$

When $\tilde{\mathbf{w}}$ consists of samples from a Pth-order autoregressive (AR) process, then a Pth-order prediction filter is sufficient to completely decorrelate the elements of $\tilde{\mathbf{w}}$. In this situation, assuming that the first P symbols constitute a known training sequence, (2.223) can be written as

$$\min_j \eta_j = \sum_{k=P}^{L-1} \left|\tilde{z}_k^{(j)}\right|^2 \tag{2.226}$$

where we have ignored the first P prediction error terms, and also ignored $\sigma^2_{e,k}$ since it is constant ($= \sigma^2_{e,P}$) for $k \geq P$.

Equation (2.226) now be implemented recursively using the Viterbi algorithm (VA). For uncoded M-ary signalling, the trellis would have M^P states, where P is the order of the prediction filter required to decorrelate the noise. The trellis diagram is illustrated in Figure 2.14(a) for the case when the prediction filter order is one ($P = 1$) and uncoded QPSK ($M = 4$) signalling is used. The topmost transition from each of the states is due to symbol 0 and bottom transition is due to symbol 3. The jth trellis state is represented by an M-ary P-tuple as given below.

$$\mathcal{S}_j = \left\{\mathcal{S}_{j,1} \ldots \mathcal{S}_{j,P}\right\} \tag{2.227}$$

where the digits

$$\mathcal{S}_{j,k} \in \{0, \ \ldots, \ M-1\}. \tag{2.228}$$

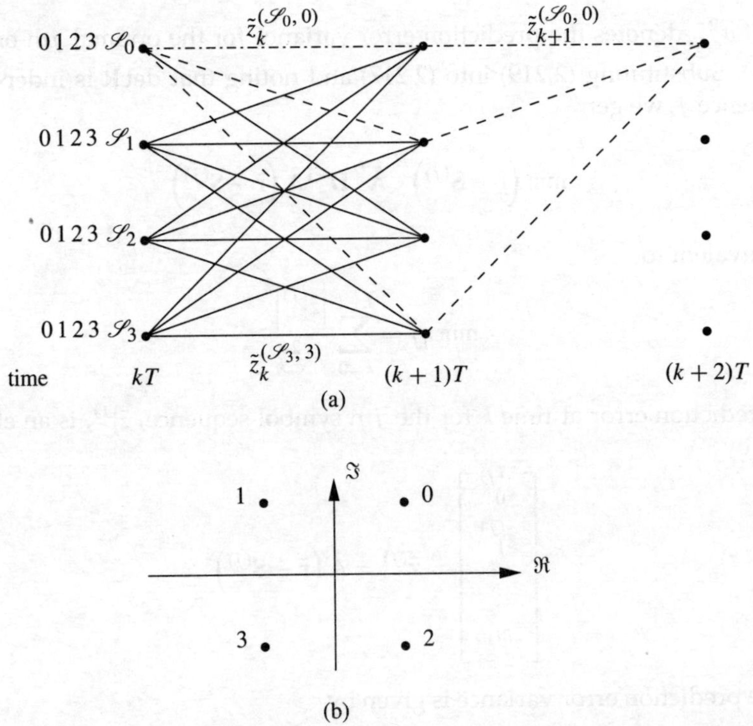

Figure 2.14 *(a) Trellis diagram for the predictive VA when $P = 1$ and $M = 4$. (b) Labelling of the symbols in the QPSK constellation*

There is a one-to-one mapping between the digits and the symbols of the M-ary constellation. Let us denote the mapping by $\mathscr{M}(\cdot)$. For example, in Figure 2.14(b)

$$\mathscr{M}(0) = 1 + j. \tag{2.229}$$

Given the present state $\mathscr{S}_j$ and input l ($l \in \{0, \ldots, M-1\}$), the next state is given by

$$\mathscr{S}_k = \left\{l\, \mathscr{S}_{j,1} \ldots \mathscr{S}_{j,P-1}\right\}. \tag{2.230}$$

The branch metric at time k, from state $\mathscr{S}_j$ due to input symbol l ($0 \le l \le M-1$) is given by

$$\left|\tilde{z}_k^{(\mathscr{S}_j,l)}\right|^2 = \left|(\tilde{r}_k - \mathscr{M}(l)) + \sum_{n=1}^{P} \tilde{a}_{P,n}\left(\tilde{r}_{k-n} - \mathscr{M}(\mathscr{S}_{j,n})\right)\right|^2 \tag{2.231}$$

where $\tilde{a}_{P,n}$ denotes the nth predictor coefficient of the optimal Pth-order predictor. Since the prediction filter is used in the metric computation, this is referred to as the predictive VA. A detector similar to the predictive VA has also been derived in [41–43] in the context of magnetic recording.

Note that when noise is white (elements of $\tilde{\mathbf{w}}$ are uncorrelated), then (2.216) reduces to

$$\max_j \frac{1}{(2\pi\sigma_w^2)^L} \exp\left(-\frac{1}{2\sigma_w^2}\sum_{k=0}^{L-1}\left|\tilde{r}_k - S_k^{(j)}\right|^2\right) \qquad \text{for } 1 \le j \le M^L \tag{2.232}$$

where $\tilde{r}_k$ and $S_k^{(j)}$ are elements of $\tilde{\mathbf{r}}$ and $\mathbf{S}^{(j)}$ respectively. Taking the natural logarithm of the above equation and ignoring constants, we get

$$\min_j \sum_{k=0}^{L-1}\left|\tilde{r}_k - S_k^{(j)}\right|^2 \qquad \text{for } 1 \le j \le M^L. \tag{2.233}$$

When the symbols are uncoded, all the M^L symbol sequences are valid and the sequence detection in (2.233) reduces to symbol-by-symbol detection

$$\min_j \left|\tilde{r}_k - S_k^{(j)}\right|^2 \qquad \text{for } 1 \le j \le M \tag{2.234}$$

where M denotes the size of the constellation. The above detection rule implies that each symbol can be detected *independently* of the other symbols. However, when the symbols are coded, as in Trellis Coded Modulation (TCM) (see Chapter 3), all symbol sequences are not valid and the detection rule in (2.233) must be implemented using the VA.

2.7.1 Performance analysis

In this section we consider the probability of symbol error for uncoded signalling for the case of predictive VA as well as conventional symbol-by-symbol detection in ACGN.

Predictive VA

At high SNR the probability of symbol error is governed by the probability of the *minimum distance error event*[2]. We assume M-ary signalling and that a Pth-order prediction filter is required to completely decorrelate the noise. Consider a transmitted symbol sequence **i**:

$$\mathbf{S}^{(i)} = \{\ldots,\ S_k^{(i)},\ S_{k+1},\ S_{k+2},\ldots\}. \tag{2.235}$$

Typically, a minimum distance error event is generated by a sequence **j**

$$\mathbf{S}^{(j)} = \{\ldots,\ S_k^{(j)},\ S_{k+1},\ S_{k+2},\ldots\} \tag{2.236}$$

where $S_k^{(j)}$ is the symbol closest to $S_k^{(i)}$ in the M-ary constellation. Observe that the sequence in (2.236) is different from (2.235) only at time instant k. The notation we have used here is as follows: the superscript i in $S_k^{(i)}$ denotes the ith symbol in the M-ary constellation ($0 \le i \le M-1$), occurring at time k. The superscript i in $\mathbf{S}^{(i)}$ denotes the ith sequence. The two minimum distance error events are denoted by a dashed line in Figure 2.14. The transmitted (or reference) sequence is denoted by a dot-dashed line in the same figure.

For the correct sequence the prediction error at time $k+n$ is given by $(0 \le n \le P)$

$$\tilde{z}_{k+n} = \sum_{m=0}^{P} \tilde{a}_{P,\,m}\, \tilde{w}_{k+n-m}. \tag{2.237}$$

For the erroneous sequence we have the prediction error at time $k+n$ as $(0 \le n \le P)$

$$\begin{aligned} \tilde{z}_{e,\,k+n} &= \sum_{m=0,\, m\neq n}^{P} \tilde{a}_{P,\,m}\, \tilde{w}_{k+n-m} + \tilde{a}_{P,\,n}\left(S_k^{(i)} - S_k^{(j)} + \tilde{w}_k\right) \\ &= \tilde{z}_{k+n} + \tilde{a}_{P,\,n}\left(S_k^{(i)} - S_k^{(j)}\right). \end{aligned} \tag{2.238}$$

Hence, the probability of an error event, which is the probability of the receiver deciding in favour of the jth sequence, given that the ith sequence was transmitted is given by

$$\begin{aligned} P\,(\mathbf{j}|\mathbf{i}) &= P\left(\sum_{m=0}^{P} |\tilde{z}_{k+m}|^2 > \sum_{m=0}^{P} |\tilde{z}_{e,\,k+m}|^2\right) \\ &= P\left(\sum_{m=0}^{P}\left[|\tilde{g}_{k+m}|^2 + 2\Re\left\{\tilde{g}_{k+m}\, \tilde{z}_{k+m}^{*}\right\}\right] < 0\right) \end{aligned} \tag{2.239}$$

where for the sake of brevity we have used the notation $\mathbf{j}|\mathbf{i}$ instead of $\mathbf{S}^{(j)}|\mathbf{S}^{(i)}$, $P(\cdot)$ denotes probability and

$$\tilde{g}_{k+m} \stackrel{\Delta}{=} \tilde{a}_{P,\,m}\left(S_k^{(i)} - S_k^{(j)}\right). \tag{2.240}$$

Let us define

$$Z \stackrel{\Delta}{=} 2\sum_{m=0}^{P} \Re\left\{\tilde{g}_{k+m}\, \tilde{z}_{k+m}^{*}\right\}. \tag{2.241}$$

Observe that the noise terms $\tilde{z}_{k+m}$ are uncorrelated with zero mean and variance $\sigma_{e,\,P}^2$. It is clear that Z is a real Gaussian random variable obtained at the output of a filter with coefficients $\tilde{g}_{k+m}$. Hence, the mean and variance of Z is given by

$$\begin{aligned} E[Z] &= 0 \\ E[Z^2] &= 4d_{\text{min},\,1}^2\, \sigma_{e,\,P}^2 \end{aligned} \tag{2.242}$$

where

$$d_{\text{min},\,1}^2 \stackrel{\Delta}{=} \sum_{m=0}^{P} |\tilde{g}_{k+m}|^2. \tag{2.243}$$

The probability of error event in (2.239) can now be written as

$$\begin{aligned} P\left(\mathbf{j}|\mathbf{i}\right) &= P\left(Z < -d_{\text{min},\,1}^2\right) \\ &= \frac{1}{2}\,\text{erfc}\left(\sqrt{\frac{d_{\text{min},\,1}^4}{8d_{\text{min},\,1}^2\sigma_{e,\,P}^2}}\right) \\ &= \frac{1}{2}\,\text{erfc}\left(\sqrt{\frac{d_{\text{min},\,1}^2}{8\sigma_{e,\,P}^2}}\right). \end{aligned} \tag{2.244}$$

When there are $M_{1,\,i}$ sequences that are at a distance $d_{\text{min},\,1}^2$ from the sequence i in (2.235), the probability of symbol error, given that the ith sequence has been transmitted, can be written as

$$P\left(e|\mathbf{i}\right) = \frac{M_{1,\,i}\,P\left(\mathbf{j}|\mathbf{i}\right)}{P(e|i) = M_{1,\,i}P(j/i)} \tag{2.245}$$

since there is only one erroneous symbol in the error event. Observe that from our definition of the error event, $M_{1,\,i}$ is also the number of symbols that are closest to the transmitted symbol $S_k^{(i)}$. The quantity $M_{1,\,i}$ is also referred to as *multiplicity*[44]. The lower bound (based on the squared minimum distance) on the *average* probability of symbol error is given by (for M-ary signalling)

$$\begin{aligned} P(e) &= \sum_{i=0}^{M-1} P\left(e|\mathbf{i}\right) P\left(S_k^{(i)}\right) \\ &= \sum_{i=0}^{M-1} \frac{M_{1,\,i}\,P\left(\mathbf{j}|\mathbf{i}\right)}{M} \end{aligned} \tag{2.246}$$

where we have assumed that $S_k^{(i)}$ in (2.235) could be any one of the symbols in the M-ary constellation and that all symbols are equally likely (probability of occurrence is $1/M$).

Symbol-by-symbol detection

Let us now consider the probability of symbol error for the symbol-by-symbol detector in correlated noise. Recall that for uncoded signalling, the symbol-by-symbol detector is optimum for white noise. Following the derivation in Section 2.1.1, it can be easily shown that the probability of deciding in favour of $S_k^{(j)}$ given that $S_k^{(i)}$ is transmitted is given by

$$P\left(j|i\right) = \frac{1}{2}\,\text{erfc}\left(\sqrt{\frac{d_{\text{min},\,2}^2}{8\sigma_w^2}}\right) \tag{2.247}$$

where, for the sake of brevity we have used the notation $j|i$ instead of $S_k^{(j)}|S_k^{(i)}$,

$$d^2_{\text{min},\,2} \stackrel{\Delta}{=} \left|S_k^{(i)} - S_k^{(j)}\right|^2 \tag{2.248}$$

and

$$\sigma_w^2 \stackrel{\Delta}{=} \frac{1}{2} E\left[|\tilde{w}_k|^2\right]. \tag{2.249}$$

Assuming all symbols are equally likely and the earlier definition for $M_{1,\,i}$, the average probability of symbol error is given by

$$P(e) = \sum_{i=0}^{M-1} \frac{M_{1,\,i}\, P(j|i)}{M}. \tag{2.250}$$

In deriving (2.247) we have assumed that the in-phase and quadrature components of $\tilde{w}_k$ are uncorrelated. This implies that

$$\frac{1}{2} E\left[\tilde{w}_n\, \tilde{w}^*_{n-m}\right] = \frac{1}{2} E\left[w_{n,\,I}\, w_{n-m,\,I}\right] + \frac{1}{2} E\left[w_{n,\,Q}\, w_{n-m,\,Q}\right] = R_{ww,\,m} \tag{2.251}$$

where the subscripts I and Q denote the in-phase and quadrature components respectively. Observe that the last equality in (2.251) follows when the in-phase and quadrature components have identical autocorrelation.

Example To find out the performance improvement of the predictive VA over the symbol-by-symbol detector (which is optimum when the additive noise is white), let us consider uncoded QPSK as an example. Let us assume that the samples of $\tilde{\mathbf{w}}$ in (2.214) are obtained at the output of a first-order IIR filter. We normalize the energy of the IIR filter to unity so that the variance of correlated noise is identical to that of the input. Thus, the in-phase and quadrature samples of correlated noise are generated by the following equation:

$$w_{n,\,I\{Q\}} = \sqrt{(1 - a^2)}\, u_{n,\,I\{Q\}} - a\, w_{n-1,\,I\{Q\}} \tag{2.252}$$

where $u_{n,\,I\{Q\}}$ denotes either the in-phase or the quadrature component of white noise at time n. Since $u_{n,\,I}$ and $u_{n,\,Q}$ are mutually uncorrelated, $w_{n,\,I}$ and $w_{n,\,Q}$ are also mutually uncorrelated and (2.251) is valid.

In this case it can be shown that

$$\begin{aligned}
\tilde{a}_{1,\,1} &= a \\
\sigma^2_{e,\,P} &= \sigma^2_w(1 - a^2) \\
d^2_{\text{min},\,1} &= d^2_{\text{min},\,2}(1 + a^2) \\
M_{1,\,i} &= 2 \qquad \text{for } 0 \le i \le 3.
\end{aligned} \tag{2.253}$$

Hence (2.246) reduces to

$$P_e = \frac{1}{2}\,\text{erfc}\left(\sqrt{\frac{d_{\text{min},\,2}^2(1+a^2)}{8\sigma_w^2(1-a^2)}}\right) \tag{2.254}$$

and (2.250) becomes

$$P_e = \text{erfc}\left(\sqrt{\frac{d_{\text{min},\,2}^2}{8\sigma_w^2}}\right). \tag{2.255}$$

Comparing (2.255) and (2.254), we can define the SNR gain as

$$\text{SNR}_{\text{gain}} \stackrel{\Delta}{=} 10\log\left(\frac{1+a^2}{1-a^2}\right). \tag{2.256}$$

From the above expression it is clear that detection schemes that are optimal in white noise are suboptimal in coloured noise.

2.8 Coherent Detectors for Frequency Nonselective (Flat) Fading Channels

We have so far dealt with the detection of signals in additive Gaussian noise (both white and coloured) channels. Such channels are *non-fading* or *time-invariant*. However, in wireless communication channels, there is additional distortion to the signal in the form of fading. Early papers on fading channels can be found in [45–47]. Some good tutorials on fading channel communications can be found in [48,50].

Consider the model shown in Figure 2.15. The transmit antenna emits a symbol $S_n^{(i)}$, where as usual n denotes time and i denotes the ith symbol in an M-ary constellation. The signal received at the N_r receive antennas can be written in vector form as

$$\begin{aligned}\tilde{\mathbf{r}}_n \stackrel{\Delta}{=} \begin{bmatrix}\tilde{r}_{n,\,1}\\ \vdots \\ \tilde{r}_{n,\,N_r}\end{bmatrix} &= S_n^{(i)}\begin{bmatrix}\tilde{h}_{n,\,1}\\ \vdots \\ \tilde{h}_{n,\,N_r}\end{bmatrix} + \begin{bmatrix}\tilde{w}_{n,\,1}\\ \vdots \\ \tilde{w}_{n,\,N_r}\end{bmatrix}\\ &\stackrel{\Delta}{=} S_n^{(i)}\tilde{\mathbf{h}}_n + \tilde{\mathbf{w}}_n\end{aligned} \tag{2.257}$$

where $\tilde{h}_{n,\,j}$ denotes the time-varying channel gain (or fade coefficient) between the transmit antenna and the jth receive antenna. The signal model given in (2.257) is typically encountered in wireless communication.

This kind of a channel that introduces multiplicative distortion in the transmitted signal besides additive noise is called a fading channel. When the received signal at time n is a function of the transmitted symbol at time n, the channel is said to be frequency nonselective (flat). On the other hand, when the received signal at time n is a function of

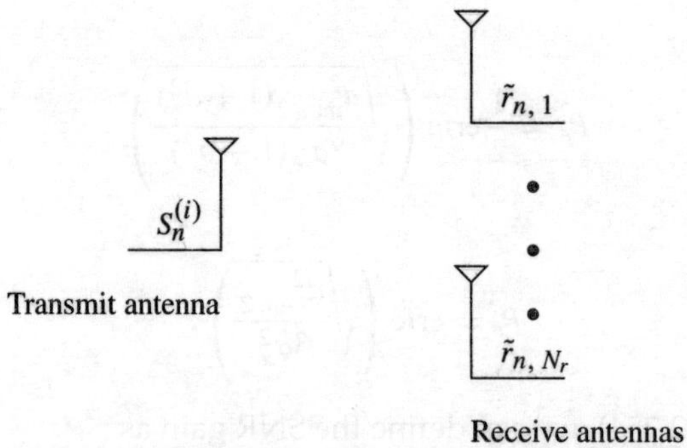

Figure 2.15 *Signal model for fading channels with receive diversity*

the present as well as the past transmitted symbols, the channel is said to be frequency selective.

We assume that the channel gains in (2.257) are zero-mean Gaussian random variables whose in-phase and quadrature components are independent of each other, that is

$$\begin{aligned}\tilde{h}_{n,j} &\triangleq \tilde{h}_{n,j,I} + \mathrm{j}h_{n,j,Q}\\ E[h_{n,j,I}h_{n,j,Q}] &= E[h_{n,j,I}]E[h_{n,j,Q}] = 0.\end{aligned} \tag{2.258}$$

We also assume the following relations:

$$\begin{aligned}\frac{1}{2}E\left[\tilde{h}_{n,j}\tilde{h}^*_{n,k}\right] &= \sigma_f^2\delta_K(j-k)\\ \frac{1}{2}E\left[\tilde{w}_{n,j}\tilde{w}^*_{n,k}\right] &= \sigma_w^2\delta_K(j-k)\\ \frac{1}{2}E\left[\tilde{h}_{n,j}\tilde{h}^*_{m,j}\right] &= \sigma_f^2\delta_K(n-m)\\ \frac{1}{2}E\left[\tilde{w}_{n,j}\tilde{w}^*_{m,j}\right] &= \sigma_w^2\delta_K(n-m).\end{aligned} \tag{2.259}$$

Since the channel gain is zero-mean Gaussian, the magnitude of the channel gain given by

$$\left|\tilde{h}_{n,j}\right| = \sqrt{h^2_{n,j,I} + h^2_{n,j,Q}} \quad \text{for } 1 \le j \le N_r \tag{2.260}$$

is Rayleigh distributed. Due to the independence assumption on the channel gains, it is quite unlikely that at any time n, all $|\tilde{h}_{n,j}|$ are close to zero simultaneously. Thus intuitively we can expect a receiver with multiple antennas to perform better than a single antenna receiver.

This method of improving the receiver performance by using multiple antennas is known as antenna diversity. Other commonly used forms of diversity are frequency, time and polarization diversity. In all cases the signal model in (2.257) is valid.

The task of the receiver is to optimally detect the transmitted symbol given $\mathbf{r}_n$. This is given by the MAP rule

$$\max_j P\left(S^{(j)}|\tilde{\mathbf{r}}_n\right) \qquad \text{for } 1 \leq j \leq M, \tag{2.261}$$

where M denotes an M-ary constellation. When all symbols in the constellation are equally likely, the MAP detector becomes an ML detector with the detection rule:

$$\max_j p\left(\tilde{\mathbf{r}}_n|S^{(j)}\right) \qquad \text{for } 1 \leq j \leq M. \tag{2.262}$$

Since we have assumed a coherent detector, the receiver has perfect knowledge of the fade coefficients. Therefore, the conditional pdf in (2.262) can be written as

$$\max_d p(\tilde{\mathbf{r}}_n|S^j, \tilde{h}_n) \quad \text{for} \quad 1 \leq j \leq M. \tag{2.263}$$

Following the method given in (2.83), (2.263) becomes

$$\max_j \frac{1}{\left(2\pi\sigma_w^2\right)^{N_r}} \exp\left(-\frac{\sum_{l=1}^{N_r}\left|\tilde{r}_{n,l} - S^{(j)}\tilde{h}_{n,l}\right|^2}{2\sigma_w^2}\right) \tag{2.264}$$

which after simplification reduces to

$$\min_j \sum_{l=1}^{N_r}\left|\tilde{r}_{n,l} - S^{(j)}\tilde{h}_{n,l}\right|^2. \tag{2.265}$$

When

$$\left|S^{(j)}\right| = \text{a constant independent of } j \tag{2.266}$$

as in the case of M-ary PSK constellations, the detection rule reduces to

$$\max_j \sum_{l=1}^{N_r} \Re\left\{\tilde{r}_{n,l}^* S^{(j)}\tilde{h}_{n,l}\right\}. \tag{2.267}$$

The detection rule in (2.267) for M-ary PSK signalling is also known as *maximal ratio combining*.

2.8.1 Performance analysis

In order to compute the average probability of symbol error, we proceed as follows.

1. We first compute the pairwise probability of symbol error for a given $\tilde{\mathbf{h}}_n$.
2. Next we compute the average pairwise probability of symbol error by averaging over all $\tilde{\mathbf{h}}_n$.
3. Finally we use the union bound to compute the average probability of symbol error.

Given that $S^{(i)}$ has been transmitted, the receiver decides in favour of $S^{(j)}$ when

$$\sum_{l=1}^{N_r} \left|\tilde{r}_{n,l} - S^{(j)}\tilde{h}_{n,l}\right|^2 < \sum_{l=1}^{N_r} \left|\tilde{r}_{n,l} - S^{(i)}\tilde{h}_{n,l}\right|^2 . \tag{2.268}$$

Substituting for $\tilde{r}_{n,l}$ on both sides and simplifying, we get

$$P\left(S^{(j)}|S^{(i)}, \tilde{\mathbf{h}}_n\right) = P\left(Z < -d^2\right) \tag{2.269}$$

where

$$Z = 2\Re\left\{\sum_{l=1}^{N_r}\left(S^{(i)} - S^{(j)}\right)\tilde{h}_{n,l}\tilde{w}_{n,l}^*\right\}$$

$$d^2 = \left|S^{(i)} - S^{(j)}\right|^2 \sum_{l=1}^{N_r}\left|\tilde{h}_{n,l}\right|^2 . \tag{2.270}$$

Clearly, Z is a real-valued Gaussian random variable with respect to $\tilde{\mathbf{w}}_n$ (since in the first step $\tilde{\mathbf{h}}_n$ is assumed known) with

$$\begin{aligned} E[Z|\tilde{h}_n] &= 0 \\ E[Z^2|\tilde{h}_n] &= 4d^2\sigma_w^2 . \end{aligned} \tag{2.271}$$

Therefore

$$\begin{aligned} P\left(S^{(j)}|S^{(i)}, \tilde{\mathbf{h}}_n\right) &= \frac{1}{\sqrt{\pi}}\int_{x=y}^{\infty} \mathrm{e}^{-x^2}\,dx \\ &\stackrel{\Delta}{=} P\left(.S^{(j)}|S^{(i)}, y\right) \end{aligned} \tag{2.272}$$

where

$$y = \frac{d}{2\sqrt{2}\sigma_w} = \frac{|S^{(i)} - S^{(j)}|}{2\sqrt{2}\sigma_w}\sqrt{\sum_{l=1}^{N_r} h_{n,l,I}^2 + h_{n,l,Q}^2} . \tag{2.273}$$

Thus

$$\begin{aligned} P\left(S^{(j)}|S^{(i)}\right) &= \int_{y=0}^{\infty} P\left(S^{(j)}|S^{(i)}, y\right) p_Y(y)\,dy \\ &= \frac{1}{\sqrt{\pi}}\int_{y=0}^{\infty}\int_{x=y}^{\infty} \mathrm{e}^{-x^2}\, p_Y(y)\,dx\,dy. \end{aligned} \tag{2.274}$$

We know that if R is a random variable given by

$$R = \sqrt{\sum_{i=1}^{N} X_i^2} \tag{2.275}$$

where X_i are real-valued independent zero-mean Gaussian random variables each with variance σ^2, the pdf of R is given by the *generalized Rayleigh distribution* as follows[2]

$$p_R(r) = \frac{r^{n-1}}{2^{(n-2)/2}\sigma^n\Gamma(n/2)} e^{-r^2/(2\sigma^2)} \qquad \text{for } r \geq 0 \tag{2.276}$$

where $\Gamma(\cdot)$ denotes the gamma function which takes on values:

$$\begin{aligned} \Gamma(0.5) &= \sqrt{\pi} \\ \Gamma(1.5) &= \sqrt{\pi}/2 \\ \Gamma(k) &= (k-1)! \qquad \text{where } k > 0 \text{ is an integer.} \end{aligned} \tag{2.277}$$

For the special case when $N = 2M$, the cumulative distribution function (cdf) of R is given by[2]

$$\begin{aligned} F_R(r) &= \int_{\alpha=0}^{r} p_R(\alpha)\, d\alpha \\ &= 1 - e^{-r^2/(2\sigma^2)} \sum_{k=0}^{M-1} \frac{1}{k!}\left(\frac{r^2}{2\sigma^2}\right)^k. \end{aligned} \tag{2.278}$$

Now, interchanging the order of the integrals in (2.274), we get

$$\begin{aligned} P\left(S^{(j)}|S^{(i)}\right) &= \frac{1}{\sqrt{\pi}} \int_{x=0}^{\infty} e^{-x^2}\, dx \int_{y=0}^{x} p_Y(y)\, dy \\ &= \frac{1}{\sqrt{\pi}} \int_{x=0}^{\infty} e^{-x^2} F_Y(x)\, dx \end{aligned} \tag{2.279}$$

where $F_Y(x)$ is the cdf of Y. For the given problem, the cdf of Y is given by (2.278) with r replaced by x and

$$\begin{aligned} N &= 2N_r \\ \sigma^2 &= \frac{\sigma_f^2}{8\sigma_w^2}\left|S^{(i)} - S^{(j)}\right|^2 \\ &= \frac{\sigma_f^2}{8\sigma_w^2}\left|S^{(i)} - S^{(j)}\right|^2. \end{aligned} \tag{2.280}$$

Substituting for $F_Y(x)$ in (2.279) we get

$$
\begin{aligned}
P\left(S^{(j)}|S^{(i)}\right) &= \frac{1}{\sqrt{\pi}}\int_{x=0}^{\infty} e^{-x^2}\left[1 - e^{-x^2/(2\sigma^2)}\sum_{k=0}^{N_r-1}\frac{1}{k!}\left(\frac{x^2}{2\sigma^2}\right)^k\right]dx \\
&= \frac{1}{\sqrt{\pi}}\int_{x=0}^{\infty}\left[e^{-x^2} - e^{-x^2(1+1/(2\sigma^2))}\sum_{k=0}^{N_r-1}\frac{1}{k!}\left(\frac{x^2}{2\sigma^2}\right)^k\right]dx \\
&= \frac{1}{2} - \frac{1}{\sqrt{\pi}}\int_{x=0}^{\infty} e^{-x^2(1+1/(2\sigma^2))}\sum_{k=0}^{N_r-1}\frac{1}{k!}\left(\frac{x^2}{2\sigma^2}\right)^k dx. \qquad (2.281)
\end{aligned}
$$

Substitute

$$
\begin{aligned}
x\sqrt{1+1/(2\sigma^2)} &= \alpha \\
\Rightarrow dx\sqrt{1+1/(2\sigma^2)} &= d\alpha \qquad (2.282)
\end{aligned}
$$

in (2.281) to get

$$
P\left(S^{(j)}|S^{(i)}\right) = \frac{1}{2} - \sqrt{\frac{2\sigma^2}{1+2\sigma^2}}\sum_{k=0}^{N_r-1}\frac{1}{k!}\frac{1}{\sqrt{\pi}}\int_{\alpha=0}^{\infty} e^{-\alpha^2}\left(\frac{\alpha^2}{1+2\sigma^2}\right)^k d\alpha. \qquad (2.283)
$$

We know that if X is a zero-mean Gaussian random variable with variance σ_1^2, then for $n > 0$,

$$
\begin{aligned}
\frac{1}{\sigma_1\sqrt{2\pi}}\int_{x=-\infty}^{\infty} x^{2n} e^{-x^2/(2\sigma_1^2)}\,dx &= 1 \times 3 \times \cdots \times (2n-1)\sigma_1^{2n} \\
\Rightarrow \frac{1}{\sigma_1\sqrt{2\pi}}\int_{x=0}^{\infty} x^{2n} e^{-x^2/(2\sigma_1^2)}\,dx &= \frac{1}{2} \times 1 \times 3 \times \cdots \times (2n-1)\sigma_1^{2n}. \qquad (2.284)
\end{aligned}
$$

Note that in (2.283) $2\sigma_1^2 = 1$. Thus for $N_r = 1$ we have

$$
P\left(S^{(j)}|S^{(i)}\right) = \frac{1}{2} - \frac{1}{2}\sqrt{\frac{2\sigma^2}{1+2\sigma^2}}. \qquad (2.285)
$$

For $N_r > 1$ we have

$$
P\left(S^{(j)}|S^{(i)}\right) = \frac{1}{2} - \frac{1}{2}\sqrt{\frac{2\sigma^2}{1+2\sigma^2}} - \frac{1}{2}\sqrt{\frac{2\sigma^2}{1+2\sigma^2}}\sum_{k=1}^{N_r-1}\frac{1 \times 3 \ldots (2k-1)}{k!\,2^k}\left(\frac{1}{1+2\sigma^2}\right)^k. \qquad (2.286)
$$

Thus we find that the average pairwise probability of symbol error depends on the squared Euclidean distance between the two symbols.

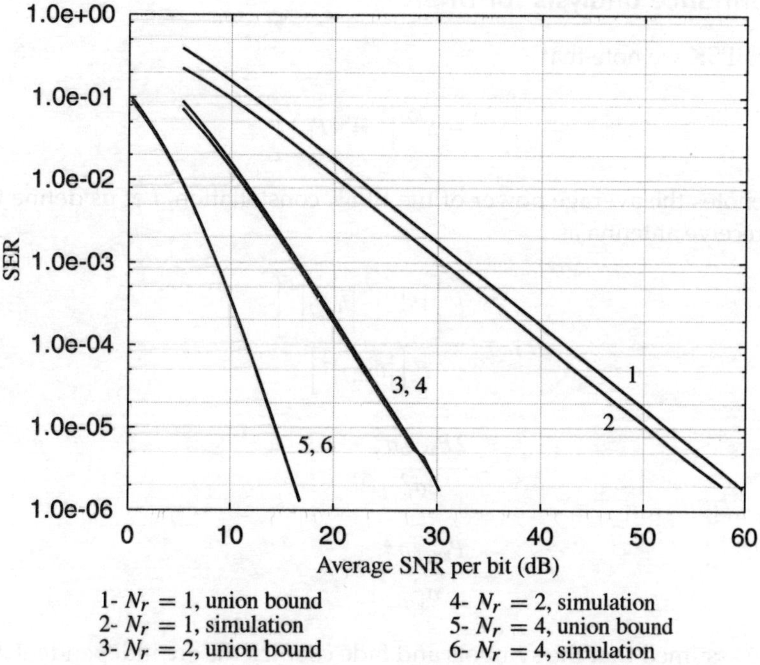

Figure 2.16 *Theoretical and simulation results for 8-PSK in Rayleigh flat fading channel for various diversities*

Finally, the average probability of error is upper bounded by the union bound as follows.

$$P(e) \leq \sum_{i=1}^{M} P\left(S^{(i)}\right) \sum_{\substack{j=1 \\ j\neq i}}^{M} P\left(S^{(j)}|S^{(i)}\right). \tag{2.287}$$

If we assume that all symbols are equally likely, then the average probability of error reduces to

$$P(e) \leq \frac{1}{M} \sum_{i=1}^{M} \sum_{\substack{j=1 \\ j\neq i}}^{M} P\left(S^{(j)}|S^{(i)}\right). \tag{2.288}$$

The theoretical and simulation results for 8-PSK are plotted in Figure 2.16. Note that there is a slight difference between the theoretical and simulated curves for first-order diversity. However, for second and fourth-order diversity the theoretical and simulated curves overlap, which demonstrates the accuracy of the union bound.

2.8.2 Performance analysis for BPSK

For the case of BPSK we note that

$$\left|S^{(1)} - S^{(2)}\right|^2 = 4P_{\text{av},\,b} \tag{2.289}$$

where $P_{\text{av},\,b}$ denotes the average power of the BPSK constellation. Let us define the average SNR for each receive antenna as

$$\begin{aligned}\gamma &= \frac{E\left[\left|S_n^{(i)}\right|^2 \left|\tilde{h}_{n,\,l}\right|^2\right]}{E\left[\left|\tilde{w}_{n,\,l}\right|^2\right]} \\ &= \frac{2P_{\text{av},\,b}\sigma_f^2}{2\sigma_w^2} \\ &= \frac{P_{\text{av},\,b}\sigma_f^2}{\sigma_w^2}\end{aligned} \tag{2.290}$$

where we have assumed that the symbols and fade coefficients are independent. Comparing (2.280) and (2.290), we find that

$$2\sigma^2 = \gamma. \tag{2.291}$$

We also note that when both the symbols are equally likely, the pairwise probability of error is equal to the average probability of error. Hence, substituting (2.291) in (2.286), we get (for $N_r = 1$)

$$P(e) = \frac{1}{2} - \frac{1}{2}\sqrt{\frac{\gamma}{1+\gamma}}. \tag{2.292}$$

For $N_r > 1$ we have

$$P(e) = \frac{1}{2} - \frac{1}{2}\sqrt{\frac{\gamma}{1+\gamma}} - \frac{1}{2}\sqrt{\frac{\gamma}{1+\gamma}}\sum_{k=1}^{N_r-1}\frac{1\times 3\ldots(2k-1)}{k!\,2^k}\left(\frac{1}{1+\gamma}\right)^k. \tag{2.293}$$

Further, if we define

$$\mu = \sqrt{\frac{\gamma}{1+\gamma}} \tag{2.294}$$

the average probability of error is given by (for $N_r = 1$)

$$P(e) = \frac{1}{2}(1-\mu). \tag{2.295}$$

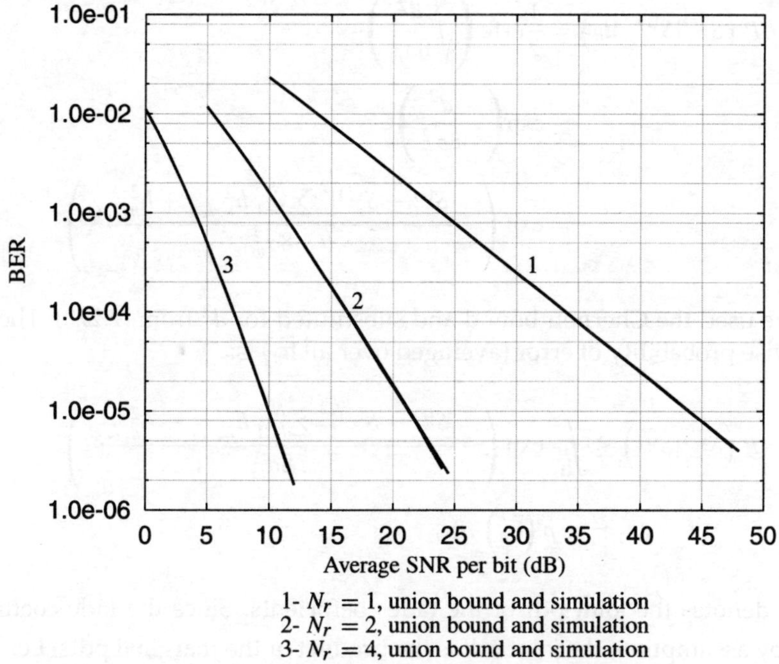

Figure 2.17 *Theoretical and simulation results for BPSK in Rayleigh flat fading channels for various diversities*

For $N_r > 1$ the average probability of error is given by

$$P(e) = \frac{1}{2}(1-\mu) - \frac{\mu}{2} \sum_{k=1}^{N_r-1} \frac{1 \times 3 \ldots (2k-1)}{k!\, 2^k} \left(1-\mu^2\right)^k. \tag{2.296}$$

Interestingly, the average probability of error is also given by[2]

$$P(e) = \left[\frac{1}{2}(1-\mu)\right]^{N_r} \sum_{k=0}^{N_r-1} \binom{N_r-1+k}{k} \left[\frac{1}{2}(1+\mu)\right]^k. \tag{2.297}$$

Both formulas are identical. The theoretical and simulated curves for BPSK are shown in Figure 2.17. Observe that the theoretical and simulated curves overlap.

2.8.3 Approximate performance analysis

In this section we obtain the expression for the average probability of symbol error using the Chernoff bound. From (2.272) we have

$$
\begin{aligned}
P\left(S^{(j)}|S^{(i)}, \tilde{\mathbf{h}}_n\right) &= \frac{1}{2}\text{erfc}\left(\sqrt{\frac{d^2}{8\sigma_w^2}}\right) \\
&\le \exp\left(-\frac{d^2}{8\sigma_w^2}\right) \\
&= \exp\left(-\frac{\left|S^{(i)} - S^{(j)}\right|^2 \sum_{l=1}^{N_r} h_{n,\,l,\,I}^2 + h_{n,\,l,\,Q}^2}{8\sigma_w^2}\right)
\end{aligned} \tag{2.298}
$$

where we have used the Chernoff bound and substituted for d^2 from (2.270). Therefore the average pairwise probability of error (averaged over all $\tilde{\mathbf{h}}_n$) is:

$$
\begin{aligned}
P\left(S^{(j)}|S^{(i)}\right) \le \int_{\tilde{\mathbf{h}}_n} &\exp\left(-\frac{\left|S^{(i)} - S^{(j)}\right|^2 \sum_{l=1}^{N_r} h_{n,\,l,\,I}^2 + h_{n,\,l,\,Q}^2}{8\sigma_w^2}\right) \\
&\times p\left(\tilde{\mathbf{h}}_n\right)\, d\tilde{\mathbf{h}}_n
\end{aligned} \tag{2.299}
$$

where $p\left(\tilde{\mathbf{h}}_n\right)$ denotes the joint pdf of the fade coefficients. Since the fade coefficients are independent by assumption, the joint pdf is the product of the marginal pdfs. Let

$$
x = \int_{h_{n,\,l,\,I}=-\infty}^{\infty} \exp\left(-\frac{\left|S^{(i)} - S^{(j)}\right|^2 h_{n,\,l,\,I}^2}{8\sigma_w^2}\right) p\left(h_{n,\,l,\,I}\right)\, dh_{n,\,l,\,I}. \tag{2.300}
$$

It is clear that (2.299) reduces to:

$$
P\left(S^{(j)}|S^{(i)}\right) = x^{2N_r}. \tag{2.301}
$$

Substituting for $p(h_{n,\,l,\,I})$ in (2.300) we get:

$$
\begin{aligned}
x &= \frac{1}{\sigma_f\sqrt{2\pi}} \int_{h_{n,\,l,\,I}=-\infty}^{\infty} \exp\left(-\frac{\left|S^{(i)} - S^{(j)}\right|^2 h_{n,\,l,\,I}^2}{8\sigma_w^2} - \frac{h_{n,\,l,\,I}^2}{2\sigma_f^2}\right) dh_{n,\,l,\,I} \\
&= \frac{1}{\sqrt{1 + 2A\sigma_f^2}}
\end{aligned} \tag{2.302}
$$

where

$$
A = \frac{\left|S^{(i)} - S^{(j)}\right|^2}{8\sigma_w^2}. \tag{2.303}
$$

The average probability of error is obtained by substituting (2.301) in (2.287).

2.9 Differential Detectors with Diversity for Flat Fading Channels

Consider the signal model in (2.257). Let us assume that $S_n^{(i)}$ is drawn from an M-ary PSK constellation with

$$P_{\text{av}} = C. \tag{2.304}$$

Furthermore, we assume that the symbols are differentially encoded so that the received vector over two consecutive symbol durations is given by

$$\begin{aligned} \tilde{\mathbf{r}}_{n-1} &= \sqrt{C}\tilde{\mathbf{h}}_{n-1} + \tilde{\mathbf{w}}_{n-1} \\ \tilde{\mathbf{r}}_n &= \sqrt{C}\mathrm{e}^{\mathrm{j}\phi_i}\tilde{\mathbf{h}}_n + \tilde{\mathbf{w}}_n \end{aligned} \tag{2.305}$$

where,

$$\phi_i = \frac{2\pi i}{M} \quad \text{for } 1 \le i \le M \tag{2.306}$$

is the transmitted phase change. In the signal model given by (2.305) we assume that the channel gains are correlated over a given diversity path (receive antenna). However, we continue to assume the channel gains to be uncorrelated across different receive antennas. In view of the above assumptions, the third equation in (2.259) must be rewritten as

$$\frac{1}{2}E[\tilde{h}_{n,j}\tilde{h}^*_{n-m,j}] = R_{\tilde{h}\tilde{h},m} \tag{2.307}$$

which is assumed to be real-valued. In other words, we assume that the inphase and quadrature components of the channel gain are independent of each other[51] as given in (2.258). Let

$$R_{\tilde{h}\tilde{h},0} = \sigma_f^2, \qquad \frac{R_{\tilde{h}\tilde{h},1}}{R_{\tilde{h}\tilde{h},0}} = \rho. \tag{2.308}$$

Define the signal-to-noise ratio as

$$\gamma_s = \frac{2C\sigma_f^2}{2\sigma_w^2} = \frac{C\sigma_f^2}{\sigma_w^2}. \tag{2.309}$$

Consider the differential detection rule given by[51]:

$$\max_j \sum_{l=1}^{N_r} \Re\,\{\tilde{r}_{n,l}\tilde{r}^*_{n-1,l}\mathrm{e}^{-\mathrm{j}\phi_j}\}. \tag{2.310}$$

We wish to compute the probability of deciding in favour of ϕ_j given that ϕ_i was transmitted. This happens when

$$
\begin{aligned}
&\sum_{l=1}^{Nr} \Re\left\{\tilde{r}_{n,l}\tilde{r}^{*}_{n-1,l}(\mathrm{e}^{-\mathrm{j}\phi_i} - \mathrm{e}^{-\mathrm{j}\phi_j})\right\} < 0 \\
&\Rightarrow \sum_{l=1}^{Nr} \Re\left\{\tilde{r}_{n,l}\tilde{r}^{*}_{n-1,l}\mathrm{e}^{-\mathrm{j}\phi_i}(1 - \mathrm{e}^{\mathrm{j}\delta_{i,j}})\right\} < 0 \\
&\Rightarrow \sum_{l=1}^{Nr} v\,\Re\left\{\tilde{r}_{n,l}\tilde{r}^{*}_{n-1,l}\mathrm{e}^{-\mathrm{j}\phi_i}\,B\mathrm{e}^{\mathrm{j}\alpha}\right\} < 0 \\
&\Rightarrow \sum_{l=1}^{Nr} \Re\left\{\tilde{r}_{n,l}\tilde{r}^{*}_{n-1,l}\mathrm{e}^{-\mathrm{j}\phi_i}\mathrm{e}^{\mathrm{j}\alpha}\right\} < 0.
\end{aligned}
\tag{2.311}
$$

where $\delta_{i,j}$ $B\mathrm{e}^{\mathrm{j}\alpha}$ are defined in (2.202) and (2.204) respectively. Let

$$
Z \Rightarrow \sum_{l=1}^{Nr} \Re\left\{\tilde{r}_{n,l}\tilde{r}^{*}_{n-1,l}\mathrm{e}^{-\mathrm{j}\phi_i}\mathrm{e}^{\mathrm{j}\alpha}\right\}.
\tag{2.312}
$$

Then

$$
\begin{aligned}
P(\phi_j|\phi_i &= P(Z < 0|\phi_i) \\
&= \int_{\tilde{\mathbf{r}}_{n-1}} P(Z < 0|\tilde{\mathbf{r}}_{n-1}, \phi_i)\,p(\tilde{\mathbf{r}}_{n-1})\,d\tilde{\mathbf{r}}_{n-1}.
\end{aligned}
\tag{2.313}
$$

Given the vector $\tilde{\mathbf{r}}_{n-1}$, Z is a Gaussian distributed random variable, since it is a linear combination of the elements of $\tilde{\mathbf{r}}_n$. Let us now compute the conditional mean and variance of Z.

We begin by making the following observations:

1. The elements of $\tilde{\mathbf{r}}_n$ are independent of each other for a given value of ϕ_i.
2. The elements of $\tilde{\mathbf{r}}_{n-1}$ are independent of each other.
3. The random variables $\tilde{r}_{n,l}$ and $\tilde{r}_{n-1,j}$ are independent for $j \neq l$. However, $\tilde{r}_{n,l}$ and $\tilde{r}_{n-1,l}$ are correlated. Therefore the following relations hold:

$$
\begin{aligned}
p(\tilde{r}_{n,l}|\tilde{\mathbf{r}}_{n-1}, \phi_i) &= p(\tilde{r}_{n,l}|\tilde{r}_{n-1,l}, \phi_i) \\
\Rightarrow E(\tilde{r}_{n,l}|\tilde{\mathbf{r}}_{n-1}, \phi_i) &= E[\tilde{r}_{n,l}|\tilde{r}_{n-1,l}, \phi_i] \\
&\triangleq \tilde{m}_1.
\end{aligned}
\tag{2.314}
$$

4. Again, due to the independence between $\tilde{r}_{n,l}$ and $\tilde{r}_{n-1,j}$, we have

$$
\begin{aligned}
&E[(\tilde{r}_{n,l} - \tilde{m}_l)(\tilde{r}_{n,j} - \tilde{m}_j)|\tilde{\mathbf{r}}_{n-1}, \phi_i] \\
&= E[(\tilde{r}_{n,l} - \tilde{m}_l)(\tilde{r}_{n,j} - \tilde{m}_j)|\tilde{r}_{n-1,l}, \tilde{r}_{n-1,j}, \phi_i] \\
&= E[(\tilde{r}_{n,l} - \tilde{m}_l)|\tilde{r}_{n-1,l}, \phi_i]E[(\tilde{r}_{n,j} - \tilde{m}_j)|\tilde{r}_{n-1,j}, \phi_i] \\
&= 0.
\end{aligned}
\tag{2.315}
$$

Now,

$$
\begin{aligned}
p(\tilde{r}_{n,l}|\tilde{r}_{n-1,l}, \phi_i) &= \frac{p(\tilde{r}_{n,l}, \tilde{r}_{n-1,l}|\phi_i)}{p(\tilde{r}_{n-1,l}|\phi_i)} \\
&= \frac{p(\tilde{r}_{n,l}, \tilde{r}_{n-1,l}|\phi_i)}{p(\tilde{r}_{n-1,l})}
\end{aligned}
\tag{2.316}
$$

since $\tilde{r}_{n-1,l}$ is independent of ϕ_i. Let

$$
\tilde{\mathbf{x}} = [\tilde{r}_{n,l} \quad \tilde{r}_{n-1,l}]^T. \tag{2.317}
$$

Clearly,

$$
E[\tilde{\mathbf{x}}|\phi_i] = [0 \quad 0]^T. \tag{2.318}
$$

Then the covariance matrix of $\tilde{\mathbf{x}}$ is given by

$$
\tilde{\mathbf{R}}_{\tilde{x}\tilde{x}} = \frac{1}{2}E[\tilde{\mathbf{x}}\tilde{\mathbf{x}}^H|\phi_i] = \begin{bmatrix} \tilde{R}_{\tilde{x}\tilde{x},0} & \tilde{R}_{\tilde{x}\tilde{x},1} \\ \tilde{R}^*_{\tilde{x}\tilde{x},1} & \tilde{R}_{\tilde{x}\tilde{x},0} \end{bmatrix} \tag{2.319}
$$

where

$$
\begin{aligned}
\tilde{R}_{\tilde{x}\tilde{x},0} &= \frac{1}{2}E[\tilde{r}_{n,l}\tilde{r}^*_{n,l}|\phi_i] \\
&= \frac{1}{2}E[\tilde{r}_{n-1,l}\tilde{r}^*_{n-1,l}] = C\sigma_f^2 + \sigma_w^2 \\
\tilde{R}_{\tilde{x}\tilde{x},1} &= \frac{1}{2}E[\tilde{r}_{n,l}\tilde{r}^*_{n-1,l}|\phi_i] = C\mathrm{e}^{\mathrm{j}\phi_i} R_{\tilde{h}\tilde{h},l}.
\end{aligned}
\tag{2.320}
$$

Now,

$$
p(\tilde{r}_{n,l}, \tilde{r}_{n-1,l}|\phi_i) = \frac{1}{(2\pi)^2\Delta}\exp\left(-\frac{1}{2}\tilde{\mathbf{x}}^H\tilde{\mathbf{R}}^{-1}_{\tilde{x}\tilde{x}}\tilde{\mathbf{x}}\right) \tag{2.321}
$$

where

$$
\Delta = \tilde{R}^2_{\tilde{x}\tilde{x},0} - |\tilde{R}_{\tilde{x}\tilde{x},1}|^2 = \det(\tilde{\mathbf{R}}_{\tilde{x}\tilde{x}}). \tag{2.322}
$$

Observe that $\tilde{r}_{n-1,l}$ is a Gaussian random variable with

$$
\begin{aligned}
E[\tilde{r}_{n-1,l}] &= 0 \\
E[r^2_{n-1,l,I}] &= \tilde{R}_{\tilde{x}\tilde{x},0} \\
&= E[r^2_{n-1,l,Q}].
\end{aligned}
\tag{2.323}
$$

Therefore,

$$p(\tilde{r}_{n-1,l}) = \frac{1}{(2\pi\,\tilde{R}_{\tilde{x}\tilde{x},0})}\exp\left(-\frac{|\tilde{r}_{n-1,l}|^2}{2\tilde{R}_{\tilde{x}\tilde{x},0}}\right). \tag{2.324}$$

Then it can be shown from (2.316), (2.321) and (2.324) that

$$p(\tilde{r}_{n,l}|\tilde{r}_{n-1,l,}\phi_i) = \frac{\tilde{R}_{\tilde{x}\tilde{x},0}}{(2\pi\,\Delta)}\exp\left(-\frac{\tilde{R}_{\tilde{x}\tilde{x},0}}{2\Delta}\left|\tilde{r}_{n,l} - \frac{\tilde{r}_{n-1,l}\,\tilde{R}_{\tilde{x}\tilde{x},1}}{\tilde{R}_{\tilde{x}\tilde{x},0}}\right|^2\right). \tag{2.325}$$

Hence $\tilde{r}_{n,l}$ is conditionally Gaussian with (conditional) mean and variance given by

$$\begin{aligned}
E[\tilde{r}_{n,l}|\tilde{r}_{n-1,l},\phi_i] &= \frac{\tilde{r}_{n-1,l}\,\tilde{R}_{\tilde{x}\tilde{x},1}}{\tilde{R}_{\tilde{x}\tilde{x},0}}\\
&= \tilde{m}_l\\
&= m_{l,I} + \mathrm{j}m_{l,Q}\\
\mathrm{var}\,(\tilde{r}_{n,l}|\tilde{r}_{n-1,l},\phi_i) &= \frac{1}{2}E[|\tilde{r}_{n,l} - \tilde{m}_l|^2|\tilde{r}_{n-1,l},\phi]\\
&= E[(r_{n,l,I} - m_{l,I})^2|\tilde{r}_{n-1,l},\phi_i]\\
&= E[(r_{n,l,Q} - m_{l,Q})^2|\tilde{r}_{n-1,l},\phi_i]\\
&= \frac{\Delta}{\tilde{R}_{\tilde{x}\tilde{x},0}}
\end{aligned} \tag{2.326}$$

which is obtained by the inspection of (2.325). Note that (2.325) and the pdf in (2.13) have a similar form. Hence we observe from (2.325) that the in-phase and quadrature components of $\tilde{r}_{n,l}$ are conditionally uncorrelated, that is,

$$E[(r_{n,l,I} - m_{l,I})(r_{n,l,Q} - m_{l,Q})|\tilde{r}_{n-1,l},\phi_i] = 0 \tag{2.327}$$

and being Gaussian, they are also statistically independent.

Having obtained these results, we are now in a position to evaluate the conditional mean and variance of Z as defined in (2.312). Using (2.314), the conditional mean is[51]

$$\begin{aligned}
E[Z|\tilde{\mathbf{r}}_{n-1},\phi_i] &= \sum_{l=1}^{Nr}\Re\left\{E[\tilde{r}_{n,l}|\tilde{\mathbf{r}}_{n-1},\phi_i]\tilde{r}^*_{n-1,l}\mathrm{e}^{-\mathrm{j}\phi_i}\mathrm{e}^{\mathrm{j}\alpha}\right\}\\
&= \sum_{l=1}^{Nr}\Re\left\{E[\tilde{r}_{n,l}|\tilde{r}_{n-1,l},\phi_i]\tilde{r}^*_{n-1,l}\mathrm{e}^{-\mathrm{j}\phi_i}\mathrm{e}^{\mathrm{j}\alpha}\right\}\\
&= \sum_{l=1}^{Nr}|\tilde{r}_{n-1,l}|^2\,\Re\left\{\frac{\tilde{R}_{\tilde{x}\tilde{x},1}}{\tilde{R}_{\tilde{x}\tilde{x},0}}\mathrm{e}^{-\mathrm{j}\phi_i}\mathrm{e}^{\mathrm{j}\alpha}\right\}
\end{aligned}$$

$$= \sum_{l=1}^{Nr} |\tilde{r}_{n-1,l}|^2 \Re \left\{ \frac{CR_{\tilde{h}\tilde{h},1}}{CR_{\tilde{h}\tilde{h},0} + \sigma_w^2} e^{j\alpha} \right\}$$

$$= \sum_{l=1}^{Nr} |\tilde{r}_{n-1,l}|^2 \frac{CR_{\tilde{h}\tilde{h},1}}{C\sigma_f^2 + \sigma_w^2} \cos(\alpha)$$

$$= \frac{\rho\gamma_s}{1+\gamma_s} \cos(\alpha) \sum_{l=1}^{Nr} |\tilde{r}_{n-1,l}|^2$$

$$\triangleq m_Z. \tag{2.328}$$

Now we need to compute the conditional variance of Z.

Consider a set of independent complex-valued random variables $\tilde{x}_1$ with mean $\tilde{m}_1$ for $1 \leq l \leq N_r$. Let $\tilde{A}_l (1 \leq l \leq N_r)$ denote a set of complex constants. We also assume that the in-phase and quadrature components of $\tilde{x}_1$ are uncorrelated, that is,

$$E[(x_{l,I} - m_{l,I})(x_{l,Q} - m_{l,Q})] = 0. \tag{2.329}$$

Let the variance of $\tilde{x}_l$ be denoted by

$$\text{var}\,(\tilde{x}_l) = \frac{1}{2} E[|\tilde{x}_l - \tilde{m}_l|^2]$$

$$= E[(x_{l,I} - m_{l,I})^2]$$

$$= E[(x_{l,Q} - m_{l,Q})^2]$$

$$\triangleq \sigma_x^2. \tag{2.330}$$

Then

$$E\left[\sum_{l=1}^{N_r} \Re\,\{\tilde{x}_l \tilde{A}_l\}\right] = \sum_{l=1}^{Nr} \Re\,\{E[\tilde{x}_1]\tilde{A}_l\} = \sum_{l=1}^{Nr} \Re\,\{\tilde{m}_l \tilde{A}_l\}$$

$$= \sum_{l=1}^{Nr} m_{l,I} \tilde{A}_{l,I} - m_{l,Q} A_{l,Q}. \tag{2.331}$$

Therefore using (2.329) and independence between $\tilde{x}_l$ and $\tilde{x}_j$ for $j \neq l$, we have

$$\text{var}\left(\sum_{l=1}^{N_r} \Re\,\{\tilde{x}_l \tilde{A}_l\}\right)$$

$$= \text{var}\left(\sum_{l=1}^{N_r} x_{l,I} A_{l,I} - x_{l,Q} A_{l,Q}\right)$$

$$= E\left[\left(\sum_{l=1}^{N_r}(x_{l,I} - m_{l,I})A_{l,I} - (x_{l,Q} - m_{l,Q})A_{l,Q}\right)^2\right]$$

$$= \sigma_x^2 \sum_{l=1}^{N_r} |\tilde{A}_l|^2. \tag{2.332}$$

Using the above analogy for the computation of the conditional variance of Z, we have, from (2.312) and (2.326),

$$\begin{aligned}
\tilde{x}_l &= \tilde{r}_{n,l} \\
\sigma_x^2 &= \frac{\Delta}{\tilde{R}_{\tilde{x}\tilde{x},0}} \\
\tilde{A}_l &= \tilde{r}_{n-1,l}^* \mathrm{e}^{-\mathrm{j}\phi_i} \mathrm{e}^{\mathrm{j}\alpha} \\
\tilde{m}_l &= \frac{\tilde{r}_{n-1,l} \tilde{R}_{\tilde{x}\tilde{x},1}}{\tilde{R}_{\tilde{x}\tilde{x},0}}
\end{aligned} \tag{2.333}$$

Therefore using (2.315) and (2.327) we have[51]

$$\begin{aligned}
\mathrm{var}\,(Z|\tilde{\mathbf{r}}_{n-1}, \phi_i) &= \frac{\Delta}{\tilde{R}_{\tilde{x}\tilde{x},0}} \sum_{l=1}^{Nr} |\tilde{r}_{n-1,l}|^2 \\
&= \sigma_w^2 \left[\frac{(1+\gamma_s)^2 - (\rho\gamma_s)^2}{1+\gamma_s}\right] \sum_{l=1}^{N_r} |\tilde{r}_{n-1,l}|^2 \\
&\triangleq \sigma_Z^2.
\end{aligned} \tag{2.334}$$

Hence the conditional probability in (2.313) can be written as

$$P(Z < 0|\tilde{\mathbf{r}}_{n-1}, \phi_i) = \frac{1}{\sigma_Z\sqrt{2\pi}} \int_{Z=-\infty}^{0} \exp\left(\frac{(Z-m_Z)^2}{2\sigma_Z^2}\right) dZ. \tag{2.335}$$

Substituting

$$\frac{(Z-m_Z)}{\sigma_z\sqrt{2}} = x \tag{2.336}$$

we get

$$\begin{aligned}
P(Z < 0|\tilde{\mathbf{r}}_{n-1}, \phi_i) &= \frac{1}{\sqrt{\pi}} \int_{x=y}^{\infty} \mathrm{e}^{-x^2}\, dx \\
&= \frac{1}{2}\mathrm{erfc}(y)
\end{aligned} \tag{2.337}$$

where

$$
\begin{aligned}
y &= \frac{m_Z}{\sigma_Z\sqrt{2}} \\
&= \frac{\rho\gamma_s\cos(\alpha)}{\sigma_w\sqrt{2(1+\gamma_s)((1+\gamma_s)^2-(\rho\gamma_s)^2)}}\sqrt{\sum_{l=1}^{N_r}|\tilde{r}_{n-1,l}|^2}
\end{aligned}
\tag{2.338}
$$

which is similar to (2.273). Finally,

$$
\begin{aligned}
P(\phi_j|\phi_i) &= P(Z<0|\phi i) \\
&= \int_{\tilde{\mathbf{r}}_{n-1}} P(Z<0|\tilde{\mathbf{r}}_{n-1},\phi_i)p(\tilde{\mathbf{r}}_{n-1})d\tilde{\mathbf{r}}_{n-1} \\
&= \int_{y=0}^{\infty} P(Z<0|y,\phi_i)p_Y(y)dy \\
&= \frac{1}{\sqrt{\pi}}\int_{y=0}^{\infty}\int_{x=y}^{\infty} \mathrm{e}^{-x^2}p_Y(y)dxdy
\end{aligned}
\tag{2.339}
$$

which is similar to the right-hand-side of (2.274). Hence the solution to (2.339) is given by (2.285) and (2.286) with

$$
\begin{aligned}
\sigma^2 &= \frac{(\rho\gamma_s\cos(\alpha))^2}{2\sigma_w^2(1+\gamma_s)((1+\gamma_s)^2-(\rho\gamma_s)^2)}E[r_{n-1,l,I}^2] \\
&= \frac{(\rho\gamma_s\cos(\alpha))^2}{2\sigma_w^2(1+\gamma_s)((1+\gamma_s)^2-(\rho\gamma_s)^2)}\tilde{R}_{\tilde{x}\tilde{x},0}
\end{aligned}
\tag{2.340}
$$

Note that when $\rho = 0$ (the channel gains are uncorrelated), from (2.285) and (2.286) we get

$$
P(\phi_j|\phi_i) = \frac{1}{2}. \tag{2.341}
$$

Thus it is clear that the detection rule in (2.310) makes sense only when the channels gains are correlated.

The average probability of error is given by (2.288). However, due to symmetry in the M-ary PSK constellation (2.288) reduces to

$$
P(e) \leq \sum_{\substack{j=1\\ j\neq 1}}^{M} P(\phi_j|\phi_i). \tag{2.342}
$$

There is an alternate solution for the last integral in (2.339). Define

$$
\mu = \sqrt{\frac{2\sigma^2}{1+2\sigma^2}} \tag{2.343}
$$

where σ^2 is defined in (2.340). Then[2,51],

$$P(\phi_j|\phi_i) = \left(\frac{1-\mu}{2}\right)^{N_r} \sum_{l=0}^{N_r-1} \binom{N_r - 1 + l}{l} \left(\frac{1+\mu}{2}\right)^l. \tag{2.344}$$

2.10 Summary

In this chapter we have derived and analyzed the performance of coherent detectors for both two-dimensional and multidimensional signalling schemes. A procedure for optimizing a binary two-dimensional constellation is discussed. The error-rate analysis for non-equiprobable symbols is done. The minimum SNR required for error-free coherent detection of multi-dimensional orthogonal signals is studied. We have also derived and analyzed the performance of noncoherent detectors for multidimensional orthogonal signals and M-ary PSK signals. The problem of optimum detection of signals in coloured Gaussian noise is investigated. Finally, the performance of coherent and differential detectors in Rayleigh flat-fading channels is analyzed. A notable feature of this chapter is that the performance of various detectors is obtained in terms of the minimum Euclidean distance (d), instead of the usual signal-to-noise ratio. In fact, by adopting the minimum Euclidean distance measure, we have demonstrated that the average probability of error for coherent detection is $(A/2)\text{erfc}\,(\sqrt{d^2/(8\sigma_w^2)})$, where A is a scale factor that depends of the modulation scheme.

The next chapter is devoted to the study of error control coding schemes which result in improved symbol-error-rate or bit-error-rate performance over the uncoded schemes discussed in this chapter.

Observe that all the detection rules presented in this chapter can be implemented in software.

3 Channel Coding

The purpose of error control coding or *channel coding* is to reduce the bit-error-rate (BER) compared to that of an uncoded system for a given SNR. The channel coder achieves the BER improvement by introducing redundancy in the uncoded data. Channel coders can be broadly classified into two groups:

(a) Block coders
(b) Convolutional coders

In this chapter we will deal with only convolutional codes since it has got several interesting extensions like the two-dimensional trellis coded modulation (TCM), multidimensional trellis coded modulation (MTCM) and turbo codes.

There are two different strategies for decoding convolutional codes:

(a) Maximum likelihood (ML) decoding
(b) Sequential decoding

The Viterbi decoder corresponds to maximum likelihood decoding and the Fano decoder corresponds to sequential decoding. In this chapter we will deal with only ML decoding and the Viterbi decoder, which is by far the most popularly used decoder for convolutional codes.

The block diagram of the communication system under consideration is shown in Figure 3.1. The subscript m in the figure denotes time index. Observe that the uncoded bit sequence is grouped into *non-overlapping* blocks of k bits by the serial-to-parallel converter, and n coded bits are generated for every k-bit uncoded block. The *code rate* is defined as $k/n < 1$. Thus if the uncoded bit rate is R bits/s then the coded bit rate is Rn/k bits/sec. Hence it is clear that channel coding results in an expansion of bandwidth. Note that the receiver can be implemented in many ways, which will be taken up in the later sections.

It is often necessary to compare the performance of different coding schemes. It is customary to select uncoded BPSK with average power denoted by $P_{\text{av},b}$, as the reference. We now make the following proposition:

Proposition 3.0.1 *The energy transmitted by the coded and uncoded modulation schemes over the same time duration must be identical.*

The above proposition looks intuitively satisfying, since it would be unfair for a coding scheme to increase the energy above that of uncoded BPSK and then claim a coding gain.

As an example, assume that k bits are encoded at a time. If the uncoded bit-rate is R then the duration of k uncoded bits is $T_k = k/R$. The transmitted energy of uncoded BPSK in the duration T_k is then $P_{\text{av},b}k$. Then the transmitted energy of *any* coding scheme in the duration

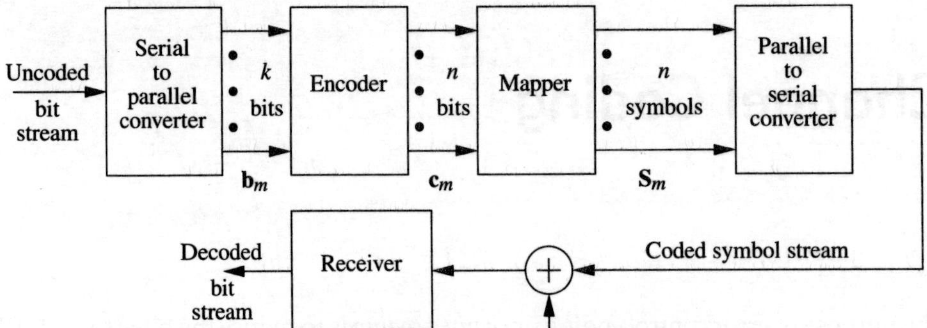

$$\mathbf{b}_m = \left[b_{1,m} \cdots b_{k,m}\right]^T$$
$$\mathbf{c}_m = \left[c_{1,m} \cdots c_{n,m}\right]^T$$
$$\mathbf{S}_m = \left[S_{1,m} \cdots S_{n,m}\right]^T$$

Uncoded bit stream: $\cdots \underbrace{1011 \cdots 11}_{k \text{ bits}}\,\underbrace{1100 \cdots 10}_{k \text{ bits}} \cdots$

Coded bit stream: $\cdots \underbrace{1010 \cdots 01}_{n \text{ bits}}\,\underbrace{0010 \cdots 00}_{n \text{ bits}} \cdots$

Figure 3.1 *Block diagram of a general convolutional coder*

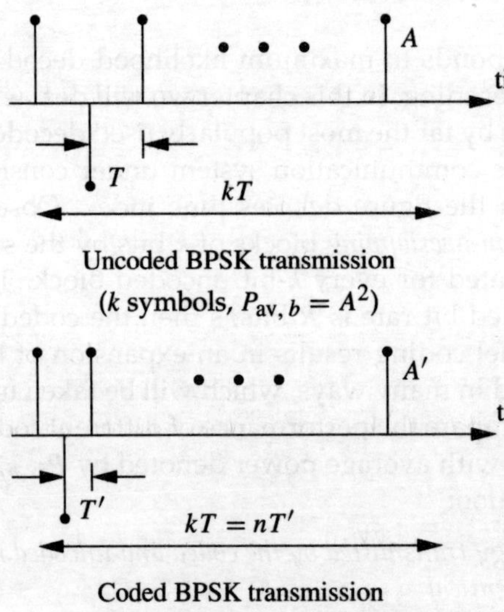

Figure 3.2 *Illustrating Proposition 3.0.1. Note that* $kA^2 = nA'^2$

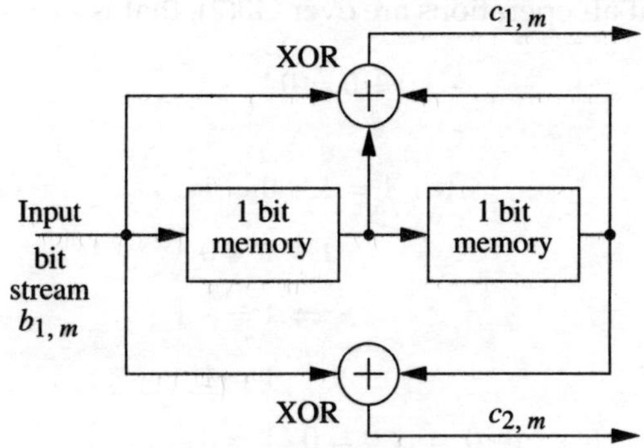

$$\mathbf{b}_m = [b_{1,m}]^T$$
$$\mathbf{c}_m = [c_{1,m} \;\; c_{2,m}]^T$$

Figure 3.3 *A rate-1/2 convolutional encoder*

T_k should be $P_{\text{av},b}k$. This is illustrated in Figure 3.2. A formal proof of the above proposition using continuous-time signals is given in Chapter 4, Section 4.1.3.

Proposition 3.0.2 *The average decoded bit error rate performance of any coding scheme must be expressed in terms of* $P_{\text{av},\,b}$.

This proposition will not only tell us of the improvement of a coding scheme with respect to uncoded BPSK, but will also give information about the relative performance of different coding schemes.

In the next section, we describe the implementation of the convolutional encoder. The reader is also advised to go through Appendix C for a brief introduction to groups and fields.

3.1 The Convolutional Encoder

Consider the encoder shown in Figure 3.3[4]. For every uncoded bit, the encoder generates two coded bits, hence the code rate is 1/2. The encoded outputs at time m are given by

$$\begin{aligned} c_{1,m} &= b_{1,m}g_{1,1,0} + b_{1,m-1}g_{1,1,1} + b_{1,m-2}g_{1,1,2} \\ &\stackrel{\Delta}{=} \sum_{l=0}^{2} g_{1,1,l}b_{1,m-l}, \\ c_{2,m} &= b_{1,m}g_{1,2,0} + b_{1,m-1}g_{1,2,1} + b_{1,m-2}g_{1,2,2} \\ &\stackrel{\Delta}{=} \sum_{l=0}^{2} (g_{1,2,l}b_{1,m-l}), \end{aligned} \tag{3.1}$$

where it is understood that all operations are over GF(2), that is

$$\begin{aligned} 0+0 &= 0 \\ 0+1 = 1+0 &= 1 \\ 1+1 &= 0 \\ \Rightarrow 1 &= -1 \\ 1\cdot 1 &= 1 \\ 0\cdot 0 = 1\cdot 0 = 0\cdot 1 &= 0. \end{aligned} \tag{3.2}$$

Observe that addition in GF(2) is an XOR operation whereas multiplication is an AND operation. Moreover, subtraction in GF(2) is the same as addition. It must be emphasized that whether '+' denotes real addition or addition over GF(2), will be clear from the context. Where there is scope for ambiguity, we explicitly use '$\oplus$' to denote over GF(2).

In (3.1), $b_{i,\,m}$ denotes the ith parallel input at time m, $c_{j,\,m}$ denotes the jth parallel output at time m, and $g_{i,\,j,\,l}$ denotes a connection from the lth memory element *along* the ith parallel input to the jth parallel output. More specifically, $g_{i,\,j,\,l} = 1$ denotes a connection and $g_{i,\,j,\,l} = 0$ denotes no connection. Note also that $b_{i,\,m}$ and $c_{j,\,m}$ are elements of the set {0, 1}. In the above example, there is one parallel input, two parallel outputs and the connections are:

$$\begin{aligned} g_{1,\,1,\,0} &= 1 \\ g_{1,\,1,\,1} &= 1 \\ g_{1,\,1,\,2} &= 1 \\ g_{1,\,2,\,0} &= 1 \\ g_{1,\,2,\,1} &= 0 \\ g_{1,\,2,\,2} &= 1. \end{aligned} \tag{3.3}$$

Since the expressions in (3.1) denote a convolution sum, the D-transform of the encoded outputs can be written as

$$\begin{aligned} C_1(D) &= B_1(D)G_{1,\,1}(D), \\ C_2(D) &= B_1(D)G_{1,\,2}(D), \end{aligned} \tag{3.4}$$

where $B_1(D)$ denotes the D-transform of $b_{1,\,m}$ and $G_{1,\,1}(D)$ and $G_{1,\,2}(D)$ denote the D-transforms of $g_{1,\,1,\,l}$ and $g_{1,\,2,\,l}$ respectively. $G_{1,\,1}(D)$ and $G_{1,\,2}(D)$ are also called the generator polynomials. For example, the generator polynomials for the top and bottom XOR gates of Figure 3.3 are given by

$$\begin{aligned} G_{1,\,1}(D) &= 1 + D + D^2, \\ G_{1,\,2}(D) &= 1 + D^2. \end{aligned} \tag{3.5}$$

For example, if

$$B_1(D) = 1 + D + D^2 + D^3, \tag{3.6}$$

then using the generator polynomials in (3.5)

$$\begin{aligned} C_1(D) &= (1 + D + D^2 + D^3)(1 + D + D^2) \\ &= 1 + D^2 + D^3 + D^5 \\ &\stackrel{\Delta}{=} \sum_{m=0}^{5} c_{1,m} D^m, \\ C_2(D) &= (1 + D + D^2 + D^3)(1 + D^2) \\ &= 1 + D + D^4 + D^5 \\ &\stackrel{\Delta}{=} \sum_{m=0}^{5} c_{2,m} D^m. \end{aligned} \tag{3.7}$$

The *state* of the convolutional encoder depends on the contents of the memory elements. In Figure 3.3 there are two memory elements, hence there are $2^2 = 4$ states which can be labelled 00, 01, 10, 11. According to our convention, the left bit denotes the contents of the left memory element and the right bit denotes the contents of the right memory element of Figure 3.3. This convention is arbitrary; what we wish to emphasize here is that whatever be the convention used, it must be consistently followed.

Each encoded bit is a function of the encoder state and the input bit(s). The encoded bits that are obtained due to different combinations of the encoder state and the input bit(s), can be represented by a *trellis diagram*. The trellis diagram for the encoder in Figure 3.3 is shown in Figure 3.4. The black dots denote the state of the encoder and the lines connecting the dots denote the transitions of the encoder from one state to the other. The transitions are labelled $b_{1,m}/c_{1,m}c_{2,m}$. The reader's attention is drawn to the notation used here: at time m, the input $b_{1,m}$ in combination with the encoder state yields the encoded bits $c_{1,m}$ and $c_{2,m}$.

With these basic definitions, we are now ready to generalize the convolutional encoder. A k/n convolutional encoder can be represented by a $k \times n$ generator matrix:

$$\mathbf{G}(D) = \begin{bmatrix} G_{1,1}(D) & \cdots & G_{1,n}(D) \\ G_{2,1}(D) & \cdots & G_{2,n}(D) \\ \vdots & \vdots & \vdots \\ G_{k,1}(D) & \cdots & G_{k,n}(D) \end{bmatrix} \tag{3.8}$$

where $G_{i,j}(D)$ denotes the generator polynomial corresponding to the ith input and the jth output. Thus the code vector $\mathbf{C}(D)$ and the input vector $\mathbf{B}(D)$ are related by:

$$\mathbf{C}(D) = \mathbf{G}^T(D)\mathbf{B}(D) \tag{3.9}$$

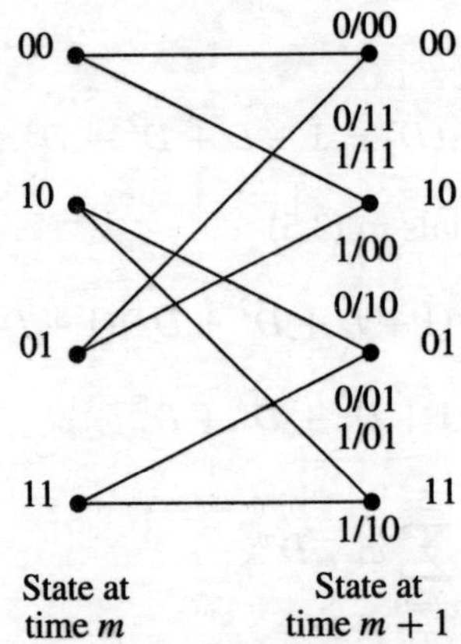

Figure 3.4 *Trellis diagram for the convolutional encoder in Figure 3.3*

where

$$\begin{aligned} \mathbf{C}(D) &= \left[\begin{array}{ccc} C_1(D) & \ldots & C_n(D) \end{array} \right]^T \\ \mathbf{B}(D) &= \left[\begin{array}{ccc} B_1(D) & \ldots & B_k(D) \end{array} \right]^T . \end{aligned} \tag{3.10}$$

The generator matrix for the rate-1/2 encoder in Figure 3.3 is given by

$$\mathbf{G}(D) = \left[\begin{array}{cc} 1 + D + D^2 & 1 + D^2 \end{array} \right]. \tag{3.11}$$

A rate-2/3 convolutional encoder is shown in Figure 3.5. The corresponding generator matrix is given by

$$\mathbf{G}(D) = \begin{bmatrix} D^2 + D^3 & D + D^3 & 1 + D^2 \\ 1 + D^2 & D^2 & D + D^2 \end{bmatrix}. \tag{3.12}$$

The encoder in Figure 3.5 has $2^5 = 32$ states, since there are five memory elements.

Any convolutional encoder designed using XOR gates is *linear* since the following condition is satisfied:

$$\begin{aligned} \mathbf{C}_1(D) &= \mathbf{G}^T(D)\mathbf{B}_1(D) \\ \mathbf{C}_2(D) &= \mathbf{G}^T(D)\mathbf{B}_2(D) \\ \Rightarrow (\mathbf{C}_1(D) + \mathbf{C}_2(D)) &= \mathbf{G}^T(D)\left(\mathbf{B}_1(D) + \mathbf{B}_2(D)\right) \\ \Rightarrow \mathbf{C}_3(D) &= \mathbf{G}^T(D)\mathbf{B}_3(D). \end{aligned} \tag{3.13}$$

The above property implies that the sum of two codewords is a codeword. Linearity also implies that if

$$\begin{aligned} \mathbf{C}_3(D) &= \mathbf{C}_1(D) + \mathbf{C}_2(D), \\ \mathbf{B}_3(D) &= \mathbf{B}_1(D) + \mathbf{B}_2(D), \end{aligned} \tag{3.14}$$

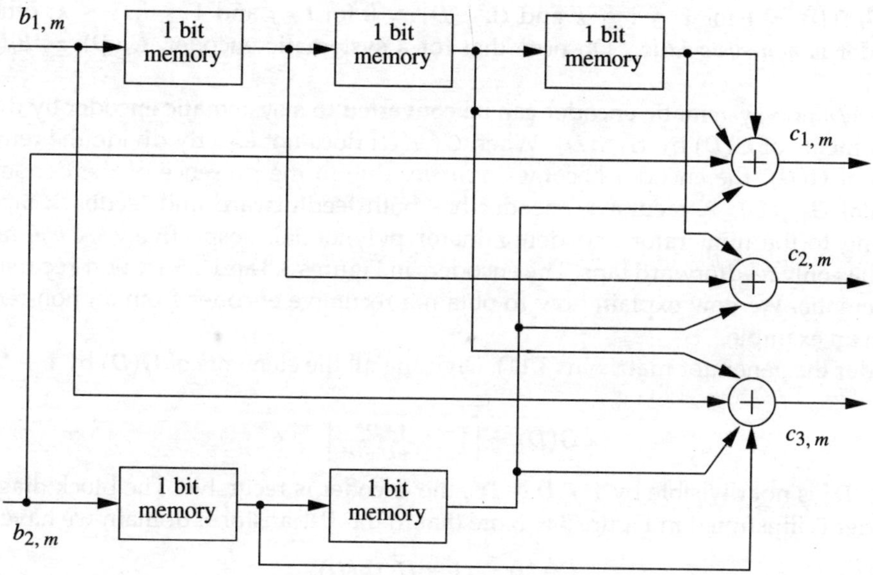

$$\mathbf{b}_m = \left[b_{1,m}\ b_{2,m}\right]^T$$
$$\mathbf{c}_m = \left[c_{1,m}\ c_{2,m}\ c_{3,m}\right]^T$$

Figure 3.5 *A rate-2/3 convolutional encoder*

then

$$\begin{aligned}
&\mathbf{C}_3(D) + (-\mathbf{C}_2(D)) = \mathbf{G}^T(D)\left(\mathbf{B}_3(D) + (-\mathbf{B}_2(D))\right) \\
&\Rightarrow \mathbf{C}_3(D) + \mathbf{C}_2(D) = \mathbf{G}^T(D)\left(\mathbf{B}_3(D) + \mathbf{B}_2(D)\right) \\
&\Rightarrow \mathbf{C}_1(D) = \mathbf{G}^T(D)\mathbf{B}_1(D)
\end{aligned} \tag{3.15}$$

since in GF(2), subtraction is the same as addition. Thus, subtraction of two codewords gives another codeword.

Note that the XOR operation cannot be replaced by an OR operation, since, even though the OR operation satisfies (3.13), it does not satisfy (3.15). This is because subtraction (additive inverse) is not defined in OR operation. Technically speaking, the OR operation does not constitute a field, in fact, it does not even constitute a group. Thus, an encoder implemented using OR gates is not linear.

A rate-k/n convolutional encoder is *systematic* if

$$\mathbf{G}(D) = \begin{bmatrix} 1 & 0 & \cdots & 0 & G_{1,k+1}(D) & \cdots & G_{1,n}(D) \\ 0 & 1 & \cdots & 0 & G_{2,k+1}(D) & \cdots & G_{2,n}(D) \\ \vdots & \vdots & \vdots & \vdots & \vdots & \vdots & \vdots \\ 0 & 0 & \cdots & 1 & G_{k,k+1}(D) & \cdots & G_{k,n}(D) \end{bmatrix} \tag{3.16}$$

that is, $G_{i,i}(D) = 1$ for $1 \leq i \leq k$ and $G_{i,j}(D) = 0$ for $i \neq j$ and $1 \leq i, j \leq k$; otherwise the encoder is *non-systematic*. Observe that for a systematic encoder, $C_i(D) = B_i(D)$ for $1 \leq i \leq k$.

A rate-$1/n$ non-systematic encoder can be converted to a systematic encoder by dividing all the elements of $\mathbf{G}(D)$ by $G_{1,1}(D)$. When $G_{1,1}(D)$ does not exactly divide the remaining elements of $\mathbf{G}(D)$, the encoder becomes *recursive* due to the presence of the denominator polynomial $G_{1,1}(D)$. A recursive encoder has both feedforward and feedback taps, corresponding to the numerator and denominator polynomials respectively. A *non-recursive* encoder has only feedforward taps. The encoders in Figures 3.3 and 3.5 are non-recursive and non-systematic. We now explain how to obtain a recursive encoder from an non-recursive one, with an example.

Consider the generator matrix in (3.11). Dividing all the elements of $\mathbf{G}(D)$ by $1 + D + D^2$, we get

$$\mathbf{G}(D) = \begin{bmatrix} 1 & \frac{1+D^2}{1+D+D^2} \end{bmatrix}. \tag{3.17}$$

Since $1 + D^2$ is not divisible by $1 + D + D^2$, the encoder is recursive. The block diagram of the encoder is illustrated in Figure 3.6. Note that in the D-transform domain we have

$$C_2(D) = (1 + D^2)Y(D). \tag{3.18}$$

However,

$$\begin{aligned} Y(D) &= B_1(D) + DY(D) + D^2Y(D) \\ \Rightarrow Y(D) - DY(D) - D^2Y(D) &= B_1(D) \\ \Rightarrow Y(D) + DY(D) + D^2Y(D) &= B_1(D) \\ \Rightarrow Y(D) &= \frac{B_1(D)}{1 + D + D^2}. \end{aligned} \tag{3.19}$$

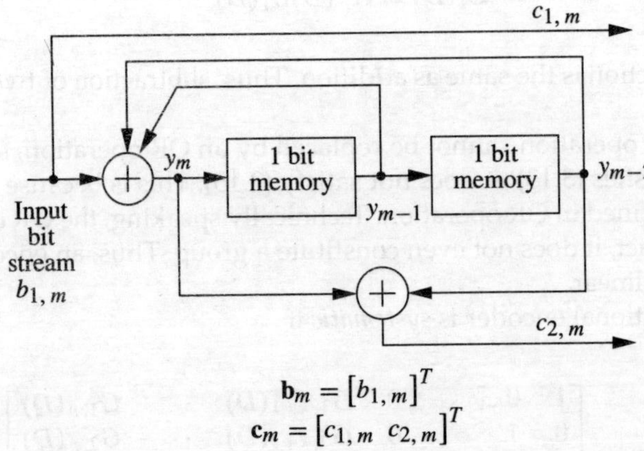

Figure 3.6 *Block diagram of a rate-1/2 recursive systematic encoder*

Substituting (3.19) in (3.18), we get

$$G_{1,2}(D) = \frac{C_2(D)}{B_1(D)} = \frac{1+D^2}{1+D+D^2}. \tag{3.20}$$

Since

$$\frac{1+D^2}{1+D+D^2} = 1 + D + D^2 + D^4 + D^5 + \ldots \tag{3.21}$$

the encoder has infinite memory.

A convolutional encoder is *non-catastrophic* if there exists at least one $k \times n$ decoding matrix $\mathbf{H}(D)$ whose elements have no denominator polynomials such that

$$\mathbf{H}(D)\mathbf{G}^T(D) = D^i \cdot \mathbf{I}_k. \tag{3.22}$$

Note that $\mathbf{H}(D)$ has kn unknowns, whereas we have only k^2 equations (the right-hand-side is a $k \times k$ matrix), hence there are in general infinite solutions for $\mathbf{H}(D)$. However, only certain solutions (if such a solution exists) yield $\mathbf{H}(D)$ whose elements have no denominator polynomials.

The absence of any denominator polynomials in $\mathbf{H}(D)$ ensures that the decoder is feedback-free, hence there is no propagation of errors in the decoder[52]. Conversely, if there does not exist any 'feedback-free' $\mathbf{H}(D)$ that satisfies (3.22), then the encoder is said to be catastrophic.

One of the solutions for $\mathbf{H}(D)$ is obtained by noting that

$$\left(\mathbf{G}(D)\mathbf{G}^T(D)\right)^{-1}\mathbf{G}(D)\mathbf{G}^T(D) = \mathbf{I}_k. \tag{3.23}$$

Hence

$$\mathbf{H}(D) = \left(\mathbf{G}(D)\mathbf{G}^T(D)\right)^{-1}\mathbf{G}(D). \tag{3.24}$$

Such a decoding matrix is known as the *left pseudo-inverse* and almost always has denominator polynomials (though this does not mean that the encoder is catastrophic).

Theorem 3.1.1 *A necessary and sufficient condition for the existence of a feedback-free* $\mathbf{H}(D)$ *is that the greatest common divisor of the minors (the determinants of the* $\binom{n}{k}$, $k \times k$ *matrices) of* $\mathbf{G}(D)$ *should be of equal to* D^l *for* $l \geq 0$[52,53].

Example 3.1.1 Let

$$\mathbf{G}(D) = \begin{bmatrix} 1+D & 1 & 1+D \\ D & 1+D & 0 \end{bmatrix}. \tag{3.25}$$

Check if the corresponding encoder is catastrophic.

Solution: The minors are:

$$D_1 = \begin{vmatrix} 1+D & 1 \\ D & 1+D \end{vmatrix} = 1 + D + D^2$$

$$D_2 = \begin{vmatrix} 1 & 1+D \\ 1+D & 0 \end{vmatrix} = 1 + D^2$$

$$D_3 = \begin{vmatrix} 1+D & 1+D \\ D & 0 \end{vmatrix} = D + D^2. \tag{3.26}$$

Since

$$\text{GCD}\left(1 + D + D^2,\ 1 + D^2,\ D + D^2\right) = 1 \tag{3.27}$$

the encoder specified by (3.25) is not catastrophic.

Obviously, a systematic encoder cannot be catastrophic since the input (uncoded) bits are directly available. In other words, *one of the solutions* for the decoding matrix is:

$$\mathbf{H}(D) = \begin{bmatrix} 1 & 0 & & 0 & 0 & \cdots & 0 \\ 0 & 1 & \cdots & 0 & 0 & \cdots & 0 \\ \vdots & \vdots & & \vdots & \vdots & & \vdots \\ 0 & 0 & \cdots & 1 & 0 & \cdots & 0 \end{bmatrix} \tag{3.28}$$

Thus, as a corollary, a non-systematic, non-catastrophic convolutional encoder can always be converted to a systematic convolutional encoder by a series of matrix operations.

Consider two code sequences $C_1(D)$ and $C_2(D)$. The error sequence $E(D)$ is defined as

$$\begin{aligned} E(D) &= C_1(D) + (-C_2(D)) \\ &= C_1(D) + C_2(D) \end{aligned} \tag{3.29}$$

since subtraction in GF(2) is the same as addition. The *Hamming* distance between $C_1(D)$ and $C_2(D)$ is equal to the number of non-zero terms in $E(D)$. A more intuitive way to understand the concept of Hamming distance is as follows. Let

$$L - 1 = \max\left\{\text{degree of } C_1(D), \text{ degree of } C_2(D)\right\} \tag{3.30}$$

Then $E(D)$ can be represented as a $L \times 1$ vector $\mathbf{e}$, as follows:

$$\mathbf{e} = \begin{bmatrix} e_0 \\ e_1 \\ \vdots \\ e_{L-1} \end{bmatrix} \tag{3.31}$$

where $e_i \in \{0, 1\}$, for $0 \le i \le L-1$. Then

$$d_{H, c_1, c_2} \stackrel{\Delta}{=} \mathbf{e}^T \cdot \mathbf{e} = \sum_{i=0}^{L-1} e_i \cdot e_i \tag{3.32}$$

where the superscript T denotes the transpose and the subscript H denotes the Hamming distance. Note that in the above equation, the addition and multiplication are real. The reader is invited to compare the definition of the Hamming distance defined above with that of the Euclidean distance defined in (2.96). Observe in particular, the consistency in the definitions. In the next section we describe hard-decision decoding of convolutional codes.

3.2 Are the Encoded Symbols Correlated?

In this section we analyze the correlation properties of the encoded symbol stream. This is necessary because we will show in Chapter 4 that the power spectral density of the transmitted signal depends on the correlation between the symbols. In fact, it is desirable that the symbols are uncorrelated. In order to analyze the correlation properties of the encoded bit stream, it is convenient to develop an alternate structure for the convolutional encoder.

An example is shown in Figure 3.7. Note that the XOR gates have been replaced by real multiplication and the mapper has been shifted *before* the convolutional encoder. Bit 0 gets mapped to +1 and bit 1 gets mapped to −1. The encoded symbols are related to the input symbols as follows:

$$\begin{aligned} S_{1,m} &= S_{b,1,m} S_{b,1,m-1} S_{b,1,m-2} \\ S_{2,m} &= S_{b,1,m} S_{b,1,m-2}. \end{aligned} \tag{3.33}$$

The important point to note here is that *every* convolutional encoder (that uses XOR gates) followed by a mapper can be replaced by a mapper followed by an alternate 'encoder' that uses multipliers instead of XOR gates. Moreover, the mapping operation must be defined as indicated in Figure 3.7.

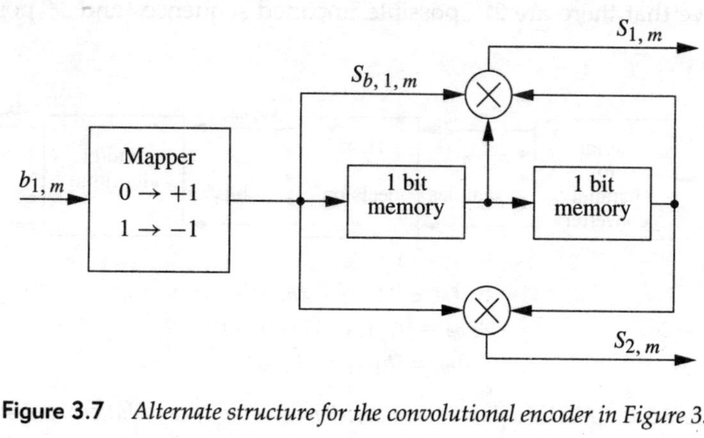

Figure 3.7 *Alternate structure for the convolutional encoder in Figure 3.3*

Let us assume that the input symbols are statistically independent and equally likely. Then,

$$E[S_{b,1,m}S_{b,1,m-i}] = \delta_K(i). \tag{3.34}$$

Then, clearly,

$$E[S_{1,m}] = E[S_{2,m}] = 0. \tag{3.35}$$

The various covariances of the encoded symbols are computed as

$$\begin{aligned} E[S_{1,m}S_{1,m-i}] &= \delta_K(i) \\ E[S_{2,m}S_{2,m-i}] &= \delta_K(i) \\ E[S_{1,m}S_{2,m-i}] &= 0 \qquad \text{for all } i. \end{aligned} \tag{3.36}$$

Thus we see that the encoded symbols are uncorrelated. This leads us to conclude that error control coding does not in general imply that the encoded symbols are correlated, though the encoded symbols are not statistically independent. We will use this result later in Chapter 4.

3.3 Hard-Decision Decoding of Convolutional Codes

Figure 3.8 shows the block diagram for hard-decision decoding of convolutional codes. The encoder is assumed to be rate-k/n. We do not make any assumptions about the initial state of the encoder.

Let us assume that L uncoded blocks are transmitted. Each block consists of k bits. Then the uncoded bit sequence can be written as

$$\mathbf{b}^{(i)} = \begin{bmatrix} b_{1,1}^{(i)} & \ldots & b_{k,1}^{(i)} & \ldots & b_{1,L}^{(i)} & \ldots & b_{k,L}^{(i)} \end{bmatrix}^T \tag{3.37}$$

where $b_{l,m}^{(i)}$ is taken from the set $\{0, 1\}$ and the superscript (i) denotes the ith possible sequence. Observe that there are 2^{kL} possible uncoded sequences and $\mathscr{S}$ possible starting

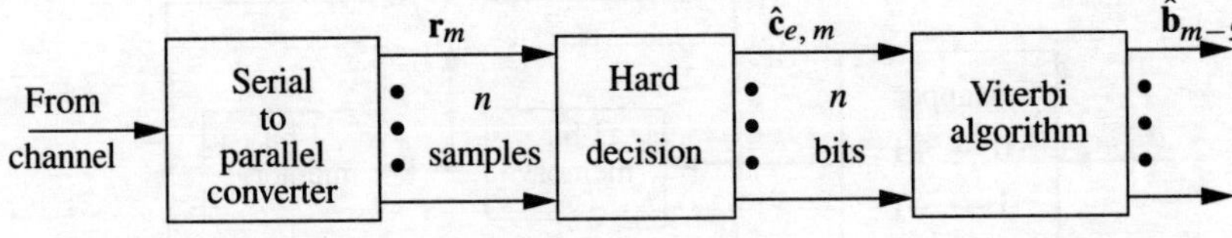

$$\mathbf{r}_m = [r_{1,m} \ldots r_{n,m}]^T$$
$$\mathbf{c}_{e,m} = [c_{e,1,m} \ldots c_{e,n,m}]^T$$
$$\hat{\mathbf{b}}_m = [\hat{b}_{1,m} \ldots \hat{b}_{k,m}]^T$$

Figure 3.8 *Block diagram of hard-decision decoding of convolutional codes*

states, where $\mathscr{S}$ denotes the total number of states in the trellis. Hence the superscript i in (3.37) lies in the range

$$1 \le i \le \mathscr{S} \times 2^{kL}. \tag{3.38}$$

The corresponding coded bit and symbol sequences can be written as

$$\begin{aligned}\mathbf{c}^{(i)} &= \begin{bmatrix} c_{1,1}^{(i)} & \ldots & c_{n,1}^{(i)} & \ldots & c_{1,L}^{(i)} & \ldots & c_{n,L}^{(i)} \end{bmatrix}^T \\ \mathbf{S}^{(i)} &= \begin{bmatrix} S_{1,1}^{(i)} & \ldots & S_{n,1}^{(i)} & \ldots & S_{1,L}^{(i)} & \ldots & S_{n,L}^{(i)} \end{bmatrix}^T\end{aligned} \tag{3.39}$$

where the symbols $S_{l,m}^{(i)}$ are taken from the set $\{\pm a\}$ (antipodal constellation) and again the superscript (i) denotes the ith possible sequence. Just to be specific, we assume that the mapping from an encoded bit to a symbol is given by

$$S_{l,m}^{(i)} = \begin{cases} +a & \text{if } c_{l,m}^{(i)} = 0 \\ -a & \text{if } c_{l,m}^{(i)} = 1. \end{cases} \tag{3.40}$$

Note that for the code sequence to be *uniquely decodeable* we must have

$$\mathscr{S} \times 2^{kL} \le 2^{nL}. \tag{3.41}$$

In other words, there must be a *one-to-one* mapping between an input sequence-starting state combination and the encoded sequence. Note that when

$$\mathscr{S} \times 2^{kL} = 2^{nL} \tag{3.42}$$

the *minimum* Hamming distance between the encoded sequences is unity (which is also equal to the minimum Hamming distance between the uncoded sequences) and there is *no* coding gain. Thus, a uniquely decodeable code can achieve any coding gain only when

$$\mathscr{S} \times 2^{kL} < 2^{nL}. \tag{3.43}$$

Since

$$\mathscr{S} = 2^{\mathscr{M}} \tag{3.44}$$

where $\mathscr{M}$ is the number of memory elements in the encoder, (3.43) can be written as

$$\begin{aligned} 2^{kL+\mathscr{M}} &< 2^{nL} \\ \Rightarrow kL + \mathscr{M} &< nL \\ \Rightarrow L &> \left\lfloor \frac{\mathscr{M}}{n-k} \right\rfloor. \end{aligned} \tag{3.45}$$

Thus, the above equation sets a lower limit on the block length L that can be considered for decoding.

For example, let us consider the encoder in Figure 3.3 having the trellis diagram of Figure 3.4. When the received encoded sequence is 00 ($L = 1$), clearly, we cannot decide whether a 0 or a 1 has been transmitted. When the received encoded sequence is 00 00 ($L = 2$), we can uniquely decode the sequence to 00. However, note that there are two encoded sequences given by 00 01 and 00 10 which are at the minimum distance of 1 from 00 00. Thus we cannot get any coding gain by decoding a length two sequence. In other words, to achieve any coding gain, L must be greater than 2.

The received signal can be written as

$$\mathbf{r} = \mathbf{S}^{(i)} + \mathbf{w} \tag{3.46}$$

where

$$\begin{aligned} \mathbf{r} &= \begin{bmatrix} r_{1,1} & \ldots & r_{n,1} & \ldots & r_{1,L} & \ldots & r_{n,L} \end{bmatrix}^T \\ &= \begin{bmatrix} \mathbf{r}_1^T & \ldots & \mathbf{r}_L^T \end{bmatrix}^T, \\ \mathbf{w} &= \begin{bmatrix} w_{1,1} & \ldots & w_{n,1} & \ldots & w_{1,L} & \ldots & w_{n,L} \end{bmatrix}^T. \end{aligned} \tag{3.47}$$

$\mathbf{r}_m$ is defined in Figure 3.8. We assume that $w_{l,m}$ are samples of AWGN with zero mean and variance σ_w^2. Observe that all signals in the above equation are real.

The hard-decision device shown in Figure 3.8 optimally detects $S_{l,m}^{(i)}$ from $r_{l,m}$ as discussed in section 2.1 and de-maps them to bits (1s and 0s). Hence the output of the hard-decision device can be written as

$$\mathbf{c}_e = \mathbf{c}^{(i)} \oplus \mathbf{e} \tag{3.48}$$

where $\mathbf{c}_e$ is *not* necessarily a code sequence and

$$\mathbf{e} = \begin{bmatrix} e_{1,1} & \ldots & e_{n,1} & \ldots & e_{1,L} & \ldots & e_{n,L} \end{bmatrix}^T \tag{3.49}$$

denotes the error sequence. Obviously,

$$e_{l,m} = \begin{cases} 0 & \text{denotes 'no error'} \\ 1 & \text{denotes 'an error'.} \end{cases} \tag{3.50}$$

The probability of error (which is equal to the probability that $e_{l,m} = 1$) will be denoted by p and is given by (2.20) with $\tilde{d} = 2a$.

Now, the maximum *a posteriori* detection rule can be written as (for $1 \le j \le \mathscr{S} \times 2^{kL}$):

$$\text{Choose } \hat{\mathbf{c}} = \mathbf{c}^{(j)} \text{ if } P(\mathbf{c}^{(j)}|\mathbf{c}_e) \text{ is the maximum.} \tag{3.51}$$

Or more simply,

$$\max_j P(\mathbf{c}^{(j)}|\mathbf{c}_e). \tag{3.52}$$

Using Bayes' rule, the above maximization can be rewritten as

$$\max_j \frac{P(\mathbf{c}_e|\mathbf{c}^{(j)})P(\mathbf{c}^{(j)})}{P(\mathbf{c}_e)}. \tag{3.53}$$

Once again, assuming that all code sequences are equally likely and noting that the denominator term in the above equation is independent of j, the MAP detection rule can be simplified to the ML detection rule as follows:

$$\max_j P(\mathbf{c}_e|\mathbf{c}^{(j)}). \tag{3.54}$$

Assuming that the errors occur independently, the above maximization reduces to

$$\max_j \prod_{m=1}^{L}\prod_{l=1}^{n} P(c_{e,\,l,\,m}|c_{l,\,m}^{(j)}). \tag{3.55}$$

Let

$$P(c_{e,\,l,\,m}|c_{l,\,m}^{(j)}) = \begin{cases} p & \text{for } c_{e,\,l,\,m} \neq c_{l,\,m}^{(j)} \\ 1-p & \text{for } c_{e,\,l,\,m} = c_{l,\,m}^{(j)} \end{cases} \tag{3.56}$$

where p denotes the probability of error in the coded bit. If $d_{H,\,j}$ denotes the Hamming distance between c_e and $c^{(j)}$, that is,

$$d_{H,\,j} = \left(\mathbf{c}_e \oplus \mathbf{c}^{(j)}\right)^T \cdot \left(\mathbf{c}_e \oplus \mathbf{c}^{(j)}\right) \tag{3.57}$$

then (3.55) reduces to

$$\begin{aligned} &\max_j p^{d_{H,j}}(1-p)^{nL-d_{H,j}} \\ &\Rightarrow \max_j \left(\frac{p}{1-p}\right)^{d_{H,\,j}} (1-p)^{nL} \\ &\Rightarrow \max_j \left(\frac{p}{1-p}\right)^{d_{H,\,j}}. \end{aligned} \tag{3.58}$$

If $p < 0.5$ (which is usually the case), then the above maximization is equivalent to

$$\min_j d_{H,\,j} \qquad \text{for } 1 \leq j \leq \mathscr{S} \times 2^{kL}. \tag{3.59}$$

In other words, the maximum likelihood detector decides in favour of that code sequence $\mathbf{c}^{(j)}$ which is nearest in the Hamming distance sense to $\mathbf{c}_e$.

The channel 'as seen' by the maximum likelihood detector is called the *binary symmetric channel* (BSC). This is illustrated in Figure 3.9.

From (3.59), it is clear that the complexity of the ML detector increases exponentially with the length of the sequence to be detected. The Viterbi algorithm is a practical implementation of the ML detector whose complexity increases linearly with the sequence length. This is described in the next section.

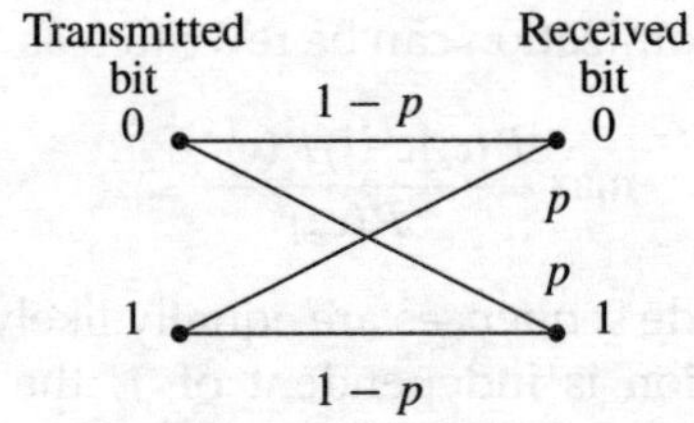

$$P(1|1) = P(0|0) = 1 - p$$
$$P(0|1) = P(1|0) = p$$

Figure 3.9 *The binary symmetric channel. The transition probabilities are given by p and* $1 - p$

3.3.1 The Viterbi algorithm (VA)

Though the decoding matrix **H** in (3.22) can be used for hard-decision decoding of convolutional codes, we will nevertheless describe the Viterbi decoding algorithm in this section since it has got applications elsewhere. However, it must be emphasized that using the decoding matrix may not always be optimal, in the sense of minimizing the uncoded bit error rate. A typical example is the decoding matrix in (3.28), since it does not utilize the parity bits at all.

Consider a rate-k/n convolutional code. Then k is the number of parallel inputs and n is the number of parallel outputs. To develop the Viterbi algorithm we use the following terminology.

(a) Let $\mathscr{S}$ denote the number of states in the trellis.
(b) Let $\mathscr{D}_v$ denote the detection delay of the Viterbi algorithm.
(c) Let `Weight[S][T]` denote an array representing the accumulated Hamming weight, or more generally, the accumulated metric at state `S` and time `T`.
(d) Let `PrevState[S][T]` denote the previous state (at time `T-1`) that leads to state `S` at time `T`.
(e) Let `PrevInput[S][T]` denote the previous input (at time `T-1`) that leads to state `S` at time `T`.

The Viterbi algorithm is now explained below:

1. For `State=1` to $\mathscr{S}$
   set `Weight[State][0]=0`
2. From time `T1=0`, do forever:
   - 2.1 For `State=1` to $\mathscr{S}$
     set `Weight[State][T1+1]=A very large value`
   - 2.2 Get the next n bits from the hard-decision device.
   - 2.3 For `State=1` to $\mathscr{S}$, do the following:
     - 2.3.1 For `Input=1` to 2^k, do the following:
       - 2.3.1.1 Compute the n code bits corresponding to `State` and `Input`.

2.3.1.2 Compute the Hamming distance between the received n bits in item (2.2) and the code bits in item (2.3.1.1). Call this distance as d_H (d_H is also called the branch metric or branch weight).

2.3.1.3 Compute the `NextState` corresponding to `State` and `Input`.

2.3.1.4 Let $w_H =$ `Weight[State][T1]` $+ d_H$. Note that "+" denotes real addition.

2.3.1.5 If `Weight[NextState][T1+1]` $> w_H$ then set `Weight[NextState][T1+1]` $= w_H$. Note down the `State` that leads to `NextState` as follows: `PrevState[NextState][T1+1]=State.` Note down the `Input` as follows: `PrevInput[NextState][T1+1]=Input.` The path leading from `State` to `NextState` is called the surviving path and `Input` is called the surviving input.

2.4 If `T1` $> \mathscr{D}_v$ then do the following:

2.4.1 For `State=1` to $\mathscr{S}$ find the minimum of `Weight[State][T1+1]`. Denote the minimum weight state as `MinWghtState`.

2.4.2 Set `State=MinWghtState` and `T=T1+1`.

2.4.3 For `index=1` to $\mathscr{D}_v + 1$ do the following:

2.4.3.1 `PreviousState=PrevState[State][T]`

2.4.3.2 `input=PrevInput[State][T]`

2.4.3.3 `State=PreviousState`

2.4.3.4 `T=T-1`

2.4.4 De-map `input` to bits and declare these bits as the estimated uncoded bits that occurred at time `T1` $- \mathscr{D}_v$.

Since the accumulated metrics are real numbers, it is clear that an eliminated path cannot have a lower weight than the surviving path at a later point in time. The branch metrics and survivor computation as the VA evolves in time is illustrated in Figure 3.10 for the encoder in Figure 3.3.

Let us now compare the computational complexity of the VA with that of the ML decoder for a block length L. For every block of n received bits, the VA requires $O(\mathscr{S} \times 2^k)$ operations to compute the survivors. There is an additional $\mathscr{D}_v$ operations for backtracking. Thus for a block length of L the total operations required by the VA is $O(L(\mathscr{S} \times 2^k + \mathscr{D}_v))$. However, the computational complexity of the ML decoder is $\mathscr{S} \times 2^{kL}$. Thus we see that the complexity of the VA is linear in L whereas the complexity of the ML detector is exponential in L.

In Figure 3.11, we illustrate the concept of *error events* and the reason why the VA requires a detection delay for obtaining reliable decisions. An error event occurs when the VA decides in favour of an incorrect path. This happens when an incorrect path has a lower weight than the correct path. We also observe from Figure 3.11 that the survivors at all states at time m

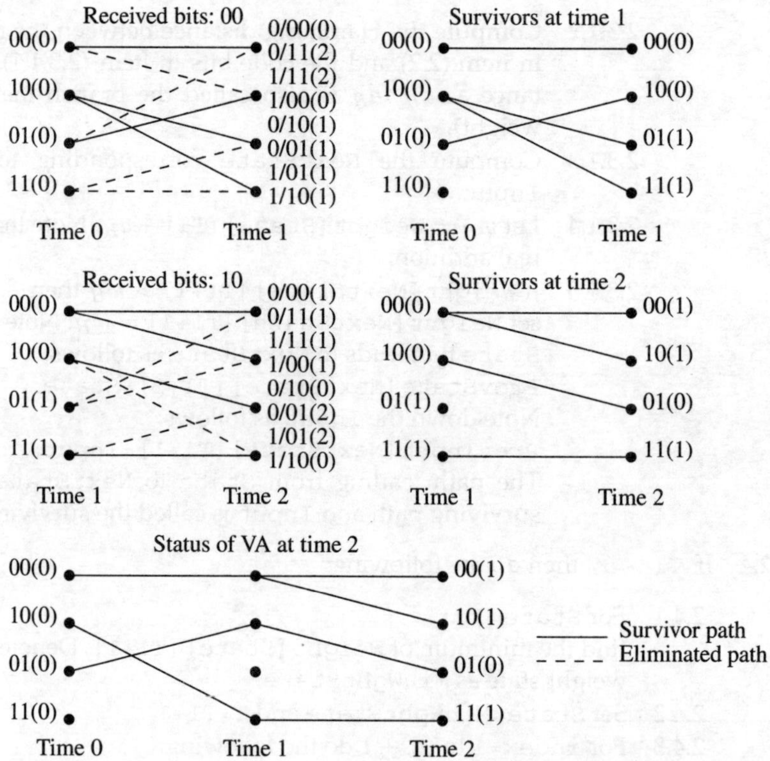

Figure 3.10 *Survivor computation in the Viterbi algorithm. Number in bracket denotes Hamming weight of a branch or state*

have diverged from the correct path at some previous instant of time. Hence it is quite clear that if $\mathscr{D}_v$ is made sufficiently large[3], then all the survivors at time m would have merged back to the correct path, resulting in correct decisions by the VA. Typically, $\mathscr{D}_v$ is equal to five times the memory of the encoder[2].

In the next section we provide an analysis of hard decision Viterbi decoding of convolutional codes.

3.3.2 Performance analysis of hard-decision decoding

In this section we provide a performance analysis of hard-decision decoding of the rate-1/2 encoder shown in Figure 3.3. We begin by first studying the *distance properties* of the code words generated by the encoder in Figure 3.3. The study of distance properties of a code involves the following:

(a) To find out the minimum (Hamming) distance between any two code sequences that constitute an error event.

(b) Given a transmitted sequence, to find out the number of code sequences (constituting an error event) that are at a minimum distance from the transmitted sequence.

(c) To find out the number of code sequences (constituting an error event) that are at other distances from the transmitted sequence.

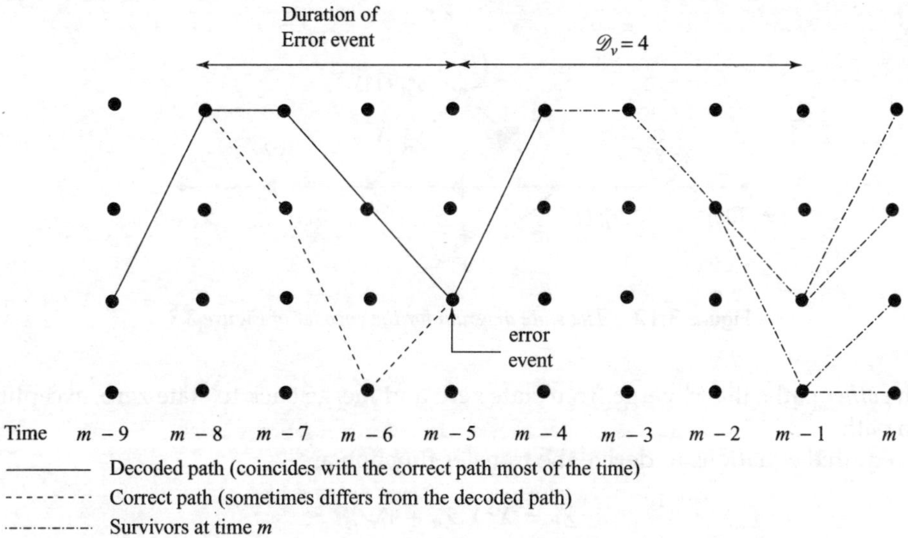

Figure 3.11 *Illustration of the error events and the detection delay of the Viterbi algorithm*

To summarize, we need to find out the *distance spectrum*[44] with the respect to the transmitted sequence. Note that for linear convolutional encoders, the distance spectrum is *independent* of the transmitted sequence. The reasoning is as follows. Consider (3.13). Let $\mathbf{B}_1(D)$ denote the reference sequence of length kL bits that generates the code sequence $\mathbf{C}_1(D)$. Similarly $\mathbf{B}_2(D)$, also of length kL, generates $\mathbf{C}_2(D)$. Now, the Hamming distance between $\mathbf{C}_3(D)$ and $\mathbf{C}_1(D)$ is equal to the Hamming weight of $\mathbf{C}_2(D)$, which in turn is dependent only on $\mathbf{B}_2(D)$. Extending this concept further, we can say that all the 2^{kL} combinations of $\mathbf{B}_2(D)$ would generate all the valid codewords $\mathbf{C}_2(D)$. In other words, the distance spectrum is generated merely by taking different combinations of $\mathbf{B}_2(D)$. Thus, it is clear that the distance spectrum is independent of $\mathbf{B}_1(D)$ or the reference sequence.

At this point it will be worthwhile to emphasize that only a subset of the 2^{kL} combinations of $\mathbf{B}_2(D)$ generates the distance spectrum. This is because only those codewords $\mathbf{C}_3(D)$ that merges back to $\mathbf{C}_1(D)$ (and does not diverge again) within L blocks are to be considered. It is assumed that $\mathbf{C}_1(D)$ and $\mathbf{C}_3(D)$ start from the same state.

Hence, we will assume for convenience that the all-zero uncoded sequence has been transmitted. The resulting coded sequence is also an all-zero sequence. We now proceed to compute the distance spectrum of the codes generated by the encoder in Figure 3.3.

In Figure 3.12 we show the state diagram for the encoder in Figure 3.3. The state diagram is just an alternate way to represent the trellis. The transitions are labelled as exponents of the dummy variables X and Y. The exponent of X denotes the number of 1s in the encoded bits and the exponent of Y denotes the number of 1s in the uncoded (input) bit. Observe that state 00 has been repeated twice in Figure 3.12. The idea here is to find out the transfer function between the output state 00 and the input state 00 with the path gains represented as $X^i Y^j$. Moreover, since the reference path is the all-zero path, the self-loop about state zero is not shown in the state diagram. In other words, we are interested in knowing the characteristics

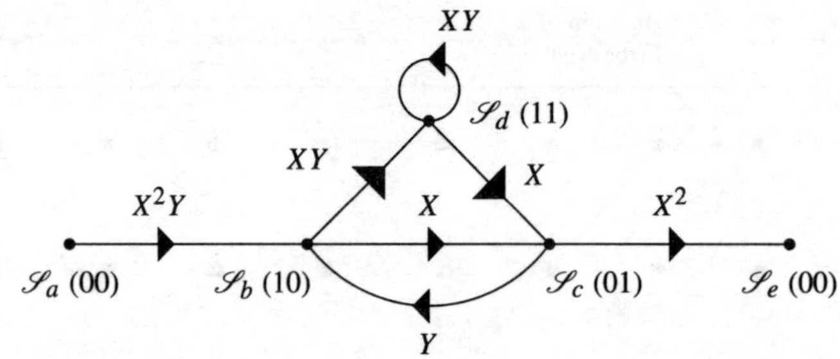

Figure 3.12 *The state diagram for the encoder of Figure 3.3*

of all the *other* paths that diverge from state zero and merge back to state zero, excepting the all-zero path.

The required equations to derive the transfer function are

$$\begin{aligned}
\mathscr{S}_b &= X^2Y\mathscr{S}_a + Y\mathscr{S}_c \\
\mathscr{S}_c &= X\mathscr{S}_b + X\mathscr{S}_d \\
\mathscr{S}_d &= XY\mathscr{S}_b + XY\mathscr{S}_d \\
\mathscr{S}_e &= X^2\mathscr{S}_c.
\end{aligned} \tag{3.60}$$

From the above set of equations, we have

$$\begin{aligned}
\frac{\mathscr{S}_e}{\mathscr{S}_a} &= \frac{X^5Y}{1-2XY} \\
&= (X^5Y)\cdot(1+2XY+4X^2Y^2+8X^3Y^3+\ldots) \\
&= X^5Y+2X^6Y^2+4X^7Y^3+\ldots \\
&= \sum_{d_H=d_{H,\min}}^{\infty} A_{d_H}X^{d_H}Y^{d_H-d_{H,\min}+1}
\end{aligned} \tag{3.61}$$

where A_{d_H} is the multiplicity[44] which denotes the number of sequences that are at a Hamming distance d_H from the transmitted sequence. The series obtained in the above equation is interpreted as follows (recall that the all-zero sequence is taken as the reference):

(a) There is one encoded sequence of weight 5 and the corresponding weight of the uncoded (input) sequence is 1.
(b) There are two encoded sequences of weight 6 and the corresponding weight of the uncoded sequence is 2.
(c) There are four encoded sequences of weight 7 and the corresponding weight of the uncoded sequence is 3 and so on.

From the above discussion it is clear that the minimum distance between any two code sequences is 5. A *minimum distance error event* (MDEE) is said to occur when the VA decides in

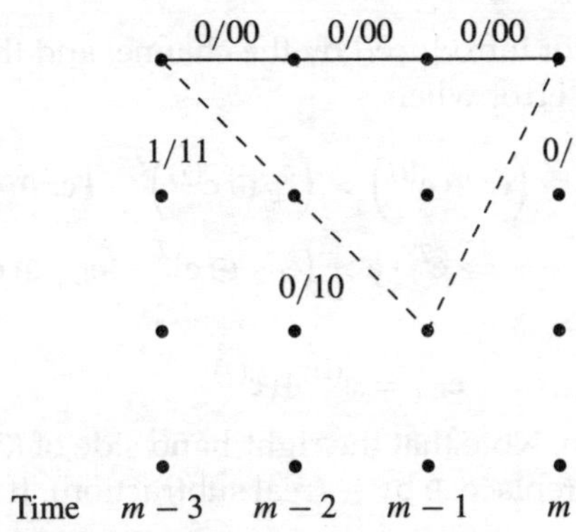

Figure 3.13 *The minimum distance error event for the encoder in Figure 3.3*

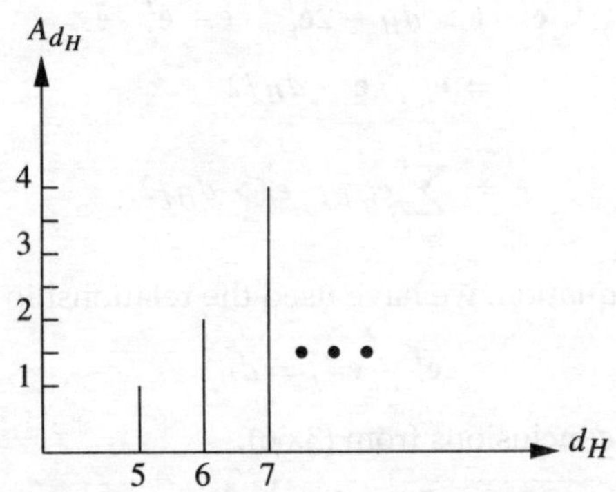

Figure 3.14 *The distance spectrum for the code generated by encoder in Figure 3.3*

favour of a code sequence that is at a minimum distance from the transmitted code sequence. The MDEE for the encoder in Figure 3.3 is shown in Figure 3.13. The distance spectrum for the code generated by the encoder in Figure 3.3 is shown in Figure 3.14. We emphasize that for more complex convolutional encoders (having a large number of states), it may be too difficult to obtain closed-form expressions for the distance spectrum, like the one given in (3.61). In such situations, one has to resort to a computer search through the trellis to arrive at the distance spectrum for the code.

We now derive a general expression for the probability of an uncoded bit error when the Hamming distance between code sequences constituting an error event is d_H. We assume that the error event extends over L blocks, each block consisting of n coded bits.

Let $\mathbf{c}^{(i)}$ be a $nL \times 1$ vector denoting a transmitted code sequence (see (3.39)). Let $\mathbf{c}^{(j)}$ be another $nL \times 1$ vector denoting a a code sequence at a distance d_H from $\mathbf{c}^{(i)}$. Note that the elements of $\mathbf{c}^{(i)}$ and $\mathbf{c}^{(j)}$ belong to the set $\{0, 1\}$. We assume that $\mathbf{c}^{(i)}$ and $\mathbf{c}^{(j)}$ constitute an error event. Let the received sequence be denoted by $\mathbf{c}_e$. Then (see also (3.48))

$$\mathbf{c}_e = \mathbf{c}^{(i)} \oplus \mathbf{e}, \tag{3.62}$$

where $\mathbf{e}$ is the $nL \times 1$ error vector introduced by the channel and the elements of $\mathbf{e}$ belong to the set $\{0, 1\}$. The VA makes an error when

$$\left(\mathbf{c}_e \oplus \mathbf{c}^{(i)}\right)^T \cdot \left(\mathbf{c}_e \oplus \mathbf{c}^{(i)}\right) > \left(\mathbf{c}_e \oplus \mathbf{c}^{(j)}\right)^T \cdot \left(\mathbf{c}_e \oplus \mathbf{c}^{(j)}\right)$$
$$\Rightarrow \mathbf{e}^T \cdot \mathbf{e} > \left(\mathbf{e}_{i,\,j} \oplus \mathbf{e}\right)^T \cdot \left(\mathbf{e}_{i,\,j} \oplus \mathbf{e}\right) \tag{3.63}$$

where

$$\mathbf{e}_{i,\,j} = \mathbf{c}^{(i)} \oplus \mathbf{c}^{(j)} \tag{3.64}$$

and $\cdot$ denotes real multiplication. Note that the right-hand side of (3.63) cannot be expanded. To overcome this difficulty, we replace $\oplus$ by $-$ (real subtraction). It is easy to see that

$$\left(\mathbf{e}_{i,\,j} \oplus \mathbf{e}\right)^T \cdot \left(\mathbf{e}_{i,\,j} \oplus \mathbf{e}\right) = \left(\mathbf{e}_{i,\,j} - \mathbf{e}\right)^T \cdot \left(\mathbf{e}_{i,\,j} - \mathbf{e}\right). \tag{3.65}$$

Thus (3.63) can be simplified to:

$$\begin{aligned} \mathbf{e}^T \cdot \mathbf{e} &> d_H - 2\mathbf{e}_{i,\,j}^T \cdot \mathbf{e} + \mathbf{e}^T \cdot \mathbf{e} \\ &\Rightarrow \mathbf{e}_{i,\,j}^T \cdot \mathbf{e} > d_H/2 \\ &\Rightarrow \sum_{l=1}^{nL} e_{i,\,j,\,l} \cdot e_l > d_H/2. \end{aligned} \tag{3.66}$$

Observe that in the above equation, we have used the relationship

$$\mathbf{e}_{i,\,j}^T \cdot \mathbf{e}_{i,\,j} = d_H. \tag{3.67}$$

We can draw the following conclusions from (3.66).

(a) When $e_{i,\,j,\,l} = 0$, there is no contribution to the summation *independent* of whether e_l is equal to one or zero (independent of whether the channel introduces an error or not).

(b) When $e_{i,\,j,\,l} = 1$, then $e_l = 1$ contributes to the summation. This statement and the statement in item (a) imply that only those encoded bit errors are considered, which occur in locations where the ith and jth codewords differ. Note that according to (3.67), the ith and jth codewords differ in d_H locations. Suppose there are k ($k \le d_H$) locations where $e_l = e_{i,\,j,\,l} = 1$. This can happen in $\binom{d_H}{k}$ ways.

(c) The maximum value of the summation is d_H.

Assuming that d_H is odd, let

$$d_{H,\,1} = (d_H + 1)/2. \tag{3.68}$$

Based on the conclusions in items (a)–(c), the probability of the error event can be written as

$$\begin{aligned} P\left(\mathbf{c}^{(j)} | \mathbf{c}^{(i)}\right) &= \sum_{k=d_{H,\,1}}^{d_H} \binom{d_H}{k} p^k (1-p)^{d_H - k} \\ &\approx \binom{d_H}{d_{H,\,1}} p^{d_{H,\,1}} \qquad \text{for } p \ll 1. \end{aligned} \tag{3.69}$$

Substituting for p from (2.20) with $\tilde{d} \doteq 2a$ (refer to (3.40)), we get

$$P\left(\mathbf{c}^{(j)}|\mathbf{c}^{(i)}\right) = \binom{d_H}{d_{H,1}}\left[0.5 \times \operatorname{erfc}\left(\sqrt{\frac{a^2}{2\sigma_w^2}}\right)\right]^{d_{H,1}}. \tag{3.70}$$

Using the Chernoff bound for the complementary error function, we get

$$P(\mathbf{c}^{(j)}|\mathbf{c}^{(i)}) < \binom{d_H}{d_{H,1}} \exp\left(-\frac{a^2 d_{H,1}}{2\sigma_w^2}\right). \tag{3.71}$$

Next we observe that a^2 is the average transmitted power for *every encoded bit*. Following Propositions 3.0.1 and 3.0.2, we must have

$$kP_{\text{av},\,b} = a^2 n. \tag{3.72}$$

Substituting for a^2 from the above equation into (3.71), we get

$$P(\mathbf{c}^{(j)}|\mathbf{c}^{(i)}) < \binom{d_H}{d_{H,1}} \exp\left(-\frac{P_{\text{av},\,b} k d_{H,1}}{2n\sigma_w^2}\right). \tag{3.73}$$

When d_H is even, it can be similarly shown that

$$P(\mathbf{c}^{(j)}|\mathbf{c}^{(i)}) < \frac{1}{2}\binom{d_H}{d_{H,1}} \exp\left(-\frac{P_{\text{av},\,b} k d_{H,1}}{2n\sigma_w^2}\right) \tag{3.74}$$

where the factor $1/2$ is due to the fact that the VA decides in favour of $\mathbf{c}^{(i)}$ or $\mathbf{c}^{(j)}$ with equal probability and

$$d_{H,1} = d_H/2. \tag{3.75}$$

From equations (3.73) and (3.74) it is clear that $P(\mathbf{c}^{(j)}|\mathbf{c}^{(i)})$ is *independent* of $\mathbf{c}^{(i)}$ and $\mathbf{c}^{(j)}$, and is dependent only on the Hamming distance d_H between the two code sequences. Hence, for simplicity we write

$$P(\mathbf{c}^{(j)}|\mathbf{c}^{(i)}) = P_{\text{ee, HD}}(d_H) \tag{3.76}$$

where $P_{\text{ee, HD}}(d_H)$ denotes the probability of error event characterized by Hamming distance d_H between the code sequences. The subscript 'HD' denotes hard decision.

We now proceed to compute the probability of bit error. Let $\mathbf{b}^{(i)}$ denote the $kL \times 1$ uncoded vector that yields $\mathbf{c}^{(i)}$. Similarly, let $\mathbf{b}^{(j)}$ denote the $kL \times 1$ uncoded vector that yields $\mathbf{c}^{(j)}$. Let

$$\left(\mathbf{b}^{(i)} \oplus \mathbf{b}^{(j)}\right)^T \cdot \left(\mathbf{b}^{(i)} \oplus \mathbf{b}^{(j)}\right) = w_H(d_H). \tag{3.77}$$

Now consider Figure 3.15, where we have shown a sequence of length L_1 blocks (nL_1 coded bits), where L_1 is a very large number. Let us assume that m identical (in the sense that $\mathbf{c}^{(j)}$ is detected instead of $\mathbf{c}^{(i)}$) error events have occurred. We assume that the Hamming distance between the code sequences constituting the error event is d_H and the corresponding Hamming distance between the information sequences is $w_H(d_H)$. Observe that the error events occur at distinct time instants, namely $t_1, \ldots, t_m$. In computing the probability of

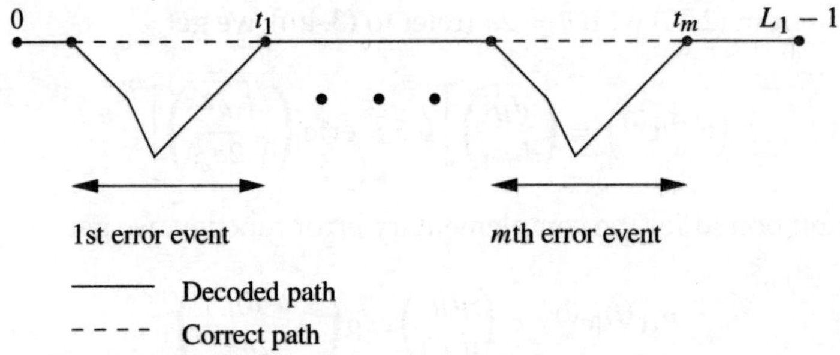

Figure 3.15 *Relation between the probability of error event and bit-error probability*

bit error, we assume that the error event is a random process[18,54–57] which is stationary and ergodic. Stationarity implies that the probability of the error event is independent of time, that is, $t_1, \ldots, t_m$. Ergodicity implies that the ensemble average is equal to the time average. Note that the error event probability computed in (3.74) is actually an ensemble average.

Using ergodicity, the probability of error event is

$$P_{\text{ee, HD}}(d_H) = \frac{m}{L_1}. \tag{3.78}$$

The probability of bit error is

$$P_{b,\,\text{HD}}(d_H) = \frac{m w_H(d_H)}{k L_1} \tag{3.79}$$

since there are kL_1 information bits in a block length of L_1 and each error event contributes $w_H(d_H)$ errors in the information bits. Thus the probability of bit error is

$$P_{b,\,\text{HD}}(d_H) = \frac{w_H(d_H)}{k} P_{\text{ee, HD}}(d_H). \tag{3.80}$$

Observe that this procedure of relating the probability of bit error with the probability of error event is identical to the method of relating the probability of symbol error and bit error for Gray coded PSK constellations. Here, an error event can be considered as a 'symbol' in an M-PSK constellation.

Let us now assume that there are A_{d_H} sequences that are at a distance d_H from the transmitted sequence i. In this situation, applying the union-bound argument, (3.80) must be modified to

$$P_{b,\,\text{HD}}(d_H) \le \frac{P_{\text{ee, HD}}(d_H)}{k} \sum_{l=1}^{A_{d_H}} w_{H,l}(d_H) \tag{3.81}$$

where $w_{H,l}(d_H)$ denotes the Hamming distance between $\mathbf{b}^{(i)}$ and any other sequence $\mathbf{b}^{(j)}$ such that (3.67) is satisfied.

The average probability of uncoded bit error is given by the union bound:

$$P_{b,\,\mathrm{HD}}(e) \leq \sum_{d_H=d_{H,\,\min}}^{\infty} P_{b,\,\mathrm{HD}}(d_H). \tag{3.82}$$

When $p \ll 1$, $P_{b,\,\mathrm{HD}}(e)$ is dominated by the minimum distance error event and can be approximated by

$$P_{b,\,\mathrm{HD}}(e) \approx P_{b,\,\mathrm{HD}}(d_{H,\,\min}). \tag{3.83}$$

For the encoder in Figure 3.3, $d_{H,\,\min} = 5$, $d_{H,\,1} = 3$, $k = 1$, $n = 2$, $w_{H,\,1}(5) = 1$, and $A_{d_{H,\,\min}} = 1$. Hence (3.83) reduces to

$$P_{b,\,\mathrm{HD}}(e) < 10 \exp\left(-\frac{3P_{\mathrm{av},\,b}}{4\sigma_w^2}\right). \tag{3.84}$$

Note that the average probability of bit error for uncoded BPSK is given by (from (2.20) and the Chernoff bound)

$$P_{b,\,\mathrm{BPSK,\;UC}}(e) < \exp\left(-\frac{P_{\mathrm{av},\,b}}{2\sigma_w^2}\right) \tag{3.85}$$

where the subscript 'UC' denotes uncoded and we have substituted

$$\left|\tilde{d}\right|^2 = 4P_{\mathrm{av},\,b} \tag{3.86}$$

in (2.20). Ignoring the term outside the exponent (for high SNR) in (3.84), we find that the performance of the convolutional code in Figure 3.3 with hard-decision decoding is better than uncoded BPSK by

$$10 \log\left(\frac{0.75}{0.5}\right) = 1.761\ \mathrm{dB}. \tag{3.87}$$

However, this improvement has been obtained at the expense of *doubling* the transmitted bandwidth.

In Figure 3.16 we compare the theoretical and simulated performance of hard-decision decoding for the convolutional encoder in Figure 3.3. In the figure, $\mathrm{SNR}_{\mathrm{av},\,b}$ denotes the SNR for uncoded BPSK, and is computed as (see also (2.31))

$$\mathrm{SNR}_{\mathrm{av},\,b} = \frac{P_{\mathrm{av},\,b}}{2\sigma_w^2}. \tag{3.88}$$

The theoretical performance was obtained as follows. Note that both $d_H = 5, 6$ yield $d_{H,\,1} = 3$. Hence we need to consider the first two spectral lines in the expression for the bit error probability. From (3.61) we note that the multiplicity of the first spectral line ($d_H = 5$) is one and the Hamming weight of the information sequence is also one. The multiplicity of the second spectral line ($d_H = 6$) is two ($A_6 = 2$) and the corresponding Hamming weight of the information sequence is also two ($w_{H,\,l}(6) = 2$ for $l = 1, 2$). Thus the average probability of bit error can be obtained from the union-bound as

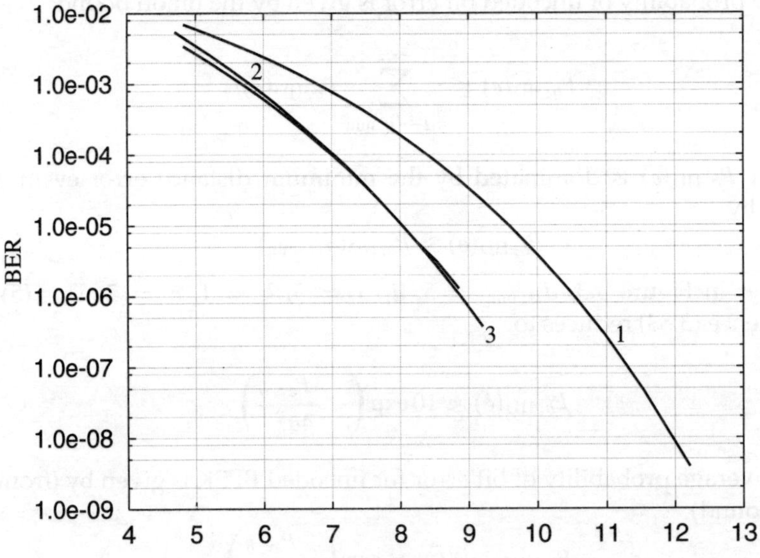

Figure 3.16 *Theoretical and simulated performance of hard decision decoding*

$$P_{b,\,\mathrm{HD}}(e) \approx \binom{5}{3} p^3 + \frac{1}{2}\binom{6}{3} p^3 \sum_{l=1}^{A_6} w_{H,\,l}(6) \tag{3.89}$$

where p is the probability of error at the output of the hard-decision device and is given by

$$\begin{aligned} p &= 0.5 \times \operatorname{erfc}\left(\sqrt{\frac{a^2}{2\sigma_w^2}}\right) \\ &= 0.5 \times \operatorname{erfc}\left(\sqrt{\frac{P_{\mathrm{av},\,b}}{4\sigma_w^2}}\right). \end{aligned} \tag{3.90}$$

We have not used the Chernoff bound for p in the plot since the bound is loose for small values of $\mathrm{SNR}_{\mathrm{av},\,b}$.

Substituting $A_6 = 2$ and $w_{H,\,l}(6) = 2$ for $l = 1, 2$ in (3.89), we get

$$P_{b,\,\mathrm{HD}}(e) \approx 50p^3. \tag{3.91}$$

We find that the theoretical performance given by (3.91) coincides with the simulated performance.

In Figure 3.17 we illustrate the performance of the VA using hard decisions for different decoding delays. We find that there is no difference in performance for $\mathcal{D}_v = 10, 40$. Note that

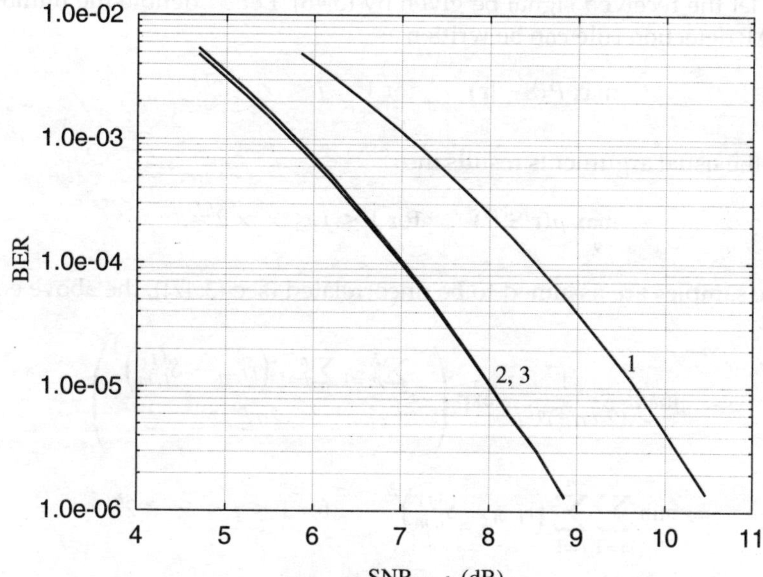

Figure 3.17 *Simulated performance of VA hard-decision for different decoding delays*

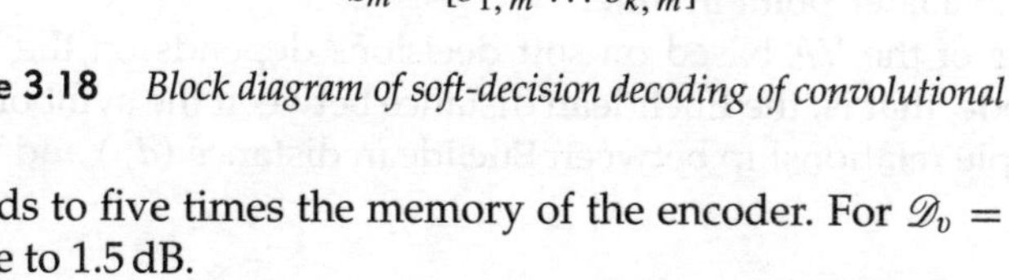

$$\mathbf{r}_m = [r_{1,m} \cdots r_{n,m}]^T$$
$$\hat{\mathbf{b}}_m = [\hat{b}_{1,m} \cdots \hat{b}_{k,m}]^T$$

Figure 3.18 *Block diagram of soft-decision decoding of convolutional codes*

$\mathscr{D}_v = 10$ corresponds to five times the memory of the encoder. For $\mathscr{D}_v = 4$ the performance degradation is close to 1.5 dB.

In the next section we study the performance of soft-decision decoding of convolutional codes which achieves a better performance than hard decision decoding.

3.4 Soft-Decision Decoding of Convolutional Codes

The block diagram of soft-decision decoding of convolutional codes is given in Figure 3.18. Note that the VA operates directly on the received samples $\mathbf{r}$. Following the developments in Section 3.3, let the received signal be given by (3.46). Let $\mathscr{S}$ denote the number of trellis states. The MAP detection rule can be written as

$$\max_j P(\mathbf{S}^{(j)}|\mathbf{r}) \qquad \text{for } 1 \le j \le \mathscr{S} \times 2^{kL} \tag{3.92}$$

which, due to the usual arguments results in

$$\max_j p(\mathbf{r}|\mathbf{S}^{(j)}) \qquad \text{for } 1 \le j \le \mathscr{S} \times 2^{kL}. \tag{3.93}$$

Since the noise samples are assumed to be uncorrelated (see (3.47)), the above equation can be written as

$$\max_j \frac{1}{(2\pi\sigma_w^2)^{nL/2}} \exp\left(-\frac{\sum_{m=1}^{L}\sum_{l=1}^{n}\left(r_{l,m} - S_{l,m}^{(j)}\right)^2}{2\sigma_w^2}\right)$$

$$\Rightarrow \min_j \sum_{m=1}^{L}\sum_{l=1}^{n}\left(r_{l,m} - S_{l,m}^{(j)}\right)^2 \qquad \text{for } 1 \le j \le \mathscr{S} \times 2^{kL}. \tag{3.94}$$

Thus the soft-decision ML detector decides in favour of the sequence that is closest, in terms of the Euclidean distance, to the received sequence.

Once again, we notice that the complexity of the ML detector increases exponentially with the length of the sequence (kL) to be detected. The Viterbi algorithm is a practical way to implement the ML detector. The only difference is that the branch metrics are given by the inner summation of (3.94), that is,

$$\sum_{l=1}^{n}(r_{l,m} - S^{(j)})^2 \quad \text{for } 1 \le j \le \mathscr{I} \times 2^k \tag{3.95}$$

where the superscript j now varies over all possible states and all possible inputs. Observe that due to the periodic nature of the trellis, the subscripts l and m are not required in $S^{(j)}$. It is easy to see that a path eliminated by the VA cannot have a lower metric (or weight) than the surviving path at a later point in time.

The performance of the VA based on soft decisions depends on the Euclidean distance properties of the code, that is, the Euclidean distance between the symbol sequences $\mathbf{S}^{(i)}$ and $\mathbf{S}^{(j)}$. There is a simple relationship between Euclidean distance (d_E^2) and Hamming distance d_H as given below.

$$\left(\mathbf{S}^{(i)} - \mathbf{S}^{(j)}\right)^T \cdot \left(\mathbf{S}^{(i)} - \mathbf{S}^{(j)}\right) = 4a^2 \cdot \left(\mathbf{c}^{(i)} \oplus \mathbf{c}^{(j)}\right)^T \cdot \left(\mathbf{c}^{(i)} \oplus \mathbf{c}^{(j)}\right)$$

$$\Rightarrow d_E^2 = 4a^2 d_H. \tag{3.96}$$

Due to the above equation, it is easy to verify that the distance spectrum is independent of the reference sequence. In fact, the distance spectrum is similar to that for the VA based on hard decisions (see for example Figure 3.14), except that the distances have to be scaled by $4a^2$. The relationship between multiplicities is simple:

$$A_{d_E} = A_{d_H} \tag{3.97}$$

where A_{d_E} denotes the number of sequences at a Euclidean distance d_E from the reference sequence. It is customary to consider the symbol sequence $\mathbf{S}^{(i)}$ corresponding to the all-zero code sequence, as the reference.

3.4.1 Performance analysis of soft-decision decoding

In this section we compute the probability that the VA decides in favour of sequence $\mathbf{S}^{(j)}$ given that sequence $\mathbf{S}^{(i)}$ has been transmitted. We assume that $\mathbf{S}^{(i)}$ and $\mathbf{S}^{(j)}$ constitute an error event. The VA decides in favour of $\mathbf{S}^{(j)}$ when

$$\begin{aligned}
\sum_{m=1}^{L}\sum_{l=1}^{n}\left(r_{l,m} - S_{l,m}^{(j)}\right)^2 &< \sum_{m=1}^{L}\sum_{l=1}^{n}\left(r_{l,m} - S_{l,m}^{(i)}\right)^2 \\
\Rightarrow \sum_{m=1}^{L}\sum_{l=1}^{n}\left(e_{l,m} + w_{l,m}\right)^2 &< \sum_{m=1}^{L}\sum_{l=1}^{n} w_{l,m}^2 \\
\Rightarrow \sum_{m=1}^{L}\sum_{l=1}^{n}\left(e_{l,m}^2 + 2e_{l,m}w_{l,m}\right) &< 0
\end{aligned} \tag{3.98}$$

where $w_{l,m}$ are the noise samples in (3.47) and

$$e_{l,m} = S_{l,m}^{(i)} - S_{l,m}^{(j)}. \tag{3.99}$$

Let

$$Z \triangleq 2\sum_{m=1}^{L}\sum_{l=1}^{n} e_{l,m}w_{l,m}. \tag{3.100}$$

Then Z is a Gaussian random variable with mean and variance given by

$$\begin{aligned}
E[Z] &= 0, \\
E\left[Z^2\right] &= 4\sigma_w^2 d_E^2
\end{aligned} \tag{3.101}$$

where

$$d_E^2 \triangleq \sum_{m=1}^{L}\sum_{l=1}^{n} e_{l,m}^2. \tag{3.102}$$

The probability of the error event is given by

$$P\left(\mathbf{S}^{(j)}|\mathbf{S}^{(i)}\right) = P\left(Z < -d_E^2\right)$$
$$= \frac{1}{2}\text{erfc}\left(\sqrt{\frac{d_E^2}{8\sigma_w^2}}\right). \tag{3.103}$$

Substituting for d_E^2 from (3.96) and for a^2 from (3.72) and using the Chernoff bound in the above equation, we get

$$\begin{aligned} P\left(\mathbf{S}^{(j)}|\mathbf{S}^{(i)}\right) &= \frac{1}{2}\text{erfc}\left(\sqrt{\frac{4a^2 d_H}{8\sigma_w^2}}\right) \\ &= \frac{1}{2}\text{erfc}\left(\sqrt{\frac{P_{\text{av},\,b} k d_H}{2n\sigma_w^2}}\right) \\ &< \exp\left(-\frac{P_{\text{av},\,b} k d_H}{2n\sigma_w^2}\right) \\ &= P_{\text{ee, SD}}(d_H) \qquad \text{(say).} \end{aligned} \tag{3.104}$$

The subscript 'SD' in $P_{\text{ee, SD}}(\cdot)$ denotes soft decision. Comparing (3.104) and (3.73), we see that the VA based on soft decisions straightaway gives approximately 3 dB improvement in performance over the VA based on hard decisions.

Once again, if $\mathbf{b}^{(i)}$ denotes the input (uncoded) sequence that maps to $\mathbf{S}^{(i)}$, and similarly if $\mathbf{b}^{(j)}$ maps to $\mathbf{S}^{(j)}$, the probability of uncoded bit error corresponding to the error event in (3.104) is given by

$$P_{b,\,\text{SD}}(d_H) = \frac{w_H(d_H)}{k} P_{\text{ee, SD}}(d_H) \tag{3.105}$$

which is similar to (3.80) with $w_H(d_H)$ given by (3.77). When the multiplicity at distance d_H is equal to A_{d_H}, the probability of bit error in (3.105) must be modified to

$$P_{b,\,\text{SD}}(d_H) \le \frac{P_{\text{ee, SD}}(d_H)}{k} \sum_{l=1}^{A_{d_H}} w_{H,\,l}(d_H) \tag{3.106}$$

where $w_{H,\,l}(d_H)$ denotes the Hamming distance between $\mathbf{b}^{(i)}$ and any other sequence $\mathbf{b}^{(j)}$ such that the Hamming distance between the corresponding code sequences is d_H.

The average probability of uncoded bit error is given by the union bound

$$P_{b,\,\text{SD}}(e) \le \sum_{d_H = d_{H,\,\min}}^{\infty} P_{b,\,\text{SD}}(d_H) \tag{3.107}$$

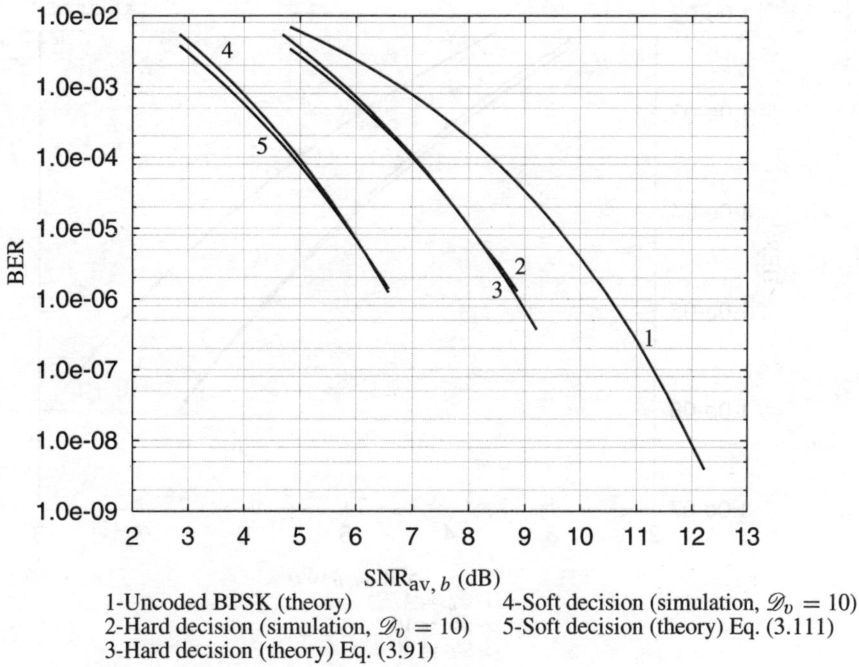

Figure 3.19 *Theoretical and simulated performance of VA with soft decision*

which, for large values of signal-to-noise ratios, $P_{\text{av}, b}/(2\sigma_w^2)$, is well approximated by

$$P_{b,\,\text{SD}}(e) \approx P_{b,\,\text{SD}}(d_{H,\,\text{min}}). \tag{3.108}$$

Let us once again consider the encoder in Figure 3.3. Noting that $w_H(5) = 1$, $A_{d_{H,\text{min}}} = 1$, $k = 1, n = 2$ and $d_{H,\,\text{min}} = 5$, we get the average probability of bit error as:

$$P_{b,\,\text{SD}}(e) < \exp\left(-\frac{5P_{\text{av},\,b}}{4\sigma_w^2}\right). \tag{3.109}$$

Ignoring the term outside the exponent in the above equation and comparing with (3.85), we find that the performance of the convolutional code in Figure 3.3 is better than uncoded BPSK by

$$10\log\left(\frac{5\times 2}{4}\right) = 3.98 \text{ dB} \tag{3.110}$$

which is a significant improvement over hard-decision decoding. However, note that the improvement is still at the expense of doubling the bandwidth.

In Figure 3.19 we have plotted the theoretical and simulated performance of VA with soft decision for the encoder in Figure 3.3. The theoretical performance was plotted using the first three spectral lines ($d_H = 5, 6, 7$) in (3.61). Using the union-bound we get

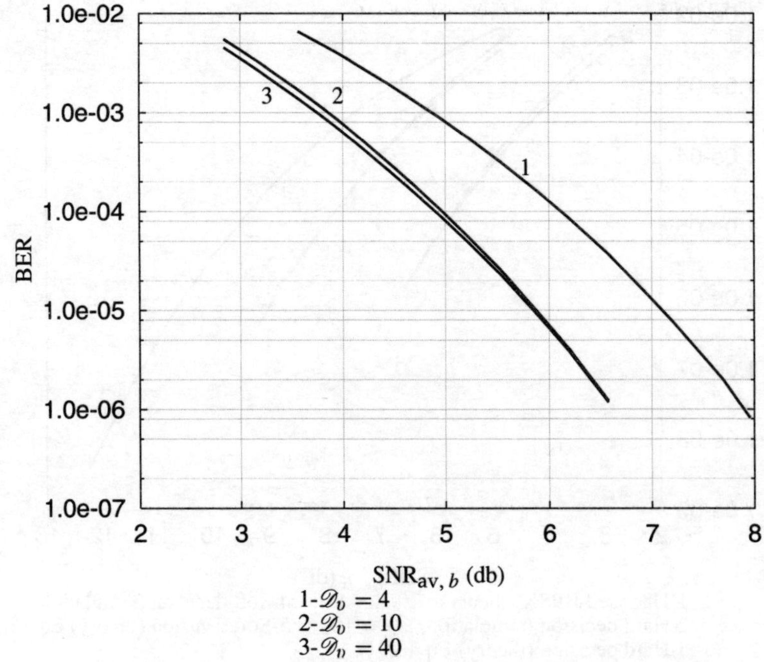

Figure 3.20 *Simulated performance of VA with soft decision for different decoding delays*

$$P_{b,\,\text{SD}}(e) \approx \frac{1}{2}\text{erfc}\left(\sqrt{\frac{5P_{\text{av},\,b}}{4\sigma_w^2}}\right) + \frac{4}{2}\text{erfc}\left(\sqrt{\frac{6P_{\text{av},\,b}}{4\sigma_w^2}}\right) + \frac{12}{2}\text{erfc}\left(\sqrt{\frac{7P_{\text{av},\,b}}{4\sigma_w^2}}\right). \tag{3.111}$$

Once again we find that the theoretical and simulated curves nearly overlap.

In Figure 3.20 we have plotted the performance of the VA with soft decisions for different decoding delays. It is clear that $\mathscr{D}_v$ must be equal to five times the memory of the encoder to obtain the best performance.

We have so far discussed coding schemes that increase the bandwidth of the transmitted signal, since n coded bits are transmitted in the same duration as k uncoded bits. This results in bandwidth expansion. In the next section we discuss Trellis Coded Modulation (TCM) wherein the n coded bits are mapped onto a symbol in a 2^n-ary constellation. Thus, the transmitted bandwidth remains unchanged.

3.5 Trellis Coded Modulation (TCM)

The concept of trellis coded modulation was introduced by Ungerboeck in [58]. A tutorial exposition can be found in [59,60]. A more general class of TCM codes known as coset codes is discussed in [61–63]. An interesting review of trellis codes can also be found in [64,65]. A detailed performance analysis of trellis codes can be found in [66]. In practical situations,

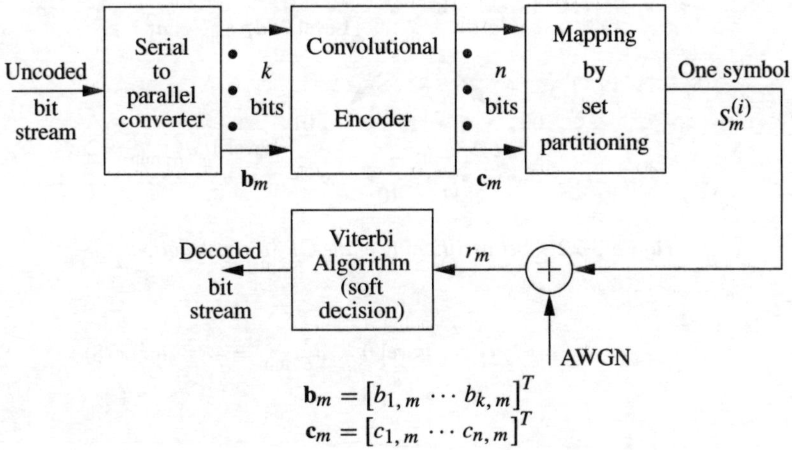

Figure 3.21 *Block diagram of a trellis coded modulation scheme (TCM)*

the carrier synchronization procedures at the receiver exhibit 90°-phase ambiguities. This implies that the received symbol sequence gets multiplied by $e^{j\theta}$ where θ is an integer multiple of 90°. The decoder at the receiver should be able to correctly estimate the symbol sequence, in spite of this impairment. This calls for proper design of trellis codes such that they are insensitive to such rotations. These aspects are discussed in detail in [67,68]. The concept of *rotational invariance* is also required in the design of convolutional codes, and this is dealt with in [69,70].

Comparing Figures 3.21 and 3.18 we find that a new block called mapping by set partitioning as been included. This block maps the n coded bits to a symbol in a 2^n-ary constellation. The mapping is done in such a way that the Euclidean distance between symbol sequences is maximized. Note that if TCM was not used, the k uncoded bits would get mapped onto a 2^k-ary constellation. From Proposition 3.0.1 we have:

$$kP_{\text{av},b} = \text{Average power of the } M = 2^n\text{-ary constellation.} \tag{3.112}$$

Using (3.112) it can be shown that the minimum Euclidean distance of the M-ary constellation is less than that of uncoded BPSK. This suggests that symbol-by-symbol detection would be suboptimal, and we need to go for sequence detection (detecting a sequence of symbols) using the Viterbi algorithm.

We now proceed to describe the concept of mapping by set partitioning.

3.5.1 Mapping by set partitioning

Set partitioning essentially involves dividing the constellation into subsets with increasing minimum distance between symbols. This is illustrated in Figure 3.22 for the QPSK constellation, in Figure 3.23 for the 8-PSK constellation and in Figure 3.24 for the 16-QAM constellation. The number of *levels* into which a constellation is to be partitioned is determined by the encoder design, as we shall see below[66].The next step is to map the n coded bits into symbols in the partitioned constellation.

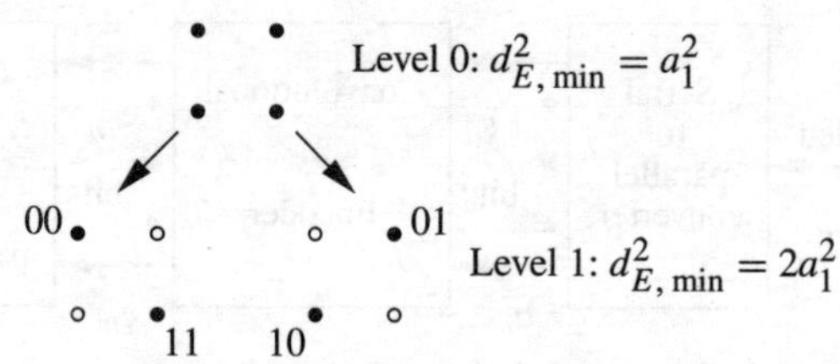

Figure 3.22 *Set partitioning of the QPSK constellation*

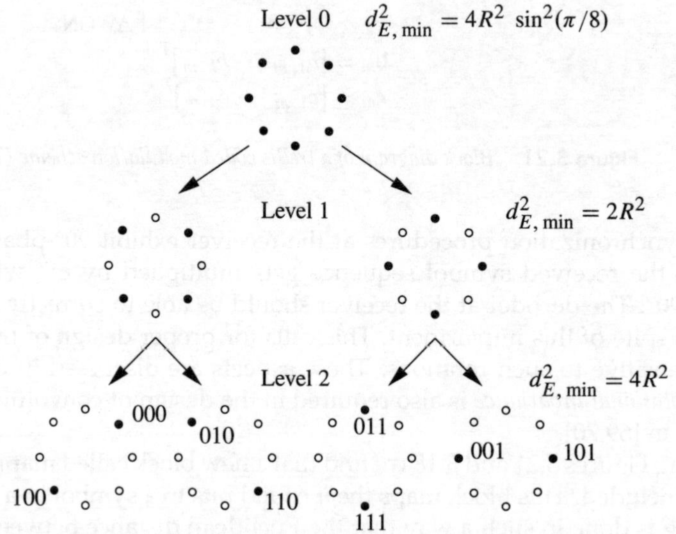

Figure 3.23 *Set partitioning of the 8-PSK constellation*

At this point we need to identify two kinds of TCM encoders. The first kind of encoder has systematic bits, as illustrated in Figure 3.25. Here there are k_2 systematic (uncoded) bits. Observe that the k_2 uncoded bits result in 2^{k_2} parallel transitions between states, since these bits have no effect on the encoder state. Here the maximum level of partitioning required is equal to $n - k_2$. There are 2^{k_2} points in each subset at partition level $n - k_2$. The total number of subsets at partition level $n - k_2$ is equal to 2^{n-k_2}.

We now have to discuss the rules for mapping the codewords to symbols. These rules are enumerated below for the first type of encoder (having systematic bits).

(a) In the trellis diagram there are 2^k distinct encoder outputs diverging from any state. Hence, all encoder outputs that diverge from a state must be mapped to points in a subset at partition level $n - k$.

(b) The encoded bits corresponding to parallel transitions must be mapped to points in a subset at the partition level $n - k_2$. The subset at partition level $n - k_2$ to which they

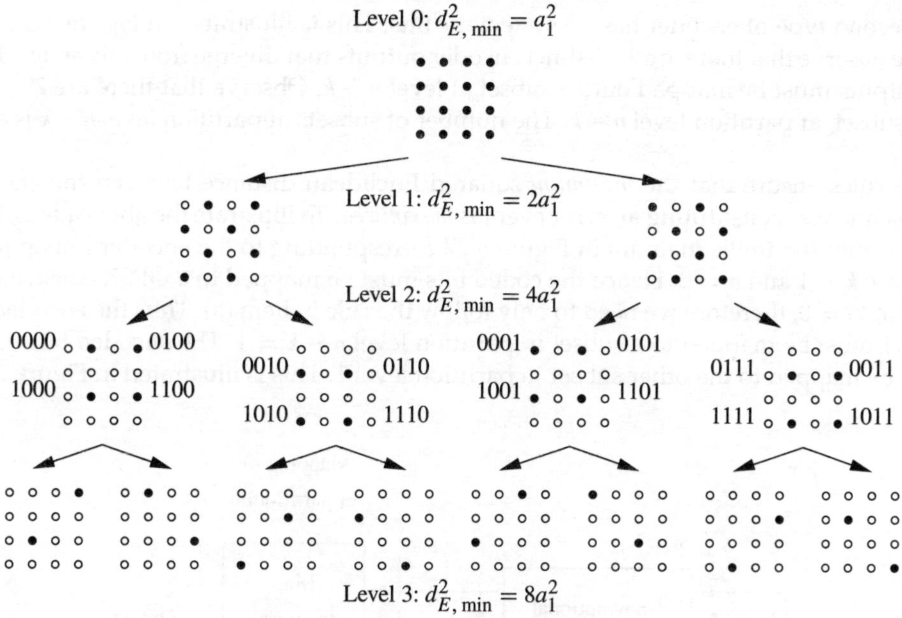

Figure 3.24 *Set partitioning of the 16-QAM constellation*

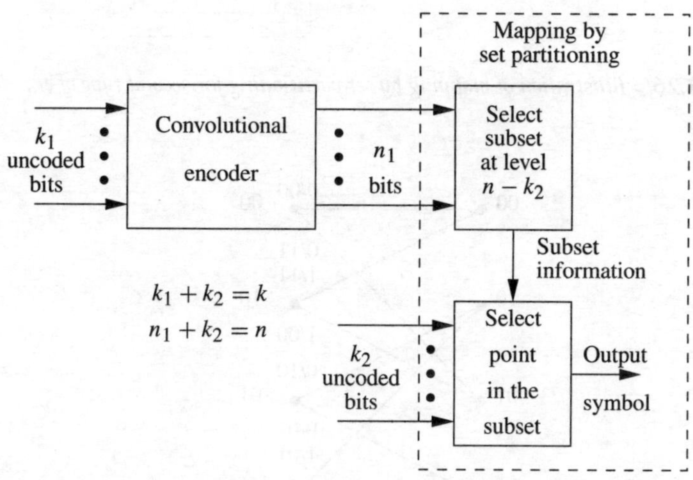

Figure 3.25 *Illustration of mapping by set partitioning for first type of encoder*

are assigned is determined by the n_1 coded bits. The point in the subset is selected by the k_2 uncoded bits. The subsets selected by the n_1 coded bits must be such that the rule in item (a) is not violated. In other words, the subset at partition level $n - k$ must be a parent of the subset at partition level $n - k_2$.

The second type of encoder has no systematic bits. This is illustrated in Figure 3.26. Here again we observe that there are 2^k distinct encoder outputs that diverge from any state. Hence these outputs must be mapped onto a subset at level $n-k$. Observe that there are 2^k points in each subset, at partition level $n-k$. The number of subsets at partition level $n-k$ is equal to 2^{n-k}.

These rules ensure that the *minimum* squared Euclidean distance between the encoded symbol sequences constituting an error event is *maximized*. To illustrate the above ideas, let us again consider the trellis diagram in Figure 3.27 corresponding to the encoder in Figure 3.3. In this case $k = 1$ and $n = 2$. Hence the coded bits must be mapped to a QPSK constellation. Moreover, $k_2 = 0$, therefore we need to only follow the rule in item (a). Thus the encoded bits 00 and 11 must be mapped to a subset in partition level $n-k=1$. The encoded bits 01 and 10 must be mapped to the other subset in partition level 1. This is illustrated in Figure 3.22.

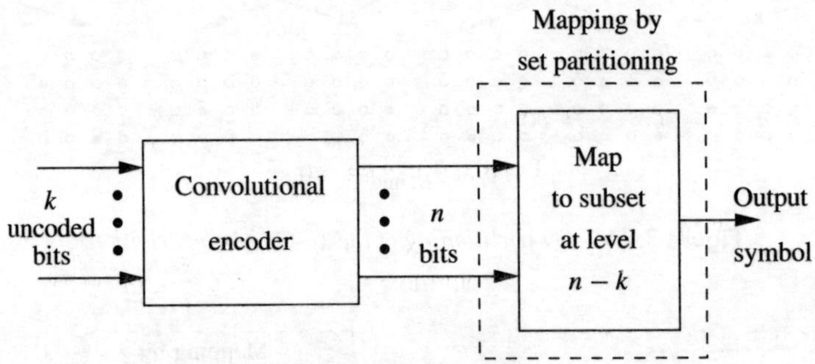

Figure 3.26 *Illustration of mapping by set partitioning for second type of encoder*

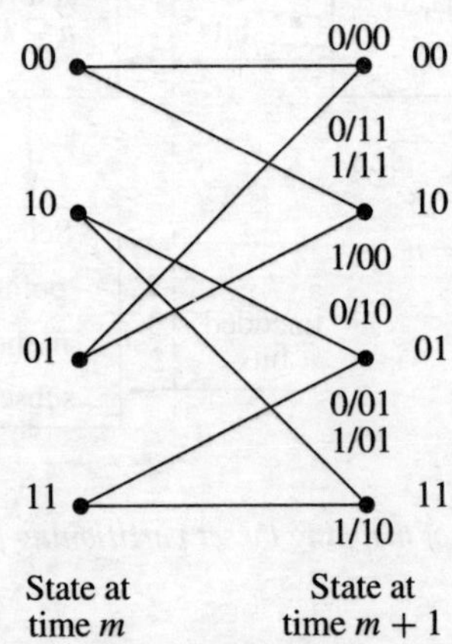

Figure 3.27 *Trellis diagram for the convolutional encoder in Figure 3.3*

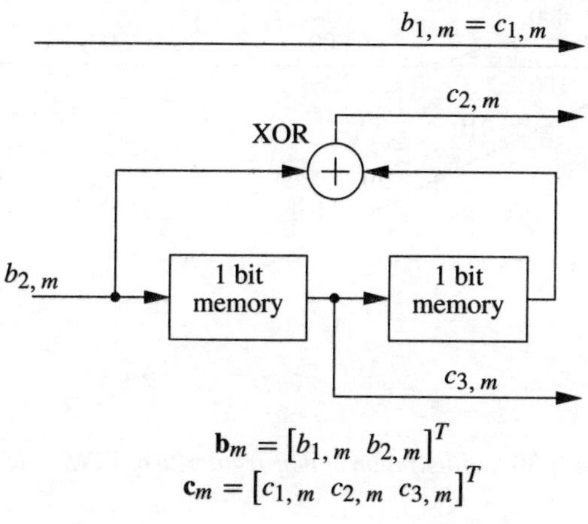

Figure 3.28 *A rate-2/3 convolutional encoder*

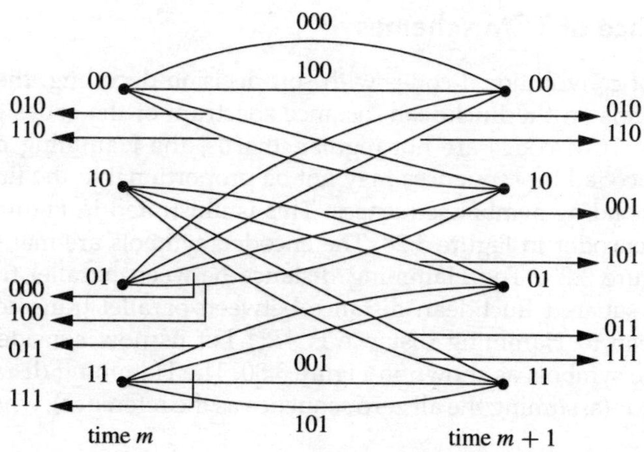

Figure 3.29 *Trellis diagram for encoder in Figure 3.28*

As another example, consider the encoder in Figure 3.28. The corresponding trellis diagram is shown in Figure 3.29. Since $n = 3$, the coded bits must be mapped to an 8-PSK constellation (note that the 8-QAM constellation cannot be used since it cannot be set partitioned). In this case $k_2 = 1$ and the rules in item (a) and (b) are applicable. Thus, following rule (a), the encoded bits 000, 100, 010 and 110 must be mapped to a subset in partition level $n - k = 1$. The encoded bits 001, 101, 011 and 111 must be mapped to the other subset in partition level 1. Following rule (b), the encoded bits 000 and 100 must be mapped to a subset in partition level $n - k_2 = 2$. The encoded bits 010 and 110 must be mapped to another subset in partition level 2 such that rule (a) is satisfied. This is illustrated in Figure 3.23. Note that once the subset is selected, the mapping of the k_2 uncoded bits to points within the

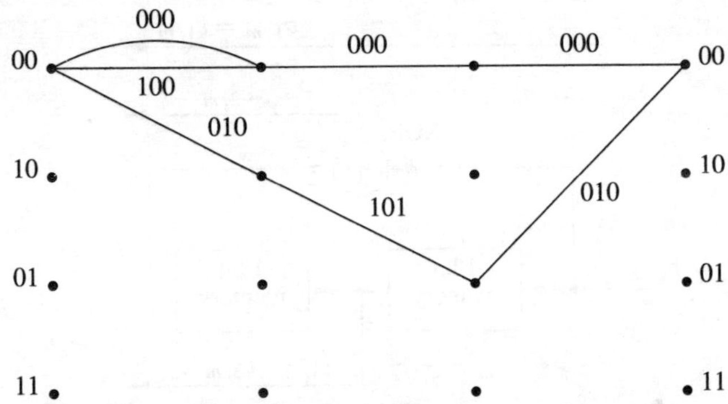

Figure 3.30 *Illustration of non-regularity of TCM codes*

subset can be done arbitrarily. In the next section we study the performance of some TCM schemes.

3.5.2 Performance of TCM schemes

Just as in the case of convolutional codes with soft-decision decoding, the performance of TCM schemes depends on the Euclidean distance spectrum of the codes generated by the encoder. In general, TCM codes are not regular, that is, the Hamming distance between between any two encoded bit sequences may not be proportional to the Euclidean distance between the corresponding symbol sequences. This is illustrated in Figure 3.30. The trellis corresponds to the encoder in Figure 3.28. The encoded symbols are mapped to the 8-PSK constellation in Figure 3.23. The Hamming distance between parallel transitions is one. The corresponding squared Euclidean distance between parallel transitions is $4R^2$. Thus the ratio of Euclidean to Hamming distance is $4R^2$. Let us now consider an error event extending over three symbols as shown in Figure 3.30. The Hamming distance between the code sequences is four (assuming the all zero sequence as the reference), whereas the squared Euclidean distance is

$$d_E^2 = 4R^2\left(1 + \sin^2(\pi/8)\right). \tag{3.113}$$

The ratio of Euclidean to Hamming distance in this case is

$$\frac{4R^2\,(1 + \sin^2(\pi/8))}{4} \neq 4R^2. \tag{3.114}$$

Hence the TCM code specified by Figure 3.28 and the mapping in Figure 3.23 is not regular.

In general, for TCM codes (3.96) is not satisfied excepting for a special case where a rate-1/2 encoder is used and the two code bits are mapped to a QPSK constellation. This will be clear from the following theorems.

Theorem 3.5.1 *The necessary and sufficient condition for a TCM code (using a rate-k/n encoder) to be regular is that the mapping of the n-bit codeword to the 2^n-ary constellation should be regular.*

Proof: Consider the mapping

$$\mathbf{c}^{(i)} \rightarrow \tilde{S}^{(i)} \quad \text{for } 1 \leq i \leq 2^n \tag{3.115}$$

where $\mathbf{c}^{(i)}$ is a $n \times 1$ codeword and $\tilde{S}^{(i)}$ is a symbol in a 2^n-ary two-dimensional constellation. The mapping of codewords to symbols is said to be regular if

$$\left|\tilde{S}^{(i)} - \tilde{S}^{(j)}\right|^2 = C\left(\mathbf{c}^{(i)} \oplus \mathbf{c}^{(j)}\right)^T \left(\mathbf{c}^{(i)} \oplus \mathbf{c}^{(j)}\right) \tag{3.116}$$

where C is a constant. Let us now consider the ith code sequence denoted by the $nL \times 1$ vector

$$\mathbf{C}^{(i)} = \left[\left(\mathbf{c}_1^{(i)}\right)^T \quad \cdots \quad \left(\mathbf{c}_L^{(i)}\right)^T\right]^T \tag{3.117}$$

and the corresponding symbol sequence

$$\tilde{\mathbf{S}}^{(i)} = \left[\tilde{S}_1^{(i)} \quad \ldots \quad \tilde{S}_L^{(i)}\right]^T. \tag{3.118}$$

Then clearly,

$$\begin{aligned}
\left(\tilde{\mathbf{S}}^{(i)} - \tilde{\mathbf{S}}^{(j)}\right)^H \left(\tilde{\mathbf{S}}^{(i)} - \tilde{\mathbf{S}}^{(j)}\right) &= \sum_{k=1}^{L} \left|\tilde{S}_k^{(i)} - \tilde{S}_k^{(j)}\right|^2 \\
&= C \sum_{k=1}^{L} \left(\mathbf{c}_k^{(i)} \oplus \mathbf{c}_k^{(j)}\right)^T \left(\mathbf{c}_k^{(i)} \oplus \mathbf{c}_k^{(j)}\right) \\
&= C\left(\mathbf{C}^{(i)} \oplus \mathbf{C}^{(j)}\right)^T \left(\mathbf{C}^{(i)} \oplus \mathbf{C}^{(j)}\right).
\end{aligned} \tag{3.119}$$

Thus if the mapping is regular, the Euclidean distance between symbols sequences is proportional to the Hamming distance between the corresponding code sequences (sufficient condition). The condition in (3.116) is also necessary because if the mapping is not regular then the TCM code is also not regular ((3.119) is not satisfied). In [66], this property is referred to as *strong sense* regularity. Note that *weak sense* regularity[66] (as opposed to strong sense regularity) implies that the Euclidean distance is proportional to the Hamming distance between the symbols in a *subset* of the constellation. This property is valid for the first type of encoder having at most two systematic bits $k_2 \leq 2$. Thus, it is easy to see that for any subset at level $n - k_2$, the Euclidean distance is proportional to the Hamming distance.

Regularity is a property that is nice to have, and since we are guaranteed that the Euclidean distance spectrum is independent of the reference sequence, therefore we can take the all-zero information sequence ($\mathbf{b}^{(i)}$) as the reference. However, this may not be always possible as we shall see below. □

Theorem 3.5.2 *There cannot be a regular mapping of n-bit codeword to a two-dimensional constellation for* $n \geq 3$[44].

Proof: The number of nearest neighbours for an n-bit codeword is n (at a Hamming distance of unity). This is true for all the 2^n codewords. However, in two-dimensional space there cannot be n nearest neighbours for all the 2^n symbols, for $n \geq 3$. Hence proved. As a corollary, TCM codes for $n \geq 3$ are not regular, therefore the Euclidean distance spectrum cannot be obtained from the Hamming distance spectrum. □

However, most TCM codes are *quasiregular*, that is, the Euclidean distance spectrum is independent of the reference sequence even though (3.96) is not satisfied. Quasiregular codes are also known as geometrically uniform codes[71]. Hence we can once again assume that the all-zero information sequence to be the reference sequence. We now proceed to compute the probability of an error event. We assume that the error event extends over L symbol durations.

Let the received symbol sequence be denoted by

$$\tilde{\mathbf{r}} = \mathbf{S}^{(i)} + \tilde{\mathbf{w}} \tag{3.120}$$

where

$$\mathbf{S}^{(i)} = \begin{bmatrix} S_1^{(i)} & \ldots & S_L^{(i)} \end{bmatrix}^T \tag{3.121}$$

denotes the ith possible $L \times 1$ vector of complex symbols drawn from an M-ary constellation and

$$\tilde{\mathbf{w}} = \begin{bmatrix} \tilde{w}_1 & \ldots & \tilde{w}_L \end{bmatrix}^T \tag{3.122}$$

denotes an $L \times 1$ vector of AWGN samples having zero mean and variance

$$\frac{1}{2} E\left[|\tilde{w}_i|^2 \right] = \sigma_w^2. \tag{3.123}$$

Let

$$\mathbf{S}^{(j)} = \begin{bmatrix} S_1^{(j)} & \ldots & S_L^{(j)} \end{bmatrix}^T \tag{3.124}$$

denote the jth possible $L \times 1$ vector that forms an error event with $\tilde{\mathbf{S}}^{(i)}$. Let

$$\left(\mathbf{S}^{(i)} - \mathbf{S}^{(j)} \right)^H \left(\mathbf{S}^{(i)} - \mathbf{S}^{(j)} \right) = d_E^2 \tag{3.125}$$

denote the squared Euclidean distance between sequences $\mathbf{S}^{(i)}$ and $\mathbf{S}^{(j)}$. Then the probability that the VA decides in favour of $\mathbf{S}^{(j)}$ given that $\mathbf{S}^{(i)}$ was transmitted is

$$\begin{aligned} P\left(\mathbf{S}^{(j)} | \mathbf{S}^{(i)} \right) &= \frac{1}{2} \operatorname{erfc} \left(\sqrt{\frac{d_E^2}{8\sigma_w^2}} \right) \\ &= P_{\text{ee, TCM}}\left(d_E^2 \right) \quad \text{(say).} \end{aligned} \tag{3.126}$$

Assuming that $\mathbf{b}^{(i)}$ maps to $\mathbf{S}^{(i)}$ and $\mathbf{b}^{(j)}$ maps to $\mathbf{S}^{(j)}$, the probability of uncoded bit error corresponding to the above error event is given by

$$P_{b,\,\mathrm{TCM}}(d_E^2) = \frac{w_H(d_E^2)}{k} P_{\mathrm{ee},\,\mathrm{TCM}}(d_E^2) \tag{3.127}$$

where $w_H(d_E^2)$ is again given by (3.77). Note that $w_H(d_E^2)$ denotes the Hamming distance between the information sequences when the squared Euclidean distance between the corresponding symbol sequences is d_E^2.

When the multiplicity at d_E^2 is A_{d_E}, (3.127) must be modified to

$$P_{b,\,\mathrm{TCM}}(d_E^2) \le \frac{P_{\mathrm{ee},\,\mathrm{TCM}}(d_E^2)}{k} \sum_{l=1}^{A_{d_E}} w_{H,\,l}(d_E^2). \tag{3.128}$$

The average probability of uncoded bit error is given by the union bound (assuming that the code is quasiregular)

$$P_{b,\,\mathrm{TCM}}(e) \le \sum_{d_E^2 = d_{E,\,\min}^2}^{\infty} P_{b,\,\mathrm{TCM}}(d_E^2) \tag{3.129}$$

which at high signal-to-noise ratio is well approximated by

$$P_{b,\,\mathrm{TCM}}(e) \approx P_{b,\,\mathrm{TCM}}(d_{E,\,\min}^2). \tag{3.130}$$

3.5.3 Analysis of a QPSK TCM scheme

Let us now analyze the performance of the TCM code characterized by the encoder in Figure 3.3. The two encoded bits are mapped to the QPSK constellation, as shown in Figure 3.22. The minimum distance error event is given in Figure 3.13 with $d_{E,\,\min}^2 = 5a_1^2$. The multiplicity at the minimum Euclidean distance is $A_{d_{E,\,\min}} = 1$ and the corresponding distance between the information sequences is $w_{H,\,1}(5a_1^2) = 1$. Substituting these values in (3.130) and using the Chernoff bound, we get

$$\begin{aligned} P_{b,\,\mathrm{TCM}}(e) &\approx \frac{1}{2}\mathrm{erfc}\left(\sqrt{\frac{5a_1^2}{8\sigma_w^2}}\right) \\ &< \exp\left(-\frac{5a_1^2}{8\sigma_w^2}\right). \end{aligned} \tag{3.131}$$

We now need to compare the performance of the above TCM scheme with uncoded BPSK.

Firstly we note that the average power of the QPSK constellation is $a_1^2/2$. Since $k = 1$, we must have (see Propositions 3.0.1 and 3.0.2 in Section 3.1)

$$P_{\mathrm{av},\,b} = a_1^2/2. \tag{3.132}$$

Substituting for a_1^2 from the above equation into (3.131) we get

$$P_{b,\,\mathrm{TCM}}(e) < \exp\left(-\frac{5P_{\mathrm{av},\,b}}{4\sigma_w^2}\right) \tag{3.133}$$

which is identical to (3.109). Therefore, for *this particular example* we see that the performance of TCM is identical to the rate-1/2 convolutional code with soft decisions. The difference however lies in the transmission bandwidth. Whereas the bandwidth of the TCM scheme is identical to that of uncoded BPSK, the bandwidth of the rate-1/2 convolutional code is double that of uncoded BPSK.

When a TCM scheme uses a rate-k/n encoder, it may not make sense to compare the performance of TCM with uncoded BPSK. This is because if the uncoded bit-rate is R, then the baud-rate of TCM is R/k. Thus, we need to compare the performance of TCM with uncoded signalling having the same baud-rate. This motivates us to introduce the concept of *asymptotic coding gain* of a TCM scheme. This is defined as

$$G_a \stackrel{\Delta}{=} 10\log\left(\frac{d_{E,\,\text{min, TCM}}^2}{d_{E,\,\text{min, UC}}^2}\right) \tag{3.134}$$

where $d_{E,\,\text{min, TCM}}^2$ denotes the minimum squared Euclidean distance of the rate-k/n TCM scheme (that uses a 2^n-ary constellation) and $d_{E,\,\text{min, UC}}^2$ denotes the minimum squared Euclidean distance of the uncoded scheme (that uses a 2^k-ary constellation) transmitting the *same* average power as the TCM scheme. In other words,

$$P_{\text{av, TCM}} = P_{\text{av, UC}} = kP_{\text{av}, b} \tag{3.135}$$

where we have used Proposition 3.0.1; $P_{\text{av, TCM}}$ is the average power of the 2^n-ary constellation and $P_{\text{av, UC}}$ is the average power of the 2^k-ary constellation (see the definition for average power in (2.29)).

For the QPSK TCM scheme discussed in this section, the coding gain is over uncoded BPSK. In this example we have (refer to Figure 3.22),

$$P_{\text{av, TCM}} = a_1^2/2 = P_{\text{av, UC}}. \tag{3.136}$$

Hence

$$\begin{aligned} d_{E,\,\text{min, UC}}^2 &= 2a_1^2 \\ d_{E,\,\text{min, TCM}}^2 &= 5a_1^2 \end{aligned} \tag{3.137}$$

and the asymptotic coding gain is

$$G_a = 10\log\left(\frac{5a_1^2}{2a_1^2}\right) = 3.98\text{ dB}. \tag{3.138}$$

In the next section, we analyze the performance of a 16-QAM TCM scheme.

3.5.4 Analysis of a 16-QAM TCM scheme

Consider the rate-3/4 encoder shown in Figure 3.31. The corresponding trellis is shown in Figure 3.32. Since there are two uncoded bits, there are four parallel transitions between

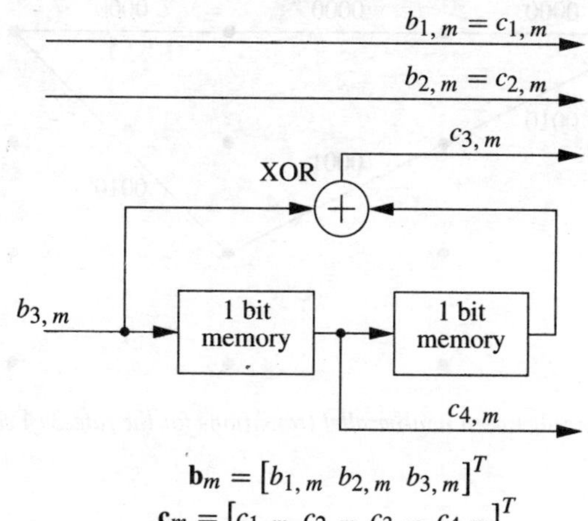

Figure 3.31 *A rate-3/4 convolutional encoder*

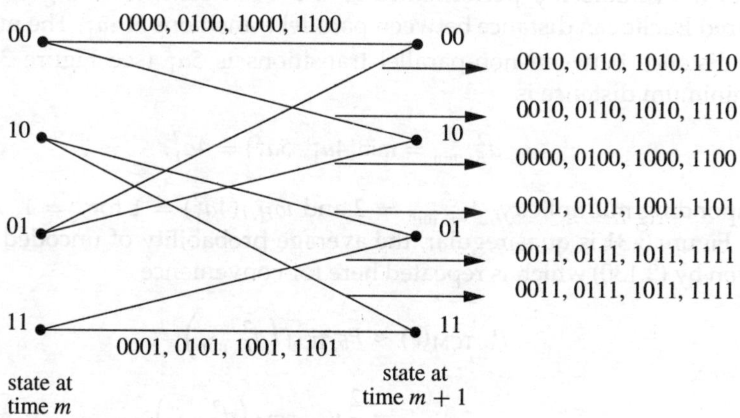

Figure 3.32 *Trellis diagram for the rate-3/4 convolutional encoder in Figure 3.31*

states. For the sake of clarity, the parallel transitions are represented by a single transition and labelled by the four encoded bits.

Let us first discuss the mapping of encoded bits on to symbols in the 16-QAM constellation. According to the set partition rule (a) in section 3.5.1, the encoded bits 0000, 0100, 1000, 1100, 0010, 0110, 1010, 1110 emerge from or merge into a common state in the trellis. Hence they must be mapped onto a subset in partition level $n - k = 4 - 3 = 1$ in Figure 3.24. Similarly, the encoded bits 0001, 0101, 1001, 1101, 0011, 0111, 1011, 1111 must be mapped onto the other subset in partition level 1.

Next, according to set partition rule (b), the encoded bits corresponding to parallel transitions must be mapped to the same subset in partition level $n - k_2 = 4 - 2 = 2$. The subset is

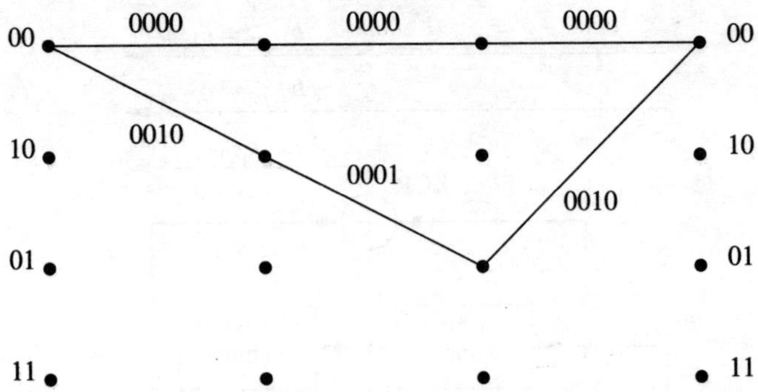

Figure 3.33 *Minimum distance between non-parallel transitions for the rate-3/4 convolutional encoder in Figure 3.31*

selected by the n_1 coded bits such that rule (a) is not violated. This is illustrated in Figure 3.24. The k_2 uncoded bits are used to select a point in the subset in partition level 2, and this can be done by Gray coding so that the nearest neighbours differ by at most one bit.

Let us now evaluate the performance of the TCM scheme in Figure 3.31. The minimum squared Euclidean distance between parallel transitions is $4a_1^2$. The minimum squared Euclidean distance between non-parallel transitions is $5a_1^2$ (see Figure 3.33). Hence, the effective minimum distance is

$$d_{E,\,\min}^2 = \min\{4a_1^2,\, 5a_1^2\} = 4a_1^2. \tag{3.139}$$

The corresponding multiplicity, $A_{d_{E,\,\min}} = 2$ and $w_{H,\,l}(4a_1^2) = 1$ for $l = 1, 2$. Since the TCM scheme in Figure 3.31 is quasiregular, the average probability of uncoded bit error at high SNR is given by (3.130) which is repeated here for convenience.

$$\begin{aligned} P_{b,\,\mathrm{TCM}}(e) &\approx P_{b,\,\mathrm{TCM}}\left(d_{E,\,\min}^2\right) \\ &= \frac{2}{3} P_{\mathrm{ee},\,\mathrm{TCM}}\left(d_{E,\,\min}^2\right) \\ &= \frac{2}{3}\cdot\frac{1}{2}\mathrm{erfc}\left(\sqrt{\frac{4a_1^2}{8\sigma_w^2}}\right) \\ &< \frac{2}{3}\exp\left(-\frac{a_1^2}{2\sigma_w^2}\right) \end{aligned} \tag{3.140}$$

where we have used the Chernoff bound.

The average transmit power for the 16-QAM constellation in Figure 3.24 is $5a_1^2/2$. Hence, following Proposition 3.0.1 in Section 3.1, we have (note that $k = 3$)

$$P_{\mathrm{av},\,b} = 5a_1^2/6. \tag{3.141}$$

Substituting for a_1^2 from the above equation into (3.140), we get

$$P_{b,\,\mathrm{TCM}}(e) < \frac{2}{3}\exp\left(-\frac{6P_{\mathrm{av},\,b}}{10\sigma_w^2}\right). \tag{3.142}$$

Comparing the above equation with (3.85), we find that at high SNR the performance of the 16-QAM TCM scheme considered here is better than uncoded BPSK by only

$$10\log\left(\frac{0.6}{0.5}\right) = 0.792 \text{ dB}. \tag{3.143}$$

Note however that the bandwidth of the TCM scheme is *less* than that of uncoded BPSK by a factor of *three* (since three uncoded bits are mapped onto a symbol).

Let us now compute the asymptotic coding gain of the 16-QAM TCM scheme with respect to uncoded 8-QAM. Since (3.135) must be satisfied, we get (refer to the 8-QAM constellation in Figure 2.3)

$$d^2_{E,\,\mathrm{min,\,UC}} = \frac{12P_{\mathrm{av},\,b}}{3+\sqrt{3}}. \tag{3.144}$$

Similarly, from Figure 3.24,

$$d^2_{E,\,\mathrm{min,\,TCM}} = 4a_1^2 = \frac{24P_{\mathrm{av},\,b}}{5}. \tag{3.145}$$

Therefore the asymptotic coding gain of the 16-QAM TCM scheme over uncoded 8-QAM is

$$G_a = 10\log\left(\frac{2(3+\sqrt{3})}{5}\right) = 2.77 \text{ dB}. \tag{3.146}$$

From this example it is quite clear that TCM schemes result in *bandwidth reduction* at the expense of BER performance (see (3.143)) with respect to uncoded BPSK. Though the 16-QAM TCM scheme using a rate-3/4 encoder discussed in this section may not be the best (there may exist other rate-3/4 encoders that may give a larger minimum squared Euclidean distance between symbol sequences), it is clear that if the minimum squared Euclidean distance of the 16-QAM constellation had been increased, the BER performance of the TCM scheme would have improved. However, according to Proposition 3.0.1, the average transmit power of the TCM scheme cannot be increased arbitrarily. However, it is indeed possible to increase the minimum squared Euclidean distance of the 16-QAM constellation by *constellation shaping*.

Constellation shaping involves modifying the probability distribution of the symbols in the TCM constellation. In particular, symbols with larger energy are made to occur less frequently. Thus, for a *given* minimum squared Euclidean distance, the average transmit power is *less* than the situation where all symbols are equally likely. Conversely, for a *given* average transmit power, the minimum squared Euclidean distance can be *increased* by constellation shaping. This is the primary motivation behind multidimensional TCM (MTCM)[72–76]. The study of MTCM requires knowledge of lattices, which can be found in [77]. An overview of multidimensional constellations is given in [78]. Constellation shaping can also be achieved by another approach called *shell mapping*[79–85]. However, before we discuss shell mapping, it is useful to compute the maximum possible reduction in transmit power that can be achieved by constellation shaping. This is described in the next section.

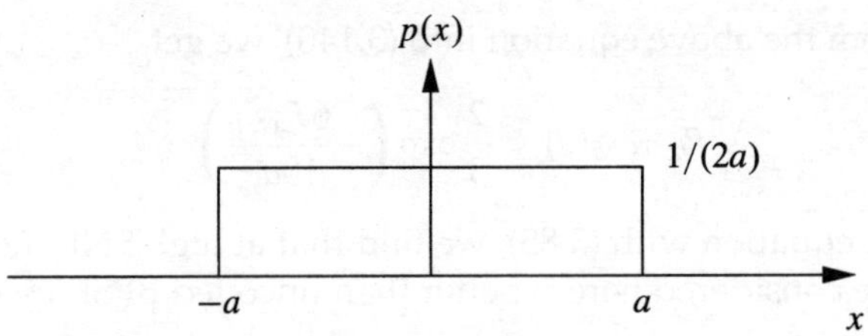

Figure 3.34 *A source with a uniform probability density function*

3.6 Maximization of the Shape Gain

For the purpose of computing the maximum attainable shape gain, we need to consider continuous sources. Note that an information source that emits symbols from an M-ary constellation is a discrete source. As a reference, we consider a source $\mathscr{X}$ that has a uniform probability density function (pdf) in the interval $[-a, a]$. This is illustrated in Figure 3.34 where x denotes the amplitude of the transmitted symbol and $p(x)$ denotes the pdf of x. Note that we have not assumed quadrature modulation, that is, all symbols transmitted by the source are real-valued. However, it can be shown that an identical shape gain can be achieved in two dimensions (and for that matter, in N dimensions) as well. The average transmit power of the source $\mathscr{X}$ is

$$\begin{aligned} P_{\text{av}, \mathscr{X}} &= \frac{1}{2a}\int_{x=-a}^{a} x^2\, dx \\ &= \frac{a^2}{3}. \end{aligned} \tag{3.147}$$

The entropy of $\mathscr{X}$ is

$$\begin{aligned} H_{\mathscr{X}} &= \frac{1}{2a}\log_2(2a)\int_{x=-a}^{a} dx \\ &= \log_2(2a). \end{aligned} \tag{3.148}$$

Note that entropy signifies the number of bits required to represent the source. For example, in the case of a discrete source that emits symbols from the 16-QAM constellation with equal probability, the entropy is

$$\sum_{k=1}^{16}\frac{1}{16}\log_2(16) = 4 \text{ bits}. \tag{3.149}$$

Let us now consider any other source $\mathscr{Y}$ with pdf $p(y)$. The statement of the problem is as follows: Find out the pdf $p(y)$ such that the transmit power of $\mathscr{Y}$ is minimized for the *same* entropy $H(\mathscr{X})$. Mathematically, the problem can be stated as

$$\min \int_y y^2 p(y)\, dy \tag{3.150}$$

subject to the constraints

$$\int_y p(y)\,dy = 1$$
$$H_{\mathscr{Y}} = H_{\mathscr{X}}. \tag{3.151}$$

This is a constrained optimization problem which can be solved using Lagrange multipliers. Thus the given problem can be reformulated as

$$\min\left[\int_y y^2 p(y)\,dy + \lambda_1\left(\int_y p(y)\,dy - 1\right) + \lambda_2\left(\int_y p(y)\log_2\left(\frac{1}{p(y)}\right)dy - \log_2(2a)\right)\right] \tag{3.152}$$

where the minimization is done with respect to $p(y)$ and λ_1 and λ_2 are constants. Differentiating the above equation with respect to $p(y)$ we get

$$\int_y y^2\,dy + \lambda_1\int_y dy + \lambda_2\int_y\left(\log_2\left(\frac{1}{p(y)}\right) - \log_2(e)\right)dy = 0$$
$$\Rightarrow \int_y\left(y^2 + \lambda_2\log_2\left(\frac{1}{p(y)}\right) + \lambda_1 - \lambda_2\log_2(e)\right)dy = 0. \tag{3.153}$$

Now, the simplest possible solution to the above integral is to make the integrand equal to zero. Thus (3.153) reduces to

$$y^2 + \lambda_2\log_2\left(\frac{1}{p(y)}\right) + \lambda_1 - \lambda_2\log_2(e) = 0$$
$$\Rightarrow p(y) = \exp\left(\frac{y^2}{\lambda_2\log_2(e)} + \frac{\lambda_1}{\lambda_2\log_2(e)} - 1\right) \tag{3.154}$$

which is similar to the Gaussian pdf with zero mean. Let us write $p(y)$ as

$$p(y) = \frac{1}{\sigma\sqrt{2\pi}}\exp\left(-\frac{y^2}{2\sigma^2}\right) \tag{3.155}$$

where the variance σ^2 is to be determined. We now need to satisfy the entropy constraint

$$\int_{y=-\infty}^{\infty} p(y)\log_2\left(\frac{1}{p(y)}\right)dy = \log_2(2a). \tag{3.156}$$

Substituting for $p(y)$ in the above equation and simplifying, we get

$$\begin{aligned}
\int_{y=-\infty}^{\infty} \frac{-\log_2(\mathrm{e})}{\sigma\sqrt{2\pi}} \exp\left(\frac{-y^2}{2\sigma^2}\right) \ln\left(\frac{1}{\sigma\sqrt{2\pi}} \exp\left(\frac{-y^2}{2\sigma^2}\right)\right) dy &= \log_2(2a) \\
\Rightarrow \log_2(\mathrm{e}) \left(\frac{1}{2} - \ln\left(\frac{1}{\sigma\sqrt{2\pi}}\right)\right) &= \log_2(2a) \\
\Rightarrow \exp\left(\frac{1}{2} - \ln\left(\frac{1}{\sigma\sqrt{2\pi}}\right)\right) &= 2a \\
\Rightarrow \sigma^2 &= \frac{2a^2}{\pi \mathrm{e}} \\
\Rightarrow \int_{y=-\infty}^{\infty} y^2 p(y)\, dy &= \frac{2a^2}{\pi \mathrm{e}}.
\end{aligned} \tag{3.157}$$

Thus the Gaussian pdf achieves a reduction in transmit power over the uniform pdf (for the same entropy) by

$$\frac{a^2}{3} \times \frac{\pi \mathrm{e}}{2a^2} = \frac{\pi \mathrm{e}}{6}. \tag{3.158}$$

Thus the limit of the shape gain in dB is given by

$$10 \log\left(\frac{\pi \mathrm{e}}{6}\right) = 1.53 \text{ dB}. \tag{3.159}$$

For an alternate derivation on the limit of the shape gain, see [73]. In the next section we discuss constellation shaping by shell mapping.

The important conclusion that we arrive at is that shaping can only be done on an *expanded* constellation (having more number of points than the original constellation). In other words, the peak-to-average power ratio increases over the original constellation due to shaping (the peak power is defined as the square of the maximum amplitude). Observe that the Gaussian distribution that achieves the maximum shape gain has an infinite peak-to-average power ratio, whereas for the uniform distribution, the peak-to-average power ratio is 3.

Example 3.6.1 Consider a one-dimensional continuous (amplitude) source $\mathscr{X}$ having a uniform pdf in the range $[-a, a]$. Consider another source $\mathscr{Y}$ whose entropy is the same as $\mathscr{X}$ and having a pdf

$$p(y) = b\mathrm{e}^{-c|y|} \quad for - \infty < y < \infty.$$

1. Find b and c in terms of a.
2. Compute the shape gain.

Solution: Firstly we observe that

$$\begin{aligned}
\int_{y=-\infty}^{\infty} p(y)dy &= 1 \\
\Longrightarrow 2b\int_{y=0}^{\infty} e^{-cy}dys &= 1 \\
\Longrightarrow 2b/c &= 1.
\end{aligned} \tag{3.160}$$

Next we equate the entropies

$$\begin{aligned}
-\int_{y=-\infty}^{\infty} p(y)\log_2(p(y))dy &= \log_2(2a) \\
\Longrightarrow -\log_2(\mathrm{e})\int_{y=-\infty}^{\infty} p(y)\mathrm{ln}(p(y))dy &= \log_2(2a) \\
\Longrightarrow 2c\log_2(\mathrm{e})\int_{y=0}^{\infty} yp(y)dy - \log_2(b) &= \log_2(2a) \\
\Longrightarrow 2bc\log_2(\mathrm{e})\left\{\left|\frac{ye^{cy}}{-c}\right|_{y=0}^{\infty} - \int_{y=0}^{\infty}\frac{\mathrm{e}^{-cy}}{-c}dy\right\} &= \log_2(2ab) \\
\Longrightarrow 2(b/c)\log_2(\mathrm{e}) &= \log_2(2ab) \\
\Longrightarrow \mathrm{e} &= 2ab
\end{aligned} \tag{3.161}$$

where we have used integration by parts. The average power of $\mathscr{Y}$ can similarly found to be:

$$\begin{aligned}
P_{av,\mathscr{Y}} &= \int_{y=-\infty}^{\infty} y^2\, p(y)dy \\
&= \frac{2}{c^2} \\
&= \frac{2a^2}{\mathrm{e}^2}.
\end{aligned} \tag{3.162}$$

Therefore the shape gain in decibels is

$$\begin{aligned}
G_{\text{shape}} &= 10\log_{10}\left(\frac{P_{av,\mathscr{X}}}{P_{av,\mathscr{Y}}}\right) \\
&= 10\log_{10}(\mathrm{e}^2/6) \\
&= 0.9\ \mathrm{dB}
\end{aligned} \tag{3.163}$$

where $P_{av,X}$ is given by (3.147).

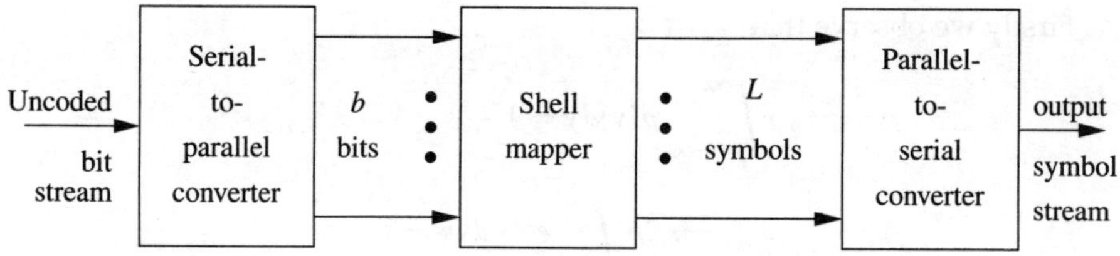

Figure 3.35 *Block diagram of shell mapping*

3.7 Constellation Shaping by Shell Mapping

The shell mapping procedure is used in the *V.34* voiceband modem[79] for date transmission of upto 33.6 kbps over the telephone network (whose typical bandwidth is 3 kHz). Voiceband modems are commonly used in fax machines.

The basic idea behind shell mapping is to make the symbols with larger energy occur less frequently than the symbols with smaller energy, thus reducing the average transmit power for the *same* minimum distance between the symbols. At this point it must be emphasized that shell mapping has got nothing to to with error control coding. In fact, shell mapping is done on an uncoded bit stream and error control coding is done *after* shell mapping. The block diagram of the shell mapping scheme is shown in Figure 3.35.

The shell mapping concept is best explained with an example. Consider a 5-ary, 2 tuple $\{R_1\ R_0\}$, where $R_1,\ R_0 \in [0,\ 1,\ 2,\ 3,\ 4]$. All the $5^2 = 25$ possible combinations of $R_1\ R_0$ are illustrated in Table 3.1. We assume that R_1 denotes the most significant digit and R_0 denotes the least significant digit. Observe that the $R_1\ R_0$ combination is arranged in the ascending order of their sum. In case the sums are identical, the $R_1\ R_0$ combinations are arranged in the ascending order of their decimal representation. For example, the decimal representation of $R_1\ R_0 = (13)_5$ is $1 \cdot 5^1 + 3 \cdot 5^0 = 8_{10}$. From Table 3.1 it is clear that the probability of occurrence of all the digits is equal to 10/50.

Let us now consider the first 2^k entries in Table 3.1, with $k = 4$. The number of occurrences of each of the digits in the truncated table is given in Table 3.2. Clearly, the probability of occurrence of the digits is not uniform.

Now consider the 20-point constellation in Figure 3.36. This is essentially the 16-QAM constellation in Figure 2.3 plus four additional points on the axes. The constellation consists of five rings, each ring having four points. We will see later that it is essential that each ring have the *same* number of points. Though the rings $\mathcal{R}_1$ and $\mathcal{R}_2$ are identical; they can be visualized as two different rings, with each ring having four of the alternate points as indicated in Figure 3.36. The minimum distance between the points is equal to unity. The mapping of the rings to the digits is also shown. It is now clear from Table 3.2 that rings with larger radius (larger power) occur with less probability than the rings with smaller radius. The exception is of course the rings $\mathcal{R}_1$ and $\mathcal{R}_2$ which have the same radius and yet occur with different probabilities. Having discussed the basic concept, let us now see how shell mapping is done.

The incoming uncoded bit stream is divided into frames of b bits each. Out of the b bits, k bits are used to select the L-tuple ring sequence denoted by $R_{L-1} \ldots R_0$. Observe that $R_i \in \mathcal{D}$, where $\mathcal{D}$ denotes the set

Table 3.1 *Illustrating the concept of shell mapping*

Index	R_1	R_0	$\sum_{i=0}^{1} R_i$
0	0	0	0
1	0	1	1
2	1	0	1
3	0	2	2
4	1	1	2
5	2	0	2
6	0	3	3
7	1	2	3
8	2	1	3
9	3	0	3
10	0	4	4
11	1	3	4
12	2	2	4
13	3	1	4
14	4	0	4
15	1	4	5
16	2	3	5
17	3	2	5
18	4	1	5
19	2	4	6
20	3	3	6
21	4	2	6
22	3	4	7
23	4	3	7
24	4	4	8

Occurrences of 0 in R_1 R_0: 10

Occurrences of 1 in R_1 R_0: 10

Occurrences of 2 in R_1 R_0: 10

Occurrences of 3 in R_1 R_0: 10

Occurrences of 4 in R_1 R_0: 10

Table 3.2 *Number of occurrences of various digits in the first 16 entries of Table 3.1*

Digit	Number of occurrences	Probability of occurrence
0	10	10/32
1	9	9/32
2	6	6/32
3	4	4/32
4	3	3/32

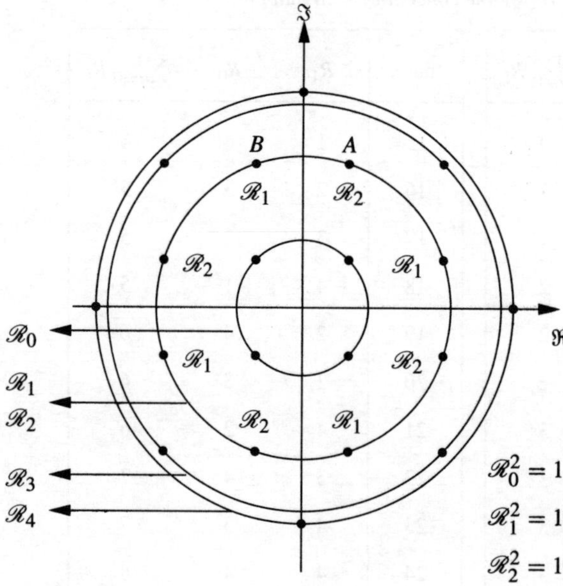

Radius	Mapping to digit
$\mathscr{R}_0$	0
$\mathscr{R}_1$	1
$\mathscr{R}_2$	2
$\mathscr{R}_3$	3
$\mathscr{R}_4$	4

$\mathscr{R}_0^2 = 1/2$ $\quad\mathscr{R}_3^2 = 18/4$

$\mathscr{R}_1^2 = 10/4$ $\quad\mathscr{R}_4^2 = (3+\sqrt{3})^2/4$

$\mathscr{R}_2^2 = 10/4$

Figure 3.36 *A 20-point constellation. The minimum distance between two points is unity*

$$\mathscr{D} = \{0, 1, \ldots, N-1\}. \tag{3.164}$$

In the example considered, $L = 2$, $N = 5$, with a one-to-one mapping between the elements of $\mathscr{D}$ and the radii (or rings) of the constellation in Figure 3.36. The remaining $b - k$ bits are used to select the points in each of the L rings. In general there are 2^P points in each ring (P bits are required to select a point in the ring). Hence we must have

$$b - k = P \times L. \tag{3.165}$$

In the example that we have considered, $P = 2$, $L = 2$, $k = 4$, hence $b = 8$. Hence if the uncoded bit sequence is 1000 11 01, then the ring sequence to be selected corresponds to $1000 \equiv 8$ in Table 3.1. Hence $R_1\ R_0 = 2\ 1$, which correspond to rings $\mathscr{R}_2$ and $\mathscr{R}_1$ respectively. The last four bits are used to select a point in the two rings (this is precisely the reason why we require each ring to have the same number of points). Thus finally the points A and B in Figure 3.36 may be transmitted. Note that we are transmitting $L = 2$ 'shaped symbols' in b bit durations. The other important inequality that needs to be satisfied is

$$2^k < N^L \tag{3.166}$$

that is, the number of ring combinations must be strictly greater than the number of k-bit combinations.

The average transmitted power due to shaping is given by

$$P_{\text{av}} = \sum_{i=0}^{N-1} \mathscr{R}_i^2 P(\mathscr{R}_i) \tag{3.167}$$

where $P(\mathscr{R}_i)$ denotes the probability of occurrence of ring $\mathscr{R}_i$ which is equal to the probability of occurrence of the digit i. In order to compare the power saving due to constellation shaping, we need to compare it with a reference constellation that does not use shaping. The criteria used to select the reference constellation are as follows:

1. We require the reference scheme to have the *same* symbol rate as the shaping scheme, which implies that the reference scheme must also transmit L symbols in b-bit durations. Hence, the reference scheme must use a $2^{b/L}$-ary constellation.
2. The additional constraint that needs to be imposed is that the minimum distance of the reference constellation must be identical to that used by the shaping scheme. This ensures that the probability of symbol error for the two schemes are identical (ignoring the factor outside the erfc $(\cdot)$ term). Thus for the same probability of error, the shaping scheme would require less transmit power than the reference scheme.

In the example considered, it is clear that the reference scheme must use a 16-QAM constellation shown in Figure 2.3. In the reference scheme, all points in the constellation occur with equal probability, since all the 2^b bit combinations occur with equal probability. For the rectangular 16-QAM constellation in Figure 2.3, the average transmit power is (assuming that the minimum distance between the points is unity)

$$P_{\text{av, ref, 16-QAM}} = 2.5. \tag{3.168}$$

For the 20-point constellation shown in Figure 3.36, the average transmit power is (with minimum distance between points equal to unity and probability distribution of the rings given in Table 3.2)

$$P_{\text{av, shape, 20-point}} = 2.4154. \tag{3.169}$$

Thus the shape gain over the reference scheme is a modest

$$G_{\text{shape}} = 10\log\left(\frac{2.5}{2.4154}\right) = 0.15\text{dB}. \tag{3.170}$$

The shape gain can however be improved by increasing L. Let $L = 8$, that is, we wish to transmit eight symbols in b bit durations. Our reference scheme continues to be 16-QAM, hence $b/L = 4$, which in turn implies $b = 32$. If we continue to assume four points in a ring, then $b - k = 2L = 16$. This implies that $k = 16$. To compute the number of rings (N) required in the 'shaped' constellation, we need to use (3.166) to obtain

$$\begin{aligned} 2^{16} &< N^8 \\ \Rightarrow N &> 2^2. \end{aligned} \tag{3.171}$$

Let us take $N = 5$. Hence we can continue to use the 20-point constellation in Figure 3.36. However, it is clear that we need a lookup table of size $2^{16} = 65536$. In fact in the V.34 modem, k is as large as 30, hence the table size is 2^{30}. Obviously the lookup table method of finding the ring sequence becomes infeasible. Hence we need an algorithmic approach to compute the ring sequence. We now proceed to describe the shell mapping algorithm[79].

Let us now summarize the important points in this section.

- The size of the constellation after shell mapping is larger than the reference constellation.
- The size of the expanded constellation is no longer a power of two (in the example considered, the size of the expanded constellation is 20).
- The entropy of the 16-QAM constellation (with all symbols equally likely) is 4 bits (see (3.149)). However, assuming that the probability of occurrence of a symbol is one-fourth the probability of occurrence of the corresponding ring, the entropy of the 20-point constellation is 4.187 bits. Thus we find that the entropies are slightly different. This is because, it is not possible to incorporate the entropy constraint in the shell mapping algorithm. It is due to this reason that we had to introduce constraints on the symbol-rate and the minimum distance to determine the reference constellation, in lieu of the entropy constraint.

3.7.1 The shell mapping algorithm

In this section, we assume that $L = 8$[79]. In particular, for the shell mapping algorithm described below, L must be a power of 2. Let $G_2(p)$ denote the number of two-ring combinations of weight p. Then we have,

$$G_2(p) = \begin{cases} p+1 & \text{for } 0 \le p \le N-1 \\ N-(p-N+1) & \text{for } N \le p \le 2(N-1) \\ 0 & \text{for } p > 2(N-1). \end{cases} \tag{3.172}$$

For example, in Table 3.1, $G_2(2) = 2 + 1 = 3$ and $G_2(6) = 5 - (6 - 5 + 1) = 3$. Let $G_4(p)$ denote the number of four-ring combinations of weight p. Since a four-ring combination can be broken up into two two-ring combinations, we have

$$G_4(p) = \begin{cases} \sum_{k=0}^{p} G_2(k)G_2(p-k) & \text{for } 0 \le p \le 4(N-1) \\ 0 & \text{for } p > 4(N-1). \end{cases} \tag{3.173}$$

Similarly, let $G_8(p)$ denote the number of eight-ring combinations of weight p. Clearly,

$$G_8(p) = \sum_{k=0}^{p} G_4(k)G_4(p-k) \qquad \text{for } 0 \le p \le 8(N-1). \tag{3.174}$$

Let $Z_8(p)$ denote the number of eight-ring combinations of weight less than p. Then we have

$$Z_8(p) = \sum_{k=0}^{p-1} G_8(k) \qquad \text{for } 1 \le p \le 8(N-1). \tag{3.175}$$

Note that

$$Z_8(0) = 0. \tag{3.176}$$

The construction of the eight-ring table is evident from equations (3.172)–(3.176). Eight ring sequences of weight p are placed before eight-ring sequences of weight $p+1$. Amongst the eight-ring sequences of weight p, the sequences whose first four rings have a weight zero and next four rings have a weight p, are placed before the sequences whose first four rings have a weight of one and the next four rings have a weight of $p-1$, and so on. Similarly, the four-ring sequences of weight p are constructed according to (3.173).

The shell mapping algorithm involves the following steps:

(1) First convert the k bits to a decimal. Call this number I_0. We now need to find out the ring sequence corresponding to index I_0 in the table. In what follows, we assume that the arrays $G_2(\cdot)$, $G_4(\cdot)$, $G_8(\cdot)$ and $Z_8(\cdot)$ have been precomputed and stored, as depicted in Table 3.3 for $N = 5$ and $L = 8$. Note that the sizes of these arrays are insignificant compared to 2^k.

(2) Find the largest number A such that $Z_8(A) \leq I_0$. This implies that the index I_0 corresponds to the eight-ring combination of weight A. Let

$$I_1 = I_0 - Z_8(A). \tag{3.177}$$

We have thus restricted the search to those entries in the table with weight A. Let us re-index these entries starting from zero, that is, the first ring sequence of weight A is indexed zero, and so on. We now have to find the ring sequence of weight A corresponding to the I_1th index in the reduced table.

(3) Next, find the largest number B such that

$$\sum_{k=0}^{B-1} G_4(k)G_4(A-k) \;\leq\; I_1. \tag{3.178}$$

Note that

$$\begin{aligned} G_4(0)G_4(A) &> I_1 \\ \Rightarrow B &= 0. \end{aligned} \tag{3.179}$$

Now, (3.178) and (3.179) together imply that the first four rings corresponding to index I_1 have a weight of B and the next four rings have a weight of $A-B$. Let

$$I_2 = \begin{cases} I_1 - \sum_{k=0}^{B-1} G_4(k)G_4(A-k) & \text{for } B > 0 \\ I_1 & \text{for } B = 0. \end{cases} \tag{3.180}$$

We have now further restricted the search to those entries in the table whose first four rings have a weight of B and the next four rings have a weight of $A-B$. We again re-index the reduced table, starting from zero, as illustrated in Table 3.4. We now have to find out the ring sequence corresponding to the $I_{2\text{th}}$ index in this reduced table.

Table 3.3 *Table of entries for $G_2(p)$, $G_4(p)$, $G_8(p)$ and $Z_8(p)$ for $N = 5$ and $L = 8$.*

p	$G_2(p)$	$G_4(p)$	$G_8(p)$	$Z_8(p)$
0	1	1	1	0
1	2	4	8	1
2	3	10	36	9
3	4	20	120	45
4	5	35	330	165
5	4	52	784	495
6	3	68	1652	1279
7	2	80	3144	2931
8	1	85	5475	6075
9		80	8800	11550
10		68	13140	20350
11		52	18320	33490
12		35	23940	51810
13		20	29400	75750
14		10	34000	105150
15		4	37080	139150
16		1	38165	176230
17			37080	214395
18			34000	251475
19			29400	285475
20			23940	314875
21			18320	338815
22			13140	357135
23			8800	370275
24			5475	379075
25			3144	384550
26			1652	387694
27			784	389346
28			330	390130
29			120	390460
30			36	390580
31			8	390616
32			1	390624

Table 3.4 *Illustration of step 4 of the shell mapping algorithm with $B = 4$, $A - B = 5$ and $N = 5$. Here $G_4(A - B) = x$, $G_4(B) = y$*

Index	Index in Table 1	R_7	R_6	R_5	R_4	R_3	R_2	R_1	R_0	Index in Table 2
0	0	0	0	0	4	0	0	1	4	0
⋮	⋮									⋮
$x-1$	0	0	0	0	4	4	1	0	0	$x-1$
x	1	0	0	1	3	0	0	1	4	0
⋮	⋮									⋮
$2x-1$	1	0	0	1	3	4	1	0	0	$x-1$
⋮										⋮
I_2	I_4			?			?			I_3
⋮										⋮
$xy-1$	$y-1$	4	0	0	0	4	1	0	0	$x-1$

(4) Note that according to our convention, the first four rings of weight B correspond to the most significant rings and last four rings of weight $A - B$ correspond to the lower significant rings. We can also now obtain two tables, the first table corresponding to the four ring combination of weight B and the other table corresponding to the four ring combination of weight $A - B$. Once again, these two tables are indexed starting from zero. The next task is to find out the indices in the two tables corresponding to I_2. These indices are given by:

$$\begin{aligned} I_3 &= I_2 \bmod G_4(A-B) \\ I_4 &= \text{the quotient of } (I_2/G_4(A-B)). \end{aligned} \tag{3.181}$$

(5) Next, find out the largest integers C and D such that

$$\begin{aligned} \sum_{k=0}^{C-1} G_2(k) G_2(B-k) &\leq I_4 \\ \sum_{k=0}^{D-1} G_2(k) G_2(A-B-k) &\leq I_3. \end{aligned} \tag{3.182}$$

Again note that

$$\begin{aligned}
G_2(0)G_2(B) &> I_4 \\
&\Rightarrow C = 0 \\
G_2(0)G_2(A-B) &> I_3 \\
&\Rightarrow D = 0.
\end{aligned} \tag{3.183}$$

Equations (3.182) and (3.183) together imply that index I_4 corresponds to that four ring combination whose first two rings have a weight C and the next two rings have a weight $B - C$. Likewise, index I_3 corresponds to that four ring combination whose first two rings have a weight of D and the next two rings have a weight of $A - B - D$. The indices I_3 and I_4 have to re-initialized as follows:

$$I_5 = \begin{cases} I_3 - \sum_{k=0}^{D-1} G_2(k)G_2(A-B-k) & \text{for } D > 0 \\ I_3 & \text{for } D = 0. \end{cases}$$

$$I_6 = \begin{cases} I_4 - \sum_{k=0}^{C-1} G_2(k)G_2(B-k) & \text{for } C > 0 \\ I_4 & \text{for } C = 0. \end{cases} \tag{3.184}$$

(6) We can now construct four tables of two ring combinations. In the first table, we compute the index corresponding to I_6, of the two ring combination of weight C. Denote this index as I_{10}. In the second table we compute the index corresponding to I_6, of the two ring combination of weight $B - C$. Denote this index as I_9. This is illustrated in Table 3.5. Similarly, from the third and fourth tables, we compute the indices corresponding to I_5 of the two ring combination of weight D and $A - B - D$ respectively. Denote these indices as I_8 and I_7 respectively. Then we have the following relations.

$$\begin{aligned}
I_7 &= I_5 \bmod G_2(A-B-D) \\
I_8 &= \text{the quotient of } (I_5/G_2(A-B-D)) \\
I_9 &= I_6 \bmod G_2(B-C) \\
I_{10} &= \text{the quotient of } (I_6/G_2(B-C))
\end{aligned} \tag{3.185}$$

We now have the scenario shown in Table 3.6.

(7) In the final step, we use the ring indices and their corresponding weights to arrive at the actual two-ring combinations. For example, with the ring index I_{10} corresponding to weight C in Table 3.6, rings R_7 and R_6 are given by

$$R_7 = \begin{cases} I_{10} & \text{if } C \le N-1 \\ C-(N-1)+I_{10} & \text{if } C > N-1 \end{cases}$$

$$R_6 = C - R_7. \tag{3.186}$$

Table 3.5 *Illustration of step 6 of the shell mapping algorithm with $B = 11$, $C = 6$ and $N = 5$. Here $G_2(B - C) = x$, $G_2(C) = y$*

Index	Index in Table 1	R_7	R_6	R_5	R_4	Index in Table 2
0	0	2	4	1	4	0
⋮	⋮					⋮
$x - 1$	0	2	4	4	1	$x - 1$
x	1	3	3	1	4	0
⋮	⋮					⋮
$2x - 1$		3	3	4	1	$x - 1$
⋮						⋮
I_6	I_9	?		?		I_9
⋮						⋮
$xy - 1$	$y - 1$	4	2	4	1	$x - 1$

Table 3.6 *Situation after computing the indices I_7, I_8, I_9 and I_{10}*

	Most significant two ring combination (R_7, R_6)	(R_5, R_4)	(R_3, R_2)	Least significant two ring combination (R_1, R_0)
Weight	C	$B - C$	D	$A - B - D$
Index in the corresponding two ring table	I_9	I_9	I_8	I_7

The above relation between the ring numbers, indices and the weights is shown in Table 3.7 for $C = 4$ and $C = 6$. The expressions for the other rings, from R_0 to R_5, can be similarly obtained by substituting the ring indices and their corresponding weights in (3.186). This completes the shell mapping algorithm.

Table 3.7 *Illustration of step 7 of the shell mapping algorithm for $N = 5$ for two different values of C*

$C = 4$

Index	R_7	R_6
0	0	4
1	1	3
2	2	2
3	3	1
4	4	0

$C = 6$

Index	R_7	R_6
0	2	4
1	3	3
2	4	2

Table 3.8 *Probability of occurrence of various digits for $L = 8$ and $k = 16$*

Digit	Number of occurrences	Probability of occurrence
0	192184	0.366562
1	139440	0.265961
2	95461	0.182077
3	60942	0.116238
4	36261	0.069162

Example 3.7.1 Compute the eight-ring sequence corresponding to the index 100.

Solution: From Table 3.3 we get:

$$
\begin{aligned}
A &= 3 & I_1 &= 55 \\
B &= 1 & I_2 &= 35 \\
I_3 &= 5 & I_4 &= 3 \\
C &= 1 & D &= 1 \\
I_6 &= 1 & I_5 &= 2 \\
I_{10} &= 1 & I_9 &= 0 \\
I_8 &= 1 & I_7 &= 0.
\end{aligned}
\tag{3.187}
$$

Therefore the eight-ring sequence is: 1 0 0 0 1 0 0 1.

Using the shell mapping algorithm, the probability of occurrence of various digits (and hence the corresponding rings in Figure 3.36) is given in Table 3.8.

Hence the average transmit power is obtained by substituting the various probabilities in (3.167), which results in

$$P_{\text{av, shape, 20-point}} = 2.2136 \tag{3.188}$$

and the shape gain becomes

$$G_{\text{shape}} = 10 \log \left(\frac{2.5}{2.2136} \right) = 0.528 \text{ dB}. \tag{3.189}$$

Thus, by increasing L (the number of dimensions) we have improved the shape gain. In fact, as L and N (the number of rings) tend to infinity, the probability distribution of the rings approaches that of a Gaussian pdf and shape gain approaches the maximum value of 1.53 dB.

3.8 Turbo Codes

Turbo codes are a class of powerful error correcting codes that achieve very low bit-error-rates at signal-to-noise ratios that are close to 0 dB. These codes were proposed by Berrou *et. al.* in [86,87]. There are some recent books on turbo-codes[9,10,88] which are recommended for further reading. The turbo principle has been applied to other areas like equalization, which has been effectively dealt with in [8,89–91]. Bandwidth efficient turbo-coding schemes (also known as turbo trellis coded modulation (TTCM)) are discussed in [92–99]. Noncoherent iterative decoding of turbo coded signals is presented in [100–102]. Noncoherent iterative decoding of turbo trellis coded modulation is presented in [103]. The performance of noncoherent iterative decoding on Rayleigh fading channels is investigated in [104]. The problem of turbo decoding in coloured noise has been addressed recently in [105–107]. We begin with a description of the turbo encoder.

Consider the encoder shown in Figure 3.37. It consists of two recursive systematic encoders (similar to the one shown in Figure 3.6) and an interleaver. Thus, at any time instant m there are three output bits, one is the input (systematic) bit denoted by $b_{1,m}$ and the other two are the encoded bits, denoted by $c_{1,m}$ and $c_{2,m}$. The interleaver is used to randomly shuffle the input bits. The interleaved input bits, denoted by $b_{2,m}$, are not transmitted (see Figure 3.38 for an illustration of the interleaving operation). Mathematically, the relationship between $b_{2,m}$ and $b_{1,n}$ can be written as

$$b_{2,m} = b_{2,\pi(n)} = b_{1,n} = b_{1,\pi^{-1}(m)} \tag{3.190}$$

where $\pi(\cdot)$ denotes the interleaving operation. The turbo encoder operates on a frame of L input bits and generates $3L$ bits at the output. Thus the code-rate is $1/3$. Thus, if the input bit-rate is R, the output bit-rate is $3R$. A reduction in the output bit-rate (or an increase in the code-rate) is possible by *puncturing*. Puncturing is a process of discarding some of the output bits in every frame. A commonly used puncturing method is to discard $c_{1,m}$ for every even m and $c_{2,m}$ for every odd m, increasing the code-rate to $1/2$.

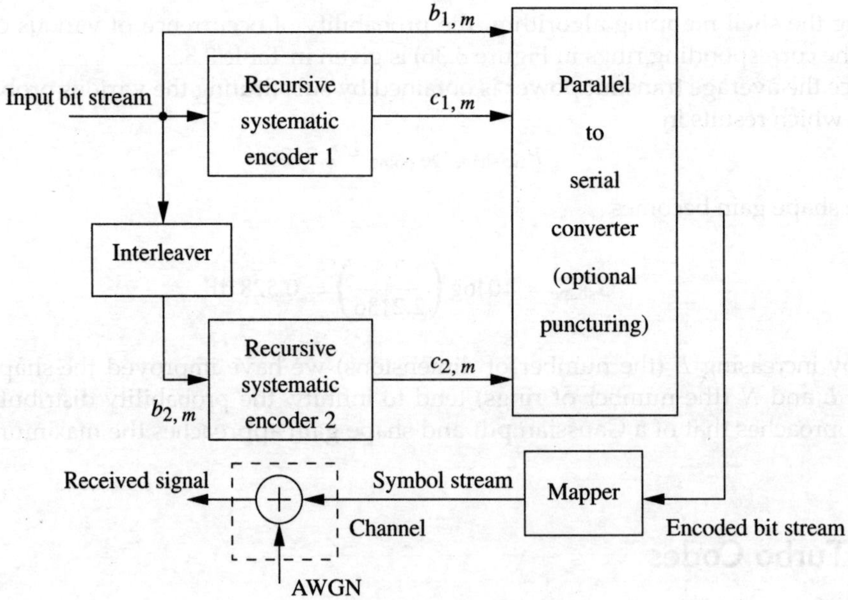

Figure 3.37 *Block diagram of a turbo encoder*

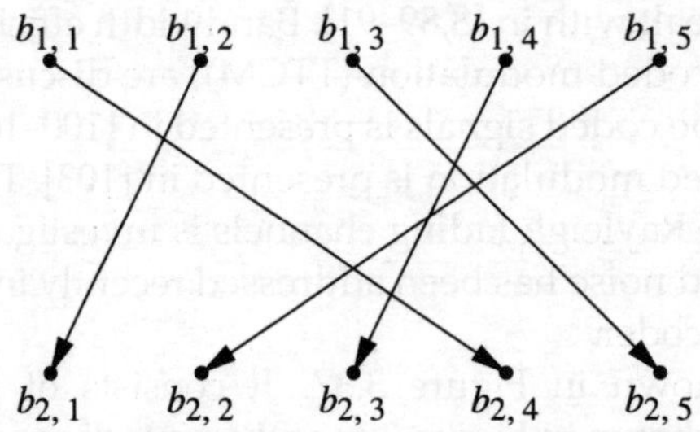

Figure 3.38 *Illustration of the interleaving operation*

The output bits are mapped onto a BPSK constellation with amplitudes ± 1 and sent to the channel which adds samples of AWGN with zero mean and variance σ_w^2. The mapping is done as follows:

$$
\begin{aligned}
b_{1,m} &\rightarrow S_{b1,m} \\
c_{1,m} &\rightarrow S_{c1,m} \\
c_{2,m} &\rightarrow S_{c2,m}.
\end{aligned}
\tag{3.191}
$$

We now turn our attention to the turbo decoder.

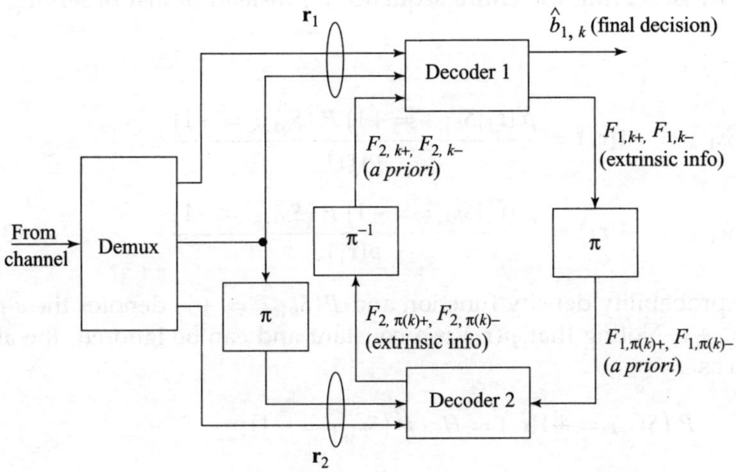

Figure 3.39 *The turbo decoder*

3.8.1 The turbo decoder

The turbo decoder is shown in Figure 3.39. Assuming a code-rate of 1/3 and a frame size of L, the output of the demultiplexer is

$$
\begin{aligned}
r_{b1,\,m} &= S_{b1,\,m} + w_{b1,\,m} \\
r_{c1,\,m} &= S_{c1,\,m} + w_{c1,\,m} \\
r_{c2,\,m} &= S_{c2,\,m} + w_{c2,\,m} \\
r_{b2,\,m} &= r_{b2,\,\pi(n)} = r_{b1,\,n} = r_{b1,\,\pi^{-1}(m)} \qquad \text{for } 0 \le m,\ n \le L-1
\end{aligned}
\tag{3.192}
$$

where $w_{b1,\,m}$, $w_{c1,\,m}$ and $w_{c2,\,m}$ are samples of zero-mean AWGN with variance σ_w^2. Note that all quantities in (3.192) are real-valued. The first decoder computes the *a posteriori* probabilities

$$
P\left(S_{b1,\,k} = +1|\mathbf{r}_1\right) \text{ and } P\left(S_{b1,\,k} = -1|\mathbf{r}_1\right) \tag{3.193}
$$

for $0 \le k \le L-1$ and $\mathbf{r}_1$ is a $2L \times 1$ matrix denoted by

$$
\mathbf{r}_1 = \left[r_{b1,\,0} \quad \dots \quad r_{b1,\,L-1} \quad r_{c1,\,0} \quad \dots \quad r_{c1,\,L-1}\right]^T. \tag{3.194}
$$

In the above equation, $r_{b1,\,k}$ and $r_{c1,\,k}$ respectively denote the received samples corresponding to the uncoded symbol and the parity symbol emanating from the first encoder at time k. Note that the *a posteriori* probabilities in (3.193) make sense because the constituent encoders are recursive (they have infinite memory). Thus $c_{1,\,i}$ for $k \le i \le L-1$ depends on $b_{1,\,i}$ for $k \le i \le L-1$ and the encoder state at time k. However, the encoder state at time k depends on all the past inputs $b_{1,\,i}$ for $0 \le i \le k-1$. Thus, intuitively we can expect to get better information about $b_{1,k}$ by observing the entire sequence $\mathbf{r}_1$, instead of just observing $r_{b1,k}$ and $r_{c1,k}$.

Now (for $0 \le k \le L-1$),

$$
\begin{aligned}
P\left(S_{b1,k} = +1 | \mathbf{r}_1\right) &= \frac{p\left(\mathbf{r}_1 | S_{b1,k} = +1\right) P\left(S_{b1,k} = +1\right)}{p(\mathbf{r}_1)} \\
P\left(S_{b1,k} = -1 | \mathbf{r}_1\right) &= \frac{p\left(\mathbf{r}_1 | S_{b1,k} = -1\right) P\left(S_{b1,k} = -1\right)}{p(\mathbf{r}_1)}
\end{aligned}
\tag{3.195}
$$

where $p(\cdot)$ denotes the probability density function and $P(S_{b1,k} = +1)$ denotes the *a priori* probability that $S_{b1,k} = +1$. Noting that $p(\mathbf{r}_1)$ is a constant and can be ignored, the above equation can be written as

$$
\begin{aligned}
P\left(S_{b1,k} = +1 | \mathbf{r}_1\right) &= H_{k+} P\left(S_{b1,k} = +1\right) \\
P\left(S_{b1,k} = -1 | \mathbf{r}_1\right) &= H_{k-} P\left(S_{b1,k} = -1\right)
\end{aligned}
\tag{3.196}
$$

where

$$
\begin{aligned}
H_{1,k+} &\stackrel{\Delta}{=} p(\mathbf{r}_1 | S_{b1,k} = +1) \\
&= \sum_{j=1}^{\mathscr{S} \times 2^{L-1}} p(\mathbf{r}_1 | \mathbf{S}_{b1,k+}^{(j)}, \mathbf{S}_{c1,k+}^{(j)}) P_{\bar{k}}^{(j)} \\
H_{1,k-} &\stackrel{\Delta}{=} p(\mathbf{r}_1 | S_{b1,k} = -1) \\
&= \sum_{j=1}^{\mathscr{S} \times 2^{L-1}} p(\mathbf{r}_1 | \mathbf{S}_{b1,k-}^{(j)}, \mathbf{S}_{c1,k-}^{(j)}) P_{\bar{k}}^{(j)}
\end{aligned}
\tag{3.197}
$$

$\mathscr{S}$ denotes the number of encoder states and the $L \times 1$ vectors

$$
\begin{aligned}
\mathbf{S}_{b1,k+}^{(j)} &= \begin{bmatrix} S_{b1,0}^{(j)} & \ldots & +1 & \ldots & S_{b1,L-1}^{(j)} \end{bmatrix}^T \\
\mathbf{S}_{b1,k-}^{(j)} &= \begin{bmatrix} S_{b1,0}^{(j)} & \ldots & -1 & \ldots & S_{b1,L-1}^{(j)} \end{bmatrix}^T
\end{aligned}
\tag{3.198}
$$

are constrained such that the kth symbol is $+1$ or -1 respectively, for all j. Similarly the $L \times 1$ vectors $\mathbf{S}_{c1,k+}^{(j)}$ and $\mathbf{S}_{c1,k-}^{(j)}$ denote the parity sequences corresponding to $\mathbf{S}_{b1,k+}^{(j)}$ and $\mathbf{S}_{b1,k-}^{(j)}$ respectively. Note that the parity sequence depends not only on the input bits, but also on the starting state. Hence the summation in (3.197) is over $\mathscr{S} \times 2^{L-1}$ possibilities. Assuming that the uncoded symbols occur independently,

$$
P_{\bar{k}}^{(j)} = \prod_{\substack{i=0 \\ i \neq k}}^{L-1} P\left(S_{b1,i}^{(j)}\right). \tag{3.199}
$$

Since the noise terms are independent, the joint conditional pdf in (3.197) can be written as the marginal pdfs, as shown by:

$$p\left(\mathbf{r}_1 | \mathbf{S}^{(j)}_{bl,k+}, \mathbf{S}^{(j)}_{cl,k+}\right) = \prod_{i=0}^{L-1} \gamma^{(j)}_{1,\text{sys},i,k+} \gamma^{(j)}_{1,\text{par},i,k+}$$

$$p\left(\mathbf{r}_1 | \mathbf{S}^{(j)}_{bl,k-}, \mathbf{S}^{(j)}_{cl,k-}\right) = \prod_{i=0}^{L-1} \gamma^{(j)}_{1,\text{sys},i,k-} \gamma^{(j)}_{1,\text{par},i,k-} \tag{3.200}$$

where $\gamma^{(j)}_{1,\,\text{sys},\,i,\,k+}$ and $\gamma^{(j)}_{1,\,\text{sys},\,i,\,k-}$ denote *intrinsic* information; $\gamma^{(j)}_{1,\,\text{par},\,i,\,k+}$ and $\gamma^{(j)}_{1,\,\text{par},\,i,\,k-}$ constitute *extrinsic* information (to be defined later) at decoder 1 (represented by the subscript '1') and are calculated as:

$$\gamma^{(j)}_{1,\,\text{sys},\,i,\,k+} = \exp\left[-\frac{\left(r_{b1,\,i} - S^{(j)}_{b1,\,i}\right)^2}{2\sigma_w^2}\right]$$

$$= \gamma^{(j)}_{1,\,\text{sys},\,i,\,k-} \qquad \text{for } 0 \le i \le L-1, i \ne k$$

$$\gamma^{(j)}_{1,\,\text{sys},\,k,\,k+} = \exp\left[-\frac{\left(r_{b1,\,k} - 1\right)^2}{2\sigma_w^2}\right] \qquad \forall j$$

$$\gamma^{(j)}_{1,\,\text{sys},\,k,\,k-} = \exp\left[-\frac{\left(r_{b1,\,k} + 1\right)^2}{2\sigma_w^2}\right] \qquad \forall j$$

$$\gamma^{(j)}_{1,\,\text{par},\,i,\,k+} = \exp\left[-\frac{\left(r_{c1,\,i} - S^{(j)}_{c1,\,i,\,k+}\right)^2}{2\sigma_w^2}\right]$$

$$\gamma^{(j)}_{1,\,\text{par},\,i,\,k-} = \exp\left[-\frac{\left(r_{c1,\,i} - S^{(j)}_{c1,\,i,\,k-}\right)^2}{2\sigma_w^2}\right]. \tag{3.201}$$

The terms $S^{(j)}_{c1,\,i,\,k+}$ and $S^{(j)}_{c1,\,i,\,k-}$ are used to denote the parity symbols at time i that is generated by the first encoder when $S^{(j)}_{b1,\,k}$ is a $+1$ or a -1 respectively.

Substituting (3.200) in (3.197), we get

$$H_{1,k+} = \sum_{j=1}^{\mathscr{S}\times 2^{L-1}} \prod_{i=0}^{L-1} \gamma^{(j)}_{1,\,\text{sys},\,i,\,k+} \gamma^{(j)}_{1,\,\text{par},\,i,\,k+} P^{(j)}_{\bar{k}}$$

$$H_{1,k-} = \sum_{j=1}^{\mathscr{S}\times 2^{L-1}} \prod_{i=0}^{L-1} \gamma^{(j)}_{1,\,\mathrm{sys},\,i,\,k-} \gamma^{(j)}_{1,\,\mathrm{par},\,i,\,k-} P^{(j)}_{\bar{k}}. \tag{3.202}$$

Due to practical considerations, the *a posteriori* probability computed using (3.196) is *not* fed as *a priori* probability to the second decoder since $\gamma^{(j)}_{1,\,\mathrm{sys},\,k,\,k+}$ and $\gamma^{(j)}_{1,\,\mathrm{sys},\,k,\,k-}$ are common to all the terms in the two summations in (3.202). In fact, the *extrinsic information* that is to be fed as *a priori* probabilities to the second decoder are actually computed as F_{k+} and F_{k-} as follows (the common term is removed):

$$\begin{aligned}
G_{1,k+} &= H_{1,k+}/\gamma^{(j)}_{1,\,\mathrm{sys},\,k,\,k+} \\
G_{1,k-} &= H_{1,k-}/\gamma^{(j)}_{1,\,\mathrm{sys},\,k,\,k-} \\
F_{1,k+} &= G_{1,k+}/(G_{1,k+}+G_{1,k-}) \\
F_{1,k-} &= G_{1,k-}/(G_{1,k+}+G_{1,k-}).
\end{aligned} \tag{3.203}$$

Note that F_{k+} and F_{k-} are the *normalized* values of G_{k+} and G_{k-} respectively, such that they satisfy the fundamental law of probability:

$$F_{1,k+} + F_{1,k-} = 1. \tag{3.204}$$

The probabilities in (3.196) is computed only in the last iteration, and again after appropriate normalization, are used as the final values of the symbol probabilities.

The equations for the second decoder are identical, excepting that the received vector is given by:

$$\mathbf{r}_2 = \begin{bmatrix} r_{b2,\,0} & \cdots & r_{b2,\,L-1} & r_{c2,\,0} & \cdots & r_{c2,\,L-1} \end{bmatrix}. \tag{3.205}$$

Clearly, the computation of G_{k+} and G_{k-} is prohibitively expensive for large values of L (L is typically about 1000). Let us now turn our attention to the recursive computation of G_{k+} and G_{k-} using the BCJR algorithm[108] (also known as the forward-backward algorithm).

3.8.2 The BCJR algorithm

The BCJR algorithm has the following components:

1. The forward recursion
2. The backward recursion
3. The computation of the extrinsic information and the final *a posteriori* probabilities.

Note that G_{k+} and G_{k-} are nothing but a sum-of-products (SOP) and can be efficiently computed by using the encoder trellis. Let $\mathscr{S}$ denote the number of states in the encoder trellis. Let $\mathscr{D}_n$ denote the set of states that diverge from state n. For example

$$\mathscr{D}_0 = \{0,\ 3\} \tag{3.206}$$

implies that states 0 and 3 can be reached from state 0. Similarly, let $\mathscr{C}_n$ denote the set of states that converge to state n. Let $\alpha_{i,n}$ denote the forward SOP at time i ($0 \le i \le L-2$) at state n $(0 \le n \le \mathscr{S} - 1)$. Then the forward SOP for decoder 1 can be recursively computed as follows:

$$\alpha'_{i+1,n} = \sum_{m \in \mathscr{C}_n} \alpha_{i,m} \gamma_{1,\text{sys},i,m,n} \gamma_{1,\text{par},i,m,n} P\left(S_{b,i,m,n}\right)$$

$$\alpha_{0,n} = 1 \qquad \text{for } 0 \le n \le \mathscr{S} - 1$$

$$\alpha_{i+1,n} = \alpha'_{i+1,n} \Big/ \left(\sum_{n=0}^{\mathscr{S}-1} \alpha'_{i+1,n} \right) \tag{3.207}$$

where

$$P(S_{b,i,m,n}) = \begin{cases} F_{2,t+} & \text{if } S_{b,i,m,n} = +1 \\ F_{2,t-} & \text{if } S_{b,i,m,n} = -1 \end{cases} \tag{3.208}$$

denotes the *a priori* probability of the systematic bit corresponding to the transition from state m to state n at decoder 1 at time i obtained from the 2nd decoder at time l after deinterleaving, (that is, $i = \pi^{-1}(l)$ for some $0 \le l \le L - 1, l \ne i$) and

$$\gamma_{1,\text{sys},i,m,n} = \exp\left[-\frac{\left(r_{b1,i} - S_{b,m,n}\right)^2}{2\sigma_w^2} \right]$$

$$\gamma_{1,\text{par},i,m,n} = \exp\left[-\frac{\left(r_{c1,i} - S_{c,m,n}\right)^2}{2\sigma_w^2} \right]. \tag{3.209}$$

The terms $S_{b,m,n} \in \pm 1$ and $S_{c,m,n} \in \pm 1$ denote the uncoded symbol and the parity symbol respectively that are associated with the transition from state m to state n. The normalization step in the last equation of (3.207) is done to prevent numerical instabilities[90].

Similarly, let $\beta_{i,n}$ denote the backward SOP at time i $(1 \le i \le L - 1)$ at state n $(0 \le n \le \mathscr{S} - 1)$. Then the recursion for the backward SOP at decoder 1 can be written as

$$\beta'_{i,n} = \sum_{m \in \mathscr{D}_n} \beta_{i+1,m} \gamma_{1,\text{sys},i,n,m} \gamma_{1,\text{par},i,n,m} P\left(S_{b,i,n,m}\right)$$

$$\beta_{L,n} = 1 \qquad \text{for } 0 \le n \le \mathscr{S} - 1,$$

$$\beta_{i,n} = \beta'_{i,n} \Big/ \left(\sum_{n=0}^{\mathscr{S}-1} \beta'_{i,n} \right). \tag{3.210}$$

Once again, the normalization step in the last equation of (3.210) is done to prevent numerical instabilities.

Let $\rho^+(n)$ denote the state that is reached from state n when the input symbol is $+1$. Similarly, let $\rho^-(n)$ denote the state that can be reached from state n when the input symbol is -1. Then

$$G_{1,\,\text{norm},\,k+} = \sum_{n=0}^{\mathscr{S}-1} \alpha_{k,\,n}\gamma_{1,\,\text{par},\,k,\,n,\,\rho^+(n)}\beta_{k+1,\,\rho^+(n)}$$

$$G_{1,\,\text{norm},\,k-} = \sum_{n=0}^{\mathscr{S}-1} \alpha_{k,\,n}\gamma_{1,\,\text{par},\,k,\,n,\,\rho^-(n)}\beta_{k+1,\,\rho^-(n)}. \tag{3.211}$$

Note that

$$\begin{aligned} G_{1,\,\text{norm},\,k+} &= A_k G_{1,\,k+} \\ G_{1,\,\text{norm},\,k-} &= A_k G_{1,\,k-} \end{aligned} \tag{3.212}$$

where A_k is a constant and $G_{1,\,k+}$ and $G_{1,\,k-}$ are defined in (3.203). It can be shown that in the absence of the normalization step in (3.207) and (3.210), $A_k = 1$ for all k. It can also be shown that

$$\begin{aligned} F_{1,\,k+} &= G_{1,\,\text{norm},\,k+}/(G_{1,\,\text{norm},\,k+} + G_{1,\,\text{norm},\,k-}) \\ F_{1,\,k-} &= G_{1,\,\text{norm},\,k-}/(G_{1,\,\text{norm},\,k+} + G_{1,\,\text{norm},\,k-}) \end{aligned} \tag{3.213}$$

is identical to $F_{1,\,k+}$ and $F_{1,\,k-}$ in (3.203). Equations (3.207), (3.209), (3.210), (3.211) and (3.213) constitute the MAP recursions for the first decoder. The MAP recursions for the second decoder are similar.

After several iterations, the final decision regarding the kth information bit obtained at the output of the first decoder is computed as:

$$\begin{aligned} P\left(S_{b1,\,k} = +1|\mathbf{r}_1\right) &= \sum_{n=0}^{\mathscr{S}-1} \alpha_{k,\,n}\gamma_{1,\,\text{par},\,k,\,n,\,\rho^+(n)}\gamma_{1,\,\text{sys},\,k,\,n,\,\rho^+(n)}F_{2,\,k+}\,\beta_{k+1,\,\rho^+(n)} \\ &= F_{1,\,k+}F_{2,\,k+}\exp\left(-\frac{(r_{b1,k}-1)^2}{2\sigma_w^2}\right) \\ P\left(S_{b1,\,k} = -1|\mathbf{r}_1\right) &= \sum_{n=0}^{\mathscr{S}-1} \alpha_{k,\,n}\gamma_{1,\,\text{par},\,k,\,n,\,\rho^-(n)}\gamma_{1,\,\text{sys},\,k,\,n,\,\rho^-(n)}F_{2,k-}\,\beta_{k+1,\,\rho^-(n)} \\ &= F_{1,\,k-}F_{2,\,k-}\exp\left(-\frac{(r_{b1,k}+1)^2}{2\sigma_w^2}\right) \end{aligned} \tag{3.214}$$

where again F_{k+} and F_{k-} denote the *a priori* probabilities obtained at the output of the second decoder (after deinterleaving) in the previous iteration. Note that:

1. One iteration involves decoder 1 followed by decoder 2.
2. Since the terms $\alpha_{k,\,n}$ and $\beta_{k,\,n}$ depend on F_{k+} and F_{k-}, they have to be recomputed for every decoder in every iteration according to the recursion given in (3.207) and (3.210) respectively.

We have so far discussed the BCJR algorithm for a rate-1/3 encoder. In the case of a rate-1/2 encoder, the following changes need to be incorporated in the BCJR algorithm (we assume that $c_{1,i}$ is not transmitted for $i = 2k$ and $c_{2,i}$ is not transmitted for $i = 2k+1$).

$$\gamma_{1,\,\mathrm{par},\,i,\,m,\,n} = \begin{cases} \exp\left[-\dfrac{\left(r_{c1,\,i} - S_{c,\,m,\,n}\right)^2}{2\sigma_w^2}\right] & \text{for } i = 2k+1 \\ 1 & \text{for } i = 2k. \end{cases}$$

$$\gamma_{2,\,\mathrm{par},\,i,\,m,\,n} = \begin{cases} \exp\left[-\dfrac{\left(r_{c2,\,i} - S_{c,\,m,\,n}\right)^2}{2\sigma_w^2}\right] & \text{for } i = 2k \\ 1 & \text{for } i = 2k+1. \end{cases} \tag{3.215}$$

Figure 3.40 shows the simulation results for a rate-1/3 and rate-1/2 turbo code. The generating matrix for the constituent encoders is given by

$$\mathbf{G}(D) = \begin{bmatrix} 1 & \dfrac{1 + D^2 + D^3 + D^4}{1 + D + D^4} \end{bmatrix}. \tag{3.216}$$

The frame size $L = 1000$ and the number of frames simulated is 10^4. Three kinds of initializing procedures for $\alpha_{0,n}$ and $\beta_{L,n}$ are considered:

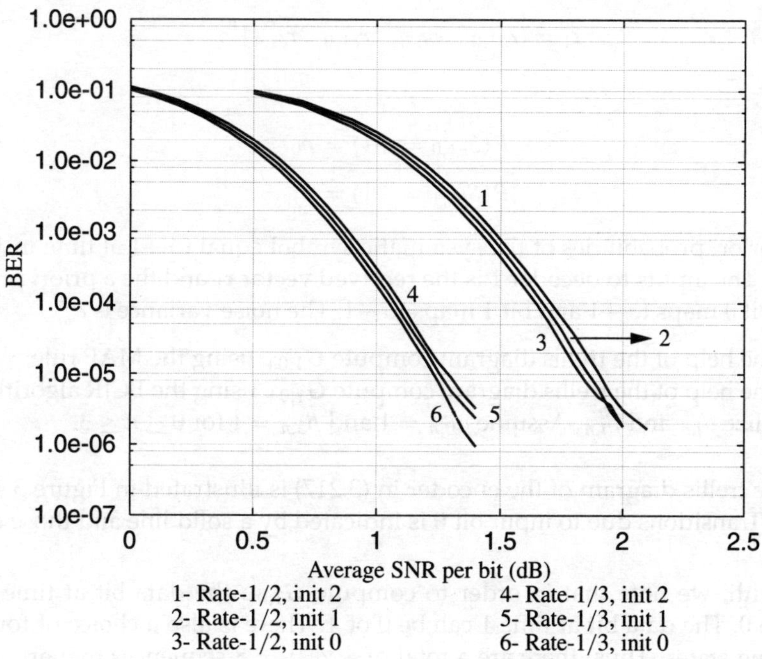

Figure 3.40 *Simulation results for turbo codes with 4 iterations*

1. The starting and ending states of both encoders are assumed to be known at the receiver (this is a hypothetical situation). Thus only one of $\alpha_{0,n}$ and $\beta_{L,n}$ is set to unity for both decoders, the rest of $\alpha_{0,n}$ and $\beta_{L,n}$ are set to zero. We refer to this as initialization type 0. Note that in the case of *tailbiting* turbo codes, the encoder start and end states are constrained to be identical[109].
2. The starting states of both encoders are assumed to be known at the receiver (this corresponds to the real-life situation). Here only one of $\alpha_{0,n}$ is set to unity for both decoders, the rest of $\alpha_{0,n}$ are set to zero. However, $\beta_{L,n}$ is set to unity for all n for both decoders. We refer to this as initialization type 1.
3. The receiver has no information about the starting and ending states (this is a pessimistic assumption). Here $\alpha_{0,n}$ and $\beta_{L,n}$ are set to unity for all n for both decoders. This is referred to as initialization type 2.

From the simulation results it is clear that there is not much difference in the performance between the three types of initialization, and type 1 lies midway between type 0 and type 2.

Example 3.8.1 Consider a turbo code employing a generator matrix of the form

$$\mathbf{G}(D) = \begin{bmatrix} 1 & \frac{1+D^2}{1+D+D^2} \end{bmatrix}. \tag{3.217}$$

Assume that the turbo code employs a frame length $L = 2$. Let

$$\mathbf{r}_1 = [r_{b1,0} \quad r_{b1,1} \quad r_{c1,0} \quad r_{c1,1}]^T. \tag{3.218}$$

Let

$$\begin{aligned} P(S_{b1,0} = +1) &= p_0 \\ P(S_{b1,1} = +1) &= p_1 \end{aligned} \tag{3.219}$$

denote the a priori probabilities of the systematic symbol equal to $+1$ at time instants 0 and 1 respectively. The inputs to decoder 1 is the received vector $\mathbf{r}_1$ and the a priori probabilities. Assume that bit 0 maps to $+1$ and bit 1 maps to -1. The noise variance is σ_w^2.

1. With the help of the trellis diagram compute $G_{1,0+}$ using the MAP rule.
2. With the help of the trellis diagram compute $G_{1,0+}$ using the BCJR algorithm. Do not normalize $\alpha_{i,n}$ and $\beta_{i,n}$. Assume $\alpha_{0,n} = 1$ and $\beta_{3,n} = 1$ for $0 \le n \le 3$.

Solution: The trellis diagram of the encoder in (3.217) is illustrated in Figure 3.41 for three time instants. Transitions due to input bit 0 is indicated by a solid line and those due to 1 by a dashed line.

To begin with, we note that in order to compute $G_{1,0+}$ the data bit at time 0 must be constrained to 0. The data bit at time 1 can be 0 or 1. There is also a choice of four different encoder starting states. Thus, there are a total of $4 \times 2^1 = 8$ sequences that are involved in the computation of $G_{1,0+}$. These sequences are shown in Table 3.9. Next we observe that p_0 and $\gamma^{(j)}_{1,\text{sys},0,0+}$ are not involved in the computation of $G_{1,0+}$. Finally we have

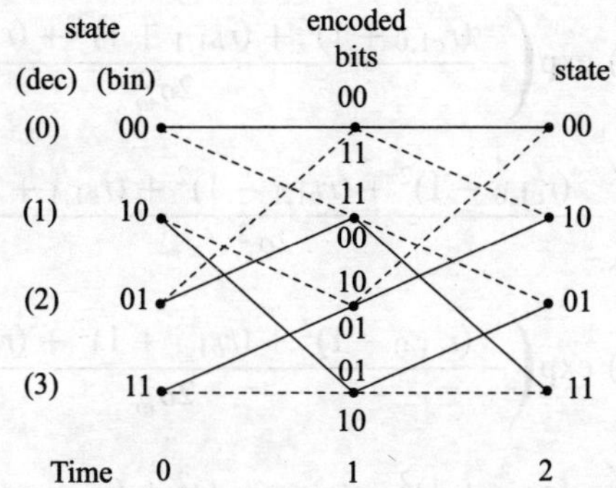

Figure 3.41 *Trellis diagram for the convolutional encoder in (3.217)*

Table 3.9 *Valid code sequences for $G_{1,0+}$.*

Starting state	Data seq.	Encoded seq.
00	00	00 00
00	01	00 11
10	00	01 01
10	01	01 10
01	00	00 01
01	01	00 10
11	00	01 00
11	01	01 11

$$P(S_{b1,1} = -1) = 1 - p_1. \tag{3.220}$$

With these observations, let us now compute $G_{1,0+}$ using the MAP rule. Using (3.197) and (3.203) we get:

$$\begin{aligned} G_{1,0+} = {} & p_1 \exp\left(-\frac{(r_{c1,0}-1)^2 + (r_{b1,1}-1)^2 + (r_{c1,1}-1)^2}{2\sigma_w^2}\right) \\ & + (1-p_1)\exp\left(-\frac{(r_{c1,0}-1)^2 + (r_{b1,1}+1)^2 + (r_{c1,1}+1)^2}{2\sigma_w^2}\right) \\ & + p_1 \exp\left(-\frac{(r_{c1,0}+1)^2 + (r_{b1,1}-1)^2 + (r_{c1,1}+1)^2}{2\sigma_w^2}\right) \end{aligned}$$

$$+ (1 - p_1) \exp\left(-\frac{(r_{c1,0} + 1)^2 + (r_{b1,1} + 1)^2 + (r_{c1,1} - 1)^2}{2\sigma_w^2}\right)$$

$$+ p_1 \exp\left(-\frac{(r_{c1,0} - 1)^2 + (r_{b1,1} - 1)^2 + (r_{c1,1} + 1)^2}{2\sigma_w^2}\right)$$

$$+ (1 - p_1) \exp\left(-\frac{(r_{c1,0} - 1)^2 + (r_{b1,1} + 1)^2 + (r_{c1,1} - 1)^2}{2\sigma_w^2}\right)$$

$$+ p_1 \exp\left(-\frac{(r_{c1,0} + 1)^2 + (r_{b1,1} - 1)^2 + (r_{c1,1} - 1)^2}{2\sigma_w^2}\right)$$

$$+ (1 - p_1) \exp\left(-\frac{(r_{c1,0} + 1)^2 + (r_{b1,1} + 1)^2 + (r_{c1,1} + 1)^2}{2\sigma_w^2}\right) \tag{3.221}$$

Let us now compute $G_{1,0+}$ using the BCJR algorithm. Note that we need not compute $\alpha_{1,n}$. Only $\beta_{1,n}$ needs to be computed. Using the initial conditions we have:

$$\begin{aligned}\beta_{1,0} &= p_1 \exp\left(-\frac{(r_{b1,1} - 1)^2 + (r_{c1,1} - 1)^2}{2\sigma_w^2}\right) \\ &\quad + (1 - p_1) \exp\left(-\frac{(r_{b1,1} + 1)^2 + (r_{c1,1} + 1)^2}{2\sigma_w^2}\right) \\ &= \beta_{1,2}\end{aligned} \tag{3.222}$$

and

$$\begin{aligned}\beta_{1,1} &= p_1 \exp\left(-\frac{(r_{b1,1} - 1)^2 + (r_{c1,1} - 1)^2}{2\sigma_w^2}\right) \\ &\quad + (1 - p_1) \exp\left(-\frac{(r_{b1,1} + 1)^2 + (r_{c1,1} - 1)^2}{2\sigma_w^2}\right) \\ &= \beta_{1,3}.\end{aligned} \tag{3.223}$$

Finally, $G_{1,0+}$ is computed using the BCJR algorithm as follows:

$$\begin{aligned}G_{1,0+} &= \beta_{1,0} \exp\left(-\frac{(r_{c1,0} - 1)^2}{2\sigma_w^2}\right) \\ &\quad + \beta_{1,3} \exp\left(-\frac{(r_{c1,0} + 1)^2}{2\sigma_w^2}\right)\end{aligned}$$

$$+ \beta_{1,1} \exp\left(-\frac{(r_{c1,0} - 1)^2}{2\sigma_w^2}\right)$$

$$+ \beta_{1,2} \exp\left(-\frac{(r_{c1,0} + 1)^2}{2\sigma_w^2}\right). \tag{3.224}$$

It can be verified that $G_{1,0+}$ in (3.221) and (3.224) are identical.

Once $G_{1,0+}$ has been computed, the a *posteriori* probability can be computed as:

$$P(S_{b1,0} = +1|\mathbf{r}_1) = G_{1,0+} p_0 \exp\left(-\frac{(r_{b1,0} - 1)^2}{2\sigma_w^2}\right). \tag{3.225}$$

3.8.3 Performance of ML decoding of turbo codes

The analysis of iterative decoding of turbo codes using the BCJR algorithm is rather involved. The reader is referred to [110,111] for a detailed treatment on this subject. The convergence analysis of iterative decoding using extrinsic information transfer (EXIT) charts is presented in [112–114]. Instead, we analyze the performance of ML decoding of turbo codes using the procedure outlined in [115]. We assume that the code-rate is 1/3.

Firstly, we observe that the constituent recursive systematic encoders are linear since they are implemented using XOR gates. The interleaver is also linear since

$$\mathbf{b}_1^{(i)} \xrightarrow{\pi} \mathbf{b}_2^{(i)} \qquad \text{for } 1 \le i \le 2^L$$

$$\mathbf{b}_1^{(j)} \xrightarrow{\pi} \mathbf{b}_2^{(j)} \qquad \text{for } 1 \le j \le 2^L$$

$$\Rightarrow \mathbf{b}_1^{(i)} \oplus \mathbf{b}_1^{(j)} \xrightarrow{\pi} \mathbf{b}_2^{(i)} \oplus \mathbf{b}_2^{(j)} \tag{3.226}$$

where $\mathbf{b}_1^{(i)}$ and $\mathbf{b}_1^{(j)}$ are $L \times 1$ vectors vectors denoting the input bits and $\mathbf{b}_2^{(i)}$ and $\mathbf{b}_2^{(j)}$ denote the corresponding interleaved input vector. turbo encoder is linear and the analysis can be carried out without any loss of generality assuming that the transmitted sequence $\mathbf{b}_1^{(i)}$ is an all zero sequence. Let us denote the transmitted symbol sequences by the $L \times 1$ vectors:

$$\mathbf{S}_{b1}^{(i)} = \left[S_{b1,0}^{(i)} \quad \cdots \quad S_{b1,L-1}^{(i)}\right]^T$$

$$\mathbf{S}_{c1}^{(i)} = \left[S_{c1,0}^{(i)} \quad \cdots \quad S_{c1,L-1}^{(i)}\right]^T$$

$$\mathbf{S}_{c2}^{(i)} = \left[S_{c2,0}^{(i)} \quad \cdots \quad S_{c2,L-1}^{(i)}\right]^T. \tag{3.227}$$

Assuming that the constituent encoders start from the all-zero state, both $\mathbf{S}_{c1}^{(i)}$ and $\mathbf{S}_{c2}^{(i)}$ correspond to the all-zero parity vectors. Let us denote the $3L \times 1$ received vector by

$$\mathbf{r} = \left[r_{b1,0} \quad \cdots \quad r_{b1,L-1} \quad r_{c1,0} \quad \cdots \quad r_{c1,L-1} \quad r_{c2,0} \quad \cdots \quad r_{c2,L-1}\right]^T \tag{3.228}$$

Applying the MAP detection rule on $\mathbf{r}$, we get

$$\max_j P\left(\mathbf{S}_{b1}^{(j)}, \mathbf{S}_{c1}^{(j)}, \mathbf{S}_{c2}^{(j)} | \mathbf{r}\right) \qquad \text{for } 1 \le j \le 2^L \tag{3.229}$$

where we have assumed that both encoders start from the all-zero state, and hence there are only 2^L possibilities of j (and not $\mathscr{S} \times 2^L$). Assuming that all the input sequences are equally likely, the MAP rule reduces to the ML rule which is given by

$$\max_j p\left(\mathbf{r} | \mathbf{S}_{b1}^{(j)}, \mathbf{S}_{c1}^{(j)}, \mathbf{S}_{c2}^{(j)}\right) \qquad \text{for } 1 \le j \le 2^L \tag{3.230}$$

Now, given $\mathbf{S}_{b1}^{(j)}$, the other vectors $\mathbf{S}_{c1}^{(j)}$ and $\mathbf{S}_{c2}^{(j)}$ are uniquely determined. Therefore, (3.229) is equivalent to

$$\max_j p\left(\mathbf{r} | \mathbf{S}_{b1}^{(j)}, \mathbf{S}_{c1}^{(j)}, \mathbf{S}_{c2}^{(j)}\right) \qquad \text{for } 1 \le j \le 2^L. \tag{3.231}$$

Since the noise terms are assumed to be independent, with zero mean and variance σ_w^2, maximizing the pdf in (3.231) is equivalent to

$$\min_j \sum_{k=0}^{L-1} \left(r_{b1,\,k} - S_{b1,\,k}^{(j)}\right)^2 + \left(r_{c1,\,k} - S_{c1,\,k}^{(j)}\right)^2 + \left(r_{c2,\,k} - S_{c2,\,k}^{(j)}\right)^2 \qquad \text{for } 1 \le j \le 2^L. \tag{3.232}$$

Assuming ML soft-decision decoding, we have (see also (3.104) with $a = 1$)

$$P\left(\mathbf{b}_1^{(j)} | \mathbf{b}_1^{(i)}\right) = \frac{1}{2}\operatorname{erfc}\left(\sqrt{\frac{4d_H}{8\sigma_w^2}}\right) \tag{3.233}$$

where

$$d_H = d_{H,\,b1} + d_{H,\,c1} + d_{H,\,c2} \tag{3.234}$$

denotes the combined Hamming distance between the ith and jth sequences. Note that $d_{H,\,b1}$ denotes the Hamming distance between the ith and jth systematic bit sequence and so on.

Let us now consider an example. Let each of the constituent encoders have the generating matrix

$$\mathbf{G}(D) = \begin{bmatrix} 1 & \frac{1+D^2}{1+D+D^2} \end{bmatrix}. \tag{3.235}$$

Now,

$$\begin{aligned} \mathbf{b}_1^{(j)}(D) &= 1 + D + D^2 \\ \Rightarrow \mathbf{C}_1^{(j)}(D) &= 1 + D^2. \end{aligned} \tag{3.236}$$

Thus (recall that the reference sequence is the all-zero sequence),

$$\begin{aligned} d_{H,\,b1} &= 3 \\ d_{H,\,c1} &= 2. \end{aligned} \tag{3.237}$$

However, when $\mathbf{B}_1^{(j)}(D)$ is randomly interleaved to $\mathbf{B}_2^{(j)}(D)$, then typically $d_{H,\,c2}$ is very large (note that L is typically 1000). Thus, due to random interleaving, at least one term in (3.234) is very large, leading to a large value of d_H and consequently a small value of the probability of sequence error.

3.9 Summary

In this chapter, we have shown how the performance of an uncoded scheme can be improved by incorporating error correcting codes. The emphasis of this chapter was on convolutional codes. The early part of the chapter was devoted to the study of the structure and properties of convolutional codes. The later part dealt with the decoding aspects. We have studied the two kinds of maximum likelihood decoders – one based on hard decision and the other based on soft decision. We have shown that soft decision results in about 3 dB improvement in the average bit error rate performance over hard decision. The Viterbi algorithm was described as an efficient alternative to maximum likelihood decoding.

Convolutional codes result in an increase in transmission bandwidth. Trellis coded modulation (TCM) was shown to be a bandwidth efficient coding scheme. The main principle behind TCM is to maximize the Euclidean distance between coded symbol sequences. This is made possible by using the concept of mapping by set partitioning. The shell mapping algorithm was discussed, which resulted in the reduction in the average transmit power, at the cost of an increased peak power.

The chapter concludes with the discussion of turbo codes and the BCJR algorithm for iterative decoding of turbo codes. The analysis of ML decoding of turbo codes was presented, and an intuitive explanation regarding the good performance of turbo codes was given.

4 Transmission of Signals through Distortionless Channels

In the last two chapters we studied how to optimally detect points that are corrupted by additive white Gaussian noise (AWGN). We now graduate to a real-life scenario where we deal with the transmission of signals that are functions of time. This implies that the sequences of points that were considered in the last two chapters have to be converted to continuous-time signals. How this is done is the subject of this chapter. We will however assume that the channel is *distortionless*, which means that the received signal is *exactly* the transmitted signal plus white Gaussian noise. This could happen only when the channel characteristics correspond to *one* of the items below.

(a) The impulse response of the channel is given by a *Dirac-delta* function, e.g. $\delta_D(t - t_0)$, where t_0 is the delay. The magnitude and phase response of this channel is shown in Figure 4.1.

(b) The magnitude response of the channel is flat and the phase response of the channel is *linear* over the bandwidth (B) of the transmitted signal. This is illustrated in Figure 4.2. Many channels encountered in real-life fall into this category, *for sufficiently small values of B*. Examples include telephone lines, terrestrial line-of-sight wireless communication and the communication link between an earth station and a geostationary satellite.

In this chapter, we describe the transmitter and receiver structures for both linear as well as nonlinear modulation schemes. A modulation scheme is said to be linear if the message signal modulates the amplitude of the carrier. In the nonlinear modulation schemes, the message signal modulates the frequency or the phase of the carrier. An important feature of linear modulation schemes is that the carrier merely translates the spectrum of the message signal. This is however not the case with nonlinear modulation schemes—the spectrum of the modulated carrier is completely different from that of the message signal. Whereas linear modulation schemes require linear amplifiers, nonlinear modulation schemes are immune to nonlinearities in the amplifiers. Linear modulation schemes are easy to analyze even when they are passed through a distorting channel. Analysis of nonlinear modulating schemes transmitted through a distorting channel is rather involved.

The next section deals with linear modulation. In this part, the emphasis is on implementing the transmitter and the receiver using discrete-time signal processing techniques. We also derive the bandpass sampling theorem which has many practical applications.

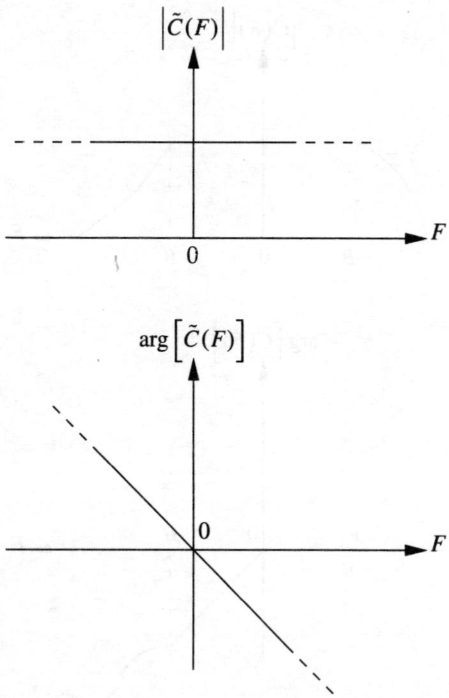

Figure 4.1 *Magnitude and phase response of a channel that is ideal over the entire frequency range. $\tilde{C}(F)$ is the Fourier transform of the channel impulse response*

4.1 Linear Modulation

4.1.1 Transmitter

Consider the signal

$$\tilde{s}_1(t) = \sum_{k=-\infty}^{\infty} S_k \, \delta_D(t - kT) = s_{1,\,I}(t) + \mathrm{j}\, s_{1,\,Q}(t), \tag{4.1}$$

where S_k denotes a complex symbol occurring at time kT and drawn from an M-ary PSK/QAM constellation, $\delta_D(t)$ is the Dirac delta function defined by

$$\delta_D(t) = 0 \qquad \text{if } t \neq 0$$

$$\int_{t=-\infty}^{\infty} \delta_D(t) = 1 \tag{4.2}$$

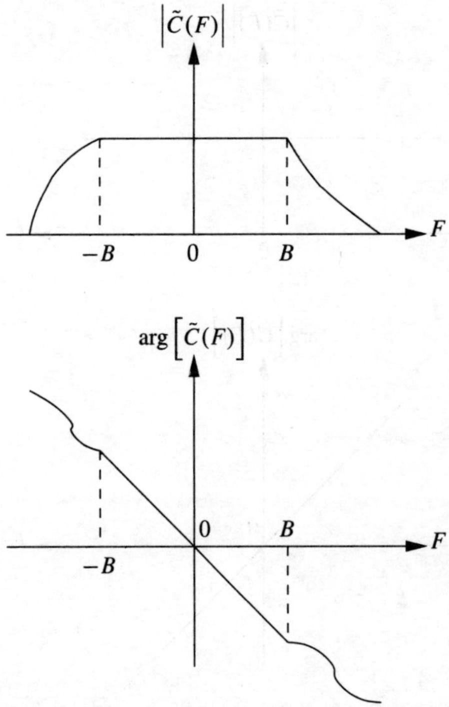

Figure 4.2 *Magnitude and phase response of a channel that is ideal in the frequency range* $\pm B$. $\tilde{C}(F)$ *is the Fourier transform of the channel impulse response*

and T denotes the symbol period. Note the $1/T$ is the symbol rate. The symbols could be uncoded or coded. Now, if $s_1(t)$ is input to a filter with the complex impulse response $\tilde{p}(t)$, the output is given by

$$\begin{aligned} \tilde{s}(t) &= \sum_{k=-\infty}^{\infty} S_k\, \tilde{p}(t-kT) \\ &= s_I(t) + \mathrm{j}\, s_Q(t) \qquad \text{(say).} \end{aligned} \tag{4.3}$$

The signal $\tilde{s}(t)$ is referred to as the complex lowpass equivalent or the *complex envelope* of the transmitted signal and $\tilde{p}(t)$ is called the *transmit filter* or the *pulse shaping filter*. Note that $|\tilde{s}(t)|$ is referred to as the *envelope* of $\tilde{s}(t)$. The transmitted (passband) signal is given by

$$\begin{aligned} s_p(t) &= \Re\{\tilde{s}(t)\exp(\mathrm{j}\,2\pi F_c t)\} \\ &= s_I(t)\cos(2\pi F_c t) - s_Q(t)\sin(2\pi F_c t) \end{aligned} \tag{4.4}$$

where F_c denotes the carrier frequency. In practice, it is not possible to obtain Dirac-delta functions, hence the discrete-time approach is adopted.

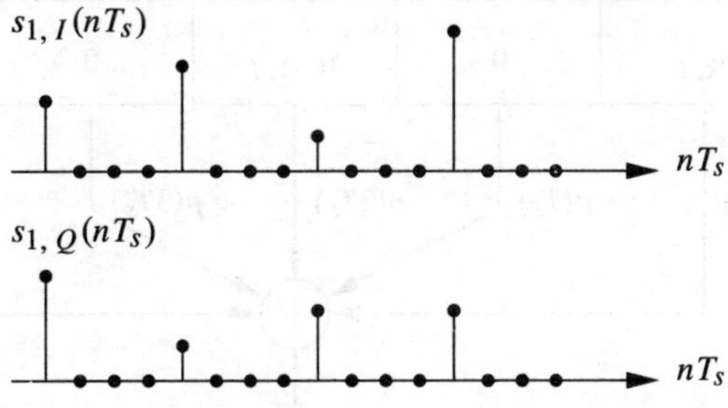

Figure 4.3 *The real and imaginary parts of $\tilde{s}_1(nT_s)$ for $M = 4$*

Let $\tilde{p}(t)$ be bandlimited to $\pm B$. Let $\tilde{p}(nT_s)$ denote the samples of $\tilde{p}(t)$ obtained by sampling $\tilde{p}(t)$ at $F_s = 1/T_s \geq 2B$. Construct the discrete-time signal

$$\begin{aligned}
\tilde{s}_1(nT_s) &= \sum_{k=-\infty}^{\infty} S_k\, \delta_K(nT_s - kT) \\
&= \sum_{k=-\infty}^{\infty} S_k\, \delta_K(nT_s - kNT_s) \\
&= s_{1,I}(nT_s) + \mathrm{j}\, s_{1,Q}(nT_s) \qquad \text{(say)}
\end{aligned} \tag{4.5}$$

where

$$\frac{T}{T_s} = N \tag{4.6}$$

is an integer. The real and imaginary parts of $\tilde{s}_1(nT_s)$ for $M = 4$ is shown in Figure 4.3.

If $\tilde{s}_1(nT_s)$ is input to $\tilde{p}(nT_s)$, then the output is given by

$$\begin{aligned}
\tilde{s}(nT_s) &= \sum_{k=-\infty}^{\infty} S_k\, \tilde{p}(nT_s - kNT_s) \\
&\stackrel{\Delta}{=} s_I(nT_s) + \mathrm{j}\, s_Q(nT_s).
\end{aligned} \tag{4.7}$$

In the above equation, it is assumed that the transmit filter has infinite length, hence the limits of the summation are from minus infinity to infinity.

In practice, the transmit filter is causal and time-limited. In this situation the transmit filter coefficients are denoted by $\tilde{p}(nT_s)$ for $0 \leq nT_s \leq (L-1)T_s$. The complex baseband signal $\tilde{s}(nT_s)$ can be written as

$$\begin{aligned}
\tilde{s}(nT_s) &= \sum_{k=k_1}^{k_2} S_k\, \tilde{p}(nT_s - kNT_s) \\
&\stackrel{\Delta}{=} s_I(nT_s) + \mathrm{j}\, s_Q(nT_s),
\end{aligned} \tag{4.8}$$

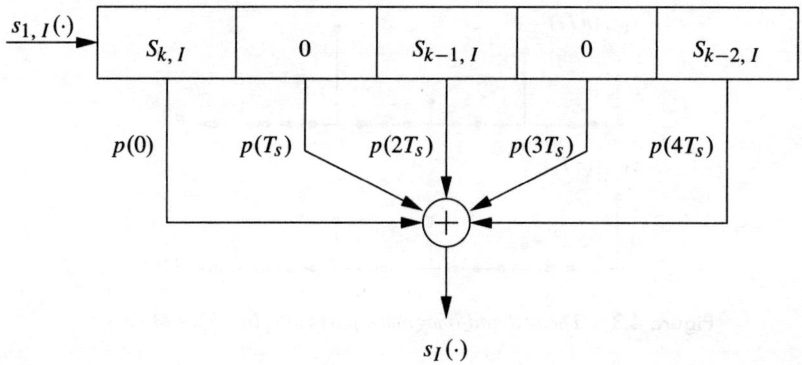

Figure 4.4 *Tapped delay line implementation of the transmit filter for $N = 2$. The transmit filter coefficients are assumed to be real-valued.*

where

$$k_1 = \left\lceil \frac{n - L + 1}{N} \right\rceil$$

$$k_2 = \left\lfloor \frac{n}{N} \right\rfloor. \tag{4.9}$$

The limits k_1 and k_2 are obtained using the fact that $\tilde{p}(\cdot)$ is time-limited, that is,

$$0 \le nT_s - kNT_s \le (L-1)T_s. \tag{4.10}$$

The transmit filter can be implemented as a tapped delay line to obtain $s_I(\cdot)$ and $s_Q(\cdot)$ as shown in Figure 4.4 for $N = 2$.

The discrete-time passband signal is then

$$\begin{aligned} s_p(nT_s) &= \Re\{\tilde{s}(nT_s)\exp(\mathrm{j}\,2\pi F_c nT_s)\} \\ &= s_I(nT_s)\cos(2\pi F_c nT_s) - s_Q(nT_s)\sin(2\pi F_c nT_s) \end{aligned} \tag{4.11}$$

which is converted to $s_p(t)$ by a digital-to-analog converter.

For the sake of implementation simplicity, $1/(F_c T_s) = P$ is chosen to be an integer so that the sinusoidal terms in the above equation are periodic with a period of P samples. Hence the sinusoidal terms can be precomputed and stored in the memory of the DSP, thus saving on real-time computation. The block diagram of the transmitter when $\tilde{p}(t)$ is real-valued is shown in Figure 4.5. The simplified block diagram is shown in Figure 4.6. In the next section we compute the power spectrum of the transmitted signal.

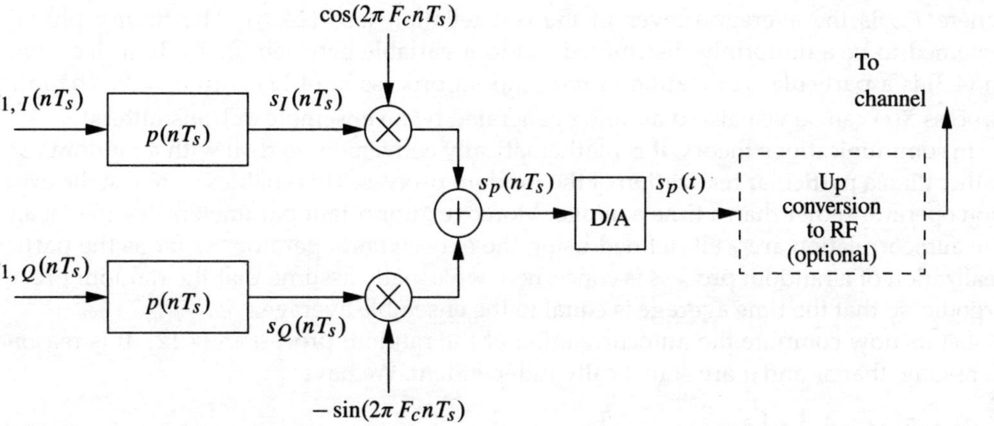

Figure 4.5 *Block diagram of the discrete-time implementation of the transmitter for linear modulation when $\tilde{p}(t)$ is real-valued*

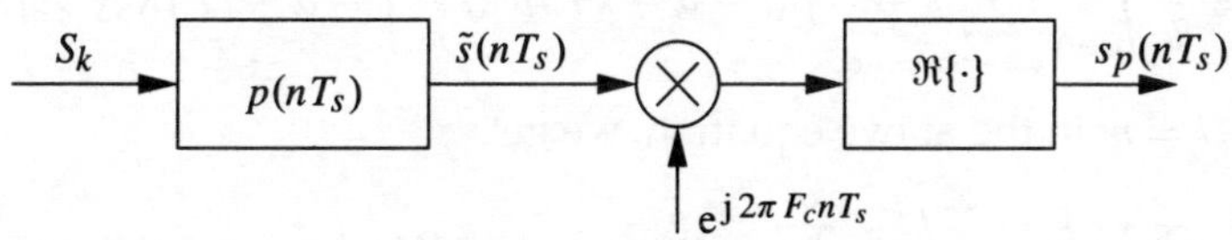

Figure 4.6 *Simplified block diagram of the discrete-time transmitter for linear modulation*

4.1.2 Power spectral density of the transmitted signal

Consider the random process given by

$$\tilde{S}(t) = \sum_{k=-\infty}^{\infty} S_k \, \tilde{p}(t - \alpha - kT)$$

$$\stackrel{\Delta}{=} S_I(t) + \mathrm{j}\, S_Q(t) \qquad \text{(say)}. \tag{4.12}$$

In (4.12), there are two random variables, the symbol S_k and the timing phase α. Such a random process can be visualized as being obtained from a large ensemble (collection) of transmitters. We assume that the symbols have a discrete-time autocorrelation given by

$$\tilde{R}_{SS,\,l} \stackrel{\Delta}{=} \frac{1}{2} E\left[S_k S_{k-l}^*\right]. \tag{4.13}$$

Note that

$$P_{\text{av}} = 2\tilde{R}_{SS,\,0} \tag{4.14}$$

where P_{av} is the average power in the constellation (see (2.29)). The timing phase α is assumed to be a uniformly distributed random variable between $[0, T)$. It is clear that $\tilde{s}(t)$ in (4.3) is a particular realization of the random process in (4.12) with $\alpha = 0$. The random process $\tilde{S}(t)$ can be visualized as being generated by an ensemble of transmitters.

In communications theory, it is mathematically convenient to deal with a random process rather than a particular realization of the random process. This enables us to use the expectation operator rather than a time average. Moreover, important parameters like the mean and the autocorrelation are well defined using the expectation operator. As far as the particular realization of a random process is concerned, we usually assume that the random process is ergodic, so that the time average is equal to the ensemble average.

Let us now compute the autocorrelation of the random process in (4.12). It is reasonable to assume that S_k and α are statistically independent. We have

$$\begin{aligned}
\tilde{R}_{\tilde{S}\tilde{S}}(\tau) &\stackrel{\Delta}{=} \frac{1}{2}E\left[\tilde{S}(t)\tilde{S}^*(t-\tau)\right] \\
&= \frac{1}{2}E\left[\left(\sum_{k=-\infty}^{\infty} S_k\tilde{p}(t-\alpha-kT)\right)\left(\sum_{l=-\infty}^{\infty} S_l^*\tilde{p}^*(t-\tau-\alpha-lT)\right)\right] \\
&= \frac{1}{T}\int_{\alpha=0}^{T}\sum_{k=-\infty}^{\infty}\sum_{l=-\infty}^{\infty}\tilde{p}(t-\alpha-kT)\tilde{p}^*(t-\tau-\alpha-lT)\tilde{R}_{SS,\,k-l}\,d\alpha. \qquad (4.15)
\end{aligned}$$

Substituting $k - l = m$ in the above equation, we get

$$\tilde{R}_{\tilde{S}\tilde{S}}(\tau) = \frac{1}{T}\sum_{m=-\infty}^{\infty}\tilde{R}_{SS,\,m}\int_{\alpha=0}^{T}\sum_{k=-\infty}^{\infty}\tilde{p}(t-\alpha-kT)\tilde{p}^*(t-\tau-\alpha-kT+mT)\,d\alpha. \qquad (4.16)$$

Substituting $t - \alpha - kT = x$ and combining the integral and the summation over k, we get

$$\begin{aligned}
\tilde{R}_{\tilde{S}\tilde{S}}(\tau) &= \frac{1}{T}\sum_{m=-\infty}^{\infty}\tilde{R}_{SS,\,m}\int_{x=-\infty}^{\infty}\tilde{p}(x)\tilde{p}^*(x-\tau+mT)\,dx \\
&= \frac{1}{T}\sum_{m=-\infty}^{\infty}\tilde{R}_{SS,\,m}\tilde{R}_{\tilde{p}\tilde{p}}(\tau-mT), \qquad (4.17)
\end{aligned}$$

where $\tilde{R}_{\tilde{p}\tilde{p}}(\cdot)$ is the autocorrelation of $\tilde{p}(t)$.

The power spectral density of $\tilde{S}(t)$ in (4.12) is simply the Fourier transform of the autocorrelation and is given by

$$\begin{aligned}
S_{\tilde{S}}(F) &= \frac{1}{T}\int_{\tau=-\infty}^{\infty}\sum_{m=-\infty}^{\infty}\tilde{R}_{SS,\,m}\tilde{R}_{\tilde{p}\tilde{p}}(\tau-mT)\exp(-\mathrm{j}\,2\pi F\tau)\,d\tau \\
&= \frac{1}{T}\int_{y=-\infty}^{\infty}\sum_{m=-\infty}^{\infty}\tilde{R}_{SS,\,m}\tilde{R}_{\tilde{p}\tilde{p}}(y)\exp(-\mathrm{j}\,2\pi F(y+mT))\,dy \\
&= \frac{1}{T}S_{\mathscr{P},\,S}(F)\left|\tilde{P}(F)\right|^2 \qquad (4.18)
\end{aligned}$$

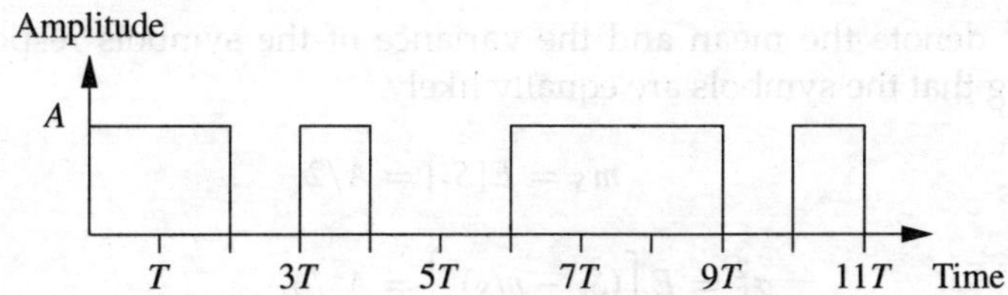

Figure 4.7 *A random binary wave*

where

$$\tilde{P}(F) = \int_{t=-\infty}^{\infty} \tilde{p}(t) \exp(-\mathrm{j}\, 2\pi Ft)\, dt \tag{4.19}$$

is the continuous-time Fourier transform of $\tilde{p}(t)$ and

$$S_{\mathcal{P},S}(F) = \sum_{l=-\infty}^{\infty} \tilde{R}_{SS,l} \exp(-\mathrm{j}\, 2\pi FlT) \tag{4.20}$$

denotes the discrete-time Fourier transform of the autocorrelation of the symbol sequence (see Appendix E). Note that the power spectral density is real valued.

Example 4.1.1 Compute the power spectral density of a random binary wave shown in Figure 4.7, with symbols $+A$ and 0 occurring with equal probability. Assume that the symbols are independent.

Solution: Here the transmit filter is

$$p(t) = \begin{cases} 1 & \text{for } 0 < t < T \\ 0 & \text{elsewhere} \end{cases}$$

$$\stackrel{\Delta}{=} \operatorname{rect}\left(\frac{t - T/2}{T}\right). \tag{4.21}$$

Hence

$$|\tilde{P}(F)| = T \left|\frac{\sin(\pi FT)}{\pi FT}\right| \stackrel{\Delta}{=} T\, |\operatorname{sinc}(FT)|. \tag{4.22}$$

The constellation has two points, namely $\{0, A\}$. Since the signal in this example is real-valued, we do not use the factor of half in the autocorrelation. Hence we have

$$R_{SS,l} = \begin{cases} A^2/2 & \text{for } l = 0 \\ A^2/4 & \text{for } l \neq 0 \end{cases}$$

$$= \begin{cases} \sigma_S^2 + m_S^2 & \text{for } l = 0 \\ m_S^2 & \text{for } l \neq 0 \end{cases}$$

$$= m_S^2 + \sigma_S^2 \delta_K(l) \tag{4.23}$$

where m_S and σ_S^2 denote the mean and the variance of the symbols respectively. In this example, assuming that the symbols are equally likely,

$$m_S = E[S_k] = A/2$$

$$\sigma_S^2 = E\left[(S_k - m_S)^2\right] = A^2/4. \tag{4.24}$$

The discrete-time Fourier transform of $R_{SS,l}$ is

$$S_{\mathscr{P},S}(F) = \sigma_S^2 + m_S^2 \sum_{k=-\infty}^{\infty} \exp(-\mathrm{j}\, 2\pi FkT). \tag{4.25}$$

However from (E.5) in Appendix E, we have

$$\sum_{k=-\infty}^{\infty} \exp(-\mathrm{j}\, 2\pi FkT) = \frac{1}{T} \sum_{k=-\infty}^{\infty} \delta_D\left(F - \frac{k}{T}\right). \tag{4.26}$$

Hence

$$S_{\mathscr{P},S}(F) = \sigma_S^2 + \frac{m_S^2}{T} \sum_{k=-\infty}^{\infty} \delta_D\left(F - \frac{k}{T}\right). \tag{4.27}$$

The overall power spectrum is given by

$$S_{\tilde{S}}(F) = \frac{1}{T}\left(\sigma_S^2 + \frac{m_S^2}{T} \sum_{k=-\infty}^{\infty} \delta_D\left(F - \frac{k}{T}\right)\right)\left|\tilde{P}(F)\right|^2. \tag{4.28}$$

Substituting for $\tilde{P}(F)$ from (4.22), we get

$$S_{\tilde{S}}(F) = \frac{1}{T}\left(\sigma_S^2 + \frac{m_S^2}{T} \sum_{k=-\infty}^{\infty} \delta_D\left(F - \frac{k}{T}\right)\right) T^2 \operatorname{sinc}^2(FT). \tag{4.29}$$

However,

$$\delta_D\left(F - \frac{k}{T}\right) \operatorname{sinc}^2(FT) = \begin{cases} 0 & \text{for } F = k/T, k \neq 0 \\ \delta_D(F) & \text{for } F = 0 \\ 0 & \text{elsewhere.} \end{cases} \tag{4.30}$$

Hence

$$S_{\tilde{S}}(F) = \frac{A^2 T}{4} \operatorname{sinc}^2(FT) + \frac{A^2}{4} \delta_D(F). \tag{4.31}$$

Equation (4.28) suggests that to avoid the spectral lines at k/T (the summation term in (4.28)), the constellation must have zero mean, in which case $R_{SS,l}$ becomes a Kronecker delta function.

To find out the power spectral density of the transmitted signal $s_p(t)$, once again consider the random process

$$\tilde{A}(t) = \tilde{S}(t) \exp\left(\mathrm{j}\ (2\pi F_c t + \theta)\right) \tag{4.32}$$

where $\tilde{S}(t)$ is the random process in (4.12) and θ is a uniformly distributed random variable in the interval $[0, 2\pi)$. Define the random process

$$\begin{aligned} S_p(t) &\stackrel{\Delta}{=} \Re\left\{\tilde{A}(t)\right\} \\ &= \frac{1}{2}\left(\tilde{A}(t) + \tilde{A}^*(t)\right). \end{aligned} \tag{4.33}$$

Note that $s_p(t)$ in (4.4) is a particular realization of the random process in (4.33) for $\alpha = 0$ and $\theta = 0$. Now, the autocorrelation of the random process in (4.33) is given by (since $S_p(t)$ is real-valued, we do not use the factor $1/2$ in the autocorrelation function)

$$\begin{aligned} R_{S_pS_p}(\tau) &= E\left[S_p(t)S_p(t-\tau)\right] \\ &= \frac{1}{4}E\left[\left(\tilde{A}(t) + \tilde{A}^*(t)\right)\left(\tilde{A}(t-\tau) + \tilde{A}^*(t-\tau)\right)\right] \\ &= \Re\left\{\tilde{R}_{\tilde{S}\tilde{S}}(\tau)\exp\left(\mathrm{j}\,2\pi F_c\tau\right)\right\} \end{aligned} \tag{4.34}$$

where we have used the fact that the random variables θ, α and S_k are statistically independent and hence

$$\begin{aligned} E\left[\tilde{A}(t)\tilde{A}(t-\tau)\right] &= E\left[\tilde{A}^*(t)\tilde{A}^*(t-\tau)\right] \\ &= 0 \\ \frac{1}{2}E\left[\tilde{A}(t)\tilde{A}(^*t-\tau)\right] &= \tilde{R}_{\tilde{S}\tilde{S}}(\tau)\exp\left(\mathrm{j}\,2\pi F_c\tau\right). \end{aligned} \tag{4.35}$$

Thus the power spectral density of $S_p(t)$ in (4.33) is given by

$$S_{S_p}(F) = \frac{1}{2}\left[S_{\tilde{S}}(F - F_c) + S_{\tilde{S}}(-F - F_c)\right]. \tag{4.36}$$

In the next section we give the proof of Proposition 3.0.1 of Chapter 3.

4.1.3 Proof of Proposition 3.0.1

Now that we have defined continuous-time signals, we are in a better position to understand the significance of Proposition 3.0.1 of Chapter 3. We assume that the autocorrelation in (4.13) is a Kronecker delta function, that is

$$\tilde{R}_{SS,\,l} = \frac{P_{\text{av}}}{2}\delta_K(l). \tag{4.37}$$

Fortunately, the above condition is valid for both coded and uncoded systems employing *zero-mean* constellations (see Section 3.2). Hence, the baseband power spectral density in (4.18) becomes

$$S_{\tilde{S}}(F) = \frac{P_{\text{av}}}{2T}\left|\tilde{P}(F)\right|^2. \tag{4.38}$$

As an example, let us compare uncoded BPSK with coded BPSK employing a rate-k/n code. If the uncoded bit-rate is $R = 1/T$, then the coded bit-rate is $Rn/k = 1/T_c$. We assume that the uncoded system employs a transmit filter $\tilde{p}_1(t)$, whereas the coded system employs a transmit filter $\tilde{p}_2(t)$. We constrain both transmit filters to have the same energy, that is,

$$\begin{aligned}\int_{t=-\infty}^{\infty}|\tilde{p}_1(t)|^2\,dt &= \int_{t=-\infty}^{\infty}|\tilde{p}_2(t)|^2\,dt\\ &= \int_{F=-\infty}^{\infty}\left|\tilde{P}_1(F)\right|^2\,dF\\ &= \int_{F=-\infty}^{\infty}\left|\tilde{P}_2(F)\right|^2\,dF\end{aligned} \tag{4.39}$$

where we have used the Parseval's energy theorem (refer to Appendix G). Let $P_{\text{av},\,b}$ denote the average power of the uncoded BPSK constellation and $P_{\text{av},\,\text{C},\,b}$ denote the average power of the coded BPSK constellation.

Now, in the case of uncoded BPSK, the average transmit power is

$$\begin{aligned}P_1 &= \int_{F=-\infty}^{\infty} S_{S_p}(F)\,dF\\ &= \frac{P_{\text{av},\,b}A_0}{4T}\end{aligned} \tag{4.40}$$

where

$$A_0 = \int_{F=-\infty}^{\infty}\left[\left|\tilde{P}_1(F-F_c)\right|^2 + \left|\tilde{P}_1(-F-F_c)\right|^2\right]dF. \tag{4.41}$$

The energy transmitted in the duration of k uncoded bits is

$$kT\,P_1 = \frac{P_{\text{av},\,b}A_0 k}{4}. \tag{4.42}$$

In the case of coded BPSK, the average transmit power is

$$P_2 = \frac{P_{\text{av, C}, b} A_0}{4T_c} \tag{4.43}$$

and the energy transmitted in the duration nT_c is

$$nT_c P_2 = \frac{P_{\text{av, C}, b} A_0 n}{4}. \tag{4.44}$$

Since $kT P_1 = nT_c P_2$,

$$\Rightarrow n P_{\text{av, C}, b} = k P_{\text{av}, b}. \tag{4.45}$$

Thus proved. In the next section we derive the optimum receiver for linearly modulated signals.

4.1.4 Receiver

The received signal is given by

$$r(t) = S_p(t) + w(t) \tag{4.46}$$

where $S_p(t)$ is the random process defined in (4.33) and $w(t)$ is an AWGN process with zero mean and power spectral density $N_0/2$. This implies that

$$E\left[w(t)w(t-\tau)\right] = \frac{N_0}{2}\delta_D(\tau). \tag{4.47}$$

Now consider the receiver shown in Figure 4.8. The signals $u_I(t)$ and $u_Q(t)$ are given by

$$\begin{aligned} u_I(t) &= 2r(t)\cos(2\pi F_c t + \phi) \\ &= \left[S_I(t)\cos(\theta - \phi) - S_Q(t)\sin(\theta - \phi)\right] + v_I(t) + 2F_c \text{ terms,} \\ u_Q(t) &= -2r(t)\sin(2\pi F_c t + \phi) \\ &= \left[S_I(t)\sin(\theta - \phi) + S_Q(t)\cos(\theta - \phi)\right] + v_Q(t) + 2F_c \text{ terms,} \end{aligned} \tag{4.48}$$

where ϕ is a random variable in $[0, 2\pi)$, $S_I(t)$ and $S_Q(t)$ are defined in (4.12) and

$$\begin{aligned} v_I(t) &= 2w(t)\cos(2\pi F_c t + \phi) \\ v_Q(t) &= -2w(t)\sin(2\pi F_c t + \phi). \end{aligned} \tag{4.49}$$

Define the random processes

$$\tilde{v}(t) = v_I(t) + \mathrm{j}\, v_Q(t). \tag{4.50}$$

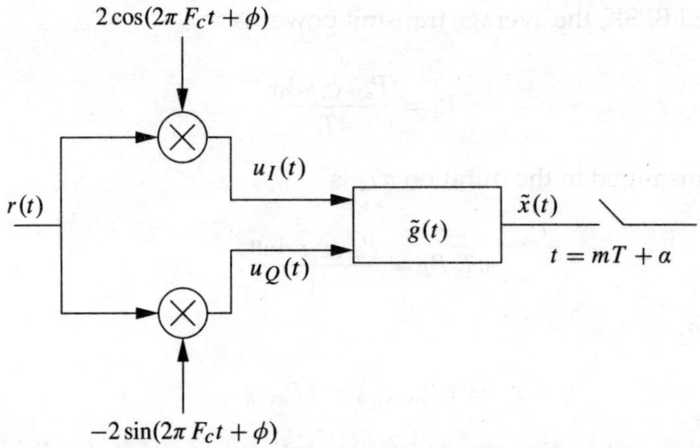

Figure 4.8 *Receiver for linear modulation schemes*

Assuming ϕ and $w(t)$ are statistically independent, it is clear that $v_I(t)$ and $v_Q(t)$ have a zero mean and an autocorrelation given by

$$E\left[v_I(t)v_I(t-\tau)\right] = E\left[v_Q(t)v_Q(t-\tau)\right] = N_0\delta_D(\tau). \tag{4.51}$$

Moreover, $v_I(t)$ and $v_Q(t)$ are uncorrelated, that is,

$$E\left[v_I(t)v_Q(t-\tau)\right] = 0 \qquad \text{for all } \tau. \tag{4.52}$$

Hence

$$R_{\tilde{v}\tilde{v}}(\tau) = \frac{1}{2}E\left[\tilde{v}(t)\tilde{v}^*(t-\tau)\right] = N_0\delta_D(\tau). \tag{4.53}$$

With these definitions, we are now ready to state the problem.

Find out a filter $\tilde{g}(t)$ such that:

(a) The signal-to-noise ratio at the sampler output is maximized.
(b) The intersymbol interference (ISI) at the sampler output is zero.

Firstly we note that the $2F_c$ terms in (4.48) must be eliminated, hence $\tilde{g}(t)$ must necessarily have a lowpass frequency response. Secondly, since the $2F_c$ terms are eliminated anyway, we might as well ignore them at the input of $\tilde{g}(t)$ itself. With these two points in mind, let us define $\tilde{u}(t)$ as

$$\begin{aligned}\tilde{u}(t) &\stackrel{\Delta}{=} u_I(t) + \mathrm{j}\,u_Q(t)\\ &= \tilde{S}(t)\exp\left(\mathrm{j}\,(\theta-\phi)\right) + \tilde{v}(t)\\ &= \left(\sum_{k=-\infty}^{\infty} S_k\tilde{p}(t-\alpha-kT)\right)\exp\left(\mathrm{j}\,(\theta-\phi)\right) + \tilde{v}(t).\end{aligned} \tag{4.54}$$

Observe that when $\theta \neq \phi$, the in-phase and quadrature parts of the signal interfere with each other. This phenomenon is called *cross-talk*. The output of the filter is given by

$$\begin{aligned}\tilde{x}(t) &= \tilde{u}(t) \star \tilde{g}(t) \\ &= \exp\left(\mathrm{j}\,(\theta - \phi)\right) \sum_{k=-\infty}^{\infty} S_k \tilde{h}(t - \alpha - kT) + \tilde{z}(t)\end{aligned} \tag{4.55}$$

where

$$\begin{aligned}\tilde{h}(t) &= \tilde{g}(t) \star \tilde{p}(t) \\ \tilde{z}(t) &= \tilde{g}(t) \star \tilde{v}(t).\end{aligned} \tag{4.56}$$

To satisfy the zero ISI constraint, we must have

$$\tilde{h}(kT) = \begin{cases} \tilde{h}(0) & \text{for } k = 0 \\ 0 & \text{for } k \neq 0. \end{cases} \tag{4.57}$$

Thus, the sampler output becomes (at time instants $mT + \alpha$)

$$\tilde{x}(mT + \alpha) = S_m \tilde{h}(0) \exp\left(\mathrm{j}\,(\theta - \phi)\right) + \tilde{z}(mT + \alpha). \tag{4.58}$$

Now, maximizing the signal-to-noise ratio implies

$$\begin{aligned}&\max \frac{E\left[|S_k|^2\right] \left|\tilde{h}(0) \exp\left(\mathrm{j}\,(\theta - \phi)\right)\right|^2}{2\tilde{R}_{\tilde{z}\tilde{z}}(0)} \\ \Rightarrow\ &\max \frac{E\left[|S_k|^2\right] \left|\tilde{h}(0) \exp\left(\mathrm{j}\,(\theta - \phi)\right)\right|^2}{E\left[|\tilde{z}(mT + \alpha)|^2\right]} \\ \Rightarrow\ &\max \frac{P_{\mathrm{av}} \left|\int_{F=-\infty}^{\infty} \tilde{P}(F) \tilde{G}(F)\, dF\right|^2}{2N_0 \int_{F=-\infty}^{\infty} \left|\tilde{G}(F)\right|^2 dF}.\end{aligned} \tag{4.59}$$

We now use the Schwarz's inequality which states that

$$\left|\int_{F=-\infty}^{\infty} \tilde{P}(F) \tilde{G}(F)\, dF\right|^2 \leq \int_{F=-\infty}^{\infty} \left|\tilde{P}(F)\right|^2 dF \int_{F=-\infty}^{\infty} \left|\tilde{G}(F)\right|^2 dF. \tag{4.60}$$

The inequality becomes an equality when

$$\begin{aligned}\tilde{G}(F) &= \tilde{P}^*(F) \\ \Rightarrow \tilde{H}(F) &= \left|\tilde{P}(F)\right|^2\end{aligned} \tag{4.61}$$

and the SNR attains the maximum value given by

$$\frac{P_{\text{av}} \int_{F=-\infty}^{\infty} \left|\tilde{P}(F)\right|^2 dF}{2N_0}. \tag{4.62}$$

From (4.61), the impulse response of $\tilde{g}(t)$ is given by

$$\tilde{g}(t) = \tilde{p}^*(-t) \tag{4.63}$$

and is called the *matched filter*[116–118]. Note that the energy in the transmit filter (and also the matched filter) is given by

$$\tilde{h}(0) = \int_{t=-\infty}^{\infty} |\tilde{p}(t)|^2 \, dt = \int_{F=-\infty}^{\infty} \left|\tilde{P}(F)\right|^2 dF \tag{4.64}$$

where we have used the Parseval's energy theorem (see Appendix G). Note also that

$$\tilde{h}(t) = \tilde{R}_{\tilde{p}\tilde{p}}(t) \tag{4.65}$$

is the autocorrelation of $\tilde{p}(t)$. For convenience, $\tilde{h}(0)$ is set to unity so that the sampler output becomes

$$\tilde{x}(mT + \alpha) = S_m \exp\left(\mathrm{j}\,(\theta - \phi)\right) + \tilde{z}(mT + \alpha) \tag{4.66}$$

and the maximum SNR is equal to

$$\frac{P_{\text{av}}}{2N_0}. \tag{4.67}$$

The noise samples $\tilde{z}(mT + \alpha)$ have zero mean with autocorrelation (see Appendix H)

$$R_{\tilde{z}\tilde{z}}(kT) = \frac{1}{2} E\left[\tilde{z}(mT + \alpha)\tilde{z}^*(mT + \alpha - kT)\right] = N_0 \tilde{R}_{\tilde{p}\tilde{p}}(kT) = N_0 \delta_K(kT) \tag{4.68}$$

Thus the noise samples at the sampler output are uncorrelated and being Gaussian, they are also statistically independent. Equation (4.66) provides the motivation for all the detection techniques (both coherent and non-coherent) discussed in Chapter 2 with $\sigma_w^2 = N_0$. At this point it must be emphasized that multidimensional orthogonal signalling is actually a non-linear modulation scheme and hence its corresponding transmitter and receiver structure will be discussed in a later section.

Equation (4.66) also provides the motivation to perform carrier synchronization (setting $\phi = \theta$) and timing synchronization (computing the value of the timing phase α). In the next section, we study some of the pulse shapes that satisfy the zero ISI condition.

4.1.5 Pulse shapes with zero ISI

From (4.65) we note that the pulse shape at the output of the matched filter is an autocorrelation function. Hence the Fourier transform of $\tilde{h}(t)$ is real-valued. Let $\tilde{H}(F)$ denote the Fourier transform of $\tilde{h}(t)$. Now, if $\tilde{h}(t)$ is sampled at a rate $1/T$ Hz, the spectrum of the sampled signal is given by (see Appendix E)

$$\tilde{H}_{\mathscr{P}}(F) = \frac{1}{T} \sum_{k=-\infty}^{\infty} \tilde{H}(F - k/T). \tag{4.69}$$

Since from (4.57) we have

$$\tilde{h}(kT) = \delta_K(kT) \tag{4.70}$$

(recall that $\tilde{h}(0)$ is set to unity), the discrete-time Fourier transform (see Appendix E) of $\tilde{h}(kT)$ is given by[119]

$$\tilde{H}_{\mathscr{P}}(F) = 1. \tag{4.71}$$

Equating (4.70) and (4.71) we get

$$\sum_{k=-\infty}^{\infty} \tilde{H}(F - k/T) = T. \tag{4.72}$$

One of the solutions to the above equation is

$$\tilde{H}(F) = \left|\tilde{P}(F)\right|^2 = \begin{cases} T & \text{for } -1/(2T) \le F \le 1/(2T) \\ 0 & \text{elsewhere.} \end{cases} \tag{4.73}$$

The corresponding pulse shape at the matched filter output is

$$h(t) = \frac{\sin(\pi t/T)}{\pi t/T} = \text{sinc}(t/T) \tag{4.74}$$

and the impulse response of the transmit filter is

$$p(t) = \frac{1}{\sqrt{T}} \frac{\sin(\pi t/T)}{\pi t/T}. \tag{4.75}$$

The other solution to (4.72) is the *raised cosine* spectrum given by

$$\begin{aligned} \tilde{H}(F) &= \begin{cases} \frac{1}{2B} & \text{for } -F_1 \le F \le F_1 \\ \frac{1}{4B}\left[1 + \cos\left(\frac{\pi(|F| - F_1)}{2B - 2F_1}\right)\right] & \text{for } F_1 \le |F| \le 2B - F_1 \\ 0 & \text{elsewhere} \end{cases} \\ &= \left|\tilde{P}(F)\right|^2 \end{aligned} \tag{4.76}$$

where

$$2B \triangleq \frac{1}{T}$$

$$\rho \triangleq 1 - \frac{F_1}{B}. \tag{4.77}$$

The term ρ is called the *roll-off factor*, which varies from zero to unity. The percentage *excess bandwidth* is specified as 100ρ. When $\rho = 0$ (0% excess bandwidth), $F_1 = B$ and (4.76) and (4.73) are identical. The pulse shape at the matched filter output is given by

$$h(t) = \text{sinc}(2Bt)\frac{\cos(2\pi\rho Bt)}{1 - 16\rho^2B^2t^2}. \tag{4.78}$$

The corresponding impulse response of the transmit filter is (see Appendix F)

$$p(t) = \frac{1}{\pi\sqrt{2B}(1 - 64B^2\rho^2t^2)}\left[8B\rho\cos(\theta_1 + \theta_2) + \frac{\sin(\theta_1 - \theta_2)}{t}\right] \tag{4.79}$$

where

$$\theta_1 = 2\pi Bt$$

$$\theta_2 = 2\pi B\rho t. \tag{4.80}$$

The Fourier transform of the impulse response in (4.79) is referred to as the *root raised cosine* spectrum[120,121]. Recently, a number of other pulses that satisfy the zero-ISI condition have been proposed[122–125].

4.1.6 Application of matched filtering in CDMA

In this section we illustrate with examples, the application of matched filtering in code division multiple access (CDMA) systems[126–128].

Example 4.1.2 Consider the baseband equivalent model of a 2-user CDMA transmitter as shown in Figure 4.9 (the process of modulation and demodulation is not shown). Here $S_{1,k}$ and $S_{2,k}$ denote the symbols drawn from a QPSK constellation originating from user 1 and user 2 respectively. Assume that the squared minimum Euclidean distance between the symbols in the constellation is d^2. Note that the transmit filters $p_1(t)$ and $p_2(t)$ are orthogonal, that is

$$\int_{t=0}^{T} p_1(t)p_2(t)\,dt = 0. \tag{4.81}$$

Compute the symbol error probability of each user using the union bound, assuming coherent detection and ideal timing synchronization.

Solution 1: The baseband equivalent of the received signal can be written as

$$\tilde{u}(t) = \sum_{k=-\infty}^{\infty} S_{1,k}p_1(t - kT) + \sum_{k=-\infty}^{\infty} S_{2,k}p_2(t - kT) + \tilde{v}(t) \tag{4.82}$$

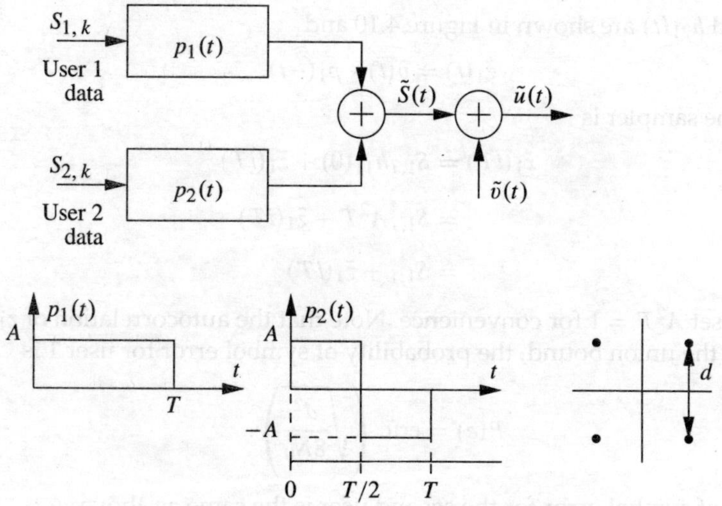

Figure 4.9 *The baseband equivalent model of a CDMA transmitter*

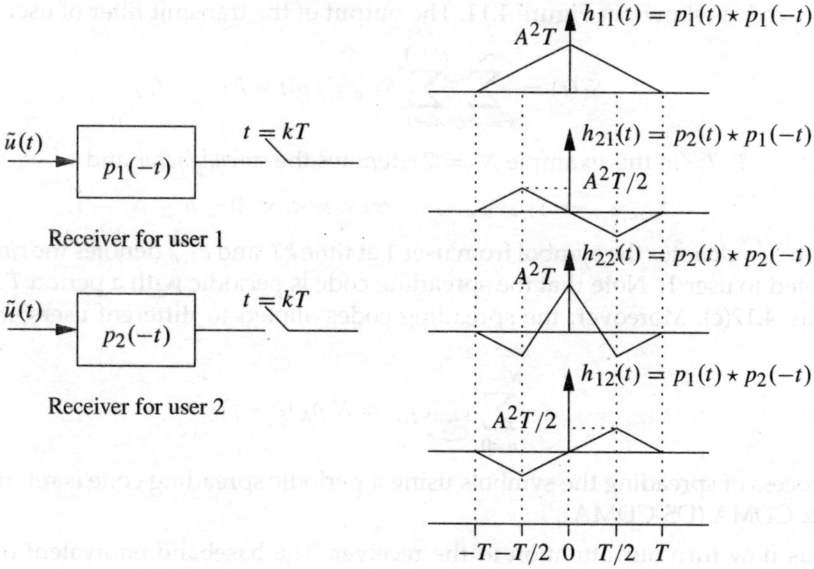

Figure 4.10 *Receiver for users 1 and 2*

where the autocorrelation of $\tilde{v}(t)$ is given by (4.53). The output of the matched filter for user 1 is

$$\tilde{x}_1(t) = \sum_{k=-\infty}^{\infty} S_{1,k} h_{11}(t-kT) + \sum_{k=-\infty}^{\infty} S_{2,k} h_{21}(t-kT) + \tilde{z}_1(t) \tag{4.83}$$

where $h_{11}(t)$ and $h_{21}(t)$ are shown in Figure 4.10 and

$$\tilde{z}_1(t) = \tilde{v}(t) \star p_1(-t). \tag{4.84}$$

The output of the sampler is

$$\begin{aligned}\tilde{x}_1(iT) &= S_{1,i}h_{11}(0) + \tilde{z}_1(iT) \\ &= S_{1,i}A^2T + \tilde{z}_1(iT) \\ &= S_{1,i} + \tilde{z}_1(iT)\end{aligned} \tag{4.85}$$

where we have set $A^2T = 1$ for convenience. Note that the autocorrelation of $\tilde{z}_1(iT)$ is given by (4.68). Using the union bound, the probability of symbol error for user 1 is

$$P(e) = \text{erfc}\left(\sqrt{\frac{d^2}{8N_0}}\right). \tag{4.86}$$

The probability of symbol error for the second user is the same as above.

Solution 2: Consider the alternate model for the CDMA transmitter as shown in Figure 4.11. Note that here the transmit filter is the *same* for both users. However, each user is alloted a *spreading code* as shown in Figure 4.11. The output of the transmit filter of user 1 is given by

$$\tilde{S}_1(t) = \sum_{k=-\infty}^{\infty} \sum_{n=0}^{N_c-1} S_{1,c,k,n}\,p(t - kT - nT_c) \tag{4.87}$$

where $N_c = T/T_c$ (in this example $N_c = 2$) denotes the *spread factor* and

$$S_{1,c,k,n} = S_{1,k}c_{1,n} \qquad -\infty < k < \infty, 0 \le n \le N_c - 1. \tag{4.88}$$

The term $S_{1,k}$ denotes the symbol from user 1 at time kT and $c_{1,n}$ denotes the *chip* at time $kT + nT_c$ alloted to user 1. Note that the spreading code is periodic with a period T, as illustrated in Figure 4.12(c). Moreover, the spreading codes alloted to different users are orthogonal, that is,

$$\sum_{n=0}^{N_c-1} c_{i,n}c_{j,n} = N_c\delta_K(i - j). \tag{4.89}$$

This process of spreading the symbols using a periodic spreading code is referred to as *direct sequence* CDMA (DS-CDMA).

Let us now turn our attention to the receiver. The baseband equivalent of the received signal is given by

$$\begin{aligned}\tilde{u}(t) = {} & \sum_{k=-\infty}^{\infty} \sum_{n=0}^{N_c-1} S_{1,c,k,n}\,p(t - kT - nT_c) \\ & + \sum_{k=-\infty}^{\infty} \sum_{n=0}^{N_c-1} S_{2,c,k,n}\,p(t - kT - nT_c) + \tilde{v}(t)\end{aligned} \tag{4.90}$$

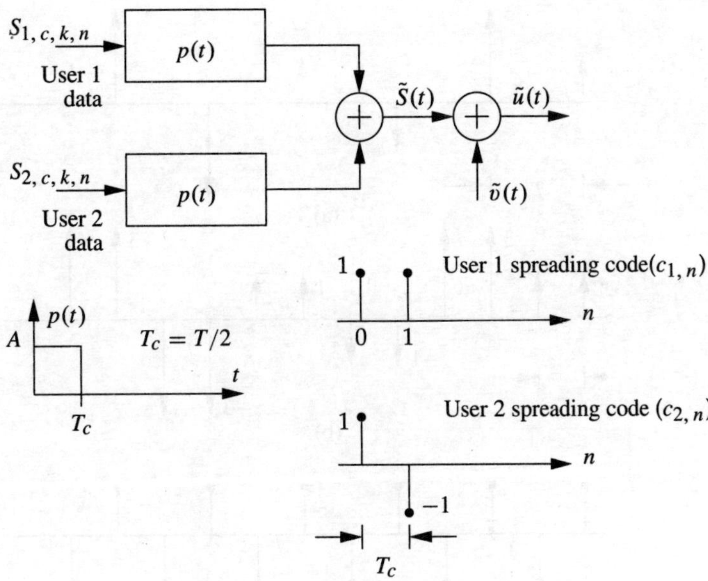

Figure 4.11 *Alternate baseband equivalent model for Figure 4.9*

where the autocorrelation of $\tilde{v}(t)$ is once again given by (4.53). The output of the matched filter for user 1 is given by

$$\begin{aligned}\tilde{x}_1(t) &= \sum_{k=-\infty}^{\infty}\sum_{n=0}^{N_c-1} S_{1,c,k,n}h(t-kT-nT_c)\\&\quad+\sum_{k=-\infty}^{\infty}\sum_{n=0}^{N_c-1} S_{2,c,k,n}h(t-kT-nT_c)+\tilde{z}(t).\end{aligned}\tag{4.91}$$

The output of the sampler is

$$\begin{aligned}\tilde{x}_1(kT+nT_c) &= S_{1,c,k,n}A^2T_c + S_{2,c,k,n}A^2T_c + \tilde{z}_1(kT+nT_c)\\&= S_{1,c,k,n}/N_c + S_{2,c,k,n}/N_c + \tilde{z}_1(kT+nT_c)\end{aligned}\tag{4.92}$$

where we have substituted $A^2T_c = 1/N_c$ (since $A^2T = 1$ by assumption). The autocorrelation of $\tilde{z}_1(kT+nT_c)$ is given by

$$\begin{aligned}R_{\tilde{z}_1\tilde{z}_1}(lT+mT_c) &= \frac{1}{2}E\left[\tilde{z}_1(kT+nT_c)\tilde{z}_1^*((k-l)T+(n-m)T_c)\right]\\&= N_0A^2T_c\delta_K(lT+mT_c)\\&= \frac{N_0}{N_c}\delta_K(lT+mT_c).\end{aligned}\tag{4.93}$$

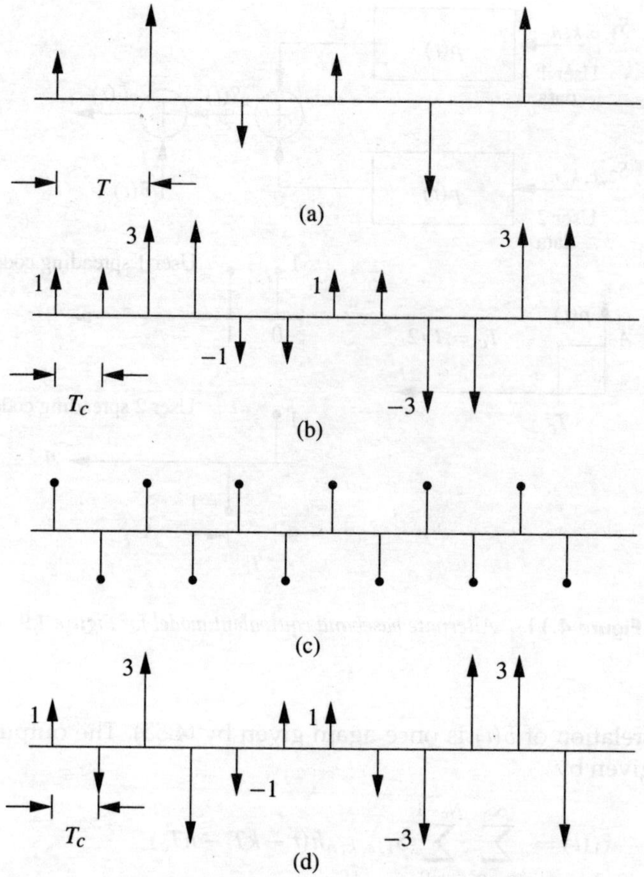

Figure 4.12 *(a) Delta train weighted by symbols. (b) Modified delta train. Each symbol is repeated N_c times. (c) Periodic spreading sequence. (d) Delta train after spreading (multiplication with the spreading sequence). This is used to excite the transmit filter $p(t)$.*

The signal at the output of the summer is

$$\begin{aligned}\tilde{y}_1(kT) &= \sum_{n=0}^{N_c-1} \tilde{x}_1(kT + nT_c)c_{1,n}\\ &= S_{1,k} + \tilde{a}(kT)\end{aligned} \tag{4.94}$$

where we have made use of the orthogonality of the code sequences. Note that

$$\tilde{a}(kT) = \sum_{n=0}^{N_c-1} \tilde{z}_1(kT + nT_c)c_{1,n}. \tag{4.95}$$

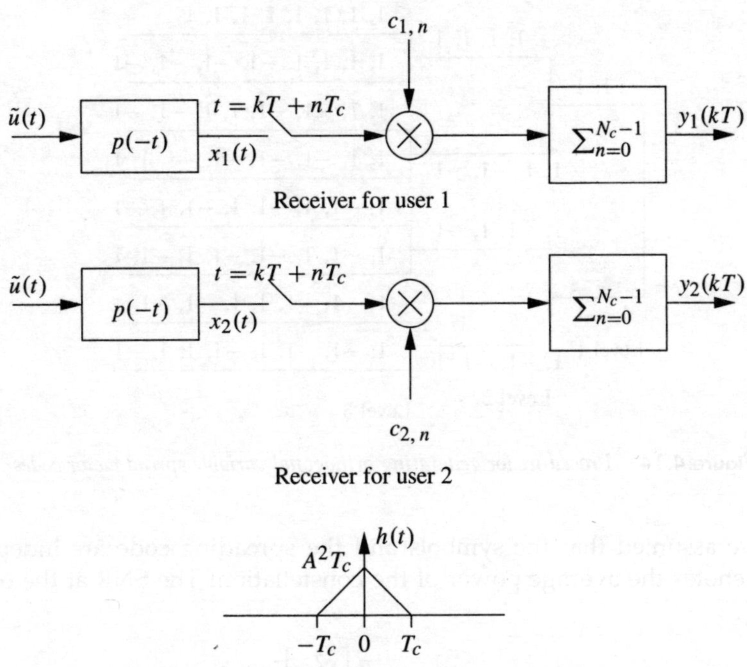

Figure 4.13 *Modified receivers for users 1 and 2*

The autocorrelation of $\tilde{a}(kT)$ is given by

$$R_{\tilde{a}\tilde{a}}(mT) = \frac{1}{2}E\left[\tilde{a}(kT)\tilde{a}^*(kT - mT)\right] = N_0\delta_K(mT). \tag{4.96}$$

Comparing (4.95) and (4.85) we find that both detection strategies are optimal and yield the same symbol error rate performance.

The signal-to-noise ratio at the input to the summer is defined as the ratio of the *desired* signal power to the noise power, and is equal to

$$\begin{aligned}
\text{SNR}_{\text{in}} &= \frac{E\left[S_{1,c,k,n}^2\right]}{2N_c^2 R_{\tilde{z}_1\tilde{z}_1}(0)} \\
&= \frac{E\left[S_{1,k}^2\right]c_{1,n}^2}{2N_c^2 R_{\tilde{z}_1\tilde{z}_1}(0)} \\
&= \frac{P_{\text{av}}}{2N_c N_0}
\end{aligned} \tag{4.97}$$

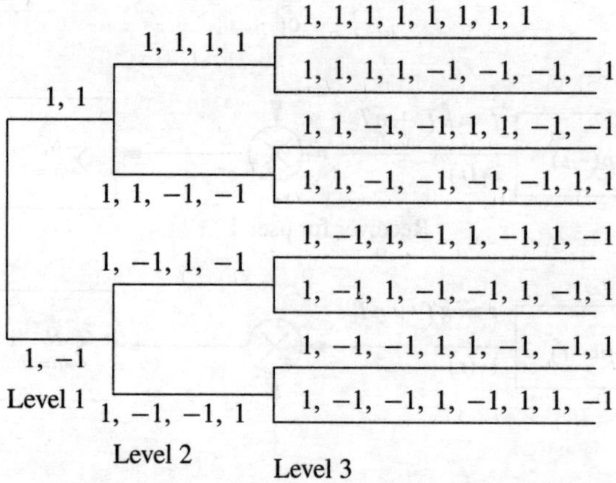

Figure 4.14 *Procedure for generating orthogonal variable spread factor codes*

where we have assumed that the symbols and the spreading code are independent and as usual P_{av} denotes the average power of the constellation. The SNR at the output of the summer is

$$\begin{aligned} \text{SNR}_{\text{out}} &= \frac{E\left[S_{1,k}^2\right]}{2R_{\tilde{a}\tilde{a}}(0)} \\ &= \frac{P_{\text{av}}}{2N_0}. \end{aligned} \tag{4.98}$$

The *processing gain* is defined as the ratio of the output SNR to the input SNR. From (4.97) and (4.98), it is clear that the processing gain is equal to N_c.

The second solution suggests that we can now use the root-raised cosine pulse as the transmit filter in order to band-limit the transmitted signal. However, now

$$2B = 1/T_c \tag{4.99}$$

where $2B$ has been previously defined in (4.77). In Figure 4.14 we illustrate the procedure for generating *orthogonal variable spread factor* (OVSF) codes that can be used in DS-CDMA. The OVSF codes are used in the 3G wireless standard[129]. In the next section we describe the discrete time receiver implementation and the *bandpass sampling theorem*.

4.1.7 Discrete-time receiver implementation

The received signal is given by (4.46) which is repeated here for convenience:

$$r(t) = S_p(t) + w_1(t) \tag{4.100}$$

where $S_p(t)$ is the random process given by (4.33) and $w_1(t)$ is an AWGN process with zero mean and power spectral density $N_0/2$. The received signal is passed through an analog bandpass filter to eliminate out-of-band noise, sampled and converted to a discrete-time signal for further processing. Recall that $S_p(t)$ is a bandpass signal centered at F_c. In many situations F_c is much higher than the sampling frequency of the analog-to-digital converter and the bandpass sampling theorem needs to be invoked to avoid aliasing. This theorem is based on the following observations:

1. The spectrum of any signal after sampling becomes periodic with a period of F_s, where F_s is the sampling frequency.
2. Aliasing, if any, occurs across integer multiples of π.
3. The analog frequency (F) in hertz and the digital frequency (ω) in radians are related by $\omega = 2\pi F/F_s$.

Assume that $S_p(t)$ is bandlimited in the range $[F_c - B_1,\ F_c + B_2]$. The statement of the bandpass sampling theorem is as follows.

Theorem 4.1.1 *Find out the smallest value of the sampling frequency F_s such that:*

$$\begin{aligned} k\pi &\leq \frac{2\pi(F_c - B_1)}{F_s} \\ (k+1)\pi &\geq \frac{2\pi(F_c + B_2)}{F_s} \end{aligned} \tag{4.101}$$

where k is a positive integer.

Let

$$F_1 = F_c - B_1,\ F_2 = F_c + B_2. \tag{4.102}$$

Given F_1 and F_2, we now illustrate how the minimum F_s can be computed.

(a)

$$\begin{aligned} k\pi &= \frac{2\pi F_1}{F_s} \\ (k+1)\pi &= \frac{2\pi F_2}{F_s}. \end{aligned} \tag{4.103}$$

In this case it is straightforward to solve for k and F_s – if there exists such a solution.

(b)

$$\begin{aligned} k\pi &< \frac{2\pi F_1}{F_s} \\ (k+1)\pi &= \frac{2\pi F_2}{F_s}. \end{aligned} \tag{4.104}$$

Solving the above equations, we get

$$F_{s,\,\min,\,1} = \frac{2F_2}{k_{\max}+1}$$

$$F_{s,\,\min,\,1} < \frac{2F_1}{k_{\max}}$$

$$\Rightarrow \frac{2F_2}{k_{\max}+1} < \frac{2F_1}{k_{\max}}$$

$$\Rightarrow k_{\max} < \frac{F_1}{F_2 - F_1} \tag{4.105}$$

for some positive integer $k_{\max}$.

(c)

$$k\pi = \frac{2\pi F_1}{F_s}$$

$$(k+1)\pi > \frac{2\pi F_2}{F_s}. \tag{4.106}$$

In this case, we again get

$$k_{\max} < \frac{F_1}{F_2 - F_1}$$

$$F_{s,\,\min,\,2} = \frac{2F_1}{k_{\max}} \tag{4.107}$$

for some positive integer $k_{\max}$. However, having found out $k_{\max}$ and $F_{s,\,\min,\,2}$, it is *always* possible to find out a *lower* sampling frequency for the *same* value of $k_{\max}$ such that (4.104) is satisfied.

(d)

$$k\pi < \frac{2\pi F_1}{F_s}$$

$$(k+1)\pi > \frac{2\pi F_2}{F_s}. \tag{4.108}$$

Once again, having found out k and F_s, it is always possible to find out a lower value of F_s for the same k such that (4.104) is satisfied.

To summarize, the minimum sampling frequency is determined either by item (a) or (b), but never by (c) or (d).

For simplicity of demodulation, the carrier and sampling frequency are usually chosen such that

$$\frac{2\pi F_c}{F_s} = \frac{(2m+1)\pi}{2} \tag{4.109}$$

where m is a positive integer. It is important to note that the condition in (4.109) is *not* mandatory, and aliasing can be avoided even if it is not met. However, the conditions in (4.101) are mandatory in order to avoid aliasing.

Example 4.1.3 A real-valued bandpass signal occupies the frequency band $50.25 \le |F| \le 52.5$ MHz.

1. Find out the minimum sampling frequency such that there is no aliasing.
2. Find the carrier frequency in the range $50.25 \le |F| \le 52.5$ MHz such that it maps to an odd multiple of $\pi/2$.
3. Does the carrier frequency map of $\pi/2$ or $3\pi/2$ mod-2π?

Solution: Substituting $F_1 = 50.25$ and $F_2 = 52.5$ in (4.130) we have:

$$\begin{aligned} F_s &= 2(F_2 - F_1) \\ &= 4.5\,\text{MHz} \\ k &= \frac{2F_1}{F_s} \\ &= 22.33. \end{aligned} \tag{4.110}$$

Since k is not an integer, condition (a) is not satisfied. Let us now try condition (b). From (4.105) we have:

$$\begin{aligned} k_{\text{max}} &< \frac{F_1}{F_2 - F_1} \\ \Rightarrow k_{\text{max}} &= 22 \\ F_{s,\text{min},1} &= \frac{2F2}{k_{\text{max}} + 1} \\ &= 4.5652\,\text{MHz} \end{aligned} \tag{4.111}$$

Since the signal spectrum lies in the range

$$22\pi < \frac{2\pi|F|}{F_s} \le 23\pi \tag{4.112}$$

the carrier frequency F_c must be at:

$$\begin{aligned} 22\pi + \frac{\pi}{2} &= \frac{2\pi F_c}{F_s} \\ \Rightarrow F_c &= 51.359\,\text{MHz}. \end{aligned} \tag{4.113}$$

From (4.112) it is clear that the carrier frequency maps to $\pi/2$ mod-2π.

Let us now assume, for mathematical simplicity, that the analog bandpass filter has ideal characteristics in the frequency range $[F_c - B,\ F_c + B]$, where

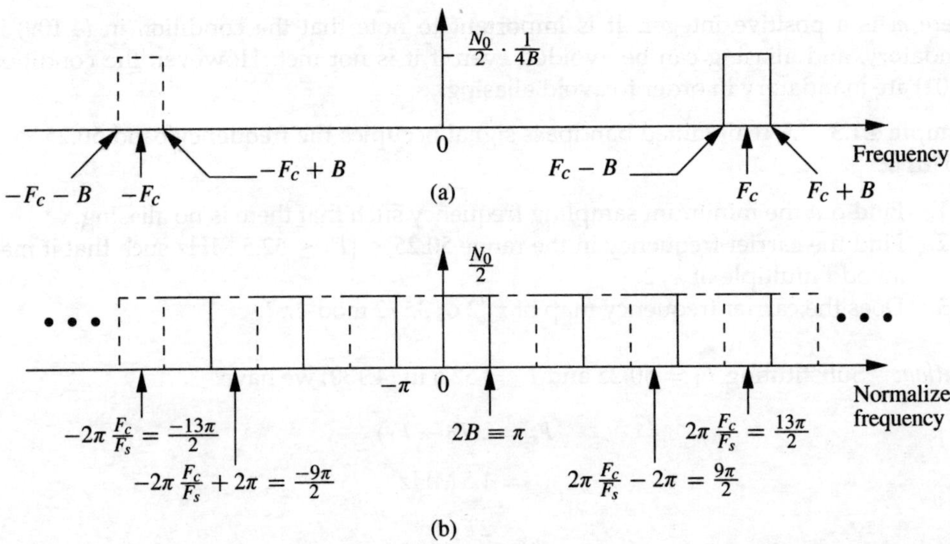

Figure 4.15 *(a) Power spectral density of noise at the output of the bandpass filter. (b) Power spectral density of noise after bandpass sampling.*

$$B = \max[B_1, \; B_2]. \tag{4.114}$$

The bandpass sampling rules in (4.101) can now be invoked with B_1 and B_2 replaced by B and the inequalities replaced by equalities. This ensures that the power spectral density of noise after sampling is flat. This is illustrated in Figure 4.15. Note that in this example, the sampling frequency $F_s = 1/T_s = 4B$. We further assume that the energy of the bandpass filter is unity so that the noise power at the bandpass filter output is equal to $N_0/2$. This implies that the gain of the BPF is $1/\sqrt{4B} = \sqrt{T_s}$. Therefore, for the case of subsequent analysis, we assume that $S_p(t)$ in (4.100) is given by

$$S_p(t) = \frac{A}{\sqrt{T_S}} \Re\left\{\tilde{S}(t) \exp\left(j\left(2\pi F_c t + 0\right)\right)\right\} \tag{4.115}$$

where A is an unknown gain introduced by the channel. We also assume that the condition in (4.109) is satisfied. Now, depending on whether the variable m in (4.109) is even or odd, there are two situations.

(a) When $m = 2l$, where l is a positive integer, (4.109) becomes

$$\frac{2\pi F_c}{F_s} = 2l\pi + \frac{\pi}{2} \equiv \frac{\pi}{2} \tag{4.116}$$

and the samples of the received signal is given by

$$\begin{aligned} r(nT_s) &= \sqrt{T_s}\, S_p(nT_s) + w(nT_s) \\ &= \sqrt{T_s}\, S_I(nT_s)\cos(n\pi/2 + \theta) - \sqrt{T_s}\, S_Q(nT_s)\sin(n\pi/2 + \theta) + w(nT_s) \end{aligned} \tag{4.117}$$

where $S_I(nT_s)$ and $S_Q(nT_s)$ are samples of the random process defined in (4.12).

(b) When $m = 2l + 1$, where l is a positive integer, (4.109) becomes

$$\frac{2\pi F_c}{F_s} = 2l\pi + \frac{3\pi}{2} \equiv -\frac{\pi}{2} \tag{4.118}$$

and the samples of the received signal is given by

$$\begin{aligned} r(nT_s) &= \sqrt{T_s}\, S_p(nT_s) + w(nT_s) \\ &= \sqrt{T_s}\, S_I(nT_s)\cos(n\pi/2 - \theta) + \sqrt{T_s}\, S_Q(nT_s)\sin(n\pi/2 - \theta) + w(nT_s). \end{aligned} \tag{4.119}$$

Note that $w(nT_s)$ in (4.117) and (4.119) denotes samples of AWGN with zero mean and variance $N_0/2$. In what follows, we assume that m in (4.109) is odd. The analysis is similar when m is even.

Following the discussion in Section 4.1.4, the output of the local oscillators is given by (ignoring the $2F_c$ terms)

$$\begin{aligned} \tilde{u}(nT_s) &\stackrel{\Delta}{=} u_I(nT_s) + \mathrm{j}\, u_Q(nT_s) \\ &= \sqrt{T_s}\, \tilde{S}(nT_s) \exp\left(\mathrm{j}\,(\theta + \phi)\right) + \tilde{v}(nT_s) \\ &= \sqrt{T_s}\, \mathrm{e}^{\mathrm{j}\,(\theta+\phi)} \sum_{k=-\infty}^{\infty} S_k \tilde{p}(nT_s - \alpha - kT) + \tilde{v}(nT_s) \end{aligned} \tag{4.120}$$

where α is a uniformly distributed random variable in the interval $[0,\ T]$ and $\tilde{v}(nT_s)$ denotes samples of AWGN with zero mean and autocorrelation

$$R_{\tilde{v}\tilde{v}}(mT_s) = \frac{1}{2} E\left[\tilde{v}(nT_s)\tilde{v}^*(nT_s - mT_s)\right] = N_0 \delta_K(mT_s). \tag{4.121}$$

Note that the in-phase and quadrature components of $\tilde{v}(nT_s)$ are uncorrelated.

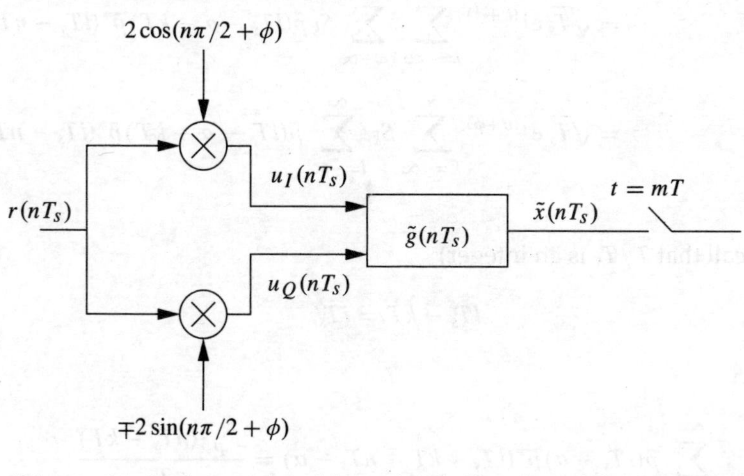

Figure 4.16 *Discrete-time implementation of the receiver for linearly modulated signals. The minus sign in the sine term is applicable when m in (4.109) is even, and the plus sign is applicable when m is odd.*

The next issue is the design of the matched filter. We assume that

$$\frac{T}{T_s} = M \tag{4.122}$$

is an integer. In other words, we assume that there are an integer number of samples per symbol duration. Consider the matched filter of the form

$$\tilde{g}(nT_s) = \tilde{p}^*(-nT_s - \alpha). \tag{4.123}$$

Let

$$\tilde{q}(nT_s) = \sqrt{T_s}\,\mathrm{e}^{\mathrm{j}\,(\theta+\phi)} \sum_{k=-\infty}^{\infty} S_k \tilde{p}(nT_s - \alpha - kT). \tag{4.124}$$

Then the matched filter output can be written as

$$\tilde{x}(nT_s) = \tilde{q}(nT_s) \star \tilde{p}^*(-nT_s - \alpha) + \tilde{z}(nT_s) \tag{4.125}$$

where

$$\tilde{z}(nT_s) = \tilde{v}(nT_s) \star \tilde{p}^*(-nT_s - \alpha). \tag{4.126}$$

Now,

$$\begin{aligned}\tilde{q}(nT_s) \star \tilde{p}^*(-nT_s - \alpha) &= \sum_{l=-\infty}^{\infty} \tilde{q}(lT_s)\tilde{p}^*(lT_s - nT_s - \alpha) \\ &= \sqrt{T_s}\,\mathrm{e}^{\mathrm{j}\,(\theta+\phi)} \sum_{l=-\infty}^{\infty} \sum_{k=-\infty}^{\infty} S_k \tilde{p}(lT_s - \alpha - kT)\tilde{p}^*(lT_s - nT_s - \alpha) \\ &= \sqrt{T_s}\,\mathrm{e}^{\mathrm{j}\,(\theta+\phi)} \sum_{k=-\infty}^{\infty} S_k \sum_{l=-\infty}^{\infty} \tilde{p}(lT_s - \alpha - kT)\tilde{p}^*(lT_s - nT_s - \alpha).\end{aligned} \tag{4.127}$$

Substituting (recall that T/T_s is an integer)

$$lT_s - kT = iT_s \tag{4.128}$$

in (4.127), we get

$$\sum_{i=-\infty}^{\infty} \tilde{p}(iT_s - \alpha)\tilde{p}^*(iT_s + kT - nT_s - \alpha) = \frac{\tilde{R}_{\tilde{p}\tilde{p}}(nT_s - kT)}{T_s} \tag{4.129}$$

where we have used (E.21) from Appendix E.

Thus the matched filter output can be written as

$$\tilde{x}(nT_s) = \exp\left(\mathrm{j}\left(\theta+\phi\right)\right)\frac{1}{\sqrt{T_s}}\sum_{k=-\infty}^{\infty} S_k \tilde{R}_{\tilde{p}\tilde{p}}(nT_s - kT) + \tilde{z}(nT_s). \tag{4.130}$$

It is now clear that the matched filter output must be sampled at instants $nT_s = mT$ so that the output of the symbol-rate sampler can be written as

$$\tilde{x}(mT) = \exp\left(\mathrm{j}\left(\theta+\phi\right)\right)\frac{1}{\sqrt{T_s}} S_m \tilde{R}_{\tilde{p}\tilde{p}}(0) + \tilde{z}(mT) \tag{4.131}$$

where we have used (4.65) and the zero ISI requirement of (4.57). Once again, for convenience we set

$$\tilde{R}_{\tilde{p}\tilde{p}}(0) = 1. \tag{4.132}$$

The autocorrelation of the noise samples at the matched filter output is given by

$$R_{\tilde{z}\tilde{z}}(mT_s) = \frac{1}{2}E\left[\tilde{z}(nT_s)\tilde{z}^*(nT_s - mT_s)\right] = \frac{N_0}{T_s}\tilde{R}_{\tilde{p}\tilde{p}}(mT_s) \tag{4.133}$$

which implies that the autocorrelation of noise at the sampler output is given by

$$R_{\tilde{z}\tilde{z}}(mT) = \frac{1}{2}E\left[\tilde{z}(nT)\tilde{z}^*(nT - mT)\right] = \frac{N_0}{T_s}\delta_K(mT) \tag{4.134}$$

and we have once again used (4.65), (4.57) and (E.21) of Appendix E.

4.2 Synchronization for Linearly Modulated Signals

Synchronization in digital communication systems is an old topic that was addressed as early as 1956 by Costas[130] who invented the Costas loop for carrier phase synchronization. This was later followed by detailed treatments of phase-locked loops (PLLs) in [131–133]. Digital implementation of PLLs is described in [134]. Timing recovery using discrete-time signal processing techniques is given in [135]. A tutorial on both carrier and timing recovery is given in [136]. Besides, a special issue of the *IEEE Transactions on Communications* covers a wide range of topics on synchronization. Books that deal specifically with synchronization in digital communication systems include [5,6,137–140]. An associated topic of carrier frequency/frequency-offset estimation is dealt with in [141–153]

As mentioned in sections 4.1.4 and 4.1.7, synchronization involves estimating the timing phase α (timing recovery) and the carrier phase-offset, $\beta = \theta \pm \phi$ (carrier recovery). In practice, for ease of implementation, ϕ is usually set to zero (see Figures 4.8 and 4.16) so that $\beta = \theta$. There exist two methods of estimating the carrier and timing, namely the *maximum* a *posteriori* (MAP) and the *maximum likelihood* (ML) estimators. When α and β are uniformly distributed over a certain range, then the MAP detector reduces to an ML detector. In this section we concentrate on ML estimators. The ML estimators for the timing and carrier phase can be further classified into *data-aided* and *non-data-aided* estimators. We begin with a discussion on the ML estimators for the carrier phase.

4.2.1 Data-aided carrier phase estimation

Throughout this section, we assume that timing synchronization has been achieved. Assuming a discrete-time receiver implementation, the output of the symbol-rate sampler is given by (4.131), which is repeated here for convenience:

$$\tilde{x}_n = Ae^{j\theta} S_n + \tilde{z}_n \tag{4.135}$$

where we have assumed that $R_{\tilde{p}\tilde{p}}(0)/T_s = 1$ (see (4.132)). Observe that we have dropped the variable T since it is understood that all samples are T-spaced. The autocorrelation of $\tilde{z}_n$ is

$$R_{\tilde{z}\tilde{z}}, m = \frac{1}{2}E[\tilde{z}_n \tilde{z}^*_{n-m}] = N_0 \delta_k(m) \triangleq \sigma_z^2 \delta_k(m). \tag{4.136}$$

Consider the vectors

$$\begin{aligned} \tilde{\mathbf{x}} &= [\tilde{x}_0 \quad \ldots \quad \tilde{x}_{L-1}]^T \\ \mathbf{S} &= [S_0 \quad \ldots \quad S_{L-1}]^T. \end{aligned} \tag{4.137}$$

At this point we need to distinguish between data-aided and non-data-aided phase estimation. In the case of data-aided estimation, the statement of the problem is to estimate θ given A, $\tilde{\mathbf{x}}$ and $\mathbf{S}$. In other words, the symbols are considered to be known at the receiver, which is a valid assumption during a *training* period. Then the ML estimate of θ maximizes the joint conditional pdf

$$p(\tilde{\mathbf{x}}|A, \mathbf{S}, \theta) = \frac{1}{(\sigma_z\sqrt{2\pi})^{2L}} \exp\left(-\frac{\sum_{n=0}^{L-1} |\tilde{x}_n - AS_n e^{j\theta}|^2}{2\sigma_z^2}\right). \tag{4.138}$$

The problem can be equivalently stated as

$$\max_\theta p(\tilde{\mathbf{x}}|A, \mathbf{S}, \theta) = \frac{1}{(\sigma_z\sqrt{2\pi})^{2L}} \exp\left(-\frac{\sum_{n=0}^{L-1} |\tilde{x}_n - AS_n e^{j\theta}|^2}{2\sigma_z^2}\right) \tag{4.139}$$

which reduces to

$$\min_\theta \sum_{n=0}^{L-1} |\tilde{x}_n - AS_n e^{j\theta}|^2. \tag{4.140}$$

Differentiating the above equation wrt θ and setting the result to zero gives

$$\sum_{n=1}^{L-1} \tilde{x}_n S_n^* e^{-j\theta} - \tilde{x}_n^* S_n e^{j\theta} = 0. \tag{4.141}$$

Let

$$\sum_{n=0}^{L-1} \tilde{x}_n S_n^* = X + jY. \tag{4.142}$$

Then the ML estimate θ is given by:

$$\hat{\theta} = \tan^{-1}\left(\frac{Y}{X}\right) \quad \text{for } 0 \le \hat{\theta} < 2\pi. \tag{4.143}$$

The following points are worth noting:

1. The phase estimate is independent of A and in the absence of noise $\hat{\theta} = \theta$, which is intuitively satisfying.
2. The phase estimate $\hat{\theta}$ lies in the range $[0, 2\pi)$ since the quadrant information can be obtained from the sign of X and Y.
3. The other solution of $\hat{\theta}$ given by

$$\hat{\theta} = \tan^{-1}\left(\frac{Y}{X}\right) + \pi \quad \text{for } 0 \le \hat{\theta} < 2\pi \tag{4.144}$$

also satisfies (4.141). However, this solution *maximizes* (4.140) and is hence incorrect.

Performance Analysis

The quality of an estimate is usually measured in terms of its bias and variance[154–157]. Since $\hat{\theta}$ in (4.143) is a random variable, it is clear that it will have its own mean and variance. With reference to the problem at hand, the estimate of θ is said to be unbiased if

$$E[\hat{\theta}] = \theta. \tag{4.145}$$

For an unbiased estimate, the variance is lower bounded by the Cramer-Rao bound (CRB):

$$E[(\hat{\theta} - \theta)^2] \ge 1/E\left[\left(\frac{\partial}{\partial\theta} \ln p(\tilde{\mathbf{x}}|\theta)\right)^2\right]. \tag{4.146}$$

An unbiased estimate whose variance is equal to the Cramér-Rao lower bound, is said to be *efficient*.

For convenience of analysis, we assume that the phase-offset to be estimated is small, i.e. $|\theta| \approx 0$, the symbols are drawn from an M-ary PSK constellation with $|S_n|^2 = 1$, the gain $A = 1$, the observation interval is large ($L \gg 1$) and the SNR is large ($\sigma_z^2 \ll 1$). Thus (4.142) becomes.

$$\begin{aligned} X + \mathrm{j}Y &= L\mathrm{e}^{\mathrm{j}\theta} + \sum_{n=0}^{L-1} \tilde{z}_n S_n^* \\ &\approx L(1 + \mathrm{j}\theta) + \mathrm{j}\sum_{n=0}^{L-1}(z_{n,Q}S_{n,I} - z_{n,I}S_{n,Q}) \end{aligned} \tag{4.147}$$

where we have substituted

$$\cos(\theta) \approx 1$$
$$\sin(\theta) \approx \theta$$
$$L + \sum_{n=0}^{L-1} (z_{n,I} S_{n,I} + z_{n,Q} S_{n,Q}) \approx L. \tag{4.148}$$

Therefore from (4.143) we have:

$$\hat{\theta} \approx \theta + \frac{1}{L} \sum_{n=0}^{L-1} (z_{n,Q} S_{n,I} - z_{n,I} S_{n,Q}) \tag{4.149}$$

where we have used the fact that for $|x| \approx 0$

$$\tan^{-1}(x) \approx x. \tag{4.150}$$

Clearly,

$$E[\hat{\theta}] = \theta \tag{4.151}$$

therefore the estimator is unbiased. Similarly, it can be shown that the variance of the estimate is

$$E\left[(\hat{\theta} - \theta)^2\right] = \frac{\sigma_z^2}{L}. \tag{4.152}$$

Now, the Cramér-Rao bound on the variance of the estimate is (assuming $A = 1$)

$$\left\{ E\left[\left(\frac{\partial}{\partial \theta} \ln\, p(\tilde{\mathbf{x}}|\theta) \right)^2 \right] \right\}^{-1} = \left\{ E\left[\left(\frac{\partial}{\partial \theta} \ln\, p(\tilde{\mathbf{x}}|\theta, \mathbf{S}) \right)^2 \right] \right\}^{-1} \tag{4.153}$$

since by assumption, the symbols are known. Substituting for the conditional pdf, the denominator of the CRB becomes:

$$\begin{aligned} &\frac{1}{4\sigma_z^4} E\left[\left(\frac{\partial}{\partial \theta} \sum_{n=0}^{L-1} |\tilde{x}_n - S_n \mathrm{e}^{\mathrm{j}\theta}|^2 \right)^2 \right] \\ &= \frac{-1}{4\sigma_z^4} E\left[\left(\sum_{n=0}^{L-1} \tilde{x}_n S_n^* \mathrm{e}^{-\mathrm{j}\theta} - \tilde{x}_n^* S_n \mathrm{e}^{\mathrm{j}\theta} \right)^2 \right] \\ &= \frac{-1}{4\sigma_z^4} E\left[\left(\sum_{n=0}^{L-1} \tilde{z}_n S_n^* \mathrm{e}^{-\mathrm{j}\theta} - \tilde{z}_n^* S_n \mathrm{e}^{\mathrm{j}\theta} \right)^2 \right]. \end{aligned} \tag{4.154}$$

Let

$$S_n^* \mathrm{e}^{-\mathrm{j}\theta} = \mathrm{e}^{\mathrm{j}\alpha_n}. \tag{4.155}$$

Then (4.154) reduces to

$$\begin{aligned}
&\frac{1}{4\sigma_z^4} E\left[\left(\frac{\partial}{\partial\theta}\sum_{n=0}^{L-1}|\tilde{x}_n - S_n e^{j\theta}|^2\right)^2\right] \\
&= \frac{1}{\sigma_z^4} E\left[\left(\sum_{n=0}^{L-1}\tilde{z}_{n,Q}\cos(\alpha_n) + \tilde{z}_{n,I}\sin(\alpha_n)\right)^2\right] \\
&= \frac{L}{\sigma_z^2}. \qquad (4.156)
\end{aligned}$$

Hence, the CRB is given by:

$$\left\{E\left[\left(\frac{\partial}{\partial\theta}\ln p(\tilde{\mathrm{x}}|\theta, \mathrm{S})\right)^2\right]\right\}^{-1} = \frac{\sigma_z^2}{L} \qquad (4.157)$$

which is identical to (4.152). Thus the data-aided ML estimator for the carrier phase-offset, is efficient under the assumptions stated earlier.

4.2.2 Non-data-aided carrier phase estimation

In the case of non-data-aided phase estimation, the problem is to estimate θ given A and $\tilde{\mathrm{x}}$. In particular, the ML estimate yields that value of θ which maximizes the joint conditional pdf:

$$\begin{aligned}
&\max_{\theta} \quad p(\tilde{\mathrm{x}}|A, \theta) \\
&\Rightarrow \max_{\theta} \quad \sum_{i=0}^{M^L-1} p(\tilde{\mathrm{x}}|A, \mathbf{S}^{(i)}, \theta)P(\mathbf{S}^{(i)}) \qquad (4.158)
\end{aligned}$$

where $P(\mathbf{S}^{(i)})$ is the probability of occurrence of the ith symbol sequence. Assuming that the symbols are independent and equally likely and the constellation is M-ary, we have:

$$P(\mathbf{S}^{(i)}) = \frac{1}{M^L} \qquad (4.159)$$

which is a constant. A general solution for θ in (4.158) may be difficult to obtain. Instead, let us look at a simple case where $L = 1$ and $M = 2$ (BPSK) with $S_0 = \pm 1$. In this case, the problem reduces to (after ignoring constants)

$$\max_{\theta} \exp\left(-\frac{|\tilde{x}_0 - Ae^{j\theta}|^2}{2\sigma_z^2}\right) + \exp\left(-\frac{|\tilde{x}_0 + Ae^{j\theta}|^2}{2\sigma_z^2}\right). \qquad (4.160)$$

Expanding the exponents in the above equation and ignoring constants we get

$$\max_{\theta} \exp\left(\frac{2\Re\left\{\tilde{x}_0 A \mathrm{e}^{-\mathrm{j}\theta}\right\}}{2\sigma_z^2}\right) + \exp\left(\frac{2\Re\left\{\tilde{x}_0 A \mathrm{e}^{-\mathrm{j}\theta}\right\}}{2\sigma_z^2}\right). \tag{4.161}$$

Now, for large values of $|x|$ we can write

$$\mathrm{e}^{x} + \mathrm{e}^{-x} \approx \mathrm{e}^{|x|}. \tag{4.162}$$

Thus for large SNR ($A \gg \sigma_z^2$) (4.161) reduces to

$$\max_{\theta} \exp\left(\frac{\left|\Re\left\{\tilde{x}_0 A \mathrm{e}^{-\mathrm{j}\theta}\right\}\right|}{\sigma_z^2}\right) \tag{4.163}$$

which is equivalent to

$$\max_{\theta} \left|\Re\left\{\tilde{x}_0 \mathrm{e}^{-\mathrm{j}\theta}\right\}\right| \tag{4.164}$$

where we have again ignored the constants. If

$$\tilde{x}_0 = P + \mathrm{j}Q \tag{4.165}$$

then the solution to (4.164) is

$$\hat{\theta} = \tan^{-1}\left(\frac{Q}{P}\right) \quad \text{for} - \pi/2 < \hat{\theta} < \pi/2. \tag{4.166}$$

The other solution to $\hat{\theta}$ is given by:

$$\hat{\theta} = \tan^{-1}\left(\frac{Q}{P}\right) + \pi \tag{4.167}$$

which also maximizes (4.164). However, it is customary to take $\hat{\theta}$ in the range $[-\pi/2, \pi/2]$. The plot of $\hat{\theta}$ vs θ is depicted in Figure 4.17 in the absence of noise, when

$$\tilde{x}_0 = A\mathrm{e}^{\mathrm{j}\theta} S_0. \tag{4.168}$$

Observe that the phase estimate exhibits 180° phase ambiguity, that is $\hat{\theta} = 0$ when θ is an integer multiple of 180°.

An alternate solution to the problem of ML non-data-aided carrier phase estimate is the following two-step procedure:

1. Estimate the data assuming that $\theta = 0$.
2. Estimate the carrier phase using the estimated data using (4.142) and (4.143).

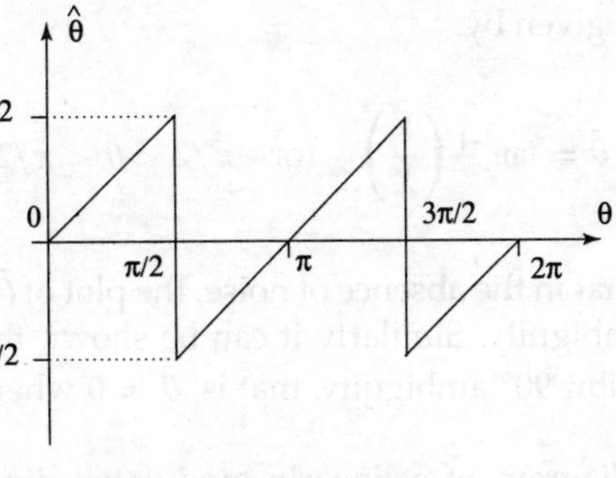

Figure 4.17 *The plot of $\hat{\theta}$ vs θ for the ML non-data-aided estimation of BPSK signals*

Mathematically, the problem can be stated as

$$\max_i p\left(\tilde{x}_0 | A, S_0^{(i)}, \theta = 0\right)$$
$$\max_\theta p\left(\tilde{x}_0 | A, S_0^{(i)}, \theta\right). \tag{4.169}$$

Once again we use BPSK with data-length $L = 1$ to demonstrate this concept. In the first step we have:

$$\max_i p\left(\tilde{x}_0 | A, S_0^{(i)}, \theta = 0\right) \quad \text{for } 1 \leq i \leq 2$$

$$\Rightarrow \max_i \frac{1}{2\pi\sigma_z^2} \exp\left(-\frac{|\tilde{x}_0 - AS_0^{(i)}|^2}{2\sigma_z^2}\right)$$

$$\Rightarrow \min_i |\tilde{x}_0 - AS_0^{(i)}|^2$$

$$\Rightarrow \max_i \Re\left\{\tilde{x}_0 S_0^{(i)}\right\}$$

$$\Rightarrow \max_i S_0^{(i)} \Re\left\{\tilde{x}_0\right\} \tag{4.170}$$

since $S_0^{(i)} = \pm 1$ and we have assumed that A is positive. There are two points to be noted in the last step of (4.170):

1. The detection rule does not require knowledge of A.
2. The detection rule is equivalent to making a hard decision on $\tilde{x}_0$, i.e., choose $S_0^{(i)} = +1$ if $\Re\left\{\tilde{x}_0\right\} > 0$, choose $S_0^{(i)} = -1$ if $\Re\left\{\tilde{x}_0\right\} < 0$.

Once the data estimate is obtained, we can use the data-aided ML rule for the phase estimate. To this end, let

$$\tilde{x}_0 S_0^i = X + \mathrm{j}Y. \tag{4.171}$$

Then the phase estimate is given by:

$$\hat{\theta} = \tan^{-1}\left(\frac{Y}{X}\right) \quad \text{for } -\pi/2 < \hat{\theta} < \pi/2. \tag{4.172}$$

Once again it can be seen that in the absence of noise, the plot of $\hat{\theta}$ vs θ is given by Figure 4.17, resulting in 180° phase ambiguity. Similarly it can be shown that for QPSK, the non-data-aided phase estimates exhibit 90° ambiguity, that is, $\hat{\theta} = 0$ when θ is an integer multiple of 90°.

The equivalent block diagram of a linearly modulated digital communication system employing carrier phase synchronization is shown in Figure 4.18. Observe that in order to overcome the problem of phase ambiguity, the data bits b_n have to be differentially encoded to c_n. The differential encoding rules and the differential encoding table are also shown in Figure 4.18. The differential decoder is the reverse of the encoder. In order to understand the principle behind differential encoding, let us consider an example.

Example 4.2.1 In Figure 4.18 assume that $\theta = 8\pi/7$. Assuming no noise, compute $\hat{\theta}$ and the sequences c_n, S_n, d_n and a_n if $b_0b_1b_2b_3 = 1011$. Assume that $c_{-1} = d_{-1} = 0$.

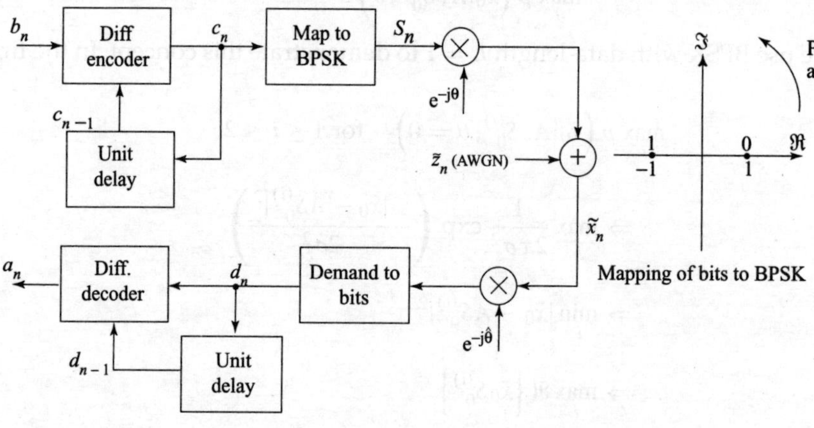

Input		Output
b_n	c_{n-1}	c_n
0	0	0
0	1	1
1	0	1
1	1	0

Differential encoding table

Data bits b_n	Rotation
0	0
1	π

Differential encoding rules

Figure 4.18 *The equivalent block diagram of a linearly modulated digital communication system employing carrier phase synchronization*

n	b_n	c_n	S_n	d_n	a_n
−1		0	+1	0	
0	1	1	−1	0	0
1	0	1	−1	0	0
2	1	0	+1	1	1
3	1	1	−1	0	1

Figure 4.19 *The sequences c_n, S_n, d_n and a_n when $b_0b_1b_2b_3 = 1011$.*

Solution: In order to estimate θ, we assume without loss of generality that $S_0 = +1$ has been transmitted. Therefore

$$\begin{aligned}\tilde{x}_0 &= AS_0\mathrm{e}^{\mathrm{j}8\pi/7} \\ &= A\mathrm{e}^{\mathrm{j}8\pi/7}.\end{aligned} \tag{4.173}$$

From step (1)we get $S^{(i)} = -1 = \mathrm{e}^{-\mathrm{j}\pi}$. Then

$$\begin{aligned}\tilde{x}_0S^{(i)} &= A\mathrm{e}^{\mathrm{j}(8\pi/7-\pi)} \\ \tilde{x}_0S^{(i)} &= A\mathrm{e}^{\mathrm{j}\pi/7}.\end{aligned} \tag{4.174}$$

Thus

$$\begin{aligned}\hat{\theta} &= \pi/7 \\ \Rightarrow \theta - \hat{\theta} &= \pi.\end{aligned} \tag{4.175}$$

It can be shown that the result in (4.175) is true even when $S_0 = -1$. The sequences c_n, S_n, d_n and a_n are shown in Figure 4.19. Observe that d_n is a 180° rotated version of c_n for $n \geq 0$.

4.2.3 Error-rate analysis

The signal at the output of the receiver multiplier in Figure 4.18 is

$$\begin{aligned}\tilde{x}_n\mathrm{e}^{-\mathrm{j}\hat{\theta}} &= A\mathrm{e}^{\mathrm{j}(\theta-\hat{\theta})}S_n + \tilde{z}_n\mathrm{e}^{-\mathrm{j}\hat{\theta}} \\ &\triangleq A\mathrm{e}^{\mathrm{j}(\theta-\hat{\theta})}S_n + \tilde{u}_n.\end{aligned} \tag{4.176}$$

It can be shown that the autocorrelation of $\tilde{u}_n$ is given by:

$$R_{\tilde{u}\tilde{u},m} = \frac{1}{2}E\left[\tilde{u}_n\tilde{u}^*_{n-m}\right] = N_0\delta_K(m) \triangleq \sigma_z^2\delta_K(m) \tag{4.177}$$

where σ_z^2 has been previously defined in (4.136).

Note that once the carrier phase has been acquired during the training period (to an integer multiple of 90°, using QPSK), the transmitter can switch over to M-ary 2-D signalling. In what follows, we assume that $\theta - \hat{\theta}$ is an integer multiple of 90°. Since the 2-D constellations that are used in practice are invariant to rotation by integer multiples of 90°, it is still possible to do coherent detection. Now, from section 2.1 it is clear that the average probability of symbol error before differential decoding remains unchanged due to rotation of the constellation. Since the differential decoder is a unit-delay *feedforward* system, a single error at its input leads to two consecutive errors at its output (there is no error propagation). Thus, the average probability of symbol error at the output of the differential decoder is twice that of the input.

Observe carefully the difference between coherent differential decoding and noncoherent differential detection (section 2.6). In the former case, we are only doubling the probability of error, as opposed to the latter case where the performance is 3 dB inferior to coherent detection. However, coherent differential decoding is possible only when $\theta - \hat{\theta}$ is an integer multiple of 90°, whereas noncoherent differential detection is possible for any value of $\theta - \hat{\theta}$. Finally, coherent differential decoding is possible for any of the 90° rotationally-invariant M-ary 2-D constellations, non-coherent differential detection is possible only for M-ary PSK constellations.

4.2.4 Data-Aided Timing Synchronization

Recall that in the previous section on carrier phase estimation, we had assumed that the timing is known. This implies that timing synchronization must be done noncoherently. The task of the timing recovery algorithm is twofold[158]:

1. To estimate the matched filter, i.e. $p(-nT_s - \alpha)$ (see(4.123)).
2. To sample the output of the matched filter at the right instants.

As far as estimating the matched filter is concerned, a possible solution is to *interpolate* the output of the local oscillators to the desired accuracy. This concept is best illustrated by an example. Let us assume for simplicity that the transmit filter has a triangular shape. The samples of the received pulse is shown in Figure 4.20(a). The corresponding matched filter is given in Figure 4.20(b). Now, let us sample $p(-t)$ at a rate $F_{s1} = 1/T_{s1}$, where

$$\frac{T_s}{T_{s1}} = I \quad \text{(an integer).} \tag{4.178}$$

We find that in our example with I = 4, one set of samples indicated by solid lines in Figure 4.20(c), correspond to the matched filter. This has been possible because α is an integer multiple of T_{s1}. In Figure 4.20, $\alpha = 3T_{s1}$. In practice, since α is uniformly distributed between $[0, T)$, it may only be possible to get close to the exact matched filter, if I is taken to be sufficiently large. The final output signal is obtained by first up-sampling the received pulse $p(nT_s - \alpha)$ by a factor of I and convolving it with $p(-nT_{s1})$. This output signal is guaranteed to contain the peak, $R_{pp}(0)/T_s$, and the zerocrossing. Note that when α is not an integer multiple of T_{s1}, we can only get close to the peak.

The process of up-sampling and convolution can also be explained in the frequency domain as shown in Figure 4.21. We assume that $p(t)$ is bandlimited to $[-B, B]$ and $F_s = 4B$. We have[158]

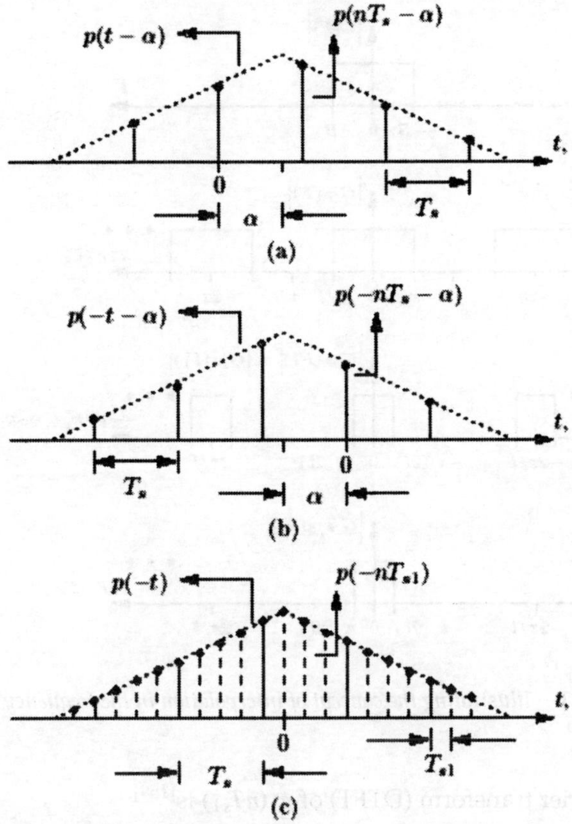

Figure 4.20 *Matched filter estimation using interpolation. (a) Samples of the received pulse. (b) Filter matched to the received pulse. (c) Transmit filter $p(t)$ sampled at a higher frequency. Observe that one set of samples (shown by solid lines) correspond to the matched filter.*

$$p(t-\alpha) = g(t) \rightleftharpoons \tilde{G}(F) = \begin{cases} \tilde{P}(F)\mathrm{e}^{-\mathrm{j}2\pi F\alpha} & -B \le F \le B \\ 0 & \text{otherwise} \end{cases}$$

$$\Rightarrow p(nT_s-\alpha) = g(nT_s) \rightleftharpoons \tilde{G}_{\mathscr{P}}(F) = \begin{cases} \tilde{G}(F)/T_s & 0 \le |2\pi F/F_s| \le \pi/2 \\ 0 & \pi/2 \le |2\pi F/F_s| \le \pi. \end{cases} \tag{4.179}$$

Construct the up-sampled sequence

$$g_1(nT_{s1}) = \begin{cases} g(nT_s/I) & \text{for } n = mI \\ 0 & \text{otherwise.} \end{cases} \tag{4.180}$$

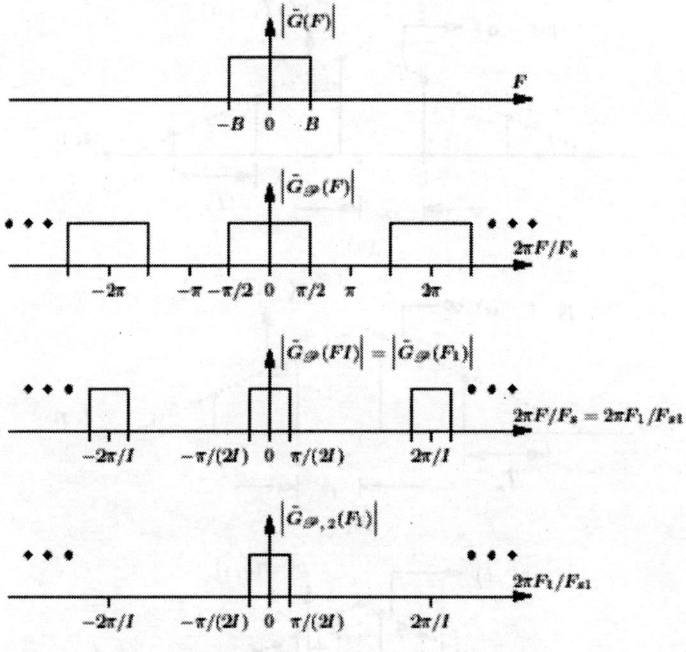

Figure 4.21 *Illustrating the concept of interpolation in the frequency domain*

The discrete-time Fourier transform (DTFT) of $g_1(nT_{s1})$ is[159]:

$$g_1(nT_{s1}) \rightleftharpoons G_{\mathscr{P}}(FI). \tag{4.181}$$

Let us define a new frequency variable

$$F_1 = FI \tag{4.182}$$

with respect to the new sampling frequency F_{s1}. Now, if $p(-t)$ is sampled at a rate F_{s1} the DTFT of the resulting sequence is:

$$\begin{aligned} p(-nT_{s1}) &= g_2(nT_{s1}) \\ &\rightleftharpoons \tilde{G}_{\mathscr{P},2}(F_1) = \begin{cases} \tilde{P}^*(F_1)/T_{s1} & 0 \le \left|\frac{2\pi F_1}{F_{s1}}\right| \le \frac{\pi}{(2I)} \\ 0 & \pi/(2I) \le \left|\frac{2\pi F_1}{F_{s1}}\right| \le \pi. \end{cases} \end{aligned} \tag{4.183}$$

The convolution of $g_1(nT_{s1})$ with $g_2(nT_{s1})$ can be written as:

$$g_1(nT_{s1}) \star g_2(nT_{s1}) = \frac{1}{T_s T_{s1} F_{s1}} \int_{F_1=-B}^{B} |\tilde{P}(F_1)|^2 e^{j2\pi F_1 (nT_{s1}-\alpha)} dF_1. \tag{4.184}$$

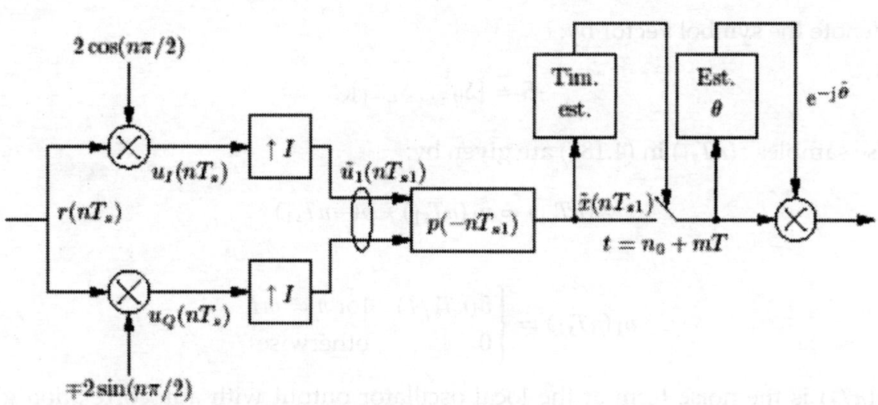

Figure 4.22 *The modified discrete-time receiver which up-samples the local oscillator output by a factor of I and then performs matched filtering at a sampling frequency F_{s1}*

Clearly, if $\alpha = n_0 T_{s1}$, then the above convolution becomes

$$g_1(nT_{s1}) \star g_2(nT_{s1}) = \frac{R_{pp}((n-n_0)T_{s1})}{T_s} \tag{4.185}$$

with a peak value equal to $R_{pp}(0)/T_s$. The modified discrete-time receiver is depicted in Figure 4.22. Note that

$$\tilde{u}_1(nT_{s1}) = \begin{cases} \tilde{u}(nT_s/I) & n = mI \\ 0 & \text{otherwise.} \end{cases} \tag{4.186}$$

Since $\tilde{u}(nT_s)$ is just a weighted linear combination of $p(nT_s - \alpha - kT)$ (refer to (4.120)), the theory explained in Figures 4.20 and 4.21 for a single pulse $p(nT_s - \alpha)$, is equally valid in Figure 4.22 for a sequence of pulses. Now it only remains to identify the peaks ($R_{pp}(0)/T_s$) of the output signal $\tilde{x}(nT_{s1})$. In what follows, we assume that $\alpha = n_0 T_{s1}$.

Firstly we rewrite the output signal as follows:

$$\tilde{x}(nT_{s1}) = \frac{A\exp(\mathrm{j}\theta)}{T_s}\sum_{k=0}^{L-1} S_k R_{pp}((n-n_0)T_{s1-kT}) + \tilde{z}(nT_{s1}) \tag{4.187}$$

where we have considered only L symbols for simplicity of derivation. This implies that the sequences $\tilde{x}(nT_{s1})$ is also finite and can be represented by a vector $\tilde{\mathrm{x}}$. The length of $\tilde{\mathrm{x}}$ is not of importance here. We assume that the symbols S_k are known (they may be a part of a training sequence) and the bandwidth of $p(t)$ is $B = 1/T$. Therefore

$$\frac{T}{T_s} = 4$$

$$\Rightarrow \frac{T}{T_{s1}} = 4I. \tag{4.188}$$

Let us denote the symbol vector by:

$$\mathbf{S} = [S_0 \ldots S_{L-1}]. \tag{4.189}$$

The noise samples $\tilde{z}(nT_{s1})$ in (4.187) are given by:

$$\tilde{z}(nT_{s1}) = \tilde{v}_1(nT_{s1}) \star p(-nT_{s1}) \tag{4.190}$$

where

$$\tilde{v}_1(nT_{s1}) = \begin{cases} \tilde{v}(nT_s/I) & \text{for } n = mI \\ 0 & \text{otherwise} \end{cases} \tag{4.191}$$

when $\tilde{v}(nT_s)$ is the noise term at the local oscillator output with autocorrelation given by (4.121). It is easy to verify that the autocorrelation of $\tilde{v}_1(nT_{s1})$ is given by:

$$R_{\tilde{v}_1\tilde{v}_1}(mT_{s1}) = \frac{1}{2}E[\tilde{v}_1(nT_{s1})\tilde{v}_1^*(nT_{s1} - mT_{s1})] = \frac{N_0}{I}\delta_K(mT_{s1}). \tag{4.192}$$

Therefore the autocorrelation of $\tilde{z}(nT_{s1})$ is given by:

$$R_{\tilde{z}\tilde{z}}(mT_{s1}) = \frac{1}{2}E[\tilde{z}(nT_{s1})\tilde{z}^*(nT_{s1} - mT_{s1})] = \frac{N_0}{IT_{s1}}R_{pp}(mT_{s1}). \tag{4.193}$$

After symbol-rate sampling, the autocorrelation of the noise samples becomes (assuming that $R_{pp}(0)/T_s = 1$):

$$\begin{aligned} R_{\tilde{z}\tilde{z}(mT)} = \frac{1}{2}E[\tilde{z}(nT)\tilde{z}^*(nT - mT)] &= \frac{N_0}{IT_{s1}}R_{pp}(mT) \\ &= \frac{N_0}{T_s}R_{pp}(0)\delta_K(mT) \\ &= N_0\delta_K(mT) \end{aligned} \tag{4.194}$$

which is identical to (4.134).

The ML timing recovery problem can now be stated as follows. Choose that sampling instant nT_{s1} which maximizes the joint conditional pdf:

$$p(\tilde{x}|\mathbf{S}, A). \tag{4.195}$$

Here we assume that A is known at the receiver, though later on we show that this information is not required. Observe that if the instant nT_{s1} is known, then the symbols can be extracted from every $(4I)^{th}$ sample of $\tilde{x}$ starting from n. Thus the problem reduces to

$$\max_n p(\tilde{x}|\mathbf{S}, A). \tag{4.196}$$

Since the timing estimation must be done non-coherently, we need to average out the effects of θ in (4.187). Thus, the timing estimation problem can be restated as[158]:

$$\max_{n} \int_{\theta=0}^{2\pi} p(\tilde{\mathrm{x}}|\mathbf{S}, A, \theta) p(\theta) d\theta. \tag{4.197}$$

Using the fact the pdf of θ is uniform over 2π and the noise terms that are $4I$ samples apart (T-spaced) are uncorrelated (see (4.194)) we get:

$$\max_{n} \frac{1}{2\pi} \frac{1}{(2\pi\sigma_z^2)^L} \int_{\theta=0}^{2\pi} \exp\left(-\frac{\sum_{k=0}^{L-1} |\tilde{x}(nT_{s1} + kT) - AS_k \mathrm{e}^{\mathrm{j}\theta}|^2}{2\sigma_z^2} \right) d\theta. \tag{4.198}$$

Observe that one of the terms in the exponent of (4.198) is

$$\frac{\sum_{k=0}^{L-1} |\tilde{x}(nT_{s1} + kT)|^2}{2\sigma_z^2} \tag{4.199}$$

which is independent of θ and hence can be taken outside the integral. Furthermore, for large values of L we can expect the summation in (4.199) to be independent of n as well. In fact for large values of L, the numerator in (4.199) approximates to:

$$\sum_{k=0}^{L-1} |\tilde{x}(nT_{s1} + kT)|^2 \approx L \times \text{the average received signal power.} \tag{4.200}$$

Moreover, if

$$|S_k|^2 = \text{a constant} = C \tag{4.201}$$

as in the case of M-ary PSK, then the problem in (4.198) simplifies to:

$$\max_{n} \frac{1}{2\pi} \int_{\theta=0}^{2\pi} \exp\left(\frac{2A \sum_{k=0}^{L-1} \Re\{\tilde{x}(nT_{s1} + +kT) S_k^* \mathrm{e}^{-\mathrm{j}\theta}\}}{2\sigma_z^2} \right) d\theta \tag{4.202}$$

which further simplifies to (refer to (2.153)):

$$\max_{n} \left| \sum_{k=1}^{L-1} \tilde{x}(nT_{s1} + kT) S_k^* \right|^2 \tag{4.203}$$

which is independent of A. At the correct sampling phase ($n = n_0$) the computation in (4.203) results in (assuming that $R_{pp}(0)/T_s = 1$):

$$\left| \sum_{k=0}^{L-1} (A|S_k|^2 \exp(j\theta) + \tilde{z}(n_0 T_{s1} + kT) S_k^*) \right|^2. \tag{4.204}$$

Since

$$E[|S_k|^2] \triangleq P_{\mathrm{av}} = C \tag{4.205}$$

the signal power in (4.204) is equal to $L^2 A^2 P_{\mathrm{av}}^2$ in two dimensions. The noise power in (4.204) is $2N_0 P_{\mathrm{av}} L$, also in two dimensions. Thus the SNR at the output of the timing recovery algorithm at the right sampling phase is

$$\text{SNR}_{\text{tim rec}} = \frac{P_{\text{av}} L A^2}{2N_0} \tag{4.206}$$

which increases linearly with the observation vector L. Therefore, we expect this method of timing recovery to perform well even at very low SNR at the sampler output (at the right timing phase). The SNR at the sampler output at the right timing phase is defined as (from(4.187)):

$$\text{SNR}_{\text{samp op}} = \frac{A^2 P_{\text{av}}}{2N_0}. \tag{4.207}$$

The SNR per bit is defined as:

$$E_b/N_0 = \frac{A^2 P_{\text{av}}}{4N_0}. \tag{4.208}$$

Once the timing is recovered, the signal model in (4.135) can be used to estimate the carrier phase and the gain A. In fact, one can immediately recognize that (4.204) is just the squared magnitude of (4.142), therefore θ can be estimated using (4.143). Finally, A is estimated as:

$$\hat{A} = (X + \text{j}Y)\text{e}^{-\text{j}\hat{\theta}}/LC \tag{4.209}$$

where $X + \text{j}Y$ is defined in (4.142) and C is defined in (4.201). It can be shown that when $\hat{\theta} = \theta$, then $E[\hat{A}] = A$ and the variance of $\hat{A}$ is:

$$\begin{aligned} \text{var}(\hat{A}) &= 2N_0 P_{\text{av}} L/(L^2 C^2) \\ &= 2N_0/(L P_{\text{av}}). \end{aligned} \tag{4.210}$$

Thus the variance of the estimate is inversely proportional to L.

4.2.5 Results for Synchronization

In this section we present some of the simulation results for carrier and timing synchronization[158]. Figure 4.23 shows the block diagram of the digital communication system under consideration. Observe that the channel is assumed to be essentially distortionless. Without loss of generality and for ease of simulation we set the channel delay $\tau = 0$. However, there is yet an overall system delay of $\mathcal{D}$ symbols due to the delay introduced by the transmit and the receive (matched) filter. Therefore, the detection delay is also $\mathcal{D}$ symbols. The symbols are uncoded and drawn from a QPSK constellation as depicted in Figure 4.23.

The input to the transmitter is a frame comprising of three components:

1. A known preamble of length L symbols. This is required for carrier and timing synchronization and AGC.
2. Data of length L_d symbols.
3. A postamble of length L_o symbols. For the purpose of simulation, it is convenient to have a postamble of length at least equal to the system delay, so that all the data symbols can be recovered.

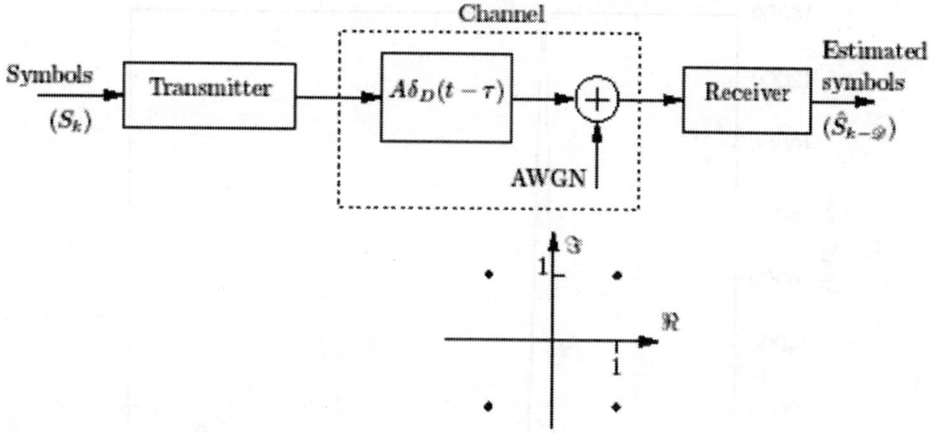

Figure 4.23 *Block diagram of the system*

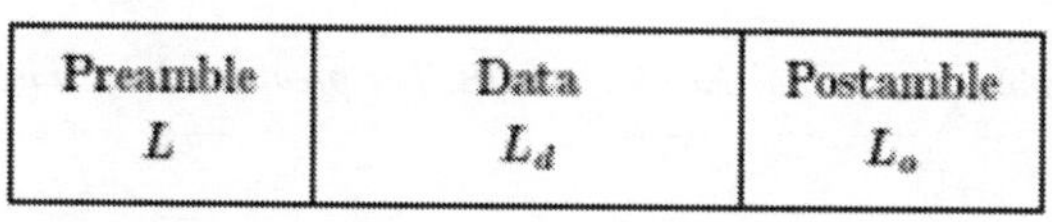

Figure 4.24 *The frame structure*

The burst structure is illustrated in Figure 4.24. Two options for the preamble length were considered, that is, $L = 64$ and $L = 128$ QPSK symbols. The datalength was taken to be $L_d = 1500$ QPSK symbols. The postamble length was fixed at 18 QPSK symbols. The channel gain A was set to unity and the average power of the QPSK constellation is $P_{\text{av}} = 2$. The transmit filter has a root-raised cosine spectrum with a roll-off equal to 0.41.

The first step in the burst acquisition system is to detect the preamble and the timing instant using (4.203). This is illustrated for two different preamble lengths in Figures 4.25 and 4.26 for an SNR of 0 dB at the sampler output.

The normalized (with respect to the symbol duration) variance of the timing error is depicted in Figure 4.27. In these plots, the timing phase α was set to zero to ensure that the correct timing instant n_0 is an integer. The expression for the normalized variance of the timing error is[158]

$$\sigma_\alpha^2 = E\left[\left(\frac{(n-n_0)T_{s1}}{T}\right)^2\right] = \frac{1}{16I^2}E[(n-n_0)^2] \tag{4.211}$$

where n_0 is the correct timing instant and n is the estimated timing instant. In practice, the expectation is replaced by a time-average.

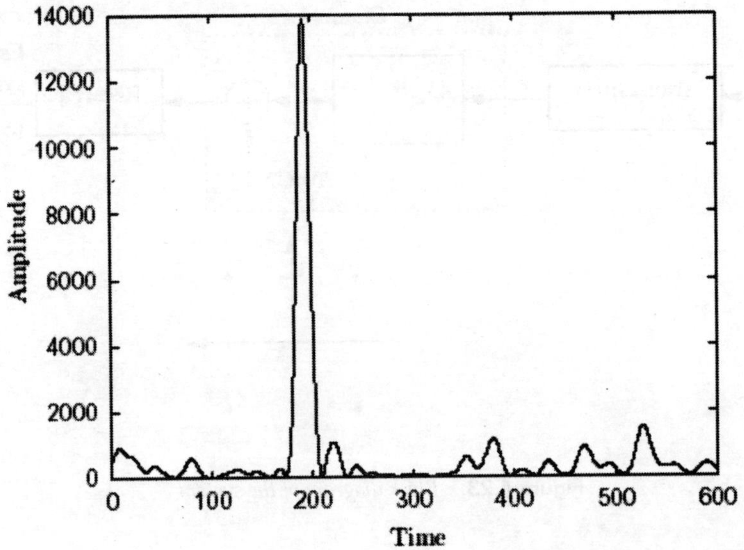

Figure 4.25 *Preamble detection at $E_b/N_0 = 0\,dB$. The preamble length is 64 QPSK symbols.*

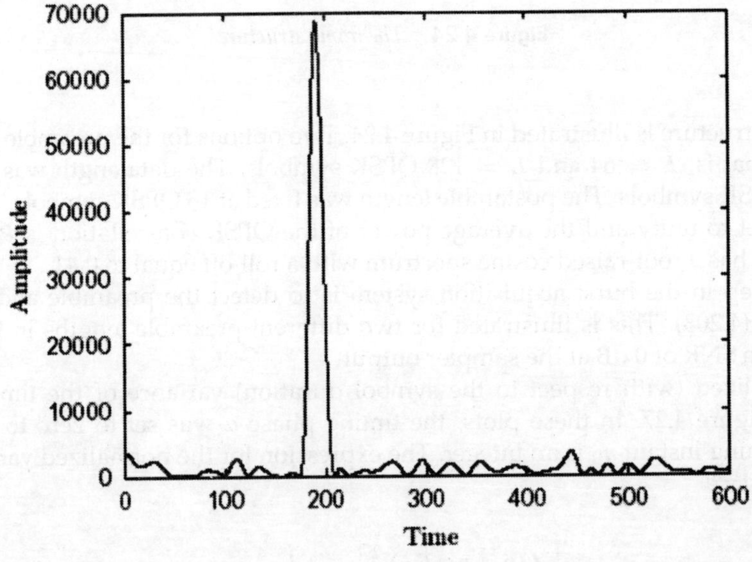

Figure 4.26 *Preamble detection at $E_b/N_0 = 0\,dB$. The preamble length is 128 QPSK symbols.*

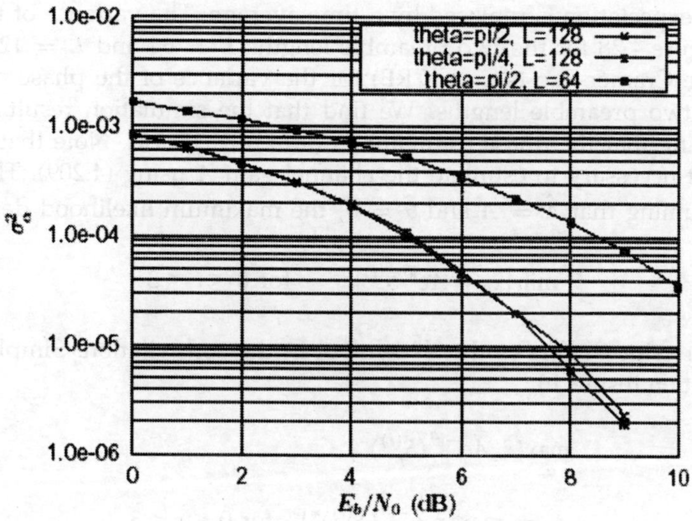

Figure 4.27 *Normalized variance of the timing error for two preamble lengths*

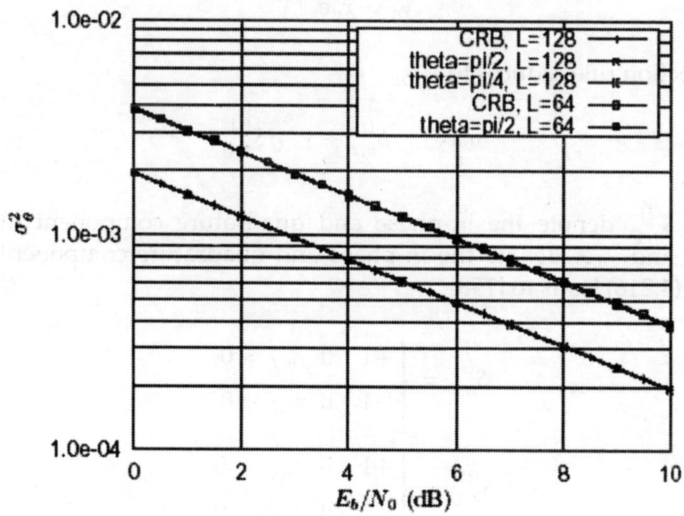

Figure 4.28 *Variance of the phase error for two preamble lengths*

The next step is to detect the carrier phase using (4.143). The variance of the phase error is given by[158]

$$\sigma_\theta^2 = E[(\theta = \hat{\theta})^2]. \tag{4.212}$$

In practice, the expectation is replaced by a time average. The variance of the phase error is plotted in Figure 4.28 for the two preamble lengths $L = 64$ and $L = 128$, for different values of θ. The Cramér-Rao bound (CRB) for the variance of the phase estimate is also plotted for the two preamble lengths. We find that the simulation results coincide with the CRB, implying that the phase estimator in (4.143) is *efficient*. Note that for QPSK signalling, it is not necessary to estimate the channel gain A using (4.209). The reasoning is as follows. Assuming that $\hat{A} = A$ and $\hat{\theta} = \theta$, the maximum likelihood detection rule for QPSK is:

$$\min_i |\tilde{x}_n - A\mathrm{e}^{\mathrm{j}\theta} S_n^{(i)}|^2 \qquad \text{for } 0 \le i \le 3 \tag{4.213}$$

where the superscript i refers to the ith symbol in the constellation. Simplification of the above minimization results in

$$\begin{aligned} &\max_i \{\tilde{x}_n A \mathrm{e}^{-\mathrm{j}\theta} (S_n^{(i)})^*\} \\ &\Rightarrow \max_i \{\tilde{x}_n \mathrm{e}^{-\mathrm{j}\theta} (S_n^{(i)})^*\} \quad \text{for } 0 \le i \le 3 \end{aligned} \tag{4.214}$$

which is independent of A. If we further define

$$\tilde{y}_n = \tilde{x}_n \mathrm{e}^{-\mathrm{j}\theta} \tag{4.215}$$

then the ML detection rule reduces to

$$\max_i y_{n,I} S_{n,I}^{(i)} + y_{n,Q} S_{n,Q}^{(i)} \tag{4.216}$$

where $S_{n,I}^{(i)}$ and $S_{n,Q}^{(i)}$ denote the in-phase and quadrature component of the ith QPSK symbol and $y_{n,I}$ and $y_{n,Q}$ denote the in-phase and quadrature component of $\tilde{y}_n$. Further simplification of (4.216) leads to [158]

$$\begin{aligned} S_{n,I}^{(i)} &= \begin{cases} +1 & \text{if } y_{n,I} > 0 \\ -1 & \text{if } y_{n,I} < 0 \end{cases} \\ S_{n,Q}^{(i)} &= \begin{cases} +1 & \text{if } y_{n,Q} > 0 \\ -1 & \text{if } y_{n,Q} < 0. \end{cases} \end{aligned} \tag{4.217}$$

Finally, the theoretical and simulated BER curves for uncoded QPSK is illustrated in Figure 4.29. In the case of random-phase and fixed-timing (RP-FT), θ was varied uniformly between $[0, 2\pi)$ from frame-to-frame (θ is fixed for each frame) and α is set to zero. In the case of random-phase and random-timing (RP-RT), α is also varied uniformly between $[0, T)$ for every frame (α is fixed for each frame). We find that the simulation results coincide with the theoretical results, indicating the accuracy of the carrier and timing recovery procedures.

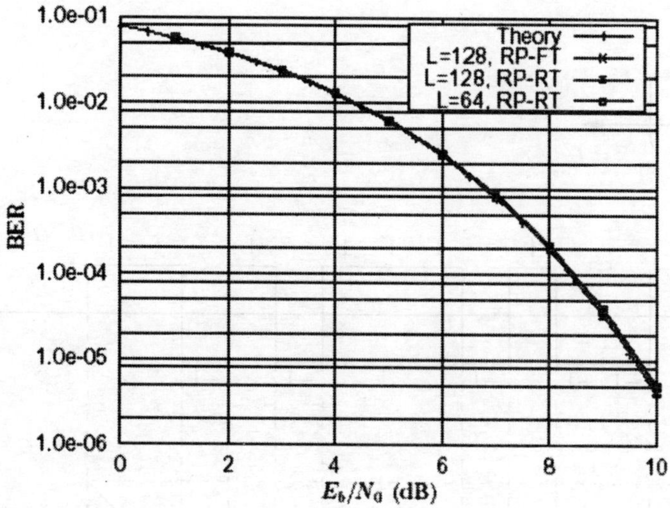

Figure 4.29 *Bit-error-rate performance of uncoded QPSK with carrier and timing recovery*

4.3 Nonlinear Modulation

In this section, we study various nonlinear modulation schemes that use coherent detection at the receiver. In particular, we concentrate on a class of nonlinear modulation schemes called continuous phase frequency modulation (CPFM). As the name suggests, the phase of the transmitted signal is continuous, and the instantaneous frequency of the transmitted signal is determined by the message signal. Frequency modulation can be done using a full response or a partial response transmit filter. Full response implies that the time span of the transmit filter is less than or equal to one symbol duration, whereas partial response implies that the time span of the transmit filter is greater than one symbol duration. Note that as in the case of linear modulation, the transmit filter controls the bandwidth of the transmitted signal.

4.3.1 CPFM with full response rectangular filters

In this section, we study two CPFM schemes that use full response rectangular (FRR) transmit filters. The first scheme uses strongly orthogonal signals while the second scheme uses weakly orthogonal signals. In the case of strongly orthogonal signals, the symbols can be *optimally* detected *without* using a phase trellis. In other words, symbol-by-symbol detection is optimal. In the case of weakly orthogonal signals, it is still possible to do symbol-by-symbol detection; however, this procedure is *suboptimal*. It is necessary to use the phase trellis for optimal detection.

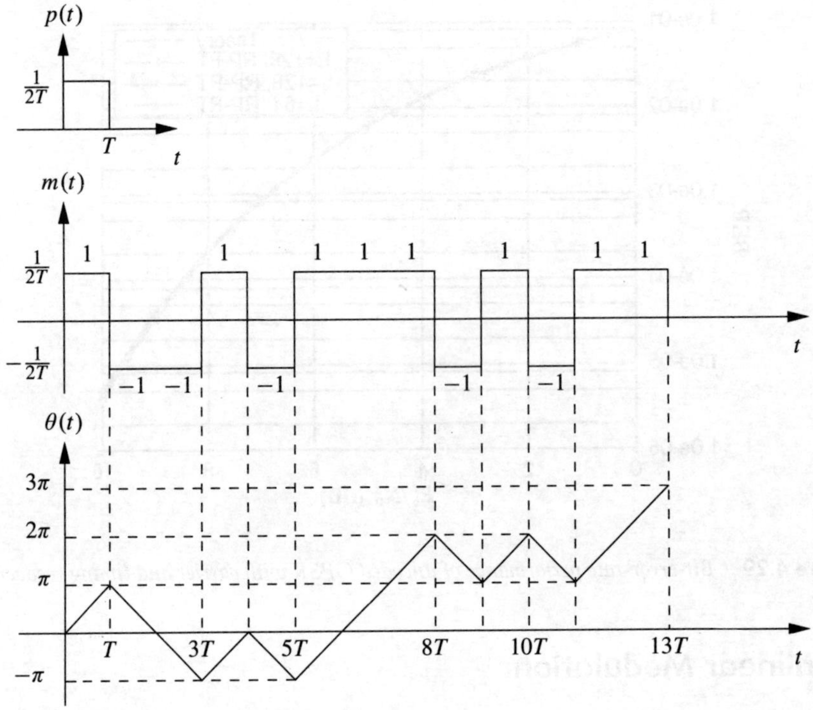

Figure 4.30 *Message and phase waveforms for a binary CPFM-FRR scheme. The initial phase θ_0 is assumed to be zero.*

Signalling with strongly orthogonal signals

Consider the message and phase waveforms in Figure 4.30. Note that $m(t)$ is real-valued and is in general given by

$$m(t) = h \sum_{k=-\infty}^{\infty} S_k p(t - kT) \tag{4.218}$$

where h denotes the modulation index, S_k is a real-valued symbol occurring at time k and drawn from an M-ary PAM constellation with points at ± 1, ± 3, ± 5 and so on, $p(t)$ is the impulse response of the transmit filter and T denotes the symbol duration. A symbol in an M-ary PAM constellation is given by $2i - M - 1$ for $1 \leq i \leq M$. In this section we set $h = 1$. As a convention, the area under the transmit filter is set to $1/2$, that is,

$$\int_{t=-\infty}^{\infty} p(t)\, dt = 1/2. \tag{4.219}$$

The maximum frequency deviation is given by

$$f_d = \max |m(t)|. \tag{4.220}$$

Observe that $m(t)$ is generated by exciting $p(t)$ by a Dirac delta train, which can be written as

$$s_1(t) = \sum_{k=-\infty}^{\infty} S_k \delta_D(t - kT). \tag{4.221}$$

In Figure 4.30, S_k is drawn from a 2-PAM constellation with points at ± 1 and $p(t)$ is a rectangular pulse given by

$$p(t) = \begin{cases} 1/(2T) & \text{for } 0 \le t \le T \\ 0 & \text{elsewhere} \end{cases} \tag{4.222}$$

as illustrated in Figure 4.30. It is clear that the maximum frequency deviation is $1/(2T)$. In general, for full response rectangular filters, the maximum frequency deviation is $h/(2T)$.

Note that when the time span of $p(t)$ is less than or equal to the symbol duration, it is referred to as *full response* signalling. When the time span of $p(t)$ is greater than the symbol duration, it is referred to as partial response signalling. We will refer to the scheme in Figure 4.30 as binary CPFM with full response rectangular pulse shape (CPFM-FRR).

In general for CPFM, the message and phase are related by

$$\theta(t) = 2\pi \int_{\tau=-\infty}^{t} m(\tau)\, dt. \tag{4.223}$$

For the case of M-ary CPFM-FRR with $p(t)$ given by (4.222), we have

$$\theta(t) = \frac{2\pi(2i - M - 1)t}{2T} \qquad \text{for } 1 \le i \le M \tag{4.224}$$

where we have assumed that $\theta(0) = 0$. Note that the phase is continuous. In the case of M-ary CPFM-FRR, the phase contributed by any symbol over the time interval T is equal to $(2m + 1)\pi$, where m is an integer. The variation in $\theta(t)$ can be represented by a phase trellis[2,160]. This is illustrated in Figure 4.31 for binary CPFM-FRR. The initial phase at time 0 is assumed to be zero. Note that the phase state is an even multiple of π (0 modulo-2π) for even time instants and an odd multiple of π (π modulo-2π) for odd time instants. It is clear that symbols 1 and -1 traverse the *same* path through the trellis. It is now easy to conclude that M-ary CPFM-FRR would also have two phase states (since all symbols contribute an odd multiple of π) and M parallel transitions between the states.

Consider the complex envelope:

$$\tilde{s}(t) = \frac{1}{\sqrt{T}} \exp\left(\mathrm{j}\,\theta(t)\right). \tag{4.225}$$

The factor $1/\sqrt{T}$ in the above equation ensures that $\tilde{s}(t)$ has unit energy over a symbol period (T seconds). Observe that the envelope of $\tilde{s}(t)$ in the above equation is a constant, that is

$$|\tilde{s}(t)| = \text{a constant}. \tag{4.226}$$

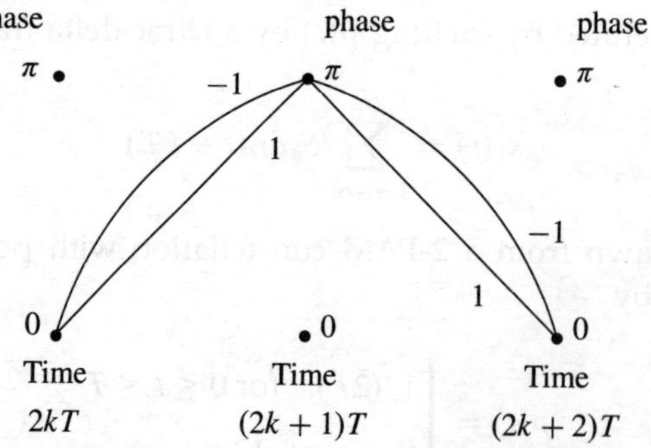

Figure 4.31 *Phase trellis for the binary CPFM-FRR scheme in Figure 4.30*

This is in contrast to the envelope of a linear modulation scheme where the envelope is *not* constant (refer to (4.3)).

For an M-ary CPFM-FRR modulation using the transmit filter in (4.222), the complex envelope corresponding to the ith symbol ($1 \le i \le M$) is given by

$$\tilde{s}(t) = \frac{1}{\sqrt{T}} \mathrm{e}^{\,\mathrm{j}\,2\pi(2i-M-1)t/(2T)}. \tag{4.227}$$

Two signals $\tilde{\beta}^{(i)}(t)$ and $\tilde{\beta}^{(j)}(t)$ are said to be *strongly* orthogonal over a time interval $[kT,\ (k+1)T]$ if

$$\int_{t=kT}^{(k+1)T} \tilde{\beta}^{(i)}(t) \left(\tilde{\beta}^{(j)}(t)\right)^* dt = \delta_K(i-j). \tag{4.228}$$

Two signals are weakly orthogonal in $[kT,\ (k+1)T]$ if

$$\Re\left\{\int_{t=kT}^{(k+1)T} \tilde{\beta}^{(i)}(t) \left(\tilde{\beta}^{(j)}(t)\right)^* dt\right\} = \delta_K(i-j). \tag{4.229}$$

Define

$$\tilde{\beta}^{(i)}(t,\ kT) = \begin{cases} \frac{1}{\sqrt{T}} \mathrm{e}^{\,\mathrm{j}\,2\pi(2i-M-1)t/(2T)} & \text{for } kT \le t \le (k+1)T \\ 0 & \text{elsewhere.} \end{cases} \tag{4.230}$$

From the above equation it is clear that $\tilde{\beta}^{(i)}(\cdot)$ and $\tilde{\beta}^{(j)}(\cdot)$ are strongly orthogonal over one symbol duration for $i \neq j$, and $1 \le i,\ j \le M$. Moreover, $\tilde{\beta}^{(i)}(\cdot)$ has unit energy for all i. Observe also that the phase of $\tilde{\beta}^{(i)}(\cdot)$ is 0 for even values of k and π for odd values of k, consistent with the trellis in Figure 4.31.

The transmitted signal is given by

$$\begin{aligned} s_p(t) &= \Re\{\tilde{s}(t)\exp(\mathrm{j}\,(2\pi F_c t + \theta_0))\} \\ &= \frac{1}{\sqrt{T}} \cos(2\pi F_c t + \theta(t) + \theta_0) \end{aligned} \tag{4.231}$$

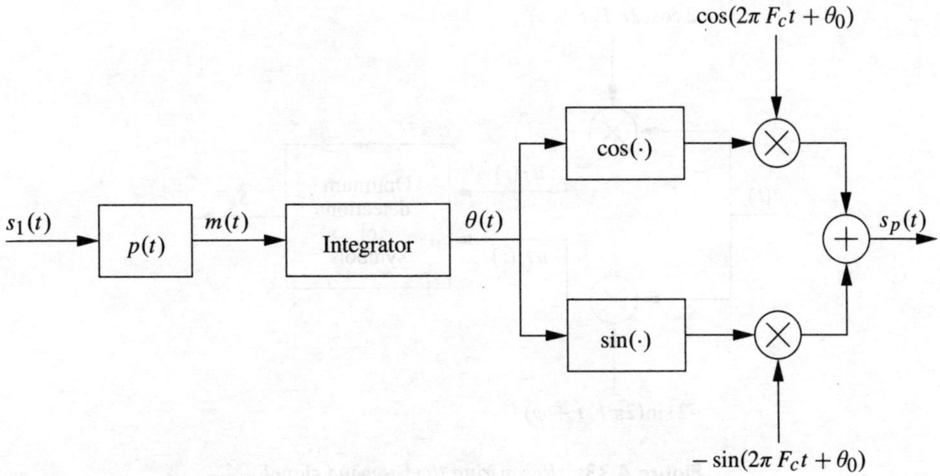

Figure 4.32 *Transmitter block diagram for CPFM schemes*

where F_c denotes the carrier frequency and θ_0 denotes the initial carrier phase at time $t = 0$. The transmitter block diagram is shown in Figure 4.32. Note that for M-ary CPFM-FRR with $h = 1$, there are M transmitted frequencies given by

$$F_c + \frac{2(2i - M - 1)}{2T} \quad \text{for } 1 \le i \le M. \tag{4.232}$$

Hence, this modulation scheme is commonly known as M-ary FSK.

The received signal is given by

$$r(t) = s_p(t) + w(t), \tag{4.233}$$

where $w(t)$ is AWGN with zero mean and psd $N_0/2$. The first task of the receiver is to recover the baseband signal. This is illustrated in Figure 4.33. The block labelled 'optimum detection of symbols' depends on the transmit filter $p(t)$ as will be seen later. The received complex baseband signal can be written as

$$\begin{aligned} \tilde{u}(t) &= \tilde{s}(t) \exp\left(\mathrm{j}\,(\theta_0 - \phi)\right) + \tilde{v}(t) + \tilde{d}(t) \\ &= \frac{1}{\sqrt{T}} \exp\left(\mathrm{j}\,(\theta(t) + \theta_0 - \phi)\right) + \tilde{v}(t) + \tilde{d}(t) \end{aligned} \tag{4.234}$$

where $\tilde{v}(t)$ is complex AWGN as defined in (4.50) and $\tilde{d}(t)$ denotes terms at twice the carrier frequency. The next step is to optimally detect the symbols from $\tilde{u}(t)$. Firstly, we assume that the detector is *coherent* and hence in (4.234) substitute $\theta_0 = \phi$. Let us assume that $\tilde{s}(t)$ extends over L symbols. The optimum detector (which is the maximum likelihood sequence

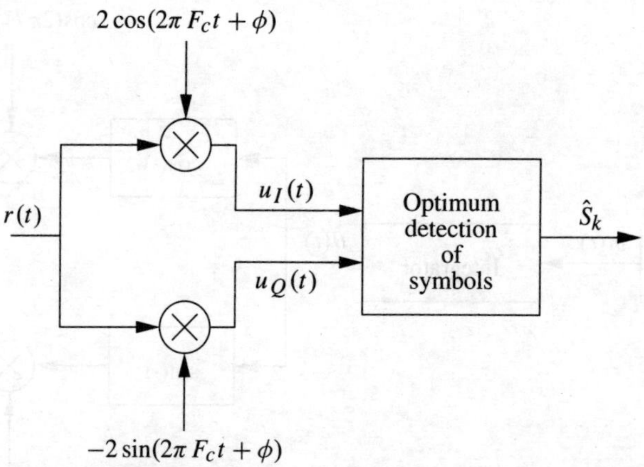

Figure 4.33 *Recovering the baseband signal*

detector) decides in favour of that sequence which is closest to the received sequence $\tilde{u}(t)$. Mathematically, this can be written as

$$\min_i \int_{t=0}^{LT} \left|\tilde{u}(t) - \tilde{s}^{(i)}(t)\right|^2 dt \qquad \text{for } 1 \le i \le M^L \tag{4.235}$$

where $\tilde{s}^{(i)}(t)$ denotes the complex envelope due to the ith possible symbol sequence. Note that the above equation also represents the squared Euclidean distance between two continuous-time signals. Note also that there are M^L possible sequences of length L. Expanding the integrand and noting that $|\tilde{u}(t)|^2$ is independent of i and $\left|\tilde{s}^{(i)}(t)\right|^2$ is a constant independent of i, and ignoring the constant 2, we get

$$\max_i \int_{t=0}^{LT} \Re\left\{\tilde{u}(t)\left(\tilde{s}^{(i)}(t)\right)^*\right\} dt \qquad \text{for } 1 \le i \le M^L. \tag{4.236}$$

Using the fact that the integral of the real part is equal to the real part of the integral, the above equation can be written as

$$\max_i \Re\left\{\int_{t=0}^{LT} \tilde{u}(t)\left(\tilde{s}^{(i)}(t)\right)^* dt\right\} \qquad \text{for } 1 \le i \le M^L. \tag{4.237}$$

The integral in the above equation can be immediately recognized as the convolution of $\tilde{u}(t)$ with $\left(\tilde{s}^{(i)}(LT - t)\right)^*$, evaluated at time LT. Moreover, since $\left(\tilde{s}^{(i)}(LT - t)\right)^*$ is a low-pass signal, it automatically eliminates the terms at twice the carrier frequency. Note that the above detection rule is valid for *any* CPFM signal and not just for CPFM-FRR schemes.

We also observe from the above equation that the complexity of the maximum likelihood (ML) detector increases exponentially with the sequence length, since it has to decide from amongst M^L sequences. The Viterbi algorithm (VA) is a practical way to implement the ML detector. The recursion for the VA is given by

$$\Re\left\{\int_{t=0}^{LT} \tilde{u}(t)\left(\tilde{s}^{(i)}(t)\right)^* dt\right\} = \Re\left\{\int_{t=0}^{(L-1)T} \tilde{u}(t)\left(\tilde{s}^{(i)}(t)\right)^* dt\right\} + \Re\left\{\int_{t=(L-1)T}^{LT} \tilde{u}(t)\left(\tilde{s}^{(i)}(t)\right)^* dt\right\}. \tag{4.238}$$

The first integral on the right-hand-side of the above equation represents the 'accumulated metric' whereas the second integral represents the 'branch metric'. Once again, the above recursion is valid for any CPFM scheme.

Let us now consider the particular case of M-ary CPFM-FRR scheme. We have already seen that the trellis contains two phase states and all the symbols traverse the same path through the trellis. Hence the VA reduces to a symbol-by-symbol detector and is given by

$$\max_m \Re\left\{\int_{t=(L-1)T}^{LT} \tilde{u}(t)\left(\tilde{\beta}^{(m)}(t,\ (L-1)T)\right)^* dt\right\} \qquad \text{for } 1 \le m \le M \tag{4.239}$$

where we have replaced $\tilde{s}^{(i)}(t)$ in the interval $[(L-1)T,\ LT]$ by $\tilde{\beta}^{(m)}(t,\ (L-1)T)$ which is defined in (4.230). Since (4.239) is valid for every symbol interval, it can be written as (for all integer k)

$$\max_m \Re\left\{\int_{t=kT}^{(k+1)T} \tilde{u}(t)\left(\tilde{\beta}^{(m)}(t,\ kT)\right)^* dt\right\} \qquad \text{for } 1 \le m \le M. \tag{4.240}$$

Note that since $\tilde{\beta}^{(m)}(\cdot)$ is a lowpass signal, the term corresponding to twice the carrier frequency is eliminated. Hence $\tilde{u}(t)$ can be effectively written as (in the interval $[kT,\ (k+1)T]$)

$$\tilde{u}(t) = \frac{1}{\sqrt{T}} \exp\left(\mathrm{j}\, 2\pi(2p - M - 1)t/(2T)\right) + \tilde{v}(t). \tag{4.241}$$

Substituting for $\tilde{u}(t)$ from the above equation and $\tilde{\beta}^{(m)}(\cdot)$ from (4.230) into (4.239), we get

$$\max_m x_m((k+1)T) = y_m((k+1)T) + z_{m,\,I}((k+1)T) \qquad \text{for } 1 \le m \le M \tag{4.242}$$

where

$$y_m((k+1)T) = \begin{cases} 1 & \text{for } m = p \\ 0 & \text{for } m \ne p \end{cases} \tag{4.243}$$

and

$$z_{m,\,I}((k+1)T) = \Re\left\{\int_{kT}^{(k+1)T} \tilde{v}(t)\left(\tilde{\beta}^{(m)}(t,\ kT)\right)^* dt\right\}. \tag{4.244}$$

Note that all the terms in (4.242) are real-valued. Since $\tilde{v}(t)$ is zero-mean, we have

$$E\left[z_{m,\,I}(iT)\right] = 0. \tag{4.245}$$

Let us define

$$\tilde{z}_m((k+1)T) = \int_{kT}^{(k+1)T} \tilde{v}(t) \left(\tilde{\beta}^{(m)}(t,\, kT)\right)^* \, dt$$
$$\stackrel{\Delta}{=} z_{m,\,I}((k+1)T) + \mathrm{j}\, z_{m,\,Q}((k+1)T). \tag{4.246}$$

Then, since $\tilde{v}(t)$ satisfies (4.53) and

$$\int_{-\infty}^{\infty} \tilde{\beta}^{(m)}(t,\, iT) \left(\tilde{\beta}^{(m)}(t,\, jT)\right)^* \, dt = \begin{cases} 1 & \text{for } i = j \\ 0 & \text{for } i \neq j \end{cases} \tag{4.247}$$

we have

$$E\left[\tilde{z}_m(iT)\tilde{z}_m^*(jT)\right] = \begin{cases} 0 & \text{for } i \neq j \\ 2N_0 & \text{for } i = j. \end{cases} \tag{4.248}$$

It can be shown that the in-phase and quadrature components of $\tilde{z}_m(iT)$ have the same variance, hence

$$E\left[z_{m,\,I}(iT) z_{m,\,I}(jT)\right] = \begin{cases} 0 & \text{for } i \neq j \\ N_0 & \text{for } i = j. \end{cases} \tag{4.249}$$

Similarly, it can be shown that

$$E\left[z_{m,\,I}(iT) z_{n,\,I}(iT)\right] = \begin{cases} 0 & \text{for } m \neq n \\ N_0 & \text{for } m = n. \end{cases} \tag{4.250}$$

Thus from (4.243) and (4.250), it is clear that the receiver 'sees' an M-ary multidimensional orthogonal constellation corrupted by AWGN. We can hence conclude that M-ary CPFM-FRR using strongly orthogonal signals is equivalent to M-ary multidimensional orthogonal signalling. The block diagram of the optimum detector for M-ary CPFM-FRR is shown in Figure 4.34.

Note that for the CPFM-FRR scheme considered in this section, the minimum frequency separation is $1/T$. In the next section, we show that by considering weakly orthogonal signals, the minimum frequency separation can be reduced to $1/(2T)$. Observe that the detection rule in (4.239) is such that it is sufficient to consider only weakly orthogonal signals.

Signalling with weakly orthogonal signals

In the case of weakly orthogonal signals, the modulation index is set to $1/2$ and the transmit filter is again given by

$$p(t) = \begin{cases} 1/(2T) & \text{for } 0 \le t \le T \\ 0 & \text{elsewhere.} \end{cases} \tag{4.251}$$

The maximum frequency deviation in this case is $1/(4T)$.

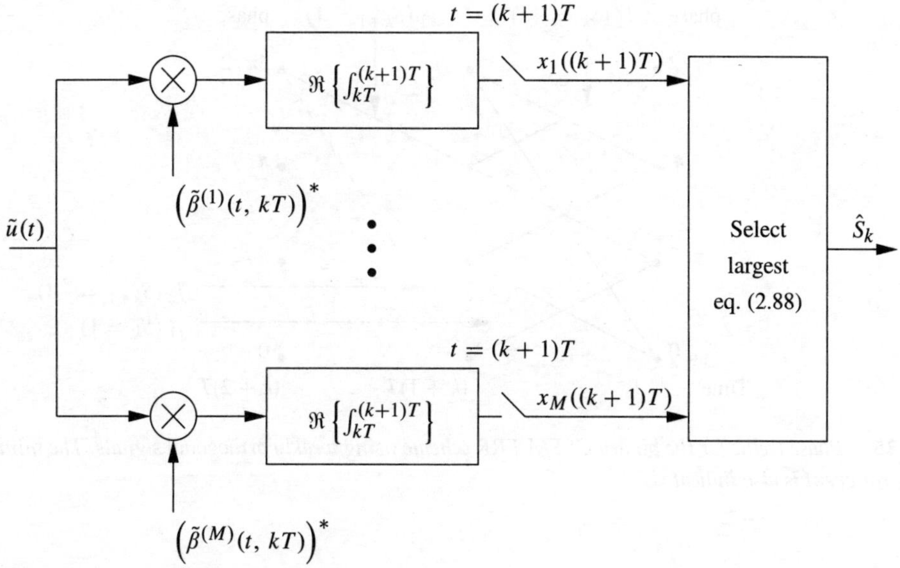

Figure 4.34 *Optimum detection of symbols for M-ary CPFM-FRR schemes using strongly orthogonal signals*

The symbols are once again drawn from an M-ary PAM constellation. The complex envelope of the transmitted signal corresponding to the ith symbol ($1 \le i \le M$) in the interval $[kT \le t \le (k+1)T]$ is given by

$$\tilde{\beta}^{(i)}(t, kT, \alpha_k) = \begin{cases} \frac{1}{\sqrt{T}} e^{\mathrm{j}\theta^{(i)}(t, kT, \alpha_k)} & \text{for } kT \le t \le (k+1)T \\ 0 & \text{elsewhere} \end{cases} \tag{4.252}$$

where

$$\theta^{(i)}(t, kT, \alpha_k) = \left(2\pi(2i - M - 1)(t - kT)\right)/(4T) + \alpha_k \tag{4.253}$$

and α_k is the initial phase at time kT. Note that the phase contributed by any symbol over a time interval T is either $\pi/2$ (modulo-2π) or $3\pi/2$ (modulo-2π). The phase trellis is given in Figure 4.35 for the particular case when $M = 2$. When $M > 2$, the phase trellis is similar, except that each transition now corresponds to $M/2$ parallel transitions.

Note also that the complex envelopes corresponding to distinct symbols are weakly orthogonal:

$$\Re\left\{\int_{t=kT}^{(k+1)T} \tilde{\beta}^{(i)}(t, kT, \alpha_k)\left(\tilde{\beta}^{(j)}(t, kT, \alpha_k)\right)^* dt\right\} = \delta_K(i - j). \tag{4.254}$$

The transmitted signal is given by (4.231) with

$$\tilde{s}(t) = \tilde{\beta}^{(i)}(t, kT, \alpha_k) \qquad \text{for } kT \le t \le (k+1)T \tag{4.255}$$

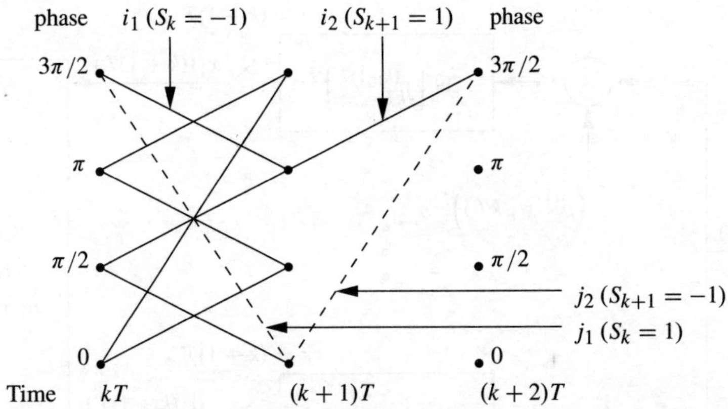

Figure 4.35 *Phase trellis for the binary CPFM-FRR scheme using weakly orthogonal signals. The minimum distance error event is also indicated.*

and the received signal is given by (4.233). Observe that the set of transmitted frequencies in the passband signal are given by

$$F_c + \frac{(2i - M - 1)}{4T}. \tag{4.256}$$

The complex baseband signal, $\tilde{u}(t)$, can be recovered using the procedure illustrated in Figure 4.33. The next step is to optimally recover the symbols from $\tilde{u}(t)$.

Observe that since the trellis in Figure 4.35 is non-trivial; the Viterbi algorithm (VA) with recursions similar to (4.238) needs to be used with the branch metrics given by (in the time interval $[kT,\ (k+1)T]$)

$$\Re\left\{\int_{t=kT}^{(k+1)T} \tilde{u}(t) \left(\tilde{\beta}^{(i)}(t,\ kT,\ \alpha_k)\right)^* dt\right\} \qquad \text{for } 1 \le i \le M. \tag{4.257}$$

Let us now compute the probability of the minimum distance error event. It is clear that when $M > 2$, the minimum distance is due to the parallel transitions. Note that when $M = 2$, there are *no* parallel transitions and the minimum distance is due to non-parallel transitions. Figure 4.35 shows the minimum distance error event corresponding to non-parallel transitions. The solid line denotes the transmitted sequence **i** and the dashed line denotes an erroneous sequence **j**. The branch metrics corresponding to the transitions in **i** and **j** are given by:

$$\begin{aligned} i_1 &: \quad 1 + w_{i_1, I} \\ i_2 &: \quad 1 + w_{i_2, I} \\ j_1 &: \quad w_{j_1, I} \\ j_2 &: \quad w_{j_2, I}. \end{aligned} \tag{4.258}$$

Once again, it can be shown that $w_{i_1,I}$, $w_{i_2,I}$, $w_{j_1,I}$ and $w_{j_2,I}$ are mutually uncorrelated with zero-mean and variance N_0. The VA makes an error when

$$\begin{aligned} 2 + w_{i_1,I} + w_{i_2,I} &< w_{j_1,I} + w_{j_2,I} \\ \Rightarrow 2 &< w_{j_1,I} + w_{j_2,I} - w_{i_1,I} - w_{i_2,I}. \end{aligned} \tag{4.259}$$

Let

$$Z = w_{j_1,I} + w_{j_2,I} - w_{i_1,I} - w_{i_2,I}. \tag{4.260}$$

It is clear that

$$\begin{aligned} E[Z] &= 0 \\ E\left[Z^2\right] &= 4N_0 \\ &= \sigma_Z^2 \quad \text{(say)}. \end{aligned} \tag{4.261}$$

Then the probability of minimum distance error event due to non-parallel transitions is given by

$$\begin{aligned} P(\mathbf{j}|\mathbf{i}) &= P(Z > 2) \\ &= \frac{1}{2}\operatorname{erfc}\left(\sqrt{\frac{1}{2N_0}}\right). \end{aligned} \tag{4.262}$$

When the sequences $\mathbf{i}$ and $\mathbf{j}$ correspond to parallel transitions, it can be shown that the probability of the error event is given by

$$P(\mathbf{j}|\mathbf{i}) = \frac{1}{2}\operatorname{erfc}\left(\sqrt{\frac{1}{4N_0}}\right) \tag{4.263}$$

which is 3 dB worse than (4.262). Hence we conclude that the average probability of symbol error when $M > 2$ is dominated by the error event due to parallel transitions. Moreover, since there are $M/2$ parallel transitions, the number of nearest neighbours with respect to the correct transition, is $(M/2) - 1$. Hence the average probability of symbol error when $M > 2$ is given by the union bound

$$P(e) \leq \left(\frac{M}{2} - 1\right)\frac{1}{2}\operatorname{erfc}\left(\sqrt{\frac{1}{4N_0}}\right). \tag{4.264}$$

When $M = 2$, there are no parallel transitions, and the average probability of symbol error is dominated by the minimum distance error event corresponding to non-parallel transitions, as illustrated in Figure 4.35. Moreover, the multiplicity at the minimum distance is one, that is, there is just one erroneous sequence which is at the minimum distance from the correct sequence. Observe also that the number of symbol errors corresponding to the error event is two. Hence, following the logic of (3.80), the average probability of symbol error when $M = 2$ is given by

$$
\begin{aligned}
P(e) &= \frac{2}{2} \operatorname{erfc}\left(\sqrt{\frac{1}{2N_0}}\right) \\
&= \operatorname{erfc}\left(\sqrt{\frac{1}{2N_0}}\right).
\end{aligned} \tag{4.265}
$$

The particular case of $M = 2$ is commonly called *minimum shift keying* (MSK) and the above expression gives the average probability of symbol (or bit) error for MSK.

4.4 Summary

This chapter dealt with the transmission of signals through a distortionless AWGN channel. In the case of linear modulation, the structure of the transmitter and the receiver in both continuous-time and discrete-time was discussed. A general expression for the power spectral density of linearly modulated signals was derived. The optimum receiver was shown to consist of a matched filter followed by a symbol-rate sampler. Pulse shapes that result in zero intersymbol interference (ISI) were given. In the context of discrete-time receiver implementation, the bandpass sampling theorem was discussed. Synchronization techniques for linearly modulated signals were explained.

In the case of non-linear modulation, we considered continuous phase frequency modulation with full response rectangular filters (CPFM-FRR). By changing the amplitude of the rectangular filters, we get either strongly orthogonal or weakly orthogonal signals. Minimum shift keying was shown to be a particular case of M-ary CPFM-FRR using weakly orthogonal signals.

5 Transmission of Signals Through Distorting Channels

This chapter is devoted to the study of different receiver implementations when the transmitted signal passes through a channel that introduces distortion and additive white Gaussian noise. We will consider only transmitted signals that are *linearly modulated;* signals that are nonlinearly modulated (e.g. CPM signals) are difficult to analyze when passed through a channel.

A channel is said to introduce distortion if its amplitude response is *not* flat and the phase response is *not* linear over the bandwidth of the transmitted signal. In this situation, due to the presence of *intersymbol interference* (ISI), the matched filter alone is no longer sufficient to recover the symbols.

There are three approaches to combat the effects of ISI:

(a) The first approach is to use an *equalizer* which minimizes the mean squared error between the desired symbol and the received symbol. There are two kinds of equalizers – *linear* and *nonlinear*. Linear equalizers can further be classified into symbol-spaced and fractionally-spaced equalizers. The decision-feedback equalizer falls in the category of nonlinear equalizers.

(b) The second approach is based on maximum likelihood (ML) detection which directly minimizes the symbol-error-rate for a given SNR.

(c) The third approach is multicarrier communication which is also known as orthogonal frequency division multiplexing (OFDM) or discrete multitone (DMT).

The block diagram of the digital communication system under study in this chapter is shown in Figure 5.1. We begin with the discussion on equalization. For the sake of simplicity,

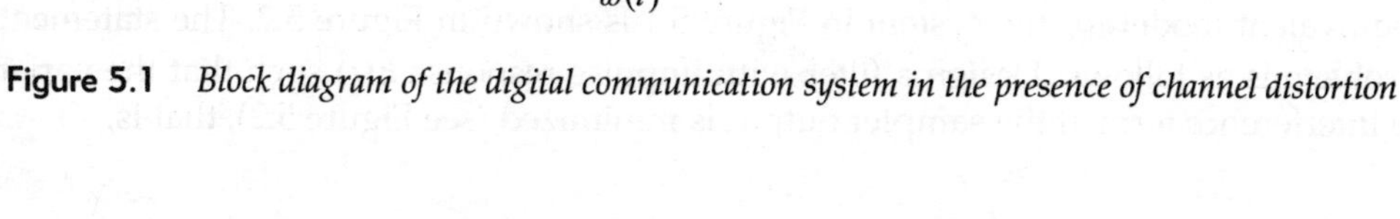

Figure 5.1 *Block diagram of the digital communication system in the presence of channel distortion*

we consider only the complex lowpass equivalent of the communication system. The justification for this approach is given in Appendix I.

5.1 Receivers Based on Equalization

The concept of equalization was first introduced by Lucky in [161]. A good tutorial on equalizer can be found in [162]. As discussed earlier, equalizers can be classified as linear and nonlinear. In the next section we take up linear equalization schemes.

5.1.1 Linear equalization – symbol-spaced equalizers

Let the complex lowpass equivalent of the transmitted signal be given by

$$\tilde{s}(t) = \sum_{k=-\infty}^{\infty} S_k\, \tilde{p}(t - kT - \alpha) \tag{5.1}$$

where S_k denotes a complex symbol drawn from an M-ary constellation occurring at time instant k, $\tilde{p}(t)$ denotes the complex-valued impulse response of the pulse shaping filter at the transmitter, α denotes the random timing phase uniformly distributed in $[0, T)$ and $1/T$ denotes the symbol-rate. The received signal is given by

$$\tilde{r}(t) = \tilde{s}(t) \star \tilde{c}(t) + \tilde{w}(t) \tag{5.2}$$

where $\star$ denotes convolution, $\tilde{c}(t)$ denotes the complex lowpass equivalent (complex envelope) of the channel[4] and $\tilde{w}(t)$ denotes a complex additive white Gaussian noise process with zero mean and autocorrelation given by (refer to (4.53))

$$R_{\tilde{w}\tilde{w}}(\tau) \stackrel{\Delta}{=} \frac{1}{2} E\left[\tilde{w}(t)\tilde{w}^*(t-\tau)\right] = N_0 \delta_D(\tau). \tag{5.3}$$

For convenience of presentation we assume that $\tilde{p}(t)$ and $\tilde{c}(t)$ are *non-causal* and hence extend from $-\infty$ to ∞. We also assume that $\tilde{p}(t)$ and $\tilde{c}(t)$ have finite energy, that is,

$$\begin{aligned} \int_{t=-\infty}^{\infty} |\tilde{p}(t)|^2 &= \text{a constant} \\ \int_{t=-\infty}^{\infty} |\tilde{c}(t)|^2 &= \text{a constant.} \end{aligned} \tag{5.4}$$

It is easy to see that (5.2) can be written as

$$\tilde{r}(t) = \sum_{k=-\infty}^{\infty} S_k\, \tilde{q}(t - kT) + \tilde{w}(t) \tag{5.5}$$

where

$$\tilde{q}(t) = \tilde{p}(t - \alpha) \star \tilde{c}(t). \tag{5.6}$$

The equivalent model for the system in Figure 5.1 is shown in Figure 5.2. The statement of the problem is as follows: Design a filter with impulse response $\tilde{h}(t)$ such that the variance of the interference term at the sampler output is minimized (see Figure 5.2), that is,

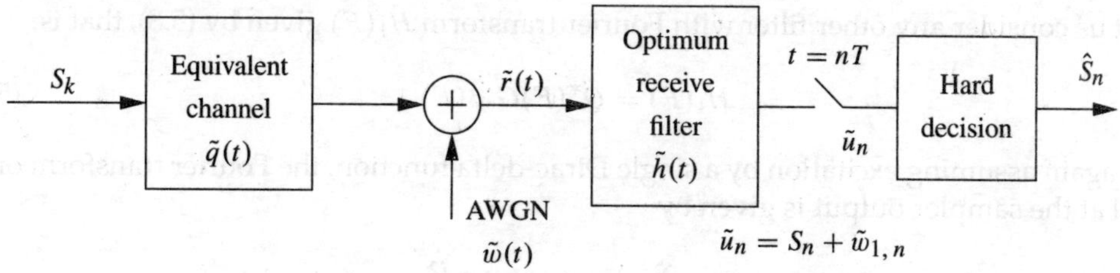

Figure 5.2 *Equivalent model for the digital communication system shown in Figure 5.1*

$$\text{minimize } E\left[\left|\tilde{w}_{1,n}\right|^2\right]. \tag{5.7}$$

The term $\tilde{w}_{1,n}$ denotes the combination of both Gaussian noise as well as residual intersymbol interference.

We will attempt to solve the above problem in two steps:

(a) Firstly design a filter, $\tilde{h}(t)$, such that the variance of the Gaussian noise component *alone* at the sampler output is minimized.

(b) In the second step, impose further constraints on $\tilde{h}(t)$ such that the variance of the interference, $\tilde{w}_{1,k}$, (this includes both Gaussian noise and intersymbol interference) at the sampler output is minimized.

We now show that the *unique* optimum filter that satisfies condition (a), has a frequency response of the type

$$\tilde{H}_{\text{opt}}(F) = \tilde{Q}^*(F)\tilde{G}_{\mathscr{P}}(F) \tag{5.8}$$

where $\tilde{Q}^*(F)$ denotes the complex conjugate of the Fourier transform of $\tilde{q}(t)$ (that is, $\tilde{Q}^*(F)$ is the Fourier transform of the filter *matched* to $\tilde{q}(t)$) and $\tilde{G}_{\mathscr{P}}(F)$ (the subscript $\mathscr{P}$ denotes 'periodic') is a *periodic* frequency response with period $1/T$, that is,

$$\tilde{G}_{\mathscr{P}}\left(F + \frac{k}{T}\right) = \tilde{G}_{\mathscr{P}}(F) \qquad \text{for all integer } k. \tag{5.9}$$

We prove the above result by contradiction[163].

Let $\tilde{H}(F)$ denote the Fourier transform of the optimum filter that satisfies condition (a). Let us also assume that the whole system in Figure 5.2 is excited by a single Dirac delta function. The Fourier transform of the signal component at the output of the sampler is given by

$$\tilde{Y}_{\mathscr{P},\tilde{H}}(F) = \frac{1}{T}\sum_{k=-\infty}^{\infty} \tilde{Q}\left(F - \frac{k}{T}\right)\tilde{H}\left(F - \frac{k}{T}\right). \tag{5.10}$$

The power spectral density of noise at the sampler output is given by

$$S_{\mathscr{P},\tilde{H}}(F) = \frac{N_0}{T}\sum_{k=-\infty}^{\infty}\left|\tilde{H}\left(F - \frac{k}{T}\right)\right|^2. \tag{5.11}$$

Observe that the power spectral density is real and that $S_{\mathscr{P},\tilde{H}}(F)$ is *not* the power spectral density of $\tilde{w}_{1,k}$.

Let us consider any other filter with Fourier transform $\tilde{H}_1(F)$ given by (5.8), that is,

$$\tilde{H}_1(F) = \tilde{Q}^*(F)\tilde{G}_{\mathscr{P}}(F). \tag{5.12}$$

Once again assuming excitation by a single Dirac-delta function, the Fourier transform of the signal at the sampler output is given by

$$\tilde{Y}_{\mathscr{P},\,\tilde{H}_1}(F) = \frac{1}{T}\sum_{k=-\infty}^{\infty}\left|\tilde{Q}\left(F-\frac{k}{T}\right)\right|^2 \tilde{G}_{\mathscr{P}}\left(F-\frac{k}{T}\right) \tag{5.13}$$

and the power spectral density of noise is given by

$$S_{\mathscr{P},\,\tilde{H}_1}(F) = \frac{N_0}{T}\sum_{k=-\infty}^{\infty}\left|\tilde{Q}\left(F-\frac{k}{T}\right)\right|^2 \left|\tilde{G}_{\mathscr{P}}\left(F-\frac{k}{T}\right)\right|^2. \tag{5.14}$$

Using the fact that $\tilde{G}_{\mathscr{P}}(F)$ is periodic with period $1/T$, (5.13) becomes

$$\tilde{Y}_{\mathscr{P},\,\tilde{H}_1}(F) = \frac{\tilde{G}_{\mathscr{P}}(F)}{T}\sum_{k=-\infty}^{\infty}\left|\tilde{Q}\left(F-\frac{k}{T}\right)\right|^2 \tag{5.15}$$

and (5.14) becomes

$$S_{\mathscr{P},\,\tilde{H}_1}(F) = \frac{N_0\left|\tilde{G}_{\mathscr{P}}(F)\right|^2}{T}\sum_{k=-\infty}^{\infty}\left|\tilde{Q}\left(F-\frac{k}{T}\right)\right|^2. \tag{5.16}$$

Now, if

$$\tilde{G}_{\mathscr{P}}(F) = \frac{\sum_{k=-\infty}^{\infty}\tilde{Q}\left(F-\frac{k}{T}\right)\tilde{H}\left(F-\frac{k}{T}\right)}{\sum_{k=-\infty}^{\infty}\left|\tilde{Q}\left(F-\frac{k}{T}\right)\right|^2} \tag{5.17}$$

then it is clear that

$$\tilde{Y}_{\mathscr{P},\,\tilde{H}_1}(F) = \tilde{Y}_{\mathscr{P},\,\tilde{H}}(F) \tag{5.18}$$

and

$$S_{\mathscr{P},\,\tilde{H}_1}(F) = \frac{N_0}{T}\frac{\left|\sum_{k=-\infty}^{\infty}\tilde{Q}\left(F-\frac{k}{T}\right)\tilde{H}\left(F-\frac{k}{T}\right)\right|^2}{\sum_{k=-\infty}^{\infty}\left|\tilde{Q}\left(F-\frac{k}{T}\right)\right|^2}. \tag{5.19}$$

We now invoke the Schwarz's inequality which states that

$$\left|\sum_{k=-\infty}^{\infty}\tilde{Q}\left(F-\frac{k}{T}\right)\tilde{H}\left(F-\frac{k}{T}\right)\right|^2 \le \left(\sum_{k=-\infty}^{\infty}\left|\tilde{Q}\left(F-\frac{k}{T}\right)\right|^2\right)\times\left(\sum_{k=-\infty}^{\infty}\left|\tilde{H}\left(F-\frac{k}{T}\right)\right|^2\right). \tag{5.20}$$

Thus from Schwarz's inequality we have,

$$S_{\mathscr{P},\tilde{H}_1}(F) \le \frac{N_0}{T} \sum_{k=-\infty}^{\infty} \left| \tilde{H}\left(F - \frac{k}{T}\right)\right|^2$$

$$\Rightarrow S_{\mathscr{P},\tilde{H}_1}(F) \le S_{\mathscr{P},\tilde{H}}(F). \tag{5.21}$$

The above equation implies that the noise variance at the output of the sampler due to $\tilde{H}_1(F)$ is *less* than that due to $\tilde{H}(F)$ since

$$\int_{F=-1/(2T)}^{+1/(2T)} S_{\mathscr{P},\tilde{H}_1}(F)\,dF \le \int_{F=-1/(2T)}^{+1/(2T)} S_{\mathscr{P},\tilde{H}}(F)\,dF. \tag{5.22}$$

Thus, we have found out a filter $\tilde{H}_1(F)$ that yields a lesser noise variance than $\tilde{H}(F)$ for the same signal power. However, this contradicts our original statement that $\tilde{H}(F)$ is the optimum filter. To conclude, given any filter $\tilde{H}(F)$, we can find out another filter $\tilde{H}_1(F)$ *in terms of* $\tilde{H}(F)$ that yields a *lower* noise variance than $\tilde{H}(F)$. It immediately follows that when $\tilde{H}(F)$ is optimum, $\tilde{H}_1(F)$ must be identical to $\tilde{H}(F)$.

The next question is: What is the optimum $\tilde{H}(F)$? Notice that the inequality in (5.20) becomes an equality only when

$$\tilde{H}(F) = \tilde{Q}^*(F)\tilde{J}_{\mathscr{P}}(F) \tag{5.23}$$

for some frequency response $\tilde{J}_{\mathscr{P}}(F)$ that is periodic with period $1/T$. Substituting the above equation in (5.17), we get

$$\tilde{G}_{\mathscr{P}}(F) = \tilde{J}_{\mathscr{P}}(F). \tag{5.24}$$

Thus we have proved that $\tilde{H}(F)$ and $\tilde{H}_1(F)$ are identical and correspond to the *unique* optimum filter given by (5.8).

An important consequence of the above proof is that we have found out a general expression for the filter frequency response which maximizes the signal-to-Gaussian noise ratio at the output of the sampler. In fact, the matched filter given by $\tilde{Q}^*(F)$ (see also (4.61)) is a particular case of (5.8) with $\tilde{G}_{\mathscr{P}}(F) = 1$. Having proved that

$$\tilde{H}_{\text{opt}}(F) = \tilde{Q}^*(F)\tilde{G}_{\mathscr{P}}(F) \tag{5.25}$$

we now have to find out the exact expression for $\tilde{G}_{\mathscr{P}}(F)$ that minimizes the variance of the combined effect of Gaussian noise as well as residual intersymbol interference. Note that since $\tilde{G}_{\mathscr{P}}(F)$ is periodic with period $1/T$, the cascade of $\tilde{G}_{\mathscr{P}}(F)$ followed by a rate-$1/T$ sampler can be replaced by a rate-$1/T$ sampler followed by a *discrete-time* filter whose frequency response is $\tilde{G}_{\mathscr{P}}(F)$. This is illustrated in Figure 5.3. Note that the input to the matched filter is given by (5.5), which is repeated here for convenience.

$$\tilde{r}(t) = \sum_{k=-\infty}^{\infty} S_k\,\tilde{q}(t - kT) + \tilde{w}(t). \tag{5.26}$$

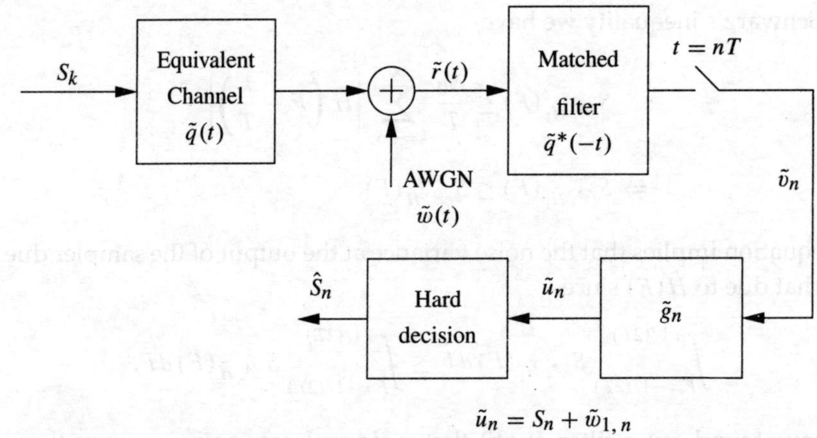

Figure 5.3 *Structure of the optimum receive filter*

The output of the matched filter is

$$\tilde{v}(t) = \sum_{k=-\infty}^{\infty} S_k \tilde{R}_{\tilde{q}\tilde{q}}(t - kT) + \tilde{w}_2(t) \tag{5.27}$$

where

$$\tilde{R}_{\tilde{q}\tilde{q}}(t) = \tilde{q}(t) \star \tilde{q}^*(-t)$$

$$\tilde{w}_2(t) = \tilde{w}(t) \star \tilde{q}^*(-t). \tag{5.28}$$

The signal at the output of the sampler is given by

$$\tilde{v}_n = \sum_{k=-\infty}^{\infty} S_k \tilde{R}_{\tilde{q}\tilde{q},\, n-k} + \tilde{w}_{2,\, n} \tag{5.29}$$

where $\tilde{R}_{\tilde{q}\tilde{q},\, k}$ denotes the sampled autocorrelation of $\tilde{q}(t)$ *with sampling phase equal to zero.* We will discuss the importance of zero sampling phase at a later stage. The discrete-time equivalent system at the sampler output is shown in Figure 5.4.

The autocorrelation of $\tilde{w}_{2,\, n}$ is given by

$$\begin{aligned}
\frac{1}{2} E\left[\tilde{w}_{2,\, n} \tilde{w}^*_{2,\, n-m}\right] &= \frac{1}{2} E\left[\int_{x=-\infty}^{\infty} \tilde{q}^*(x - nT)\tilde{w}(x)\, dx \times \int_{y=-\infty}^{\infty} \tilde{q}(y - nT + mT)\tilde{w}^*(y)\, dy\right] \\
&= N_0 \tilde{R}_{\tilde{q}\tilde{q}}(mT) \\
&\stackrel{\Delta}{=} N_0 \tilde{R}_{\tilde{q}\tilde{q},\, m}.
\end{aligned} \tag{5.30}$$

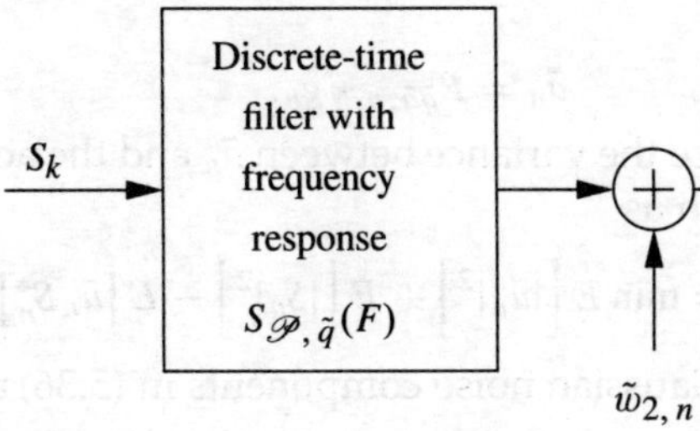

Figure 5.4 *The discrete-time equivalent system at the output of the sampler in Figure 5.3*

The (periodic) power spectral density of $\tilde{w}_{2,n}$ is given by

$$\begin{aligned} S_{\mathscr{P},\tilde{w}_2}(F) &\stackrel{\Delta}{=} N_0 \sum_{m=-\infty}^{\infty} \tilde{R}_{\tilde{q}\tilde{q},m} \exp(-\mathrm{j}2\pi F m T) \\ &= \frac{N_0}{T} \sum_{m=-\infty}^{\infty} \left| \tilde{Q}\left(F - \frac{m}{T}\right) \right|^2 \end{aligned} \tag{5.31}$$

where $\tilde{Q}(F)$ is the Fourier transform of $\tilde{q}(t)$. Define

$$S_{\mathscr{P},\tilde{q}}(F) \stackrel{\Delta}{=} \frac{1}{T} \sum_{m=-\infty}^{\infty} \left| \tilde{Q}\left(F - \frac{m}{T}\right) \right|^2. \tag{5.32}$$

Then (5.31) becomes

$$S_{\mathscr{P},\tilde{w}_2}(F) \stackrel{\Delta}{=} N_0 S_{\mathscr{P},\tilde{q}}(F). \tag{5.33}$$

Note that the condition of zero intersymbol interference is

$$\tilde{R}_{\tilde{q}\tilde{q},k} = \delta_K(k). \tag{5.34}$$

The above condition also implies that $\tilde{w}_{2,k}$ is uncorrelated.

Let $\tilde{g}_n$ denote the discrete-time impulse response corresponding to the periodic spectrum, $\tilde{G}_{\mathscr{P}}(F)$. Note that

$$G_{\mathscr{P}}(F) \stackrel{\Delta}{=} \sum_{n=-\infty}^{\infty} \tilde{g}_n \exp(-\mathrm{j}2\pi F n T). \tag{5.35}$$

The output of $\tilde{g}_n$ is given by

$$\begin{aligned} \tilde{u}_n &= \tilde{v}_n \star \tilde{g}_n \\ &= \sum_{k=-\infty}^{\infty} S_k \tilde{a}_{n-k} + \sum_{k=-\infty}^{\infty} \tilde{g}_k \tilde{w}_{2,n-k} \end{aligned} \tag{5.36}$$

where

$$\tilde{a}_n = \tilde{R}_{\tilde{q}\tilde{q},n} \star \tilde{g}_n. \tag{5.37}$$

Our objective now is to minimize the variance between $\tilde{u}_n$ and the actual transmitted symbol S_n (see (5.7)). This can be written as

$$\min E\left[|\tilde{u}_n - S_n|^2\right] = \min E\left[|\tilde{u}_n|^2\right] + E\left[|S_n|^2\right] - E\left[\tilde{u}_n S_n^*\right] - E\left[\tilde{u}_n^* S_n\right]. \tag{5.38}$$

Assuming that the signal and Gaussian noise components in (5.36) are statistically independent, we get

$$E\left[|\tilde{u}_n|^2\right] = P_{\text{av}} \sum_{k=-\infty}^{\infty} |\tilde{a}_k|^2 + 2N_0 T \int_{F=-1/(2T)}^{1/(2T)} S_{\mathscr{P},\tilde{q}}(F) \left|\tilde{G}_{\mathscr{P}}(F)\right|^2 dF \tag{5.39}$$

where $S_{\mathscr{P},\tilde{q}}(F)$ is given by (5.32), $\tilde{G}_{\mathscr{P}}(F)$ is given by (5.35) and we have made use of the fact that the symbols are uncorrelated, that is,

$$E\left[S_k S_j^*\right] = P_{\text{av}} \delta_K(k-j). \tag{5.40}$$

Note that the second term on the right-hand side of (5.39) is obtained by by using the the fact that the noise variance is equal to the inverse discrete-time Fourier transform (see (E.14)) of the power spectral density evaluated at time zero. We now use the *Parseval's* theorem which states that

$$\sum_{k=-\infty}^{\infty} |\tilde{a}_k|^2 = T \int_{F=-1/(2T)}^{1/(2T)} \left|\tilde{A}_{\mathscr{P}}(F)\right|^2 dF \tag{5.41}$$

where we once again note that the left-hand side of the above equation corresponds to the autocorrelation of $\tilde{a}_k$ at zero lag, which is nothing but the inverse Fourier transform of the power spectral density evaluated at time zero (note the factor T which follows from (E.14)). Note also that

$$\begin{aligned} \tilde{A}_{\mathscr{P}}(F) &\stackrel{\Delta}{=} \sum_{k=-\infty}^{\infty} \tilde{a}_k \exp(-\mathrm{j}2\pi FkT) \\ &= S_{\mathscr{P},\tilde{q}}(F)\tilde{G}_{\mathscr{P}}(F). \end{aligned} \tag{5.42}$$

Using (5.40) it can be shown that

$$\begin{aligned} E\left[|S_n|^2\right] &= P_{\text{av}} \\ E\left[\tilde{u}_n S_n^*\right] &= \tilde{a}_0 P_{\text{av}} \\ &= P_{\text{av}} T \int_{F=-1/(2T)}^{1/(2T)} S_{\mathscr{P},\tilde{q}}(F)\tilde{G}_{\mathscr{P}}(F)\, dF \\ E\left[\tilde{u}_n^* S_n\right] &= \tilde{a}_0^* P_{\text{av}} \\ &= P_{\text{av}} T \int_{F=-1/(2T)}^{1/(2T)} S_{\mathscr{P},\tilde{q}}(F)\tilde{G}_{\mathscr{P}}^*(F)\, dF. \end{aligned} \tag{5.43}$$

Thus we have[162]

$$E\left[|\tilde{u}_n - S_n|^2\right] = T\int_{F=-1/(2T)}^{1/(2T)} \left[P_{\text{av}}\left|1 - S_{\mathscr{P},\tilde{q}}(F)\tilde{G}_{\mathscr{P}}(F)\right|^2 + 2N_0 S_{\mathscr{P},\tilde{q}}(F)\left|\tilde{G}_{\mathscr{P}}(F)\right|^2\right] dF. \tag{5.44}$$

Since the integrand in the above equation is real and non-negative, minimizing the integral is equivalent to minimizing the integrand. Hence, ignoring the factor T, we get

$$\min E\left[|\tilde{u}_n - S_n|^2\right]$$

$$\Rightarrow \min\left[P_{\text{av}}\left|1 - S_{\mathscr{P},\tilde{q}}(F)\tilde{G}_{\mathscr{P}}(F)\right|^2 + 2N_0 S_{\mathscr{P},\tilde{q}}(F)\left|\tilde{G}_{\mathscr{P}}(F)\right|^2\right]. \tag{5.45}$$

Differentiating the above expression with respect to $\tilde{G}^*_{\mathscr{P}}(F)$ (see Appendix A) and setting the result to zero, we get the solution for the *symbol-spaced, minimum mean squared error* (MMSE) equalizer as

$$\tilde{G}_{\mathscr{P},\,\text{opt, MMSE}}(F) = \frac{P_{\text{av}}}{P_{\text{av}} S_{\mathscr{P},\tilde{q}}(F) + 2N_0} \qquad \text{for } -1/(2T) \le F \le 1/(2T). \tag{5.46}$$

Substituting the above expression in (5.44), we obtain the expression for the minimum variance of $\tilde{w}_{1,k}$ as

$$\begin{aligned}\min E\left[\left|\tilde{w}_{1,k}\right|^2\right] &= \int_{F=-1/(2T)}^{1/(2T)} \frac{N_0 P_{\text{av}} T}{P_{\text{av}} S_{\mathscr{P},\tilde{q}}(F) + 2N_0}\, dF \\ &= \mathscr{J}_{\text{MMSE}}(\text{linear}) \qquad (\text{say})\end{aligned} \tag{5.47}$$

where $\mathscr{J}_{\text{MMSE}}(\text{linear})$ denotes the minimum mean squared error that is achieveable by a linear equalizer. (At a later stage we show that a fractionally-spaced equalizer also achieves the same MMSE). Note that since $\tilde{w}_{1,k}$ consists of both Gaussian noise and residual ISI, the pdf of $\tilde{w}_{1,k}$ is *not* Gaussian.

We have thus obtained the complete solution for detecting symbols at the receiver with the minimum possible error that can be achieved with equalization (henceforth we will differentiate between the matched filter, $\tilde{Q}^*(F)$ and the equalizer, $\tilde{G}_{\mathscr{P}}(F)$). We emphasize at this point that equalization is by no means the best approach to detect symbols in the presence of ISI.

It is also possible to compute the expression for a *zero-forcing* (ZF) equalizer. A ZF equalizer by definition, ensures that the ISI at its output is zero. It is easy to see that

$$\tilde{G}_{\mathscr{P},\,\text{opt, ZF}}(F) = \frac{1}{S_{\mathscr{P},\tilde{q}}(F)} \qquad \text{for } -1/(2T) \le F \le 1/(2T) \tag{5.48}$$

and the noise variance at its output is

$$\begin{aligned}E\left[\left|\tilde{w}_{1,k}\right|^2\right] &= \int_{F=-1/(2T)}^{1/(2T)} \frac{2N_0 T}{S_{\mathscr{P},\tilde{q}}(F)}\, dF \\ &= \mathscr{J}_{\text{ZF}}(\text{linear}) \qquad (\text{say}).\end{aligned} \tag{5.49}$$

Note that in the case of a ZF equalizer, $\tilde{w}_{1,\,k}$ consists of only Gaussian noise (since ISI is zero) with variance given by the above equation. Note that

$$\mathscr{J}_{\text{ZF}}(\text{linear}) > \mathscr{J}_{\text{MMSE}}(\text{linear}). \tag{5.50}$$

In the next section we discuss some of the issues related to implementation of the equalizer.

5.1.2 Finite length equalizer

In the previous section we derived the frequency response of the optimum MMSE equalizer. In general, such an equalizer would have an infinite time-span. In practice however, we have to deal with a finite length equalizer. This section is devoted to the implementation of an optimum finite length equalizer and the study of its convergence properties. Note that an optimum finite length equalizer is inferior to an optimum infinite length equalizer.

Let $\tilde{g}_n$ denote the impulse response of the equalizer spanning over L symbols. Let $\tilde{v}_n$ denote the input to the equalizer (see (5.29)) and let $\tilde{u}_n$ denote the equalizer output (see (5.36)). Then we have

$$\tilde{u}_n = \sum_{k=0}^{L-1} \tilde{g}_k \tilde{v}_{n-k} \tag{5.51}$$

Let S_n denote the desired symbol at time n. The optimum equalizer taps must be chosen such that the error variance is minimized, that is,

$$\min E\left[|\tilde{e}_n|^2\right] \tag{5.52}$$

where

$$\begin{aligned}\tilde{e}_n &\stackrel{\Delta}{=} S_n - \tilde{u}_n \\ &= S_n - \sum_{k=0}^{L-1} \tilde{g}_k \tilde{v}_{n-k}.\end{aligned} \tag{5.53}$$

To find out the optimum tap weights, we need to compute the gradient with respect to each of the tap weights and set the result to zero. Thus we have (see Appendix A)

$$\frac{\partial E\left[|\tilde{e}_n|^2\right]}{\partial \tilde{g}_j^*} = 0 \qquad \text{for } 0 \le j \le L-1. \tag{5.54}$$

Interchanging the order of the expectation and the partial derivative, we get

$$E\left[\tilde{v}_{n-j}^* \tilde{e}_n\right] = 0 \qquad \text{for } 0 \le j \le L-1. \tag{5.55}$$

The above condition is called the *principle of orthogonality*, which states the following: if the mean-squared estimation error at the equalizer output is to be minimized, then the estimation error at time n must be orthogonal to all the input samples that are involved in the estimation process at time n. Substituting for $\tilde{e}_n$ from (5.53) and ignoring the factor -2, we get

$$E\left[\tilde{v}_{n-j}^* S_n\right] = \sum_{k=0}^{L-1} \tilde{g}_k^* E\left[\tilde{v}_{n-j}^* \tilde{v}_{n-k}\right] \qquad \text{for } 0 \leq j \leq L-1. \tag{5.56}$$

Substituting for $\tilde{v}_{n-j}$ from (5.29) and using the fact that the symbols are uncorrelated (see (5.40)), we get

$$E\left[\tilde{v}_{n-j}^* S_n\right] = \sum_{k=0}^{L-1} \tilde{g}_k E\left[\tilde{v}_{n-j}^* \tilde{v}_{n-k}\right]$$

$$\Rightarrow \frac{P_{\text{av}}}{2} \tilde{R}_{\tilde{q}\tilde{q},\,-j}^* = \sum_{k=0}^{L-1} \tilde{g}_k \tilde{R}_{\tilde{v}\tilde{v},\,j-k} \qquad \text{for } 0 \leq j \leq L-1, \tag{5.57}$$

where

$$\begin{aligned} E\left[\tilde{v}_{n-j}^* \tilde{v}_{n-k}\right] \stackrel{\Delta}{=} 2\tilde{R}_{\tilde{v}\tilde{v},\,j-k} &= P_{\text{av}} \sum_{l=-\infty}^{\infty} \tilde{R}_{\tilde{q}\tilde{q},\,n-j-l}^* \tilde{R}_{\tilde{q}\tilde{q},\,n-k-l} + 2N_0 \tilde{R}_{\tilde{q}\tilde{q},\,j-k} \\ &= P_{\text{av}} \sum_{i=-\infty}^{\infty} \tilde{R}_{\tilde{q}\tilde{q},\,i} \tilde{R}_{\tilde{q}\tilde{q},\,i+k-j}^* + 2N_0 \tilde{R}_{\tilde{q}\tilde{q},\,j-k}. \end{aligned} \tag{5.58}$$

We can rewrite (5.57) in the form of a set of linear equations as follows:

$$\begin{bmatrix} \tilde{R}_{\tilde{v}\tilde{v},\,0} & \tilde{R}_{\tilde{v}\tilde{v},\,-1} & \cdots & \tilde{R}_{\tilde{v}\tilde{v},\,-L+1} \\ \tilde{R}_{\tilde{v}\tilde{v},\,1} & \tilde{R}_{\tilde{v}\tilde{v},\,0} & \cdots & \tilde{R}_{\tilde{v}\tilde{v},\,-L+2} \\ \vdots & \vdots & \vdots & \vdots \\ \tilde{R}_{\tilde{v}\tilde{v},\,L-1} & \tilde{R}_{\tilde{v}\tilde{v},\,L-2} & \cdots & \tilde{R}_{\tilde{v}\tilde{v},\,0} \end{bmatrix} \begin{bmatrix} \tilde{g}_0 \\ \tilde{g}_1 \\ \vdots \\ \tilde{g}_{L-1} \end{bmatrix} = P_{\text{av},\,1} \begin{bmatrix} \tilde{R}_{\tilde{q}\tilde{q},\,0} \\ \tilde{R}_{\tilde{q}\tilde{q},\,1} \\ \vdots \\ \tilde{R}_{\tilde{q}\tilde{q},\,L-1} \end{bmatrix} \tag{5.59}$$

where on the right-hand side of the above equation we have used the fact that

$$\tilde{R}_{\tilde{q}\tilde{q},\,-m}^* = \tilde{R}_{\tilde{q}\tilde{q},\,m}$$

$$P_{\text{av},\,1} = \frac{P_{\text{av}}}{2}. \tag{5.60}$$

The above system of equations can be written more compactly in matrix form:

$$\tilde{\mathbf{R}}_{\tilde{v}\tilde{v}}\tilde{\mathbf{g}} = P_{\text{av},\,1}\tilde{\mathbf{R}}_{\tilde{q}\tilde{q}}. \tag{5.61}$$

The solution for the optimum tap weights for the finite length equalizer is obviously

$$\tilde{\mathbf{g}}_{\text{opt, FL}} = P_{\text{av},\,1}\tilde{\mathbf{R}}_{\tilde{v}\tilde{v}}^{-1}\tilde{\mathbf{R}}_{\tilde{q}\tilde{q}}, \tag{5.62}$$

where the subscript "FL" denotes finite length. The minimum mean-squared error corresponding to the optimum tap weights is given by

$$
\begin{aligned}
E\left[\tilde{e}_n\tilde{e}_n^*\right] &= E\left[\left(S_n^* - \sum_{k=0}^{L-1}\tilde{g}_k^*\tilde{v}_{n-k}^*\right)\tilde{e}_n\right] \\
&= E\left[S_n^*\tilde{e}_n\right] \qquad (5.63)
\end{aligned}
$$

where we have made use of (5.55). Substituting for $\tilde{e}_n$ in the above equation, we have

$$
\begin{aligned}
E\left[\tilde{e}_n\tilde{e}_n^*\right] &= E\left[S_n^*\left(S_n - \sum_{k=0}^{L-1}\tilde{g}_k\tilde{v}_{n-k}\right)\right] \\
&= P_{\text{av}} - P_{\text{av}}\sum_{k=0}^{L-1}\tilde{g}_k\tilde{R}_{\tilde{q}\tilde{q},\,-k} \\
&= P_{\text{av}}\left(1 - \tilde{\mathbf{g}}_{\text{opt, FL}}^{\text{T}}\tilde{\mathbf{R}}_{\tilde{q}\tilde{q}}^*\right) \\
&= P_{\text{av}}\left(1 - \tilde{\mathbf{g}}_{\text{opt, FL}}^{\text{H}}\tilde{\mathbf{R}}_{\tilde{q}\tilde{q}}\right) \\
&= P_{\text{av}}\left(1 - P_{\text{av}}\tilde{\mathbf{R}}_{\tilde{q}\tilde{q}}^{\text{H}}\tilde{\mathbf{R}}_{\tilde{v}\tilde{v}}^{-1}\tilde{\mathbf{R}}_{\tilde{q}\tilde{q}}\right) \\
&= \mathscr{J}_{\text{MMSE}}(\text{linear, FL}) \quad \text{(say)} \qquad (5.64)
\end{aligned}
$$

where we have used the fact that the mean-squared error is real and $\tilde{\mathbf{R}}_{\tilde{v}\tilde{v}}$ is *Hermitian*, that is,

$$
\tilde{\mathbf{R}}_{\tilde{v}\tilde{v}}^{H} = \tilde{\mathbf{R}}_{\tilde{v}\tilde{v}}. \qquad (5.65)
$$

The superscript H denotes Hermitian (transpose conjugate) and the superscript T denotes transpose.

Example 5.1.1 Consider the communication system shown in Figure 5.5. The symbols S_n are independent and equally likely and drawn from a BPSK constellation with amplitude ± 2. The channel output can be written as

$$
v_n = S_n h_0 + S_{n-1}h_1 + w_n \qquad (5.66)
$$

where h_n is real-valued, and w_n denotes discrete-time, zero-mean real-valued AWGN with variance σ_w^2. The equalizer output can be written as

$$
u_n = v_n g_0 + v_{n-1}g_1. \qquad (5.67)
$$

1. Compute the optimum linear MMSE equalizer coefficients (g_0 and g_1) in terms of h_n and σ_w^2.
2. Compute the MMSE in terms of h_n and σ_w^2.

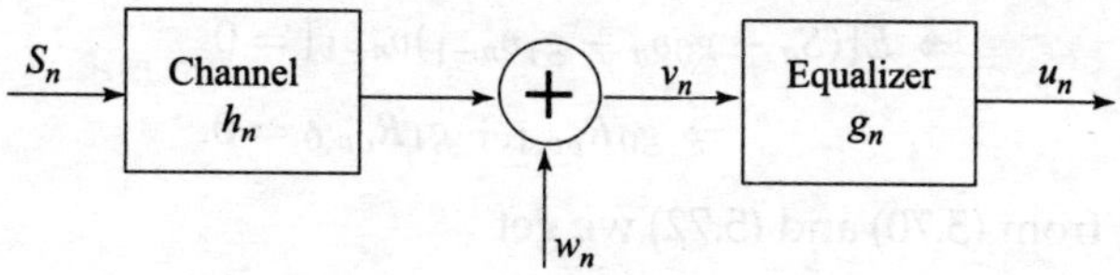

Figure 5.5 *Figure for Example 5.1.1*

Solution: Since all the parameters in this problem are real-valued, we expect the equalizer coefficients also to be real-valued. Define

$$\begin{aligned} e_n &= S_n - u_n \\ &= S_n - v_n g_0 + v_{n-1} g_1. \end{aligned} \tag{5.68}$$

We need to find g_0 and g_1 which minimizes

$$E[e_n^2]. \tag{5.69}$$

Differentiating (5.69) wrt g_0 and equating to zero we get

$$\begin{aligned} \frac{\partial}{\partial g_0} E[e_n^2] &= E\left[2e_n \frac{\partial e_n}{\partial g_0}\right] \\ &= -2E[e_n v_n] \\ &= 0 \\ \Rightarrow E[(S_n - g_0 v_n - g_1 v_{n-1}) v_n] &= 0 \\ \Rightarrow g_0 R_{vv,0} + g_1 R_{vv,1} &= h_0 P_{\text{av}} \end{aligned} \tag{5.70}$$

where

$$\begin{aligned} R_{vv,m} &= E[v_n v_{n-m}] \\ P_{\text{av}} &= E[S_n^2] \\ &= 4. \end{aligned} \tag{5.71}$$

Observe the absence of the factor of $1/2$ in the definition of $R_{vv,m}$, since v_n is a real-valued random variable.

Similarly differentiating (5.69) wrt g_1 and equating to zero we get

$$\begin{aligned} \frac{\partial}{\partial g_1} E[e_n^2] &= E\left[2e_n \frac{\partial e_n}{\partial g_1}\right] v \\ &= -2E[e_n v_{n-1}] \\ &= 0 \end{aligned}$$

$$\Rightarrow E[(S_n - g_0 v_n - g_1 v_{n-1}) v_{n-1}] = 0$$
$$\Rightarrow g_0 R_{vv,1} + g_1 R_{vv,0} = 0. \tag{5.72}$$

Solving for g_0 and g_1 from (5.70) and (5.72) we get

$$g_0 = \frac{R_{vv,0} h_0 P_{av}}{R^2_{vv,0} - R^2_{vv,1}}$$
$$g_1 = \frac{-R_{vv,1} h_0 P_{av}}{R^2_{vv,0} - R^2_{vv,1}} \tag{5.73}$$

where

$$R_{vv,0} = P_{\text{av}}(h_0^2 + h_1^2 + h_2^2) + \sigma_w^2$$
$$R_{vv,1} = P_{\text{av}}(h_0 h_1 + h_1 h_2). \tag{5.74}$$

Using the principle of orthogonality, the MMSE is

$$\begin{aligned} E[e_n^2] &= E[e_n(S_n - g_0 v_n - g_1 v_{n-1})] \\ &= E[e_n S_n] \\ &= E[(S_n - g_0 v_n - g_1 v_{n-1}) S_n] \\ &= P_{\text{av}} - g_0 E[v_n S_n] \\ &= P_{\text{av}} - g_0 E[S_n(h_0 S_n + h_1 S_{n-1} + h_2 S_{n-2} + w_n)] \\ &= P_{\text{av}} - g_0 h_0 P_{\text{av}} \\ &= P_{\text{av}} \left[1 - \frac{R_{vv,0} h_0^2 P_{av}}{R^2_{vv,0} - R^2_{vv,1}} \right]. \end{aligned} \tag{5.75}$$

Note that the MMSE can be reduced by increasing the number of equalizer coefficients.

From the above discussion it is clear that computing the optimum equalizer tab weights is computationally complex, especially when L is large. In the next section, we discuss the steepest descent algorithm and the least mean square algorithm which are used in practice to obtain near-optimal equalizer performance at a reduced complexity.

5.1.3 The steepest descent algorithm

Consider the equation

$$y = x^2 \tag{5.76}$$

where x and y are real variables. Starting from an arbitrary point x_0, we are required to find out the value of x that minimizes y, using some kind of a recursive algorithm. This can be done as follows. We compute the gradient

$$\frac{dy}{dx} = 2x. \tag{5.77}$$

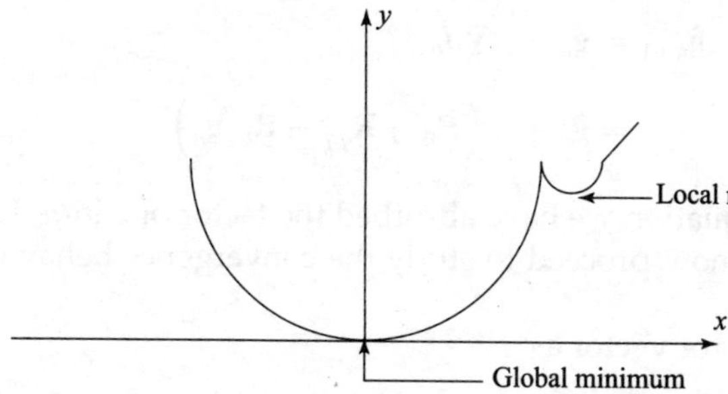

Figure 5.6 *Function having both local and global minimum. Depending on the starting point, the steepest descent algorithm may converge to the local or global minimum.*

It is easy to see that the following recursion achieves the purpose:

$$x_{n+1} = x_n - \mu(x)_n. \tag{5.78}$$

where $\mu > 0$ is called the *step-size*, and x_n at time zero is equal to x_0. Observe that we have absorbed the factor of 2 in μ and the gradient at time n is x_n. It is important to note that in the above recursion, x_n is updated with the negative value of the gradient or in the direction of *steepest descent*. It is also clear that for $x_n \to 0$ as $n \to \infty$ we require:

$$|1 - \mu| < 1. \tag{5.79}$$

This simple analogy is used to derive the steepest descent algorithm that makes the equalizer taps converge to the optimum values. When the function to be minimized contains local minima, there is possibility for the steepest descent algorithm to converge to one of the local minima, instead of the global minimum. This is illustrated in Figure 5.6.

Define the gradient vector at time n as

$$\begin{aligned}\nabla J_n &= \left[\frac{\partial E\left[|\tilde{e}_n|^2\right]}{\partial \tilde{g}^*_{n,0}} \quad \cdots \quad \frac{\partial E\left[|\tilde{e}_n|^2\right]}{\partial \tilde{g}^*_{n,L-1}}\right]^T \\ &= -E\left[\tilde{\mathbf{v}}^*_n \tilde{e}_n\right] \\ &= -\left(P_{\text{av}}\tilde{\mathbf{R}}_{\tilde{q}\tilde{q}} - 2\tilde{\mathbf{R}}_{\tilde{v}\tilde{v}}\tilde{\mathbf{g}}_n\right)\end{aligned} \tag{5.80}$$

where $\tilde{e}_n$ is given by (5.53) and

$$\begin{aligned}\tilde{\mathbf{v}}_n &= \left[\tilde{v}_n \quad \tilde{v}_{n-1} \quad \cdots \quad \tilde{v}_{n-L+1}\right]^T, \\ \tilde{\mathbf{g}}_n &= \left[\tilde{g}_{n,0} \quad \tilde{g}_{n,1} \quad \cdots \quad \tilde{g}_{n,L-1}\right]^T.\end{aligned} \tag{5.81}$$

Note that $\tilde{g}_{n,i}$ denotes the ith tap at time nT. Note also that the gradient vector is zero only for the *optimum* tap weights (see (5.55)). The tap update equations can now be written as

$$\tilde{\mathbf{g}}_{n+1} = \tilde{\mathbf{g}}_n - \mu \nabla J_n$$
$$= \tilde{\mathbf{g}}_n + \mu \left(P_{\text{av, 1}} \tilde{\mathbf{R}}_{\tilde{q}\tilde{q}} - \tilde{\mathbf{R}}_{\tilde{v}\tilde{v}} \tilde{\mathbf{g}}_n \right). \tag{5.82}$$

Notice that in the above equation we have absorbed the factor of 2 in μ. Having derived the tap update equations, we now proceed to study the convergence behaviour of the steepest descent algorithm[164].

Define the tap weight error vector as

$$\tilde{\mathbf{g}}_{e,\,n} \stackrel{\Delta}{=} \tilde{\mathbf{g}}_n - \tilde{\mathbf{g}}_{\text{opt, FL}} \tag{5.83}$$

where $\tilde{\mathbf{g}}_{\text{opt, FL}}$ denotes the optimum tap weight vector. The tap update equation in (5.82) can be written as

$$\tilde{\mathbf{g}}_{e,\,n+1} = \tilde{\mathbf{g}}_{e,\,n} + \mu \left(P_{\text{av}} \tilde{\mathbf{R}}_{\tilde{q}\tilde{q}} - \tilde{\mathbf{R}}_{\tilde{v}\tilde{v}} \tilde{\mathbf{g}}_{e,\,n} - \tilde{\mathbf{R}}_{\tilde{v}\tilde{v}} \tilde{\mathbf{g}}_{\text{opt, FL}} \right)$$
$$= \tilde{\mathbf{g}}_{e,\,n} - \mu \tilde{\mathbf{R}}_{\tilde{v}\tilde{v}} \tilde{\mathbf{g}}_{e,\,n}$$
$$= \left(\mathbf{I}_L - \mu \tilde{\mathbf{R}}_{\tilde{v}\tilde{v}} \right) \tilde{\mathbf{g}}_{e,\,n}$$
$$= \left(\mathbf{I}_L - \mu \tilde{\mathbf{Q}} \mathbf{\Lambda} \tilde{\mathbf{Q}}^H \right) \tilde{\mathbf{g}}_{e,\,n}. \tag{5.84}$$

In the above equation, we have used the unitary similarity transformation (see Appendix D) to decompose $\tilde{\mathbf{R}}_{\tilde{v}\tilde{v}}$ as

$$\tilde{\mathbf{R}}_{\tilde{v}\tilde{v}} = \tilde{\mathbf{Q}} \mathbf{\Lambda} \tilde{\mathbf{Q}}^H \tag{5.85}$$

where $\tilde{\mathbf{Q}}$ is an $L \times L$ matrix consisting of the eigenvectors of $\tilde{\mathbf{R}}_{\tilde{v}\tilde{v}}$ and $\mathbf{\Lambda}$ is an $L \times L$ diagonal matrix consisting of the eigenvalues of $\tilde{\mathbf{R}}_{\tilde{v}\tilde{v}}$. Pre-multiplying both sides of (5.84) by $\tilde{\mathbf{Q}}^H$ and using the fact that $\tilde{\mathbf{Q}}^H \tilde{\mathbf{Q}} = \mathbf{I}_L$, we get

$$\tilde{\mathbf{Q}}^H \tilde{\mathbf{g}}_{e,\,n+1} = \left(\tilde{\mathbf{Q}}^H - \mu \mathbf{\Lambda} \tilde{\mathbf{Q}}^H \right) \tilde{\mathbf{g}}_{e,\,n}$$
$$= \left(\mathbf{I}_L - \mu \mathbf{\Lambda} \right) \tilde{\mathbf{Q}}^H \tilde{\mathbf{g}}_{e,\,n}. \tag{5.86}$$

Let

$$\tilde{\mathbf{h}}_n \stackrel{\Delta}{=} \tilde{\mathbf{Q}}^H \tilde{\mathbf{g}}_{e,\,n} \tag{5.87}$$

denote another $L \times 1$ vector. Then (5.86) becomes

$$\tilde{\mathbf{h}}_{n+1} = \left(\mathbf{I}_L - \mu \mathbf{\Lambda} \right) \tilde{\mathbf{h}}_n. \tag{5.88}$$

It is clear that as $n \to \infty$, $\tilde{\mathbf{h}}_n$ must tend to zero. Let $\tilde{h}_{k,\,n}$ denote the kth element of $\tilde{\mathbf{h}}_n$. Then the recursion for the kth element of $\tilde{\mathbf{h}}_n$ is given by

$$\tilde{h}_{k,\,n+1} = (1 - \mu \lambda_k)\, \tilde{h}_{k,\,n} \qquad \text{for } 1 \le k \le L. \tag{5.89}$$

The required condition for $\tilde{h}_{k,n}$ to approach zero as $n \to \infty$ is

$$\begin{aligned} -1 &< 1 - \mu\lambda_k < 1 \\ \Rightarrow 2 &> \mu\lambda_k \\ \Rightarrow \frac{2}{\lambda_k} &> \mu \qquad \text{for } 1 \le k \le L. \end{aligned} \tag{5.90}$$

As mentioned earlier, μ must also be strictly positive (it has been shown in Appendix D that the eigenvalues of a correlation matrix are positive and real). Obviously, if

$$0 < \mu < \frac{2}{\lambda_{\max}} \tag{5.91}$$

where $\lambda_{\max}$ is the maximum eigenvalue of $\tilde{\mathbf{R}}_{\tilde{v}\tilde{v}}$, then the condition in (5.90) is automatically satisfied for all k.

Example 5.1.2 In Example 5.1.1, it is given that $h_0 = 1, h_1 = 2, h_2 = 3$ and $\sigma_w^2 = 4$. Determine the largest step-size that can be used in the steepest descent algorithm, based on the maximum eigenvalue.

Solution: For the given values

$$\begin{aligned} R_{vv,0} &= 60 \\ R_{vv,1} &= 32. \end{aligned} \tag{5.92}$$

Therefore

$$R_{vv} = \begin{bmatrix} 60 & 32 \\ 32 & 60 \end{bmatrix}. \tag{5.93}$$

The eigenvalues of this matrix are given by

$$\begin{vmatrix} 60-\lambda & 32 \\ 32 & 60-\lambda \end{vmatrix} = 0$$

$$\begin{aligned} \Rightarrow \lambda_1 &= 28 \\ \lambda_2 &= 92. \end{aligned} \tag{5.94}$$

Therefore from (5.91) the step-size for the steepest descent algorithm must lie in the range

$$0 < \mu < \frac{2}{92}. \tag{5.95}$$

The main drawback of the steepest gradient algorithm is that it requires estimation of $\tilde{\mathbf{R}}_{\tilde{v}\tilde{v}}$ and $\tilde{\mathbf{R}}_{\tilde{q}\tilde{q}}$, which again could be computationally complex for large values of L. In the next section we discuss the least mean square algorithm which provides a simple way to update the equalizer taps.

5.1.4 The least mean square (LMS) algorithm

The LMS algorithm belongs to the family of *stochastic (or estimated) gradient algorithms* as opposed to the steepest descent algorithm which uses a *deterministic (or exact) gradient*. The tap update equations for the LMS algorithm is given by

$$\tilde{\mathbf{g}}_{n+1} = \tilde{\mathbf{g}}_n + \mu\left(\tilde{\mathbf{v}}_n^* \tilde{e}_n\right). \tag{5.96}$$

Note that the only difference between (5.82) and (5.96) is in the presence or absence of the expectation operator. In other words, the LMS algorithm uses the *instantaneous* value of the gradient instead of the *exact* value of the gradient.

It can be shown that μ should satisfy the condition in (5.91) for the LMS algorithm to converge. However, since in practice it is difficult to estimate the eigenvalues of the correlation matrix, we resort to a more conservative estimate of μ which is given by:

$$0 < \mu < \frac{2}{\sum_{i=1}^{L} \lambda_i} \tag{5.97}$$

where λ_i are the eigenvalues of $\tilde{\mathbf{R}}_{\tilde{v}\tilde{v}}$. However, from matrix theory we know that the sum of the eigenvalues of $\tilde{\mathbf{R}}_{\tilde{v}\tilde{v}}$ is equal to the trace of $\tilde{\mathbf{R}}_{\tilde{v}\tilde{v}}$ (this result is proved in Appendix D with reference to the correlation matrix). Thus (5.97) becomes:

$$0 < \mu < \frac{2}{L\tilde{R}_{\tilde{v}\tilde{v},0}}. \tag{5.98}$$

Note that $\tilde{R}_{\tilde{v}\tilde{v},0}$ is the power of the signal, $\tilde{v}_n$ in (5.29), that is input to the equalizer.

In the next section, we discuss the fractionally-spaced equalizer, which is a better way to implement the symbol-spaced equalizer.

5.1.5 Linear equalization – fractionally-spaced equalizers

From an implementation point of view, the symbol-spaced equalizer suffers from two major disadvantages[2,162,165]:

(a) It is sensitive to the sampling phase of the symbol-rate sampler.
(b) It is sensitive to imperfectness in the matched filter.

We now discuss these two issues in detail.

Recall that the output of the matched filter is given by (5.27) which is repeated here for convenience:

$$\tilde{v}(t) = \sum_{k=-\infty}^{\infty} S_k \tilde{R}_{\tilde{q}\tilde{q}}(t - kT) + \tilde{w}_2(t). \tag{5.99}$$

Let us assume that $\tilde{v}(t)$ is sampled at instants $nT - t_0$ where $t_0 \in [0, T)$ denotes the sampling phase. Note that in (5.29) the sampling phase is zero. The sampler output for a sampling phase of t_0 can be written as

$$\tilde{v}(nT - t_0) = \sum_{k=-\infty}^{\infty} S_k \tilde{R}_{\tilde{q}\tilde{q}}(nT - t_0 - kT) + \tilde{w}_2(nT - t_0). \tag{5.100}$$

The autocorrelation of $\tilde{w}_2(nT - t_0)$ is *independent* of t_0 and is given by (5.30), that is,

$$\frac{1}{2}E\left[\tilde{w}_2(nT - t_0)\tilde{w}_2^*(nT - mT - t_0)\right] = N_0\tilde{R}_{\tilde{q}\tilde{q},\,m}. \tag{5.101}$$

Hence the power spectral density of $\tilde{w}_2(nT - t_0)$ is given by (5.33). Let us denote the discrete-time Fourier transform of $\tilde{R}_{\tilde{q}\tilde{q}}(mT - t_0)$ in (5.100) by $\tilde{S}_{\mathscr{P},\tilde{q}}(F,\, t_0)$. Then,

$$\tilde{S}_{\mathscr{P},\tilde{q}}(F,\, t_0) = \frac{1}{T}\sum_{k=-\infty}^{\infty}\left|\tilde{Q}\left(F + \frac{k}{T}\right)\right|^2 \exp\left(-\mathrm{j}\,2\pi t_0\left(F + \frac{k}{T}\right)\right). \tag{5.102}$$

Observe that $\tilde{R}_{\tilde{q}\tilde{q}}(mT - t_0)$ is *not* a discrete-time autocorrelation sequence for $t_0 \neq 0$, hence its Fourier transform is *not* real-valued.

From the above developments, (5.38) can be written as

$$E\left[|\tilde{u}_n - S_n|^2\right] = T\int_{F=-1/(2T)}^{1/(2T)}\left[P_{\mathrm{av}}\left|1 - \tilde{S}_{\mathscr{P},\tilde{q}}(F,\, t_0)\tilde{G}_{\mathscr{P}}(F)\right|^2 + 2N_0 S_{\mathscr{P},\tilde{q}}(F)\left|\tilde{G}_{\mathscr{P}}(F)\right|^2\right]dF. \tag{5.103}$$

Differentiating the integrand in the above equation with respect to $\tilde{G}^*_{\mathscr{P}}(F)$, we get the optimum equalizer frequency response as

$$\tilde{G}_{\mathscr{P},\,\mathrm{opt,\,MMSE}}(F,\, t_0) = \frac{P_{\mathrm{av}}\tilde{S}^*_{\mathscr{P},\tilde{q}}(F,\, t_0)}{P_{\mathrm{av}}\left|\tilde{S}_{\mathscr{P},\tilde{q}}(F,\, t_0)\right|^2 + 2N_0 S_{\mathscr{P},\tilde{q}}(F)} \quad \text{for } -1/(2T) \le F < 1/(2T). \tag{5.104}$$

The corresponding mean square error is given by

$$\mathscr{J}_{\mathrm{MMSE}}(\text{linear},\, t_0) = \int_{F=-1/(2T)}^{1/(2T)}\frac{2N_0P_{\mathrm{av}}T}{P_{\mathrm{av}}\left|\tilde{S}_{\mathscr{P},\tilde{q}}(F,\, t_0)\right|^2\cdot\dfrac{1}{S_{\mathscr{P},\tilde{q}}(F)} + 2N_0}\,dF. \tag{5.105}$$

Let us now compare the MMSE obtained in (5.47) and (5.105) for the real-life situation where the (two-sided) bandwidth of $\tilde{Q}(F)$ extends over the frequency range $[-1/T,\, 1/T]$. In this case $\tilde{Q}(F)$ is said to have an *excess bandwidth* and (5.102) reduces to

$$\tilde{S}_{\mathscr{P},\tilde{q}}(F,\, t_0) = \frac{\mathrm{e}^{-\mathrm{j}\,2\pi F t_0}}{T}\left[\left|\tilde{Q}(F)\right|^2 + \left|\tilde{Q}\left(F - \frac{1}{T}\right)\right|^2\mathrm{e}^{\mathrm{j}\,2\pi t_0/T}\right] \quad \text{for } 0 \le F < 1/T. \tag{5.106}$$

The above model is justified since in most communication standards employing linear modulation, the transmit filter is specified to be pulse corresponding to the root-raised cosine spectrum with at most 100% excess bandwidth.

Note that if we had taken the frequency interval to be $-1/(2T) \le F \le 1/(2T)$, there would have been three terms on the right-hand side of (5.106), which would have made analysis more complicated. In other words,

$$\tilde{S}_{\mathscr{P},\tilde{q}}(F, t_0) = \frac{e^{-j2\pi F t_0}}{T}\left[\left|\tilde{Q}\left(F+\frac{1}{T}\right)\right|^2 e^{-j2\pi t_0/T} + \left|\tilde{Q}(F)\right|^2 + \left|\tilde{Q}\left(F-\frac{1}{T}\right)\right|^2 e^{j2\pi t_0/T}\right]$$

$$\text{for } -1/(2T) \leq F < 1/(2T). \tag{5.107}$$

Hence, for ease of analysis, we prefer to use $\tilde{S}_{\mathscr{P},\tilde{q}}(F, t_0)$ given by (5.106) in the frequency range $0 \leq F \leq 1/T$. Observe also that the frequency ranges specified in (5.106) and (5.107) correspond to an interval of 2π.

However $S_{\mathscr{P},\tilde{q}}(F)$ is given by

$$S_{\mathscr{P},\tilde{q}}(F) = \frac{1}{T}\left[\left|\tilde{Q}(F)\right|^2 + \left|\tilde{Q}\left(F-\frac{1}{T}\right)\right|^2\right] \qquad \text{for } 0 \leq F < 1/T. \tag{5.108}$$

Clearly,

$$S^2_{\mathscr{P},\tilde{q}}(F) > \left|\tilde{S}_{\mathscr{P},\tilde{q}}(F, t_0)\right|^2 \qquad \text{for } 0 \leq F < 1/T$$

$$\Rightarrow S_{\mathscr{P},\tilde{q}}(F) > \frac{\left|\tilde{S}_{\mathscr{P},\tilde{q}}(F, t_0)\right|^2}{S_{\mathscr{P},\tilde{q}}(F)} \qquad \text{for } 0 \leq F < 1/T$$

$$\Rightarrow \mathscr{J}_{\text{MMSE}}(\text{linear}, t_0) > \mathscr{J}_{\text{MMSE}}(\text{linear}). \tag{5.109}$$

Thus, the above analysis shows that an incorrect choice of sampling phase results in a larger-than-minimum mean squared error.

The other problem with the symbol-spaced equalizer is that there is a marked degradation in performance due to inaccuracies in the matched filter. It is difficult to obtain closed form expressions for performance degradation due to a "mismatched" filter. However, experimental results have shown that on an average telephone channel, the filter matched to the transmitted pulse (instead of the received pulse) performs poorly[162].

The solution to both the problems of timing phase and matched filtering, is to combine the matched filter $\tilde{Q}^*(F)$ and $\tilde{G}_{\mathscr{P}}(F)$ to form a single filter, $\tilde{H}_{\text{opt}}(F)$, as given in (5.8). The advantage behind this combination is that $\tilde{H}_{\text{opt}}(F)$ can be *adapted* to minimize the MSE arising due

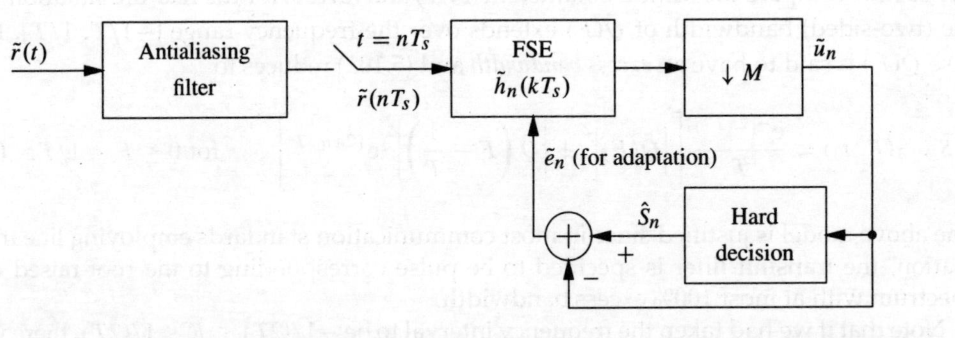

Figure 5.7 *A digital communication system employing a fractionally-spaced equalizer (FSE)*

to timing offset and inaccuracies in the matched filter. This is in contrast to the symbol-spaced equalizer where only $\tilde{G}_{\mathscr{P}}(F)$ is adapted.

Since $\tilde{H}_{\text{opt}}(F)$ has a finite (one-sided) bandwidth, say B, its discrete-time impulse response can be obtained by sampling $\tilde{h}_{\text{opt}}(t)$ at Nyquist-rate ($2B$) or above. Thus $\tilde{h}_{\text{opt}}(nT_s)$, where $T_s = 1/(2B)$, is the impulse response of the optimum fractionally-spaced equalizer (FSE). It is clear that the minimum mean-squared error for the optimum (infinitely long) fractionally-spaced equalizer is *exactly* identical to that of the optimum (infinitely long) symbol-spaced equalizer[128] and is given by (5.47).

In practice, the FSE is of finite length and is adapted using the LMS algorithm. The block diagram of a digital communication system employing a discrete-time adaptive FSE is shown in Figure 5.7. Here $T/T_s = M$ is assumed to be an integer, where $1/T$ denotes the symbol-rate. The signal $\tilde{r}(t)$ is given by (5.5). Let L denote the length of the FSE and $\tilde{h}_n(kT_s)$ denote the kth equalizer tap coefficient at time nT (note that the equalizer taps are time-varying due to the adaptation algorithm). Let

$$\tilde{u}(nMT_s) = \sum_{k=0}^{L-1} \tilde{h}_n(kT_s)\tilde{r}(nMT_s - kT_s) \stackrel{\Delta}{=} \tilde{u}_n \tag{5.110}$$

denote the decimated output of the FSE. The error signal is computed as

$$\tilde{e}_n = \hat{S}_n - \tilde{u}_n \tag{5.111}$$

where $\hat{S}_n$ denotes the estimate of the symbol, which we assume is equal to the transmitted symbol S_n. The LMS algorithm for updating the equalizer taps is given by

$$\tilde{\mathbf{h}}_{n+1} = \tilde{\mathbf{h}}_n + \mu\left(\tilde{\mathbf{r}}_n^* \tilde{e}_n\right) \tag{5.112}$$

where

$$\tilde{\mathbf{h}}_n = \left[\tilde{h}_n(0) \quad \cdots \quad \tilde{h}_n((L-1)T_s)\right]^T$$

$$\tilde{\mathbf{r}}_n = \left[\tilde{r}(nMT_s) \quad \cdots \quad \tilde{r}((nM-L+1)T_s)\right]^T$$

$$0 < \mu < \frac{2}{LE\left[|\tilde{r}(nT_s)|^2\right]}. \tag{5.113}$$

Having discussed the performance of the FSE, the question arises whether we can do better. From (5.47) we note that the power spectral density of the interference at the equalizer output is not flat. In other words, we are dealing with the problem of detecting symbols in correlated interference, which has been discussed earlier in Section 2.7 in Chapter 2. Whereas the interference at the equalizer output is not Gaussian, the interference considered in Section 2.7 of Chapter 2 is Gaussian. Nevertheless, in both cases, the prediction filter needs to be used to reduce the variance of the interference at the equalizer output and hence improve the bit-error-rate performance. We have thus motivated the need for using a *decision-feedback* equalizer (DFE).

5.1.6 Nonlinear equalization – the predictive DFE

The decision feedback equalizer (DFE) was introduced by Austin in [166]. The performance analysis of the DFE can be found in [167–173]. In [174], the DFE is used for detecting trellis coded modulation signals. A reduced complexity DFE for channels having large delay spreads is discussed in [175]. A technique to reduce the effect of error propagation in the DFE is given in [176]. In [89,91] the DFE is used in connection with turbo equalization.

From (5.47) it is clear that the periodic power spectral density of the interference at the equalizer output (assuming that the matched filter output is sampled at the correct instants) is given by

$$S_{\mathcal{P},\tilde{w}_1}(F) = \frac{2N_0 P_{\text{av}} T}{P_{\text{av}} S_{\mathcal{P},\tilde{q}}(F) + 2N_0}. \tag{5.114}$$

Let us consider a discrete-time filter having a frequency response $\tilde{\Gamma}_{\mathcal{P}}(F)$ such that[162]:

$$\left|\tilde{\Gamma}_{\mathcal{P}}(F)\right|^2 = \frac{1}{S_{\mathcal{P},\tilde{w}_1}(F)}. \tag{5.115}$$

Note that when $N_0 \neq 0$, $S_{\mathcal{P},\tilde{w}_1}(F)$ has no nulls (zeros), and hence $\tilde{\Gamma}_{\mathcal{P}}(F)$ always exists. We refer to $\tilde{\Gamma}_{\mathcal{P}}(F)$ as the *whitening* filter. Thus, when the interference at the equalizer output is passed through $\tilde{\Gamma}_{\mathcal{P}}(F)$, the power spectral density at the filter output is flat with value equal to unity. This further implies that the variance of the interference at the output of the whitening filter is also unity. Note that since the whitening filter must be causal,

$$\tilde{\Gamma}_{\mathcal{P}}(F) \stackrel{\Delta}{=} \sum_{k=0}^{\infty} \tilde{\gamma}_k \exp\left(-\mathrm{j}\, 2\pi F k T\right), \tag{5.116}$$

where $\tilde{\gamma}_k$ are the whitening filter coefficients.

However, due to reasons that will be explained later, what we require is a discrete-time *forward prediction* filter (see Appendix J) of the form

$$\tilde{A}_{\mathcal{P}}(F) \stackrel{\Delta}{=} 1 + \sum_{k=1}^{\infty} \tilde{a}_k \exp\left(-\mathrm{j}\, 2\pi F k T\right). \tag{5.117}$$

It is easy to see that the above filter can be obtained by dividing all coefficients of $\tilde{\Gamma}_{\mathcal{P}}(F)$ by $\tilde{\gamma}_0$. Hence

$$\tilde{A}_{\mathcal{P}}(F) = \frac{\tilde{\Gamma}_{\mathcal{P}}(F)}{\tilde{\gamma}_0}. \tag{5.118}$$

Thus the power spectral density of the interference at the output of the prediction filter is flat with value equal to $1/|\tilde{\gamma}_0|^2$, which is also equal to the variance of the interference. Note that since $A_{\mathcal{P}}(F)$ is minimum phase (see section J.4), $\tilde{\Gamma}_{\mathcal{P}}(F)$ must also be minimum phase.

Let us now try to express $\tilde{\gamma}_0$ in terms of the power spectral density of $\tilde{w}_{1,n}$. Computing the squared magnitude of both sides of (5.118), we get

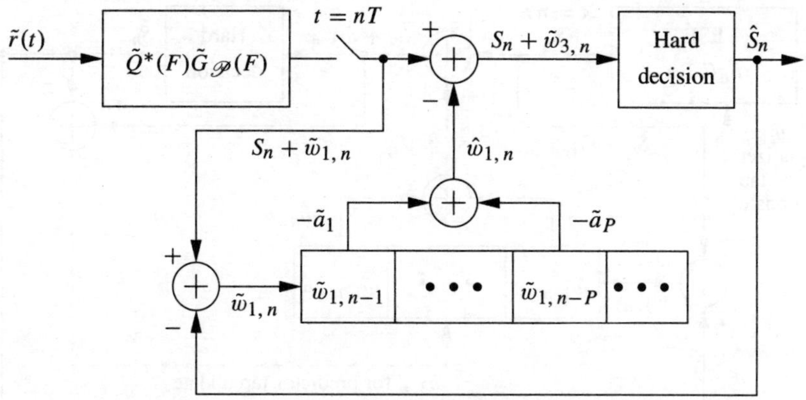

Figure 5.8 *Structure of the optimum predictive decision feedback equalizer*

$$|\tilde{\gamma}_0|^2 = \frac{\left|\tilde{\Gamma}_{\mathscr{P}}(F)\right|^2}{\left|\tilde{A}_{\mathscr{P}}(F)\right|^2} \tag{5.119}$$

Taking the natural logarithm of both sides and integrating,

$$\ln|\tilde{\gamma}_0|^2 = T\int_0^{1/T} \ln\left|\tilde{\Gamma}_{\mathscr{P}}(F)\right|^2 dF - T\int_0^{1/T} \ln\left|\tilde{A}_{\mathscr{P}}(F)\right|^2 dF. \tag{5.120}$$

Since the second integral on the right-hand side of the above equation is zero (see (J.89)) we get[162]:

$$\begin{aligned}
\ln|\tilde{\gamma}_0|^2 &= T\int_0^{1/T} \ln\left|\tilde{\Gamma}_{\mathscr{P}}(F)\right|^2 dF \\
\Rightarrow \frac{1}{|\gamma_0|^2} &= \exp\left(T\int_0^{1/T} \ln\left(S_{\mathscr{P},\,\tilde{w}_1}(F)\right) dF\right) \\
&= \frac{1}{2}E\left[\left|\tilde{w}_{3,n}\right|^2\right] \qquad \text{(say)}
\end{aligned} \tag{5.121}$$

where $\tilde{w}_{3,n}$ denotes the noise sequence at the output of the optimum (infinite-order) predictor given by (5.118).

Figure 5.8 shows the structure of the equalizer that uses a forward prediction filter of order P. Note the use of a hard-decision device to subtract out the symbol. This structure is referred to as the *predictive decision feedback* equalizer (predictive DFE). The predictive DFE operates as follows. At time nT, the estimate of the interference $\hat{w}_{1,n}$ is obtained using the past values of the interference (this is *not* the estimate of the past values, but the actual past values), $\tilde{w}_{1,n-1}, \ldots, \tilde{w}_{1,n-P}$. This estimate, $\hat{w}_{1,n}$ is subtracted out from the equalizer output at time nT to obtain

$$\tilde{u}_n - \hat{w}_{1,n} = S_n + \tilde{w}_{1,n} - \hat{w}_{1,n} = S_n + \tilde{w}_{3,n} = \tilde{r}_{2,n} \qquad \text{(say)}. \tag{5.122}$$

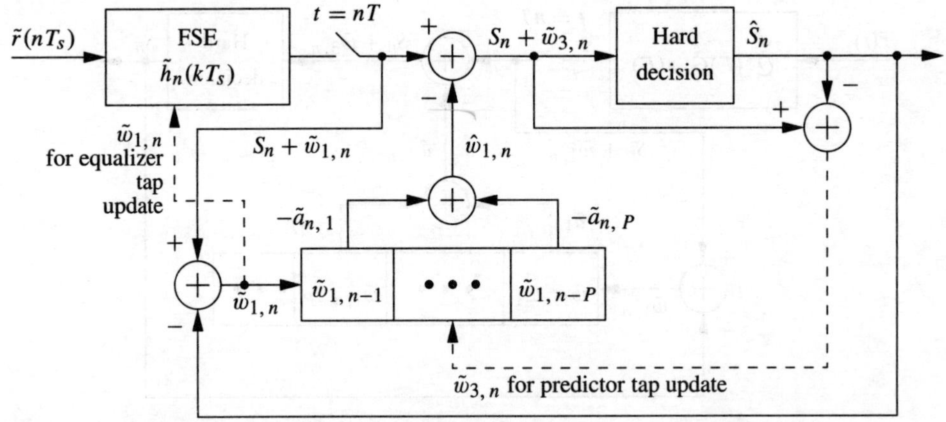

Figure 5.9 *Implementation of the predictive decision feedback equalizer*

Since the variance of $\tilde{w}_{3,n}$ is less than $\tilde{w}_{1,n}$ (see Appendix J), the hard decisions that are obtained using $\tilde{r}_{2,n}$ are more reliable than those obtained from $\tilde{u}_n$. Hence we expect the bit-error-rate performance of the ideal DFE to be better than even the optimum linear equalizer. Having obtained the estimate of the symbol, which we assume to be equal to S_n, it is straightforward to obtain $\tilde{w}_{1,n}$ from $\tilde{u}_n$, which is fed to the forward prediction filter to estimate $\hat{w}_{1,n+1}$. It is clear that the effectiveness of this equalizer depends on the correctness of the hard decision. In the next section we discuss the practical implementation of the DFE.

5.1.7 Implementation of the predictive DFE

As usual in a practical implementation, we have to deal with finite-length filters. Moreover, we also require the filters to be adaptive so that they can be *trained* to attain the optimum tap coefficients. Let us assume that the fractionally-spaced equalizer (feedforward part) has L taps and the prediction filter (feedback part) has P taps. The output of the FSE is given by (5.110) which is repeated here for convenience:

$$\tilde{u}_n = \sum_{k=0}^{L-1} \tilde{h}_n(kT_s)\tilde{r}(nMT_s - kT_s) = S_n + \tilde{w}_{1,n}. \tag{5.123}$$

The error signal at the equalizer output is given by

$$\tilde{u}_n - S_n = \tilde{w}_{1,n}. \tag{5.124}$$

The prediction error is given by

$$\tilde{w}_{3,n} = \tilde{w}_{1,n} - \hat{w}_{1,n} = \sum_{k=0}^{P} \tilde{a}_{n,k}\tilde{w}_{1,n-k} \tag{5.125}$$

where $\tilde{a}_{n,k}$ denotes the kth coefficient of the predictor at time nT with

$$\tilde{a}_{n,0} = 1. \tag{5.126}$$

Note that we have dropped the subscript P in labelling the predictor coefficients since it is understood that we are using a Pth-order predictor (in Appendix J the subscript was explicitly used to differentiate between the Pth-order and $P-1$th-order predictor).

The LMS algorithm for the equalizer tap updates is

$$\tilde{\mathbf{h}}_{n+1} = \tilde{\mathbf{h}}_n - \mu_1 \left(\tilde{\mathbf{r}}_n^* \tilde{w}_{1,\,n}\right) \tag{5.127}$$

where again

$$\begin{aligned}
\tilde{\mathbf{h}}_n &= \left[\tilde{h}_n(0) \quad \cdots \quad \tilde{h}_n((L-1)T_s)\right]^T \\
\tilde{\mathbf{r}}_n &= \left[\tilde{r}(nMT_s) \quad \cdots \quad \tilde{r}((nM-L+1)T_s)\right]^T \\
0 &< \mu_1 < \frac{2}{LE\left[|\tilde{r}(nT_s)|^2\right]}.
\end{aligned} \tag{5.128}$$

Note the difference between the tap update equations in (5.127) and (5.112) and also the expression for the error signal in (5.124) and (5.111).

The LMS tap update equation for the prediction filter is given by

$$\tilde{\mathbf{a}}_{n+1} = \tilde{\mathbf{a}}_n - \mu_2 \left(\tilde{\mathbf{w}}_{1,\,n}^* \tilde{w}_{3,\,n}\right) \tag{5.129}$$

where

$$\begin{aligned}
\tilde{\mathbf{a}}_n &= \left[\tilde{a}_{n,\,1} \quad \cdots \quad \tilde{a}_{n,\,P}\right]^T \\
\tilde{\mathbf{w}}_{1,\,n} &= \left[\tilde{w}_{1,\,n-1} \quad \cdots \quad \tilde{w}_{1,\,n-P}\right]^T \\
0 &< \mu_2 < \frac{2}{PE\left[\left|\tilde{w}_{1,\,n}\right|^2\right]}.
\end{aligned} \tag{5.130}$$

The main problem with the predictive DFE is that the tap update equations (5.127) and (5.129) *independently* minimize the variance of $\tilde{w}_{1,\,n}$ and $\tilde{w}_{3,\,n}$ respectively. In practical situations, this would lead to a suboptimal performance, that is, the variance of $\tilde{w}_{3,\,n}$ would be higher than the minimum. Moreover, $\tilde{\mathbf{a}}_n$ in (5.129) can be updated only after $\tilde{\mathbf{h}}_n$ in (5.127) has converged to the optimum value. If both the tap update equations minimized the variance of just one term, say, $\tilde{w}_{3,\,n}$, this would yield a better performance than the predictive DFE. This motivates us to discuss the conventional decision feedback equalizer.

5.1.8 The conventional DFE

For the purpose of deriving the conventional DFE,[172] we assume an infinitely long equalizer and predictor. Note that

$$\hat{w}_{1,\,n} = -\sum_{k=1}^{\infty} \tilde{a}_k \tilde{w}_{1,\,n-k}$$

$$= -\sum_{k=1}^{\infty} \tilde{a}_k \left(\tilde{u}_{n-k} - S_{n-k}\right) \tag{5.131}$$

where as usual $\tilde{a}_k$ denotes the forward predictor coefficients. The final error $\tilde{w}_{3,\,n}$ is given by

$$\tilde{w}_{3,\,n} = \tilde{w}_{1,\,n} - \hat{w}_{1,\,n}$$

$$= \tilde{u}_n - S_n + \sum_{k=1}^{\infty} \tilde{a}_k \left(\tilde{u}_{n-k} - S_{n-k}\right)$$

$$\Rightarrow S_n + \tilde{w}_{3,\,n} = \sum_{k=0}^{\infty} \tilde{a}_k \tilde{u}_{n-k} - \sum_{k=1}^{\infty} \tilde{a}_k S_{n-k}. \tag{5.132}$$

At this point, we need to go back to the symbol-spaced equalizer structure given in Figure 5.3 (we have already shown that the optimum FSE is identical to the optimum symbol-spaced equalizer). Hence $\tilde{u}_n$ is given by (5.36) which is repeated here for convenience:

$$\tilde{u}_n = \tilde{v}_n \star \tilde{g}_n$$

$$= \sum_{j=-\infty}^{\infty} \tilde{v}_j \tilde{g}_{n-j} \tag{5.133}$$

where $\tilde{v}_n$ is given by (5.29). Substituting for $\tilde{u}_n$ from the above equation into (5.132), we get

$$S_n + \tilde{w}_{3,\,n} = \sum_{j=-\infty}^{\infty} \sum_{k=0}^{\infty} \tilde{a}_k \tilde{v}_j \tilde{g}_{n-k-j} - \sum_{k=1}^{\infty} \tilde{a}_k S_{n-k}$$

$$= \sum_{j=-\infty}^{\infty} \tilde{v}_j \sum_{k=0}^{\infty} \tilde{a}_k \tilde{g}_{n-k-j} - \sum_{k=1}^{\infty} \tilde{a}_k S_{n-k}$$

$$= \sum_{j=-\infty}^{\infty} \tilde{v}_j \tilde{g}_{1,\,n-j} - \sum_{k=1}^{\infty} \tilde{a}_k S_{n-k} \tag{5.134}$$

where $\tilde{g}_{1,\,n}$ denotes the convolution of the original symbol-spaced equalizer with the prediction filter. Let $\tilde{G}_{\mathscr{P},\,1}(F)$ denote the discrete-time Fourier transform of $\tilde{g}_{1,\,n}$. Then,

$$\tilde{G}_{\mathscr{P},\,1}(F) = \tilde{A}_{\mathscr{P}}(F) \tilde{G}_{\mathscr{P}}(F) \tag{5.135}$$

where $\tilde{G}_{\mathscr{P}}(F)$ is given by (5.35) and

$$\tilde{A}_{\mathscr{P}}(F) = \sum_{k=0}^{\infty} \tilde{a}_k \exp\left(-\mathrm{j}\, 2\pi FnT\right). \tag{5.136}$$

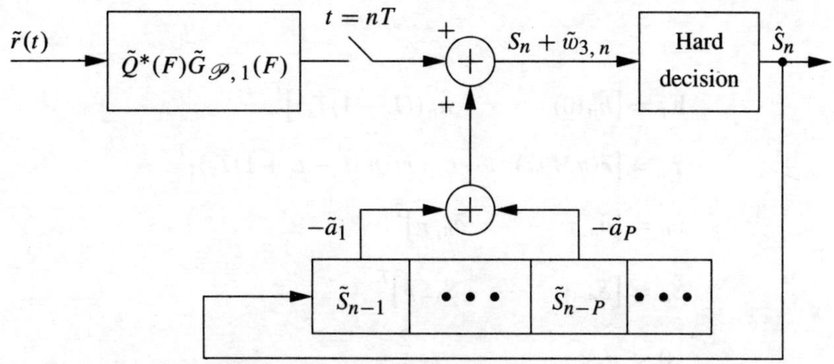

Figure 5.10 *Structure of the optimum conventional decision feedback equalizer*

With this development, the structure of the optimum conventional DFE is presented in Figure 5.10. In a practical implementation, we would have a finite length fractionally-spaced feedforward filter (FSE) and a finite length symbol-spaced feedback filter. Let $\tilde{h}_n(kT_s)$ denote the kth tap of the FSE at time nT. Let $\tilde{a}_{n,k}$ denote the kth tap of the predictor at time nT. Then the DFE output can be written as

$$\begin{aligned} S_n + \tilde{w}_{3,n} &= \sum_{k=0}^{L-1} \tilde{h}_n(kT_s)\tilde{r}(nMT_s - kT_s) - \sum_{k=1}^{P} \tilde{a}_{n,k} S_{n-k} \\ &= \tilde{u}_{1,n} \qquad \text{(say)}. \end{aligned} \tag{5.137}$$

Since we are interested in minimizing $|\tilde{w}_{3,n}|^2$ with respect to $\tilde{h}_n(kT_s)$ and $\tilde{a}_{n,k}$, the corresponding gradient equations are given by

$$\begin{aligned} \frac{\partial\left(w_{3,n}w_{3,n}^*\right)}{\partial\tilde{h}_n^*(jT_s)} &= \tilde{w}_{3,n}\tilde{r}^*(nMT_s - jT_s) \qquad \text{for } 0 \le j \le L-1 \\ \frac{\partial\left(w_{3,n}w_{3,n}^*\right)}{\partial\tilde{a}_{n,i}^*} &= -\tilde{w}_{3,n}\tilde{S}_{n-i}^* \qquad \text{for } 1 \le i \le P. \end{aligned} \tag{5.138}$$

The LMS tap update equations can be summarized in vector form as follows:

$$\begin{aligned} \tilde{\mathbf{h}}_{n+1} &= \tilde{\mathbf{h}}_n - \mu\left(\tilde{\mathbf{r}}_n^*\tilde{w}_{3,n}\right) \\ \tilde{\mathbf{a}}_{n+1} &= \tilde{\mathbf{a}}_n + \mu\left(\mathbf{S}_n^*\tilde{w}_{3,n}\right) \end{aligned} \tag{5.139}$$

where

$$\tilde{\mathbf{h}}_n = \left[\tilde{h}_n(0) \quad \cdots \quad \tilde{h}_n((L-1)T_s)\right]^T$$

$$\tilde{\mathbf{r}}_n = \left[\tilde{r}(nMT_s) \quad \cdots \quad \tilde{r}((nM-L+1)T_s)\right]^T$$

$$\tilde{\mathbf{a}}_n = \left[\tilde{a}_{n,\,1} \quad \cdots \quad \tilde{a}_{n,\,P}\right]^T$$

$$\tilde{\mathbf{S}}_n = \left[S_{n-1} \quad \cdots \quad S_{n-P}\right]^T$$

$$0 < \mu < \frac{2}{LE\left[|\tilde{r}(kT_s)|^2\right] + PE\left[|S_n|^2\right]}. \tag{5.140}$$

This completes the discussion on various equalization techniques. In the next section, we take up the discussion on maximum likelihood detectors. Observe that since the interference at the equalizer output is *not* Gaussian, we cannot in principle evaluate the symbol-error-rate performance at the equalizer output. We can only compute the minimum mean squared error at the equalizer output. Hence, communication systems that employ equalizers must rely on computer simulations to obtain the symbol-error-rate performance.

5.2 Receivers Based on Maximum Likelihood Sequence Estimation (MLSE)

The maximum likelihood sequence estimation approach is based on directly minimizing the symbol-error-rate. This is in contrast to the equalization approach, which relies on minimizing the noise variance at its output (this indirectly minimizes the symbol-error-rate). However, the ML approach is computationally more complex compared to the equalization approach. As in the case of equalization, ML detectors can also be classified into two categories:

(a) Symbol-spaced[177]
(b) Fractionally-spaced

While the symbol-spaced ML detectors are useful for the purpose of analysis, it is the fractionally-spaced ML detectors that are used in practice. Under ideal conditions (perfect matched filter and correct timing phase), the symbol-error-rate performance of the symbol-spaced ML detector is identical to that of the fractionally-spaced ML detector.

An efficient ML detector based on truncating the channel impulse response is discussed in [178]. ML detection for passband systems is described in [179]. In [180], aDFE is used in combination with an ML detector. ML detection for time-varying channels is given in [181,182]. An efficient MLdetector based on set-partitioning the constellation is given in [183]. In [184,185], the set-*partioning approach* is extended to trellis coded signals. Efficient ML detectors based on per-survivor processing is given in [186].

5.2.1 Symbol-spaced MLSE

At the outset, we assume that the equivalent channel $\tilde{q}(t)$ in (5.6) is finite in time. This assumption is valid in practical situations, since most of the channel energy is concentrated over a finite time interval. Hence the discrete-time signal at the sampler output which was given by (5.29) must be modified to

$$\tilde{v}_n = \sum_{k=-L}^{L} \tilde{R}_{\tilde{q}\tilde{q},k} S_{n-k} + \tilde{w}_{2,n} \tag{5.141}$$

where $\tilde{R}_{\tilde{q}\tilde{q},k}$ denotes the sampled autocorrelation of $\tilde{q}(t)$ *with sampling phase equal to zero.* Note that

(a) Due to the assumption that $\tilde{q}(t)$ is finite in time, $\tilde{R}_{\tilde{q}\tilde{q},k}$ is also finite, that is,

$$\tilde{R}_{\tilde{q}\tilde{q},k} = 0 \qquad \text{for } k < -L \text{ and } k > L \tag{5.142}$$

for some integer L.

(b) Zero sampling phase implies that $\tilde{R}_{\tilde{q}\tilde{q},m}$ is a valid discrete-time autocorrelation sequence which satisfies

$$\tilde{R}_{\tilde{q}\tilde{q},-m} = \tilde{R}^*_{\tilde{q}\tilde{q},m}. \tag{5.143}$$

(c) Zero sampling phase also implies that the autocorrelation peak is sampled. Here the autocorrelation peak occurs at index $k = 0$, that is, $\tilde{R}_{\tilde{q}\tilde{q},0}$ is real-valued and

$$\tilde{R}_{\tilde{q}\tilde{q},0} \geq \left|\tilde{R}_{\tilde{q}\tilde{q},k}\right| \qquad \text{for } k \neq 0. \tag{5.144}$$

The autocorrelation of $\tilde{w}_{2,n}$ is given by (5.30), which is repeated here:

$$\begin{aligned}
\frac{1}{2}E\left[\tilde{w}_{2,n}\tilde{w}^*_{2,n-m}\right] &= \frac{1}{2}E\left[\int_{x=-\infty}^{\infty} \tilde{q}^*(x-nT)\tilde{w}(x)\,dx \times \int_{y=-\infty}^{\infty} \tilde{q}(y-nT+mT)\tilde{w}^*(y)\,dy\right] \\
&= N_0 \tilde{R}_{\tilde{q}\tilde{q}}(mT) \\
&\stackrel{\Delta}{=} N_0 \tilde{R}_{\tilde{q}\tilde{q},m}
\end{aligned} \tag{5.145}$$

where $\tilde{R}_{\tilde{q}\tilde{q},m}$ is given by (5.142).

The first step towards implementing the ML detector is to whiten the noise. Let $\tilde{R}_{\tilde{q}\tilde{q}}(\tilde{z})$ denote the $\tilde{z}$-transform of $\tilde{R}_{\tilde{q}\tilde{q},m}$, that is

$$\tilde{R}_{\tilde{q}\tilde{q}}(\tilde{z}) = \sum_{m=-L}^{L} \tilde{R}_{\tilde{q}\tilde{q},m}\tilde{z}^{-m}. \tag{5.146}$$

Then due to (5.143) we must have

$$\begin{aligned}
\tilde{R}_{\tilde{q}\tilde{q},m} &= \tilde{b}_m \star \tilde{b}^*_{-m} \\
\Rightarrow \tilde{R}_{\tilde{q}\tilde{q}}(\tilde{z}) &= \tilde{B}(\tilde{z})\tilde{B}^*(1/\tilde{z}^*) \\
&= \tilde{R}^*_{\tilde{q}\tilde{q}}(1/\tilde{z}^*)
\end{aligned} \tag{5.147}$$

for some discrete-time causal impulse response $\tilde{b}_n$, and $\tilde{B}(\tilde{z})$ is the $\tilde{z}$-transform of $\tilde{b}_n$ as given by

$$\tilde{B}(\tilde{z}) = \sum_{n=0}^{L} \tilde{b}_n \tilde{z}^{-n}. \tag{5.148}$$

Note that

$$\tilde{R}_{\tilde{q}\tilde{q}}(\tilde{z})\Big|_{\tilde{z}=e^{j2\pi FT}} = S_{\mathscr{P},\tilde{q}}(F) = \tilde{B}_{\mathscr{P}}(F)\tilde{B}^*_{\mathscr{P}}(F) \tag{5.149}$$

where $S_{\mathscr{P},\tilde{q}}(F)$ is defined in (5.32) and $\tilde{B}_{\mathscr{P}}(F)$ is the discrete-time Fourier transform of $\tilde{b}_n$. Observe also that if $\tilde{z}_0$ is a zero of $\tilde{R}_{\tilde{q}\tilde{q}}(\tilde{z})$, so is $1/\tilde{z}_0^*$. We assume that $\tilde{R}_{\tilde{q}\tilde{q}}(\tilde{z})$ does not have any zeros on the unit circle. This is equivalent to saying that $S_{\mathscr{P},\tilde{q}}(F)$ does not have any spectral nulls, that is

$$\tilde{S}_{\mathscr{P},\tilde{q}}(F) \neq 0 \qquad \text{for all } F. \tag{5.150}$$

Let the $\tilde{z}$-transform of the whitening filter be

$$\tilde{W}(\tilde{z}) = \frac{1}{\tilde{B}^*(1/\tilde{z}^*)}. \tag{5.151}$$

Note that $\tilde{W}(\tilde{z})$ is anti-causal. Hence, for stability we require all the zeros of $\tilde{B}^*(1/\tilde{z}^*)$ to be outside the unit circle (maximum phase).

Now, if $\tilde{v}_n$ in (5.141) is passed through the whitening filter, the pulse-shape at the output is simply $\tilde{B}(\tilde{z})$, which is minimum phase (all the zeros lie inside the unit circle). Thus, the signal at the output of the whitening filter is given by

$$\tilde{x}_n = \sum_{k=0}^{L} \tilde{b}_k S_{n-k} + \tilde{w}_{4,n} \tag{5.152}$$

where $\tilde{w}_{4,n}$ denotes samples of additive white Gaussian noise with variance N_0, that is

$$\frac{1}{2} E\left[\tilde{w}_{4,n}\tilde{w}^*_{4,n-m}\right] = N_0 \delta_K(m). \tag{5.153}$$

This is shown in Figure 5.11. The combination of the matched filter, the symbol-rate sampler and the whitening is usually refused to as the whitened matched filter (WMF)[177]. The

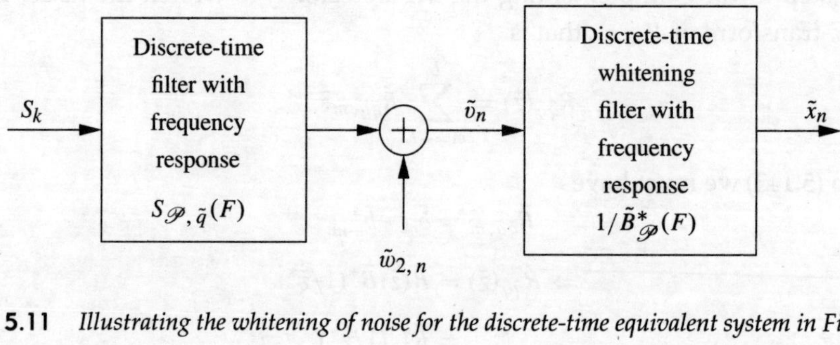

Figure 5.11 *Illustrating the whitening of noise for the discrete-time equivalent system in Figure 5.4*

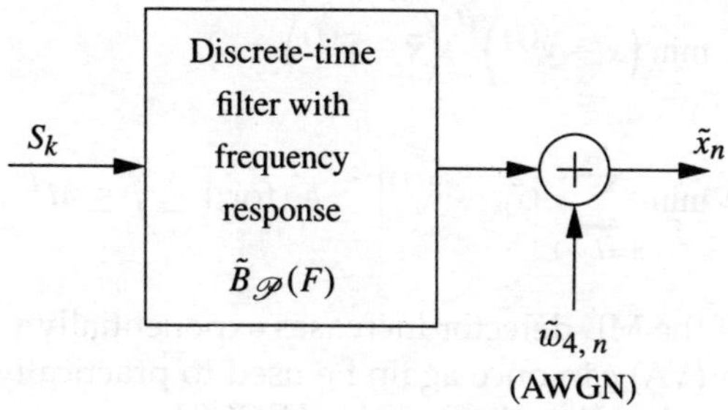

Figure 5.12 *The discrete-time equivalent (minimum phase) channel at the output of the whitening filter*

discrete-time equivalent system at the output of the whitening filter is shown in Figure 5.12. From (5.152) we note that the span (length) of the discrete-time equivalent channel at the output of the whitening filter is $L+1$ (T-spaced) samples. The stage is now set for deriving the ML detector. We assume that L_s symbols have been transmitted. Typically, $L_s \gg L$. We also assume that the symbols are uncoded and drawn from an M-ary constellation. The ith possible symbol vector is denoted by

$$\mathbf{S}_v^{(i)} = \begin{bmatrix} S_1^{(i)} & S_2^{(i)} & \ldots & S_{L_s}^{(i)} \end{bmatrix}^T \qquad \text{for } 1 \le i \le M^{L_s}. \tag{5.154}$$

The received sample sequence can be written as an $(L_s - L) \times 1$ vector as follows.

$$\begin{bmatrix} \tilde{x}_{L+1} \\ \tilde{x}_{L+2} \\ \vdots \\ \tilde{x}_{L_s} \end{bmatrix} = \begin{bmatrix} S_{L+1}^{(i)} & \cdots & S_1^{(i)} \\ S_{L+2}^{(i)} & \cdots & S_2^{(i)} \\ \vdots & \vdots & \vdots \\ S_{L_s}^{(i)} & \cdots & S_{L_s-L}^{(i)} \end{bmatrix} \begin{bmatrix} \tilde{b}_0 \\ \tilde{b}_1 \\ \vdots \\ \tilde{b}_L \end{bmatrix} + \begin{bmatrix} \tilde{w}_{4,\,L+1} \\ \tilde{w}_{4,\,L+2} \\ \vdots \\ \tilde{w}_{4,\,L_s} \end{bmatrix}. \tag{5.155}$$

Note that when the symbol sequence in (5.154) is convolved with the $(L+1)$-tap discrete-time equivalent channel in Figure 5.12, the length of the output sample sequence is $L_s+L+1-1 = L_s + L$. However, the first and the last L samples correspond to the 'transient response' of the channel (all channel taps are not excited). Hence the number of 'steady-state' samples is only $L_s + L - 2L = L_s - L$ samples. This explains why $\tilde{\mathbf{x}}$ is an $(L_s - L) \times 1$ vector.

The above equation can be compactly written as

$$\begin{aligned} \tilde{\mathbf{x}} &= \mathbf{S}^{(i)}\tilde{\mathbf{B}} + \tilde{\mathbf{w}}_4 \\ &\stackrel{\Delta}{=} \tilde{\mathbf{y}}^{(i)} + \tilde{\mathbf{w}}_4. \end{aligned} \tag{5.156}$$

Note that since there are M^{L_s} distinct symbol sequences, there are also an equal number of sample sequences, $\tilde{\mathbf{y}}^{(i)}$. Since the noise samples are uncorrelated, the ML detector reduces to (see also (2.86) for a similar derivation)

$$\min_j \left(\tilde{\mathbf{x}} - \tilde{\mathbf{y}}^{(j)}\right)^H \left(\tilde{\mathbf{x}} - \tilde{\mathbf{y}}^{(j)}\right)$$

$$\Rightarrow \min_j \sum_{n=L+1}^{L_s} \left|\tilde{x}_n - \tilde{y}_n^{(j)}\right|^2 \qquad \text{for } 1 \le j \le M^{L_s}. \tag{5.157}$$

Clearly, the complexity of the ML detector increases exponentially with the sequence length L_s. The Viterbi algorithm (VA) can once again be used to practically implement (5.157). An efficient implementation of the VA is discussed in [187]. The recursion for the VA is given by

$$\sum_{n=L+1}^{N} \left|\tilde{x}_n - \tilde{y}_n^{(j)}\right|^2 = \sum_{n=L+1}^{N-1} \left|\tilde{x}_n - \tilde{y}_n^{(j)}\right|^2 + \left|\tilde{x}_N - \tilde{y}_N^{(j)}\right|^2. \tag{5.158}$$

Whereas the first term in the right-hand-side of the above equation denotes the accumulated metric, the second term denotes the branch metric. The trellis would have M^L states, and the complexity of the VA in detecting L_s symbols would be $L_s M^L$, compared to M^{L_s} for the ML detector in (5.157). Following the notation in (2.227), the jth state would be represented by an M-ary L-tuple

$$\mathcal{S}_j = \left\{\mathcal{S}_{j,1} \ldots \mathcal{S}_{j,L}\right\} \tag{5.159}$$

where the digits

$$\mathcal{S}_{j,k} \in \{0, \ldots, M-1\}. \tag{5.160}$$

The trellis diagram for $M = 4$ and $L = 2$ is exactly identical to Figure 2.14. Given the present state $\mathcal{S}_j$ and input l ($l \in \{0, \ldots, M-1\}$), the next state is given by

$$\mathcal{S}_k = \left\{l\, \mathcal{S}_{j,1} \ldots \mathcal{S}_{j,L-1}\right\}. \tag{5.161}$$

Once again, let $\mathcal{M}(\cdot)$ denote the one-to-one mapping between the digits and the symbols. The branch metric at time kT, from state $\mathcal{S}_j$ due to input symbol l ($0 \le l \le M-1$) is given by

$$\tilde{z}_k^{(\mathcal{S}_j, l)} = \left|\tilde{x}_k - \tilde{y}^{(\mathcal{S}_j, l)}\right|^2 \tag{5.162}$$

where

$$\tilde{y}^{(\mathcal{S}_j, l)} = \tilde{b}_0 \mathcal{M}(l) + \sum_{n=1}^{L} \tilde{b}_n \mathcal{M}(\mathcal{S}_{j,n}). \tag{5.163}$$

Note carefully, the difference in metric computation in (2.231) and (5.162). The trellis diagram for $M = 2$ and $L = 2$ is depicted in Figure 5.13, for $b_0 = 1$, $b_1 = 2$ and $b_2 = 3$. The branches are labelled as $l/\tilde{y}^{(\mathcal{S}_j, l)}$, where l denotes the input digit. The evolution of the VA over two bit durations is depicted in Figure 5.14.

It is interesting to note that each row of $\mathbf{S}^{(i)}$ in (5.155) denotes the contents of the tapped delay line. The first element of each row represents the input symbol and the remaining elements define the state of the trellis. In the next section we discuss the performance of the ML detector.

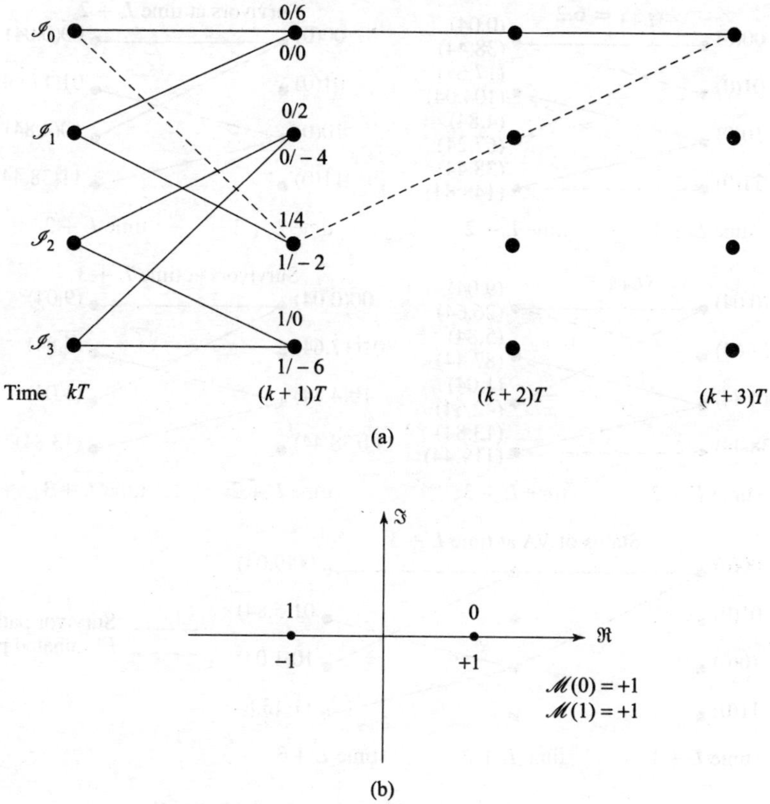

Figure 5.13 *(a) Trellis diagram for BPSK modulation with $L = 2$. The minimum distance error event is shown in dashed lines. (b) Mapping of binary digits to symbols.*

Performance analysis of the symbol-spaced ML detector

In this section, we derive the expression for the average probability of symbol error when ML detection is used. We assume that the symbols are uncoded. First, we derive the expression for the probability of an error event. Consider the ith symbol sequence given by

$$\mathbf{S}^{(i)} = \{\ldots,\, S_{k-1}^{(i)},\, S_k^{(i)},\, S_{k+1}^{(i)},\, \ldots,\, S_{k+L_{i,j}}^{(i)},\, S_{k+L_{i,j}+1}^{(i)},\, \ldots\}. \tag{5.164}$$

Now consider the jth symbol sequence given by

$$\mathbf{S}^{(j)} = \{\ldots,\, S_{k-1}^{(j)},\, S_k^{(j)},\, S_{k+1}^{(j)},\, \ldots,\, S_{k+L_{i,j}}^{(j)},\, S_{k+L_{i,j}+1}^{(j)},\, \ldots\}. \tag{5.165}$$

with the constraint that

$$S_n^{(i)} = S_n^{(j)} \qquad \text{for } n < k \text{ and } n > (k + L_{i,j}). \tag{5.166}$$

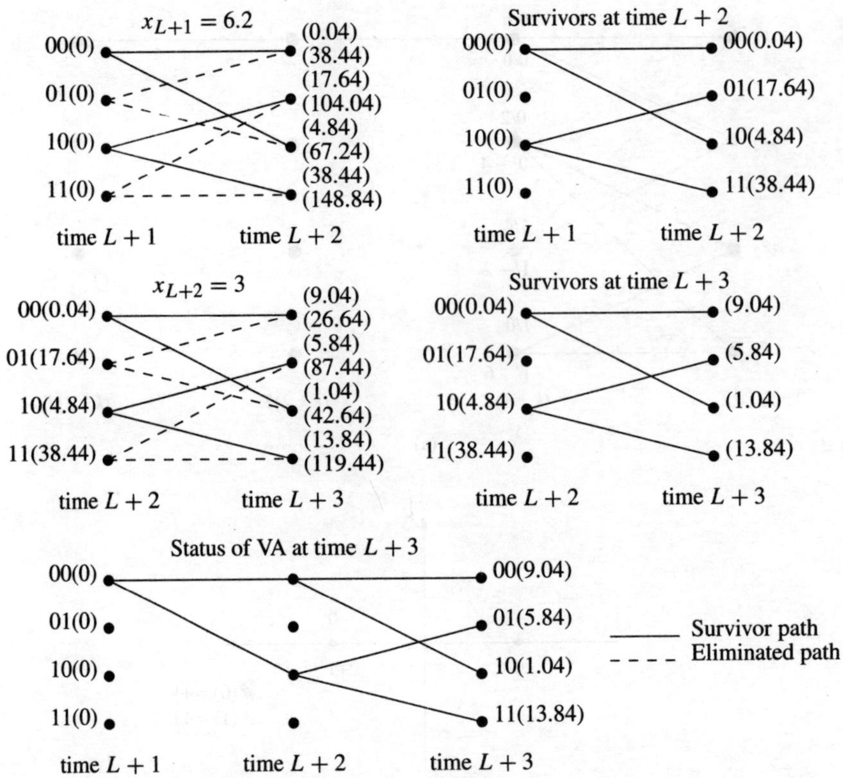

Figure 5.14 *Evolution of the VA over two bit durations*

We also wish to emphasize that

$$S_n^{(i)} \neq S_n^{(j)} \qquad \text{for } n = k \text{ and } n = (k + L_{i,j}) \tag{5.167}$$

and

$$S_n^{(i)} \stackrel{?}{=} S_n^{(j)} \qquad \text{for } n > k \text{ and } n < (k + L_{i,j}). \tag{5.168}$$

In other words, the ith and j^{th} sequences are identical for all times less than kT and greater than $(k + L_{i,j})T$. The sequences may or may not be identical in between the times kT and $(k + L_{i,j})T$. Thus, the ith and j^{th} sequences diverge from a common state at time kT and remerge back *only* at time $(k + L_{i,j} + L + 1)T$. This implies that at time $(k + L_{i,j} + L + 1)T$, the ML detector must decide between the ith and the jth sequence. This also implies that the length of the error event is

$$L_{e,i,j} \stackrel{\Delta}{=} L_{i,j} + L + 1. \tag{5.169}$$

Let us now assume that the ith sequence was transmitted. The ML detector decides in favour of the jth sequence when

$$\sum_{n=k}^{k+L_{e,i,j}-1} \left|\tilde{w}_{4,n}\right|^2 > \sum_{n=k}^{k+L_{e,i,j}-1} \left|\tilde{y}_{i,j,n} + \tilde{w}_{4,n}\right|^2 \tag{5.170}$$

where

$$\tilde{y}_{i,j,n} = \sum_{l=0}^{L} \tilde{b}_l \left(S_{n-l}^{(i)} - S_{n-l}^{(j)}\right) \qquad \text{for } k \le n \le (k + L_{e,i,j} - 1). \tag{5.171}$$

From (5.170), the expression for the probability of error event reduces to

$$P\left(\mathbf{S}^{(j)}|\mathbf{S}^{(i)}\right) = P\left(Z < -d_{i,j}^2\right) \tag{5.172}$$

where

$$Z = \sum_{n=k}^{k+L_{e,i,j}-1} 2\Re\left\{\tilde{y}_{i,j,n}\tilde{w}_{4,n}^*\right\}$$

$$d_{i,j}^2 = \sum_{n=k}^{k+L_{e,i,j}-1} \left|\tilde{y}_{i,j,n}\right|^2. \tag{5.173}$$

Clearly,

$$E[Z] = 0$$

$$E[Z^2] = 4N_0 d_{i,j}^2. \tag{5.174}$$

Hence (5.172) reduces to

$$P\left(\mathbf{S}^{(j)}|\mathbf{S}^{(i)}\right) = \frac{1}{2}\,\text{erfc}\left(\sqrt{\frac{d_{i,j}^2}{8N_0}}\right)$$

$$= P_{\text{ee}}\left(d_{i,j}^2\right) \qquad \text{(say)}. \tag{5.175}$$

Having found out the probability of an error event at a distance $d_{i,j}^2$ from the reference sequence, we now turn our attention to computing the average probability of symbol error.

Unfortunately, this issue is complicated by the fact that when QAM constellations are used the distance spectrum depends on the reference sequence. To see why, let us consider a simple example with $L_{i,j} = 0$ in (5.164) and (5.165). That is, the sequences i and j differ in only one symbol, occurring at time k. If the reference symbol is $S_k^{(i)}$, then for QAM constellations, the number of nearest neighbours depends on the reference symbol. Thus, even though the minimum distance is independent of the reference symbol, the multiplicity is different. To summarize, the distance spectrum is dependent on the reference sequence when QAM constellations are used. However, for PSK constellations, the distance spectrum is independent of the reference sequence.

In any case, in order to solve the problem at hand, we assume that we have at our disposal the distance spectra with respect to all possible reference symbol sequences of length $\mathscr{L}$. Since the performance of the ML detector is dominated by the first few spectral lines, it is sufficient to consider

$$\mathscr{L} = 5L \tag{5.176}$$

where L is the memory of the discrete-time equivalent channel at the output of the whitening filter. The probability of symbol error given that $\mathbf{S}^{(i)}$ was transmitted and $\mathbf{S}^{(j)}$ is detected is given by

$$N_{i,\,j}\, P_{\text{ee}}\left(d_{i,\,j}^2\right) = \frac{N_{i,\,j}}{2}\, \text{erfc}\left(\sqrt{\frac{d_{i,\,j}^2}{8N_0}}\right) \tag{5.177}$$

where $N_{i,\,j}$ is the number of symbol errors when sequence $\mathbf{S}^{(j)}$ is detected instead of $\mathbf{S}^{(i)}$. Note that due to (5.166), (5.167) and (5.168),

$$N_{i,\,j} \leq L_{i,\,j} + 1. \tag{5.178}$$

Now, for convenience of representation, let us denote

$$\begin{aligned} N_{i,\,j} &= N_{l,\,d_{i,\,m}} \\ d_{i,\,j}^2 &= d_{i,\,m}^2 \end{aligned} \tag{5.179}$$

where $d_{i,\,m}^2$ denotes the mth squared Euclidean distance with respect to sequence i and $N_{l,\,d_{i,\,m}}$ denotes the number of symbol errors corresponding to the lth multiplicity at a squared distance of $d_{i,\,m}^2$ with respect to sequence i.

In order to explain the above notation, let us consider an example. Let the distance spectrum (distances are arranged strictly in ascending order) with respect to sequence i be

$$\{1.5,\ 2.6,\ 5.1\} \tag{5.180}$$

and the corresponding set of multiplicities be

$$\{1,\ 4,\ 5\}. \tag{5.181}$$

Let M_i denote the cardinality of the set of distances with respect to sequence i. Then,

$$\begin{aligned} C_i &= 3 \\ d_{i,\,1}^2 &= 1.5 \\ d_{i,\,2}^2 &= 2.6 \\ d_{i,\,3}^2 &= 5.1 \\ A_{d_{i,\,1}} &= 1 \\ A_{d_{i,\,2}} &= 4 \\ A_{d_{i,\,3}} &= 5. \end{aligned} \tag{5.182}$$

We wish to emphasize at this point that since we have considered the reference sequence to be of finite length ($\mathscr{L}$), the set of distances is also finite. The true distance spectrum (which has infinite spectral lines) can be obtained only as $\mathscr{L} \to \infty$. In practice the first few spectral lines can be correctly obtained by taking $\mathscr{L} = 5L$.

With these basic definitions, the average probability of symbol error *given* that the ith sequence is transmitted is union bounded (upper bounded) by

$$P_{e|i} \le \sum_{m=1}^{M_i} P_{\text{ee}}(d_{i,m}^2) \sum_{l=1}^{A_{d_{i,m}}} N_{l,\, d_{i,m}}. \tag{5.183}$$

The average probability of symbol error is then

$$P_e \le \sum_{i=1}^{M^{\mathscr{L}}} P(i) P_{e|i} \tag{5.184}$$

where $P(i)$ denotes the probability of occurrence of the ith reference sequence. If all sequences are equally likely, then

$$P(i) = \frac{1}{M^{\mathscr{L}}}. \tag{5.185}$$

Note that when PSK constellations are used, the distance spectrum is independent of the reference sequence with $C_i = C$, and the average probability of symbol error is directly given by (5.183), that is,

$$P_e \le \sum_{m=1}^{M} P_{\text{ee}}(d_m^2) \sum_{l=1}^{A_{d_m}} N_{l,\, d_m}. \tag{5.186}$$

At high SNR, the probability of symbol error is dominated by the minimum distance error event.

Having discussed the symbol-spaced ML detector,let us now look into the implementation issues. Just as in the case of the equalizer, the symbol-spaced ML detector too is sensitive to the inaccuracies in the matched filter, the timing phase and above all, the realizability of the whitening filter. Observe from (5.150) that the whitening filter can be implemented only when $\tilde{B}_{\mathscr{P}}(F)$ does not have any spectral nulls. This in turn implies that $S_{\mathscr{P},q}(F)$ must also not contain any spectral nulls. This is a serious constraint in the implementation of the symbol-spaced ML detector. Observe that the whitening filter cannot be avoided, since otherwise the ML detection rule will not take the simple form given in (5.157). The other problem is related to a non-zero timing phase. As a consequence, the discrete-time equivalent channel at the output of the whitening filter has an infinite impulse response, which renders the ML detector to be impractical. These issues motivate us to discuss the fractionally-spaced ML detector, which overcomes all the problems associated with symbol-spaced ML detection.

5.2.2 Fractionally-spaced MLSE

Consider the digital communication system shown in Figure 5.2. Since the transmit filter $\tilde{p}(t)$ is usually a root-raised cosine pulse and is bandlimited to $[-1/T,\, 1/T]$ ($1/T$ is the symbol-rate), $\tilde{q}(t)$ is also bandlimited to $[-1/T, 1/T]$. Let us pass $\tilde{r}(t)$ in (5.5) through an ideal lowpass filter having unit energy and extending over $[-1/T, 1/T]$. The lowpass filter output can be written as

$$\tilde{x}(t) = \sqrt{\frac{T}{2}} \sum_{k=-\infty}^{\infty} S_k \, \tilde{q}(t - kT) + \tilde{w}_1(t) \tag{5.187}$$

where $\tilde{w}_1(t)$ denotes bandlimited noise having a flat psd of height $N_0T/2$ in the range $[-1/T, 1/T]$. Now if $\tilde{x}(t)$ is sampled at Nyquist-rate $(2/T = 1/T_s)$ the output is

$$\tilde{x}(nT_s) = \sqrt{\frac{T}{2}} \sum_{k=-\infty}^{\infty} S_k \, \tilde{q}(nT_s - kT) + \tilde{w}_1(nT_s) \tag{5.188}$$

where $\tilde{w}_1(nT_s)$ has the autocorrelation (see also Figure 5.15)

$$\frac{1}{2} E\left[\tilde{w}_1(nT_s)\tilde{w}_1^*(nT_s - mT_s)\right] = N_0 \delta_K(mT_s). \tag{5.189}$$

The samples $\tilde{x}(nT_s)$ are fed to the fractionally-spaced ML detector, which estimates the symbols. This is illustrated in Figure 5.16.

In order to derive the ML detector, we need to assume that $\tilde{q}(t)$ is time-limited. Strictly speaking, it is not possible for $\tilde{q}(t)$ to be both time-limited and band-limited. However for practical purposes this is a valid assumption, since most of the energy of $\tilde{q}(t)$ is concentrated over a finite time-span. Let $\tilde{q}(t)$ span over L_qT symbol durations. Let us also assume that $\tilde{q}(t)$ is causal. Further, since we have assumed that $T/T_s = 2$, the discrete-time equivalent channel has $2L_q$ coefficients denoted by $\tilde{q}(kT_s)$ for $0 \le k \le 2L_q - 1$. With these assumptions, (5.188) can be written as

$$\tilde{x}(nT_s) = \sqrt{\frac{T}{2}} \sum_{k=k_1}^{k_2} S_k \, \tilde{q}(nT_s - 2kT_s) + \tilde{w}_1(nT_s) \tag{5.190}$$

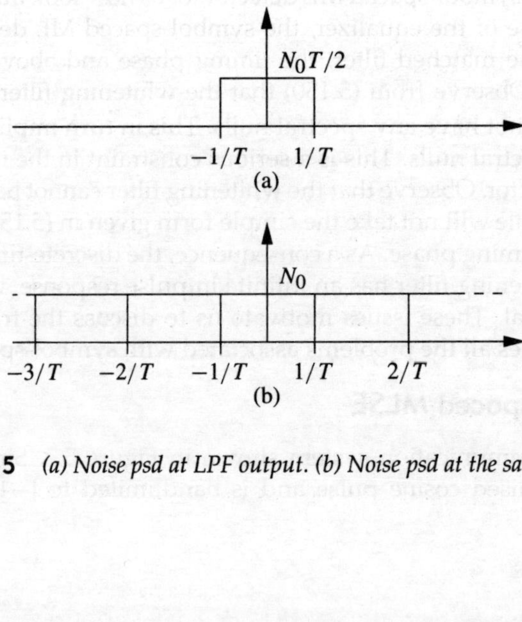

Figure 5.15 *(a) Noise psd at LPF output. (b) Noise psd at the sampler output*

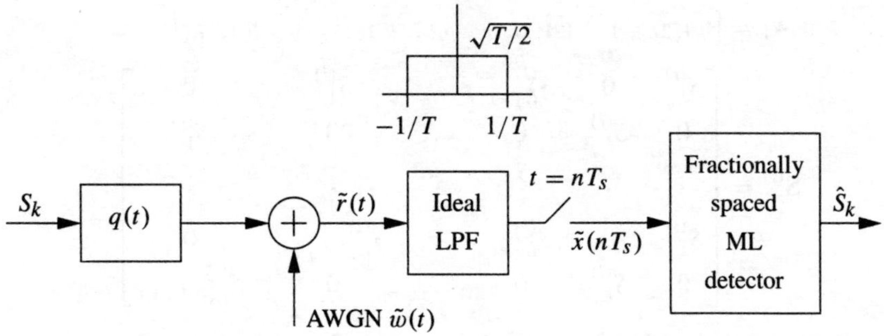

Figure 5.16 *Model for the digital communication system employing fractionally-spaced ML detector*

where (see also (4.9))

$$k_1 = \left\lceil \frac{n - 2L_q + 1}{2} \right\rceil$$

$$k_2 = \left\lfloor \frac{n}{2} \right\rfloor. \tag{5.191}$$

The limits k_1 and k_2 are obtained using the fact that $\tilde{q}(\cdot)$ is time-limited, that is,

$$0 \le nT_s - 2kT_s \le (2L_q - 1)T_s. \tag{5.192}$$

Note that the signal component of $\tilde{x}(nT_s)$ in (5.190) can be obtained using the tapped-delay line approach shown in Figure 4.4.

Let us now assume that L_s symbols have been transmitted. Let us denote the ith interpolated symbol sequence by a $2L_s \times 1$ column vector as follows.

$$\mathbf{S}_v^{(i)} = \begin{bmatrix} S_1^{(i)} & 0 & S_2^{(i)} & \ldots & S_{L_s}^{(i)} & 0 \end{bmatrix}^T \quad \text{for } 1 \le i \le M^{L_s}. \tag{5.193}$$

The received sequence $\tilde{x}(nT_s)$ can be represented in vector form as follows.

$$\tilde{\mathbf{x}} = \sqrt{\frac{T}{2}}\mathbf{S}^{(i)}\tilde{\mathbf{Q}} + \tilde{\mathbf{w}}_1$$

$$\stackrel{\Delta}{=} \tilde{\mathbf{y}}^{(i)} + \tilde{\mathbf{w}}_1 \tag{5.194}$$

where

$$\tilde{\mathbf{x}} = \begin{bmatrix} \tilde{x}_{2L_q-1} & \tilde{x}_{2L_q} & \ldots & \tilde{x}_{2L_s-1} & \tilde{x}_{2L_s} \end{bmatrix}^T,$$

$$\tilde{\mathbf{Q}} = \begin{bmatrix} \tilde{q}(0) & \tilde{q}(T_s) & \ldots & \tilde{q}((2L_q-2)T_s) & \tilde{q}((2L_q-1)T_s) \end{bmatrix}^T$$

$$\tilde{\mathbf{w}}_1 = \left[\tilde{w}_{1,\,2L_q-1} \quad \tilde{w}_{1,\,2L_q} \quad \ldots \quad \tilde{w}_{1,\,2L_s-1} \quad \tilde{w}_{1,\,2L_s}\right]^T$$

$$\mathbf{S}^{(i)} = \begin{bmatrix} S_{L_q}^{(i)} & 0 & S_{L_q-1}^{(i)} & \ldots & S_1^{(i)} & 0 \\ 0 & S_{L_q}^{(i)} & 0 & \ldots & 0 & S_1^{(i)} \\ \vdots & \vdots & \vdots & \vdots & \vdots & \vdots \\ S_{L_s}^{(i)} & 0 & S_{L_s-1}^{(i)} & \ldots & S_{L_s-L_q+1}^{(i)} & 0 \\ 0 & S_{L_s}^{(i)} & 0 & \ldots & 0 & S_{L_s-L_q+1}^{(i)} \end{bmatrix}. \tag{5.195}$$

As before we have considered only the steady-state values of $\tilde{x}(nT_s)$. Since the noise terms are uncorrelated, the ML detector reduces to

$$\min_j \left(\tilde{\mathbf{x}} - \tilde{\mathbf{y}}^{(j)}\right)^H \left(\tilde{\mathbf{x}} - \tilde{\mathbf{y}}^{(j)}\right)$$

$$\Rightarrow \min_j \sum_{n=2L_q-1}^{2L_s} \left|\tilde{x}_n - \tilde{y}_n^{(j)}\right|^2 \qquad \text{for } 1 \le j \le M^{L_s} \tag{5.196}$$

which can be efficiently implemented using the VA. Here the first non-zero element of each row of $\mathbf{S}^{(i)}$ in (5.195) denotes the input symbol and the remaining $L_q - 1$ non-zero elements determine the trellis state. Thus, the number of trellis states is equal to M^{L_q-1}.

The important point that needs to be mentioned here is that the VA must process two samples of $\tilde{x}(nT_s)$ every symbol interval, unlike the symbol-spaced ML detector, where the VA takes only one sample of $\tilde{x}(nT_s)$ (see the branch computation in (5.158)). The reason is not hard to find. Referring to the matrix $\mathbf{S}^{(i)}$ in (5.195) we find that the first two rows have the same non-zero elements (symbols). Since the non-zero elements determine the trellis state, it is clear that the trellis state does not change over two input samples. This is again in contrast to the symbol-spaced ML detector where the trellis state changes every input sample.

To summarize, for both the symbol-spaced as well as the fractionally-spaced ML detector, the VA changes state every symbol. The only difference is that, for the symbol-spaced ML detector there is only one sample every symbol, whereas for the fractionally-spaced ML detector there are two samples every symbol. Hence the recursion for the VA for the fractionally-spaced ML detector can be written as

$$\sum_{n=2L_q-1}^{2N} \left|\tilde{x}_n - \tilde{y}_n^{(j)}\right|^2 = \sum_{n=2L_q-1}^{2N-2} \left|\tilde{x}_n - \tilde{y}_n^{(j)}\right|^2 + \sum_{n=2N-1}^{2N} \left|\tilde{x}_n - \tilde{y}_n^{(j)}\right|^2. \tag{5.197}$$

The first term in the right-hand-side of the above equation denotes the accumulated metric and the second term denotes the branch metric.

This concludes the discussion on the fractionally-spaced ML detector. We now proceed to prove the equivalence between the symbol-spaced and fractionally-spaced ML detectors. By establishing this equivalence, we can indirectly prove that the performance of the fractionally-spaced ML detector is identical to that of the symbol-spaced ML detector.

We now present a few examples that compare the performance of the symbol-spaced and fractionally-spaced ML detectors.

5.2.3 Equivalence between T-spaced and $T/2$-spaced ML detectors

We will establish the equivalence by demonstrating that the distance spectrum 'seen' by the two detectors are identical. Since the noise variance for both the detectors is N_0, establishing the equivalence of the distance spectrum amounts to proving that their performance will also be identical. Let us first consider the symbol-spaced (T-spaced) ML detector.

Recall that the squared Euclidean distance between two symbol sequences is given by the second equation in (5.173). Let

$$\tilde{e}_n^{(ij)} = S_n^{(i)} - S_n^{(j)} \tag{5.198}$$

denote the error sequence. Then the squared Euclidean distance between $S_n^{(i)}$ and $S_n^{(j)}$ can be written as

$$d_{T,i,j}^2 = \text{energy of the sequence } (\tilde{e}_n^{(ij)} \star \tilde{b}_n) \tag{5.199}$$

where the subscript T denotes a T-spaced ML detector and $\tilde{b}_n$ denotes the resultant pulse shape at the output of the whitening filter. Let

$$\tilde{E}_{\mathscr{P}}^{(ij)}(F) = \sum_n \tilde{e}_n^{(ij)} \mathrm{e}^{-\mathrm{j}2\pi FnT} \tag{5.200}$$

denote the discrete-time Fourier transform of the error sequence. Similarly, let $\tilde{B}_{\mathscr{P}}(F)$ denote the discrete-time Fourier transform of $\tilde{b}_n$. Then using Parseval's theorem in (5.199), we get

$$\begin{aligned} d_{T,i,j}^2 &= T \int_{F=0}^{1/T} \left|\tilde{E}_{\mathscr{P}}^{(ij)}(F)\right|^2 \left|\tilde{B}_{\mathscr{P}}(F)\right|^2 dF \\ &= T \int_{F=0}^{1/T} \left|\tilde{E}_{\mathscr{P}}^{(ij)}(F)\right|^2 S_{\mathscr{P},\tilde{q}}(F)\, dF \end{aligned} \tag{5.201}$$

where $S_{\mathscr{P},\tilde{q}}(F)$ is defined in (5.32). If $\tilde{Q}(F)$ is bandlimited to $[-1/T, 1/T]$, then

$$S_{\mathscr{P},\tilde{q}}(F) = \frac{1}{T}\left[\left|\tilde{Q}(F)\right|^2 + \left|\tilde{Q}\left(F - \frac{1}{T}\right)\right|^2\right] \quad \text{for } 0 \le F \le 1/T. \tag{5.202}$$

Thus we have

$$d_{T,i,j}^2 = \int_{F=0}^{1/T} \left|\tilde{E}_{\mathscr{P}}^{(ij)}(F)\right|^2 \left[\left|\tilde{Q}(F)\right|^2 + \left|\tilde{Q}\left(F - \frac{1}{T}\right)\right|^2\right] dF. \tag{5.203}$$

Let us now consider the fractionally-spaced ML detector. Recall from (5.194) and (5.195) that the discrete-time equivalent channel is represented by the $2L_q \times 1$ vector

$$\sqrt{\frac{T}{2}}\tilde{\mathbf{Q}} = \sqrt{\frac{T}{2}}\left[\tilde{q}(0) \quad \tilde{q}(T_s) \quad \ldots \quad \tilde{q}((2L_q-2)T_s) \quad \tilde{q}((2L_q-1)T_s)\right]^T. \tag{5.204}$$

Let us compute the squared Euclidean distance generated by the *same* error sequence $\tilde{e}_n^{(ij)}$ defined in (5.198).

To do this we first note that the samples of $\tilde{e}_n^{(ij)}$ are T-spaced, whereas the channel coefficients are $T/2$-spaced. Therefore, every alternate channel coefficient is involved in the computation of each output sample (refer also to Figure 4.4). Let us denote the even indexed channel coefficients by $\tilde{q}_e(nT)$ and the odd indexed coefficients by $\tilde{q}_o(nT)$, that is,

$$\begin{aligned}\tilde{q}_e(nT) &\stackrel{\Delta}{=} \tilde{q}_{e,\,n} = \tilde{q}(2nT_s)\\ \tilde{q}_o(nT) &\stackrel{\Delta}{=} \tilde{q}_{o,\,n} = \tilde{q}((2n+1)T_s).\end{aligned} \tag{5.205}$$

Then the distance generated by $\tilde{e}_n^{(ij)}$ is equal to

$$\begin{aligned}d^2_{T/2,\,i,\,j} &= (T/2) \times \text{energy of the sequence } \left(\tilde{e}_n^{(ij)} \star \tilde{q}_{e,\,n}\right)\\ &\quad + (T/2) \times \text{energy of the sequence } \left(\tilde{e}_n^{(ij)} \star \tilde{q}_{o,\,n}\right)\end{aligned} \tag{5.206}$$

where the subscript $T/2$ denotes a $T/2$-spaced ML detector. Observe that all the terms in the right-hand-side of the above equation are T-spaced. Using Parseval's theorem, we have

$$d^2_{T/2,\,i,\,j} = (T/2)T \int_{F=0}^{1/T} \left|\tilde{E}_{\mathscr{P}}^{(ij)}(F)\right|^2 \left|\tilde{Q}_{\mathscr{P},\,e}(F)\right|^2 dF + (T/2)T \int_{F=0}^{1/T} \left|\tilde{E}_{\mathscr{P}}^{(ij)}(F)\right|^2 \left|\tilde{Q}_{\mathscr{P},\,o}(F)\right|^2 dF \tag{5.207}$$

where

$$\begin{aligned}\tilde{Q}_{\mathscr{P},\,e}(F) &= \sum_n \tilde{q}_{e,\,n} \mathrm{e}^{-\mathrm{j}\,2\pi FnT}\\ \tilde{Q}_{\mathscr{P},\,o}(F) &= \sum_n \tilde{q}_{o,\,n} \mathrm{e}^{-\mathrm{j}\,2\pi FnT}.\end{aligned} \tag{5.208}$$

Now, it only remains to express $\tilde{Q}_{\mathscr{P},\,e}(F)$ and $\tilde{Q}_{\mathscr{P},\,o}(F)$ in terms of $\tilde{Q}(F)$.

Note that

$$\begin{aligned}\tilde{q}_{e,\,n} &= \tilde{q}(t)|_{t=nT}\\ \Rightarrow \tilde{Q}_{\mathscr{P},\,e}(F) &= \frac{1}{T} \sum_{k=-\infty}^{\infty} \tilde{Q}\left(F - \frac{k}{T}\right).\end{aligned} \tag{5.209}$$

Once again, if we assume that $\tilde{Q}(F)$ is bandlimited to $[-1/T,\ 1/T]$, then

$$\tilde{Q}_{\mathscr{P},\,e}(F) = \frac{1}{T}\left[\tilde{Q}(F) + \tilde{Q}\left(F - \frac{1}{T}\right)\right] \qquad \text{for } 0 \le F \le 1/T. \tag{5.210}$$

Similarly,

$$\begin{aligned}\tilde{q}_{o,\,n} &= \tilde{q}(t + T/2)|_{t=nT}\\ \Rightarrow \tilde{Q}_{\mathscr{P},\,o}(F) &= \frac{1}{T} \sum_{k=-\infty}^{\infty} \tilde{Q}\left(F - \frac{k}{T}\right) \mathrm{e}^{\mathrm{j}\,2\pi(T/2)(F-k/T)}\end{aligned} \tag{5.211}$$

which reduces to

$$\tilde{Q}_{\mathscr{P},o}(F) = \frac{e^{j\pi FT}}{T}\left[\tilde{Q}(F) - \tilde{Q}\left(F - \frac{1}{T}\right)\right] \qquad \text{for } 0 \le F \le 1/T. \tag{5.212}$$

Substituting (5.212) and (5.210) in (5.207), we readily obtain the result

$$d^2_{T/2,\,i,\,j} = d^2_{T,\,i,\,j} \tag{5.213}$$

which in turn proves that the fractionally-spaced and symbol-spaced ML detectors have the same performance.

Example 5.2.3 Consider a real-valued channel $q(t)$ of the form

$$q(t) = \text{sinc}\left(\frac{t}{T_s}\right) + 2\,\text{sinc}\left(\frac{t - T_s}{T_s}\right) + 3\,\text{sinc}\left(\frac{t - 2T_s}{T_s}\right) \tag{5.214}$$

where

$$\text{sinc}\,(x) \stackrel{\Delta}{=} \frac{\sin(\pi x)}{\pi x}. \tag{5.215}$$

Assume $T/T_s = 2$ and BPSK signalling. Compare the performance of the fractionally-spaced and symbol-spaced ML detectors.

Solution: The Fourier transform of the channel is

$$Q(F) = T_s\text{rect}\,(FT_s) + 2T_s\text{rect}\,(FT_s)e^{-j2\pi FT_s} + 3T_s\text{rect}\,(FT_s)e^{-j4\pi} \tag{5.216}$$

where

$$\text{rect}\,(FT_s) \stackrel{\Delta}{=} \begin{cases} 1 & \text{for } -1/(2T_s) < F < 1/(2T_s) \\ 0 & \text{elsewhere.} \end{cases} \tag{5.217}$$

Thus the channel is bandlimited to $[-1/(2T_s),\ 1/(2T_s)]$, hence it can be sampled at a rate of $1/T_s$ without any aliasing. The (real-valued) channel coefficients obtained after passing through the unit energy LPF and Nyquist-rate sampling are

$$\begin{aligned} q(0)\sqrt{T/2} &= \sqrt{T/2} \\ q(T_s)\sqrt{T/2} &= 2\sqrt{T/2} \\ q(2T_s)\sqrt{T/2} &= 3\sqrt{T/2}. \end{aligned} \tag{5.218}$$

Thus, the discrete-time channel coefficients seen by the $T/2$-spaced ML detector are given by (5.218). Consequently, the trellis has two states, as illustrated in Figure 5.17. The trellis branches are labeled by $a/(b_1,\ b_2)$, where $a \in \{-1,\ 1\}$ denotes the input symbol and b_1, b_2 denote the two $T/2$-spaced output samples. The states are labeled 0 and 1 with the mapping from digits to symbols as

$$\mathscr{M}(0) = 1, \quad \mathscr{M}(1) = -1. \tag{5.219}$$

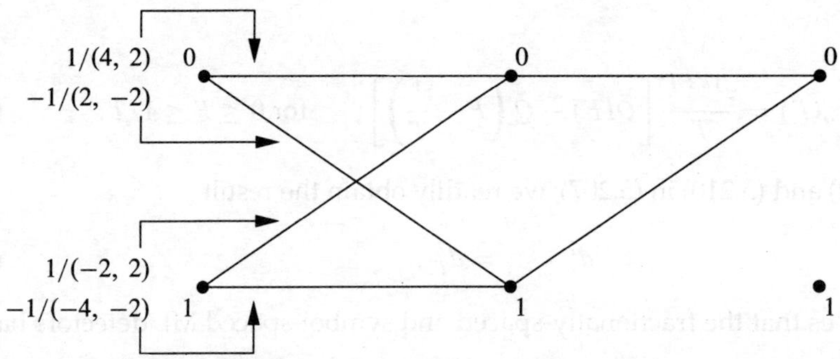

Figure 5.17 *Trellis diagram for the $T/2$-spaced ML detector with $T = 2$ seconds*

In this example, the minimum distance error event is obtained when the error sequence is given by

$$e_n^{(ij)} = 2\delta_K(n). \tag{5.220}$$

The minimum distance error event is shown in Figure 5.17. Assuming that $T = 2$ second, the squared minimum distance can be found from (5.206) to be

$$d^2_{T/2,\,\min} = \text{energy of}\left(e_n^{(ij)} \star q(nT_s)\right) = 56. \tag{5.221}$$

The multiplicity of the minimum distance $A_{d_{\min}} = 1$, and the number of symbol errors corresponding to the minimum distance error event is $N_{d_{\min}} = 1$. Therefore, the performance of the $T/2$-spaced ML detector is well approximated by the minimum distance error event as

$$P(e) = \frac{1}{2}\,\text{erfc}\left(\sqrt{\frac{56}{8N_0}}\right). \tag{5.222}$$

Let us now obtain the equivalent symbol-spaced channel as shown in Figure 5.12. The pulse-shape at the matched filter output is

$$\begin{aligned} R_{qq}(t) &= q(t) \star q(-t) \\ &= 14T_s\ \text{sinc}\left(\frac{t}{T_s}\right) + 8T_s\ \text{sinc}\left(\frac{t-T_s}{T_s}\right) + 8T_s\ \text{sinc}\left(\frac{t+T_s}{T_s}\right) \\ &\quad + 3T_s\ \text{sinc}\left(\frac{t-2T_s}{T_s}\right) + 3T_s\ \text{sinc}\left(\frac{t+2T_s}{T_s}\right). \end{aligned} \tag{5.223}$$

After symbol-rate sampling, the resultant pulse-shape is (recall from the discussion following (5.29), that the autocorrelation peak has to be sampled):

$$R_{qq}(0) = 14T_s, \quad R_{qq}(T) = 3T_s = R_{qq}(-T). \tag{5.224}$$

We now have to find out the pulse-shape at the output of the whitening filter. We have

$$R_{qq,\,n} = b_n \star b_{-n}. \tag{5.225}$$

Note that we have switched over to the subscript notation to denote time, since the samples are T-spaced. Since the span of $R_{qq,\,n}$ is three samples, the span of b_n must be two samples (recall that when two sequences of length L_1 and L_2 are convolved, the resulting sequence is of length $L_1 + L_2 - 1$). Let us denote the (real-valued) coefficients of b_n by b_0 and b_1. We have,

$$\begin{aligned} R_{qq,\,0} &= 14T_s = b_0^2 + b_1^2 \\ R_{qq,\,1} &= 3T_s = b_0 b_1. \end{aligned} \tag{5.226}$$

Solving for b_0 and b_1, we get two sets of solutions namely

$$\begin{aligned} b_0 &= 0.8218\sqrt{T_s} \quad \text{or} \quad b_0 = 3.65\sqrt{T_s} \\ b_1 &= 3.65\sqrt{T_s} \quad \text{or} \quad b_1 = 0.8218\sqrt{T_s}. \end{aligned} \tag{5.227}$$

We select the minimum phase solution, which is

$$\begin{aligned} b_0 &= 3.65\sqrt{T_s} = 3.65\sqrt{T/2} \\ b_1 &= 0.8218\sqrt{T_s} = 0.8218\sqrt{T/2}. \end{aligned} \tag{5.228}$$

The corresponding trellis has two states, as shown in Figure 5.18, where it is assumed that $T = 2$. The branches are labeled as a/b where $a \in \{-1, 1\}$ denotes the input symbol and b denotes the T-spaced output sample.

Here again the minimum distance error event is caused by

$$e_n^{(ij)} = 2\delta_K(n). \tag{5.229}$$

The minimum distance error event is shown in Figure 5.18 and the squared minimum distance is given by (5.199) which is equal to

$$d_{T,\,\min}^2 = 56. \tag{5.230}$$

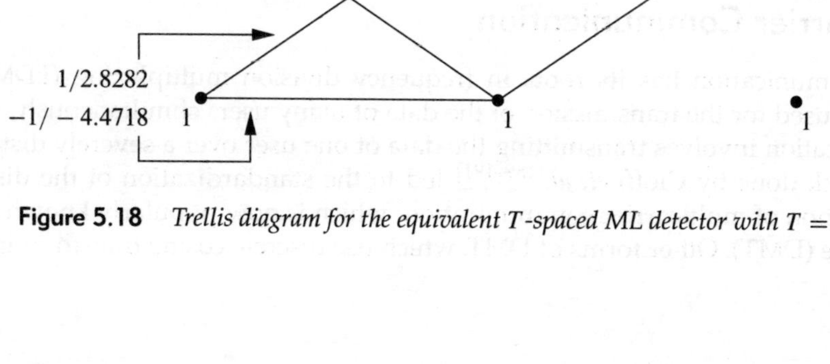

Figure 5.18 *Trellis diagram for the equivalent T-spaced ML detector with $T = 2$ seconds*

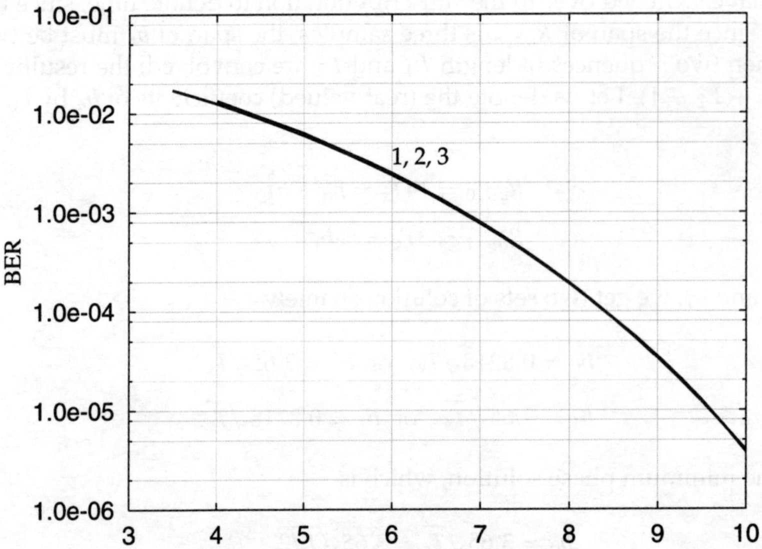

1-$T/2$-spaced MLSE (simulation)
2-T-spaced MLSE (simulation)
3-T, $T/2$-spaced MLSE (theory)

Figure 5.19 *Performance comparison of $T/2$-spaced and T-spaced MLSE for Example 5.2.1*

From the trellis in Figure 5.18, we find that $A_{d_{\min}} = 1$ and $N_{d_{\min}} = 1$. Therefore the average probability of symbol error is well approximated by the minimum distance error event and is given by

$$P(e) = \frac{1}{2} \operatorname{erfc}\left(\sqrt{\frac{56}{8N_0}}\right) \tag{5.231}$$

which is identical to the $T/2$-spaced ML detector. The simulated performance of both kinds of ML detectors along with the theoretical curve given by (5.231) are plotted in Figure 5.19. Observe that the curves overlap, which demonstrates the accuracy of the simulations and the theoretical analysis.

5.3 Multicarrier Communication

Multicarrier communication has its roots in frequency division multiplexing (FDM)[188]. Whereas FDM is used for the transmission of the data of many users simultaneously, multicarrier communication involves transmitting the data of one user over a severely distorting channel. The work done by Cioffi *et. al.*[189–191] led to the standardization of the discrete-time implementation of multicarrier communication, which is now popularly known as the discrete multitone (DMT). Other forms of DMT, which use discrete cosine transform instead

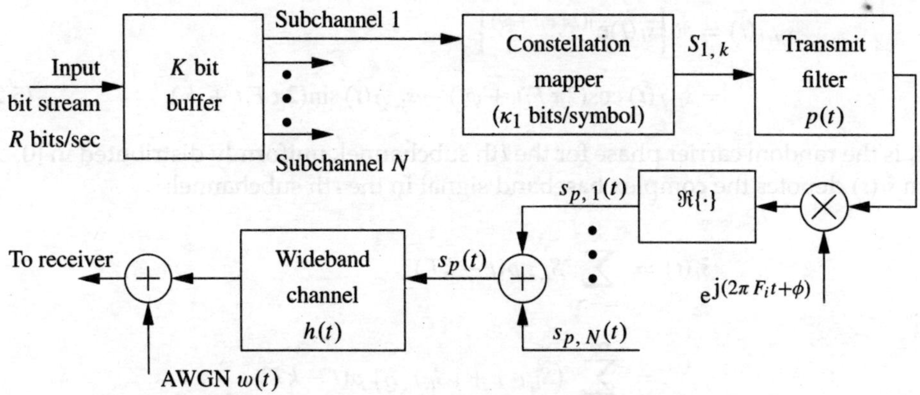

Figure 5.20 *Block diagram of an multicarrier communication transmitter*

of the discrete Fourier transform can be found in[192,193]. A variant of DMT is orthogonal frequency division multiplexing (OFDM) which is used in wireless communications.

The basic idea behind multicarrier communication is to divide the spectrum of a non-ideal wideband channel into small nonoverlapping subchannels such that the characteristics of each subchannel can be considered to be ideal (flat magnitude response and a linear phase response). Thus, any communication that takes place in a subchannel is essentially distortionless.

Consider the block diagram in Figure 5.20. The input bit-stream is fed to a buffer of size K bits, where K is a large integer. We assume that the input bit-rate is $R = 1/T_b$ bits/sec. The ith subchannel is alloted κ_i bits, which is mapped onto a symbol from a 2^{κ_i}-ary constellation (the question of how many bits are allocated to each subchannel is taken up later). The symbol-rate of each subchannel is a constant equal to $1/T$. In order to prevent buffer overflow or underflow we require

$$KT_b = T. \tag{5.232}$$

In other words, one symbol is transmitted simultaneously from all the subchannels over T seconds. Since K is large, the output symbol-rate is much smaller than the input bit-rate. We also require

$$K = \sum_{i=1}^{N} \kappa_i. \tag{5.233}$$

The overall transmitted signal is given by

$$s_p(t) = \sum_{i=1}^{N} s_{p,\,i}(t) \tag{5.234}$$

where the subscript 'p' denotes a passband signal. The passband signal for the ith subchannel is given by

$$\begin{aligned} s_{p,\,i}(t) &= \Re\left\{\tilde{s}_i(t)\mathrm{e}^{\mathrm{j}(2\pi F_i t+\phi_i)}\right\} \\ &= s_{i,\,I}(t)\cos(2\pi F_i t+\phi_i) - s_{i,\,Q}(t)\sin(2\pi F_i t+\phi_i) \end{aligned} \tag{5.235}$$

where ϕ_i is the random carrier phase for the ith subchannel, uniformly distributed in $[0, 2\pi)$. The term $\tilde{s}_i(t)$ denotes the complex baseband signal in the ith subchannel:

$$\begin{aligned} \tilde{s}_i(t) &= \sum_{k=-\infty}^{\infty} S_{i,\,k}\, p(t-kT) \\ &= \sum_{k=-\infty}^{\infty} \left(S_{i,\,k,\,I} + \mathrm{j}\, S_{i,\,k,\,Q}\right) p(t-kT) \\ &= s_{i,\,I}(t) + \mathrm{j}\, s_{i,\,Q}(t) \end{aligned} \tag{5.236}$$

where $S_{i,\,k} = S_{i,\,k,\,I} + \mathrm{j}\, S_{i,\,k,\,Q}$ denotes complex symbols from an $M = 2^{\kappa_i}$-ary two-dimensional constellation in the ith subchannel and $p(t)$ is the transmit filter, assumed to be real-valued. For convenience of analysis, we can express the ith passband signal as follows:

$$\begin{aligned} s_{p,\,i}(t) &= \Re\left\{\tilde{s}_{1,\,i}(t)\mathrm{e}^{\mathrm{j}\,2\pi F_i t}\right\} \\ &= s_{1,\,i,\,I}(t)\cos(2\pi F_i t) - s_{1,\,i,\,Q}(t)\sin(2\pi F_i t) \end{aligned} \tag{5.237}$$

where

$$\tilde{s}_{1,\,i}(t) = \tilde{s}_i(t)\mathrm{e}^{\mathrm{j}\,\phi_i}. \tag{5.238}$$

We assume that $p(t)$ is strictly bandlimited to $[-1/T, 1/T]$. Therefore,

$$F_i = \frac{2i}{T} \qquad \text{for } 1 \le i \le N. \tag{5.239}$$

We also assume

$$p(t) \star p(-t)|_{t=kT} = R_{pp}(kT) = \delta_K(kT). \tag{5.240}$$

The received signal can be written as

$$\begin{aligned} r(t) &= s_p(t) \star h(t) + w(t) \\ &= \sum_{i=1}^{N} s_{p,\,i}(t) \star h(t) + w(t) \\ &= \sum_{i=1}^{N} y_{p,\,i}(t) + w(t) \end{aligned} \tag{5.241}$$

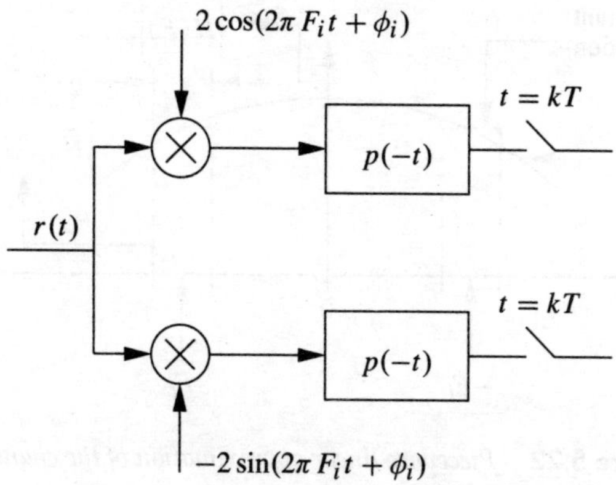

Figure 5.21 *Block diagram of the multicarrier communication receiver for the ith subchannel*

where $y_{p,i}(t) = s_{p,i}(t) \star h(t)$ and $w(t)$ denotes a zero-mean AWGN process with psd $N_0/2$.

We now consider the recovery of symbols from the ith subchannel of $r(t)$. This is illustrated in Figure 5.21. Observe that the Fourier transform of $y_{p,i}(t)$ in (5.241) is given by

$$\tilde{Y}_{p,i}(F) = \tilde{S}_{p,i}(F)\tilde{H}(F) \tag{5.242}$$

where

$$\begin{aligned} s_{p,i}(t) &\rightleftharpoons \tilde{S}_{p,i}(F) \\ h(t) &\rightleftharpoons \tilde{H}(F). \end{aligned} \tag{5.243}$$

Now, the Fourier transform of the passband signal in the ith subchannel is

$$\begin{aligned} \tilde{S}_{p,i}(F) = &\frac{1}{2}\left[\tilde{S}_{1,i,I}(F - F_i) + \tilde{S}_{1,i,I}(F + F_i)\right] \\ &- \frac{1}{2\mathrm{j}}\left[\tilde{S}_{1,i,Q}(F - F_i) - \tilde{S}_{1,i,Q}(F + F_i)\right] \end{aligned} \tag{5.244}$$

where

$$\begin{aligned} \tilde{S}_{1,i,I}(F) &= \tilde{P}(F) \sum_{k=-\infty}^{\infty} \left(S_{i,k,I}\cos(\phi_i) - S_{i,k,Q}\sin(\phi_i)\right) \mathrm{e}^{-\mathrm{j}2\pi FkT} \\ \tilde{S}_{1,i,Q}(F) &= \tilde{P}(F) \sum_{k=-\infty}^{\infty} \left(S_{i,k,I}\sin(\phi_i) + S_{i,k,Q}\cos(\phi_i)\right) \mathrm{e}^{-\mathrm{j}2\pi FkT} \end{aligned} \tag{5.245}$$

denotes the Fourier transform of the in-phase and quadrature components of the complex baseband signal in the ith subchannel respectively and

$$p(t) \rightleftharpoons \tilde{P}(F). \tag{5.246}$$

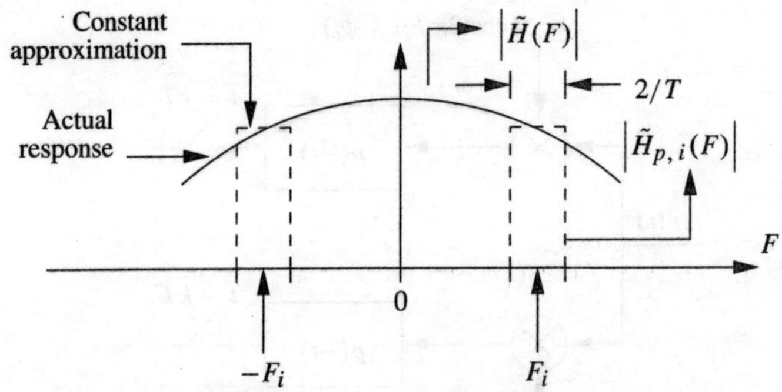

Figure 5.22 *Piecewise linear approximation of the channel*

Observe that the summation terms in (5.245) denote the discrete-time Fourier transform of the symbol sequence, which in general does not exist when the sequence length is infinity. This problem can be alleviated by assuming that the limits of the summation extend from $-L$ to L, where L is very large, but finite. Since $\tilde{P}(F)$ is bandlimited to $[-1/T,\ 1/T]$, $\tilde{S}_{p,i}(F)$ in (5.244) is bandlimited to the range $F_i - 1/T \le |F| \le F_i + 1/T]$, with bandwidth equal to $2/T$. If this bandwidth is sufficiently small, we can assume the channel magnitude response to be approximately constant in the range $F_i - 1/T \le |F| \le F_i + 1/T$ and equal to $|H(F_i)|$, as depicted in Figure 5.22. Hence we can write

$$\tilde{Y}_{p,i}(F) \approx \begin{cases} \tilde{S}_{p,i}(F)\tilde{H}(F_i) & \text{for } F > 0 \\ \tilde{S}_{p,i}(F)\tilde{H}^*(F_i) & \text{for } F < 0. \end{cases} \tag{5.247}$$

where we have used the fact that $h(t)$ is real-valued, hence

$$\tilde{H}(-F_i) = \tilde{H}^*(F_i). \tag{5.248}$$

Thus the channel is approximated by a piecewise linear characteristic and the frequency response of the ith subchannel is given by

$$\tilde{H}_{p,i}(F) = \begin{cases} \tilde{H}(F_i) & \text{for } F_i - 1/T < F < F_i + 1/T \\ \tilde{H}^*(F_i) & \text{for } -F_i - 1/T < F < -F_i + 1/T \end{cases} \tag{5.249}$$

It can be shown that the corresponding impulse response is

$$h_{p,i}(t) = \frac{4}{T}\,\text{sinc}\left(\frac{2t}{T}\right)[A\cos(2\pi F_i t) - B\sin(2\pi F_i t)] \tag{5.250}$$

where

$$A + \mathrm{j}\,B = \tilde{H}(F_i). \tag{5.251}$$

The corresponding complex envelope of the ith subchannel is given by (see Appendix I)

$$\tilde{h}_i(t) = \frac{4\tilde{H}(F_i)}{T}\,\text{sinc}\left(\frac{2t}{T}\right) \rightleftharpoons 2\tilde{H}(F_i)\,\text{rect}\,(FT/2) = \tilde{H}_i(F). \tag{5.252}$$

The complex envelope of the ith subchannel output is given by

$$\tilde{y}_i(t) = \frac{1}{2}\left(\tilde{s}_{1,i}(t) \star \tilde{h}_i(t)\right)$$
$$= \tilde{H}(F_i)\tilde{s}_{1,i}(t). \tag{5.253}$$

The passband signal corresponding to the ith subchannel output is (see Appendix I)

$$y_{p,i}(t) = \Re\left\{\tilde{y}_i(t)\mathrm{e}^{\mathrm{j}\,2\pi F_i t}\right\}$$
$$= \Re\left\{\tilde{H}(F_i)\tilde{s}_{1,i}(t)\mathrm{e}^{\mathrm{j}\,2\pi F_i t}\right\}. \tag{5.254}$$

At the receiver for the ith subchannel, the signal component at the multiplier output is (assuming coherent detection)

$$2\sum_{l=1}^{N} y_{p,l}(t)\mathrm{e}^{-\mathrm{j}(2\pi F_i t+\phi_i)} = 2\sum_{l=1}^{N}\left[\tilde{H}(F_l)\tilde{s}_{1,l}(t)\mathrm{e}^{\mathrm{j}2\pi F_l t}\right.$$
$$\left. + \tilde{H}^*(F_l)\tilde{s}^*_{1,l}(t)\mathrm{e}^{-\mathrm{j}2\pi F_l t}\right]\mathrm{e}^{-\mathrm{j}(2\pi F_i t+\phi_i)}$$
$$= \left[\tilde{H}(F_i)\tilde{s}_i(t) + \tilde{H}^*(F_i)\tilde{s}^*_i(t)\mathrm{e}^{-\mathrm{j}(4\pi F_i t+2\phi_i)}\right]$$
$$+ \sum_{\substack{l=1 \\ l\neq i}}^{N}\left[\tilde{H}(F_l)\tilde{s}_{1,l}(t)\mathrm{e}^{\mathrm{j}2\pi F_l t}\right.$$
$$\left. + \tilde{H}^*(F_l)\tilde{s}^*_{1,l}(t)\mathrm{e}^{-\mathrm{j}2\pi F_l t}\right]\mathrm{e}^{-\mathrm{j}(2\pi F_{i,t}+\phi_i)} \tag{5.255}$$

The noise component at the multiplier output is

$$2w(t)\mathrm{e}^{-\mathrm{j}(2\pi F_i t+\phi)} = \tilde{v}_i(t)$$
$$= v_{i,I}(t) + \mathrm{j}\,v_{i,Q}(t) \tag{5.256}$$

with autocorrelation (refer to (4.53))

$$R_{\tilde{v}\tilde{v}}(\tau) = \frac{1}{2}E\left[\tilde{v}_i(t)\tilde{v}^*_i(t-\tau)\right] = N_0\delta_D(\tau). \tag{5.257}$$

The composite complex baseband signal at the output of the matched filter corresponding to the ith subchannel is given by (note that the component at $2F_i$ in (5.255) and the remaining subchannels $l \neq i$ get eliminated by the matched filter)

$$\tilde{x}_i(t) = \tilde{H}(F_i)\tilde{s}_i(t) \star p(-t) + \tilde{z}_i(t)$$
$$= \tilde{H}(F_i)\sum_{k=-\infty}^{\infty} S_{i,k}R_{pp}(t-kT) + \tilde{z}_i(t) \tag{5.258}$$

where

$$\tilde{z}_i(t) = \tilde{v}_i(t) \star p(-t) \tag{5.259}$$

with autocorrelation

$$R_{\tilde{z}\tilde{z}}(\tau) = N_0 R_{pp}(\tau). \tag{5.260}$$

Finally, the output of the sampler in the ith subchannel is

$$\tilde{x}_i(nT) = \tilde{H}(F_i) S_{i,n} + \tilde{z}_i(nT). \tag{5.261}$$

Thus we have succeeded in recovering a scaled version of the symbol corrupted by noise.

The next issue that needs to be addressed is the allocation of bits to various subchannels. This procedure is known as channel loading [194].

5.3.1 Channel loading

We begin this section with the Shannon's information capacity theorem[1] (also known as the Shannon-Hartley law[195]) for a bandlimited, distortionless channel as follows:

$$C = B \log_2 \left(1 + \frac{P_{\text{av}}}{N_0 B}\right) \tag{5.262}$$

where C is the channel capacity (maximum possible data rate) in bits/sec, P_{av} is the average transmitted power, the channel bandwidth extends over $[-B,\ B]$ Hz and $N_0/2$ is the two-sided power spectral density (psd) of Gaussian noise, which is also bandlimited to $[-B,\ B]$. The above expression tells us about the maximum data-rate that can be transmitted for a given signal-to-noise (SNR) ratio. If the *actual* data-rate is less than C then it is possible to achieve an arbitrarily small error probability, using some error correcting code. If the actual data-rate exceeds C, then it is not possible to make the error probability tend to zero with any error correcting code.

The SNR is defined as

$$\text{SNR} = \frac{P_{\text{av}}}{N_0 B}. \tag{5.263}$$

The purpose of this section is to derive the optimum psd of the transmitted signal for a non-ideal bandlimited channel and an arbitrary noise psd, such that the channel capacity (transmission rate) is maximized.

To this end, let us assume that the psd of the transmitted signal is $S_{s_p}(F)$, the channel frequency response is $\tilde{H}(F)$ and the noise psd is $S_w(F)$. We assume that the signal and noise psds and the channel frequency response is constant over any subchannel. Then, the capacity of the ith subchannel is

$$\begin{aligned} C_i &= \Delta F \log_2 \left(1 + \frac{S_{s_p}(F_i)|\tilde{H}(F_i)|^2 \Delta F}{S_w(F_i)\Delta F}\right) \\ &= \Delta F \log_2 \left(1 + \frac{S_{s_p}(F_i)|\tilde{H}(F_i)|^2}{S_w(F_i)}\right) \end{aligned} \tag{5.264}$$

where

$$\Delta F = 2/T \tag{5.265}$$

is the bandwidth of each subchannel. The overall capacity is given by

$$\begin{aligned} C &= \sum_{i=1}^{N} C_i \\ &= \sum_{i=1}^{N} \Delta F \log_2\left(1 + \frac{S_{s_p}(F_i)|\tilde{H}(F_i)|^2}{S_w(F_i)}\right). \end{aligned} \tag{5.266}$$

In the limit as $\Delta F \to 0$, C takes an integral form

$$C = \int_F \log_2\left(1 + \frac{S_{s_p}(F)|\tilde{H}(F)|^2}{S_w(F)}\right) dF \tag{5.267}$$

The problem can now be mathematically formulated as follows: maximize C subject to the constraint

$$\int_F S_{s_p}(F)\,dF = P_{\text{av}} \qquad \text{a constant.} \tag{5.268}$$

This problem can be solved using the method of Lagrange multipliers. Thus, the above problem can be reformulated as

$$\max \int_F \log_2\left(1 + \frac{S_{s_p}(F)|\tilde{H}(F)|^2}{S_w(F)}\right) dF + \lambda\left(\int_F S_{s_p}(F)\,dF - P_{\text{av}}\right). \tag{5.269}$$

Since λP_{av} is a constant, maximizing (5.269) is equivalent to

$$\max \int_F \log_2\left(1 + \frac{S_{s_p}(F)|\tilde{H}(F)|^2}{S_w(F)}\right) dF + \lambda \int_F S_{s_p}(F)\,dF. \tag{5.270}$$

Since the integrand is real and positive, maximizing the integral is equivalent to maximizing the integrand. Differentiating the integrand with respect to $S_{s_p}(F)$ and setting the result to zero yields

$$S_{s_p}(F) = C - \frac{S_w(F)}{|\tilde{H}(F)|^2} \tag{5.271}$$

where

$$C = -\frac{\log_2(e)}{\lambda} \tag{5.272}$$

is a constant. This result is known as the water-pouring solution to the channel loading problem, as illustrated in Figure 5.23.

Example 5.3.1 The piecewise linear approximation for the squared magnitude response of the channel and the noise psd is shown in Figure 5.24. Compute the optimum power allocation for each subchannel. The total transmit power is 10 watts.

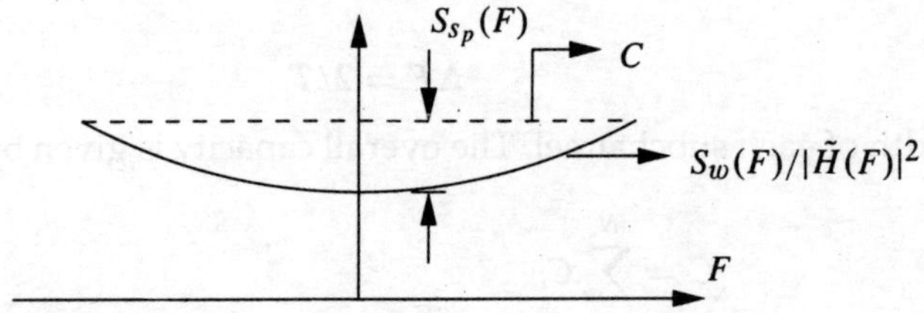

Figure 5.23 *Optimum psd of the transmitted signal*

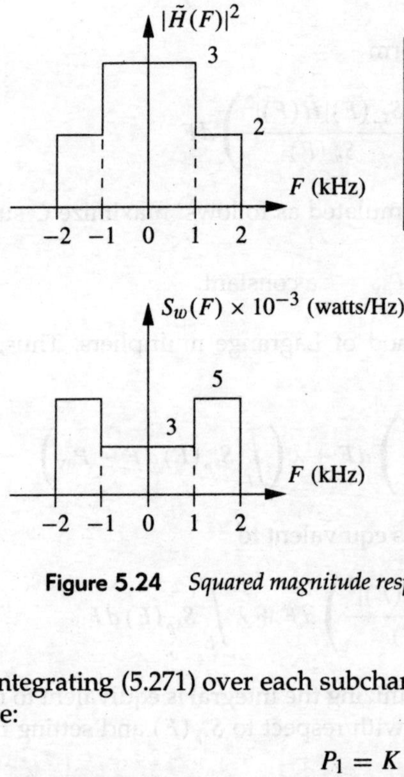

Subchannel	Freq. range (kHz)
1	0-1
2	1-2

Figure 5.24 *Squared magnitude response of the channel and noise psd*

Solution: Integrating (5.271) over each subchannel for both positive and negative frequencies, we have:

$$P_1 = K - 2$$

$$P_2 = K - 5 \tag{5.273}$$

where P_1 and P_2 are the power allocated to subchannel 1 and 2 respectively and K is a constant to be determined. We also have

$$P_1 + P_2 = 10. \tag{5.274}$$

Solving for P_1 and P_2, we get

$$P_1 = 6.5 \quad \text{watts}$$

$$P_2 = 3.5 \quad \text{watts}. \tag{5.275}$$

To summarize, we have optimally allocated power to each subchannel such that the overall transmission rate is maximized. We now give an intuitive explanation to determine how many bits/symbol (κ_i) have to be allocated to each subchannel. Recall from section 4.1.2 that the psd of a linearly modulated signal is proportional to the average power of the constellation, assuming that the symbols are uncorrelated. We assume that all subchannels use the same transmit filter. We further impose the constraint that the symbol-error-rate of all subchannels are nearly identical. This implies that the minimum Euclidean distance of the constellation is identical for all the subchannels. This leads us to conclude that a subchannel requiring larger power must be allocated more bits/symbol (implying a larger constellation).

The multicarrier communication system discussed in section 5.3 suffers from two disadvantages. Firstly, the system is too complex to implement in discrete-time for large values of N, since each subchannel requires a transmit filter and a matched filter. Secondly, the assumption that the channel characteristics is ideal over each subchannel is only approximately true. This motivates us to look for more efficient techniques to implement the multicarrier communication system. This is discussed in the next section.

5.3.2 The discrete multitone (DMT)

Let $\tilde{s}_n$ and $\tilde{h}_n$ be two complex-valued, discrete-time periodic sequences having a period N. That is,

$$\begin{aligned}\tilde{s}_n &= \tilde{s}_{n+N}\\ \tilde{h}_n &= \tilde{h}_{n+N}.\end{aligned} \tag{5.276}$$

Let S_k and $\tilde{H}_k$ denote the corresponding N-point discrete Fourier transforms (DFT), that is (for $0 \leq k \leq N-1$)

$$\begin{aligned}S_k &= \sum_{n=0}^{N-1} \tilde{s}_n \mathrm{e}^{-\mathrm{j}\,2\pi kn/N}\\ \tilde{H}_k &= \sum_{n=0}^{N-1} \tilde{h}_n \mathrm{e}^{-\mathrm{j}\,2\pi kn/N}.\end{aligned} \tag{5.277}$$

Then, the N-point circular convolution of $\tilde{s}_n$ with $\tilde{h}_n$ yields another periodic sequence $\tilde{z}_n$ whose DFT is

$$\tilde{Z}_k = S_k \tilde{H}_k \qquad \text{for } 0 \leq k \leq N-1. \tag{5.278}$$

Now consider Figure 5.25. Let S_k denote a symbol drawn from an M-ary QAM constellation corresponding to the kth subchannel. We assume that S_k and the channel $\tilde{h}_n$ is periodic with period N. Observe that we have assumed the symbols S_k to be the DFT coefficients of some time sequence $\tilde{s}_n$. In other words, $\tilde{s}_n$ is the inverse discrete Fourier transform of S_k and is given by (for $0 \leq n \leq N-1$)

$$\tilde{s}_n = \frac{1}{N} \sum_{k=0}^{N-1} S_k \mathrm{e}^{\mathrm{j}\,2\pi kn/N}. \tag{5.279}$$

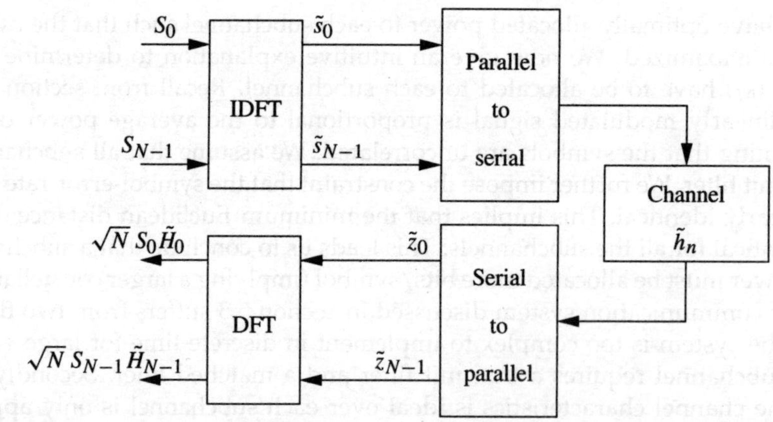

Figure 5.25 *Illustrating the concept of DMT*

From Figure 5.25 it is clear that the output of the DFT block is equal to the symbols scaled by the DFT coefficients of the channel. Thus, ISI has been neatly eliminated. The only problem is that in practical situations, neither the data nor the channel are periodic. This is overcome by inserting what is known as a *cyclic prefix* on a non-periodic data set.

In particular, let us assume that a (non-periodic) "frame" of data consists of N samples $(\tilde{s}_0, \ldots, \tilde{s}_{N-1})$ and the (non-periodic) discrete-time equivalent channel is time limited to $L+1$ coefficients $(\tilde{h}_0, \ldots, \tilde{h}_L)$ where in practice $L \ll N$. Note that $\tilde{s}_n$ is the IDFT of the input data frame S_k. Once again let $\tilde{z}_n$ denote the N-point circular convolution of $\tilde{s}_n$ with $\tilde{h}_n$ (the output we would have obtained by assuming $\tilde{s}_n$ and $\tilde{h}_n$ are periodic with period N). Then the N samples of $\tilde{z}_n$ can be obtained by the *linear* convolution of $\tilde{h}_n$ with the data sequence

$$\tilde{s}_{N-L}, \ldots, \tilde{s}_{N-1}, \tilde{s}_0, \ldots, \tilde{s}_{N-1}. \tag{5.280}$$

Observe that we have prefixed the original data sequence with the last L samples. Note also that what takes place in real-life is linear convolution and what we require is circular convolution. We are able to "simulate" a circular covolution by using the cyclic prefix. This is illustrated in Figure 5.26 for $N = 4$ and $L = 1$. We find that by using the cyclic prefix, the steady-state output of the linear convolution is identical to that of circular convolution.

With the introduction of the basic concept, we are now ready to generalize the theory of DMT. Due to (5.280), the steady-state part of the received signal can be written in the matrix form as

$$\begin{bmatrix} \tilde{r}_{N-1} \\ \tilde{r}_{N-2} \\ \vdots \\ \tilde{r}_0 \end{bmatrix} = \begin{bmatrix} \tilde{h}_0 & \tilde{h}_1 & \ldots & \tilde{h}_L & 0 & 0 & \ldots & 0 \\ 0 & \tilde{h}_0 & \ldots & \tilde{h}_{L-1} & \tilde{h}_L & 0 & \ldots & 0 \\ \vdots & \vdots & \vdots & \vdots & \vdots & \vdots & \vdots & \vdots \\ \tilde{h}_1 & \tilde{h}_2 & \ldots & 0 & 0 & 0 & \ldots & \tilde{h}_0 \end{bmatrix} \begin{bmatrix} \tilde{s}_{N-1} \\ \tilde{s}_{N-2} \\ \vdots \\ \tilde{s}_0 \end{bmatrix} + \begin{bmatrix} \tilde{w}_{N-1} \\ \tilde{w}_{N-2} \\ \vdots \\ \tilde{w}_0 \end{bmatrix} \tag{5.281}$$

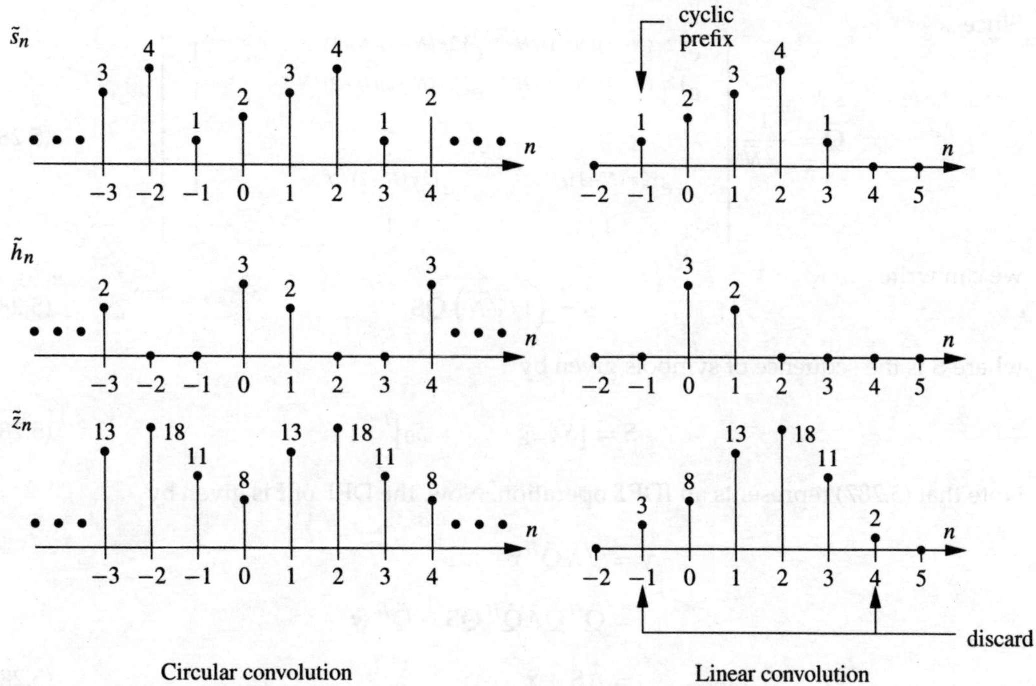

Figure 5.26 *Comparison of circular convolution with linear convolution using a cyclic prefix*

where $\tilde{w}_n$ denotes complex-valued samples of zero-mean AWGN with variance σ_w^2, that is,

$$\frac{1}{2}E\left[\tilde{w}_n\tilde{w}_{n-m}^*\right] = \sigma_w^2\delta_K(m). \tag{5.282}$$

The equation in (5.281) can be written in matrix form as

$$\tilde{\mathbf{r}} = \tilde{\mathbf{h}}\tilde{\mathbf{s}} + \tilde{\mathbf{w}}. \tag{5.283}$$

Since $\tilde{\mathbf{h}}$ is a circulant matrix, we can perform eigendecomposition (see (Appendix K)) to obtain

$$\tilde{\mathbf{r}} = \tilde{\mathbf{Q}}\tilde{\Lambda}\tilde{\mathbf{Q}}^H\tilde{\mathbf{s}} + \tilde{\mathbf{w}} \tag{5.284}$$

where

$$\tilde{\Lambda} = \begin{bmatrix} \tilde{H}_{N-1} & 0 & \dots & 0 \\ 0 & \tilde{H}_{N-2} & \dots & 0 \\ \vdots & \vdots & \vdots & \vdots \\ 0 & 0 & \dots & \tilde{H}_0 \end{bmatrix}. \tag{5.285}$$

Since

$$\tilde{\mathbf{Q}} = \frac{1}{\sqrt{N}} \begin{bmatrix} e^{j\,2\pi(N-1)(N-1)/N} & e^{j\,2\pi(N-2)(N-1)/N} & \dots & 1 \\ e^{j\,2\pi(N-1)(N-2)/N} & e^{j\,2\pi(N-2)(N-2)/N} & \dots & 1 \\ \vdots & \vdots & \vdots & \vdots \\ e^{j\,2\pi(N-1)/N} & e^{j\,2\pi(N-2)/N} & \dots & 1 \\ 1 & 1 & \dots & 1 \end{bmatrix} \tag{5.286}$$

we can write

$$\tilde{\mathbf{s}} = \left(1/\sqrt{N}\right) \tilde{\mathbf{Q}}\mathbf{S} \tag{5.287}$$

where $\mathbf{S}$ is the sequence of symbols given by

$$\mathbf{S} = \begin{bmatrix} S_{N-1} & \dots & S_0 \end{bmatrix}^T . \tag{5.288}$$

Note that (5.287) represents an IDFT operation. Now, the DFT of $\tilde{\mathbf{r}}$ is given by

$$\begin{aligned} \tilde{\mathbf{y}} &= \sqrt{N}\tilde{\mathbf{Q}}^H\tilde{\mathbf{r}} \\ &= \tilde{\mathbf{Q}}^H\tilde{\mathbf{Q}}\tilde{\Lambda}\tilde{\mathbf{Q}}^H\tilde{\mathbf{Q}}\mathbf{S} + \tilde{\mathbf{Q}}^H\tilde{\mathbf{w}} \\ &= \tilde{\Lambda}\mathbf{S} + \tilde{\mathbf{z}} \end{aligned} \tag{5.289}$$

where we have used the fact that $\tilde{\mathbf{Q}}$ is a unitary matrix and

$$\begin{aligned} \tilde{\mathbf{y}} &\stackrel{\Delta}{=} [\ \tilde{y}_{N-1} \ \ \dots \ \ \tilde{y}_0\ ]^T \\ \tilde{\mathbf{z}} &\stackrel{\Delta}{=} [\ \tilde{z}_{N-1} \ \ \dots \ \ \tilde{z}_0\ ]^T . \end{aligned} \tag{5.290}$$

Thus, we have

$$\tilde{y}_k = \tilde{H}_k S_k + \tilde{z}_k \qquad \text{for } 0 \le k \le N-1. \tag{5.291}$$

In other words, the detected symbol is a scaled version of the transmitted symbol plus noise. We have thus mitigated the problem of intersymbol interference.

From (5.283) we observe that the transmitted signal $\tilde{s}_n$ is complex-valued and it requires at least three wires for transmission. However, in practice only real-valued signals are transmitted, since they require only two wires. This is obtained by taking a $2N$-point DFT as follows:

$$s_n = \frac{1}{2N} \sum_{k=0}^{2N-1} S_k e^{j\,2\pi nk/(2N)} \tag{5.292}$$

with the constraint that

$$S_{2N-k} = S_k^* \qquad \text{for } 0 \le k \le N-1. \tag{5.293}$$

The block diagram of a practical DMT system is shown in Figure 5.27. Note that N must be a power of two.

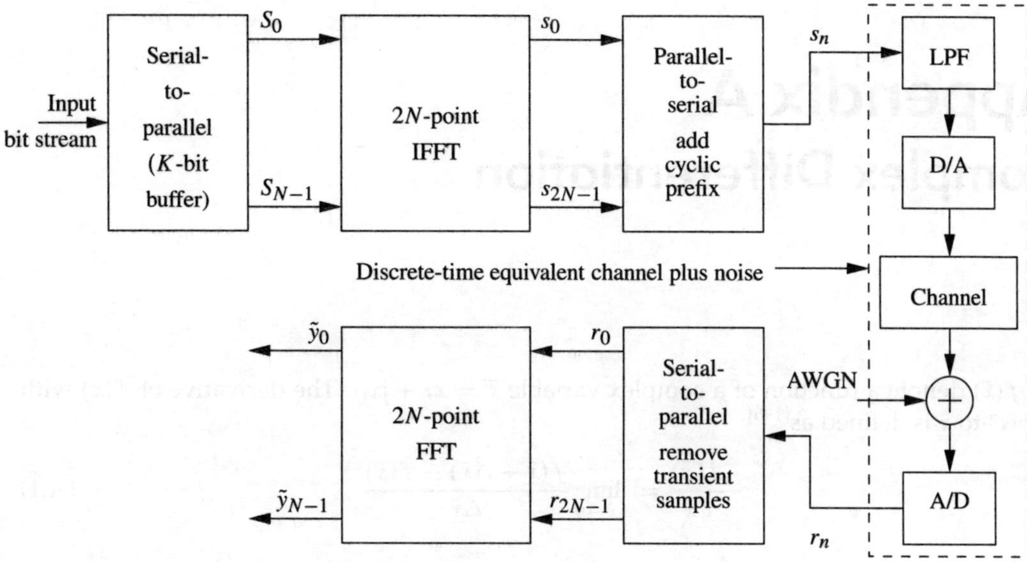

Figure 5.27 *Block diagram of a DMT system*

5.4 Summary

This chapter addressed the issue of detecting signals transmitted through channels that introduce distortion. Broadly speaking, three methods were discussed:the first method is based on equalization, the second approach is to use the maximum likelihood (ML) detector and the third is based on multicarrier communication discrete multitone (DMT) . The equalizer is simple to implement whereas the ML detector is fairly complex involving the use of a trellis. In fact, the number of states in the trellis increases exponentially with the length of the channel. The discrete multitone (DMT) is an elegant way to combat ISI.

The equalizer, on the other hand can be classified into two types – linear and non-linear. The symbol-spaced and fractionally-spaced equalizers come under the class of linear equalizers. The decision-feedback equalizers belong to the class of non-linear equalizers. It was shown that the fractionally-spaced equalizers are more robust than symbol-spaced equalizers. Amongst all kinds of equalizers, it is the decision-feedback equalizer that gives the best performance. They however suffer from the drawback of error propagation.

The ML detectors can also be classified as symbol-spaced or fractionally-spaced. It was shown that both types have the same performance, however the fractionally-spaced ML detector is expected to be more robust. The chapter concludes with the discussion of multicarrier communication systems and its practical implementation using discrete multitone (DMT).

Appendix A
Complex Differentiation

Let $f(\tilde{x})$ denote a function of a complex variable $\tilde{x} = x_I + jx_Q$. The derivative of $f(\tilde{x})$ with respect to $\tilde{x}$ is defined as[196]:

$$\frac{df\tilde{x})}{d\tilde{x}} = \lim_{\Delta\tilde{x}\to 0} \frac{f(\tilde{x}+\Delta\tilde{x}) - f(\tilde{x})}{\Delta\tilde{x}} \tag{A.1}$$

where

$$\Delta\tilde{x} = \Delta x_I + j\Delta x_Q. \tag{A.2}$$

When $f(\cdot)$ is a function of more than one complex variable, the derivative must be replaced by the partial derivative.

The function $f(\tilde{x})$ is said to be analytic (or holomorphic) at some point $\tilde{x}$, if $f(\tilde{x})$ is differentiable (the derivative exists and is unique) at $\tilde{x}$.

For example, consider

$$f(\tilde{x}) = \tilde{x}. \tag{A.3}$$

Clearly,

$$\frac{df(\tilde{x})}{d\tilde{x}} = 1 \tag{A.4}$$

for all $\tilde{x}$, therefore the function in (A.3) is analytic for all $\tilde{x}$. Let us now consider

$$f(\tilde{x}) = \tilde{x}^*. \tag{A.5}$$

We have

$$\frac{df(\tilde{x})}{d\tilde{x}} = \lim_{\substack{\Delta x_I \to 0 \\ \Delta x_Q \to 0}} \frac{\Delta x_I - j\Delta x_Q}{\Delta x_I + j\Delta x_Q} \tag{A.6}$$

which is not unique. For example when $\Delta x_I = 0$, (A.6) is equal to -1 and when $\Delta x_Q = 0$, (A.6) equals 1. Therefore the function in (A.5) is not analytic for any $\tilde{x}$. Many complex functions that are encountered in engineering are not analytic. However, they can be converted to analytic functions by making the following assumptions:

$$\begin{aligned} \frac{\partial\tilde{x}}{\partial\tilde{x}} &= \frac{\partial\tilde{x}^*}{\partial\tilde{x}^*} = 1 \\ \frac{\partial\tilde{x}^*}{\partial\tilde{x}} &= \frac{\partial\tilde{x}}{\partial\tilde{x}^*} = 0. \end{aligned} \tag{A.7}$$

These assumptions are based on the fact that $\tilde{x}$ and $\tilde{x}^*$ are two different vectors and one can be changed independently of the other. In other words $\tilde{x}^*$ can be kept constant while $\tilde{x}$ is varied, and vise versa, resulting in the derivative going to zero in (A.7).

Let $J(\tilde{x})$ be a real-valued scalar function of a complex variable $\tilde{x}$. The gradient of $J(x)$ with respect to $\tilde{x}$ is defined as:

$$\nabla J(\tilde{x}) = \frac{\partial J(\tilde{x})}{\partial \tilde{x}^*}. \tag{A.8}$$

It is immediately clear that at the maxima and minima points of $J(x)$

$$\nabla J(\tilde{x}) = 0. \tag{A.9}$$

Let us now try to justify the definition of the gradient in (A.8) using a simple example. Consider the minimization of the cost function

$$\begin{aligned} J(\tilde{x}) &= |\tilde{x}|^2 \\ &= \tilde{x} \cdot \tilde{x}^* \\ &= x_I^2 + x_Q^2 \end{aligned} \tag{A.10}$$

using the LMS algorithm (see sections 5.1.3 and 5.1.4). Clearly, $J_{\min}(\tilde{x})$ occurs when $x_1 = x_Q = 0$. The LMS algorithm starts from an arbitrary point $x_{0,I}, x_{0,Q}$ and eventually converges to the correct solution. From (A.10) we have:

$$\begin{aligned} \nabla J(\tilde{x}) &= \frac{\partial J(\tilde{x})}{\partial \tilde{x}^*} \\ &= \tilde{x}^* \frac{\partial \tilde{x}}{\partial \tilde{x}^*} + \tilde{x} \frac{\partial \tilde{x}^*}{\partial \tilde{x}^*} \\ &= \tilde{x}. \end{aligned} \tag{A.11}$$

Let $\tilde{x}_n = x_{n,I} + j x_{n,Q}$ denote the value of $\tilde{x}$ at the nth iteration. Then the update equation for $\tilde{x}_n$ is given by:

$$\begin{aligned} \tilde{x}_n &= \tilde{x}_{n-1} - \mu \nabla J(\tilde{x}_{n-1}) \\ &= \tilde{x}_{n-1} - \mu \tilde{x}_{n-1} \end{aligned} \tag{A.12}$$

where μ denotes the step-size and $\nabla J(\tilde{x}_{n-1})$ is the gradient at $\tilde{x}_{n-1}$. The update equation in (A.12) guarantees convergence to the optimum solution for:

$$|1 - \mu| < 1. \tag{A.13}$$

Thus we have justified the definition of the gradient in (A.8). Note that at the optimum point

$$\frac{\partial J(\tilde{x})}{\partial \tilde{x}} = \frac{\partial J(\tilde{x})}{\partial \tilde{x}^*} = 0. \tag{A.14}$$

However $\partial J(\tilde{x})/\partial \tilde{x}$ is not the gradient of $J(\tilde{x})$.

Appendix B
The Chernoff Bound

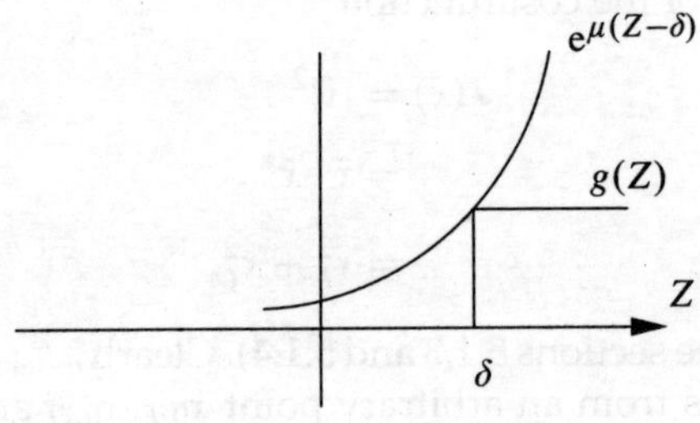

Figure B.1 *The function* $e^{\mu(Z-\delta)}$ *overbounds* $g(Z)$

In many applications, it is required to find out *closed form* expressions for the probability of $Z \geq \delta$, given that Z is a real, zero-mean Gaussian random variable. Similar problems have already been encountered in (2.20) and (2.95). In this Appendix, we derive the Chernoff bound for $P(Z \geq \delta)$ which is extremely tight.

Define the function $g(Z)$ such that

$$g(Z) = \begin{cases} 1 & \text{for } Z \geq \delta \\ 0 & \text{for } Z < \delta. \end{cases} \tag{B.1}$$

It is clear from Figure B.1 that

$$g(Z) \leq \exp\left(\mu(Z-\delta)\right) \qquad \text{for all } \mu > 0. \tag{B.2}$$

Let $p(Z)$ denote the pdf of Z. It follows that

$$E\left[g(Z)\right] \leq E\left[\exp\left(\mu(Z-\delta)\right)\right]$$

$$\Rightarrow \int_{Z=-\infty}^{\infty} g(Z)p(Z)\,dZ \leq E\left[\exp\left(\mu(Z-\delta)\right)\right]$$

$$\Rightarrow \frac{1}{\sigma_Z\sqrt{2\pi}}\int_{Z=\delta}^{\infty}\exp\left(-\frac{Z^2}{2\sigma_Z^2}\right)dZ \le E\left[\exp\left(\mu(Z-\delta)\right)\right]$$

$$\Rightarrow \frac{1}{2}\,\mathrm{erfc}\left(\sqrt{\frac{\delta^2}{2\sigma_Z^2}}\right) \le E\left[\exp\left(\mu(Z-\delta)\right)\right]. \tag{B.3}$$

We now need to find out the value of μ that minimizes the right-hand-side (RHS) of the above equation. Differentiating the RHS of the above equation with respect to μ (this can be done by first interchanging the order of differentiation and expectation) and setting the result to zero, we get

$$E\left[Z\exp\left(\mu(Z-\delta)\right)\right] = \delta E\left[\exp\left(\mu(Z-\delta)\right)\right]. \tag{B.4}$$

Computing the expectations in the above equation we get

$$\mu\sigma_Z^2\exp\left(\frac{\mu^2\sigma_Z^2}{2}\right) = \delta\exp\left(\frac{\sigma_Z^2\mu^2}{2}\right)$$

$$\Rightarrow \mu\sigma_Z^2 = \delta$$

$$\Rightarrow \mu = \frac{\delta}{\sigma_Z^2}. \tag{B.5}$$

Substituting the value of μ obtained in the above equation in (B.3) we get

$$\frac{1}{2}\,\mathrm{erfc}\left(\sqrt{\frac{\delta^2}{2\sigma_Z^2}}\right) \le \exp\left(-\frac{\delta^2}{2\sigma_Z^2}\right). \tag{B.6}$$

Appendix C
On Groups and Finite Fields

The purpose of this appendix is to introduce a new system of algebra that is useful in the area of error control coding. An exhaustive treatment of modern algebra can be found in [197]. A brief introduction can be found in [53].

C.1 Groups

Let G denote a set of elements. Let $*$ denote a binary operation on G. For any two elements a, b in G, let there exist a unique element c in G such that

$$a * b = c. \tag{C.1}$$

Then the set G is said to be *closed* under $*$.

Definition C.1.2 A set G in which a binary operation $*$ is defined, is called a *group* if the following conditions are satisfied:

(a) The binary operation is associative, that is, $a * (b * c) = (a * b) * c$.
(b) G contains an identity element e such that $a * e = e * a = a$.
(c) For every element a in G there exists another element a' also in G such that $a * a' = a' * a = e$. a' is called the inverse of a.

The group G is said to be *commutative* or *abelian* if $a * b = b * a$ for all a, b in G. The set of integers is a commutative group under real addition. Zero is the identity element and $-i$ is the inverse of i. The set of all rational numbers excluding zero is a commutative group under real multiplication. One is the identity element and b/a is the inverse of a/b.

Theorem C.1.1 *The identity element in a group is unique.*

Proof: Let there be two identity elements e and e'. Then we have $e = e * e' = e' * e = e'$. Hence $e' = e$, that is, there is one and only one identity element.

Theorem C.1.2 *The inverse of any element in a group is unique.*

Proof: Let the element a in G have two inverses, e and e'. Then we have $a' = a' * e = a' * (a * a'') = e * a'' = a''$. Hence $a' = a''$, that is, there is one and only one inverse of a.

The number of elements in a group is called the *order* of the group. A group of finite order is called a *finite* group. We now illustrate examples of finite groups.

Consider a set

$$G = \{0, 1, \ldots, m-1\}. \tag{C.2}$$

Define an operator $\oplus$ such that

$$a \oplus b \triangleq r \tag{C.3}$$

where r is the reminder when $a+b$ is divided by m. Here $+$ denotes real addition. It is clear that 0 is the identity element and the inverse of an element i in G is $m-i$ which is also in G. It is also clear that $\oplus$ is commutative. We now show that $\oplus$ is also associative, that is,

$$a \oplus (b \oplus c) = (a \oplus b) \oplus c. \tag{C.4}$$

Let

$$a + b + c = pm + r \tag{C.5}$$

and

$$b + c = p_1 m + r_1. \tag{C.6}$$

Then,

$$b \oplus c = r_1. \tag{C.7}$$

Hence

$$\begin{aligned} a \oplus (b \oplus c) &= a \oplus r_1 \\ &= \text{reminder of } (a + r_1) \\ &= \text{reminder of } (a + b + c - p_1 m) \\ &= \text{reminder of } (pm + r - p_1 m) \\ &= r. \end{aligned} \tag{C.8}$$

Similarly, let

$$a + b = p_2 m + r_2. \tag{C.9}$$

Then

$$a \oplus b = r_2. \tag{C.10}$$

Hence

$$\begin{aligned} (a \oplus b) \oplus c &= r_2 \oplus c \\ &= \text{reminder of } (r_2 + c) \\ &= \text{reminder of } (a + b + c - p_2 m) \end{aligned}$$

$$= \text{reminder of } (pm + r - p_2 m)$$
$$= r. \tag{C.11}$$

Thus we have proved that $\oplus$ is associative, that is,

$$a \oplus (b \oplus c) = (a \oplus b) \oplus c = r. \tag{C.12}$$

Hence the set G given in (C.2) is a commutative group under the operation $\oplus$. In general, the operator $\oplus$ as defined above is referred to as modulo-m addition. The group G in (C.2) is also called the *additive group*.

We now give an example of a *multiplicative group*. Let us now consider the set

$$G = \{1, \ldots, p - 1\} \tag{C.13}$$

where p is a *prime* number greater than unity. Recall that a prime number has only two factors, 1 and itself. Define an operator $\odot$ such that

$$a \odot b \stackrel{\Delta}{=} r \tag{C.14}$$

where r is the reminder when $a \cdot b$ is divided by p. Here $\cdot$ denotes real multiplication. It is immediately obvious that $\odot$ is commutative. We now show that r is in G for all a, b in G. It is obvious that $r < p$. We only need to show that $r \neq 0$.

Let us assume that there exists a, b, $1 \leq a,\ b \leq p - 1$, such that $r = 0$. This implies that

$$a \cdot b = kp \qquad \text{where } k > 1 \text{ is an integer.} \tag{C.15}$$

Observe that since p is prime, k cannot be equal to unity. If k was equal to unity, then it implies that either a or b is equal to p, since p is a prime. However, by assumption $a < p$ and $b < p$. Therefore we have a contradiction and k cannot be equal to unity. If $k > 1$ then either a or b or both a and b must have p as a factor, which is again not possible since $a < p$ and $b < p$. Thus we have shown that $r \neq 0$. We now need to show that every element in G has a *unique* inverse which is also in G.

Consider two elements a and b in G. Let

$$a \odot b = r_1 \qquad \text{where } 0 < r_1 < p. \tag{C.16}$$

Consider also

$$a \odot (b \oplus c) \tag{C.17}$$

where $\oplus$ denotes modulo-p addition and c is an element of G such that $b \oplus c \in G$. This implies that $c \neq p - b$, where $-$ denotes real subtraction. It is also clear that $b \oplus c \neq b$. In fact, if $b \oplus c = b$ then it implies that

$$b + c = p + b$$
$$\Rightarrow c = p \tag{C.18}$$

which is a contradiction since $0 < c < p$.

In the next section we show that $\odot$ is distributive over $\oplus$. Hence (C.17) can be written as

$$(a \odot b) \oplus (a \odot c) = r_1 \oplus r_2 \quad \text{(say)} \tag{C.19}$$

where

$$a \odot c = r_2 \quad \text{where } 0 < r_2 < p. \tag{C.20}$$

Once again it is clear that $r_1 \oplus r_2 \neq r_1$ since

$$\begin{aligned} r_1 \oplus r_2 &= r_1 \\ \Rightarrow r_1 + r_2 &= p + r_1 \\ \Rightarrow r_2 &= p \end{aligned} \tag{C.21}$$

which is a contradiction. Thus $r_1 \oplus r_2 \neq r_1$. Let $b \oplus c = d$. Thus we have shown that

$$a \odot b \neq a \odot d \quad \text{for } b \neq d. \tag{C.22}$$

Now, as b varies from 1 to $p - 1$, we must get $p - 1$ *distinct* values of $a \odot b$ in G, out of which one and only one result must be equal to unity. The corresponding value of b is the multiplicative inverse of a. Thus, we have shown that there exists one and only one multiplicative inverse of a.

Thus the set G in (C.13) is a commutative group under $\odot$. In Figure C.1, we show an example of modulo-2 addition and multiplication. In Figure C.2, we illustrate an example of modulo-3 addition and multiplication. In the next section, we introduce the concept of a *field*.

$\oplus$	0	1
0	0	1
1	1	0

$\odot$	1
1	1

Figure C.1 *Modulo-2 addition and multiplication*

$\oplus$	0	1	2
0	0	1	2
1	1	2	0
2	2	0	1

$\odot$	1	2
1	1	2
2	2	1

Figure C.2 *Modulo-3 addition and multiplication*

C.2 Fields

A field is a set of elements in which we can do addition, subtraction, multiplication and division such that the result is also an element in the set. Formally, a field is defined as follows:

Definition C.2.1 Let F be a set of elements on which two binary operators $\oplus$ (addition) and $\odot$ (multiplication) are defined. Then the set F together with the two binary operators is a field if the following conditions are satisfied:

(a) F is a commutative group under $\oplus$. The identity element with respect to $\oplus$ is 0, is the additive identity of F.
(b) The set of non-zero elements in F is a commutative group under $\odot$. The identity element with respect to $\odot$ is 1. It is also the multiplicative identity of F.
(c) Multiplication is distributive over addition, that is, for any three elements a, b, c in F

$$a \odot (b \oplus c) = (a \odot b) \oplus (a \odot c). \tag{C.23}$$

The number of elements in a field is called the order of the field. A field with a finite number of elements is called a finite field. In a field, the additive inverse of an element a is denoted by $-a$, hence $a \oplus (-a) = 0$. The multiplicative inverse is denoted by a^{-1}, hence $a \odot (a^{-1}) = 1$. We now state some of the basic properties of a field:

Property C.2.1 For every element a in a field $a \odot 0 = 0 \odot a = 0$.

Proof: Note that:

$$a = 1 \odot a = (1 \oplus 0) \odot a = a \oplus (0 \odot a). \tag{C.24}$$

Adding $-a$ to both sides of the above equation, we get the required result.

Property C.2.2 For any two non-zero elements $a, b, a \odot b \neq 0$.

Proof: This is a consequence of the fact that non-zero elements of a field form a group under multiplication. Hence the product of two non-zero elements must be non-zero. Recall that zero is not an element of a multiplicative group since it does not have an inverse.

Property C.2.3 If $a \odot b = 0$, then either a or b or both a and b are zero.

Proof: This is a consequence of Property C.2.2.

Property C.2.4 For any two elements a and b in a field, $-(a \odot b) = (-a) \odot b = a \odot (-b)$.

Proof: Observe that

$$0 = 0 \odot b = (a \oplus (-a)) \odot b = a \odot b \oplus (-a) \odot b. \tag{C.25}$$

Therefore $(-a) \odot b$ must be the additive inverse of $a \odot b$. Hence $-(a \odot b) = (-a) \odot b$. Similarly it can be shown that $-(a \odot b) = a \odot (-b)$.

Property C.2.5 For $a \neq 0$, $a \odot b = a \odot c$ implies $b = c$.

Proof: Since a is non-zero, it must have a multiplicative inverse denoted by a^{-1}. Hence we have

$$a \odot b = a \odot c$$

$$\Rightarrow a^{-1} \odot (a \odot b) = a^{-1} \odot (a \odot c)$$

$$\Rightarrow (a^{-1} \odot a) \odot b = (a^{-1} \odot a) \odot c$$

$$\Rightarrow 1 \odot b = 1 \odot c$$

$$\Rightarrow b = c. \tag{C.26}$$

We now consider examples of fields.

Let

$$F = \{0, 1, \ldots, p-1\} \tag{C.27}$$

where p is a prime number. In the previous section we have seen that F is a commutative group under $\oplus$ (modulo-P) addition. The non-zero elements of F constitute a commutative group under $\odot$ (modulo-P multiplication). To prove that F is a field, we only need to show that $\odot$ is distributive over $\oplus$ that is,

$$a \odot (b \oplus c) = (a \odot b) \oplus (a \odot c). \tag{C.28}$$

Let

$$b + c = x_1 \cdot p + r_1$$

$$\Rightarrow b \oplus c = r_1 \tag{C.29}$$

where, as usual $+$ denotes real addition and $\cdot$ denotes real multiplication. Therefore

$$a \odot (b \oplus c) = a \odot r_1$$

$$= \text{reminder of } (a \cdot r_1)$$

$$= \text{reminder of } (a \cdot (b + c - x_1 p)). \tag{C.30}$$

Let

$$a \cdot b = x_2 \cdot p + r_2 \quad \Rightarrow a \odot b = r_2$$

$$a \cdot c = x_3 \cdot p + r_3 \quad \Rightarrow a \odot c = r_3$$

$$r_2 + r_3 = x_4 \cdot p + r_4 \quad \Rightarrow r_2 \oplus r_3 = r_4. \tag{C.31}$$

Substituting the above equations in (C.30), we get

$$a \odot (b \oplus c) = \text{reminder of } ((x_2 + x_3 + x_4 - x_1) \cdot p + r_4).$$

$$= r_4. \tag{C.32}$$

Now, from (C.31),

$$(a \odot b) \oplus (a \odot c) = r_2 \oplus r_3 = r_4. \tag{C.33}$$

Thus we have proved (C.28). Therefore the set F given by (C.27) is a field of order p under modulo-p addition and multiplication. F is also called a *prime* field and is denoted by GF(p).The term 'GF' is an acronym for *Galois field*. For $p = 2$ we obtain the binary field GF(2) which is used in convolutional codes. Note that in GF(2),

$$1 \oplus 1 = 0 \quad \Rightarrow -1 = 1. \tag{C.34}$$

In the next section we explain the D-transform.

C.2.1 The D-transform

Consider the summation

$$\begin{aligned} A(D) &= a_0 + a_1 D + a_2 D^2 + \cdots \\ &= \sum_{n=0}^{\infty} a_n D^n, \end{aligned} \tag{C.35}$$

where a_n is an element from GF(p) (p is a prime number) occurring at time instant n. The symbol D denotes a unit delay and D^n represents a delay of n units. Note that for simplicity of notation we have used '+' and a space to denote addition and multiplication over GF(p) respectively. Whether '+' denotes real addition or addition over GF(p) will henceforth be clear from the context. $A(D)$ is called the D-transform of a_n. We now study some properties of the D-transform.

Property C.2.6 Convolution in the time domain over GF(p) is equivalent to multiplication in the frequency domain over GF(p).

Proof: Consider the element c_n for $n \geq 0$, given by the convolution sum

$$\begin{aligned} c_n &= a_0 b_n + a_1 b_{n-1} + a_2 b_{n-2} + \cdots \\ &= \sum_{k=0}^{\infty} a_k b_{n-k} \end{aligned} \tag{C.36}$$

where $\oplus$ and $\odot$ denote modulo-p addition and multiplication in GF(p) respectively and a_n and b_n are elements in GF(p). We assume that $a_n = b_n = 0$ for $n < 0$. Then the D-transform of c_n is given by

$$\begin{aligned} C(D) &= \sum_{n=0}^{\infty} \sum_{k=0}^{\infty} a_k b_{n-k} D^n \\ &= \sum_{n=0}^{\infty} \sum_{k=0}^{\infty} a_k b_{n-k} D^k D^{n-k}. \end{aligned} \tag{C.37}$$

Interchanging the order of summation, we get

$$C(D) = \sum_{k=0}^{\infty} a_k D^k \left(\sum_{n=0}^{\infty} b_{n-k} D^{n-k} \right). \tag{C.38}$$

Substituting $n - k = m$ and noting that $b_m = 0$ for $m < 0$, we get

$$\begin{aligned} C(D) &= \sum_{k=0}^{\infty} a_k D^k \left(\sum_{m=0}^{\infty} b_m D^m \right) \\ &= \sum_{k=0}^{\infty} a_k D^k B(D) \\ &= A(D)B(D). \end{aligned} \tag{C.39}$$

Thus we have proved that convolution in the time domain over GF(p) is equivalent to multiplication in the transform domain over GF(p).

Property C.2.7 If $A(D)$ is the D-transform of a_n, then $D^{n_0}A(D)$ is the D-transform of a_{n-n_0}.

Proof: Let $b_n = a_{n-n_0}$. We also assume that $a_n = 0$ for $n < 0$. Then,

$$\begin{aligned} B(D) &= \sum_{n=0}^{\infty} b_n \cdot D^n \\ &= \sum_{n=0}^{\infty} a_{n-n_0} \cdot D^n. \end{aligned} \tag{C.40}$$

Substituting $m = n - n_0$, we get

$$\begin{aligned} B(D) &= \sum_{m=-n_0}^{\infty} a_m \cdot D^{m+n_0} \\ &= D^{n_0} \sum_{m=0}^{\infty} a_m \cdot D^n \\ &= D^{n_0} A(D). \end{aligned} \tag{C.41}$$

Note that $A(D)$ in (C.35) can be considered as a polynomial with coefficients from GF(p). The *degree* of a polynomial is the highest power of D whose coefficient is non-zero. In the next section, we study operations on polynomials, with coefficients from GF(2).

C.2.2 Polynomials over GF(2)

In this section we illustrate with the help of examples, how polynomials with coefficients from GF(2) can be added, subtracted, multiplied and divided. Let

$$\begin{aligned} G_1(D) &= 1 + D + D^2 \\ G_2(D) &= 1 + D^2. \end{aligned} \tag{C.42}$$

Once again, observe that in the above equation, the + sign does not have any specific meaning. Then

$$G_1(D) + G_2(D) = G_1(D) + (-G_2(D))D. \tag{C.43}$$

Since subtraction is the same as addition in GF(2). The result of multiplying the polynomials is

$$\begin{aligned} G_1(D)G_2(D) &= 1 + D + D^2 + D^2 + D^3 + D^4 \\ &= 1 + D + D^3 + D^4. \end{aligned} \tag{C.44}$$

Consider the polynomial

$$G(D) = 1 + D. \tag{C.45}$$

Then $g^{-1}(D)$ is given by

$$\begin{aligned} G^{-1}(D) &\stackrel{\Delta}{=} \frac{1}{G(D)} \\ &= 1 + D + D^2 + D^3 + D^4 + \cdots \end{aligned} \tag{C.46}$$

The above result is obtained by long division, as illustrated in Figure C.3.

$$\begin{array}{r|l} & 1 + D + D^2 + D^3 + \ldots \\ \hline 1 + D & 1 \\ & \underline{1 + D} \\ & \quad D \\ & \quad \underline{D + D^2} \\ & \qquad D^2 \\ & \qquad \underline{D^2 + D^3} \\ & \qquad\quad D^3 \\ & \qquad\quad \underline{D^3 + D^4} \\ & \qquad\qquad D^4 \\ & \qquad\qquad \vdots \end{array}$$

Figure C.3 *Division of polynomials in GF(2)*

Appendix D
Properties of the Autocorrelation Matrix

Let $\tilde{\mathbf{R}}_{\tilde{v}\tilde{v}}$ denote an $L \times L$ autocorrelation matrix of a wide sense stationary, complex, discrete-time stochastic process represented by the $L \times 1$ vector $\tilde{\mathbf{v}}$. The elements of $\tilde{\mathbf{v}}$ are given by

$$\tilde{\mathbf{v}} = \begin{bmatrix} \tilde{v}_1 & \ldots & \tilde{v}_L \end{bmatrix}. \tag{D.1}$$

We have

$$\begin{aligned} \tilde{\mathbf{R}}_{\tilde{v}\tilde{v}} &\stackrel{\Delta}{=} E\left[\tilde{\mathbf{v}}\tilde{\mathbf{v}}^H\right] \\ &= \begin{bmatrix} \tilde{R}_{\tilde{v}\tilde{v},\,0} & \tilde{R}_{\tilde{v}\tilde{v},\,-1} & \cdots & \tilde{R}_{\tilde{v}\tilde{v},\,-L+1} \\ \tilde{R}_{\tilde{v}\tilde{v},\,1} & \tilde{R}_{\tilde{v}\tilde{v},\,0} & \cdots & \tilde{R}_{\tilde{v}\tilde{v},\,-L+2} \\ \vdots & \vdots & \vdots & \vdots \\ \tilde{R}_{\tilde{v}\tilde{v},\,L-1} & \tilde{R}_{\tilde{v}\tilde{v},\,L-2} & \cdots & \tilde{R}_{\tilde{v}\tilde{v},\,0} \end{bmatrix}. \end{aligned} \tag{D.2}$$

If $\tilde{R}_{\tilde{v}\tilde{v},i,j}$ denotes the element of $\tilde{\mathbf{R}}_{\tilde{v}\tilde{v}}$ in the ith row and j^{th} column, then we have

$$\tilde{R}_{\tilde{v}\tilde{v},i,j} = \tilde{R}_{\tilde{v}\tilde{v},i-j}. \tag{D.3}$$

This is known as the *Toeplitz* property of the autocorrelation matrix. Observe that $\tilde{\mathbf{R}}_{\tilde{v}\tilde{v}}$ is also *Hermitian*, i.e.

$$\tilde{\mathbf{R}}_{\tilde{v}\tilde{v}}^H = \tilde{\mathbf{R}}_{\tilde{v}\tilde{v}}. \tag{D.4}$$

Let $\tilde{\mathbf{x}}$ be an arbitrary non-zero $L \times 1$ vector defined by

$$\tilde{\mathbf{x}} = \begin{bmatrix} \tilde{x}_1 & \ldots & \tilde{x}_L \end{bmatrix}. \tag{D.5}$$

Consider the inner product

$$\tilde{y} = \tilde{\mathbf{v}}^H \tilde{\mathbf{x}}. \tag{D.6}$$

It is clear that

$$\begin{aligned} E\left[\tilde{y}^*\tilde{y}\right] &= E\left[\tilde{y}^H\tilde{y}\right] \\ &= E\left[\tilde{\mathbf{x}}^H\tilde{\mathbf{v}}\tilde{\mathbf{v}}^H\tilde{\mathbf{x}}\right] \\ &= \tilde{\mathbf{x}}^H E\left[\tilde{\mathbf{v}}\tilde{\mathbf{v}}^H\right]\tilde{\mathbf{x}} \\ &= \tilde{\mathbf{x}}^H\tilde{\mathbf{R}}_{\tilde{v}\tilde{v}}\tilde{\mathbf{x}}. \end{aligned} \tag{D.7}$$

Since

$$E\left[\tilde{y}^*\tilde{y}\right] \geq 0 \tag{D.8}$$

from (D.7) we get

$$\tilde{\mathbf{x}}^H\tilde{\mathbf{R}}_{\tilde{v}\tilde{v}}\tilde{\mathbf{x}} \geq 0 \tag{D.9}$$

for non-zero values of $\tilde{\mathbf{x}}$. This property of the autocorrelation matrix is called positive semidefinite. In most auto situations, the autocorrelation matrix is positive definite, that is,

$$\tilde{\mathbf{x}}^H\tilde{\mathbf{R}}_{\tilde{v}\tilde{v}}\tilde{\mathbf{x}} > 0. \tag{D.10}$$

We now wish to find an $L \times 1$ vector $\tilde{\mathbf{q}}$ that satisfies:

$$\tilde{\mathbf{R}}_{\tilde{v}\tilde{v}}\tilde{\mathbf{q}} = \lambda\tilde{\mathbf{q}} \tag{D.11}$$

where λ is a constant. The above equation can be rewritten as:

$$\left(\tilde{\mathbf{R}}_{\tilde{v}\tilde{v}} - \lambda\mathbf{I}_L\right)\tilde{\mathbf{q}} = \mathbf{0} \tag{D.12}$$

where $\mathbf{I}_L$ is an $L \times L$ identity matrix. For a non-zero solution of $\tilde{\mathbf{q}}$ we require

$$\det\left(\tilde{\mathbf{R}}_{\tilde{v}\tilde{v}} - \lambda\mathbf{I}_L\right) = \mathbf{0} \tag{D.13}$$

where $\det(\cdot)$ denotes the determinant. Solving the above determinant yields an Lth degree polynomial in λ which has L roots. These roots are referred to as eigenvalues of $\tilde{\mathbf{R}}_{\tilde{v}\tilde{v}}$, and are denoted by $\lambda_1, \ldots, \lambda_L$. The corresponding values of $\tilde{\mathbf{q}}$ are known as eigenvectors and are denoted by $\tilde{\mathbf{q}}_1, \ldots, \tilde{\mathbf{q}}_L$. We now explore some of the properties of the eigenvalues and eigenvectors of an autocorrelation matrix.

Property D.0.1 The eigenvalues of $\tilde{\mathbf{R}}_{\tilde{v}\tilde{v}}$ are real and non-negative.

Proof: We have

$$\tilde{\mathbf{R}}_{\tilde{v}\tilde{v}}\tilde{\mathbf{q}}_i = \lambda_i\tilde{\mathbf{q}}_i \tag{D.14}$$

where $\tilde{\mathbf{q}}_i$ is the eigenvector corresponding to the eigenvalue λ_i. Pre-multiplying both sides of the second equation in (D.16) by $\tilde{\mathbf{q}}_i^H$ we get

$$\tilde{\mathbf{q}}_i^H \tilde{\mathbf{R}}_{\tilde{v}\tilde{v}} \tilde{\mathbf{q}}_i = \lambda_i \tilde{\mathbf{q}}_i^H \tilde{\mathbf{q}}_i$$

$$\Rightarrow \frac{\tilde{\mathbf{q}}_i^H \tilde{\mathbf{R}}_{\tilde{v}\tilde{v}} \tilde{\mathbf{q}}_i}{\tilde{\mathbf{q}}_i^H \tilde{\mathbf{q}}_i} = \lambda_i. \tag{D.15}$$

From (D.10) and the fact that $\tilde{\mathbf{q}}_i^H \tilde{\mathbf{q}}_i$ is real and positive we conclude that λ_i is positive and real.

Property D.0.2 The eigenvectors corresponding to distinct eigenvalues of $\tilde{\mathbf{R}}_{\tilde{v}\tilde{v}}$ are orthogonal.

Proof: Let λ_i and λ_j denote two distinct eigenvalues of $\tilde{\mathbf{R}}_{\tilde{v}\tilde{v}}$. Let $\tilde{\mathbf{q}}_i$ and $\tilde{\mathbf{q}}_j$ denote the eigenvectors corresponding to λ_i and λ_j. We have,

$$\tilde{\mathbf{R}}_{\tilde{v}\tilde{v}} \tilde{\mathbf{q}}_i = \lambda_i \tilde{\mathbf{q}}_i$$

$$\tilde{\mathbf{R}}_{\tilde{v}\tilde{v}} \tilde{\mathbf{q}}_j = \lambda_j \tilde{\mathbf{q}}_j. \tag{D.16}$$

Multiplying both sides of the second equation in (D.16) by $\tilde{\mathbf{q}}_i^H$ and making use of the fact that $\tilde{\mathbf{R}}^H = \tilde{\mathbf{R}}$, we get

$$\tilde{\mathbf{q}}_i^H \tilde{\mathbf{R}}_{\tilde{v}\tilde{v}} \tilde{\mathbf{q}}_j = \lambda_j \tilde{\mathbf{q}}_i^H \tilde{\mathbf{q}}_j$$

$$\Rightarrow \left(\tilde{\mathbf{R}}_{\tilde{v}\tilde{v}} \tilde{\mathbf{q}}_i\right)^H \tilde{\mathbf{q}}_j = \lambda_j \tilde{\mathbf{q}}_i^H \tilde{\mathbf{q}}_j$$

$$\Rightarrow \left(\lambda_i \tilde{\mathbf{q}}_i\right)^H \tilde{\mathbf{q}}_j = \lambda_j \tilde{\mathbf{q}}_i^H \tilde{\mathbf{q}}_j$$

$$\Rightarrow \lambda_i \tilde{\mathbf{q}}_i^H \tilde{\mathbf{q}}_j = \lambda_j \tilde{\mathbf{q}}_i^H \tilde{\mathbf{q}}_j. \tag{D.17}$$

Since $\lambda_i \neq \lambda_j$, the only possibility is that

$$\tilde{\mathbf{q}}_i^H \tilde{\mathbf{q}}_j = 0. \tag{D.18}$$

Property D.0.3 Define the $L \times L$ matrix

$$\tilde{\mathbf{Q}} = [\ \tilde{\mathbf{q}}_1 \quad \ldots \quad \tilde{\mathbf{q}}_L\ ] \tag{D.19}$$

where $\tilde{\mathbf{q}}_i$ is the eigenvector corresponding to the eigenvalue λ_i. We assume that all eigenvalues are distinct and the eigenvectors are orthonormal. Define another $L \times L$ diagonal matrix

$$\tilde{\mathbf{\Lambda}} = \text{diag}\ [\lambda_1, \ldots, \lambda_L]. \tag{D.20}$$

Then the autocorrelation matrix can be factored as

$$\tilde{\mathbf{R}}_{\tilde{v}\tilde{v}} = \tilde{\mathbf{Q}} \tilde{\mathbf{\Lambda}} \tilde{\mathbf{Q}}^H. \tag{D.21}$$

Proof: Since

$$\tilde{\mathbf{R}}_{\tilde{v}\tilde{v}}\tilde{\mathbf{q}}_i = \lambda_i\tilde{\mathbf{q}}_i \qquad \text{for } 1 \leq i \leq L \tag{D.22}$$

we can group the L equations to get

$$\tilde{\mathbf{R}}_{\tilde{v}\tilde{v}}\tilde{\mathbf{Q}} = \tilde{\mathbf{Q}}\mathbf{\Lambda}. \tag{D.23}$$

Since the L eigenvectors are orthonormal, we have

$$\begin{aligned} \tilde{\mathbf{Q}}^H\tilde{\mathbf{Q}} &= \mathbf{I}_L \\ \Rightarrow \tilde{\mathbf{Q}}^H &= \tilde{\mathbf{Q}}^{-1} \\ \Rightarrow \tilde{\mathbf{Q}}\tilde{\mathbf{Q}}^H &= \mathbf{I}_L \end{aligned} \tag{D.24}$$

where $\mathbf{I}_L$ is an $L \times L$ identity matrix. Thus $\tilde{\mathbf{Q}}$ is an unitary matrix. Pre-multiplying both sides of (D.23) by $\tilde{\mathbf{Q}}^H$ and using (D.24), we get

$$\tilde{\mathbf{Q}}^H\tilde{\mathbf{R}}_{\tilde{v}\tilde{v}}\tilde{\mathbf{Q}} = \mathbf{\Lambda}. \tag{D.25}$$

Pre-multiplying both sides of (D.25) by $\tilde{\mathbf{Q}}$ and post-multiplying both sides by $\tilde{\mathbf{Q}}^H$ and using (D.24), we get

$$\tilde{\mathbf{R}}_{\tilde{v}\tilde{v}} = \tilde{\mathbf{Q}}\mathbf{\Lambda}\tilde{\mathbf{Q}}^H. \tag{D.26}$$

This decomposition of the autocorrelation matrix is called the unitary similarity transformation.

Property D.0.4 The sum of the eigenvalues of $\tilde{\mathbf{R}}_{\tilde{v}\tilde{v}}$ is equal to the trace of $\tilde{\mathbf{R}}_{\tilde{v}\tilde{v}}$.

Proof: From (D.25) we have

$$\operatorname{tr}\left(\tilde{\mathbf{Q}}^H\tilde{\mathbf{R}}_{\tilde{v}\tilde{v}}\tilde{\mathbf{Q}}\right) = \operatorname{tr}(\mathbf{\Lambda}). \tag{D.27}$$

Using the fact that the trace of the matrix product $\mathbf{AB}$ is equal to the product $\mathbf{BA}$, and once again using (D.24), we get

$$\begin{aligned} \operatorname{tr}\left(\tilde{\mathbf{R}}_{\tilde{v}\tilde{v}}\tilde{\mathbf{Q}}\tilde{\mathbf{Q}}^H\right) &= \operatorname{tr}(\mathbf{\Lambda}) \\ \Rightarrow \operatorname{tr}\left(\tilde{\mathbf{R}}_{\tilde{v}\tilde{v}}\right) &= \sum_{i=1}^{L}\lambda_i. \end{aligned} \tag{D.28}$$

Appendix E
Some Aspects of Discrete-Time Signal Processing

E.1 The Sampling Theorem

Consider a signal $\tilde{p}(t)$ that is multiplied by a Dirac delta train $a(t)$ where

$$a(t) = \sum_{k=-\infty}^{\infty} \delta_D(t - kT_s). \tag{E.1}$$

Since $a(t)$ is periodic it can be written as a Fourier series:

$$a(t) = b_0 + \sum_{k=1}^{\infty} (c_k \cos(2\pi k F_s t) + d_k \sin(2\pi k F_s t)) \tag{E.2}$$

where

$$F_s = 1/T_s \tag{E.3}$$

and

$$\begin{aligned}
b_0 &= \frac{1}{T_s} \int_{t=0^-}^{T_s^-} a(t)\, dt \\
&= \frac{1}{T_s}, \\
c_k &= \frac{2}{T_s} \int_{t=0^-}^{T_s^-} a(t) \cos(2\pi k F_s t)\, dt \\
&= \frac{2}{T_s}, \\
d_k &= \frac{2}{T_s} \int_{t=0^-}^{T_s^-} a(t) \sin(2\pi k F_s t)\, dt \\
&= 0.
\end{aligned} \tag{E.4}$$

In the above equation, we have used the sifting property of the Dirac delta function. Thus we get

$$\begin{aligned} a(t) &= \frac{1}{T_s} + \frac{1}{T_s}\sum_{k=1}^{\infty}(\exp(\mathrm{j}\,2\pi kF_st) + \exp(-\mathrm{j}\,2\pi kF_st)) \\ &= \frac{1}{T_s}\sum_{k=-\infty}^{\infty}\exp(\mathrm{j}\,2\pi kF_st). \end{aligned} \tag{E.5}$$

The Fourier transform of $a(t)$ is given by

$$A(F) = \frac{1}{T_s}\sum_{k=-\infty}^{\infty}\delta_D(F - kF_s). \tag{E.6}$$

The Fourier transform of the product $\tilde{p}(t)a(t)$ is

$$\tilde{A}(F) \star \tilde{P}(F) = \frac{1}{T_s}\sum_{k=-\infty}^{\infty}\tilde{P}(F - kF_s) \tag{E.7}$$

where $\star$ denotes convolution, $\tilde{P}(F)$ is the Fourier transform of $\tilde{p}(t)$ and we have once again used the sifting property of the Dirac delta function. The above equation implies that multiplying $\tilde{p}(t)$ by a Dirac delta train in the time domain results in a periodic spectrum (with period F_s) in the frequency domain. However, the Fourier transform of $\tilde{p}(t)a(t)$ is also given by

$$\begin{aligned} &\int_{t=-\infty}^{\infty}\tilde{p}(t)a(t)\exp(-\mathrm{j}\,2\pi Ft)\,dt \\ &= \sum_{k=-\infty}^{\infty}\int_{t=-\infty}^{\infty}\tilde{p}(t)\delta_D(t - kT_s)\exp(-\mathrm{j}\,2\pi Ft)\,dt \\ &= \sum_{k=-\infty}^{\infty}\tilde{p}(kT_s)\exp(-\mathrm{j}\,2\pi FkT_s). \end{aligned} \tag{E.8}$$

Equating (E.7) and (E.8) we get

$$\begin{aligned} \sum_{k=-\infty}^{\infty}\tilde{p}(kT_s)\exp(-\mathrm{j}\,2\pi FkT_s) &= \frac{1}{T_s}\sum_{k=-\infty}^{\infty}\tilde{P}(F - kF_s) \\ &= \tilde{P}_{\mathscr{P}}(F) \qquad \text{(say)}. \end{aligned} \tag{E.9}$$

The summation on the left-hand-side of the above equation is referred to as the *discrete-time Fourier transform* (DTFT)[159]. The subscript $\mathscr{P}$ in $\tilde{P}_{\mathscr{P}}(F)$ is used to denote a periodic function.

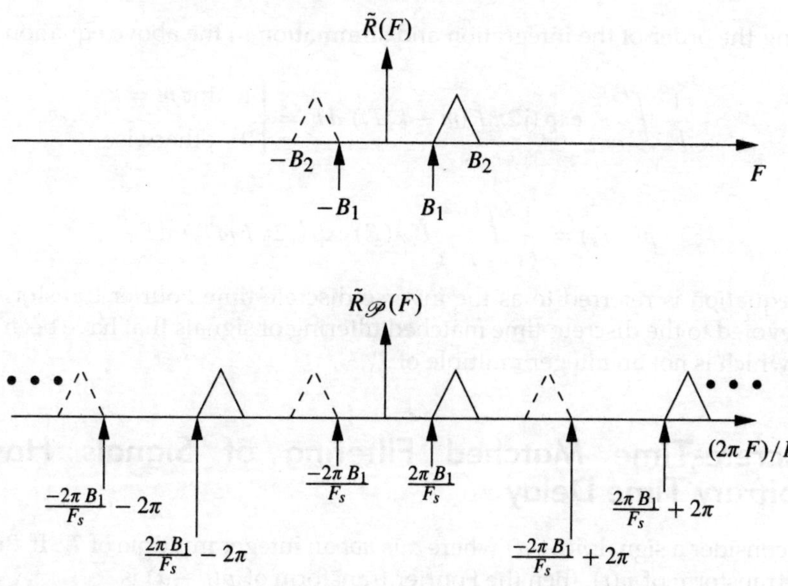

Figure E.1 *Illustrating the spectrum of a real-valued signal $r(nT_s)$ before and after sampling*

Figure E.1 illustrates the spectrum of a real-valued signal sampled at F_s. Note that the x-axis is labelled in terms of the normalized frequency in radians, that is, $2\pi F/F_s$.

Now, let

$$p(t) = \cos(2\pi F_s t) \rightleftharpoons \frac{1}{2}[\delta(F - F_s) + \delta(F + F_s)] = P(F). \tag{E.10}$$

Therefore if $T_s = 1/F_s$, then we have the important result

$$\begin{aligned} p(kT_s) &= 1 \\ \Rightarrow \sum_{k=-\infty}^{\infty} e^{-j\, 2\pi F k T_s} &= \frac{1}{2T_s} \sum_{k=-\infty}^{\infty} [\delta(F - F_s - kF_s) + \delta(F + F_s - kF_s)] \\ &= \frac{1}{T_s} \sum_{k=-\infty}^{\infty} \delta(F - kF_s). \end{aligned} \tag{E.11}$$

Let us now multiply both sides of (E.9) by $\exp(\mathrm{j}\, 2\pi F m T_s)$ and integrate the product with limits $-F_s/2$ and $F_s/2$ and divide the result by F_s. We obtain

$$\begin{aligned} &\frac{1}{F_s} \int_{-F_s/2}^{F_s/2} \sum_{k=-\infty}^{\infty} \tilde{p}(kT_s) \exp\left(\mathrm{j}\, 2\pi F(m - k)T_s\right) dF \\ &= \frac{1}{F_s} \int_{-F_s/2}^{F_s/2} \tilde{P}_{\mathcal{P}}(F) \exp\left(\mathrm{j}\, 2\pi F m T_s\right) dF. \end{aligned} \tag{E.12}$$

Interchanging the order of the integration and summation in the above equation and noting that

$$\frac{1}{F_s}\int_{-F_s/2}^{F_s/2} \exp\left(\mathrm{j}\,2\pi\,F(m-k)T_s\right)\,dF = \begin{cases} 1 & \text{for } m=k \\ 0 & \text{otherwise} \end{cases} \tag{E.13}$$

we obtain

$$\tilde{p}(mT_s) = \frac{1}{F_s}\int_{-F_s/2}^{F_s/2} \tilde{P}_{\mathscr{P}}(F)\exp\left(\mathrm{j}\,2\pi\,FmT_s\right)\,dF. \tag{E.14}$$

The above equation is referred to as the inverse discrete-time Fourier transform. The next section is devoted to the discrete-time matched filtering of signals that have been delayed by an amount which is not an integer multiple of T_s.

E.2 Discrete-Time Matched Filtering of Signals Having an Arbitrary Time Delay

Let us now consider a signal $\tilde{p}(t-\alpha)$ where α is *not* an integer multiple of T_s. If $\tilde{P}(F)$ denotes the Fourier transform of $\tilde{p}(t)$, then the Fourier transform of $\tilde{p}(t-\alpha)$ is

$$\int_{t=-\infty}^{\infty} \tilde{p}(t-\alpha)\exp\left(-\mathrm{j}\,2\pi\,Ft\right)\,dt = \exp\left(-\mathrm{j}\,2\pi\,F\alpha\right)\tilde{P}(F). \tag{E.15}$$

Now, if $\tilde{p}_1(t) = \tilde{p}(t-\alpha)$ is sampled at rate $1/T_s$, the periodic spectrum is given by

$$\tilde{P}_{\mathscr{P},1}(F) = \frac{1}{T_s}\sum_{k=-\infty}^{\infty} \exp\left(-\mathrm{j}\,2\pi\left(F-\frac{k}{T_s}\right)\alpha\right)\tilde{P}\left(F-\frac{k}{T_s}\right). \tag{E.16}$$

Let us assume that $\tilde{p}_1(t)$ is sampled at Nyquist rate or above so that there is no aliasing. In this situation we get

$$\tilde{P}_{\mathscr{P},1}(F) = \frac{1}{T_s}\exp\left(-\mathrm{j}\,2\pi\,F\alpha\right)\tilde{P}(F) \qquad \text{for } -\pi \le 2\pi\,F/F_s \le \pi. \tag{E.17}$$

Consider a filter $\tilde{p}_2(t)$, that is matched to $\tilde{p}_1(t)$. Note that

$$\tilde{p}_2(t) = p_1^*(-t) = p^*(-t-\alpha). \tag{E.18}$$

The spectrum of $\tilde{p}_2(t)$ sampled at $1/T_s$ is

$$\tilde{P}_{\mathscr{P},2}(F) = \frac{1}{T_s}\exp\left(\mathrm{j}\,2\pi\,F\alpha\right)\tilde{P}^*(F) \qquad \text{for } -\pi \le 2\pi\,F/F_s \le \pi. \tag{E.19}$$

Now, if $\tilde{p}_1(nT_s)$ is convolved with $\tilde{p}_2(nT_s)$, the result in the frequency domain is

$$\tilde{P}_{\mathscr{P},1}(F)\tilde{P}_{\mathscr{P},2}(F) = \frac{1}{T_s^2}\left|\tilde{P}(F)\right|^2 \qquad \text{for } -\pi \le 2\pi\,F/F_s \le \pi \tag{E.20}$$

which is *independent* of the time delay α.

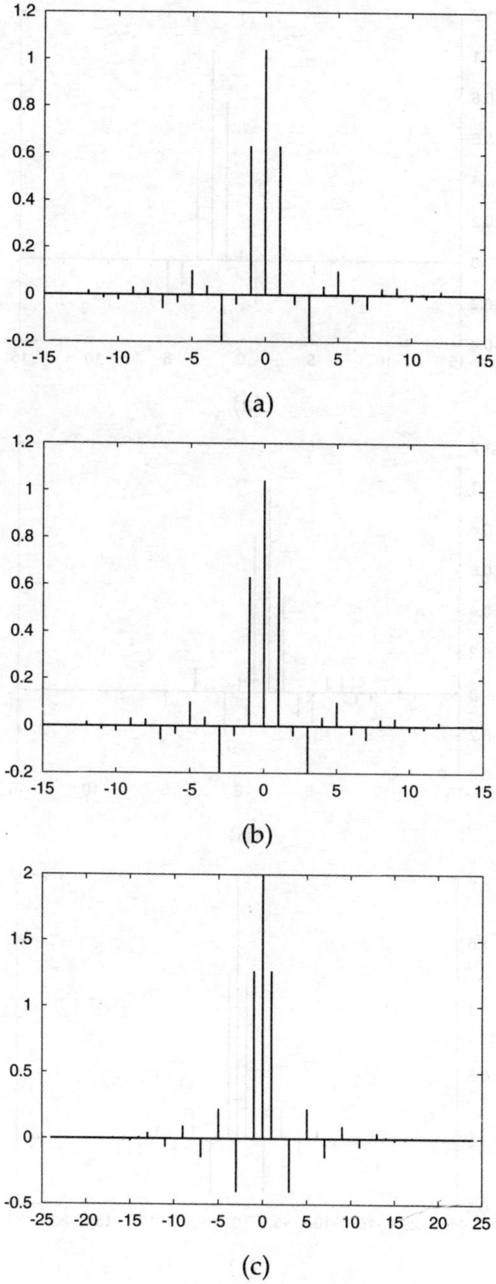

Figure E.2 *(a) Samples of the transmit filter obtained by the receiver when $\alpha = 0$. (b) Samples of the matched filter (MF). (c) MF output. Here the number of samples per symbol is 2.*

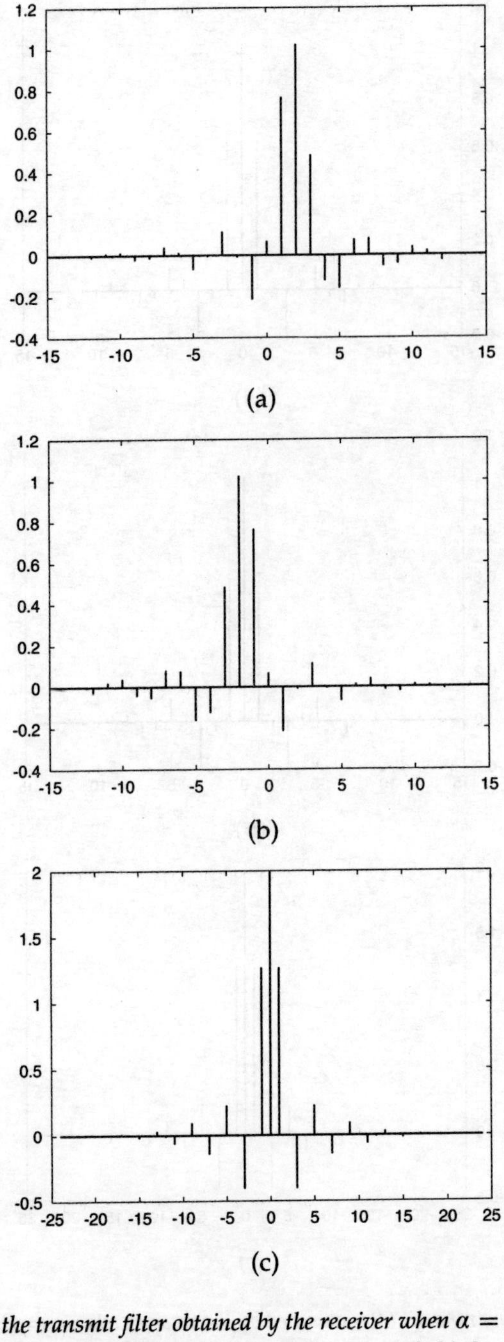

Figure E.3 *(a) Samples of the transmit filter obtained by the receiver when* $\alpha = 1.8T_s$. *(b) Samples of the matched filter (MF). (c) MF output. Here the number of samples per symbol is 2.*

Thus we have arrived at an important conclusion which is stated below.

$$\begin{aligned}
\tilde{p}(nT_s - \alpha) \star \tilde{p}^*(-nT_s - \alpha) &= \sum_{k=-\infty}^{\infty} \tilde{p}(kT_s - \alpha)\tilde{p}^*(kT_s - nT_s - \alpha) \\
&= \frac{1}{T_s^2 F_s} \int_{F=-F_s/2}^{F_s/2} \left|\tilde{P}(F)\right|^2 \exp(\mathrm{j}\, 2\pi F n T_s)\, dF \\
&= \frac{1}{T_s} \int_{F=-F_s/2}^{F_s/2} \left|\tilde{P}(F)\right|^2 \exp(\mathrm{j}\, 2\pi F n T_s)\, dF \\
&= \frac{\tilde{R}_{\tilde{p}\tilde{p}}(nT_s)}{T_s}
\end{aligned} \tag{E.21}$$

is independent of α, provided the sampling frequency is at Nyquist rate or higher. This is illustrated in Figures E.2 and E.3. Observe that the matched filter output is identical in both cases. Note that (see also (4.17))

$$\begin{aligned}
\tilde{R}_{\tilde{p}\tilde{p}}(nT_s) &= \int_{t=-\infty}^{\infty} \tilde{p}(t)\tilde{p}^*(t - nT_s)\, dt \\
&= \int_{F=-\infty}^{\infty} \left|\tilde{P}(F)\right|^2 \exp(\mathrm{j}\, 2\pi F n T_s)\, dF \\
&= \int_{F=-F_s/2}^{F_s/2} \left|\tilde{P}(F)\right|^2 \exp(\mathrm{j}\, 2\pi F n T_s)\, dF
\end{aligned} \tag{E.22}$$

since we have assumed that $\tilde{P}(F)$ is bandlimited to $[-F_s/2,\ F_s/2]$.

Appendix F
Time Domain Response for the Root-Raised Cosine Spectrum

From (4.76) we get[120,121]

$$\tilde{P}(F) = \begin{cases} \frac{1}{\sqrt{2B}} & \text{for } -F_1 \le F \le F_1 \\ \frac{1}{\sqrt{2B}} \cos\left(\frac{\pi(|F| - F_1)}{4B - 4F_1}\right) & \text{for } F_1 \le |F| \le 2B - F_1 \\ 0 & \text{elsewhere.} \end{cases} \tag{F.1}$$

Note that $\tilde{P}(F)$ is real and an even function of F. Hence its inverse Fourier transform is given by

$$\begin{aligned} p(t) &= 2\int_{0}^{2B-F_1} \tilde{P}(F)\cos(2\pi Ft)\,dF \\ &= 2\int_{0}^{F_1} P(F)\cos(2\pi Ft)\,dF + 2\int_{F_1}^{2B-F_1} P(F)\cos(2\pi Ft)\,dF. \end{aligned} \tag{F.2}$$

The first integral in the above equation equals

$$\begin{aligned} p_1(t) &= 2\int_{0}^{F_1} \frac{1}{\sqrt{2B}}\cos(2\pi Ft)\,dF \\ &= \frac{1}{\sqrt{2B}}\left[\frac{\sin(2\pi B(1-\rho)t)}{\pi t}\right] \end{aligned} \tag{F.3}$$

where we have made use of the relation

$$F_1 = B(1-\rho). \tag{F.4}$$

The second integral in (F.2) is equal to

$$p_2(t) = \frac{1}{\sqrt{2B}} \int_{B(1-\rho)}^{B(1+\rho)} \left[\cos\left(\frac{\pi F(1 + 8B\rho t - \pi F_1)}{4B\rho} \right) \right.$$

$$\left. + \cos\left(\frac{\pi F(1 - 8B\rho t - \pi F_1)}{4B\rho} \right) \right] dF. \tag{F.5}$$

Note that the upper limit of the above integral is

$$2B - F_1 = B(1 + \rho). \tag{F.6}$$

Let

$$\alpha = \frac{\pi(1 + 8B\rho t)}{4B\rho}$$

$$\gamma = \frac{\pi(1 - 8B\rho t)}{4B\rho}$$

$$\beta = \frac{\pi F_1}{4B\rho}. \tag{F.7}$$

Then the first integral in (F.5) becomes

$$p_3(t) = \frac{4B\rho}{\sqrt{2B}} \left[\frac{\sin(\alpha B(1 + \rho) - \beta) - \sin(\alpha B(1 - \rho) - \beta)}{\pi(1 + 8B\rho t)} \right]$$

$$= \frac{4B\rho}{\sqrt{2B}} \left[\frac{2\cos(\alpha B - \beta)\sin(\alpha B\rho)}{\pi(1 + 8B\rho t)} \right]. \tag{F.8}$$

Now,

$$\alpha B - \beta = \frac{\pi}{4} + 2\pi Bt$$

$$\alpha B\rho = \frac{\pi}{4} + 2\pi B\rho t. \tag{F.9}$$

Let

$$2\pi Bt = \theta_1 \quad \text{and} \quad 2\pi B\rho t = \theta_2. \tag{F.10}$$

Hence

$$p_3(t) = \frac{4B\rho}{\sqrt{2B}} \left[\frac{(\cos(\theta_1) - \sin(\theta_1))(\cos(\theta_2) + \sin(\theta_2))}{\pi(1 + 8B\rho t)} \right]$$

$$= \frac{4B\rho}{\sqrt{2B}} \left[\frac{\cos(\theta_1 + \theta_2) - \sin(\theta_1 - \theta_2)}{\pi(1 + 8B\rho t)} \right]. \tag{F.11}$$

Similarly, the second integral in (F.5) reduces to

$$p_4(t) = \frac{4B\rho}{\sqrt{2B}}\left[\frac{\cos(\theta_1+\theta_2)+\sin(\theta_1-\theta_2)}{\pi(1-8B\rho t)}\right]. \tag{F.12}$$

Adding (F.11) and (F.12) we get

$$p_2(t) = \frac{4B\rho}{\sqrt{2B}}\left[\frac{2\cos(\theta_1+\theta_2)+16B\rho t\sin(\theta_1-\theta_2)}{\pi(1-64B^2\rho^2t^2)}\right]. \tag{F.13}$$

Substituting (F.10) in (F.3) we get

$$p_1(t) = \frac{1}{\sqrt{2B}}\left[\frac{\sin(\theta_1-\theta_2)}{\pi t}\right]. \tag{F.14}$$

Adding (F.13) and (F.14), we get the final expression for the time domain response for the root raised cosine spectrum as

$$p(t) = \frac{1}{\pi\sqrt{2B}(1-64B^2\rho^2t^2)}\left[8B\rho\cos(\theta_1+\theta_2)+\frac{\sin(\theta_1-\theta_2)}{t}\right]. \tag{F.15}$$

Appendix G
Parseval's Energy Theorem

Here we show that for a finite energy signal $\tilde{p}(t)$ whose Fourier transform exists,

$$\int_{t=-\infty}^{\infty} |\tilde{p}(t)|^2 \, dt = \int_{F=-\infty}^{\infty} \left|\tilde{P}(F)\right|^2 \, dF. \tag{G.1}$$

The proof is as follows. The left-hand side of the above equation can be written as

$$\begin{aligned}
\int_{t=-\infty}^{\infty} |\tilde{p}(t)|^2 \, dt &= \int_{t=-\infty}^{\infty} \tilde{p}(t)\tilde{p}^*(t)\, dt \\
&= \int_{t=-\infty}^{\infty}\int_{x=-\infty}^{\infty}\int_{y=-\infty}^{\infty} \tilde{P}(x)\tilde{P}^*(y) \exp\left(\mathrm{j}\, 2\pi (x-y)t\right)\, dx\, dy\, dt \\
&= \int_{x=-\infty}^{\infty}\int_{y=-\infty}^{\infty} \tilde{P}(x)\tilde{P}^*(y) \int_{t=-\infty}^{\infty} \exp\left(\mathrm{j}\, 2\pi (x-y)t\right)\, dt\, dx\, dy.
\end{aligned} \tag{G.2}$$

Since the Fourier transform of the Dirac delta function is

$$\int_{t=-\infty}^{\infty} \delta_D(t) \exp\left(-\mathrm{j}\, 2\pi F t\right)\, dt = 1 \tag{G.3}$$

the inverse Fourier transform of unity is

$$\int_{F=-\infty}^{\infty} \exp\left(\mathrm{j}\, 2\pi F t\right)\, dt = \delta_D(t). \tag{G.4}$$

Using the above relation in (G.2) we get

$$\begin{aligned}
\int_{t=-\infty}^{\infty} |\tilde{p}(t)|^2 \, dt &= \int_{x=-\infty}^{\infty}\int_{y=-\infty}^{\infty} \tilde{P}(x)\tilde{P}^*(y)\delta_D(x-y)\, dx\, dy \\
&= \int_{x=-\infty}^{\infty} \left|\tilde{P}(x)\right|^2 \, dx.
\end{aligned} \tag{G.5}$$

Hence proved.

Parseval's theorem is valid for discrete-time signals as well. We know that for a discrete-time energy signal $\tilde{g}(nT_s)$,

$$\tilde{g}(nT_s) \star \tilde{g}^*(-nT_s) \rightleftharpoons \left|\tilde{G}_{\mathscr{P}}(F)\right|^2. \tag{G.6}$$

Therefore

$$\sum_n |\tilde{g}(nT_s)|^2 = \tilde{g}(nT_s) \star \tilde{g}^*(-nT_s)\big|_{n=0} \tag{G.7}$$

is also equal to the inverse discrete-time Fourier transform of $|\tilde{G}_{\mathscr{P}}(F)|^2$ evaluated at $n = 0$. Hence

$$\sum_n |\tilde{g}(nT_s)|^2 = T_s \int_{F=0}^{1/T_s} \left|\tilde{G}_{\mathscr{P}}(F)\right|^2 \, dF \tag{G.8}$$

which proves the Parseval's energy theorem in discrete time.

Appendix H
Transmission of a Random Process Through a Filter

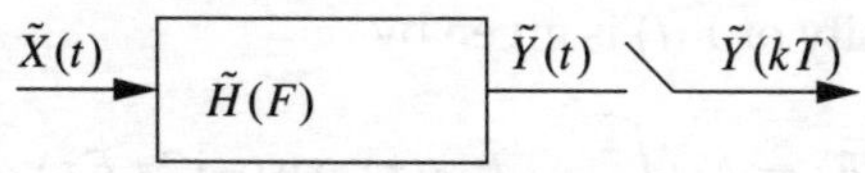

Figure H.1 *Filtering a random process followed by sampling*

Consider a complex wide sense stationary random process $\tilde{X}(t)$. Assume that $\tilde{X}(t)$ is passed through a linear time-invariant filter with complex impulse response $\tilde{h}(t)$ and Fourier transform $\tilde{H}(F)$. This is illustrated in Figure H.1. Denote the output process as $\tilde{Y}(t)$. It is clear that

$$\begin{aligned} E\left[\tilde{Y}(t)\right] &= \int_{\tau=-\infty}^{\infty} E\left[\tilde{X}(t-\tau)\right]\tilde{h}(\tau)\,d\tau \\ &= \tilde{m}_X \tilde{H}(0) \end{aligned} \tag{H.1}$$

where $\tilde{m}_X$ is the *mean* value of $\tilde{X}(t)$.

The autocorrelation of $\tilde{Y}(t)$ is given by

$$\begin{aligned} \frac{1}{2}E\left[\tilde{Y}(t)\tilde{Y}^*(t-\tau)\right] &\stackrel{\Delta}{=} \tilde{R}_{\tilde{Y}\tilde{Y}}(\tau) \\ &= \int_{\alpha=-\infty}^{\infty}\int_{\beta=-\infty}^{\infty} \frac{1}{2}E\left[\tilde{X}(t-\alpha)\tilde{X}(t-\tau-\beta)^*\right]\tilde{h}(\alpha)\tilde{h}^*(\beta)\,d\alpha\,d\beta \\ &= \int_{\alpha=-\infty}^{\infty}\int_{\beta=-\infty}^{\infty} \tilde{R}_{\tilde{X}\tilde{X}}(\tau+\beta-\alpha)\tilde{h}(\alpha)\tilde{h}^*(\beta)\,d\alpha\,d\beta. \end{aligned} \tag{H.2}$$

Taking the Fourier transform of both sides we get the power spectral density of $\tilde{Y}(t)$ as

$$S_{\tilde{Y}}(F) = S_{\tilde{X}}(F)\left|\tilde{H}(F)\right|^2. \tag{H.3}$$

In many situations, $\tilde{X}(t)$ is white, that is,

$$\tilde{R}_{\tilde{X}\tilde{X}}(\tau) = N_0 \delta_D(\tau). \tag{H.4}$$

Hence (H.2) becomes

$$\begin{aligned}
E\left[\tilde{Y}(t)\tilde{Y}^*(t-\tau)\right] &= \int_{\alpha=-\infty}^{\infty}\int_{\beta=-\infty}^{\infty} N_0 \delta_D(\tau+\beta-\alpha)\tilde{h}(\alpha)\tilde{h}(\beta)\, d\alpha\, d\beta \\
&= N_0 \int_{\alpha=-\infty}^{\infty} \tilde{h}(\alpha)\tilde{h}^*(\alpha-\tau)\, d\alpha \\
&= N_0 \tilde{R}_{\tilde{h}\tilde{h}}(\tau) \\
&= \tilde{R}_{\tilde{Y}\tilde{Y}}(\tau)
\end{aligned} \tag{H.5}$$

and the power spectral density of $\tilde{Y}(t)$ is given by

$$\begin{aligned}
S_{\tilde{Y}}(F) &= N_0 \int_{\tau=-\infty}^{\infty} \tilde{R}_{\tilde{h}\tilde{h}}(\tau)\exp(-\mathrm{j}\, 2\pi F\tau)\, d\tau \\
&= N_0 \left|\tilde{H}(F)\right|^2 .
\end{aligned} \tag{H.6}$$

Let us now assume that $\tilde{Y}(t)$ is sampled at rate $1/T$. The autocorrelation of $\tilde{Y}(kT)$ is given by

$$\frac{1}{2}E\left[\tilde{Y}(kT)\tilde{Y}^*(kT-mT)\right] = \tilde{R}_{\tilde{Y}\tilde{Y}}(mT) \tag{H.7}$$

which is equal to the autocorrelation of $\tilde{Y}(t)$ sampled at rate $1/T$. Hence the power spectral density of $\tilde{Y}(kT)$ is given by (using the sampling theorem)

$$S_{\mathscr{P},\tilde{Y}}(F) = \frac{1}{T}\sum_{k=-\infty}^{\infty} S_{\tilde{Y}}(F - \frac{k}{T}) \tag{H.8}$$

where the subscript $\mathscr{P}$ denotes 'periodic'. Note that $S_{\mathscr{P},\tilde{Y}}(F)$ has the unit of power (watts).

The variance of the samples $\tilde{Y}(kT)$ is given by

$$\begin{aligned}
\tilde{R}_{\tilde{Y}\tilde{Y}}(0) &\stackrel{\Delta}{=} T\int_{F=-1/(2T)}^{1/(2T)} S_{\mathscr{P},\tilde{Y}}(F)\, dF \\
&= \int_{-\infty}^{\infty} S_{\tilde{Y}}(F)\, dF
\end{aligned} \tag{H.9}$$

where, in the first part of the above equation we have made use of (E.14) with $m = 0$.

The above equation leads us to an important conclusion that the power of bandlimited noise (before sampling) is equal to the variance of the noise samples (obtained after sampling), *independent* of the sampling frequency.

Appendix I
Lowpass Equivalent Representation of Passband Systems

Consider the communication system shown in Figure I.1. In this sequel, we assume that $\tilde{s}_1(t)$ is a complex Dirac delta function given by

$$\begin{aligned}\tilde{s}_1(t) &= \delta_D(t)(1+\mathrm{j}) \\ &\stackrel{\Delta}{=} s_{1,I}(t) + \mathrm{j}\, s_{1,Q}(t).\end{aligned} \tag{I.1}$$

Hence $\tilde{s}(t)$ is given by

$$\begin{aligned}\tilde{s}(t) &= p(t)(1+\mathrm{j}) \\ &\stackrel{\Delta}{=} s_I(t) + \mathrm{j}\, s_Q(t).\end{aligned} \tag{I.2}$$

Note that $\tilde{s}(t)$ has a lowpass frequency response and its Fourier transform exists. The transmitted (passband) signal is given by

$$s_p(t) = s_I(t)\cos(2\pi F_c t) - s_Q(t)\sin(2\pi F_c t) \tag{I.3}$$

where the subscript 'p' in $s_p(t)$ denotes a passband signal. The channel $c_p(t)$ is given by the passband representation[4]

$$c_p(t) = c_I(t)\cos(2\pi F_c t) - c_Q(t)\sin(2\pi F_c t). \tag{I.4}$$

The complex envelope of the channel is given by

$$\tilde{c}(t) = c_I(t) + \mathrm{j}\, c_Q(t). \tag{I.5}$$

We now show that

$$\begin{aligned}s_p(t) \star c_p(t) &= \Re\{\tilde{q}(t)\exp(\mathrm{j}\, 2\pi F_c t)\} \\ &\stackrel{\Delta}{=} q_p(t) \qquad \text{(say)}\end{aligned} \tag{I.6}$$

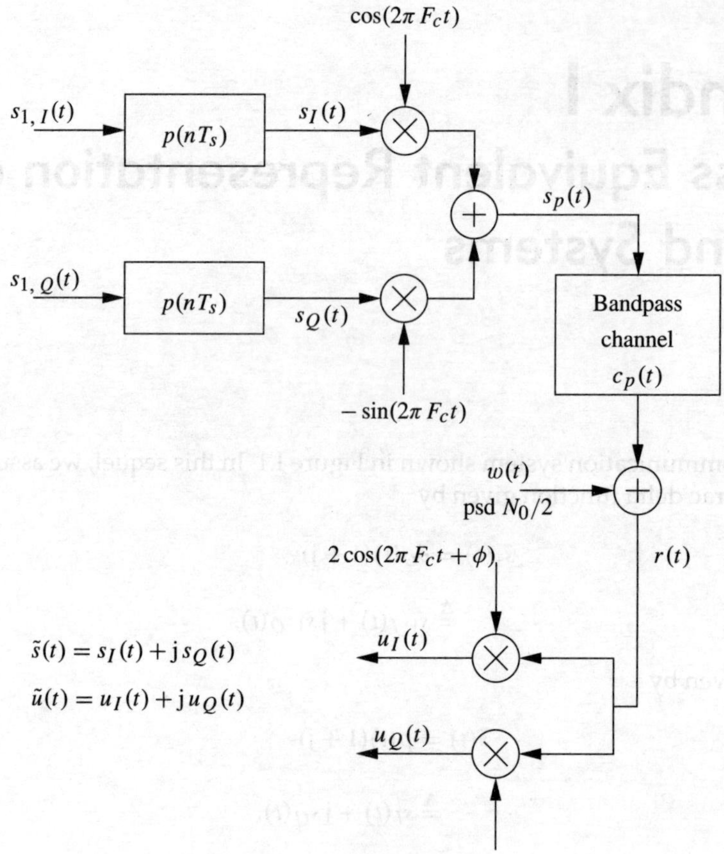

Figure I.1 *Block diagram of a digital communication system*

where

$$\tilde{q}(t) = \frac{1}{2}(\tilde{s}(t) \star \tilde{c}(t)). \tag{I.7}$$

The proof is as follows.

Let $\tilde{S}(F)$ and $\tilde{C}(F)$ denote the Fourier transforms of $\tilde{s}(t)$ and $\tilde{c}(t)$ respectively. Similarly, let $\tilde{S}_p(F)$ and $\tilde{C}_p(F)$ denote the Fourier transforms of $s_p(t)$ and $c_p(t)$ respectively. Note that

$$\begin{aligned} s_p(t) &= \Re\{\tilde{s}(t)\exp(\mathrm{j}\,2\pi F_c t)\} \\ &= \frac{1}{2}(\tilde{s}(t)\exp(\mathrm{j}\,2\pi F_c t) + \tilde{s}^*(t)\exp(-\mathrm{j}\,2\pi F_c t)) \end{aligned}$$

$$c_p(t) = \Re\{\tilde{c}(t)\exp(j2\pi F_c t)\}$$

$$= \frac{1}{2}(\tilde{c}(t)\exp(j2\pi F_c t) + \tilde{c}^*(t)\exp(-j2\pi F_c t)). \tag{I.8}$$

Hence we have

$$\tilde{S}_p(F) = \frac{1}{2}\left(\tilde{S}(F - F_c) + \tilde{S}^*(-F - F_c)\right)$$

$$\tilde{C}_p(F) = \frac{1}{2}\left(\tilde{C}(F - F_c) + \tilde{C}^*(-F - F_c)\right). \tag{I.9}$$

Now, the Fourier transform of $q_p(t)$ defined in (I.6) is given by

$$\tilde{Q}_p(F) = \tilde{S}_p(F)\tilde{C}_p(F)$$

$$= \frac{1}{4}\left(\tilde{S}(F - F_c)\tilde{C}(-F - F_c) + \tilde{S}^*(-F - F_c)\tilde{C}^*(-F - F_c)\right) \tag{I.10}$$

where we have used the fact that the product of non-overlapping frequency bands is zero, that is,

$$\tilde{S}(F - F_c)\tilde{C}^*(-F - F_c) = 0$$

$$\tilde{S}^*(-F - F_c)\tilde{C}(F - F_c) = 0. \tag{I.11}$$

By inspection, it is easy to see that the inverse Fourier transform of $\tilde{Q}_p(F)$ in (I.10) is given by

$$q_p(t) = \frac{1}{2}\Re\{(\tilde{s}(t) \star \tilde{c}(t))\exp(j2\pi F_c t)\}. \tag{I.12}$$

Comparing (I.6) and (I.12), we conclude that

$$\tilde{q}(t) = \frac{1}{2}(\tilde{s}(t) \star \tilde{c}(t)). \tag{I.13}$$

Next, we derive the signal obtained at the output of the receiver multipliers in Figure I.1. We first consider the noise term $w(t)$ in Figure I.1, which denotes an AWGN process with zero mean and psd $N_0/2$. The noise at the output of the receiver multipliers is given by

$$v_I(t) = 2w(t)\cos(2\pi F_c t + \phi)$$

$$v_Q(t) = -2w(t)\sin(2\pi F_c t + \phi) \tag{I.14}$$

where ϕ is a uniformly distributed random variable in $[0, 2\pi)$. The noise terms $v_I(t)$ and $v_Q(t)$ satisfy the relations given in (4.51) and (4.52) in Chapter 4.

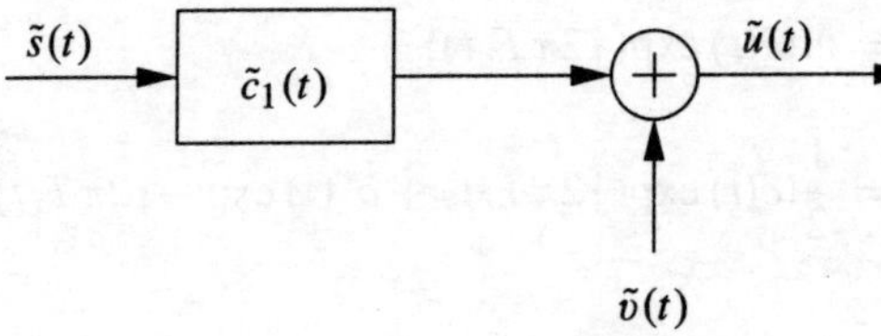

Figure I.2 *Lowpass equivalent representation for the system in Figure I.1*

Since the signal component at the input to the receiver multipliers is given by (I.6), the (complex baseband) signal at the multiplier output is equal to $\tilde{q}(t)\exp(-\mathrm{j}\,\phi)$. Thus the composite signal at the receiver multiplier output is

$$\begin{aligned}\tilde{u}(t) &\stackrel{\Delta}{=} u_I(t) + \mathrm{j}\,u_Q(t)\\ &= \tilde{q}(t)\exp(-\mathrm{j}\,\phi) + \tilde{v}(t)\\ &= \frac{1}{2}(\tilde{s}(t) \star \tilde{c}(t))\exp(-\mathrm{j}\,\phi) + \tilde{v}(t)\end{aligned} \tag{I.15}$$

where

$$\tilde{v}(t) \stackrel{\Delta}{=} v_I(t) + \mathrm{j}\,v_Q(t). \tag{I.16}$$

Hence, for the sake of analytical simplicity, we may consider the lowpass equivalent system shown in Figure I.2 where the modified complex envelope of the channel is given by

$$\tilde{c}_1(t) \stackrel{\Delta}{=} \frac{1}{2}\tilde{c}(t)\exp(-\mathrm{j}\,\phi). \tag{I.17}$$

Appendix J
Linear Prediction

In this Appendix, we derive the theory of optimum linear predictors. In particular, we discuss the principle of forward and backward prediction. Some important properties of prediction filters are also discussed.

J.1 Forward Prediction

Consider a wide sense stationary (WSS), correlated, complex-valued random process $\tilde{x}_n$ with *zero mean*. The statement of the forward prediction problem is as follows: Given the samples $\tilde{x}_{n-1}, \ldots, \tilde{x}_{n-P+1}$, try to predict $\tilde{x}_n$. Mathematically, this can be written as

$$\hat{x}_n = -\sum_{k=1}^{P-1} \tilde{a}_{P-1,\,k}\tilde{x}_{n-k}. \tag{J.1}$$

For notational simplicity, we have denoted the estimate of $\tilde{x}_n$ by $\hat{x}_n$ instead of $\hat{\tilde{x}}_n$. The terms $\tilde{a}_{P-1,\,k}$ are referred to as the forward prediction coefficients. Note that $\tilde{x}_n$ is predicted using $P-1$ past values, hence the predictor order in the above equation is $P-1$, which is also denoted by the subscript $P-1$ in $\tilde{a}_{P-1,\,k}$. The negative sign in the above equation is just for mathematical convenience, so that the $(P-1)$th-order forward prediction error can be written as

$$\begin{aligned}\tilde{e}^{f}_{P-1,\,n} &= \tilde{x}_n - \hat{x}_n \\ &= \sum_{k=0}^{P-1} \tilde{a}_{P-1,\,k}\tilde{x}_{n-k}\end{aligned} \tag{J.2}$$

with $\tilde{a}_{P-1,0} = 1$. Note that the above equation is similar to the convolution sum. Note also that $\tilde{e}^{f}_{P-1,\,n}$ denotes the error computed at time n, corresponding to the $(P-1)$th-order forward predictor which estimates $\tilde{x}_n$.

In order to compute the optimum prediction coefficients which minimize the mean squared prediction error, we set

$$\frac{\partial E\left[\left|\tilde{e}^{f}_{P-1,\,n}\right|^2\right]}{\partial \tilde{a}^{*}_{P-1,\,j}} = 0 \qquad \text{for } 1 \le j \le P-1 \tag{J.3}$$

which simplifies to

$$E\left[\tilde{e}^{f}_{P-1,n}\tilde{x}^{*}_{n-j}\right] = 0$$

$$\Rightarrow E\left[\left(\sum_{k=0}^{P-1} \tilde{a}_{P-1,k}\tilde{x}_{n-k}\right)\tilde{x}^{*}_{n-j}\right] = 0$$

$$\Rightarrow \sum_{k=0}^{P-1} \tilde{a}_{P-1,k}\tilde{R}_{\tilde{x}\tilde{x},\, j-k} = 0 \qquad \text{for } 1 \le j \le P-1 \tag{J.4}$$

where

$$\tilde{R}_{\tilde{x}\tilde{x},\, k} \triangleq \frac{1}{2}E\left[\tilde{x}_n\tilde{x}^{*}_{n-k}\right]. \tag{J.5}$$

Thus we get a set of $P - 1$ simultaneous equations, which can be used to solve for the unknowns, $\tilde{a}_{P-1,k}$ for $1 \le k \le P - 1$. The equations can be written in a matrix form as follows

$$\begin{bmatrix} \tilde{R}_{\tilde{x}\tilde{x},0} & \tilde{R}_{\tilde{x}\tilde{x},-1} & \cdots & \tilde{R}_{\tilde{x}\tilde{x},-P+2} \\ \tilde{R}_{\tilde{x}\tilde{x},1} & \tilde{R}_{\tilde{x}\tilde{x},0} & \cdots & \tilde{R}_{\tilde{x}\tilde{x},-P+3} \\ \vdots & \vdots & \vdots & \vdots \\ \tilde{R}_{\tilde{x}\tilde{x},P-2} & \tilde{R}_{\tilde{x}\tilde{x},P-3} & \cdots & \tilde{R}_{\tilde{x}\tilde{x},0} \end{bmatrix} \begin{bmatrix} \tilde{a}_{P-1,1} \\ \tilde{a}_{P-1,2} \\ \vdots \\ \tilde{a}_{P-1,P-1} \end{bmatrix} = -\begin{bmatrix} \tilde{R}_{\tilde{x}\tilde{x},1} \\ \tilde{R}_{\tilde{x}\tilde{x},2} \\ \vdots \\ \tilde{R}_{\tilde{x}\tilde{x},P-1} \end{bmatrix}. \tag{J.6}$$

The above set of linear equations are referred to as the *normal* equations. The minimum mean squared error so obtained is given by (using the fact that the error is orthogonal to the past inputs, $\tilde{x}_{n-1}, \ldots, \tilde{x}_{n-P+1}$)

$$\begin{aligned} \mathscr{E}^{f}_{P-1} &\triangleq \frac{1}{2}E\left[\left|\tilde{e}^{f}_{P-1,n}\right|^2\right] \\ &= \frac{1}{2}E\left[\tilde{e}^{f}_{P-1,n}\tilde{x}^{*}_{n}\right] \\ &= \frac{1}{2}E\left[\left(\sum_{k=0}^{P-1} \tilde{a}_{P-1,k}\tilde{x}_{n-k}\right)\tilde{x}^{*}_{n}\right] \\ &= \sum_{k=0}^{P-1} \tilde{a}_{P-1,k}\tilde{R}_{\tilde{x}\tilde{x},-k} \\ &= \sum_{k=0}^{P-1} \tilde{a}_{P-1,k}\tilde{R}^{*}_{\tilde{x}\tilde{x},k}. \end{aligned} \tag{J.7}$$

The above equation, in combination with the set of equations in (J.6) are called the Yule–Walker equations.

J.2 Backward Prediction

Let us again consider a wide sense stationary, correlated, complex random process $\tilde{x}_n$ having *zero mean*. The statement of the backward prediction problem is as follows: Given the samples $\tilde{x}_{n-1}, \ldots, \tilde{x}_{n-P+1}$, try to estimate $\tilde{x}_{n-P}$. Mathematically this can be formulated as

$$\hat{x}_{n-P} = -\sum_{k=0}^{P-2} \tilde{b}_{P-1,\,k}\tilde{x}_{n-1-k}. \tag{J.8}$$

The minus sign in the above equation is just for mathematical convenience and $\tilde{b}_{P-1,\,k}$ denotes the backward prediction coefficient. The subscript $P-1$ in $\tilde{b}_{P-1,\,k}$ denotes the predictor order. The $(P-1)$th-order backward prediction error can be written as

$$\begin{aligned}\tilde{e}^{b}_{P-1,\,n-1} &= \tilde{x}_{n-P} - \hat{x}_{n-P}\\ &= \sum_{k=0}^{P-1} \tilde{b}_{P-1,\,k}\tilde{x}_{n-1-k}\end{aligned} \tag{J.9}$$

which is again similar to the convolution sum, with $\tilde{b}_{P-1,\,P-1} = 1$. Note that $\tilde{e}^{b}_{P-1,\,n-1}$ denotes the error computed at time $n-1$, corresponding to the $(P-1)$th-order backward predictor which estimates $\tilde{x}_{n-P}$.

The optimum predictor coefficients, that minimize the mean squared error, is obtained by setting

$$\frac{\partial E\left[\left|\tilde{e}^{b}_{P-1,\,n}\right|^2\right]}{\partial \tilde{b}^{*}_{P-1,\,j}} = 0 \qquad \text{for } 0 \le j \le P-2 \tag{J.10}$$

which simplifies to

$$\begin{aligned}& E\left[\tilde{e}^{b}_{P-1,\,n-1}\tilde{x}^{*}_{n-1-j}\right] = 0\\ \Rightarrow\; & E\left[\left(\sum_{k=0}^{P-1} \tilde{b}_{P-1,\,k}\tilde{x}_{n-1-k}\right)\tilde{x}^{*}_{n-1-j}\right] = 0\\ \Rightarrow\; & \sum_{k=0}^{P-1} \tilde{b}_{P-1,\,k}\tilde{R}_{\tilde{x}\tilde{x},\,j-k} = 0 \qquad \text{for } 0 \le j \le P-2.\end{aligned} \tag{J.11}$$

The above set of equations are also called the normal equations which can be rewritten in matrix for as follows.

$$\begin{bmatrix} \tilde{R}_{\tilde{x}\tilde{x},\,0} & \tilde{R}_{\tilde{x}\tilde{x},\,-1} & \cdots & \tilde{R}_{\tilde{x}\tilde{x},\,-P+2} \\ \tilde{R}_{\tilde{x}\tilde{x},\,1} & \tilde{R}_{\tilde{x}\tilde{x},\,0} & \cdots & \tilde{R}_{\tilde{x}\tilde{x},\,-P+3} \\ \vdots & \vdots & \vdots & \vdots \\ \tilde{R}_{\tilde{x}\tilde{x},\,P-2} & \tilde{R}_{\tilde{x}\tilde{x},\,P-3} & \cdots & \tilde{R}_{\tilde{x}\tilde{x},\,0} \end{bmatrix} \begin{bmatrix} \tilde{b}_{P-1,\,0} \\ \tilde{b}_{P-1,\,1} \\ \vdots \\ \tilde{b}_{P-1,\,P-2} \end{bmatrix} = -\begin{bmatrix} \tilde{R}_{\tilde{x}\tilde{x},\,-P+1} \\ \tilde{R}_{\tilde{x}\tilde{x},\,-P+2} \\ \vdots \\ \tilde{R}_{\tilde{x}\tilde{x},\,-1} \end{bmatrix}. \tag{J.12}$$

Taking the complex conjugate of both sides in the above equation, we get

$$\begin{bmatrix} \tilde{R}^*_{\tilde{x}\tilde{x},\,0} & \tilde{R}^*_{\tilde{x}\tilde{x},\,-1} & \cdots & \tilde{R}^*_{\tilde{x}\tilde{x},\,-P+2} \\ \tilde{R}^*_{\tilde{x}\tilde{x},\,1} & \tilde{R}^*_{\tilde{x}\tilde{x},\,0} & \cdots & \tilde{R}^*_{\tilde{x}\tilde{x},\,-P+3} \\ \vdots & \vdots & \vdots & \vdots \\ \tilde{R}^*_{\tilde{x}\tilde{x},\,P-2} & \tilde{R}^*_{\tilde{x}\tilde{x},\,P-1} & \cdots & \tilde{R}^*_{\tilde{x}\tilde{x},\,0} \end{bmatrix} \begin{bmatrix} \tilde{b}^*_{P-1,\,0} \\ \tilde{b}^*_{P-1,\,1} \\ \vdots \\ \tilde{b}^*_{P-1,\,P-2} \end{bmatrix} = -\begin{bmatrix} \tilde{R}^*_{\tilde{x}\tilde{x},\,-P+1} \\ \tilde{R}^*_{\tilde{x}\tilde{x},\,-P+2} \\ \vdots \\ \tilde{R}^*_{\tilde{x}\tilde{x},\,-1} \end{bmatrix} \tag{J.13}$$

which can be rewritten as

$$\begin{bmatrix} \tilde{R}_{\tilde{x}\tilde{x},\,0} & \tilde{R}_{\tilde{x}\tilde{x},\,1} & \cdots & \tilde{R}_{\tilde{x}\tilde{x},\,P-2} \\ \tilde{R}_{\tilde{x}\tilde{x},\,-1} & \tilde{R}_{\tilde{x}\tilde{x},\,0} & \cdots & \tilde{R}_{\tilde{x}\tilde{x},\,P-3} \\ \vdots & \vdots & \vdots & \vdots \\ \tilde{R}_{\tilde{x}\tilde{x},\,-P+2} & \tilde{R}_{\tilde{x}\tilde{x},\,-P+1} & \cdots & \tilde{R}_{\tilde{x}\tilde{x},\,0} \end{bmatrix} \begin{bmatrix} \tilde{b}^*_{P-1,\,0} \\ \tilde{b}^*_{P-1,\,1} \\ \vdots \\ \tilde{b}^*_{P-1,\,P-2} \end{bmatrix} = -\begin{bmatrix} \tilde{R}_{\tilde{x}\tilde{x},\,P-1} \\ \tilde{R}_{\tilde{x}\tilde{x},\,P-2} \\ \vdots \\ \tilde{R}_{\tilde{x}\tilde{x},\,1} \end{bmatrix} \tag{J.14}$$

Comparing (J.6) and (J.14), we conclude that

$$\tilde{b}^*_{P-1,\,k} = \tilde{a}_{P-1,\,P-1-k} \qquad \text{for } 0 \le k \le P-2. \tag{J.15}$$

Since

$$\tilde{b}_{P-1,\,P-1} = \tilde{a}_{P-1,0} = 1 \tag{J.16}$$

(J.15) can be rewritten as

$$\tilde{b}^*_{P-1,\,k} = \tilde{a}_{P-1,\,P-1-k} \qquad \text{for } 0 \le k \le P-1. \tag{J.17}$$

Thus the backward prediction filter can be visualized as a 'matched filter' for the forward prediction filter.

The minimum mean squared backward prediction error is given by (using the fact that the error is orthogonal to the inputs, $\tilde{x}_{n-1}, \ldots, \tilde{x}_{n-P+1}$)

$$\begin{aligned} \mathscr{E}^b_{P-1} &\triangleq \frac{1}{2} E\left[\left|\tilde{e}^b_{P-1,\,n-1}\right|^2\right] \\ &= \frac{1}{2} E\left[\left(\sum_{k=0}^{P-1} \tilde{b}_{P-1,\,k}\tilde{x}_{n-1-k}\right)\tilde{x}^*_{n-P}\right] \end{aligned}$$

$$= \sum_{k=0}^{P-1} \tilde{b}_{P-1,k} \tilde{R}_{\tilde{x}\tilde{x},\, P-1-k}. \tag{J.18}$$

Taking the complex conjugate of both sides, we get (since the mean squared error is real)

$$\begin{aligned} \mathscr{E}^b_{P-1} &= \sum_{k=0}^{P-1} \tilde{b}^*_{P-1,k} \tilde{R}^*_{\tilde{x}\tilde{x},\, P-1-k} \\ &= \sum_{k=0}^{P-1} \tilde{b}^*_{P-1,\, P-1-k} \tilde{R}^*_{\tilde{x}\tilde{x},\, k} \\ &= \sum_{k=0}^{P-1} \tilde{a}_{P-1,k} \tilde{R}^*_{\tilde{x}\tilde{x},\, k} \\ &= \mathscr{E}^f_{P-1}. \end{aligned} \tag{J.19}$$

Thus, we have arrived at an important conclusion that the minimum mean squared error of forward and backward predictors of the same order are identical.

Having derived the basic theory behind forward and backward predictors, we now proceed to analyze them in more detail. In particular, we are interested in two important questions:

(a) Given that we have found out the optimum predictor of order $P-1$, does increasing the predictor order to P, reduce the minimum mean squared error.
(b) Given that we have found out the optimum predictor of order $P-1$, is it possible to compute the coefficients of the Pth-order predictor directly from the $(P-1)$th-order predictor, without having to solve the Yule-Walker equations.

In the next section, we discuss the Levinson–Durbin algorithm, which addresses both the above problems.

J.3 The Levinson–Durbin Algorithm

Recall that the error corresponding to the Pth-order forward predictor that estimates $\tilde{x}_n$, computed at time n is given by

$$\begin{aligned} \tilde{e}^f_{P,n} &= \tilde{x}_n - \hat{x}_n \\ &= \sum_{k=0}^{P} \tilde{a}_{P,k} \tilde{x}_{n-k}. \end{aligned} \tag{J.20}$$

The above equation can be written in terms of the $(P-1)$th-order forward and backward error as follows.

$$\tilde{e}^f_{P,n} = \tilde{e}^f_{P-1,n} + \tilde{K}_P \tilde{e}^b_{P-1,n-1} \tag{J.21}$$

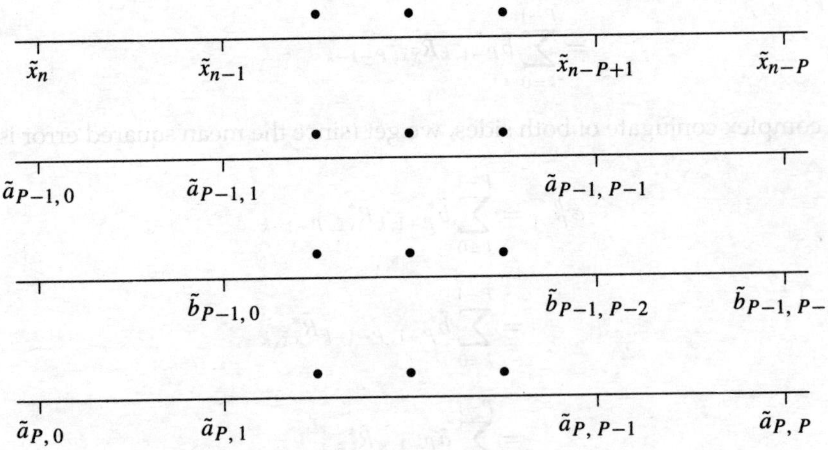

Figure J.1 *Relationship between the Pth-order forward predictor and the $(P-1)$th-order forward and backward predictors*

where $\tilde{K}_P$ is a complex constant to be determined such that the Pth-order forward mean squared error is minimized. Observe that $\tilde{e}^f_{P-1,n}$ and $\tilde{e}^b_{P-1,n-1}$ are given by (J.2) and (J.9) respectively. Moreover, from (J.20) and (J.21) we note that

$$\tilde{K}_P = \tilde{a}_{P,P}. \tag{J.22}$$

The relationship between the Pth-order forward predictor and the $(P-1)$th-order forward and backward predictors is illustrated in Figure J.1.

Thus, if $\tilde{K}_P$ is known, $\tilde{a}_{P,k}$ can be immediately found out. To compute $\tilde{K}_P$ we set

$$\frac{\partial E\left[\left|\tilde{e}^f_{P,n}\right|^2\right]}{\partial \tilde{K}^*_P} = 0. \tag{J.23}$$

Simplifying the above equation, we get

$$E\left[\tilde{e}^f_{P,n}\left(\tilde{e}^b_{P-1,n-1}\right)^*\right] = 0$$

$$\Rightarrow E\left[\left(\tilde{e}^f_{P-1,n} + \tilde{K}_P\tilde{e}^b_{P-1,n-1}\right)\left(\tilde{e}^b_{P-1,n-1}\right)^*\right] = 0. \tag{J.24}$$

Hence

$$\tilde{K}_P = -\frac{E\left[\tilde{e}^f_{P-1,n}\left(\tilde{e}^b_{P-1,n-1}\right)^*\right]}{E\left[\left|\tilde{e}^b_{P-1,n-1}\right|^2\right]}$$

$$= -\frac{E\left[\tilde{e}^{f}_{P-1,n}\left(\sum_{k=0}^{P-1}\tilde{b}^{*}_{P-1,k}\tilde{x}^{*}_{n-1-k}\right)\right]}{2\mathcal{E}^{b}_{P-1}}. \tag{J.25}$$

Once again using the principle of orthogonality we get

$$\begin{aligned}\tilde{K}_P &= -\frac{E\left[\tilde{e}^{f}_{P-1,n}\tilde{x}^{*}_{n-P}\right]}{2\mathcal{E}^{b}_{P-1}} \\ &= -\frac{E\left[\left(\sum_{k=0}^{P-1}\tilde{a}_{P-1,k}\tilde{x}_{n-k}\right)\tilde{x}^{*}_{n-P}\right]}{2\mathcal{E}^{b}_{P-1}} \\ &= -\frac{\sum_{k=0}^{P-1}\tilde{a}_{P-1,k}\tilde{R}_{\tilde{x}\tilde{x},\,P-k}}{\mathcal{E}^{b}_{P-1}}.\end{aligned} \tag{J.26}$$

Thus the minimum mean squared error corresponding to the Pth-order forward prediction filter is given by

$$\frac{1}{2}E\left[\tilde{e}^{f}_{P,n}\left(\tilde{e}^{f}_{P,n}\right)^{*}\right] = \frac{1}{2}E\left[\tilde{e}^{f}_{P,n}\left(\tilde{e}^{f}_{P-1,n}\right)^{*}\right] \tag{J.27}$$

where we have used (J.24). Simplifying the above equation we get

$$\begin{aligned}\frac{1}{2}E\left[\left(\tilde{e}^{f}_{P-1,n}+\tilde{K}_P\tilde{e}^{b}_{P-1,n-1}\right)\left(\tilde{e}^{f}_{P-1,n}\right)^{*}\right] &= \mathcal{E}^{f}_{P-1}+\frac{1}{2}\tilde{K}_P\left(-2\tilde{K}^{*}_{P}\mathcal{E}^{b}_{P-1}\right) \\ &= \left(1-\left|\tilde{K}_P\right|^{2}\right)\mathcal{E}^{f}_{P-1} \\ &= \mathcal{E}^{f}_{P}\end{aligned} \tag{J.28}$$

where we have used (J.25) and (J.19). Now, if we can prove that

$$\left|\tilde{K}_P\right| \le 1 \tag{J.29}$$

it follows that

$$\mathcal{E}^{f}_{P} \le \mathcal{E}^{f}_{P-1}. \tag{J.30}$$

In other words, the prediction error variance due to a Pth-order predictor is never greater than that due to a $(P-1)$th-order predictor. We now proceed to prove (J.29).

From (J.25) we observe that $\tilde{K}_P$ is of the form

$$\tilde{K}_P = \frac{E\left[\tilde{x}\tilde{y}^{*}\right]}{2\,\sigma_x\sigma_y} \tag{J.31}$$

where $\tilde{x}$ and $\tilde{y}$ are zero-mean, complex random variables and

$$\sigma_x = \sigma_y = \sqrt{\mathscr{E}^f_{P-1}} = \sqrt{\mathscr{E}^b_{P-1}}. \tag{J.32}$$

In other words, the expression for $\tilde{K}_P$ is identical to the correlation coefficient between two random variables. Though it is well known that the magnitude of the correlation coefficient is less than unity, nevertheless we will give a formal proof for the sake of completeness.

We begin by noting that

$$E\left[\left(a\,|\tilde{x}| - |\tilde{y}^*|\right)^2\right] \geq 0 \tag{J.33}$$

for any real constant a. Expanding the above equation we get

$$2a^2\sigma_x^2 - 2aE\left[|\tilde{x}\tilde{y}^*|\right] + 2\sigma_y^2 \geq 0. \tag{J.34}$$

The above quadratic equation in a implies that its discriminant is non-positive. Hence

$$\begin{aligned} 4E^2\left[|\tilde{x}\tilde{y}^*|\right] - 16\sigma_x^2\sigma_y^2 &\leq 0 \\ \Rightarrow E\left[|\tilde{x}\tilde{y}^*|\right] &\leq 2\sigma_x\sigma_y. \end{aligned} \tag{J.35}$$

Let

$$\tilde{x}\tilde{y}^* = \tilde{z} = \alpha + \mathrm{j}\beta \qquad \text{(say).} \tag{J.36}$$

Since in general for any real x and complex $\tilde{g}(x)$

$$\int_x |\tilde{g}(x)|\,dx \geq \left|\int_x \tilde{g}(x)\,dx\right| \tag{J.37}$$

similarly we have

$$\begin{aligned} E\left[|\tilde{z}|\right] &= \int_\alpha \int_\beta \sqrt{\alpha^2 + \beta^2}\, p(\alpha,\, \beta)\, d\alpha\, d\beta \\ &\geq \left|\int_\alpha \int_\beta (\alpha + \mathrm{j}\beta)\, p(\alpha,\, \beta)\, d\alpha\, d\beta\right| \\ &= \left|E\left[\tilde{z}\right]\right| \end{aligned} \tag{J.38}$$

where we have made use of the fact that a probability density function is real and positive, hence

$$|p(\alpha,\, \beta)| = p(\alpha,\, \beta). \tag{J.39}$$

Substituting (J.38) in (J.35) we get the desired result in (J.29). The term $\tilde{K}_P$ is commonly referred to as the *reflection coefficient* in prediction theory literature.

Finally, the Levinson–Durbin algorithm for recursively computing the optimal predictor coefficients is summarized below:

(a) Compute the reflection coefficient (which is also equal to the Pth coefficient) for the Pth-order predictor:

$$\tilde{K}_P = -\frac{\sum_{k=0}^{P-1} \tilde{a}_{P-1,k} \tilde{R}_{\tilde{x}\tilde{x},\,P-k}}{\mathscr{E}^b_{P-1}} = \tilde{a}_{P,\,P}. \tag{J.40}$$

(b) Compute the remaining forward predictor coefficients for the Pth-order (from (J.15), (J.20) and (J.21)):

$$\tilde{a}_{P,k} = \tilde{a}_{P-1,k} + \tilde{K}_P \tilde{a}^*_{P-1,\,P-k} \qquad \text{for } 1 \leq k \leq P-1 \tag{J.41}$$

(c) Compute the prediction error variance for the Pth-order predictor:

$$\mathscr{E}^f_P = \left(1 - \left|\tilde{K}_P\right|^2\right) \mathscr{E}^f_{P-1}. \tag{J.42}$$

The initial conditions for the recursion are:

$$\begin{aligned} \tilde{a}_{0,0} &= 1 \\ \tilde{K}_1 &= -\frac{\tilde{R}_{\tilde{x}\tilde{x},1}}{\tilde{R}_{\tilde{x}\tilde{x},0}} \\ \mathscr{E}^f_0 &= \tilde{R}_{\tilde{x}\tilde{x},0}. \end{aligned} \tag{J.43}$$

Thus the Levinson–Durbin algorithm is *order-recursive*, as opposed to many algorithms, e.g. the Viterbi algorithm, that are *time-recursive*.

Let us now discuss two interesting situations concerning the reflection coefficient.

(a) When $|\tilde{K}_P| = 1$ then $\mathscr{E}^f_P = 0$. This implies that $\tilde{x}_n$ can be *perfectly* estimated.
(b) When $|\tilde{K}_P| = 0$ then $\mathscr{E}^f_P = \mathscr{E}^f_{P-1}$. This implies that $\tilde{x}_n$ has been completely decorrelated (whitened), and hence increasing the predictor order would not reduce the prediction error variance any further.

In the next section we prove the minimum phase property of the optimum forward prediction filters.

Example J.3.1 Consider the system in Figure J.2. The input w_n is a real-valued, zero-mean white noise process with autocorrelation defined as:

$$R_{ww,\,m} = E[w_n w_{n-m}] = 2\delta_K(m) \tag{J.44}$$

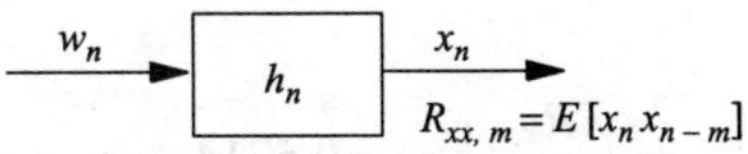

Figure J.2 *System block diagram*

where $\delta_K(\cdot)$ is the Kronecker delta function. The impulse response of the filter is given by:

$$h_n = \delta_K(n) + 2\delta_K(n-1) + 3\delta_K(n-2). \tag{J.45}$$

Using the Levinson–Durbin algorithm, compute the coefficients of the optimum 3rd-order forward predictor.

Solution: In general, the filter output x_n is given by the discrete-time convolution

$$x_n = \sum_{k=-\infty}^{\infty} h_k w_{n-k}. \tag{J.46}$$

Observe that all variables in this problem are real-valued. Therefore the autocorrelation of x_n is given by

$$\begin{aligned}
R_{xx,m} &= E\left[x_n x_{n-m}\right] \\
&= E\left[\sum_{k=-\infty}^{\infty} h_k w_{n-k} \sum_{l=-\infty}^{\infty} h_l w_{n-m-l}\right] \\
&= \sum_{k=-\infty}^{\infty}\sum_{l=-\infty}^{\infty} h_k h_l E\left[w_{n-k} w_{n-m-l}\right] \\
&= \sum_{k=-\infty}^{\infty}\sum_{l=-\infty}^{\infty} 2h_k h_l \delta_K(m+l-k) \\
&= \sum_{k=-\infty}^{\infty} 2h_k h_{k-m} \\
&= 2R_{hh,m}
\end{aligned} \tag{J.47}$$

where $R_{hh,m}$ denotes the autocorrelation of h_n. Clearly,

$$\begin{aligned}
R_{xx,0} &= 28 \\
R_{xx,1} &= 16 \\
R_{xx,2} &= 6 \\
R_{xx,m} &= 0 \qquad \text{for } |m| \geq 3.
\end{aligned} \tag{J.48}$$

Therefore

$$K_1 = -\frac{R_{xx,1}}{R_{xx,0}} = -0.5714 = a_{1,1}. \tag{J.49}$$

Hence

$$\begin{aligned}\mathcal{E}_1^f &= \left(1 - K_1^2\right)\mathcal{E}_0^f \\ &= \left(1 - K_1^2\right) R_{xx,0} \\ &= 18.8571. \end{aligned} \tag{J.50}$$

Similarly

$$K_2 = -\frac{\sum_{k=0}^{1} a_{1,k} R_{xx,2-k}}{\mathcal{E}_1^f} = 0.1666 = a_{2,2}. \tag{J.51}$$

Therefore, the second order forward predictor coefficients are

$$\begin{aligned} a_{2,0} &= 1 \\ a_{2,1} &= a_{1,1}(1 + K_2) \\ &= -0.6665 \\ a_{2,2} &= 0.1666 \end{aligned} \tag{J.52}$$

and the variance of the prediction error at the output of the second order predictor is

$$\begin{aligned}\mathcal{E}_2^f &= \left(1 - K_2^2\right)\mathcal{E}_1^f \\ &= 18.3337. \end{aligned} \tag{J.53}$$

Again

$$K_3 = -\frac{\sum_{k=0}^{2} a_{2,k} R_{xx,3-k}}{\mathcal{E}_2^f} = 0.0727 = a_{3,3} \tag{J.54}$$

and finally the coefficients of the optimum 3rd-order forward predictor are

$$\begin{aligned} a_{3,0} &= 1 \\ a_{3,1} &= a_{2,1} + K_3 a_{2,2} \\ &= -0.6543 \\ a_{3,2} &= a_{2,2} + K_3 a_{2,1} \\ &= 0.1181 \\ a_{3,3} &= 0.0727. \end{aligned} \tag{J.55}$$

Example J.3.2 Consider a random process given by

$$\tilde{x}_n = \mathrm{e}^{\mathrm{j}\,(\omega_0 n + \theta)} \tag{J.56}$$

where ω_0 is a constant and θ is uniformly distributed in $[0, 2\pi)$.

State whether $\tilde{x}_n$ is completely predictable. Justify your answer.

Solution: The autocorrelation of $\tilde{x}_n$ is given by:

$$\tilde{R}_{\tilde{x}\tilde{x},\,m} = \frac{1}{2} E\left[\tilde{x}_n \tilde{x}^*_{n-m}\right] = \frac{1}{2} \mathrm{e}^{\,\mathrm{j}\,\omega_0 m}. \tag{J.57}$$

Therefore

$$\tilde{K}_1 = -\frac{\tilde{R}_{\tilde{x}\tilde{x},\,1}}{\tilde{R}_{\tilde{x}\tilde{x},\,0}} = -\mathrm{e}^{\,\mathrm{j}\,\omega_0}. \tag{J.58}$$

Hence from (J.42) we have $\mathscr{E}_1^{\,f} = 0$, which implies that $\tilde{x}_n$ can be perfectly predicted.

In the next section we prove the minimum phase property of the optimum forward prediction filters.

J.4 Minimum Phase Property of the Forward Prediction Filter

A filter is said to be minimum phase when all its poles and zeros lie inside the unit circle. In order to prove the minimum phase property of the forward prediction filter, we first need to know some properties of all-pass filters[159]. The $\tilde{z}$-transform of an all-pass filter is of the form

$$\tilde{H}_{\mathrm{ap}}(\tilde{z}) = \frac{\tilde{a}^*_{P-1} + \tilde{a}^*_{P-2}\tilde{z}^{-1} + \ldots + \tilde{a}^*_1\tilde{z}^{-(P-2)} + \tilde{z}^{-(P-1)}}{1 + \tilde{a}_1\tilde{z}^{-1} + \ldots + \tilde{a}_{P-2}\tilde{z}^{-(P-2)} + \tilde{a}_{P-1}\tilde{z}^{-(P-1)}}. \tag{J.59}$$

It is easy to verify that

$$\tilde{H}_{\mathrm{ap}}(\tilde{z})\tilde{H}^*_{\mathrm{ap}}(\tilde{z})\Big|_{\tilde{z}=\mathrm{e}^{\mathrm{j}\,\omega}} = 1 \tag{J.60}$$

where

$$\omega = 2\pi FT \tag{J.61}$$

where T is the sampling period and F is the frequency in Hz. From (J.59) we also observe that the numerator coefficients are the complex-conjugate, time-reversed form of the denominator coefficients. This reminds us of the relation between the forward and backward predictor coefficients in (J.15). More specifically, the numerator polynomial in (J.59) corresponds to the $(P-1)$th-order backward prediction filter and the denominator polynomial corresponds to the $(P-1)$th-order forward prediction filter.

The all-pass filter in (J.59) can also be written in an alternate form as follows.

$$\tilde{H}_{\mathrm{ap}}(\tilde{z}) = \frac{\prod_{k=1}^{P-1}\left(\tilde{z}^*_k + \tilde{z}^{-1}\right)}{\prod_{k=1}^{P-1}\left(1 + \tilde{z}_k\tilde{z}^{-1}\right)}. \tag{J.62}$$

From the above equation we observe that the zeros of the $(P-1)$th-order forward prediction filter are given by $-\tilde{z}_k$.

Theorem J.4.3 *When* $|\tilde{z}_k| < 1$ *for* $1 \le k \le P-1$, *then*

$$\left|\tilde{H}_{\mathrm{ap}}(\tilde{z})\right|^2 = \tilde{H}_{\mathrm{ap}}(\tilde{z})\tilde{H}^*_{\mathrm{ap}}(\tilde{z}) \text{ is } \begin{cases} > 1 & \text{for } |\tilde{z}| < 1 \\ = 1 & \text{for } |\tilde{z}| = 1 \\ < 1 & \text{for } |\tilde{z}| > 1. \end{cases} \tag{J.63}$$

Proof: Consider a single term of $\tilde{H}_{ap}(\tilde{z})$ given by

$$\tilde{H}_{ap,\,1}(\tilde{z}) = \frac{\tilde{z}_k^* + \tilde{z}^{-1}}{1 + \tilde{z}_k \tilde{z}^{-1}} \qquad \text{for } |\tilde{z}_k| < 1. \tag{J.64}$$

Observe that $\tilde{H}_{ap,\,1}(\tilde{z})$ is also an all-pass filter and we only need to prove that

$$\tilde{H}_{ap,\,1}(\tilde{z}) \tilde{H}^*_{ap,\,1}(\tilde{z}) \text{ is } \begin{cases} > 1 & \text{for } |\tilde{z}| < 1 \\ = 1 & \text{for } |\tilde{z}| = 1 \\ < 1 & \text{for } |\tilde{z}| > 1 \end{cases} \tag{J.65}$$

since $\tilde{H}_{ap}(\tilde{z})$ is just a product of the individual terms. We have

$$\begin{aligned} \tilde{H}_{ap,\,1}(\tilde{z}) \tilde{H}^*_{ap,\,1}(\tilde{z}) &= \frac{\left(\tilde{z}_k^* + \tilde{z}^{-1}\right)\left(\tilde{z}_k + \left(\tilde{z}^{-1}\right)^*\right)}{\left(1 + \tilde{z}_k \tilde{z}^{-1}\right)\left(1 + \tilde{z}_k^* \left(\tilde{z}^{-1}\right)^*\right)} \\ &= \frac{|\tilde{z}_k|^2 + \left|\tilde{z}^{-1}\right|^2 + \tilde{z}_k^* \left(\tilde{z}^{-1}\right)^* + \tilde{z}_k \tilde{z}^{-1}}{1 + \left|\tilde{z}_k \tilde{z}^{-1}\right|^2 + \tilde{z}_k^* \left(\tilde{z}^{-1}\right)^* + \tilde{z}_k \tilde{z}^{-1}}. \end{aligned} \tag{J.66}$$

From the above equation we find that there are two common terms in the numerator and the denominator. Thus the difference between the numerator and the denominator is governed only by the terms that are *not* common. Thus the problem reduces to proving

$$\frac{|\tilde{z}_k|^2 + \left|\tilde{z}^{-1}\right|^2}{1 + \left|\tilde{z}_k \tilde{z}^{-1}\right|^2} \text{ is } \begin{cases} > 1 & \text{for } |\tilde{z}| < 1 \\ = 1 & \text{for } |\tilde{z}| = 1 \\ < 1 & \text{for } |\tilde{z}| > 1. \end{cases} \tag{J.67}$$

The proof is as follows. Obviously,

$$\left|\tilde{z}^{-1}\right| (1 - |\tilde{z}_k|) \text{ is } \begin{cases} > (1 - |\tilde{z}_k|) & \text{for } |\tilde{z}| < 1 \\ = (1 - |\tilde{z}_k|) & \text{for } |\tilde{z}| = 1 \\ < (1 - |\tilde{z}_k|) & \text{for } |\tilde{z}| > 1. \end{cases} \tag{J.68}$$

Rearranging terms in the above equation, we get

$$\left|\tilde{z}^{-1}\right| + |\tilde{z}_k| \text{ is } \begin{cases} > 1 + \left|\tilde{z}^{-1} \tilde{z}_k\right| & \text{for } |\tilde{z}| < 1 \\ = 1 + \left|\tilde{z}^{-1} \tilde{z}_k\right| & \text{for } |\tilde{z}| = 1 \\ < 1 + \left|\tilde{z}^{-1} \tilde{z}_k\right| & \text{for } |\tilde{z}| > 1. \end{cases} \tag{J.69}$$

Squaring both sides and expanding, we get

$$\left|\tilde{z}^{-1}\right|^2 + |\tilde{z}_k|^2 \text{ is } \begin{cases} > 1 + \left|\tilde{z}^{-1}\tilde{z}_k\right|^2 & \text{for } |\tilde{z}| < 1 \\ = 1 + \left|\tilde{z}^{-1}\tilde{z}_k\right|^2 & \text{for } |\tilde{z}| = 1 \\ < 1 + \left|\tilde{z}^{-1}\tilde{z}_k\right|^2 & \text{for } |\tilde{z}| > 1 \end{cases} \tag{J.70}$$

from which (J.67) follows immediately. Thus proved. □

Equipped with this fundamental result, we are now ready to prove the minimum phase property of the optimum forward prediction filter. The proof is by induction[159]. We assume that the input process $\tilde{x}_n$ is *not* deterministic. Hence

$$\left|\tilde{K}_P\right| < 1 \tag{J.71}$$

for all P.

The $\tilde{z}$-transform of the first-order prediction filter is given by:

$$\tilde{A}_1(\tilde{z}) = 1 + \tilde{K}_1\tilde{z}^{-1}. \tag{J.72}$$

The zero is at $-\tilde{K}_1$, which is inside the unit circle due to (J.71). Taking the $\tilde{z}$-transform of (J.20) and (J.21) and dividing both equations by the $\tilde{z}$-transform of the input, $\tilde{X}(\tilde{z})$, we get

$$\tilde{A}_P(\tilde{z}) = \tilde{A}_{P-1}(\tilde{z}) + \tilde{z}^{-1}\tilde{K}_P\tilde{B}_{P-1}(\tilde{z}). \tag{J.73}$$

Let $\tilde{z}_i$ denote a zero of $\tilde{A}_P(\tilde{z})$. Then,

$$\begin{aligned} \frac{1}{\tilde{K}_P} &= -\frac{\tilde{z}_i^{-1}\tilde{B}_{P-1}(\tilde{z}_i)}{\tilde{A}_{P-1}(\tilde{z}_i)} \\ &= -\tilde{z}_i^{-1}\tilde{H}_{\text{ap}}(\tilde{z}_i) \\ &= -\tilde{z}_i^{-1}\frac{\prod_{k=1}^{P-1}\left(\tilde{z}_k^* + \tilde{z}_i^{-1}\right)}{\prod_{k=1}^{P-1}\left(1 + \tilde{z}_k\tilde{z}_i^{-1}\right)} \end{aligned} \tag{J.74}$$

where $-\tilde{z}_k$, $1 \le k \le P-1$, denotes the zeros of the $(P-1)$th-order forward prediction filter. By induction we assume that the $(P-1)$th-order forward prediction filter is minimum phase, that is,

$$|\tilde{z}_k| < 1 \qquad \text{for } 1 \le k \le P-1. \tag{J.75}$$

We also assume that the $(P-1)$th-order forward prediction filter has not completely decorrelated the input process, $\tilde{x}_n$, hence

$$\left|\tilde{K}_P\right| > 0. \tag{J.76}$$

We now have to prove that

$$|\tilde{z}_i| < 1 \qquad \text{for } 1 \le i \le P. \tag{J.77}$$

The proof is as follows. Note that due to (J.71),

$$\left| \tilde{z}_i^{-1} \frac{\prod_{k=1}^{P-1} \left(\tilde{z}_k^* + \tilde{z}_i^{-1} \right)}{\prod_{k=1}^{P-1} \left(1 + \tilde{z}_k \tilde{z}_i^{-1} \right)} \right|^2 > 1. \tag{J.78}$$

Then obviously due to (J.63) and (J.78),

$$|\tilde{z}_i| \neq 1. \tag{J.79}$$

If

$$|\tilde{z}_i| > 1 \tag{J.80}$$

then due to (J.63)

$$\left| \tilde{z}_i^{-1} \frac{\prod_{k=1}^{P-1} \left(\tilde{z}_k^* + \tilde{z}_i^{-1} \right)}{\prod_{k=1}^{P-1} \left(1 + \tilde{z}_k \tilde{z}_i^{-1} \right)} \right|^2 < 1 \tag{J.81}$$

which contradicts (J.78). Hence

$$|\tilde{z}_i| < 1 \qquad \text{for } 1 \le i \le P. \tag{J.82}$$

Thus we have proved by induction that all the zeros of the optimal P^{th}-order predictor lie inside the unit circle.

Finally, we prove another important property which is given by the following equation.

$$\frac{1}{\mathrm{j}\,2\pi} \oint_C \ln \left| \tilde{A}_P(\tilde{z}) \right|^2 \tilde{z}^{-1}\, d\tilde{z} = 0 \tag{J.83}$$

where $\tilde{A}_P(\tilde{z})$ denotes the $\tilde{z}$-transform of any FIR (finite impulse response) filter of order P and the contour integral is taken in the anticlockwise direction in the region of convergence (ROC) of $\ln \left| \tilde{A}_P(\tilde{z}) \right|^2$. The proof of (J.83) is given below.

Observe that (J.83) is just the inverse $\tilde{z}$ transform of $\ln \left| \tilde{A}_P(\tilde{z}) \right|^2$ evaluated at time $n = 0$. Moreover,

$$\ln \left| \tilde{A}_P(\tilde{z}) \right|^2 = \sum_{i=1}^{P} \left(\ln \left(1 + \tilde{z}_i \tilde{z}^{-1} \right) + \ln \left(1 + \tilde{z}_i^* \left(\tilde{z}^{-1} \right)^* \right) \right) \tag{J.84}$$

where $\tilde{z}_i$ is a zero of $\tilde{A}_P(\tilde{z})$. If we can prove that when $|\tilde{z}_i| < |\tilde{z}|$

$$\frac{1}{\mathrm{j}\,2\pi} \oint_C \ln \left(1 + \tilde{z}_i \tilde{z}^{-1} \right) \tilde{z}^{-1}\, d\tilde{z} = 0 \tag{J.85}$$

where C is in the ROC of $\ln \left(1 + \tilde{z}_i \tilde{z}^{-1} \right)$, which is $|\tilde{z}| > |\tilde{z}_i|$, then the result in (J.83) follows immediately.

Using the power series expansion for $\ln(1+\tilde{x})$ for $|\tilde{x}| < 1$, we get

$$\ln\left(1+\tilde{z}_i\tilde{z}^{-1}\right) = \sum_{n=1}^{\infty} \frac{(-1)^{n+1}\tilde{z}_i^n\tilde{z}^{-n}}{n}. \tag{J.86}$$

Using the basic definition of the $\tilde{z}$-transform we get

$$\tilde{x}_n = \begin{cases} \frac{(-1)^{n+1}\tilde{z}_i^n}{n} & \text{for } n \geq 1 \\ 0 & \text{for } n \leq 1. \end{cases} \tag{J.87}$$

Thus (J.85) and hence (J.83) is proved.

When all the zeros of $\tilde{A}_P(\tilde{z})$ lie inside the unit circle, then the ROC of $\ln\left|\tilde{A}_P(\tilde{z})\right|^2$ includes the unit circle. Hence substituting

$$\tilde{z} = e^{j2\pi FT} \tag{J.88}$$

in (J.83), we get

$$\int_{F=0}^{1/T} \ln\left|\tilde{A}_P\left(e^{j2\pi FT}\right)\right|^2 dF = 0$$

$$\Rightarrow \int_{F=0}^{1/T} \ln\left|\tilde{A}_{\mathcal{P},P}(F)\right|^2 dF = 0 \tag{J.89}$$

where F denotes the frequency in Hz and T denotes the sampling period. Note that

$$\tilde{A}_P\left(e^{j2\pi FT}\right) \stackrel{\Delta}{=} \tilde{A}_{\mathcal{P},P}(F) \tag{J.90}$$

is the discrete-time Fourier transform of the sequence $\{\tilde{a}_{P,n}\}$.

Thus we have proved that in the case of an optimal P^{th}-order forward prediction filter, (J.89) is satisfied since all its zeros are inside the unit circle.

J.5 Cholesky Decomposition of the Autocovariance Matrix

Consider an $L \times 1$ noise vector $\tilde{\mathbf{w}}$ consisting of zero-mean, wide sense stationary correlated noise samples. Thus,

$$\tilde{\mathbf{w}} = \left[\ \tilde{w}_0 \ \ \ldots \ \ \tilde{w}_{L-1}\ \right]^T. \tag{J.91}$$

The autocovariance of $\tilde{\mathbf{w}}$ is given by:

$$\frac{1}{2}E\left[\tilde{\mathbf{w}}\tilde{\mathbf{w}}^H\right] = \tilde{\mathbf{\Phi}} \qquad \text{(say)}. \tag{J.92}$$

Let

$$\frac{1}{2}E\left[|\tilde{w}_j|^2\right] = \sigma_w^2 \qquad \text{for} \qquad 0 \le j \le L-1. \tag{J.93}$$

Consider another $L \times 1$ noise vector $\tilde{\mathbf{z}}$ such that

$$\tilde{\mathbf{z}} = \tilde{\mathbf{A}}\tilde{\mathbf{w}} \tag{J.94}$$

where

$$\tilde{\mathbf{A}} \stackrel{\Delta}{=} \begin{bmatrix} 1 & 0 & \ldots & 0 \\ \tilde{a}_{1,1} & 1 & \ldots & 0 \\ \vdots & \vdots & \vdots & \vdots \\ \tilde{a}_{L-1,L-1} & \tilde{a}_{L-1,L-2} & \ldots & 1 \end{bmatrix} \tag{J.95}$$

is the lower triangular matrix consisting of the optimal forward predictor coefficients and

$$\tilde{\mathbf{z}} \stackrel{\Delta}{=} \begin{bmatrix} \tilde{z}_0 & \ldots & \tilde{z}_{L-1} \end{bmatrix}^T. \tag{J.96}$$

Due to the fact that the prediction error is orthogonal to the inputs (see (J.4)), we have

$$\begin{aligned} \frac{1}{2}E\left[\tilde{z}_n\tilde{z}_{n-j}^*\right] &= E\left[\tilde{z}_n\left(\sum_{k=0}^{n-j}\tilde{a}_{n-j,k}^*\tilde{w}_{n-j-k}^*\right)\right] \\ &= \begin{cases} 0 & \text{for } 1 \le j \le n,\, 1 \le n \le L-1 \\ \sigma_{z,n}^2 & \text{for } j=0,\, 1 \le n \le L-1 \\ \sigma_{z,0}^2 = \sigma_w^2 & \text{for } j=0,\, n=0. \end{cases} \end{aligned} \tag{J.97}$$

Hence

$$\begin{aligned} \frac{1}{2}E\left[\tilde{\mathbf{z}}\tilde{\mathbf{z}}^H\right] &= \tilde{\mathbf{A}}\tilde{\mathbf{\Phi}}\tilde{\mathbf{A}}^H \\ &= \mathbf{D} \qquad \text{(say)} \end{aligned} \tag{J.98}$$

where

$$\mathbf{D} \stackrel{\Delta}{=} \begin{bmatrix} \sigma_{e,0}^2 & \ldots & 0 \\ \vdots & \vdots & 0 \\ 0 & \ldots & \sigma_{e,L-1}^2 \end{bmatrix}. \tag{J.99}$$

From (J.98) we have

$$\begin{aligned} \tilde{\mathbf{\Phi}} &= \tilde{\mathbf{A}}^{-1}\mathbf{D}\left(\tilde{\mathbf{A}}^H\right)^{-1} \\ \Rightarrow \tilde{\mathbf{\Phi}}^{-1} &= \tilde{\mathbf{A}}^H\mathbf{D}^{-1}\tilde{\mathbf{A}}. \end{aligned} \tag{J.100}$$

The first part of the above equation is referred to as the Cholesky decomposition of the autocovariance matrix $\tilde{\mathbf{\Phi}}$.

Appendix K
Eigendecomposition of a Circulant Matrix

An $N \times N$ circulant matrix $\tilde{\mathbf{A}}$ is given by

$$\tilde{\mathbf{A}} = \begin{bmatrix} \tilde{a}_0 & \tilde{a}_1 & \dots & \tilde{a}_{N-1} \\ \tilde{a}_{N-1} & \tilde{a}_0 & \dots & \tilde{a}_{N-2} \\ \vdots & \vdots & \vdots & \vdots \\ \tilde{a}_1 & \tilde{a}_2 & \dots & \tilde{a}_0 \end{bmatrix}. \tag{K.1}$$

The circulant matrix can also be expressed in terms of the permutation matrix as follows:

$$\tilde{\mathbf{A}} = \sum_{n=0}^{N-1} \tilde{a}_n \mathbf{P}_N^n \tag{K.2}$$

where $\mathbf{P}_N$ is the $N \times N$ permutation matrix given by

$$\mathbf{P}_N = \begin{bmatrix} 0 & 1 & 0 & \dots & 0 \\ 0 & 0 & 1 & \dots & 0 \\ \vdots & \vdots & \vdots & \vdots & \vdots \\ 1 & 0 & 0 & \dots & 0 \end{bmatrix}. \tag{K.3}$$

Note that

$$\begin{aligned} \mathbf{P}_N^0 &\stackrel{\Delta}{=} \mathbf{I}_N \\ \mathbf{P}_N^n &\stackrel{\Delta}{=} \mathbf{P}_N \times \cdots \times \mathbf{P}_N \qquad (n\text{-fold multiplication}). \end{aligned} \tag{K.4}$$

For example

$$\mathbf{P}_3 = \begin{bmatrix} 0 & 1 & 0 \\ 0 & 0 & 1 \\ 1 & 0 & 0 \end{bmatrix}. \tag{K.5}$$

The eigenvalues of $\mathbf{P}_3$ are given by

$$\begin{vmatrix} -\tilde{\lambda} & 1 & 0 \\ 0 & -\tilde{\lambda} & 1 \\ 1 & 0 & -\tilde{\lambda} \end{vmatrix} = 0$$

$$\Rightarrow \tilde{\lambda}^3 = 1$$

$$\Rightarrow \tilde{\lambda}^3 = \mathrm{e}^{-\mathrm{j}\,2\pi k} \tag{K.6}$$

where k is an integer. Thus the eigenvalues of $\mathbf{P}_3$ are

$$\tilde{\lambda}_k = \mathrm{e}^{-\mathrm{j}\,2\pi k/3} \quad \text{for } 0 \le k \le 2. \tag{K.7}$$

Similarly, it can be shown that the eigenvalues of $\mathbf{P}_N$ are

$$\tilde{\lambda}_k = \mathrm{e}^{-\mathrm{j}\,2\pi k/N} \qquad \text{for } 0 \le k \le N-1. \tag{K.8}$$

It can also be shown that the eigenvector of $\mathbf{P}_N$ corresponding to $\tilde{\lambda}_k$ is

$$\tilde{\mathbf{q}}_k = \frac{1}{\sqrt{N}} \begin{bmatrix} \mathrm{e}^{\mathrm{j}\,2\pi k(N-1)/N} \\ \mathrm{e}^{\mathrm{j}\,2\pi k(N-2)/N} \\ \vdots \\ \mathrm{e}^{\mathrm{j}\,2\pi k/N} \\ 1 \end{bmatrix}. \tag{K.9}$$

Note that

$$\tilde{\mathbf{q}}_n^H \tilde{\mathbf{q}}_m = \delta_K(n-m). \tag{K.10}$$

Interestingly, it turns out that all the eigenvectors of $\mathbf{P}_N$ are also eigenvectors of $\mathbf{P}_N^n$. The eigenvalue $\lambda_{1,n}$ corresponding to $\tilde{\mathbf{q}}_k$ is computed as

$$\mathbf{P}_N^n \tilde{\mathbf{q}}_k = \tilde{\lambda}_{1,k} \tilde{\mathbf{q}}_k$$

$$\Rightarrow \tilde{\lambda}_k^n \tilde{\mathbf{q}}_k = \tilde{\lambda}_{1,k} \tilde{\mathbf{q}}_k$$

$$\Rightarrow \tilde{\lambda}_k^n = \tilde{\lambda}_{1,k}. \tag{K.11}$$

Using the above result, we can conclude that $\tilde{\mathbf{q}}_k$ is also an eigenvector of $\mathbf{A}$ and the corresponding eigenvalue $\tilde{\lambda}_{2,k}$ is given by

$$\mathbf{A}\tilde{\mathbf{q}}_k = \sum_{n=0}^{N-1} \tilde{a}_n \tilde{\lambda}_k^n \tilde{\mathbf{q}}_k$$

$$= \tilde{\lambda}_{2,k} \tilde{\mathbf{q}}_k \qquad \text{for } 0 \le k \le N-1$$

$$\begin{aligned}
\Rightarrow \tilde{\lambda}_{2,k} &= \sum_{n=0}^{N-1} \tilde{a}_n \tilde{\lambda}_k^n \\
&= \sum_{n=0}^{N-1} \tilde{a}_n \mathrm{e}^{-\mathrm{j}\,2\pi nk/N} \\
&= \tilde{A}_k \qquad \text{for } 0 \le k \le N-1
\end{aligned} \tag{K.12}$$

where $\tilde{A}_k$ is the N point discrete Fourier transform (DFT) (see (5.277) for the definition of the DFT) of $\tilde{a}_n$.

Let us now construct a matrix $\tilde{\mathbf{Q}}$ and $\tilde{\mathbf{\Lambda}}$ as follows:

$$\tilde{\mathbf{Q}} = [\tilde{\mathbf{q}}_{N-1} \quad \cdots \quad \tilde{\mathbf{q}}_0]$$

$$\tilde{\mathbf{\Lambda}} = \begin{bmatrix} \tilde{\lambda}_{2,N-1} & 0 & \cdots & 0 \\ 0 & \tilde{\lambda}_{2,N-2} & \cdots & 0 \\ \vdots & \vdots & \vdots & \vdots \\ 0 & 0 & \cdots & \tilde{\lambda}_{2,0} \end{bmatrix} \tag{K.13}$$

Observe that $\tilde{\mathbf{Q}}$ is a unitary matrix, that is,

$$\begin{aligned}
\tilde{\mathbf{Q}}^H \tilde{\mathbf{Q}} &= \mathbf{I}_N \\
\Rightarrow \tilde{\mathbf{Q}}^H &= \tilde{\mathbf{Q}}^{-1}.
\end{aligned} \tag{K.14}$$

Combining the N equations in the first part of (K.12) we get

$$\begin{aligned}
\tilde{\mathbf{A}}\tilde{\mathbf{Q}} &= \tilde{\mathbf{Q}}\tilde{\mathbf{\Lambda}} \\
\Rightarrow \tilde{\mathbf{A}} &= \tilde{\mathbf{Q}}\tilde{\mathbf{\Lambda}}\tilde{\mathbf{Q}}^H
\end{aligned} \tag{K.15}$$

where we have used (K.14). The result in (K.15) is known as eigendecomposition of the circulant matrix.

References

[1] C. E. Shannon, Communication in the presence of noise, *Proc. IRE*, 37(1):10–21, January 1949.

[2] John G. Proakis, *Digital Communications*, McGraw Hill, third edition, 1995.

[3] E. A. Lee and D. G. Messerschmitt, *Digital Communication*, Kluwer Academic Publishers, first edition, 1988.

[4] Simon Haykin, *Communication Systems*, Wiley Eastern, fourth edition, 2001.

[5] H. Meyr and G. Ascheid, *Synchronization in Digital Communications vol. 1: Phase and Frequency Locked Loops and Amplitude Control*, John Wiley, 1990.

[6] Umberto Mengali and Aldo N. D'Andrea, *Synchronization Techniques for Digital Receivers (Applications of Communication Theory)*, Springer, first edition, 1997.

[7] H. Meyr and M. Moeneclaey S. A. Fechtel, *Digital Communication Receivers vol. 2: Synchronization and Channel Estimation and Signal Processing*, John Wiley, 1998.

[8] L. Hanzo, T. H. Liew, and B. L. Yeap, *Turbo Coding, Turbo Equalization and Space-Time Coding for Transmission over Fading Channels*, John Wiley, first edition, 2002.

[9] C. Heegard and Stephen B. Wicker, *Turbo Coding*, Kluwer Academic Publishers, first edition, 1999.

[10] B. Vucetic and J. Yuan, *Turbo Codes: Principles and Applications*, Kluwer Academic Publishers, first edition, 2000.

[11] B. Vucetic and J. Yuan, *Space-Time Coding*, John Wiley, first edition, 2003.

[12] M. K. Simon and Mohamed-Slim Alouini, *Digital Communication over Fading Channels*, Wiley Series in Telecommunication and Signal Processing, second edition, 2004.

[13] W. C. Jakes Jr, *Microwave Mobile Communications*, Wiley, New York, 1974.

[14] T. S. Rappaport, *Wireless Communications*, Pearson Education Inc., 2002.

[15] J. M. Wozencraft and I. M. Jacobs, *Principles of Communication Engineering*, Wiley, 1965.

[16] Thomas Kailath. A General likelihood-ratio formula for random signals in Gaussian noise, *IEEE Trans. Info. Theory*, 15(4):350–361, May 1969.

[17] G. D. Forney, Jr., R. G. Gallager, G. R. Lang, F. M. Longstaff, and S. U. H. Qureshi. Efficient modulation for bandlimited channels, *IEEE J. on Select. Areas in Commun.*, 2(5):632–647, September 1984.

[18] A. Papoulis, *Probability, Random Variables and Stochastic Processes*, McGraw-Hill, third edition, 1991.

[19] Dariush Divsalar and Marvin K. Simon. Maximum-Likelihood differential detection of uncoded and trellis coded amplitude phase modulation over AWGN and fading

channels-metrics and performance, *IEEE Trans. on Commun.*, 42(1):76–89, January 1994.

[20] M. Schwartz, W. R. Bennett, and S. Stein, *Communication Systems and Techniques*, McGraw-Hill, New York, first edition, 1966.

[21] Dariush Divsalar and Marvin K. Simon, Multiple-symbol differential detection of MPSK, *IEEE Trans. on Commun.*, 38(3):300–308, March 1990.

[22] K. Vasudevan, K. Giridhar, and Bhaskar Ramamurthi, Noncoherent sequence estimation of multilevel signals in slowly fading channels. In *Proc. of the Fourth National Conf. on Commun.*, pages 18–23, Indian Institute of Science Bangalore, India, January 1998.

[23] K. Vasudevan, K. Giridhar, and Bhaskar Ramamurthi, DSP-based noncoherent detectors for multilevel signals in flat fading channels. In *Proc. of the 7th IEEE International Conference on Universal Personal Communications*, pages 1313–1317, Florence, Italy, October 1998.

[24] K. Vasudevan, K. Giridhar, and Bhaskar Ramamurthi, Differential detection of multilevel signals in frequency nonselective Rayleigh fading channels with diversity. In *Proc. of the IEEE International Conference on Personal Wireless Communications*, pages 188–192, Jaipur, India, February 1999.

[25] K. Vasudevan, K. Giridhar, and Bhaskar Ramamurthi, Noncoherent detection of multilevel signals in frequency nonselective fading channels, *Signal Processing Journal, Elsevier Science*, 78(2):159–176, October 1999.

[26] Harry Leib and Subbarayan Pasupathy, The phase of a vector perturbed by Gaussian noise and differentially coherent receivers, *IEEE Trans. Info. Theory*, 34(6):1491–1501, November 1988.

[27] F. Edbauer, Bit error rate of binary and quaternary DPSK signals with multiple differential feedback detection, *IEEE Trans. on Commun.*, 40(3):457–460, March 1992.

[28] F. Adachi and M. Sawahashi, Viterbi-decoding differential detection of DPSK, *Electronics Letters*, 28(23):2196–2197, November 1992.

[29] Fumiyuki Adachi and Mamoru Sawahashi, Decision feedback differential detection of differentially encoded 16APSK signals, *IEEE Trans. on Commun.*, 44(4):416–418, April 1996.

[30] F. Adachi and M. Sawahashi, Decision feedback differential detection of 16-DAPSK signals, *Electronics Letters*, 29(16):1455–1456, August 1993.

[31] A. N. D'Andrea, U. Mengali, and G. M. Vitetta, Approximate ML decoding of coded PSK with no explicit carrier phase reference, *IEEE Trans. on Commun.*, 42(2/3/4): 1033–1039, February/March/April 1994.

[32] Fumiyuki Adachi, MLSE differential phase detection for M-ary DPSK, *IEE Proc. Commun.*, 141(6):407–412, December 1994.

[33] Fumiyuki Adachi and Mamoru Sawahashi, Decision feedback differential phase detection of M-ary DPSK signals, *IEEE Trans. on Veh. Technol.*, 44(2):203–210, May 1995.

[34] Fumiyuki Adachi, Reduced-state Viterbi differential detection using a recursively estimated phase reference for M-ary PSK, *IEE Proc. Commun.*, 142(4):263–270, August 1995.

[35] Fumiyuki Adachi, Bit error rate analysis of reduced-state Viterbi differential detection of M-ary DPSK signals, *Electronics Letters*, 31(24):2069–2070, November 1995.

[36] Fumiyuki Adachi, Adaptive differential detection of M-ary DPSK, *IEE Proc. Commun.*, 143(1):21–28, February 1996.

[37] Fumiyuki Adachi, Reduced state transition Viterbi differential detection of M-ary DPSK signals, *Electronics Letters*, 32(12):1064–1066, June 1996.

[38] Fumiyuki Adachi, Adaptive differential detection using linear prediction for M-ary DPSK, *IEEE Trans. on Veh. Technol.*, 47(3):909–918, August 1998.

[39] K. Vasudevan, Detection of signals in correlated interference using a predictive VA. In *Proc. of the IEEE International Conference on Communication Systems*, pages 529–533, Singapore, November 2002.

[40] K. Vasudevan, Detection of signals in correlated interference using a predictive VA, *Signal Processing Journal, Elsevier Science*, 84(12):2271–2286, December 2004.

[41] Aleksander Kavcic and Jose F. Moura, Signal dependant correlation sensitive branch metrics for Viterbi-like sequence detectors. In *Proc. of the Intl. Conf. on Commun.*, pages 657–661, 1998.

[42] J. D. Coker, E. Eleftheriou, R. L. Galbraith, and Walter Hirt, Noise predictive maximum likelihood (NPML) detection, *IEEE Trans. on Magnetics*, 34(1):110–117, January 1998.

[43] Younggyun Kim and Jaekyun Moon, Noise predictive maximum likelihood method combined with infinite impulse response equalization, *IEEE Trans. on Magnetics*, 35(6):4538–4543, November 1999.

[44] M. Rouanne and D. J. Costello, An algorithm for computing the distance spectrum of trellis codes, *IEEE J. on Select. Areas in Commun.*, 7(6):929–940, August 1989.

[45] Thomas Kailath, Correlation detection of signals perturbed by a random channel, *IRE Trans. Info. Theory*, 6(3):361–366, June 1960.

[46] Thomas Kailath, Measurements of time variant communications channels, *IRE Trans. Info. Theory*, 8(5):S229–S236, 1962.

[47] Thomas Kailath, Time variant communication channels, *IEEE Trans. Info. Theory*, 9(4):233–237, October 1963.

[48] Peter Monsen, Fading channel communications, *IEEE Commun. Mag.*, 18(1):16–25, January 1980.

[49] Donald C. Cox, Universal digital portable radio communications, *Proc. IEEE*, 75(4):436–477, April 1987.

[50] Bernard Sklar, Rayleigh fading channels in mobile digital communication systems: Parts I and II, *IEEE Commun. Mag.*, 35(7):90–109, July 1997.

[51] Pooi Yuen Kam, Bit error probabilities of MDPSK over the nonselective Rayleigh fading channel with diversity reception, *IEEE Trans. on Commun.*, 39(2):220–224, February 1991.

[52] R. Johannesson and Kamil Sh. Zigangirov, *Fundamentals of Convolutional Coding*, IEEE Press, first edition, 1999.

[53] S. Lin and D. J. Costello, *Error Control Coding: Fundamentals and Applications*, Prentice-Hall, New Jersey, first edition, 1983.

[54] L. J. Doob, *Stochastic Processes*, Wiley, New York, 1953.

[55] W. B. Davenport, *Probability and Random Processes*, McGraw-Hill, New York, 1970.

[56] Simon Haykin, *Communication Systems*, Wiley Eastern, second edition, 1983.

[57] C. W. Helstrom, *Probability and Stochastic Processes for Engineers*, Macmillan, New York, 1991.

[58] G. Ungerboeck, Channel coding with multilevel/phase Signals, *IEEE Trans. on Info. Theory*, 28(1):55–67, January 1982.

[59] G. Ungerboeck, Trellis coded modulation with redundant signal sets, Part I: Introduction, *IEEE Comm. Mag.*, 25(2):5–11, February 1987.

[60] G. Ungerboeck, Trellis coded modulation with redundant signal sets, Part II: State of the Art, *IEEE Comm. Mag.*, 25(2):12–21, February 1987.

[61] A. R. Calderbank and N. J. A. Sloane, New trellis codes based on lattices and cosets, *IEEE Trans. on Info. Theory*, 33(2):177–195, March 1987.

[62] G. D. Forney, Jr., Coset codes–Part I: Introduction and geometrical classification, *IEEE Trans. on Info. Theory*, 34(5):1123–1151, September 1988.

[63] G. D. Forney, Jr., Coset codes–Part II: Binary lattices and related codes, *IEEE Trans. on Info. Theory*, 34(5):1152–1187, September 1988.

[64] E. Biglieri, D. Divsalar, P. J. McLane, and M. K. Simon, *Introduction to Trellis Coded Modulation with Applications*, Macmillan, New York, first edition, 1991.

[65] C. Schlegel, *Trellis Coding*, IEEE Press, first edition, 1997.

[66] S. Benedetto, M. Mondin, and G. Montorsi, Performance evaluation of trellis coded modulation schemes, *Proc. IEEE*, 82(6):833–855, June 1994.

[67] M. D. Trott, S. Benedetto, R. Garello, and M. Mondin, Rotational invariance of trellis codes–Part I: Encoders and Precoders, *IEEE Trans. on Info. Theory*, 42(3):751–765, May 1996.

[68] S. Benedetto, R. Garello, M. Mondin, and M. D. Trott, Rotational invariance of trellis codes–Part II: Group codes and decoders, *IEEE Trans. on Info. Theory*, 42(3):766–778, May 1996.

[69] L. F. Wei, Rotationally invariant convolutional channel coding with expanded signal space–Part I: 180°, *IEEE J. on Select. Areas in Commun.*, 2(5):659–671, September 1984.

[70] L. F. Wei, Rotationally invariant convolutional channel coding with expanded signal space–Part II: Nonlinear codes, *IEEE J. on Select. Areas in Commun.*, 2(5):672–686, September 1984.

[71] G. D. Forney, Jr., Geometrically uniform codes, *IEEE Trans. on Info. Theory*, 37(5): 1241–1260, September 1991.

[72] Gordon R. Lang and Frederick M. Longstaff, A Leech lattice modem, *IEEE J. on Select. Areas in Commun.*, 7(6):968–972, August 1989.

[73] G. D. Forney, Jr. and L-F. Wei, Multidimensional constellations–Part I: Introduction, figures of merit, and generalized cross constellations, *IEEE J. on Select. Areas in Commun.*, 7(6):877–892, August 1989.

[74] Lee-Fang Wei, Rotationally invariant trellis-coded modulations with multidimensional M-PSK, *IEEE J. on Select. Areas in Commun.*, 7(9):1281–1295, December 1989.

[75] G. D. Forney, Jr., Multidimensional constellations–Part II: Voronoi constellations, *IEEE J. on Select. Areas in Commun.*, 7(6):941–958, August 1989.

[76] G. D. Forney, Jr., Trellis shaping, *IEEE Trans. on Info. Theory*, 38(2):281–300, March 1992.

[77] J. H. Conway and N. J. A. Sloane, *Sphere Packings, Lattices and Groups*, Springer, third edition, 1999.

[78] A. Gersho and V. B. Lawrence, Multidimensional signal constellations for voiceband data transmission, *IEEE J. on Select. Areas in Commun.*, 2(5):687–702, September 1984.

[79] ITU-T Rec V.34, *A Modem Operating at Data Signalling Rates of upto 33,600 bits/s for Use on the General Switched Telephone Network and on Leased Point-to-Point 2-Wire Telephone Type Circuits*, 1994.

[80] M. Vedat Eyuboglu, G. D. Forney, Jr., Ping Dong, and Guozhu Long, Advanced modulation techniques for V.Fast, *European Trans. on Telecommun.*, 4(3):243–256, May–June 1993.

[81] Paul Fortier, Antonio Ruiz, and John M. Cioffi, Multidimensional signal sets through the shell construction for parallel channels, *IEEE Trans. on Commun.*, 40(3):500–512, March 1992.

[82] Amir K. Khandani and Peter Kabal, Shaping multidimensional signal spaces Part–I: Optimum shaping, shell mapping, *IEEE Trans. on Info. Theory*, 39(6):1799–1808, November 1993.

[83] Amir K. Khandani, Shaping the boundary of a multidimensional signal constellation with a non flat power spectrum, *IEE Proc.–Commun.*, 145(4):213–217, August 1998.

[84] Amir K. Khandani and Peter Kabal, An efficient block-based addressing scheme for the nearly optimum shaping of multidimensional signal spaces, *IEEE Trans. on Info. Theory*, 41(6):2026–2031, November 1995.

[85] R. Laroia, N. Farvardin, and S. Tretter, On optimal shaping of multidimensional constellations, *IEEE Trans. on Info. Theory*, 40(4):1044–1056, July 1994.

[86] C. Berrou, A. Glavieux, and P. Thitimajshima, Near Shannon limit error-correcting coding and decoding: Turbo codes. In *Proc. IEEE Int. Conf. on Communications*, pages 1064–1070, Geneva, Switzerland, 1993.

[87] C. Berrou and A. Glavieux, Near optimum error correcting coding and decoding – Turbo codes, *IEEE Trans. on Commun.*, 44(10):1261–1271, October 1996.

[88] B. Sklar, A primer on turbo code concepts, *IEEE Comm. Mag.*, 35(12):94–102, December 1997.

[89] M. Tüchler, R. Koetter, and A. C. Singer, Turbo equalization: Principles and new results, *IEEE Trans. on Commun.*, 50(5):754–767, May 2002.

[90] R. Koetter, A. C. Singer, and M. Tüchler, Turbo equalization, *IEEE Sig. Proc. Mag.*, 21(1):67–80, January 2004.

[91] K. Vasudevan, Turbo equalization of serially concatenated turbo codes using a predictive DFE-based receiver, *Signal, Image and Video Processing*, 1(3):239–252, August 2007.

[92] S. Le Goff, A. Glavieux, and C. Berrou, Turbo codes and high spectral efficiency modulation. In *Proc. of the Intl. Conf. on Commun.*, pages 645–649, 1994.

[93] P. Robertson and T. Wörz, A coded modulation scheme using turbo codes, *Electronics Letters*, 31(18):1546–1547, August 1995.

[94] P. Robertson and T. Wörz, A novel bandwidth efficient coding scheme employing turbo codes. In *Proc. of the Intl. Conf. on Commun.*, pages 962–967, 1996.

[95] P. Robertson and T. Wörz, Extensions of turbo trellis coded modulation to high bandwidth efficiencies. In *Proc. of the Intl. Conf. on Commun.*, pages 1251–1255, 1997.

[96] P. Robertson and T. Wörz, Bandwidth efficient turbo trellis coded modulation using punctured component codes, *IEEE J. on Select. Areas in Commun.*, 16(2):206–218, February 1998.

[97] J. H. Gass Jr., P. J. Curry, and C. J. Langford, An application of turbo trellis coded modulation to tactical communications. In *Proc. of the Millitary Commun. Conf.*, pages 530–533, 1999.

[98] A. Chouly and O. Pothier, A non-pragmatic approach to turbo trellis coded modulations. In *Proc. of the Intl. Conf. on Commun.*, pages 1327–1331, 2002.

[99] S. Benedetto, D. Divsalar, G. Montorsi, and F. Pollara, Bandwidth efficient paralel concatenated coding schemes, *Electronics Letters*, 31(24):2067–2069, November 1995.

[100] G. Colavolpe, G. Ferrari, and R. Raheli, Noncoherent turbo decoding. In *Proc. IEEE Global Telecomm. Conf.*, pages 510–514, Rio de Janeiro, Brazil, December 1999.

[101] G. Colavolpe, G. Ferrari, and R. Raheli, Noncoherent iterative (Turbo) decoding, *IEEE Trans. on Commun.*, 48(9):1488–1498, September 2000.

[102] J. Vainappel, E. Hardy, and D. Raphaeli, Noncoherent turbo decoding. In *Proc. IEEE Global Telecomm. Conf.*, pages 952–956, San Antonio, Texas, November 2001.

[103] G. Ferrari, G. Colavolpe, and R. Raheli, Noncoherent iterative decoding of spectrally efficient coded modulations. In *Proc. IEEE Intl. Conf. on Commun.*, pages 65–69, Helsinki, Finland, June 2001.

[104] A. Ramesh, A. Chockalingam, and L. B. Milstein, Performance of non-coherent turbo detection on Rayleigh fading channels. In *Proc. IEEE Global Telecomm. Conf.*, pages 1193–1198, San Antonio, Texas, November 2001.

[105] K. Vasudevan and B. K. Rai, Predictive iterative decoding of turbo codes in coloured Gaussian noise. In *Proc. of the Tenth National Conf. on Commun.*, pages 308–312, Bangalore, India, 2004.

[106] K. Vasudevan, Detection of turbo coded signals transmitted through ISI channels using the predictive iterative decoder. In *Proc. of the seventh IEEE Intl. Conf. on Signal Proc. and Commun.*, pages 223–227, Bangalore, India, December 2004.

[107] K. Vasudevan, Optimum predictive iterative decoding of turbo codes in coloured Gaussian noise. In *Proc. of the Fourth IASTED International Multi Conf. on Wireless and Optical Commun.*, pages 306–311, Banff, Canada, July 2004.

[108] L. Bahl, J. Cocke, F. Jelinek, and J. Raviv, Optimal decoding of linear codes for minimizing symbol error rate, *IEEE Trans. on Info. Theory*, 20(2):284–287, March 1974.

[109] J. B. Anderson and S. M. Hladik, Tailbiting MAP decoders, *IEEE J. on Select. Areas in Commun.*, 16(2):297–302, February 1998.

[110] S. Benedetto and G. Montorsi, Unveiling turbo codes: Some results on parallel concatenated coding schemes, *IEEE Trans. on Info. Theory*, 42(2):409–428, March 1996.

[111] T. Richardson, The geometry of turbo decoding dynamics, *IEEE Trans. on Info. Theory*, 46(1):9–23, January 2000.

[112] Stephan ten Brink, Convergence of iterative decoding, *Electronics Letters*, 35(13): 1117–1118, June 1999.

[113] Stephan ten Brink, Convergence of iterative decoding, *Electronics Letters*, 35(10): 806–808, May 1999.

[114] Stephan ten Brink, Convergence behaviour of iteratively decoded parallel concatenated codes, *IEEE Trans. on Commun.*, 49(10):1727–1737, October 2001.

[115] W. E. Ryan, A turbo code tutorial, 1997. Available online at: http://www.ece.arizona.edu/~ryan/.

[116] G. L. Turin, An introduction to matched filters, *IRE Trans. on Info. Theory*, 6(3):311–329, June 1960.

[117] G. L. Turin, An introduction to digital matched filters, *Proc. IEEE*, 64(7):1092–1112, July 1976.

[118] J. G. Birdsall, On understanding the matched filter in the frequency domain, *IEEE Trans. on Education*, 19:168–169, November 1976.

[119] H. Nyquist, Certain topics in telegraph transmission theory, *AIEE Trans.*, 47:617–644, 1928.

[120] CCITT: Malaga-Torremolinos, *The Red Book–Data Communication over the Telephone Network–vol VIII Fascicle VIII.1*, 1984.

[121] K. Vasudevan, DSP-based algorithms for voiceband modems, 1995. Masters thesis, Indian Institute of Technology, Madras.

[122] L. E. Franks, Further results on Nyquist's problem in pulse transmission, *IEEE Trans. on Commun.*, 16(2):337–340, April 1968.

[123] N. C. Beaulieu, C. C. Tan, and M. O. Damen, A "better than" Nyquist pulse, *IEEE Commun. Lett.*, 5(9):367–368, September 2001.

[124] N. C. Beaulieu and M. O. Damen, Parametric construction of Nyquist-I pulses, *IEEE Trans. on Commun.*, 52(12):2134–2142, December 2004.

[125] S. Chandan, P. Sandeep, and A. K. Chaturvedi, A family of ISI-free polynomial pulses, *IEEE Commun. Lett.*, 9(6):496–498, June 2005.

[126] A. J. Viterbi, Spread spectrum communications: Myths and realities, *IEEE Comm. Mag.*, 17(3):11–18, May 1979.

[127] C. E. Cook and H. S. Marsh, An introduction to spread spectrum, *IEEE Comm. Mag.*, 21(2):8–16, March 1983.

[128] M. Kavehrad and P. J. McLane, Spread spectrum for indoor digital radio, *IEEE Comm. Mag.*, 25(6):32–40, June 1987.

[129] Third Generation Partnership Project, *3GPP TS 25.223 Technical Specification Group Radio Access Network: Spreading and Modulation (TDD)*, 2003. Web: http://www.3gpp.org.

[130] J. P. Costas, Synchronous communications, *Proc. IRE*, 44(12):1713–1718, December 1956.

[131] A. J. Viterbi, *Principles of Coherent Communication*, McGraw Hill, 1966.

[132] S. C. Gupta, Phase-locked loops, *Proc. IEEE*, 63(2):291–306, February 1975.

[133] F. M. Gardner, *Phaselock Techniques*, Wiley, 1979.

[134] W. C. Lindsey and C. M. Chie, A survey of digital phase locked loops, *Proc. IEEE*, 69(4):410–431, April 1981.

[135] K. H. Mueller and M. Müller, Timing recovery in digital synchronous data receivers, *IEEE Trans. on Commun.*, 24(5):516–530, May 1976.

[136] L. E. Franks, Carrier and bit synchronization in data communication – A tutorial review, *IEEE Trans. on Commun.*, 28(8):1107–1121, August 1980.

[137] J. J. Stiffler, *Theory of Synchronous Communications*, Prentice Hall, 1971.

[138] W. C. Lindsey, *Synchronization Systems in Communications*, Prentice Hall, 1972.

[139] W. C. Lindsey and M. K. Simon, *Telecommunication Systems Engineering*, Prentice Hall, 1973.

[140] L. E. Franks, *Synchronization Subsystems: Analysis and Design*, Digital Communications, Satellite/Earth Station Engineering, K. Feher, (Ed.) Prentice-Hall, 1981.

[141] D. C. Rife and R. R. Boorstyn, Single-tone parameter estimation from discrete-time observations, *IEEE Trans. Info. Theory*, 20(5):591–598, September 1974.

[142] C. R. Cahn, Improving frequency acquisition of a Costas loop, *IEEE Trans. on Commun.*, 25(12):1453–1459, December 1977.

[143] D. G. Messerschmitt, Frequency detectors for PLL acquisition in timing and carrier recovery, *IEEE Trans. on Commun.*, 27(6):1288–1295, September 1979.

[144] F. D. Natali, AFC tracking algorithms, *IEEE Trans. on Commun.*, 32(8):935–947, August 1984.

[145] F. M. Gardner, Properties of frequency difference detectors, *IEEE Trans. on Commun.*, 33(2):131–138, February 1985.

[146] H. Sari and S. Moridi, New phase and frequency detectors for carrier recovery in PSK and QAM systems, *IEEE Trans. on Commun.*, 36(9):1035–1043, September 1988.

[147] T. Alberty and V. Hespelt, A new pattern jitter free frequency error detector, *IEEE Trans. on Commun.*, 37(2):159–163, February 1989.

[148] S. Kay, A fast and accurate single frequency estimator, *IEEE Trans. on Acoust. Speech and Signal Processing*, 37(12):1987–1990, December 1989.

[149] J. C. I. Chuang and N. R. Sollenberger, Burst coherent demodulation with combined symbol timing, frequency offset estimation, and diversity selection, *IEEE Trans. on Commun.*, 39(7):1157–1164, July 1991.

[150] A. N. D'Andrea and U. Mengali, Design of quadricorrelators for automatic frequency control systems, *IEEE Trans. on Commun.*, 41(10):988–997, June 1993.

[151] A. N. D'Andrea and U. Mengali, Noise performance of two frequency-error detectors derived from maximum likelihood estimation methods, *IEEE Trans. on Commun.*, 42(2/3/4):793–802, February/March/April 1994.

[152] M. P. Fitz, Further results in the fast estimation of a single frequency, *IEEE Trans. on Commun.*, 42(2/3/4):862–864, February/March/April 1994.

[153] M. Luise and R. Reggiannini, Carrier frequency recovery in all-digital modems for burst-mode transmissions, *IEEE Trans. on Commun.*, 43(2/3/4):1169–1178, February/March/April 1995.

[154] H. Cramér, *Mathematical Methods of Statistics*, Princeton University Press, 1946.

[155] C. W. Helstrom, *Statistical Theory of Signal Detection*, Pergamon, London, 1968.

[156] H. L. Van Trees, *Detection, Estimation and Modulation Theory, Part I*, Wiley, New York, 1968.

[157] N. Mohanty, *Random Signals: Estimation and Identification*, Van Nostrand Reinhold, 1986.

[158] K. Vasudevan, Design and development of a burst acquisition system for geosynchronous SATCOM channels – first report, 2007. Project supported by Defence Electronics Applications Lab (DEAL), Dehradun (ref. no. DEAL/02/4043/2005-2006/02/016).

[159] John G. Proakis and Dimitris G. Manolakis, *Digital Signal Processing: Principles, Algorithms and Applications*, Maxwell MacMillan, second edition, 1992.

[160] J. B. Anderson, T. Aulin, and C. E. Sundberg, *Digital Phase Modulation*, New York: Plenum, 1986.

[161] R. W. Lucky, Automatic equalization for digital communication, *Bell Syst. Tech. J.*, 44(4):547–588, April 1965.

[162] Shahid. U. H. Qureshi, Adaptive equalization, *Proc. IEEE*, 73(9):1349–1387, September 1985.

[163] Thomas Ericson, Structure of optimum receiving filters in data transmission systems, *IEEE Trans. on Info. Theory*, 17(3):352–353, May 1971.

[164] Simon Haykin, *Adaptive Filter Theory*, Prentice Hall, third edition, 1996.

[165] R. D. Gitlin and S. B. Weinstein, Fractionally-spaced equalization: An improved digital transversal equalizer, *Bell System Technical Journal*, 60(2):275–296, February 1981.

[166] M. E. Austin, Decision feedback equalization for digital communication over dispersive channels, August 1967. MIT Lincoln Laboratory, Tech. Report No. 437.

[167] P. Monsen, Feedback equalization for fading dispersive channels, *IEEE Trans. on Info. Theory*, 17(1):56–64, January 1971.

[168] D. A. George, R. R Bowen, and J. R. Storey, An adaptive decision feedback equalizer, *IEEE Trans. on Commun. Tech.*, 19(6):281–293, June 1971.

[169] R. Price, Nonlinearly-feedback equalized PAM vs capacity. In *Proc. IEEE Intl. Conf. on Commun.*, pages 22.12–22.17, Philadelphia, 1972.

[170] J. Salz, Optimum mean-square decision feedback equalization, *Bell System Technical Journal*, 52(8):1341–1373, October 1973.

[171] D. L. Duttweiler, J. E. Mazo, and D. G. Messerschmitt, Error propagation in decision feedback equalizers, *IEEE Trans. on Info. Theory*, 20(4):490–497, July 1974.

[172] C. A. Belfiore and J. H. Parks, Decision-feedback equalization, *Proc. IEEE*, 67(8): 1143–1156, August 1979.

[173] S. A. Altekar and N. C. Beaulieu, Upper bounds on the error probability of decision feedback equalization, *IEEE Trans. on Info. Theory*, 39(1):145–156, January 1993.

[174] M. Vedat Eyuboğlu, Detection of coded modulation signals on linear, severely distorted channels using decision feedback noise prediction with interleaving, *IEEE Trans. on Commun.*, 36(4):401–409, April 1988.

[175] I. J. Fevrier, S. B. Gelfand, and M. P. Fitz, Reduced complexity decision feedback equalization for multipath channels with large delay spreads, *IEEE Trans. on Commun.*, 47(6):927–937, June 1999.

[176] M. Reuter, J. C. Allen, J. R. Zeidler, and R. C. North, Mitigating error propagation effects in a decision feedback equalizer, *IEEE Trans. on Commun.*, 49(11):2028–2041, November 2001.

[177] G. D. Forney, Jr., Maximum-likelihood sequence estimation of digital sequences in the presence of intersymbol interference, *IEEE Trans. Info. Theory*, 18(3):363–378, May 1972.

[178] D. D. Falconer and F. R. Magee, Adaptive channel memory truncation for maximum likelihood sequence estimation, *Bell System Technical Journal*, 52(9):1541–1562, November 1973.

[179] G. Ungerboeck, Adaptive maximum likelihood receiver for carrier modulated data transmission systems, *IEEE Trans. on Commun.*, 22(5):624–635, May 1974.

[180] Won. U. Lee and F. S. Hill, A maximum likelihood sequence estimator with decision-feedback equalization, *IEEE Trans. on Commun.*, 25(9):971–979, September 1977.

[181] Robert E. Morley, Jr. and Donald L. Snyder, Maximum likelihood sequence estimation for randomly dispersive channels, *IEEE Trans. on Commun.*, 27(6):833–839, June 1979.

[182] Gregory E. Bottomley and Sandeep Chennakesu, Unification of MLSE receivers and extension to time-varying channels, *IEEE Trans. on Commun.*, 46(4):464–472, April 1998.

[183] M. Vedat Eyuboğlu and S. U. H. Qureshi, Reduced-state sequence estimation with set partitioning and decision feedback, *IEEE Trans. on Commun.*, 36(1):13–20, January 1988.

[184] Pierre R, Chevillat and Evangelos Eleftheriou, Decoding of trellis-encoded signals in the presence of intersymbol interference and noise, *IEEE Trans. on Commun.*, 37(7):669–676, July 1989.

[185] M. Vedat Eyuboğlu and S. U. H. Qureshi, Reduced-state sequence estimation for coded modulation on intersymbol interference channels, *IEEE J. on Select. Areas in Commun.*, 7(6):989–995, August 1989.

[186] R. Raheli, A. Polydoros, and C. K. Tzou, Per-survivor processing: A general approach to MLSE in uncertain environments, *IEEE Trans. on Commun.*, 43(2/3/4):354–364, February/March/April 1995.

[187] K. Vasudevan, K. Giridhar, and Bhaskar Ramamurthi, Efficient VA for signals with ISI, *Electronics Letters*, 34(7):629–631, April 1998.

[188] John A. C. Bingham, Multicarrier modulation for data transmission: An idea whose time has come, *IEEE Comm. Mag.*, 28(5):5–14, May 1990.

[189] A. Ruiz, J. M. Cioffi, and S. Kasturia, Discrete multiple tone modulation with coset coding for spectrally shaped channel, *IEEE Trans. on Commun.*, 40(6):1012–1029, June 1992.

[190] J. M. Cioffi, V. Oksman, J-J. Werner, T. Pollet, P. M. P. Spruyt, J. S. Chow, and K. S. Jacobsen, Very-high-speed digital subscriber lines, *IEEE Comm. Mag.*, 37(4): 72–79, April 1999.

[191] T. Starr, J. M. Cioffi, and P. J. Silverman, *Understanding Digital Subscriber Line Technology*, Englewood Cliffs, N.J.: Prentice-Hall, first edition, 1999.

[192] M. A. Tzannes, M. C. Tzannes, J. G. Proakis, and P. N. Heller, DMT Systems, DWMT systems and Digital filter banks. In *Proc. IEEE Intl. Conf. on Commun.*, pages 311–315, New Orleans, Louisiana, May 1994.

[193] A. D. Rizos, J. G. Proakis, and T. Q. Nguyen, Comparision of DFT and cosine modulated filter banks in multicarrier modulation. In *Proc. IEEE Global Telecomm. Conf.*, pages 687–691, San Fransisco, California, November 1994.

[194] I. Kalet, The multitone channel, *IEEE Trans. on Commun.*, 37(2):119–124, February 1989.

[195] R. V. L. Hartley, Transmission of information, *Bell System Technical Journal*, 7(3): 535–563, July 1928.

[196] E. Kreyszig, *Advanced Engineering Mathematics*, John Wiley, 2001.

[197] G. Birkhoff and S. MacLane, *A Survey of Modern Algebra*, MacMillan, New York, first edition, 1953.

Index